JOHN G. BENNETT

ALSO BY JOSEPH AZIZE

The Phoenician Solar Theology, dissertation series, vol. 15 (2005)

Gilgameš and the World of Assyria, edited with Noel Weeks (2007, co-editor and co-contributor)

George Mountford Adie: A Gurdjieff Pupil in Australia, editor, and co-author with the late G.M. Adie (3rd edition, 2023)

Pleading Precedents, with P. El Khouri and E. Finnane (2009)

How to Spot a Fraud (2015)

John Lennon: From Pain to Harmony (2015)

Constantinople Notes on the Transition to Man Number 4 (2017)

An Introduction to the Maronite Faith (3rd edition, 2023)

Gurdjieff: Mysticism, Contemplation, and Exercises (2020)

JOHN G. BENNETT

Witness to Death and Resurrection

JOSEPH AZIZE

Red Elixir
Rhinebeck, New York

John G. Bennett: Witness to Death and Resurrection Copyright © 2024 by Joseph Azize

All rights reserved. No part of this book may be reprinted or reproduced in any form, or by any electronic, mechanical, or other means, now known or hereafter invented, including photocopying and recording, or in any information or retrieval system, without permission in writing from the publisher.

Paperback ISBN 978-1-960090-82-9
eBook ISBN 978-1-960090-83-6

Library of Congress Control Number 2024943226

Book design by Colin Rolfe

Red Elixir is an imprint of Monkfish Book Publishing Company

Red Elixir
22 East Market Street, Suite 304
Rhinebeck, New York 12572
(845) 876-4861
monkfishpublishing.com

"It is consciousness that gives us the possibility of 'hearing' things from the inside as it were instead of from the outside. Hence the idea of 'harkening'. In ancient times, people harkened to the gods, as did Utnapishtim to Ea when receiving warnings of the impending flood."

—A.G.E. Blake, *A Gymnasium of Beliefs in Higher Intelligences*, 35

"In Bennett's vision, the stars belong to a domain in which consciousness and intelligence are no longer tied to the human scale, and where creative power is exercised directly through means which we cannot comprehend with our own terrestrial, brainbound intelligence."

—Anthony Hodgson, *The Cosmic Vision of J.G. Bennett: An Appreciation*, 3

"Once Gurdjieff said: 'Judas is universal type: he can enter into all situations—but he has not type of his own'. This, at least, seemed to agree with my own estimate of myself."

—*Witness*, 1962 edition, 270

Bennett (far left) with Gurdjieff (front right) and others.

CONTENTS

Preface   *Anthony G.E. Blake*   xiii
Acknowledgments   xv
Table of the Twenty-Four Visions of John G. Bennett   xvii

Introduction   xviv
    0.1   All Discords Are Harmonized   xviv
    0.2   Of God and of Gurdjieff   xxix
    0.3   Developing "Real I" as a Mystical Endeavour   xxiv
    0.4   A Science of "Man's Relation with God and the Universe"   xxvii
    0.5   Bennett as a Pupil of Gurdjieff   xxx
    0.6   Aspects of the Edwardian Intellectual World   xxxv
    0.7   Re-evaluating Bennett within the Gurdjieff Tradition   xlii
    0.8   The Genre of Witness   xlv

Chapter 1: From Childhood to Near-Death   1
    1.1   Childhood   1
    1.2   Public Schools   12
    1.3   Bennett at King's College School   16
    1.4   Bennett in WWI   21
    1.5   The First Vision: 21 March 1918   23
    1.6   After Active Service   26

Chapter 2: Marriage, Turkey, and Gurdjieff   33
    2.1   Marriage   33

2.2   To Turkey   38
2.3   Meeting Prince Sabaheddin   43
2.4   Premonitions: The Quality of Time   46
2.5   The Second Vision: Eternity   47
2.6   Gurdjieff   56
2.7   P.D. Ouspensky   62

Chapter 3: With Gurdjieff at Fontainebleau   69
3.1   The Third Vision: Destiny   69
3.2   "Private Dreams"   76
3.3   Studying with Ouspensky   84
3.4   With Gurdjieff at Fontainebleau   88
3.5   The Lost Lecture of 1923   91
3.6   The Fourth Vision: The Great Accumulator   92
3.7   Return to London   98
3.8   Leaving Gurdjieff and the Prieuré   100

Chapter 4: With Ouspensky   105
4.1   Seeking a Career, and a Second Marriage   105
4.2   The Fifth Vision: The Past Is Undying   110
4.3   Imprisonment, March 1928   112
4.4   The Foreign Office Files   114
4.5   Return to England   119
4.6   The Sixth Vision: The Future of Humanity   123
4.7   Ouspensky on Objective Consciousness   125
4.8   The Seventh Vision: The Energy of Life   130
4.9   The Eighth Vision: Self-Observation   133
4.10 Coal Research   136

Chapter 5: Coombe Springs   141
5.1   The BCURA   141
5.2   The Ninth Vision: Redemption of the Universal Order   147
5.3   Misunderstandings between Bennett and Ouspensky   150

    5.4   Values   153

    5.5   The Tenth Vision: *Fiat Voluntas Tua*   155

    5.6   The *Institute for the Comparative Study of History, Philosophy and the Sciences*   163

    5.7   The "Unknown Builders"   165

Chapter 6: The King's College Vision, 1947   175

    6.1   The Death of Bennett's Mother   175

    6.2 *The Crisis in Human Affairs*   177

    6.3   The Eleventh, or "King's College" Vision   183

    6.4 The Death of P.D. Ouspensky   188

    6.5 Africa, from Bennett's Perspective   189

    6.6 Africa, from Lewis' Perspective   193

    6.7 Mrs Bennett, and Madame Ouspensky   196

Chapter 7: With Gurdjieff in Jerusalem   201

    7.1   The Reunion with Gurdjieff   201

    7.2   Gurdjieff Teaches Bennett Contemplation-Like Exercises   211

    7.3   The Return to Paris as a Group Leader   215

    7.4   The Twelfth Vision: Helping the Deceased   217

    7.5   With Gurdjieff in New York   221

    7.6   Paris, 1949   223

    7.7   The Thirteenth Vision: Out of Body   225

    7.8   The Fourteenth Vision: Jerusalem in 33 AD   228

    7.9   The Passing of Gurdjieff   232

    7.10 What Are We Living For?   236

    7.11 A Lost Gurdjieff Lecture   240

Chapter 8: The Secret of Everlasting Life   245

    8.1   The Fifteenth Vision: The Secret of Everlasting Life   245

    8.2   The Sixteenth Vision: No Power of Action   249

    8.3   Teaching Gurdjieff's Contemplative Exercises   250

    8.4   Further Searching in the East   257

- 8.5 The Seventeenth Vision: First Do your Duty 263
- 8.6 Separating from the Gurdjieff Society 266
- 8.7 The Djamichunatra 269
- 8.8 Bennett as Teacher 272
- 8.9 The Dramatic Universe 279

Chapter 9: The Subud Chapter 285

- 9.1 Bennett's Introduction to Subud 285
- 9.2 Pak Subuh 293
- 9.3 Opening the Djamichunatra 295
- 9.4 Bennett in Australia 298
- 9.5 The Death of the Second Mrs Bennett and Marriage to Elizabeth Mayall 299
- 9.6 The Eighteenth Vision: Christ Crucified 303
- 9.7 The Nineteenth, Twentieth and Twenty-First Visions: The Love of God 305
- 9.8 Bennett's Disaffection from Subud 309
- 9.9 Bennett, Subud, and Gurdjieff 319

Chapter 10: Bennett's Search in the 1960s 325

- 10.1 The Shivapuri Baba 325
- 10.2 The Twenty-Second Vision: Christ in the Sacrament 332
- 10.3 The Bohm-Bennett Correspondence 335
- 10.4 The Twenty-Third Vision: Work as the Will to Reality 337
- 10.5 Idries Shah 338
- 10.6 Understanding Bennett and Shah 345
- 10.7 Systematics and Education 356

Chapter 11: "I Am" and always Will Be 361

- 11.1 Hasan Shushud 361
- 11.2 The Twenty-Fourth Vision: "I Am" and always Will Be 365
- 11.3 Sherborne House 367
- 11.4 Bennett and Beelzebub 379

11.5   Death   382

Chapter 12: … And We Have Made a Beginning   387
    12.1   The Warp and the Weft   387
    12.2   As a Teacher of Contemplative Exercises   392
    12.3   The "War with Time"   399
    12.4   Christ and the "War with Time"   402
    12.5   The Sacred Image   4407
    12.6   Hazard   413
    12.7   Bennett's Achievement   417

Appendices   425
    1   Bennett's Family   425
    2   Moore on Bennett   430
    3   Idries Shah   437

Annotated Bibliography of J.G. Bennett's Work   *David Seamon*   455
Bibliography   515
Index   533

PREFACE

John Bennett met and gave accounts of many remarkable men, particularly G.I. Gurdjieff, an innovator in esoteric psychological methods offering a way to spiritual realities that went beyond what is generally thought to be either religion or science. In this book Joseph Azize has taken on the formidable task of giving an account of Bennett himself and, in particular, of his journey through a series of visions that brought him to the experience and conviction of higher realities that he then devoted his life to conveying to other people.

According to some traditions, the biography of a holy man has three levels: first, the outer story of what he did, where he went and who he met; second the story of his inner life, which one rarely finds in biographies today, and thirdly a revelation of the divine action which is the meaning of the subject's life. Joseph has faced this challenge with careful research but also with an informing passion and faith.

Bennett seems to have embraced, with equal regard, the rigours of mathematical science and mysticism of transcendental experience. In his life he was occupied in various political and commercial activities as well as industrial research. As part of his embrace of the depth and diversity of human experience, he acquired many languages and studied Scriptures from all faiths. He was faithful to his avowed principle of "integration without rejection."

The story of Bennett, his life and works, opens a window to what has become known as the fourth way, as articulated by his teacher Gurdjieff. The turn of the century, in the 1900s, brought a flood of new ideas and with it the breakdown of traditional values. Bennett was one of many who strove to make sense of it all; though he can be regarded as a remarkable and exceptional man, his story is relevant to us and what we are facing in the twenty-first century.

I was fortunate to be in his company for many years and can attest to his continuing search which I regard as an active spirituality and remained open to the unknown until his death, based on his recognition of the hazard accompanying all human endeavour and knowledge. Bennett's story is in fact the story of many people and many cultures, science and religion, past and future. Joseph's book is a repository of remarkable ideas.

—Anthony G.E. Blake
Scotland, October 2023

ACKNOWLEDGMENTS

I acknowledge all those who have assisted me in the production of this volume. The first and greatest acknowledgement is owed, and gratefully, to Anthony G.E. Blake. It is no idle thing to say that in him, Bennett found an honourable and worthy student, who has, I may be bold to think, has repaid the debt of his existence.

The second acknowledgement is owed to David Seamon, also an honourable and worthy pupil of Bennett, who generously allowed the publication here of his excellent annotated bibliography. Then, I must thank two who did not personally know Bennett: Carole Cusack, and Andrew Moyer. I am grateful for their wisdom, support and friendship. Carole's learning and impartiality are inspiring, while among other matters, Andrew saved me from making rash judgments about one important figure in this story.

I also acknowledge, in alphabetical order, the assistance of Michael Benham, Ben Bennett, George Bennett, Roberta Chromey, Tony Ingram, John Macpherson, Allen Roth, and Tim St. Clair Ford. I take the opportunity to express my appreciation of the companionship of Steven Sutcliffe, a most stimulating and erudite scholar.

My debt to all these will have been discharged if this volume plays any role in causing some people to see Bennett in a new and more favourable light, as one of the great spiritual adventurers of the twentieth century. May his example and influence shine on.

Bennett in Gurdjieff's funeral cortege (the tall figure, center).

TABLE OF THE TWENTY-FOUR VISIONS OF JOHN G. BENNETT

1. 21 March 1918	section 1.5 Near Death, France
2. September 1920	2.5 The Vision of Eternity, Rue de Péra
3. April /May 1921	3.1 Destiny, Scutari
4. August 1923	3.6 The Great Accumulator, Fontainebleau
5. August 1925	4.2 The Past Is Undying, Mycenae
6. 1929/1930	4.6 The Future of Humanity, Ostrovo swamps
7. August 1931–August 1932	4.8 The Energy of Life, Finsbury Square
8. August 1933	4.9 Self-Observation, Lyne Place
9. August 1941	5.2 Redemption of the Universal Order, Wales
10. 14 April 1944	5.5 Fiat Voluntas Tua, Coombes Springs
11. 15 September 1947	6.3 King's College, London
12. 1948	7.4 Helping the Deceased, Coombe Springs
13. 14 August 1949	7.7 Leaving the body, Paris
14. 27 August 1949	7.8 Judas, Paris
15. 1950?	8.1 Secret of Everlasting Life, en route to Paris

16. 1952	8.2	No Power of Action, Coombe Springs
17. 13 November 1953	8.5	First Do your Duty, Ceyhan in Turkey
18. 27 March 1959	9.6	Christ Crucified and Divine, Coyoacan, Mexico
19. June 1959	9.7	The Love of God, St Wandrille
20. 1959 or 1960	9.7	Submission to God's Will, Mary, St Wandrille
21. 1959, 1960, or 1961	9.7	Will and Love of God, St Wandrille
22. Summer 1961	10.2	Christ in the Sacrament, St Wandrille
23. January 1964	10.4	The infinite significance of Work
24. 28 January 1969	11.2	"I" am and always will be, England

INTRODUCTION

0.1   ALL DISCORDS ARE HARMONIZED

Death and Resurrection are the twin keys—or perhaps the one divided key—to unlock all mysteries. In death and resurrection all discords are harmonized. That is why in this book I have tried to bear witness to my conviction that death and resurrection can be experienced and verified during our present life on earth.

As I end this book, which spans forty-two years of my life, I recall Gurdjieff's saying: "Only two things have no limit—man's stupidity and the Mercy of God."[1]

In this manner, John Godolphin Bennett, born on June 6, 1897 in London, died on December 13, 1974 in Sherborne, closed "The Decisive Experience," the final chapter of the first edition of his book *Witness: The Story of a Search*. That volume was published in 1962, when he was in his sixty-fifth year. Bennett published a revised version in 1974,[2] revised because he had re-examined his life and the testimony he would bear.

---

[1] Bennett (1962) 376.
[2] The revised version was published in the U.S. in 1974, and in the United Kingdom in 1975, in small print runs. I list this in my bibliography as "Bennett (1975a)." Another edition with an epilogue by his son George Bennett, and a final note by George and his brother Ben, appeared in 1997. This latter is the edition I have generally used, since it was the most widely available version at the date of writing. The 1974, 1975, and 1997 volumes are all different editions of the revised version Bennett had completed by 1974.

That second edition has no chapter entitled "The Decisive Experience," as does the 1962. The new final chapter, "Life Begins at Seventy," closes with these words:

> More than seventy years have passed since I began to ask questions and remember the answers. I asked my mother: "Why can't we see God?" to which she replied, "I expect he doesn't want us to." This did not satisfy me then, but it satisfies me now. I can understand much better why some mysteries must remain mysteries and why others can be revealed. I am wholly convinced that there is a Providential Power at work in the world, but it cannot help us without our consent. I finish this new edition of *Witness*, as I did the first, by quoting Gurdjieff: "Only two things have no limit – man's stupidity and the Mercy of God."[3]

Between these two finales, there is significant continuity, but also significant development. Above all, both close with the imponderable message of G.I. Gurdjieff (c.1866-1949) concerning God and His Mercy, with the implication that Bennett is admitting to his own stupidity and acknowledging the grace he has received.[4] However, there is also discontinuity: the 1962 edition had been written with the conviction that Bennett had already witnessed the "decisive experience" of his life. By the time of the second edition, this settled conviction had been joyfully swept aside. In 1962, Bennett was still collaborating with Pak Subuh and helping to promote Subud. To some degree, this first iteration of *Witness* was a continuation of his 1958 protreptic, *Concerning Subud*. However, by the time of the second edition, Bennett and Subuh had separated, and he had established his "International Academy of Continuous Education" at Sherborne. Also, in the revised edition, the passage on

---

[3] Bennett (1997) 307.
[4] The best general introductions to Gurdjieff are, in my view, Ouspensky (1949), Webb (1980), and Taylor (2020).

death and resurrection with which we opened this chapter, is omitted, leaving the book's secret to be discerned by the reader; while in his redrafted farewell, Bennett remembers his mother dispensing that piece of wisdom of which he has only now perceived the value.

Through the course of the development marked by these changes, Bennett emerges, I suggest, as probably that student of Gurdjieff who most fruitfully developed Gurdjieff's system of practical mysticism; and, after P.D. Ouspensky alone, as the most penetrating exponent of Gurdjieff's ideas. Yet, Bennett is a significant thinker in his own right, with abiding value for the contemporary world.

Bennett artfully chose one stark word for the title. "Witness" is originally an abstract noun, formed from the Anglo-Saxon root *wit*- "know," and hence first meaning "knowledge" and "consciousness."[5] This volume was his testimony of the knowledge he had gained. It does more than recount what he saw, who he met, what he did, and what he heard. It skilfully places, in an autobiographical narrative, what he came to learn of the mysteries of life, death, and resurrection. However, Bennett never summarizes for us what he has concluded from his twenty-four visions. I attempt to draw this out over the course of this study, especially in the final chapter. My own view is that Bennett's chief achievement is in just the field of practical or applied mysticism: living a life oriented to the presence of God, whatever the circumstances we find ourselves in.

In *Witness*, Bennett teaches that there is no need to fear either life or death, or to regret our suffering, for God and his love are ever present, and we do survive the moment of death. But there is great need to have a care for how we live, for only to the degree that we have become conscious and developed a will which can operate independently of external influences, are we able to overcome our egoism, to experience that divine love, and to die consciously and in possession of the power of will. He aims to put heart into his readers by disclosing what he has found and illustrating its practical benefits. In declaring his own stupidity, vanity, and mistakes, he implicitly states that if someone like himself can

[5] Skeat (1910) 720.

have witnessed this, then there is hope for all of us. In *Witness*, his "book of visions," Bennett has provided a modern exemplar of the *Ars moriendi*, a guide to living a good life so as to make a good death, and this assumes that death in itself is important, a fresh departure.

0.2   OF GOD AND OF GURDJIEFF

In closing both editions of *Witness*, Bennett deliberately led up from Gurdjieff to God. For Bennett, God is the highest value, while Gurdjieff showed a practical mystical path. A path is necessary for, as Bennett stated, the Providential Power working in the world: "cannot help us without our consent."[6] Allen Roth, a student at the first Sherborne course, in 1971-72, concluded that: "Bennett was not teaching a technique: he was showing us how to surrender to God."[7] More precisely, Bennett did not teach just any technique, but one which comprised an approach to God. I would say that Gurdjieff's system as developed by Bennett, can be understood as a means to God-realization. This appears in three steps:

First, Gurdjieff was the momentous influence in Bennett's life: they shared the same values and aims, and Bennett accepted his system as fundamentally correct. In the unpublished introduction to *Gurdjieff: Making a New World*, Bennett wrote:

> As I have made it plain in the title of this book that I look to Gurdjieff and his teaching for the making of a new world, I must explain why I regard it as necessary to turn towards a teacher who stands outside of the ranks of orthodox science, philosophy and religion.... Gurdjieff is the only teacher I have met or heard of in the present century who can be called a professional in the sense of mastery of the technique of

---

[6] Bennett (1997) 307. To give that consent needs some sort of formation, hence the need for a volume like *Witness*.
[7] Roth (1998) 107.

INTRODUCTION

"making people better." He teaches not only what it means to live better and more fully, but also how this is to be done.[8]

This was probably written in 1950, shortly after Bennett had completed a series of London lectures titled *Gurdjieff: The Making of New World*.[9] While Gurdjieff was in his last months, Bennett delivered these lectures, and then at the end of his life, he gave to his fullest study of Gurdjieff exactly the same title, reaffirming his conviction that Gurdjieff's system was the key to the new world for which he had worked and hoped.

Second, Gurdjieff's importance to Bennett is illustrated by what Bennett had called the "decisive experience" of his life (the title of the final chapter in the original *Witness*):

> Gurdjieff had said to me at a prophetic meeting in his café shortly before his death: "Now you have taste of real 'I', but one day it will enter you and remain permanent. Then you will experience such happiness as you cannot imagine." After nine years, his promise was fulfilled. I knew that I was at last myself. But I also knew that this was only a beginning.[10]

Significantly, this passage is omitted from the 1997 edition,[11] I suggest because of the signal insights of the twenty-third and twenty-fourth visions, which had occurred in 1964 and 1969 respectively, after the first edition had been published. As a result of that last vision, Bennett wrote: "I was filled with joy and confidence, for I knew for certain and forever that I could lose not only my "body," but also my "mind," and still remain

---

[8] Bennett (undated and unpublished), "Introduction to *Gurdjieff: Making a New World*," 4.
[9] Email communication from Ben Young, who found and typed up the unpublished introduction, July 21, 2022. For the name and date of the lectures, see Bennett (1997) 219.
[10] Bennett (1962) 357-58.
[11] Bennett (1997) 272-73.

"myself"."[12] In Gurdjieff's terms, this means that Bennett had achieved a real "I" which stood above and beyond his functions of mind, body, and feeling.

Third, this achievement of "real I" is necessarily related to the approach to and unity with the Will of God, and hence the goal of mysticism, as understood by a Christian like Bennett, for only "real I" can be united to God. Gurdjieff once put it in a rather pithy fashion: "Behind real I lies God."[13] Or, as George Adie (1901-89), a personal pupil of Gurdjieff and Ouspensky, and a friend of Bennett, said: "A nothing cannot be related."[14] This is why I have contended that Gurdjieff can best be understood as a mystic, and his system as one for pursuing the mystic goal in daily life.[15] This is also, I shall argue, true of Bennett. I cannot here repeat my definitions and contentions, but I shall take advantage of the publication of more transcripts of meetings with Gurdjieff in 1943 and 1944 to briefly restate my pertinent conclusions.

0.3   DEVELOPING "REAL I" AS A MYSTICAL ENDEAVOR

The mystic nature of Gurdjieff's system is illustrated in his stating, in his third and esoteric series of writings, that he aimed to teach how to "touch" and even to "merge" with "reality."[16] In Christian terms, this means touching God, and, in a fashion, merging with Him; hence Gurdjieff's character Beelzebub addresses the Creator as "THOU ALL and the ALLNESS of my WHOLENESS."[17] That is, in the final analysis, God is the sole reality of the cosmos and of our own individual "real I," here alluded to by the term "my wholeness."[18] In the Paris meeting of February 29, 1944, a student said that

---

[12] Bennett (1997) 299.
[13] Nicoll (1997) 14.
[14] Personal communication, probably in 1989.
[15] Azize (2020).
[16] Gurdjieff (1975) 4. The nature of the Third Series, and that Gurdjieff intended it to be kept confidential, unless circumstances warranted publication, emerges from the "Foreword" by Jeanne de Salzmann.
[17] Gurdjieff (1950) 1183.
[18] I set out the background to this assertion in Azize (2020) 51-55.

he had been raised a Catholic, but had long ceased practising, although he believed in something which he called "God." Through this work with Gurdjieff he had come to a sense of "Me," and his idea of God had imperceptibly been replaced by that of "I am," not so much what "I" am now, but what "I" may become. To this, Gurdjieff replied:

> Stop, I have understood. You really could not be upon a better path. You have understood that God is not an old Jewish man with a beard ... but that it is precisely "I" with all the qualities which it includes. Have you read the Bible and the Gospel? We were created in the image of God. You are a miniature of God.
>
> If you always continue like that, you are God. Not you, but the sensation you have. Let this sensation become stronger and at the same time think always that God is not an old Jewish man with a beard and a comb in his pocket. You are a micro-God (micro-Dieu).... What you have to pray for now is for all the possibilities that are in you. These qualities are already within you, that is God. It is an ideal, because God is already within you.[19]

So, "God ... is precisely 'I' with all the qualities which it includes." However, in us, "I" is only potential, and to be developed by inner work. Humans are "beings having in their presences every possibility for becoming particles of a part of Divinity."[20] Gurdjieff says this in the context of deploring how we too often allow that possibility to atrophy, becoming nothing but "living flesh."[21] The esoteric nature of human potential was strikingly perceived by Bennett in his eleventh vision at King's College (section 6.3), and was used to produce his theory of "soul

---

[19] Gurdjieff (2020) 125-26. My translation from the French.
[20] Gurdjieff (1950) 452, and on the relation between the Whole and the particle, 191-92, 197, 353, and 801.
[21] Gurdjieff (1950) 452. This idea is listed in many places, but see "The Two Rivers": Gurdjieff (1950) 1227-1231.

stuff." "Real I" is thus not just naked self-affirmation. Even with "real I," we can only ever be "God" as a "micro-Dieu," a microcosm to His macrocosm. Hence, in the Third Series, Gurdjieff wrote:

> And here also is God!!! Again God!... Only He is everywhere and with Him everything is connected. I am a man, and such as I am, in contrast to all outer forms of animal life, created by Him in His image!!! For He is God and therefore I also have within myself all the possibilities and impossibilities that He has. The difference between Him and myself must lie only in scale. For He is God of all the presences in the universe! It follows that I have also to be God of some kind of presence on my scale. He is God and I am God! Whatever possibilities He has in relation to the presences of the universe, such possibilities and impossibilities I should also have in relation to the world subordinate to me. He is God of all the world, and also of my outer world. I am God also, although only of my inner world.[22]

The difference of scale between God and ourselves as God is immense, the difference between the universe and "only ... my inner world." As stated, for the analogy to be complete, one must develop the possibility of one's own "I." As Gurdjieff said on November 18, 1943: "You don't [now] have an 'I', but what fulfils the obligations of your 'I' is the idea that you wish to work and to become other than you are."[23] In this way, the work—the ideas and methods—fulfils "the obligations" of a full and permanent "I" which itself would represent God in us.

Gurdjieff also made cryptic references to being "a particle of all that exists,"[24] and of the possibility, placed in us by "Great Nature, of becoming particles of the whole of the 'Reasonable Whole',"[25] and a par-

---

[22] Gurdjieff (1975) 22-23.
[23] Gurdjieff (2017) 289.
[24] Gurdjieff (1950) 162.
[25] Gurdjieff (1950) 384.

ticle, "though an independent one, of everything existing in the Great Universe."[26] These comments seem to mean that we begin as particles of the universe ("all that exists"), and can, by working on ourselves, realise the possibility of being transformed into independent and more intelligent particles which correspond to God as an entity on a small scale corresponds to one on a larger scale. Neither Gurdjieff nor Bennett even theoretically abolished either the individual "I" or "God" by making one equivalent to another. The final mystery was that "only God has the right to call himself 'I'," as Ouspensky stated on 6 January 1938,[27] and Bennett in 1962.[28]

0.4   A SCIENCE OF "MAN'S RELATION WITH GOD AND THE UNIVERSE"

Thus, for Gurdjieff and Bennett, the way of developing the essential possibilities present in our nature is the way of *inner* work. That is, creating "real I" within ourselves is a mystical endeavour, leading to God, who is the absolute "I" to whom each individual "I" relates. Since it is a "way," something can be said of it, and how to walk it. Jeanne de Salzmann (1889-1990), Gurdjieff's lieutenant for the last ten or so years of his life, who ensured that the practical methods Gurdjieff brought were not lost, stated:

> Gurdjieff brought us a knowledge of consciousness, a science that shows what we are and our potential capacity, what needs to be developed. It is a real understanding of the energies in us. He came to bring a teaching, show a way toward consciousness. What is a "way"? And what is a *teaching* of a way?
>
> Esoteric knowledge is the science of man's relation with

---

[26] Gurdjieff (1950) 183
[27] Ouspensky (1951) 165.
[28] Bennett (1964) 219 and 227.

God and the universe.... The knowledge is passed on theoretically and through direct experience.²⁹

Kathryn Hulme (1900-81), author of *The Nun's Story*, and a personal pupil of Gurdjieff, wrote of Gurdjieff, from a more personal viewpoint, that he had: "uncovered in me a hidden longing I never knew I had—the desire for an inner life of the spirit—and taught me how to work for it as one works for one's daily bread."³⁰ The word Hulme uses, "work" is one of the defining emblems of Gurdjieff's legacy: the possibility of methodically working, with an aim and a method.

Three of Gurdjieff's most significant contributions to mystical practice are his articulation of the ideas of "self-observation," "self-remembering" ("the first conscious shock"), and what he called "the second conscious shock," an effort which even when experienced cannot be exactly described, but includes the transformation of negative emotion into positive.³¹ To be able to actualise either of these conscious shocks, one struggles, undertaking "conscious labours and intentional suffering."³² In 1949, Gurdjieff rebuked Bennett, saying: "Never once I see you struggle with *yourself*. All the time you are occupied with your cheap animal."³³ The critical fourth vision of August 1923, when Bennett penetrated to what Gurdjieff told him was the ultimate secret of human nature, was possible only after tremendous, almost life-threatening, efforts on Bennett's part, and with Gurdjieff's assistance (section 3.6). When he met the teaching of Subud, he objected when directed that he should not struggle, but rather leave all to grace. Pak Subuh papered over the question, but it would not rest, and led to Bennett's departure from Subud (section 9.8).

Bennett's own view was that the permanent changes which he believed had occurred in him were the results of his efforts to develop himself, not of the visions; although he certainly wished to understand

---

²⁹ de Salzmann (2010) 2.
³⁰ Hulme (1997) 1.
³¹ Ouspensky (1949) 188-91.
³² See the materials referred to at Azize (2020) 71.
³³ Bennett (1997) 217.

his experiences and be able to make use of them. *Witness* is Bennett's testimony to what he saw, how he struggled to understand, and what he came to. For purposes of comparison, it is instructive to consider this autobiographical account of a vision which, in Gurdjieff's and Bennett's terms, was undoubtedly one of self-remembering. In September 1980, John Lennon recalled a recent experience:

> It came out of an overwhelming feeling of loss that went right back to the womb. One night, I couldn't get through to Yoko on the telephone and I felt completely disconnected.... I think that's what the last five years were all about—to re-establish me for meself (sic). The actual moment of awareness when I remembered who I was came in a room in Hong Kong because Yoko had sent me around the world to be by meself. I hadn't done anything by meself since I was 20. I didn't know how to check into a hotel ... if someone reads this they'll think, 'These bloody popstars!' They don't understand the pain of being a freak. Whenever I got nervous about it I took a bath, and in Hong Kong I'd had about 40 baths. I was looking out over the bay when something rang a bell. It was the recognition—'My God! This relaxed person is me from way back. HE knew how to do things. It doesn't rely on any adulation or hit record. Wow!' So I called Yoko and said, 'Guess who. It's me!'
>
> I wandered around Hong Kong at dawn, alone, and it was a thrill. It was rediscovering a feeling that I once had as a youngster walking the mountains of Scotland with an Auntie. The heather, the mist ... I thought - aha! THIS is the feeling that makes you write or paint... It was with me all my life! And that's why I'm free of the Beatles, because I took time to discover that I was John Lennon before the Beatles, and will be after the Beatles. And so be it.[34]

---

[34] http://www.beatlesinterviews.org/db1980.0929.beatles.html accessed July 25, 2022

Almost all the elements in this comment are significant: the preceding feeling of loss and emptiness, the effort to physically relax allowing a new configuration of mind and feeling, the sense that one's "essence" was present in childhood,[35] and that there is something eternal in this experience of one's real self. I am not aware that Lennon had ever heard of Gurdjieff, Ouspensky, or Bennett. But the comparison is nonetheless instructive: Lennon did not know how to intentionally produce such experiences: the Gurdjieff system aims to teach just that.

0.5 BENNETT AS A PUPIL OF GURDJIEFF

Today, Bennett is remembered chiefly as one of Gurdjieff's preeminent pupils. As I have indicated, the practical side of Gurdjieff's teaching is its rationale.[36] But to consider Bennett only as a pupil of Gurdjieff would be to mistake part of the truth for the whole of it. Bennett was a mathematician and scientist, a philosopher, and above all a mystic. It is noteworthy that Bennett had attained only one qualification before propelling himself on his journey of discovery, and that was the very one he most quickly abandoned: his commission as an army officer. Gurdjieff was significantly older than Bennett, and when their paths met, they met as teacher and pupil. However, Bennett's life and work continued for a generation after Gurdjieff's death, during which time, he developed into a teacher with his own individual claim to the notice of posterity. What distinguished Bennett among Gurdjieff's pupils was arguably just his very individuality and his individual contributions to "philosophy," using that term in the wider Socratic sense.

One major difference between Gurdjieff and Bennett is the latter's achievements in mathematics and science. These were, I suggest, Bennett's means to the end of understanding large questions of the significance of life. Mathematics, especially geometry, marked Bennett's

---

[35] On "essence," its presence in childhood, and the correspondingly greater opportunities for gratuitous moments of self-remembering in childhood, Ouspensky (1949) 119, 144, 161-62, and 247.
[36]   Azize (2020).

personal path through the particulars of life to the transcendent end he pursued in common with Gurdjieff. I might venture to say that the geometry of higher dimensions provided Bennett with that intellectual grasp of the mystic visions along which the beads of *Witness* are strung. At their very first meeting in 1920 Gurdjieff impressed upon Bennett that understanding and action are of value only if they proceed in tandem.[37] Like Gurdjieff, Bennett concluded that the meaning of human life could not be divorced from human experience, and that central to this was learning from all the experiences of life, not least from our mistakes.

Bennett accordingly considered the study of human history indispensable, and he displayed a sprawling if uneven acquaintance with both the recent and distant past, including human pre-history (e.g. he was an early explorer of the Lascaux cave paintings).[38] He contemplated history not only as the story of the past but also in its future promise. Hence, he candidly writes in the "Preface to the American Edition" of the 1974/1975 editions of *Witness*:

> In the last volume of the *Dramatic Universe* published in 1965, I gave my reasons for believing that we are in the early stages of the Parousia, the Second Coming of Christ which heralds the end of the present world…. I am no less convinced than I was ten years ago and indeed discern growing evidence that the great event is in progress.[39]

Bennett's orientation towards the future, made him optimistic, however realistic he may have been about his own personal failings, and inclined him towards seeing the importance of good education. For him, the role of educator was another integral part of his mystic path, and led him in the direction of what he called "Systematics." In all this, Bennett's work appears as complementary to rather than separate from

---

[37] Bennett (1997) 46.
[38] Bennett (1997) 188.
[39] Bennett (1975a) iii.

Gurdjieff's. Yet, he is often criticised by those contemporaries who identify themselves as being within the Gurdjieff tradition. Sometimes the criticism is mild, and tempered with recognition of Bennett's abilities.[40] The most remarkable example of this may be the vignette presented by Cecil Lewis (1898-1997), one of the founders of the BBC. It is worth citing this passage, as we shall be returning to Lewis:

> To the everyday world (John Bennett) was a Director of the Coal Board and had a large house on Kingston Hill. This was the 'centre' where those who were close to him and his ideas lived. But name and address gave no idea of his personality and the magnetic quality of what he had to say and teach.
>
> In stature, he was a tall, good-looking man in his fifties, and had the air of being used to command. He spoke several languages, was widely read and seemed at much at home in philosophy or psychology as he was in higher mathematics. But all this variety was, so to speak, hidden beneath genial conversation and an evident open-hearted generosity of nature. He met all problems with assurance and authority, was never at a loss for an answer.[41]

So far so good. However, writing of the period after Gurdjieff's death in 1949, Lewis writes that, when he joined the Gurdjieff groups which had been organised in London and placed under Henriette Lannes:

> Somehow or other I had lost touch with John Bennett. In some strange way my admiration for him had faded. In fact I never saw him again and only watched from afar the bizarre developments in his own spiritual path.

[40] Opie (2011) 103-4.
[41] Lewis (1993) 136.

> To all who delve into the misty no man's land of spiritual archaeology his writings were of great interest because he brought to abstruse and difficult questions his own particular brand of articulate clarity…
>
> Unravelling the wool which Gurdjieff had effectively pulled over our eyes and reknitting it into new depths of understanding is one of the real gifts that Bennett brought to his master's work.[42]

There is a certain tension here between Lewis' evident admiration for Bennett, and his remaining at a distance to observe what he asserts, without further explanation, were "bizarre developments." Although Bennett introduced him to the Gurdjieff work, Lewis fell under the influence of other pupils of Gurdjieff, who themselves owed little to Bennett, and disapproved of some of his actions, and perhaps of the man himself. Hence, on one occasion, probably in 1955, at a meeting at which Bennett and many senior figures in the Gurdjieff groups were present, Jeanne de Salzmann (1889-1990) declared that the others should not speak with Bennett, because he was not keeping to Gurdjieff's line.[43] Bennett dates the separation to October 1955, but silently passes over the meeting.[44] Moore states that pupils at the Gurdjieff Society of London were advised "to avoid Coombe Springs like the plague."[45] Bennett was then at Coombe Springs.

The incident had precedent within the Gurdjieff tradition. A certain intra-family disdain had manifested at the time of his misunderstandings with Ouspensky in the 1930s, hence Ouspensky told pupils not to speak with Bennett, and Dr Maurice Nicoll was said to have disparaged Bennett as "The Showman,"[46] although Bennett for his part wrote of "Gurdjieff

---

[42] Lewis (1993) 152.
[43] A reminiscence of Annie-Lou Staveley who was present, and immediately afterwards offered a cup of tea to Bennett, who gratefully accepted.
[44] Bennett (1997) 256.
[45] Moore (2005) 45.
[46] Moore (2005) 170.

and his principal exponents, P.D. Ouspensky and Maurice Nicoll."[47] Taylor records that Bennett's offering a course and a diploma caused him to "suffer the scorn of many who followed Gurdjieff."[48] Michael Currer-Briggs, another personal pupil of Gurdjieff, is recorded as having stated that, to many pupils of Gurdjieff, Bennett's views about the future and its likely troubles "placed *action* before *self-questioning*."[49] Thompson notes that Bennett had relatively little personal contact with Gurdjieff until the last fourteen months of the latter's life, especially if compared to someone like Jeanne de Salzmann.[50] In 1953, Jean Toomer noted that the Wolfes, Welches, and Rita Romilly from the Foundation did not think "too well of Bennett (as he's) been out of the work too long."[51]

Yet, Bennett was never "out of the work" at all. Between 1924 and 1948, he had not been with Gurdjieff (although as we shall see he had made fruitless efforts to find Gurdjieff). However, he had been working with Ouspensky, often as an aide teaching the ideas and methods to literally hundreds of pupils. To an extent, *Witness* was effectively Bennett's apology or "reasoned defence" to de Salzmann and his critics from within the Gurdjieff tradition (and to those who deplored his association with John de Kay and the Sultan Abdul Hamid Estates). He chose, however, to make his defence indirectly, as a subsidiary and tacit aim of the volume.

Also, Bennett did not see his chief aim as being to pass on Gurdjieff's system. If I understand him correctly, his attitude was that Gurdjieff and only Gurdjieff could do that. Further, that would be to limit oneself to a given body or deposit. However, someone trained in Gurdjieff's system could do what was more important. Anthony Blake records:

> Just before he died, Mr Bennett told me that he considered his main personal task consisted in finding a way of enabling

[47] Bennett 1958) 48.
[48] Taylor (2001) 39 n.48.
[49] Opie (2011) 104.
[50] Thompson (1995) 30: a point not infrequently taken against Bennett as a pupil of Gurdjieff, let alone as a teacher in his tradition.
[51] Taylor (1998) 204 n.4. For other criticisms of Bennett by people within the Gurdjieff tradition, see Pittman (2012) 127-28.

the Western people he had to deal with to practise devotion.... In his language it is the "spiritualization of the feeling centre."[52]

0.6 ASPECTS OF THE EDWARDIAN INTELLECTUAL WORLD

It is desirable to lightly sketch some aspects of the intellectual world of Edwardian England (named for King Edward (1901-10)). I select those themes which are particularly pertinent to Bennett's interests. Darwin was the critical figure in the Edwardian intellectual world, in that the shadow of "evolution" was cast over all subsequent scientific and cultural history. Freud was significantly influenced by Darwin in several key aspects.[53] Equally influenced by the idea of evolution, and crucial for Bennett's intellectual development, was the work of scholars of mysticism such as Richard M. Bucke (1837-1902), Edward Carpenter (1844-1929), and William James (1842-1910). Bennett himself notes the critical historical importance of Einstein, Planck, Freud and Jung.[54] One of the most significant and enduring works of this period was R.M. Bucke's *Cosmic Consciousness*, published in 1901. Bucke was born the son of a Christian minister, but did not share his faith. He studied medicine, worked in mental health, became a Professor of Nervous and Mental Illness, and was an eminent member of psychological associations in both Britain and North America.[55] His thesis was that: "Cosmic Consciousness ... is a higher form of consciousness than that possessed by ordinary man."[56] He distinguished the "simple consciousness" shared by the "upper half of the animal kingdom" and humans, whereby we know are conscious of matters about us, from the "Self Consciousness" enjoyed by humans alone by which we are aware of ourselves as "distinct entit(ies) apart from all the rest of the universe," and can treat our mental states "as

---

[52] Blake (1980b) 23.
[53] Elleneberger (197) 236.
[54] Bennett (1966b) 144.
[55] Bucke (1905) 6-8; Schlosser (2018) 20-21.
[56] Bucke (1905) 1.

objects of consciousness."[57] Further, humans sometimes possess a third form of consciousness which he calls "Cosmic Consciousness." Of this he writes that:

> The prime characteristic ... is ... a consciousness of the cosmos, that is, of the life and order of the universe.... an intellectual enlightenment or illumination ... a state of moral exaltation, an indescribable feeling of elevation, elation, and joyousness ... [and] a sense of immortality, a consciousness of eternal life, not a conviction that he shall have this, but the consciousness that he has it already.[58]

Bucke believed that figures such the Buddha, St Paul, Plotinus, Muhammad, St. John of the Cross, Jacob Boehme, William Blake, Balzac, Whitman, and Edward Carpenter, but perhaps above all, Jesus Christ, possessed Cosmic Consciousness from a certain point in their lives.[59] Bucke began something of a trend of identifying "Christ" with a state of being available to other people besides Jesus, when he wrote that: "The Saviour of man is Cosmic Consciousness—in Paul's language—the Christ."[60] He made a point of including figures who stood outside Christianity, and the religious and monastic traditions of mysticism. To an extent, his vision rebrands Christianity, e.g. he writes: "Old things will be done away and all will become new,"[61] almost a direct quote of 2 Corinthians 5:17 and an echo of Revelation 21:4-5. Bucke's genealogy of cosmic consciousness would have been impossible without the mystical religious tradition. Further, his study veered towards an unverifiable occultism, when he asserted that "our descendants will sooner or later reach, as a race, the condition of cosmic consciousness, just as, long ago,

---

[57] Bucke (1905) 1.
[58] Bucke (1905) 2.
[59] Bucke (1905) *passim*, for Jesus Christ, see especially 85.
[60] Bucke (1905) 5.
[61] Bucke (1905) 4.

our ancestors passed from simple to self consciousness."[62] Accordingly, Bucke saw the human race on the cusp of an "indescribably hopeful" revolution in history, in which Socialism will abolish want, and religion will be rendered obsolete by direct experience.[63] Bucke was widely read and appreciated, not least by P.D. Ouspensky and J.G. Bennett.[64] The final chapter of Ouspensky's *Tertium Organum*, is basically a study of Bucke's volume, with lengthy quotations.[65] Robertson writes:

> Cosmic Consciousness is typical not only of turn-of-the-century interest in non-Western faiths but also of the era's efforts to reconcile religion and science. Conventional Christian doctrine suffered a staggering blow from nineteenth-century discoveries in geology and biology that contradicted the biblical account of creation.... but many intellectuals tried to find new paradigms that could accommodate both religion and science. For example, Alfred Russell Wallace, who shares credit with Charles Darwin for developing the theory of evolution by natural selection, was deeply involved in Spiritualism. In Wallace's view Spiritualist mediums were applying the same scientific methods to the immaterial realm that he had applied to natural history; he argued that Spiritualist investigation of the afterlife depended on immediate, empirical experiences that could be verified by those in attendance at a séance. The respected philosopher Paul Carus published *The Religion of Science* in 1893, which argued that scientific methods proved the immortality of the soul.... Bucke's evolutionary theory of

---

[62] Bucke (1905) 3.
[63] Bucke (1905) 3-4, see also 317-18.
[64] Ouspensky's profound interest in Bucke is noted in Schlosser (2018) 22-23, see Ouspensky (1981) ch. 23.
[65] I have checked both Ouspensky (1911), the Russian original, where it is ch. 21, and the revised English translation made by Ouspensky, where it is ch. 23.

human consciousness fits in easily with these late Victorian efforts to reconcile science and religion.⁶⁶

It is apparent from the finale of the first edition of *Witness* that this is also apt to describe Bennett's efforts in that book. Bucke included socialism in his mix of science and mysticism: the idea of "evolution" naturally embraces all human and even cosmic phenomena, and Bennett followed this natural development, rejecting any arbitrary and artificial limitation of the principles. Hence, it is striking, but not surprising that Bennett, like Ouspensky saw the summit of Bucke's book in the prophecy that a "NEW HUMANITY is at hand."⁶⁷ Ouspensky connected this to the idea of the "*superman*, who is already born and lives among us."⁶⁸ There is, of course, the influence of Nietzsche in this.⁶⁹ However, by 1929, Ouspensky had revised his views, and came to add to his stringent critique of Darwinian evolution, the conclusion that only individuals, not races, could evolve into the "Superman."⁷⁰ Bennett immediately accepted Ouspensky's ideas of the abstract division of humanity into two classes according to their conception of Superman, or the possibility of human development: it became the basis of his theory of "psychostatic," "psychokinetic" and "psychoteleios" people and orders, (i.e. asleep, seeking, and realised).⁷¹ He later came to share this opinion about individual rather than racial evolution. However, especially in his interpretation of his sixth vision at the Ostrovo swamps (section 4.6), he reflected aspects of Blavatsky's teaching in *The Secret Doctrine*:

> Now, Occult philosophy teaches that even now, under our very eyes, the new Race and Races are preparing to be

---

⁶⁶ Robertson (2008) 132.
⁶⁷ Ouspensky (1981) 277. The small capitals are in the original.
⁶⁸ Ouspensky (1981) 277-78.
⁶⁹ See chapter 3 in Ouspensky (1931).
⁷⁰ Ouspensky (1934) 21-25 and 120-21.
⁷¹ This is not a concept I pursue in any depth in this study, but see Bennett (2019) 124-34; and Blake (1980b) 19.

formed, and that it is in America that the transformation will take place, and has already silently commenced.

Pure Anglo-Saxons hardly three hundred years ago, the Americans of the United States have already become a nation apart, and, owing to a strong admixture of various nationalities and inter-marriage, almost a race *sui generis*, not only mentally, but also physically...

Thus the Americans have become in only three centuries a "primary race," *pro tem.*, before becoming a race apart, and strongly separated from all other now existing races. They are, in short, the germs of the Sixth sub-race, and in some few hundred years more, will become most decidedly the pioneers of that race which must succeed to the present European or fifth sub-race, in all its new characteristics. After this, in about 25,000 years, they will launch into preparations for the seventh sub-race.[72]

Bennett's predictions never had the same level of detail as Blavatsky endowed on hers. But this entire question of "evolution" and a coming "higher consciousness" in Blavatsky, Bucke, Ouspensky, and Bennett, shows how an avowedly scientific perspective, based on Darwinian insights, could merge into occult prophecies: after all, if humanity had evolved from non-human ancestors to this point, and evolution is progressive, then the emergence of some future race with advanced features was natural.

Gurdjieff was never affected by these ideas, but Bennett was. Bennett was also familiar with the high-profile work on mysticism of Evelyn Underhill (1875-1941), Dean Inge (1860-1954), and A.E. Waite (1857-1942), writers outside Gurdjieff's purview.[73] A good case can be made that in *Tertium Organum*, a book which made quite an impact on Bennett, Ouspensky was engaged in the quest to harmonize science and religion

---

[72] Blavatsky (1888) 444-45.
[73] Bennett (1961b) 10.

through the study of consciousness. This was possibly one of the inspirations of *The Dramatic Universe*.

Bennett makes the penetrating comment that belief in what I might call "utopian social reform schemes" had survived, although the schemes had been shown to be utterly unworkable.[74] He mentions Karl Marx (1818-83), and the *Communist Manifesto* of 1848 as "an expression of a new and essentially synergic mode of thought."[75] Marx, for Bennett, was a sign rather than an influence, a symptom of the all-permeating evolutionary principle. In the religious sphere, Bennett points to the Tai P'ing, Bab and Bahai, and Brahmo Samaj movements, in China, Persia and India, respectively.[76] He compares these to Kierkegaard, and his role in the development of philosophical existentialism, and "dialectical theology."[77] He later mentions spiritualism,[78] the importance of which in Edwardian England we can hardly appreciate today: it was no mere fringe interest. To acquire a sense of how serious a challenge spiritualism was to established religion, one might do worse than read R.H. Benson's novel *The Necromancers*, published in 1909. In art, Bennett identifies the rise of Impressionism with the passing of the dominance of Romanticism and Classicism, as a sign of "the essential unity of the artist and his subject matter."[79] Finally, according to Bennett, science and industry also reflected this synergic trend, notably in modern technology and the Hyde Park Exhibition of 1851.[80] "Evolution," then, was a cosmic principle unifying isolated fractions into a whole.

To obtain a balanced picture of how Bennett stood within his age we must note those influences to which he remained immune. For example, like Gurdjieff and Ouspensky, he was untouched by the surge of interest in eugenics and its cousin, racism:

---

[74] Bennett (1966b) 387.
[75] Bennett (1966b) 389. The *Manifesto* was, of course, co-authored by Friedrich Engels.
[76] Bennett (1966b) 388-89.
[77] Bennett (1966b) 389.
[78] Bennett (1966b) 391-92.
[79] Bennett (1966b) 391.
[80] Bennett (1966b) 390.

INTRODUCTION

> Racism obviously predated Darwinism, but during the nineteenth century—in part through the influence of Darwinism—it would undergo significant transformations. Before the nineteenth century, the intellectual dominance of Christianity militated against some of the worst excesses of racism. Christian theology taught the universal brotherhood of all races, who descended from common ancestors—Adam and Eve.[81]

There are too many examples of this view in Edwardian England for an exhaustive review, but there were loud calls to revise and overthrow traditional ideas on the family, marriage, and sex, with a view to facilitating "the upward evolution of the species,"[82] and of course to overthrow Christianity, as propagating outmoded and even dangerous views.[83] These views had an influence, weakly on Theosophy,[84] and a little more on Steiner,[85] but none whatever on Gurdjieff and Bennett. Webb is of the view that the age also saw a "flight from reason" in which those with occult leanings, fearing change, could be drawn into anti-Semitism, and people were divided into black and white categories, the former deserving nothing but hatred.[86] Bennett was free of this: he did not follow every road opened by cranks who appealed to "evolution." If social Darwinism stood for, or at least fostered the view that humans, being subject to natural laws, should discover new and natural values,[87] Bennett reaffirmed the enduring relevance of spiritual values drawn

---

[81] Weikart (2004) 103. See also Jeynes (2014), on "Race, Racism, and Darwinism."
[82] Weikart (2004) 130.
[83] Weikart (2004) 132.
[84] Blavatsky's criticism of Christianity, particularly fierce in *Isis Unveiled*, was not based on its traditional views of the family, marriage, and sex. Although she spoke of "root-races" and made many comments about "Aryans," Theosophists contend that Blavatsky was not racist since, e.g. different souls must incarnate in different races: Campbell (1980) 44-45 and 64-65, a point also made to me on July 11, 2022 by Simon O'Rourke, Education Coordinator, The Theosophical Society in Australia.
[85] Staudenmaier (2014) *passim*. Steiner's nuanced view of Christianity was not nearly so antagonistic as Blavatsky's.
[86] Webb (1976) 217-18.
[87] Weikart (2004) 123.

from the religious and mystical traditions (see the treatment of his first book, *Values*, section 5.4).

0.7 RE-EVALUATING BENNETT WITHIN THE GURDJIEFF TRADITION

This, then, indicates something of the nature of the intellectual world in which Bennett was born and grew up. I might make two further remarks. First, for those students of Gurdjieff who have studied his ideas with some care, Bennett's development of the heritage is of unmatched importance, even if his bolder flights of mind are often exploratory and suggestive rather than definitive. As an exponent of Gurdjieff's theoretical teaching, Ouspensky can never be surpassed, given not only his extraordinary abilities, but also the unique opportunities Gurdjieff gave him to learn the teaching. Yet, as Lewis indicated, there is much in Bennett's corpus which helps one to better understand Gurdjieff and his teaching. Staveley (1903-96), who was a personal pupil of Gurdjieff from 1946 to 1949 recalls that: "Bennett had been given a great deal of personal and concentrated teaching, as he was considered one of those most capable of passing Gurdjieff's ideas out to the world."[88] As we shall see, even de Salzmann shared that opinion.

Second, I think it fair to say that Bennett had some of the faculties of genius. He published a number of learned and scientific articles, wrote substantial books, and left behind many drafts, transcripts and recordings. His achievement in becoming a member of the BCURA and the Parliamentary and Scientific Committee when he had never studied at a university is more than remarkable (section 5.1). Bennett was perfectly capable of writing coherent and well-planned volumes, but his forte may have been delivering lectures and responding to questions: face to face engagement spurred him to draw on his tremendous reserves of knowledge and experience in a way he could not when alone, a point

---

[88] The foreword in Bennett (1991) 1.

well taken by George Bennett, his eldest son.[89] Much of this miscellaneous material, but not all, has been posthumously published. Most, but not all, has been collected. It is positively likely that pieces will turn up for some time. But the upshot of all this is that to judge Bennett only as a pupil of Gurdjieff, is to make a caricature of him.

This wilfully narrow perspective may be the basis of the controversy about the relationship between Bennett's teaching and Gurdjieff's, a controversy which was nourished by Bennett's championing of Pak Subuh and Idries Shah (chapters 9 and 10). Alongside those who marginalise him as a maverick, departing from the Gurdjieff line, there are those who defend him on the basis that he came back to Gurdjieff before his death. As we shall see, there are elements of truth in both the allegation and the defence. But neither of them captures the reality which was, I suggest, that even in his exploration of other teachers, Bennett was engaged upon the same search he had been on when he was a pupil of Gurdjieff, and was being as true to Gurdjieff's legacy as he could be, for Gurdjieff had never told his pupils to close their eyes to anything or anyone able to further their conscious aims. Gurdjieff told Bennett: "I am only a bridge; when you have got over the stream you can kick me away."[90]

One intriguing element of Bennett's thought and practice, affecting how one sees his relation to Gurdjieff, was the "principle of integration without rejection," within an ordered pattern.[91] For the other pupils of Gurdjieff, his helping Subuh and especially Idries Shah approximated more to "acceptance without discrimination." There is a widespread view among students of Gurdjieff, which the author shares, that Subuh was a sincere teacher from an Indonesian Islamic tradition, but that Idries Shah, on the other hand, was a *poseur*, a pretender to esoteric knowledge, who was prepared to deceive others when it was to his advantage. I trust that holding this opinion shall not prejudice the

---

[89] George Bennett (1990) 107-8.
[90] Bennett (2004) 252.
[91] I am indebted to A.G.E. Blake, one of Bennett's very closest pupils, for correctly insisting upon this point.

treatment of Bennett, but it does raise the question: did Bennett find something missing in Gurdjieff's teaching? This has necessitated a fuller study of Subuh and Shah than would otherwise have been necessary. Another aspect of this is the way that, through most of his life, Bennett was a magnet for controversy. To a significant degree, this was due to his having served in British Intelligence: it seems that few can enter that field without falling under suspicion. Jonathan Evans, Baron Evans of Weardale (Director General of MI5, 2007-13), wrote that: "Secrecy is not fashionable at the moment; it provokes suspicion."[92]

Further, Bennett made certain errors, particularly of association. The paradigm error in his life seems to have been his association with John de Kay, facilitated by Bennett's relationship and eventual marriage to Winifred Beaumont, de Kay's quondam mistress. As we shall see, Moore, in attacking Bennett, while admitting his brilliance, incidentally provides evidence that British government circles perpetuated the misunderstanding of Bennett which dogged him in the late 1920s, and leaked from there into the Gurdjieff groups. However, given his suggestibility to de Kay's persuasion, the British suspicion of Bennett was excessive but not baseless. As it happens, I am doubtful that Moore actually read the official records which he refers to but never quotes, for the simple but adequate reason that they flatly contradict his assertions. Likewise, I have been provided with a transcript from Dr. Philip Groves, who met Bennett in the 1960s, and admired his abilities, but unknowingly retailed false even vicious rumours about Bennett. For reasons of space, and its evident partiality, I have elected not to treat of it here. However, this does suggest to me that given Bennett's very prominence and capacity it was inevitable he would be both praised and traduced, and that the energy invested in these was proportionate to the strength of the impression he made. This is perhaps an exemplification of Newton's third law of motion predicting an "equal and opposite reaction."

Notwithstanding the element of what Lewis called the "bizarre," Bennett's ongoing influence has been substantial within the Gurdjieff

[92] Evans (2021) 16.

world, if not always apparent. Even today, almost fifty years after his death and over thirty years after that of Jeanne de Salzmann, there is still some bad feeling about what is seen as Bennett's straying from the way. This volume, by placing Bennett's development in context, and being able to draw on materials not available to his contemporary critics, may help to bring about a reappraisal of Bennett, and, incidentally, of Gurdjieff.

0.8   THE GENRE OF *WITNESS*

In this volume, I present my own critical interpretation of Bennett's *Witness*, setting it within the context of his life. One must be selective: the large amount of material produced at Coombe Springs and later at Sherborne would preclude a full and even coverage of Bennett's teaching, as would the complexity of his four-volume study, *The Dramatic Universe*, and his work on what he called "Systematics." However, it is possible to explore what I might call the "long concerns" of his life and his more notable achievements. In short, this is not a full study of Bennett's intellectual achievement, but it does strive to communicate the significance of the insights which Bennett intended to embed in *Witness*, while noting that at various points it also serves as a defence or *apologia* for his actions, and a sort of "educational biography." Classic examples of the reasoned self-defence available to Bennett, were Plato's *Apology* for Socrates, and John Henry Newman's *Apologia pro vita sua* ("defence of his own life"). *Witness* does bear some remote resemblances to the latter. As an educational autobiography, one thinks again of Newman, and also of *The Education of Henry Adams*, although I am not aware of any evidence that Bennett read either book.

Bennett unexpectedly passes over his childhood and school years in *Witness*, especially his interest in abstruse mathematics at an early age. His achievement at school had been substantial, and would have been especially impressive to people of his class and age. He explained that he began his account with his life just "twelve weeks before my twenty-first birthday... (because) My birth and boyhood seem irrelevant, as I have no memories that are different from those of any other boy I have known. It was only in France, when faced with death, that I began to see beyond death. From that moment I became a witness."[93] Further, he told Elizabeth Mayall, his third wife, that as a result of the near-fatal injury of March 21, 1918 (his first vision) he: "could remember only a few disconnected incidents of his childhood."[94]

I am sceptical concerning this partial amnesia, for three main reasons: first, Bennett does relate some of these memories, and they do not strike one as being merely "disconnected incidents." His sister Winifred made the acerbic remark, presumably after reading *Witness*, that it was: "as if his childhood didn't matter."[95] That is, his sister did not, apparently, believe that he had lost his memory. Second, Bennett also speculated that on March 21, 1918 his soul may have been replaced by the soul of someone who had lived in Turkey, and this is impossible to evaluate.[96] Third, as we shall see, the omission of his childhood fits in with his purpose in writing *Witness*; and there is the stubborn fact that even when recounting events after the first vision, he says next to nothing about either his own children, or his scientist brother, Arthur Lancelot (appendix 1), and they cannot have fallen under some blanket of amnesia.

I suggest that it is not that his childhood did not matter, but that nothing he could say of it mattered to the book he was writing. This presented Bennett with two dilemmas: first, to deliver his message "that death and resurrection can be experienced and verified during our present life on earth," he had to say a great deal about his life, because his life was his witness. However, if he said too much about it, readers might become lost in the details. Second, he had to mention his own errors, weakness, and vices, for the message was that everyone had real grounds for hope. However, if he painted himself in too black a hue, he might

[93] Bennett (1997) xvii.
[94] Elizabeth Bennett (2015) 67.
[95] Bennett (1997) xiii. The foreword, dated January 1997, is by George and Ben Bennett. It is of course absent from the 1962 edition.
[96] Elizabeth Bennett (2015) 67.

lose the reader's sympathy, and his entire message be rejected. Given the controversy around him, the book simply had to partake of the nature of an *apologia pro vita sua*. His solution was twofold: first, to draw limits around elements of his narrative, excluding his childhood, extensive discussion of his books, and many of his intellectual friendships (e.g. with A.N. Whitehead,[97] David Bohm and E.F. Schumacher), while hinting at rather than revealing any outright vices. Second, he adopted the voice of the wise older statesman, remaining without judgment of others, while quick to see how he himself had contributed to any misunderstanding. In this way, a cover of impartiality might fall upon the entire volume and its actors, himself included. Bennett implicitly invites the reader to adopt his compassionating and forgiving attitude. So, *Witness* is no straightforward autobiography, the subtitle of the revised edition notwithstanding.

This, I suggest, is a deeper reason why Bennett omitted from *Witness* much of the sort of material a biographer would welcome. Further, he made some errors, and sometimes, it seems, he was outright mendacious (section 6.6). Accordingly, while we are bound to use *Witness* as a framework, research is needed to fill out and sometimes correct it.

There is a related issue: Bennett's understanding of the word "witness." In the 1957 draft of *The Dramatic Universe*, he wrote: "Every event that we *witness* is an actualisation. That which is not actualised cannot belong to Fact, in just the same way as any game that is not played on a board of sixty-four squares cannot belong to chess."[98] I have italicised "witness." For Bennett, to *witness* is to perceive how the potential becomes actual, how this and higher dimensions intersect. In *The Dramatic Universe*, the "witness" was one who sought understanding, and could link "candidates" and "counsellors," which we might loosely paraphrase as "searchers" and "teachers."[99] Bennett means that he does not place himself on the same level as teachers like Gurdjieff, but believes

---

[97] Bennett (1949b) 3.
[98] Bennett (1952) 89-90.
[99] Bennett (1966a) 257.

that he can help bring others towards them. On this basis, *Witness* is also a protreptic, an exhortation and a help in seeking personal contact with a teacher. The first edition was also an exhortation to Subud. As revised, the protreptic, still implicit rather than earnestly urged, is to the mystic search for God. Hence, in both editions, he wrote:

> This book has its origin in the conviction that an essential part of man's duty upon earth is to bear witness to the truth as it has been revealed to him. Not everyone is called upon to express his vision of truth in a book or even in words at all. The finest witnesses are those whose lives are the evidence that the Reality behind outward seemings is supremely Good. My own life has certainly not been one of this kind, but I have been the witness of happenings in my own experience that have convinced me that the most interesting and the most important part of reality lies beyond the reach of our senses and our minds.[100]

This raises the fundamental question of how Bennett could know and witness to a reality beyond sense and mind. Bennett felt the reality of this challenge, and wrote: "I have sensed rather than seen, and if I can be called a witness, it is rather as a blind man who begins to see men as trees walking and is convinced, even though he does not understand."[101] It is entirely fitting, if the goal is mystical, that Bennett be a witness but a poor one, for who can fully plumb the divine mystery? Yet, he saw enough to be without fear of life or death, accepting of suffering and failure.

Therefore, as *Witness* is no straightforward autobiography, this book is no straightforward biography of Bennett, nor even an intellectual biography, or evaluation of his *apologia*. Such a study would be at

---

[100] Bennett (1997) xvii.
[101] Bennett (1997) xvii. This last metaphor is a reference to the words of a blind man healed by Christ, in Mark 8:24.

least twice as lengthy as this already considerable work, and delve into the details of his financial dealings in the 1920s. It would also have to diligently search the various editions of Bennett's published works, and the circumstances of their production, for a significant number of them were posthumously edited by various people who had differing ideas of the fidelity demanded by their roles, and in what their task consisted. Having before them a vast number of recorded talks, there were basically two options, which could be combined only if the first option was taken. The first option was to transcribe and publish all the talks, with minimal editing. The second option was to select thematic extracts from the talks but not to make the raw material available. The second option was taken, with mixed results. For instance, there is no indication that the talks at Beshara, found in *Intimations*, were edited, yet Blake, who assisted with that volume, regrets that some valuable material delivered at those lectures had been omitted.[102] Ben Bennett, J.G. Bennett's second son, wrote:

> of the books JGB published in print, a relatively small number were actually originally written down directly for publication. Bennett's very first work-related book *The Crisis in Human Affairs*, was a transcript of lectures. *The Dramatic Universe, Concerning Subud, Witness, Gurdjieff: Making a New World*, and the *Masters of Wisdom* were definitely put down in a form that could only be rendered in print. Of the remainder *A Spiritual Psychology* and *Long Pilgrimage* stand out as books that contain a substantial volume of material originally delivered orally, but extensively worked over by JGB himself. In the final years, the task of editing the books was increasingly and later wholly taken over by others, notably Tony Blake. ... Of the books edited by others, the editors had unrestricted freedom of movement (D. Seamon: *Elementary Systematics*; Blake: *Deeper Man*) ...*Transformation* stands out

[102] Bennett (1975b) vi, which refers to collection, not selection; and Blake (1980b) 18-19.

as an exception. Ken Pledge [its editor] was notorious for heavy-handed editing, and apparently the only copy of the original manuscript was destroyed after Ken's death by his nephew, so there is no possibility of verifying its authenticity. *Idiots in Paris* is of course taken from diaries. Elizabeth chose passages for publication from her own diaries and JGB's, George [JGB's eldest son] added a few more for the second edition.[103]

I have tried to note in the bibliography where a book published under the name of J.G. Bennett has been compiled and edited by someone else, usually Anthony Blake. I have enjoyed extensive correspondence with Blake, and am satisfied that he has diligently done his best to present Bennett's ideas, making minimal alterations of any description. If Blake has had a book published under the name of Bennett, then it can be taken that all of the ideas belong to Bennett, even if sometimes the formulation has been touched with Blake's pen.

It will be necessary to carefully consider Bennett's revisions of *Witness*, for they are as eloquent as anything he ever wrote about himself. He never disowned the conclusion he had come to in 1962, but it served now as a point of departure for the next stage of his voyage. He never disavowed Subud, but only the first edition, not the second, was written under the impression that he had seen all the decisive experiences of his life. The vast bulk of the two editions is identical. But there are important differences: first, Bennett added some new chapters to deal with some aspects of his life which had occurred since he wrote the first edition. Second, as we have seen, he also amended some of the final chapters of the first edition in significant ways, and in particular, he omitted the critical passage with which this introduction opened. As I suggested in section 0.1, *Witness* is, to no small extent, a modern instance of the *Ars moriendi*. I do not suggest that he was deeply read in this late medieval and early modern literature, although it is unlikely

[103] Email communication from Ben Bennett to the author and others, March 19, 2020.

he had not come across Jeremy Taylor's *The Rule and Exercises of Holy Dying*.[104] Bennett was quite capable of independently realising the value of his insights into dying.

In this introduction we have canvassed some of the reasons that Bennett's work and thought matter, noted some of the areas of controversy around him, and something of his distinctive thought. In particular, we have seen how he himself believed that an understanding of what he had witnessed would reveal something of the mystery of the "two-sided key" of death and resurrection. It is finally time to ask: to what did Bennett give witness?

---

[104] Atkinson (1992) xii-xiii.

Bennett outside the Djamichunatra at Coombe Springs.

CHAPTER 1

FROM CHILDHOOD TO NEAR-DEATH

1.1 CHILDHOOD

My ancestry is connected with England since ancient times. The name Godolphin has been given to eldest sons in my father's family for many generations. In *The Domesday Book* my Godolphin ancestors were recorded as feudal landowners since before the Norman Conquest. My Bennett ancestors for centuries owned the land where King Arthur's castle at Avalon was built and they hold to the ancient traditions that Joseph of Arimathea brought the Holy Grail to Glastonbury.[1]

Thus did John Godolphin Bennett open an unpublished autobiographical essay dated 1957. He gave pride of place to the ancient, mythological past; not only that his family had been a distinguished part of Albion, but also that they had passed the legend on to each generation as true. That belief may strike us today as quaint and fond, but it was not considered as such in 1957: the Reverend Lionel Smithett Lewis, M.A. published a book called *St Joseph of Arimathea at Glastonbury* in 1955, which was reprinted in October 1955, and again in 1958 and 1964. Lewis maintains, with vigour and self-righteousness, the thesis that the British Church was founded by Joseph of Arimathea, was preached to by St Paul (sic), and is the resting home of the Holy Grail which Joseph buried at Glastonbury.[2]

---

[1] Bennett (1957) 1.
[2] Lewis (1955) 26 and 28.

John Godolphin's brother was named "Arthur Lancelot," so it may be that this tradition was shared by his father, Basil, or possibly his mother, although she was American. Bennett's phrasing suggests that he himself probably did not believe in its literal truth, yet, it may not be fanciful to think that Bennett felt that he participated in it, and that something of its spirit was still alive in him. However, the sober reality is that the Godolphins are not mentioned in the *Domesday Book*, neither were his family "feudal landowners," and any truth behind the Arthurian legends is lost to history.[3]

According to the official birth certificate, John Godolphin Bennett was born on June 6, 1897 at 1 Pembridge Villas.[4] His father was Basil Wilfrid Bennett, and his mother Annie Caroline Bennett née Craig. Lancing College, where Basil Bennett attended school, kindly sent me the following extract from its records concerning Bennett's father:

> 1403. Bennett, Basil Wilfred, *b.* 5 June 1871, *s.* of L.W. Bennett, of 81 Westbourne Park Villas, w. School House, Left July 1889.[5]

At the time of John Godolphin's birth, Basil's profession was given as "Private Secretary," and his residence as 1 Pembridge Villas, Wimbledon Park Road, Wandsworth.[6] The Pembridge Association website states:

> The area covered by the Pembridge Ward was built on during the three decades between 1840 and 1870. An article

---

[3] I have checked the *Domesday Book*. For landholdings, see Appendix 1. For the Arthurian legend, see Hutton (2009), especially 31 and 32, that: "For much of the twentieth century, it seemed as if archaeology might succeed in locating a historical Arthur where textual analysis had failed," but that by 1975, only the year after Bennett's death, that hope had failed. I shall not here investigate the basis of Bennett's beliefs.
[4] Bennett stated that it was June 8, as did *The Times* obituary of December 18, 1974, but his birth certificate (see note 6), the military records and the 1939 UK Register, which I have seen, all have June 6.
[5] Email communication, January 26, 2021.
[6] Birth certificate 452 of 1897, from the County of London, Registrar's District of Wandsworth, Sub-District of Wandsworth.

in the Pembridge Association Newsletter in 1979 by Dr John Hayward, a noted historian, said that "the houses represent the style of a country which exercised a dominating influence throughout the world. That style was determined by the attempt to combine grandeur with economy of means. The facades, though constructed of stock brick, are covered with stucco, rusticated to imitate stonework, and are completed with complex mouldings, window frames, friezes and cornices".[7]

The area is quite desirable today: if browsing real estate agents' pages are any guide, a price of over five million pounds sterling for a freestanding house in this area is not, as of January 2021, unexpected. The Bennetts lived in a white-painted weatherboard home called "Casa Bianca."[8] In other words, it is a solidly upper middle-class area, and seems to have been much the same at the time of Bennett's birth. His father's profession of "private secretary" points to the same background. A modern web site states:

> Being a private secretary in a ministerial or senior official's office is a Whitehall rite of passage. Occupying this role is no guarantee of greatness ... but few who rise to the top make it without completing a tour of duty. Why? It pretty much goes without saying that most people working in private offices are clever. They also tend to have youth on their side, which leaves plenty of time for climbing the ranks.[9]

However, we do not know to whom B.W. Bennett served as private secretary, which limits how much we can infer. His father emerges as delightful, if feckless in some respects, perhaps even as somewhat quixotic: "I

---

[7] http://pembridgeassociation.london/our-history/ accessed January 24, 2021.
[8] Elizabeth Bennett (2015) 67.
[9] https://www.civilserviceworld.com/news/article/lurking-your-way-to-the-top-life-as-a-private-secretary accessed January 24, 2021.

was brought up in constantly changing surroundings. My father lost all his money and travelled the world, returning to tell me and my sister wonderful stories of the Amazon, the Nile and the Limpopo, of Russia and Turkey and Central Africa."[10]

Concerning his mother and her side of the family, the autobiographical note states:

> My mother was Annie Caroline Craig, descended from the Craig's and Neville's who settled in Virginia in the 17th century and with the Duquesne were the first families to own land in Pittsburgh, Pennsylvania.
>
> My great-great-grandfather was General Brown, of New England who commanded an American army in the war of 1812 and I still own the medal voted to him by a special act of Congress to commemorate his services to the nation. My great-grandfather, Major Jacob Brown, was chief mechanical engineer in the building of the Erie Railway, the first in the United States, and during its construction my grandfather, Isaac Eugene Craig was born in a houseboat on the Hudson River.
>
> At the invitation of the Czar of Russia, Major Jacob Brown went to Moscow to build the famous Moscow-St. Petersburg Railway, the first in Russia. He died of overwork at the early age of 45.
>
> My grandfather became a painter who settled in Florence where he met my grandmother who was an intimate friend of the Brownings and Rossettis, and he became a well-known member of the Pre-Raphaelite school.[11]

Perhaps items like the medal kept family memories alive in a tangible way, but details like his grandfather's birth in a houseboat will not have depended upon preservation of that worthy craft. This family, its

---

[10] Bennett (1957) 2.
[11] Bennett (1957) 1.

English scion included, was proud of its past. The memorandum continues: "When my father Basil Wilfred Bennett was in Florence in 1894 as a Reuter's correspondent in attendance on Queen Victoria, he met my mother who with her two sisters were known as the three gems of Florence."[12]

Bennett then comes to his own birth:

> I was born in London, on the 8th June, 1897, half English, half American, with strong associations for Florence. Both my father's and my mother's family numbered famous mathematicians, including Professor Arthur Cayley of Cambridge, one of the founders of modern geometry, of whom a friend wrote, "His soul too great for vulgar space, in N dimensions flourished unrestricted."[13]

Bennett's meaning is that these influences inspired him, and that the legend of Arthur Cayley (1821-95), was particularly significant. Bennett refers to a poem written by James Clerk Maxwell (1831-79) in 1874, addressing the portrait fund committee, which was commissioning a portrait of Cayley by Lowes Cato Dickinson (1819-1908). I shall not quote the entire poem, but Bennett, recalling the final lines from memory made only two small errors:

> O wretched race of men, to space confined!
> What honour can ye pay him whose mind
> To that which lies beyond hath penetrated?
> The symbols he hath formed shall sound his praise,
> And lead him on through unimagined ways
> To conquests new, in worlds not yet created.

---

[12] Bennett (1957) 1.
[13] Bennett (1957) 1-2. I cannot explain why Bennett states the date of his birth as June 8, when his birth certificate gives June 6, see note 3.

... Ye powers of the nth root of -1!
Around his head in endless circles run,
As unembodied spirits of direction.

... In two dimensions, we the form may trace
Of him whose soul, too large for vulgar space,
In n dimensions flourished unrestricted."[14]

However, as Michael Benham notes, there is no available evidence that Bennett was related to Cayley by blood.[15] Benham conjectures that the "connection is probably not through family but with Rev Henry Bennett when both families had trading interests in St. Petersburg."[16] Like Bennett, Cayley attended King's College.[17] Bennett was possibly inspired by two of Cayley's interests: "*n*-dimensional" and "non-Euclidean" geometry. Cayley "accepted the validity of models of non-Euclidean geometry," and, in his own words, contended that the problematic twelfth axiom of Euclid (the "parallel postulate") does "not need demonstration, but is part of our notion of space, of the physical space of our experience – the space, that is, which we become acquainted with by experience, but which is the representation lying at the foundation of all external experience."[18] These questions were to loom large and continuously in Bennett's intellectual life. Significantly, he tried to *visualise* how these abstruse ideas might be actualised.

The Wikipedia page, which I understand to often be edited by one of Bennett's sons, states: "In Bennett's infancy, his family were moderately wealthy and travelled frequently in Europe. In 1912, his father, who was a noted traveller, adventurer and linguist, lost all of his money and

---

[14] https://mathshistory.st-andrews.ac.uk/Extras/Cayley_poem/ accessed January 21, 2022, the story and the poem are found in Crilly (2006) 312-13.
[15] Both Benham and I conducted what registry searches we could, but these cannot be conclusive: email communication of June 30, 2022.
[16] Email communication from Michael Benham of June 30, 2022.
[17] Crilly (2006) 17.
[18] Crilly (2006) 384.

his wife's in an investment that failed."[19] This adds some details to the picture which has already emerged of a family of recently faded wealth, but continuing social claims. The travel must have included an early trip to Florence, for in volume 2 of *The Dramatic Universe*, he wrote:

> A Pietà of Michelangelo, formerly in the Florentine Bargello, was first seen by the present writer when a young child, and revisited several times at long intervals over a span of nearly sixty years. In the whole experience, a timeless quality emerges that was there from the first, and yet has deepened and been transformed into a fuller understanding of the value-experience that drew Michelangelo towards religious contemplation in his later years. It contributed to the formation in early youth of the conviction that there is an invisible reality that cannot be held within the limits of time and space.... As these lines are being written ... the present moment with its memories is one whole with innumerable impressions of Florence, recollections of the cadence of Italian poetry, and of a vivid present feeling for the direct religious insights vouchsafed to the greatest artists as their life on earth nears its close. And yet it is not any nor all these things. The emergent quality was there for the child almost too young for speech: it was renewed for the fifteen year old schoolboy who revisited Florence in 1912—it is neither the same nor is it different from what it first was.[20]

This helps explain his comment about a special affinity for Florence. His sister confided to his third wife that he was: "high spirited, highly intelligent and full of eccentricities and flights of imagination," to the extent that the local kindergarten could not handle him and he had

---

[19] https://en.wikipedia.org/wiki/John_G._Bennett accessed January 1, 2021.
[20] Bennett (1961) 4, see also 41-42.

to be sent to a day school.[21] He learned to play piano, possibly in early childhood,[22] when his family was most affluent. He would rush through his homework to get to other matters until, when he was older and he realised that his mother had little money, he applied himself to his studies, with the result that he won scholarships from that time, so that his mother never had to find the funds for his fees.[23]

Although Bennett would claim a lack of memory for events prior to March 21, 1918, he recalled that he had a non-religious upbringing, and that: "As a boy I had been revolted by the quarrels of the Christian Churches."[24] Further, at his school" (King's College, Wimbledon), there had been two Divinity teachers: "a mild but inept old clergyman" of very High Church persuasion, but the other "a ruthless fanatic" of the Low Church,[25] who "spoke of the Roman Catholic Church in terms that no schoolboy should be allowed to hear." The missionary lecturers harangued them "with such an accent of self-righteousness about the heathen … that I and many others wanted to become heathens on the spot." Bennett's mother, an American by birth, commented that the English, and especially their priests, were given to hypocrisy. His father's response was similar but more nuanced in an important respect: he drew a distinction between the religion and its representatives, saying: "Religion would be all right if it were not for the priests and missionaries; but missionaries are the worst." Perhaps his father was speaking of the Evangelical (i.e. Low Church) enthusiasm for establishing missions. Bennett adds that his father had attended Lancing College where he had undergone a "religious conversion," but that he had "afterwards reacted against institutional religion and had done his best to prevent us as children from acquiring any fixed beliefs against which we might afterwards revolt."[26]

[21] Elizabeth Bennett (2015) 67 and 69.
[22] Bennett (1962) 371.
[23] Elizabeth Bennett (2015) 69.
[24] Bennett (1997) 26.
[25] For a contemporaneous account of the High and Low Churches in the Church of England, see Benson (1910) 1-90.
[26] Bennett (1997) 26.

That Bennett's father attended Lancing College indicates that he came from an upper-middle class or professional family, and probably that his family favoured the distinctly High Church Anglican ethos of this public boarding school, which may perhaps have contributed to his father's pronounced distaste for missionaries, since English missionary activity was usually under the auspices of the Evangelical or Low wing of the Church of England.[27] That he lived in Pembridge Villas shows that he was, culturally and socially, of the upper middle class. However, we do not know whether he purchased his property, with or without a mortgage, or only leased.

Yet, if his rearing was with little direct influence of religion, there was an indirect moral effect from his mother, who: "brought me up strictly in her own mother's New England tradition of austerity, but I was an unruly boy always escaping expulsion from school by my scholastic promise and my athletic success."[28] At some time in the 1970s, while teaching at Sherborne, he recalled how his mother had disciplined their attitude to food. In an address to which the editors have given the title "The First Liberation: Freedom from Like and Dislike," Bennett said:

> If you [parents] do not from the earliest childhood instil in your children that being subject to like and dislike is slavery, you are depriving them of something that is going to be of much value. I know that I could not have come to what I have come to in myself if my mother had not done this for me. Every mother who does that for her children is really a blessing: a blessed woman.
>
> Every mother or father who gives way to their children's likes or dislikes is a curse to his or her children. That I can tell you with complete confidence from all my own life experiences and what I have seen in others…

---

[27] Gardner (1973) 176; and Gathorne-Hardy (1978) 101. On missionary activity within the Church of England, and the antipathy to High Church involvement, which nonetheless was real, see Stanley (2017) 4 and 10.
[28] Bennett (1957) 2.

> I have always been thankful to my mother for having insisted absolutely and pitilessly on eating everything that was put on the table, whether we liked it or not. We were never allowed to have an attitude of like or dislike towards food. It was equally unpardonable to like food as to dislike it. We simply had to eat what was put in front of us.[29]

Another rather illuminating reminiscence was made in the 1970s to his students at Sherborne:

> One of the powerful influences of my childhood was what we call in England a charwoman, a woman who used to come and work for my mother. Her name was Mrs Mursh, a London Cockney woman. She was so completely good and totally unselfish that in all these seventy years I still remember the influence she had on me when I was a wild, unruly child. She was one person I respected even more than my own mother, because I could not help seeing how everything that she did had no element of herself in it—like many women who are very poor and have a very hard life, she never complained.... What she had no idea of was that she was a manifestation of God, of the Work ... it couldn't have come about without much suffering and much self-discipline and a great sense of duty. I have no idea whether she had any kind of faith or not but I can't ever remember her talking about God or religion or anything like that.[30]

"Cockney" was, in Bennett's day, the dialect of the lower class, especially those of East London.[31] Mrs. Mursh perhaps impressed Bennett despite coming from such a background. Bennett would much later be

---

[29] Bennett (2006b) 12-13.
[30] Bennett (1979) 90-91.
[31] Santipolo (2003) 414.

received into the Catholic Church, and to experience something supernatural in the Eucharist. But this seemed an unlikely result for the child:

> It is hardly surprising that I grew up with very little sense of the reality of the Christian profession.... I experienced nothing in the Eucharist, and only went to church to please others. At that time, I had not met a single Christian, priest or layman, who appeared to me to have real faith in his profession.[32]

In 1943, in the foreword to his compilation *Values*, he wrote:

> The sacred literature of all ages and the speculative writings of the philosophers abound in passages which endeavour to express the ultimate values which form the goal of human striving. Some of these passages are well known—the most perfect are to be found in the Gospels—some are hidden away in obscure and ancient texts.... The object has been to give ready access to a few of the more precise and also the more pregnant statements in Eastern and Western literature. Passages from the Bible have been deliberately excluded as belonging to a different order of truth.[33]

This lofty appreciation for the Bible and especially the Gospels, needs to be taken into account when one considers his later career. It seems to me that he agreed with his mother, that it was only the hypocrisy in religion which should be rejected. He also learned from his father that religion was "all right," but rigidity was to be avoided. Having mentioned the schools attended by Bennett and his father, it is desirable to add a note on the English public schools.

---

[32] Bennett (1997) 26.
[33] Bennett (1943) 1.

1.2 PUBLIC SCHOOLS

There are two opposite errors to avoid: overstating the importance of English public schools in Bennett's career, and understating them. The schools must be mentioned, because to people who do not know anything of that system, especially as it was at the turn of the nineteenth to the twentieth century, it is hard to understand how significant they were in English life. First, from the eighteenth century, the leading established grammar schools, incorporated by English statute, began to refer to themselves as "public" schools in contradistinction to the privately owned schools, which were founded to teach subjects omitted from the curricula of the older grammar schools. The need for these private schools becomes apparent when it is realised that these new subjects included "English, arithmetic, geometry, geography, drawing and dancing."[34] By some point in the nineteenth century, this usage of the term "public school" became general, and both the revived grammar schools and the new foundations styled themselves as such "in imitation of the old leading grammar schools in order to gain something of their *cachet*."[35]

Bennett's school, the King's College School fits this mould. The King's College in London was founded in 1829, and the King's College School ("K.C.S.") first accepted pupils in 1831, preparing boys for the senior college.[36] Gardner states of K.C.S.:

> From the start the curriculum was modern as well as classical. It soon became a general school, preparing for all the universities, the services and the civil service. By the eighteen-seventies ... K.C.S. compared very favourably with any school in London. After sixty-eight years in The Strand, it was decided to move to a more open situation, with room

---

[34] Gathorne-Hardy (1978) 31-32, likewise Gardner (1973) 146.
[35] Gathorne-Hardy (1978) 32.
[36] Gardner (1973) 154-55.

for expansion; and an excellent site was found beside Wimbledon Common. In 1911 the school was separated from the College.[37]

In Bennett's time there, K.C.S. boasted a museum and its own science journal, "unrivalled in any English school."[38] It covered all sorts of scientific subjects, including the latest inventions. By 1909, it had an aeronautics editor, and it published the correspondence between its editor and Captain Scott.[39] Like some other public schools, it established a mission to the poor, and a Music Society.[40] Bennett later refers to his "school German,"[41] doubtless due to a programme, instituted by headmaster Rogers, of exchange visits between boys from K.C.S. and German lads.[42] During WWI, Rogers transferred his affections to Italy which may explain how Bennett could read Croce in Italian while recovering from his near scrape with death in 1918.[43]

Bennett's father had not been sent to K.C.S., but rather to Lancing College, the major school of the "Woodard movement," the centre of which was its extraordinary chapel. The Woodard schools were High Church, Anglican, and related to the Oxford Movement.[44] Basil Bennett belonged to the English middle class, and Canon Woodard, who founded Lancing in 1848, said that he envisioned raising a "new army of the middle classes."[45] It may be coincidence, but Rogers had taught classics to sixth form at Lancing earlier in his career.[46]

The public schools of the twentieth century formed a single system, having converged from three groups: first, the old elite establishments; then "revivified old endowed grammar schools;" and finally, the new

---

[37] Gardner (1973) 155.
[38] Hinde (1995) 63-64.
[39] Hinde (1995) 63.
[40] Hinde (1995) 65.
[41] Bennett (1997) 1.
[42] Hinde (1995) 66.
[43] Bennett (1997) 4.
[44] Gardner (1973) 174-76.
[45] Gathorne-Hardy (1978) 69 and 101.
[46] Hinde (1995) 61.

foundations of the nineteenth century.[47] Gathorne-Hardy separates the sixty-four leading public schools for the period between about 1880 and 1902 into four classes. His first group comprised twenty-two schools, such as Eton, Harrow, and Rugby. The second group numbered eight schools, including Lancing. Group three has twenty schools, and the fourth some fourteen, amongst which he places Kings College School.[48]

The importance of the public schools was manifold. First, at least from the seventeenth century, having attended a particular public school became a significant part of one's identity, and Old Boys (meaning boys who had been at the same school) would help one another in adult life. By the nineteenth century, there were "tight-knit far-flung societies" based on and contributing to "the post-school obsession that haunted many boys until they died.... it was clearly understood by the early nineteenth century that to send a boy to certain schools was to introduce him to friends who would be influential in the future."[49] As Evelyn Waugh's character Captain Grimes explained in *Decline and Fall* (1928):

> "I'm a public school man. That means everything. There's a blessed equity in the English social system," said Grimes, "that ensures the public school man against starvation. One goes through four or five years of perfect hell at an age when life is bound to be hell anyway, and after that the social system never lets one down.[50]

Gathorne-Hardy relates the rise of the public school to a burgeoning class consciousness in English society. The public schools were "annexed," as he puts it, by the upper and middle classes, providing one source of the power of those classes.[51] The upper class, as classically understood, is the titled nobility. Gathorne-Hardy acknowledges the difficulty of defining

---

[47] Gathorne-Hardy (1978) 94.
[48] Gathorne-Hardy (1978) 440-43.
[49] Gathorne-Hardy (1978) 47.
[50] Waugh (1928) 29.
[51] Gathorne-Hardy (1978) 48.

the middle class, but states that it included those who not only wanted to but had the means to send their sons to these public schools in the 19th century.[52] The Old Boys of these schools, including many land-owning aristocrats and gentry, would therefore comprise great numbers of politicians.[53] They would send their sons to their old schools; and so continue making connections and alliances.[54] The public schools became desirable destinations for the children of the middle classes, as "The avenues by which the newly rich families could join the upper classes were already—and became increasingly and soon almost solely—the public schools."[55] The scions of the middle classes who attended these schools would then adopt the dress, accent, behaviour, and manners of the upper class.[56] The aristocracy and land-owning gentry had ultimately earned their power and wealth by their military service for their feudal overlords: "The class deference of the 19th century and early 20th century had, at its heart, the hierarchical deference of a fighting machine."[57]

However, one cannot say that because Bennett, or anyone else, attended a given English public school, they were inevitably moulded a certain way. The public schools were also known to foster some people of a rebellious frame of mind, displaying: "revulsion against things—class arrogance, tyrannical authority, attempts to impose conventions and so on—experienced for so long, so intensely, when so young."[58] Thus, Bennett's education provided him with a wide range of possibilities. Like his father, Bennett had opportunities available only to privileged Englishmen. The Bennetts did not belong to the aristocracy, but they could mix with them on easy terms. The young Bennett, and more especially his father, lived in the golden age of the British Empire, when the "heaven born" Englishmen of the Indian Civil Service were sent from their gilded perches to rule over the vast Subcontinent. The

---

[52] Gathorne-Hardy (1978) 69.
[53] Gathorne-Hardy (1978) 49.
[54] Gathorne-Hardy (1978) 50.
[55] Gathorne-Hardy (1978) 51.
[56] Gathorne-Hardy (1978) 50-51.
[57] Gathorne-Hardy (1978) 52.
[58] Gathorne-Hardy (1978) 65.

world domination of the English upper and middle classes is difficult to imagine today: but glimpses are afforded through the fiction of Rudyard Kipling (1865-1936). This is the social world into which Bennett was born.

The only other anecdote I can find of his childhood is his recollection that, while a child of unspecified age, Bennett was told that each seventh wave was larger than the preceding ones, an idea which so fascinated him "that I was determined to know whether it was true or not."[59] He does not say any more about these youthful investigations.

1.3   BENNETT AT KING'S COLLEGE SCHOOL

As a child, Bennett was sent to the King's College School, Wimbledon, which has helpfully provided copies of *The King's College School Magazine*, mentioning him. Taking the pertinent articles in chronological order, in the April 1914 edition of the School Magazine, there appears this article, "Characters of the XV":

> J. BENNETT (11st. 7lbs.) A really clever, bustling forward who has come on tremendously this season. Very good both in the loose and out of touch. Makes the most of his weight in the scrum. (p. 19)

For those not initiated into Rugby, I am informed that: "In rugby, like most ball sports, possession of the ball is vital and this player [i.e. Bennett] was very good at securing possession for his team when it was being contested. In rugby when the ball goes out over the sideline they re-start play with the team not sending it out throwing it in. Several players from both sides line up 1 metre apart and the ball is thrown in between them. This is called a lineout and back in those days the taller players and good jumpers would be best for line out play to obtain the ball for their team."[60]

---

[59] Bennett (1975) 5.
[60] Email communication from Philip Azize, dated January 18, 2022.

In *The King's College School Magazine* of March 1915, page 10, we read of Bennett as: "A clever forward who has led the pack with success, but has rather spoilt his play and his leading by expressive winging. Is dashing in the loose and very good out of touch, but has lost much of his tackling power. Should make a very good captain next year." On page 13 of the same magazine, dated as the December 1914 edition, but surely a mistake for 1915, it bears the prize list of July 1915. Bennett received both the mathematical scholarship and the Maclear prize: the latter being a divinity prize in 1915.[61]

The July 1915 edition includes Bennett in a list of "Cricket Characters" on page 15: "Is very keen and has often helped the tail to wag. Is alert in the field and has safe hands, but is rather a wild throw-in." In this sport, "specialist batsmen normally bat in positions 1 to 6 and then usually the wicketkeeper bats at number 7. The specialist bowlers bat from position 8 to 11 and that is called the 'tail' ... so for 'the tail to wag' they had to bat well and score runs as they were only expected to score much less runs the top 7 batsmen. So (Bennett) could bat a bit and stay in and help the other bowlers also score runs. A "wild throw-in" ... means (that) when the fielders are standing near the boundary fence their throw back to the wicket keeper was erratic."[62]

In the April 1916 edition, page 10 features an article by Bennett titled, "Football Retrospect, 1915-1916." The retrospect presents as justly proud of solid achievement, without being self-congratulatory: "This season has been a most successful one, and the record of eight matches won out of ten played is the best for some years past. Although, as was to be expected, handicapped by youth, inexperience, and continual changes, the 1st XV has been one of the best-trained and united teams the School has known.... Thanks to the captaincy and good play of our earlier captain A.C.B. Harrison, the first half of the season was especially

---

[61] Dr. Inglis of King's College has helpfully advised that: "the prize was named in honour of the Rev Dr George Maclear, the second head master of King's College School (head from 1866 to 1880). The prizes were awarded to pupils who excelled in Divinity." Email to the author of January 21, 2022.
[62] Email communication from Philip Azize, dated January 26, 2021.

successful." Bennett was captain in the second half. Bennett was clearly a good and intelligent rugby player, as evidenced by the fact that he spent so long in the First XV. Some of the reports seem remarkably even-handed: "The team has been distinctly better outside than forward.... At fullback, Dryland has been invaluable ... The forwards have a distinct tendency to be lazy, with the exception of Roney and Peake. The work in the loose was nearly always excellent, marred only by a tendency to think that one or two are a forward rush." On the same page begins the "Characters" feature. It states:

> J.G. Bennett. Has led the forwards throughout and been captain for the second part of the season. His leadership has always been marked by brilliance, as well as by keenness. As a player he is more brilliant than sound, though latterly the development of a hard tackle has made him a much sounder player. His worst fault is hanging about, but in important games this has been entirely absent. Out of touch and in forward rushes he has been uniformly excellent." (pp. 10-11)

I am informed that this indicates that: "He was probably lazy or slack at defence/tackling but later on improved his tackling. Hanging about meant he would not get overly involved in the ruck (which is where the ball is) and get physical, but would wait for the ball to emerge from the ruck.[63] Bennett himself made the pithy comment: "I was captain of the school rugby team at King's College School, London, and second in the school's athletic championship."[64] His time at the school was therefore distinguished, both intellectually and athletically.

In July 1916, the "Valete" column featured seven Kingsmen, by far the longest entry being:

> **J.G. Bennett**, VI. Form. Prefect, Head of West House,

---

[63] Email communication from Philip Azize, dated January 26, 2021.
[64] Bennett (1957) 2.

FROM CHILDHOOD TO NEAR-DEATH

Sergeant in O.T.C., "A" Certificate, 1st XV, 1913-14-15-16. Capt. 1916. 1st XI 1915. Mathematical Postmastership at Merton College, Oxford, Dec. 1915. Edgell Hunt Science Scholarship, 1914. Mathematical Scholarship, 1915. Secretary of Chemical Society, 1913-14. Editor of School Magazine, July 1915. Games Committee. School Record for High Jump, 1916, 5ft 4¾in. Public Schools' High Jump, 1915. Passed 4th into Woolwich, 1916.

A "postmastership" is a scholarship at Merton College: the institution having been founded in that name by John Wyliot in the 1380s.[65] He was not to return to his old school until after WWII, when he received the "King's College revelation" (section 6.3). Bennett later recalled how his headmaster wrote of him: "He suffers from intellectual arrogance,"[66] and his Sixth Form Master would shake his head at him and cite 1 Samuel 15:22: "To obey is better than to sacrifice, and to hearken than the fat of rams."[67] In 1958's *Concerning Subud*, he wrote:

> When I was at school I was made by my headmaster, Lionel Rogers, a true mystic at heart, to learn by heart Robert Bridges' Lines on a Dead Child, which I quote, probably inaccurately, from memory after nearly fifty years:
>
> "Ah, little at best can all our hopes avail us
> To ease this sorrow, or cheer us when in the dark
> Unwilling, alone, we embark,
> And the things we have seen and have known
> And have heard of – fail us!"[68]

I return to this below, when I deal with Bennett's first vision. However,

---
[65] https://www.merton.ox.ac.uk/about/history-merton accessed January 20, 2022.
[66] Bennett (1997) 124.
[67] Bennett (1997) 249.
[68] Bennett (1958) 152-53. The only error is that Bennett has "ease" for "lift."

Bennett's ongoing admiration for Herbert Lionel Rogers (1871-1950), who was headmaster of Kings' College from 1910 to 1934, is apparent. He was regarded as rather too strict, and was generally unpopular with the boys.[69] However, it corresponds somewhat with Bennett's assessment that one of his students recalled: "He was completely in control of his classes because he was completely in control of himself."[70]

In *Deeper Man*, posthumously prepared by A.G.E. Blake and Brian Hartshorn from the lectures which Bennett had been delivering in his series "The Study of Man,"[71] Bennett states: "Nearly seventy years ago, when I was a boy, I read two books, both written in the 1890s that had a considerable influence on me. One was called *Flatland* and the other was ... called *The Fourth Dimension*."[72] He then describes the books, and in particular how Hinton gave "exercises to help the reader try to visualize four-dimensional bodies such as a four-dimensional cube called a "tesseract." ... When I was a boy, I was interested in all this, and used to practice a great deal trying to visualize different sorts of arrangements, different kinds of possible worlds ... I started this when I was about fourteen or fifteen years old and continued it for many years afterward."[73]

This is another sign of the ongoing significance of Bennett's childhood for him. Yet Bennett said little about his childhood. I have consulted several people who knew Bennett personally, and all stated that he was not so much reticent about his past as that it did not seem to occur in conversation. Perhaps he did not want to discuss it, or to arouse a purely personal interest in himself. It is equally possible that he felt that the type of qualification he had obtained at King's College was solely due to his natural talents and not to any special efforts which would be instructive to readers. He had grown up in the blessed green island of Edwardian England, but afterwards, something extraordinary had come

---

[69] Hinde (1995) 66-67.
[70] Hinde (1995) 80.
[71] Bennett (1978) 8.
[72] Bennett (1978) 92. Both books were by Charles H. Hinton (1853-1907), whose work was also an influence on P.D. Ouspensky.
[73] Bennett (1978) 92-93.

his way and he had participated in it. For Bennett, his engagement with the extraordinary was what deserved notice.

1.4 BENNETT IN WWI

In the autobiographical essay of 1957, Bennett wrote:

> Then came the 1914 war and I entered the Royal Military Academy, Woolwich, as a prize cadet, having achieved the highest mark ever recorded in Natural Science at the entrance examinations. Passing out first as a signal officer, I was appointed the first wireless officer of the famous Guards Division and went to France in 1917-18. In the great German offensive of March 21, 1918, I was wounded by shrapnel and sustained such a severe head injury that I was not expected to live. For five days I was in a coma and during that time had experiences that have changed the whole course of my life.[74]

Bennett was indeed commissioned as 2nd Lieutenant in the Corps of Royal Engineers.[75] Some relevant information about his experience as a soldier is found in the preface to the fourth volume of his master-work, *The Dramatic Universe*. Published in 1966, Bennett writes:

> The temerity of seeking for an explanation of all experience requires that some account be given of the genesis of the undertaking. It arose from the intense experiences that I shared with millions of others in the First World War. The waste and horror of the war convinced most young people that the static beliefs in which we had been nurtured were no answer to the problem of human foolishness and ineptitude. In my case, disillusion was tempered by my

---

[74] Bennett (1957) 2. I have been unable to locate any of the relevant records.
[75] Email communication of June 30, 2022.

faith in natural science which, at that time, seemed to offer hope of answering ultimate questions. I could see clearly enough that the general belief that the laws of nature were absolute and inviolable conflicted with the equally general, but tacit, acceptance of human responsibility and hence of human free-will; but I also believed that even this intractable problem would yield to scientific research, and thought I knew where the solution would be found. For some reason that I have never been able to discover, I had from early youth been devoted to Non-Euclidean Geometry. My favourite reading in the trenches was Coolidge's *Elements* and I spent most of my spare time trying to acquire the power to visualise constructions not allowed in conventional space and time.[76]

The book Bennett is referring to must be *The Elements of Non-Euclidean Geometry,* by Julian Coolidge (1873-1954), published by Oxford University Press in 1909. If, as he states, he had no memories which others boys did not have before the event of March 21, 1918, yet, someone who studied two- and four-dimensional worlds at the age of fourteen or fifteen, and read Non-Euclidean Geometry in the lines of WWI France, must certainly have had thoughts which other boys rarely had.

Bennett has little to report about his service in the British Army in WWI. In a tangential comment, he later mentions how "Up till then I had always been part of some large machine, such as the Army, and even if I had been independent to the verge of insubordination, I had never been alone."[77] However, he provides no further details. We turn now to the "Near Death" experience which Bennett placed in the title of the first chapter of *Witness*.

---

[76] Bennett (1966) vi-vii.
[77] Bennett (1997) 72.

1.5   THE FIRST VISION: MARCH 21, 1918

On the very first page of *Witness,* Bennett wrote: "The real beginning of life came to me with the taste of death, on the morning of 21 March 1918."[78] He begins directly with a confrontation with death as he sat in the chalk caves of Roeux listening to the Germans' field telephone by means of a new device:

> The hours passed. No one came to relieve me. Messengers came every hour to take away the notes I had made.... During this time, by a strange freak, I tuned in to hear the letters *S.O.S.* signalled.... A ship had just been torpedoed in the North Sea and was sinking.... The shock had filled me with new energy and I had lost the wish to sleep. When I was relieved, I was astonished to learn that two nights and two days had passed and I had neither slept nor stopped listening.[79]

As he was returning to his base, fatigue struck him down. He tumbled into a bath of mud, and eventually "awoke feeling very, very cold and weak."[80] He returned to his duties, and the expected heavy German attack broke out. At that time: "My state was that strange condition known to all who have experienced extreme fatigue. The physical sensation is of a kind of disembodiment. There is a headache that is painful and even frightening, but with it a sense of being set free from the limitations of ordinary existence. Under favourable circumstances, this state can pass into one of complete clarity in which the ordinary self is aware of the presence of a consciousness higher than its own."[81]

The taste of death itself came three days later, riding through a German bombardment on a motor-bike. He recalled being surprised

---

[78] Bennett (1997) 1.
[79] Bennett (1997) 1-2.
[80] Bennett (1997) 2.
[81] Bennett (1997) 2.

that he was neither afraid nor indifferent, yet he must have been struck by some shrapnel, for:

> My next memory is of waking up—not inside, but outside my own body. I knew I was not dead. I could see nothing and hear nothing, and yet I perceived that my body was lying on a white bed. I gradually became aware that there were other men present, and somehow I was seeing what they saw and even feeling what they felt. I am quite sure that my eyes did not open and that I had no sensation of my own body. Yet I was aware [of many things] ...
>
> One very clear memory is of a man in a nearby bed. I knew he was an army padre and I knew that he was afraid of dying. I knew that in some way he was stuck to his body and I was not stuck. Some thought passed through me like: "How strange—he doesn't know that it will not hurt him if his body is destroyed!"
>
> At that moment, it was perfectly clear to me that being dead is quite unlike being very ill or very weak or helpless. So far as I was concerned, there was no fear at all.... Yet I was not totally disconnected from [my body]. When my body was taken to the operating theatre, I went with it.... later I was told that I remained in a coma for six days.... there remains with me something that is not memory as when one remembers past events. It is the awareness that I entered some realm of experience where all perceptions are changed and our physical bodies are not required.[82]

Bennett muses whether a baby might be born knowing what it is like to be without a physical body, but then lose this "taste once he is well and truly fixed in the body that is to accompany him through this

---

[82] Bennett (1997) 3.

earthly life."[83] In in 1958's *Concerning Subud*, Bennett related a much shorter account of this experience. He cites the Bridges poem, extracted above in section 1.3, continuing:

> These lines were somehow a formative factor for my understanding. Two or three years after I had learned them I was severely wounded in France, and I certainly then had the experience of leaving my comatose body and entering into a state of discarnate consciousness. In this condition, I was quite unaware of the presence of other bodies, but I could perceive the inner experiences that were proceeding in people near by. I then saw without doubt that the fear of death comes from the illusion that our real existence is dependent on our bodies.
>
> Later, when I was slowly recovering and regaining the use of my paralysed left arm, I remembered Bridges' poem, and saw how true it is that the "things we have seen and have known and have heard of fail us," but that we have something in us that is unseen, unknown and unheard of, and that this will never fail us. Only, we need to be conscious of it, if we are to be delivered from fear of the unknown.[84]

To say that: "I was quite unaware of the presence of other bodies, but I could perceive the inner experiences that were proceeding in people near by," makes clear that his perceptions were somehow intuitive and not visual. Also unique to this account is the reflection that: "we have something in us that is unseen, unknown and unheard of, and that this will never fail us. Only, we need to be conscious of it, if we are to be delivered from fear of the unknown." Although omitted from *Witness*, this is germane to Bennett's message in that volume: they express his urgent message of hope, i.e. that we should fear neither death nor life.

---

[83] Bennett (1997) 3-4.
[84] Bennett (1958) 153.

However much they otherwise differ, the two accounts are alike in bringing out that he felt no fear, that neither need the army padre have felt it, and neither need we.

Although he was unaware of the passage in *Concerning Subud*, this incident was noted by Schleiter in his study of the near-death experience, Christianity, and the occult, *What Is It Like To Be Dead?* He observes that Bennett describes his experience both as "being dead" and "near death"; and that despite a certain ambiguity, this experience provides a recurring theme throughout the volume.[85] This was the first of the critically important occasions when Bennett saw "death from the inside,"[86] I suggest that his interest in higher geometry facilitated his awareness that what we perceive in this world can appear differently from the perspective of another dimension of existence. Bennett saw this experience of March 21, 1918 as being "as much a birth as a death – though I did not realize until much later that I had indeed died and been born again."[87] This explains, I suggest, the confidence which Bennett expresses in his final book, *The Masters of Wisdom*: "I am sure that we can accept literally the greater part of the accounts of miraculous healing (by Jesus) and even the raising from the dead of the daughter of Jairus."[88]

1.6   AFTER ACTIVE SERVICE

Bennett was sent to England to recuperate. He says that when he was taken to Military Hospital in Cambridge, a new life began for him.[89] Bennett later considered that, beginning in about 1929, he underwent a sustained period of death and rebirth, marked by a serious bout of tuberculosis. Bennett's experience of passing away and coming back anew may partially explain his silence on his childhood, but it is hardly adequate to explain the little space he allows for his family from whom

---

[85] Schlieter (2018) 13-14.
[86] Bennett (1997) 1.
[87] Bennett (1997) 4.
[88] Bennett (1977a) 61.
[89] Bennett (1997) 4.

he now felt a certain distance, although he was back home. Yet, at the same time, Bennett's family were quite significant in his life: his father had impressed him as a "great traveller" of South America, Africa, and Asia.[90] Fitzmaurice, former Chief Dragoman at the Sublime Porte, knew his father, and that his father knew Turkish.[91] As we shall see, his mother turns up time and again in the course of his life—even after her death (sic). Bennett notes that, when he had been sent back to the First Eastern General Military Hospital in Cambridge, his injuries were relatively mild:

> But I myself was no longer the same. The youth who had left England in 1917 was no longer living in my body. And yet I was living his life—the life of a stranger. Even though I could remember his thoughts, I could not feel his feelings.[92]

While he was recuperating in Sir Arthur Shipley's premises, Bennett had conversations with several eminent Cambridge academics, most notably for the future, the Sadleirian Professor of Pure Mathematics, E.W. Hobson (1856-1933), with whom Bennett discussed the geometry of higher dimensions. In the March 1952 draft of *The Dramatic Universe*, Bennett wrote:

> Having been inspired by the researches of Arthur Cayley—a distant cousin and boyhood hero of mine—to take an interest in non-Euclidean geometry, I had devised a geometrical calculus of imaginary rotations sufficiently promising to prompt J. A. Hobson, the late Sadleirean Professor at Cambridge, to whom I showed it in 1918, to recommend its publication. The combined influence of my mathematical speculations and my inner need to reconcile the belief in universal causality

---

[90] Bennett (1997) 6.
[91] Bennett (1997) 6.
[92] Bennett (1997) 4. Michael Benham has alerted me, via email of August 21, 2022, that Bennett was first admitted to the renowned First Eastern General Hospital https://www.youtube.com/watch?v=pAU9rzL9SME.

with an equally strong conviction that freedom is a real material agency, convinced me that most of the philosophical difficulties which men had wrestled with for centuries would disappear if the framework of space-time were to be replaced by a five-dimensional framework in which eternity plays the inverse role to time.

A few years later I met P.D. Ouspensky and found that he had come to similar conclusions as to the need for a fuller scheme of dimensions, but interpreted this in terms of the cyclicity of time, and what he called 'eternal recurrence'.

We shall return later to Ouspensky, but in *Witness*, Bennett relates his geometry to his first vision, the death and rebirth experience: "I had already begun to suspect that there might be a connection between geometrical higher space, and the world without bodies, of which evidence had been shown me on 21 March. Hobson encouraged me by saying that a theorem I discovered about rotations in a space of five dimensions was worth publishing. It was an exciting time for a young man whose life had been lived in the obscurity of a London suburb."[93]

This also raises a question: how was Bennett able to even discuss advanced geometry with Professor Hobson, electrons and relativity with Sir Joseph Thompson, and tensor calculus with Sir Joseph Larmor?[94] Whatever facilitated this prodigious theoretical achievement, it must have been related to his time at King's College and his desire to emulate Cayley, his distant relative (whether of the blood or of sympathy). This also shows that Bennett had already begun to relate his death-experience to mathematical theory. Also significant for his future, Bennett now met General Jan Smuts (1870-1950), who invited Bennett to visit him in South Africa; an invitation which was honoured some thirty years later.[95]

---

[93] Bennett (1997) 4. Hobson is mistakenly referred to as "J.A. Hobson," a different man, although also a professor.
[94] Bennett (1997) 4.
[95] Bennett (1997) 4.

Bennett's physical condition deteriorated, and he was sent to Craiglockhart Military Hospital near Edinburgh,[96] where he had another experience of being separated from his body, although on this occasion, he did not experience death and rebirth: "My body was walking and behaving foolishly: but I was not concerned—why should I be?"[97] This fearlessness is reminiscent of the earlier separation. When he tried to explain his experience to Henri Bergson he found the philosopher kind but not attentive, only interested in ideas, not people, and for a long time he did not speak of it to anyone.[98] This chance meeting, arranged by Bennett's German teacher when Bergson was speaking at Edinburgh, was to be, in some ways, repeated when Bennett later realised that his pupils would bring their suffering to him, and he, in his turn, would respond purely intellectually.[99] The autobiographical essay states:

> For some weeks [after the near death experience] I was partly paralysed but finally recovered my strength so completely that ten months later I was chosen to play Rugby for the British Army against the famous New Zealand team, the "All Blacks."[100]

The next significant episode was his learning Turkish although he "prided himself" on being a mathematician" and not at all as a linguist.[101] He worked at Turkish with real energy, taking the regular classes plus additional evening classes, and committing Turkish poetry to heart.[102] The amount of time he could work without respite was remarkable: as

---

[96] Michael Benham has advised me, by email of August 21, 2022, that Bennett misspelt the name of Craiglockhart War Hospital, a psychiatric hospital for shell shocked-officers. https://blogs.shu.edu/british-modernism-undergraduate/2017/11/24/craiglockhart-war-hospital/
[97] Bennett (1997) 5.
[98] Bennett (1997) 5.
[99] Bennett (1997) 133-34, dealt with below.
[100] Bennett (1957) 3. This is not entirely true, it was not the All Blacks, and although selected, he may not have played: see appendix 1.
[101] Bennett (1997) 5.
[102] Bennett (1997) 6.

we saw in his 48 hours of constant activity in the chalk caves. Bennett also now came to an insight into the way that language dominates without determining our thought.[103] Bennett provided more details in the autobiographical fragment, appearing to link his Turkish interests with the near-death experience:

> [M]y thoughts and interests had been opened to a new field—the search for that invisible, supra-sensible Reality from which the veil had been lifted briefly during my days of coma. I felt myself drawn to the East and by a series of rash actions—put right by strange and unmerited good fortune—I found myself passing out first in an Army course in the Turkish language, posted to the General Staff Intelligence in Constantinople, and, being the only officer in my class who had actually learned to speak Turkish reasonably fluently, appointed as assistant liaison officer in the Turkish War Office.[104]

As with achieving the highest ever mark in Natural Science at the Royal Military Academy, Woolwich, Bennett was silent in *Witness* as to his comparative excellence in Turkish: this accords with what I see as his decision that he must present himself as impartially as possible in *Witness*, a noble aim, even if it could not always be realised. Then, rather than returning to Oxford, obtaining his degree, and marrying, Bennett took the least practical course: he first married and soon went to Turkey, quite aware that he would be leaving his wife behind.[105]

A significant aspect of this which Bennett never comments upon, is simply the fact that, in the result, he did not study at any university. Given his extraordinary intellectual abilities, he may never have felt this to have been something which he had missed. However, while it

---

[103] Bennett (1997) 6.
[104] Bennett (1957) 3.
[105] Bennett (1997) 6-7.

is impossible to quantify its effects upon the course of his life, it meant that Bennett was substantially an autodidact, albeit a remarkably brilliant one. It is often remarked that one of the notes of the autodidact is that together with a broad smattering of knowledge comes an unevenness of learning due to their studying whatever interests them, but also, studying only what interests them. The breadth of knowledge is checked by a weakness in the autodidact's methodology, incomprehension as to why experts may hesitate to rush to judgment, and lack of appreciation of the presence of hidden assumptions. This renders even the precocious autodidact susceptible when encountering a thesis which fits their fancy rather than the facts. Hence the autodidact has a tendency to make bold but unwarranted statements in fields where they have not been obliged to study the basics, and to accept conclusions drawn from rather slender evidence. As we shall see, Bennett's formidable intellectual development exhibits all these advantages but also all of those limitations, especially, I shall contend, in history.

Then, there is another element which is suggestive of fate: had he studied at Oxford at the end of WWI he would not have had the Turkish adventure which so marked his life, he would not have met Islam at first hand (or at least under such extraordinary circumstances), and most of all he would not have met Gurdjieff and Ouspensky in Constantinople. Bennett's decision to pass over a university education was therefore of signal importance, even if he, being focussed on what he did do rather than the consequences of what he did not do, seems to have been oblivious.

CHAPTER 2

MARRIAGE, TURKEY, AND GURDJIEFF

2.1 MARRIAGE

In *Witness*, Bennett devotes little time to his first marriage, that to Evelyn McNeil:

> This first marriage was a strange affair. Before going to France in 1917, I had engaged myself to marry the elder sister of a school friend. Evelyn McNeil was a tall, beautiful girl.... But the bond between us was more than the vanity and possessiveness in nearly all human relationships. She was my first love, and I did not look to right or left.... My engagement had surprised me: I had not intended to propose marriage, but heard my own voice doing so during a week-end leave.[1]

When he was returned to England, wounded, he felt that his past had a dreamlike quality. In an ominous sign, when Evelyn visited him in hospital, his one effort to speak of what he had seen: "had so distressed her that I realized she was afraid that my head injury had affected my brain."[2] However, Bennett now became aware of new sexual impulses, and felt impelled to an early marriage.[3] He makes a point of saying that his inability to consider sex outside of marriage was due to his mother,

---
[1] Bennett (1997) 7.
[2] Bennett (1997) 7.
[3] Bennett (1997) 7.

although she felt the marriage would be a failure. He was, however, driven to go through with the marriage:

> The youth who was committing himself week after week to the marriage was like a wraith of my former self in strange alliance with my newly awakening man's body. The man who was to go to Turkey seemed to be living in a deeper and truer stratum of my consciousness. Behind both of them was that self – neither youth nor man – that had known the taste of death and immortality. I had not reached the point of asking myself the question: "In all this, who am I?" ... (yet) I was aware all the time that I was to find my real life in Turkey.[4]

Bennett describes different levels in his consciousness, among them a ghostly "witness" to his marriage to a woman from whom he had already become internally divorced. He later saw the failed marriage as fated to bear a child. The brief marriage itself was superseded in the unfolding of his destiny. In the collection of materials from his last years, known as *Deeper Man*, Bennett records his view that our human nature is intrinsically limited, and in those limitations we find our fate: "the way of life and experience that is fixed in us at birth."[5] A little later, Bennett describes the respective roles of "destiny," "fate," and "heredity:"

> Besides the physical pattern transmitted genetically and the "spirit pattern" or fate, there is a higher level of order that can be called "destiny." If heredity comes from World 48 and fate from World 24, destiny comes from World 12. The child's destiny is unique, given to the child independently of who his parents are.[6]

---

[4] Bennett (1997) 7.
[5] Bennett (1994) 82.
[6] Bennett (1994) 118.

Bennett means that his first marriage, whatever purpose and value it had, was not and could not be part of his given role in life: to develop his real individuality or "I," he had to move on from it. Yet, he spoke of it as a poignant and sad event, directing no reproach whatever to his wife.

His theory of fate and destiny is based on Gurdjieff's teaching of "the Ray of Creation," according to which we live simultaneously in several inter-penetrating worlds of different fineness, perhaps more precisely described as "cosmoses" or "orders." Gurdjieff named these orders of creation "Earth," "All Planets," the "Sun," "All Suns," "All World" and the "Absolute," and stated: "Man lives in all these worlds but in different ways."[7] He said that the higher the world, the higher the consciousness possible.[8] Bennett developed this, saying that in World 48 (Gurdjieff's "Earth"),[9] we live in "the world of personality, where there is a distinction between objective and subjective states, so we cannot be connected to things as they are." In terms of consciousness, "World 48 is the world of our material and reactional selves."[10] According to Bennett, we who must live in World 48 can also share in the life of World 24 by being 'aware of what is going on around us and inside us without being caught up in any of the machinery."[11] Higher, in World 12, there is Individuality; so that one who shares in that world while living in Worlds 24 and 48, also has their own "I," and a will which is a conscious "agent of creative power."[12] In 1949, when Bennett saw Gurdjieff so weak that he could no longer pretend to be other than he really was, Bennett opined that: "he was so beautiful that we felt we were looking at a being from another and better world."[13]

At this point, Bennett's father re-enters the story. His mother, who

---

[7] Ouspensky (1949) 76.
[8] Ouspensky (1949) 317-18. I conjecture that the anonymous piece relating the "development of the moon" to raising our own sensation to consciousness, was written by Ouspensky and belongs to this period: see Wertenbaker (2017) 110-11.
[9] Hence Gurdjieff states "World 48 will be the earth," and that the physical body is under "48 Laws": Ouspensky (1949) 80, 84, and 94.
[10] Bennett (1994) 107-8.
[11] Bennett (1994) 107.
[12] Bennett (1994) 105.
[13] Bennett (1997) 198.

had received a "puritanical New England upbringing," could not accept his father's sexual and financial irresponsibility, and had forbidden him the house lest the children should be "contaminated." Even when the man was dying, she went but once to see him in the "dingy boarding-house bedroom near Kensington oval, to which he had been driven by poverty."[14]

> From Armistice Day, 11 November 1918, to 20 December, the day of my wedding, my life was tense to breaking point. At least ten hours a day were spent in learning Turkish. Meanwhile my father's illness was taking a deadly serious turn. He had been invalided out of the Army with blackwater fever contracted in Central Africa. Incurably optimistic, he was convinced he would get well and was constantly making plans for new journeys and new undertakings to make us all rich.[15]

Bennett, had not realised that a living man's body could be as ravaged as his father's now was, yet his father "spoke of a great plan for going to Sicily and reorganizing the sulphur mines there."[16] Bennett would prove to indeed be his father's son when it came to schemes and plans, especially with mines. His father died the very next morning, the day appointed for Bennett's wedding. The death certificate advises that Basil Wilfred Bennett, male, aged forty-seven years, died on December 20, 1918 at 105 Vassall Road, Brixton, of two causes: ellitial disease and cardiac dilation. The informant was J.G. Bennett, his son, of 242 Temple Chambers E.C. 4,[17] rather a grim task to be engaged in on one's nuptial day. In *Witness*, Bennett observes that they were aware of their father's faults: "a very good father and a bad parent," yet "Not for anything would

---

[14] Bennett (1997) 8.
[15] Bennett (1997) 7. Nothing more is available to me about Bennett's father. Clearly, Bennett felt a deep connection with his father, even if he never felt any imperative to commit the details to writing.
[16] Bennett (1997) 8.
[17] Death certificate 400 of 1918, from the County of London, Registrar's District of Lambeth, Sub-District of Brixton.

my sister and I have had him different."[18] This suggests that his brother Arthur did not share their view (Appendix 1). The wedding went ahead:

> My mother insisted that he should be buried as a pauper and that none of us should know where or by whom he was buried. She also insisted that no one should be told of his death until after the marriage. With her lips tight and her blue eyes like sparks, she said, "I do not approve of this marriage and I would have stopped it if I could. But now it is too late. You must go through with it."[19]

The trauma was worsened by conflict between his maternal grandmother and his mother. Bennett: "felt again as I had nine months earlier—disengaged from my body. But this time my body was alive and walking to its doom."[20] Bennett insists that he "really wanted" to marry Evelyn, although he knew it wrong to be married on the day of his father's death. During the ceremony his "body moved and spoke, but it was an automaton. I had nothing to do with its actions and had no power at all to influence them."[21] This insight, redolent of Gurdjieff's ideas, need not be attributed to retrospective projection: rather, when Bennett later learned Gurdjieff's analysis, he saw its applicability.[22]

We now have three apparent out-of-body experiences: the seminal one of March 21, 1918, the incident in the English hospital, and the third on the day of his wedding on December 20, 1918. However, the second and third are presented as echoes of the first vision, so I would not count them among the revelatory experiences which are the bones of the skeleton of this book. The first two months of their marriage passed while Bennett learnt Turkish, until his posting to Salonika. His wife cried, his

---

[18] Bennett (1997) 151.
[19] Bennett (1997) 8.
[20] Bennett (1997) 8.
[21] Bennett (1997) 8-9.
[22] For Gurdjieff on the "human automaton," see Ouspensky (1949) 38, 42, 102, 112, 115, and 309.

mother laughed, but Bennett moved on, knowing, he said, less about life and people that one would expect of a man his age, yet also knowing that there was more to the mystery of life and death than people thought.[23] In Turkey, he hoped to bring his wife out, but a mission he was given soon after arrival proved so exciting that he "forgot everything."[24] When he remembered and she joined him, she did not enjoy herself, but did become pregnant. When she realised what had happened she precipitately returned to England:

> It seemed to me then, and has become even clearer since, that the true reason for our marriage was that she was destined to bear a child and I to be the father. That was the only real link between us. It is a very powerful link and I believe that neither life nor death can break it.[25]

A girl, Ann Bennett, was born on August 18, 1920.[26] Bennett wrote regularly to Evelyn in England. When he re-read the letters, he saw his selfishness and lack of any sympathetic understanding of her trials in raising their child. Strangely: "Almost immediately, I found myself unable to write home any more. England, my family, my own wife and daughter belonged to one world and I belonged to another. My letters were few and forced."[27]

2.2 TO TURKEY

Bennett's overland passage from England to Turkey was a difficult one. On being surprised to realise he was within view of Delphi, he experienced "a shock of excitement":

---

[23] Bennett (1997) 9.
[24] Bennett (1997) 13.
[25] Bennett (1997) 17.
[26] Dushka Howarth, one of Gurdjieff's natural children, was of about the same age as Ann Bennett. The two formed a friendship; see also the photograph of Ann, her husband, and Jessmin Howarth, Dushka's mother, in Howarth (1998) 277.
[27] Bennett (1997) 17.

> "This is history and I belong to it. Next time I will stay here."
> ... I am very reluctant to believe in reincarnation, at least in any of its popular forms. I am, however, inclined to believe in premonitions, and that we have some connection with the future that influences our lives more than we are aware.[28]

Bennett was posted as Assistant Liaison Officer at the Turkish War Office, Istanbul. It was an eventful period: on 8 June, not long after the Greek forces had landed in Smyrna on May 15, 1919, he was approached for visas for General Mustafa Kemal and an accompanying mission, ostensibly to keep the Turkish army out of the conflict. But the names on the list told him at once that the "peace-making mission" was in fact aiming at war. He objected, but was instructed to issue the visas. Had he not done so, the history of Turkey might have been very different. Bennett now started to become disillusioned "with the wisdom of the great."[29] This incident is accepted as historical by Kinross.[30] Further experiences at this time showed him that: "The world about me, that seemed like an incomprehensible dream, was in truth a nightmare of human vanity and love of power."[31] In Smyrna, he contracted a case of amoebic dysentery from which he would not fully recover for forty years.[32] In September 1919 he accepted the offer of a promotion to head of the Military Intelligence "B" Office in Constantinople.[33] The autobiographical essay adds that:

> In July, 1919, General Lord Milne chose me as his personal intelligence officer, and so I came to meet the Sultan of Turkey, the Grand Vizier, and to know, as few Englishmen did, the secrets of the last court of Imperial Turkey. Later,

---

[28] Bennett (1997) 10.
[29] Bennett (1997) 11.
[30] Kinross (1964) 157.
[31] Bennett (1997) 13.
[32] Bennett (1997) 16.
[33] Bennett (1997) 16.

in December 1919, I was appointed Chief of the "B" section, which required that I should get to know all the political manoeuvres from Persia to the Mediterranean.[34]

This conveys the speed of Bennett's advance through the ranks of the Intelligence Service. His reputation for knowledge and influence so far surpassed the truth that he was thought to be associated with the English Royal Family.[35] He would drive through Istanbul on most days, "and had got to know so many faces and the stories behind them, that I was able to follow the political life of the city merely by seeing people in the streets."[36] He was required to investigate the activities of the Mevlevi order, and attended a meeting or *mukabele*, complete with music and "whirling."[37] He wrote: "This is the Mevlevi zikr, or pointing of the soul towards God. It symbolizes the paradisal state of the soul when it leaves the body and enters the world of the perfected men, the *Insan i-kamil*. Later I learned how to perform the zikr myself, and could verify the state of beatitude, quite devoid of excitement, which it engenders."[38] He visited the Rufa'i or Howling Dervishes (usually known today as the Rifai Dervishes). Oddly, Bennett states that their invocation "Ya Hu" means "O Thou!"[39] but I cannot find this in Turkish, Persian, or Arabic. In Arabic, "ya" is "O" (a vocative particle), but "hu" is the third person masculine singular suffix ("his"). There he witnessed the ability of a certain dervish to subject himself to the ministrations of a blade sharp enough to slice him in half, and yet he emerged harmless.[40]

These visits to the dervishes prompted Bennett to reflect upon his Christian upbringing, and how while he had not met Christians with real faith in their religion: "It seemed different with the Muslims I met....

---

[34] Bennett (1957) 3.
[35] Bennett (1997) 16-21.
[36] Bennett (1997) 20.
[37] The Arabic word *muqābala*, written with a final t, means "encounter, meeting, reception," and was taken into other languages used by Muslims.
[38] Bennett (1997) 24.
[39] Bennett (1997) 25.
[40] Bennett (1997) 25-26.

[M]any of them really believed in God."⁴¹ His introduction to the Mevlevi Dervishes had an unexpected result: when Bennett met the Turkish Minister of Justice, he recognised him as having been one of the whirling dancers.⁴² Bennett decided to join the Ramadan fast that year. The results were not spectacular for himself or for other individuals he knew, but he saw that the atmosphere of the entire city was different during the fast, and so "I was bound to admit that, on the whole, Muslims took their religion far more seriously than the majority of Christians."⁴³ After witnessing the tremendous sight of the final night of Ramadan in the Hagia Sophia, in July 1920, he was profoundly moved but also quizzical:

> What could I make of it? The experience itself made a deep impression. But who was changed by it? Tomorrow they would all be as they were before—dominated by the same passions and weaknesses as all other men. My mind went to Rome and the same thunderous sounds at Easter, when tens of thousands of throats shout *"Tue es Petrus!"* Men and women are bathed in tears and the heavens seemed to open. Was it not the same there also; did they not all return unchanged in character to the same life dominated by the same weaknesses?⁴⁴

It is odd that Bennett should have omitted to mention a separate account, of his earlier trip to Rome, yet he had spent Easter there, and been struck by what he saw. The autobiographical essay connects his Intelligence work with both his opportunities to be among the dervishes, and with the near-death experience; his first vision:

> As the Pan-Islamic movement was then causing nearly as much anxiety to the Allies as to Bolshevism, I had to learn all

---

⁴¹ Bennett (1997) 26.
⁴² Bennett (1997) 26.
⁴³ Bennett (1997) 25-27.
⁴⁴ Bennett (1997) 27.

> I could about Islam and met numerous famous religious leaders and interviewed many pilgrims on their way to Mecca. While in Turkey on this assignment, I encountered the Dervish Brotherhoods of the Mevlevi, Bektashi and Rufa'i Orders whose spiritual exercises first showed me that it was possible to develop consciously the power that for a short time I had spontaneously experienced.[45]

Again, this is central to his agenda in *Witness*: to indicate what can be consciously developed, and how. Bennett states that while he knew the army would not be his career, neither could he abandon all he had to join the dervishes, who belonged to: "a dying world. They were a reminder that men had known how to live to the full inwardly as well as outwardly. But it was only too obvious that the ancient fire had died."[46] In the light of his later journeys through Islamic countries, and his enthusiastic collaboration with Hasan Shushud, I would think that he meant that the future of the dervishes lay only in the life of individuals now, rather than, as formerly, as a social force. Bennett pondered:

> What did I really wish to attain in my lifetime? As these questions surged in me, I could feel my heart almost breaking with the anguish of emptiness. But soon my mind, with its inveterate habit of seeking for formulae, began to assert itself.... Vanity and self-love seem to be the terrible enemies of mankind; at least I could try not to give way to them.... I vowed that I would never rest until I could find one Truth and one Faith in which all beliefs could be reconciled.... Where was I at home? In England, where I was born? In America, where my mother came from? In Turkey, where I felt at ease? Somewhere in Asia, where there might be a source of truth of which I knew nothing?... If I was to be a human being, I

[45] Bennett (1957) 3.
[46] Bennett (1997) 28.

must put aside the feeling that I was British and therefore best. Here at least was a truth that I could accept without reserve: The human race is one and indivisible, and I must live my life as a human being before all else.

A sense of peace and accomplishment came over me.... I wished to be a man free of vanity and self-love, to find the source of all religion and the unity of mankind.... For the first time in my life, the idea of search entered my consciousness. There was something that must be found, before there could be anything to be done.[47]

The searches to understand his first vision and the source of all religion would lead him to mysticism. He later told Elizabeth, his third wife, that he only felt completely at home in Turkey, while he "always felt somewhat alien" in England.[48] Probably in July 1920, he wrote to Oxford to say that he would not take up his scholarships.[49]

2.3   MEETING PRINCE SABAHEDDIN

Later that same day, someone invited him to meet Prince Sabaheddin (Sultanzade Mehmed Sabâheddin, also spelled Sabaheddin and Sabahettin, 1877-1948). Bennett declined. But he adds: "when an event is predestined, the fates have more than one shot in their locker."[50] Bennett does not mean this as just a way of speaking, for through the Prince he met Gurdjieff. A few weeks later, Bennett accepted an invitation to dine with the Prince, but almost forgot it, as he was working on an important report. Bennett comments, "Events that look like trivial accidents may appear later as evidence that there is a pattern that shapes our lives....

---

[47] Bennett (1997) 28-29.
[48] Elizabeth Bennett (2015) 67.
[49] Bennett (1997) 28.
[50] Bennett (1997) 32.

When (the go-between) came to call for me, some inner necessity took charge. I put everything aside and (went)."[51]

At this meeting, probably in July or August 1920, Bennett and the Prince impressed each other, but the latter took the initiative in the friendship, introducing Bennett to strands of European esotericism Bennett had never encountered, most notably Edouard Schuré's *Les Grands Initiés*, which, Bennett wrote: "astonished me by the suggestion that all religions are the same in their origin and that the contradictions between them are due only to our imperfect understanding."[52] Many years later, Idries Shah took the lead with Bennett, telling him that Sufism lay at the origin of world religion (sections 10.4-5).

Bennett stated in his autobiographical essay, but not *Witness*, that he considered the Prince to be his "first spiritual teacher ... a saintly little man with an extraordinary knowledge of the spiritual movements of the East and West."[53] Sabaheddin was also a friend of Rudolf Steiner (1861-1925), Colonel de Rochas (1837-1912), and Charles Lancelin (1852-1941), but the real significance of these meetings was that: "My Wednesday evening meetings with Sabaheddin brought again to life the problems and the hopes that had been aroused by my experience in the Casualty Clearing Station on 21 March 1918."[54] Again, the first vision was critical for Bennett. At these meetings, Bennett made two momentous acquaintances: that of Winifred Beaumont, whom he was to marry and remain with until her death forty years later, and G.I. Gurdjieff, "whose ideas and teaching were to become the chief concern of my inner life."[55] Bennett was enchanted by Mrs Beaumont: "her voice ... spoke within one and to one, not, as do many people's, at one and from outside.... [I]t was if it had all happened before and that we were meeting again."[56] Bennett's

---

[51] Bennett (1997) 32. On Sabaheddin, see Shaw and Shaw (1977) 258, 262, and 296.
[52] Bennett (1997) 33.
[53] Bennett (1957) 3.
[54] Bennett (1997) 33.
[55] Bennett (1997) 33.
[56] Bennett (1997) 34.

comments about predestination and the fates clearly apply to this meeting as much as to that with Gurdjieff.

One evening, the Prince, a Muslim, disclosed his great devotion to Jesus the Son of God, and to the Holy Virgin, adding the qualification that "no man ever could or ever would understand the true meaning of the relationship "Son of God."[57] Bennett was struck by the fact that Divine Love meant more for him than it did to any of the Christian clerics he had known: "I had never until that evening taken religion seriously…. But before the week was out the impression had faded. It was not until much later that I realized that no one can transmit his faith to another."[58] There is a certain correspondence between this realization and his earlier meditation that even after the stirring events in the Hagia Sophia Mosque on the final night of Ramadan, and in St Peter's Square at Easter, the faithful—no matter how high they were lifted—do not seem to permanently change as a result of such experiences, but return to their ordinary ways. A symmetry is found here: Sabaheddin was a Muslim with a profound respect for Christianity, and Bennett was to become a Christian with a profound respect for Islam. Bennett's Christian renaissance, so to speak, was to be fulfilled many years later when he converted to Catholicism.

Bennett states that at this time he counselled the British to leave a battalion in the Caucasus as a safeguard against the fall of Armenia, Azerbaijan, and Georgia to Russian Communist pressure.[59] It would be futile to envision what might have happened if his advice had been heeded—after all, as Gurdjieff said, if one thing could have been different, everything could have been different.[60] But Bennett was ignored, and the three First Independent Republics were invaded.

---

[57] Bennett (1997) 34.
[58] Bennett (1997) 34-35.
[59] Bennett (1997) 35.
[60] Ouspensky (1949) 21-22.

2.4 PREMONITIONS: THE QUALITY OF TIME

A significant event now occurred, and although it is passed over in *Witness*, it is closely related to other events there which he does mention, and the insights they led to. It is published in *The Way to Be Free*, a posthumous collection of materials from the last four years of his teaching life. Bennett told his pupils:

> While I was living in Turkey in 1919, I had a very vivid dream: I was standing with my back to a wall watching a fire. I saw a great crowd of people, and furniture was being thrown out of a window to be caught by the firemen. Then, some kind of wardrobe came out of the window, and the firemen, who obviously thought they could not catch it, got out of the way. It crashed on the ground and I saw it collapse. Five days after the dream occurred, I heard the shout of a fire warning. By then I had quite forgotten about the dream and saw the same things happen. But the moment I remember most was when I began to think, "Now, will that wardrobe come out of the window or not?" It made an extraordinary impression on me when it actually came out and I saw it crash.
>
> I said to myself: "All our understanding about time is wrong. In some way the future exists, or I couldn't have seen that fire five days before it happened." This led me to study premonitory phenomena. Later, I had various kinds of experience, but none so bright and sharp as that. I read Mire's book, *Le Phenomenon Prémonitaire*, a study of all the premonitions of the First World War that he collected.[61]

I have been unable to locate that volume. Bennett states that Mire collected and researched instances of where people claimed to have premonitions such as of the death of specific people, and of walls being

[61] Bennett (2006) 7-8.

brought down by bombardment. He was able to establish that, while these premonitions were, in a number of cases, related to actual events, yet there had been no predictions of the outcome of the war, or states of mind, or of decisions.[62] Bennett continues: "It was this that first put me on the track of different worlds, including worlds beyond prediction. The events that really matter to us are the ones belonging to the higher worlds. These events are not mechanical and do not belong to the predictable future."[63]

Bennett's understanding of "higher worlds" developed over time. It is sufficient now to observe that Bennett's questioning of the nature of time, his exploration of multi-dimensional geometry, and his study of eternity in the cosmos (*The Dramatic Universe*), are all inextricably connected. However, Bennett came to believe that it is because there are higher worlds that we have no need to fear death, for the laws of life are different there.

More prosaic, but still unusual, was his meeting with a Turkish man who was born in 1776, and remembered the massacre of the Janissaries, which he dates to 1811.[64] It was, for Bennett, another example of how unexpected phenomena may exist in traditional societies.

2.5 THE SECOND VISION: ETERNITY

Bennett moved in with Mrs Beaumont, marrying her only in 1925.[65] In the 1957 memoire, Bennett concisely states: "My [first] wife had no interest in my esoteric searches," and contrasts her with his second wife, who "took an active interest in all my researches and she has been the greatest help in all the vicissitudes of my life."[66] Under the influence of his second wife, Bennett states, he returned to his mathematical studies,

---

[62] Bennett (2006) 8.
[63] Bennett (2006) 8; see also (1998b) 26.
[64] Bennett (2014) 10-11; (1997) 306. The major slaughter of the Janissaries was the so-called "Auspicious Incident" of June 15, 1826.
[65] Bennett (1997) 36.
[66] Bennett (1957) 4.

which he now "connected ... with the problems of spiritual free will and material determinism."[67] Bennett's account of the quest is palmary: he had a conviction that both the visible (measurable and knowable) world and the invisible ("felt rather than known") were true, since he existed within them both, just as these mysteries were within him. This raised insistent questions: how are they related, and why are others not similarly obsessed with the antinomy (the fact of two equally rational yet apparently inconsistent propositions)?

> It seemed to me that people compromise too easily with the evidence before them. On the one side, the physical and biological sciences pointed towards a strictly mechanistic account in which there was no place for free will—except by some evasive subterfuge. On the one side, morality required freedom and responsibility, and religion went further and demanded faith in a mysterious world where freedom itself was not enough. Religion could only accept the conclusions of modern science by a subterfuge no less evasive than that which was offered from the other side.[68]

In the preface to the first volume of *The Dramatic Universe*, Bennett wrote: "[I]n the spring of 1920, I became convinced that many intractable problems could be resolved if we could overcome the handicap of thinking in terms of events in space and time only, and could widen our horizons to include the unseen and unexplored dimensions of eternity. I set myself to study the dilemmas of science and philosophy—such as the ether paradox or the antinomy of free will and universal law—to see if the material for knowing eternity might not be lying unnoticed before our eyes."[69]

In *Witness* he states that he one day "happened" to receive "a batch

---

[67] Bennett (1997) 36.
[68] Bennett (1997) 36-37.
[69] Bennett (1956) x.

of scientific papers."[70] Among these was a paper by Einstein on the luminiferous ether.[71] I would guess that these were received in connection with the studies he referred to in the above passage. Bennett states that Einstein argued that it was impossible for the ether to be a material substance, since this would mean that "it must have the apparently impossible property of travelling in every possible direction at once, and what is more, it must do so with the speed of light."[72] Bennett wondered whether such an impossible state of affairs could be represented geometrically. In a talk titled "The Present Moment," delivered in 1970, he adds the significant detail that he had "revolted totally" against Einstein's theories as closing the world, and making it "necessary to accept a predetermined future and this illusion surrounding decision and choice."[73]

I would suggest that this "total revolt" indicates an emotional element which may have impelled Bennett into a more than purely intellectual confrontation with the conundrum.[74] The next evening, possibly in or just after September 1920, as he was passing a hospital to return to his office and complete some reports, but just before he reached the Rue de Péra:

> the solution struck me like an electric shock. In a moment of time, I saw a whole new world. The train of thought was too rapid for words, but it was something like this: "If there is a fifth dimension not like space but like time, and if it is orthogonal to the space-time we know, then it would have

---

[70] Bennett (1997) 37.
[71] I suspect that this was "Ether and the Theory of Relativity" (1920), republished in *Sidelights on Relativity* (Methuen, London, 1922)
[72] Bennett (1997) 37.
[73] Bennett (1992) 11. He made a similar comment in 1949, that Einstein's work left him with an urgent need to find a way of: "reconciling the deterministic conclusions of physical science with our inner conviction that in some way we are free." Bennett (1949b1).
[74] Bennett (1998a) 3-7 outlines how Lawrence Bragg made a certain discovery in crystallography: the question before him was clear enough that he would know whether it was answered or not, his mind was exhausted, and he now put it out of his mind. The whole answer came before him in "a flash." Bennett actually discussed the matter with Bragg.

the required property. Any matter existing in that direction would appear from our standpoint to be travelling with the speed of light. And moreover it would travel in all directions at once. This must be the solution to Einstein's riddle. If so, the fifth dimension must be as real as the space and time we know. But the extra degree of freedom given by the fifth dimension opens all kinds of possibilities. It means that time itself is not unique, and if there is more than one time, there is more than one future. If there are many times, there should be the possibility of choosing between them. In each line of time, there can be a strict causality, but by changing from one line to another we can be free. It is like a railway passenger: so long as he remains on one train his destination is decided in advance. But he can change trains at a junction and so change his destination."[75]

In 1949 he described this incident even more vividly: "Suddenly the whole world seemed to stand still, and I can recollect with unfaded vividness all my experience of that moment—the crowd of every nationality, the smell of Pera, the weight of my revolver hanging loosely from an ill-fitting Sam Browne belt, the sunshine on the white walls of the hospital, and the dazzling flash of conviction in my own mind that I had seen the solution, and the only possible solution, of the problem."[76]

Bennett knew that readers acquainted with Gurdjieff's system would interpret this as meaning that states of self-remembering and objective consciousness came upon him, and thus he was able to grasp an objective truth about reality, and to recall it with some accuracy when he returned to his normal state.[77] Both he and Ouspensky had

---

[75] Bennett (1997) 37. It can only be given an approximate date, by reference to "the spring of 1920" at Bennett (1956) x. Gurdjieff arrived in Constantinople in July 1920: Taylor (2008) 226. Since the vision seems to have occurred not long before Bennett met him, it cannot have occurred after July 1920.
[76] Bennett (1949b) 1.
[77] Ouspensky (1949) 141-45, 279, 282 and 298.

independently concluded that the theoretical answer to many apparently insoluble problems would be found in the existence of dimensions of space/time which we cannot perceive, but for which antinomies and paradoxes provide indirect evidence. They both found in Gurdjieff's system the key to making the theory a practical reality. When Bennett told Gurdjieff of his vision, the latter taught him: "that to **know** more is not enough, and that it is necessary to **be** more if we would penetrate beyond the veil of space and time."[78] This brings us to Bennett's understanding of Gurdjieff's theories of higher centres (or brains) and bodies. A short treatment of this will allow us to better understand Bennett's autobiography, and the terms he used. In *Gurdjieff: Making a New World*, Bennett states:

> We have already considered the simple presentation of man as having three types of experience: thinking, feeling and instinctive. These Gurdjieff associates with three centres which have an anatomical significance, being related of different parts of the nervous system.... Gurdjieff, however, complicated the issue by distinguishing between the moving and instinctive centre and adding a sex centre.... Then to these five centres were added two others: the Higher Emotional and the Higher Mental Centres...[79]
>
> The higher emotional centre is the organ by which man is able to know Reality as it concerns himself. It is the seat of his conscience, the seat of his 'I' and his decision-making. It is the organ of his personal individuality.... According to Ouspensky's report, the higher centres do not need to be developed, they are present in us all. It is only through the lack of development of the lower centres that we are unable to communicate with them. The higher intellectual centre (not very happily named), is the one by which we have

---

[78] Bennett (1956) x. Bold text is in the original.
[79] Bennett (1973) 247.

contact with the Cosmic Principles.... The work of this centre is wholly outside of the mind.... It is timeless and immediate and, for this reason, we cannot describe it in terms of our thought, which is a spatio-temporal faculty.[80]

Bennett thus understood himself to have been remembering himself, and to have had access to the work of higher centres. Hence, he knew exactly where and how he was at the time the revelation was vouchsafed to him: he was returning to his office with a particular aim, and passing the Franchet d'Esperey hospital. It stuck him "like an electric shock," reminiscent of how Gurdjieff described the inrush of impressions from higher intellectual centre into the lower brains.

It was only a "moment of time," but one such moment for a lower centre is a trace of a far longer period for a higher centre (perhaps analogous to a vague memory of a month's events). Higher thought is much faster than ordinary thought, hence "the train of thought was too rapid for words."[81] Bennett had therefore been prepared for Gurdjieff's teaching by some experiences which could be accommodated by those ideas but not by contemporary science. This illustrates why Gurdjieff's system can be seen as a practical and yet mystical method.

Bennett continued: "With these notions flashing through my mind, I saw that my own riddle of free will and determinism could be solved by the addition of a fifth dimension."[82] According to Gurdjieff, it is a property of higher thought that it can harmonise two contradictory ideas, at least where the contradiction is due to the limited perspective we have of them. To take a simple example: is quinine harmful or beneficial for human health? It depends upon several factors, including the dosage in which it is taken. Reason can accommodate both views by placing them in context. Bennett found something analogous for the conundrum of free will and determinism. It might be that a reconciliation of other

---

[80] Bennett (1973) 254-55.
[81] Bennett (1997) 37.
[82] Bennett (1997) 37.

philosophical antinomies can be found in that way. Bennett's second vision continued:

> I was uplifted and carried right out of myself by the excitement of these revelations; and then I saw, or rather became aware of, a vision. I saw a great sphere and knew that it was the whole universe in which we live—that is, the universe we can reach with our senses. Inside this sphere was greater and greater darkness, and outside it light and more light. I saw beings falling from the sphere of existence into the darkness. I also saw bright forms descending on to it from beyond. And I understood that this was a vision of eternity. It was a vision of freedom and determinism, and I could see that souls could fall towards a more fixed or frozen state than that of our visible universe, and also that they could rise towards a greater freedom and glory. It seemed also that free souls could enter the universe and leave it again.
>
> All this must have happened within less than a minute, for I had not reached the Rue de Péra before the vision vanished and had become a memory. I did not go to the office, but turned back, trembling under the impact of what I had experienced, and went home to tell Mrs Beaumont. I asked her to make me a picture as nearly as she could of my description. She took a board and quickly sketched my sphere of sense perception with its inner and outer regions as I had described them.[83]

While teaching at Sherborne, possibly in 1971, Bennett provided further details:

> When I was a young man, I had a vision that had a very

[83] Bennett (1997) 37-38. This research was published as Bennett, Brown and Thring (1949).

powerful effect on my life. It was shortly before I met Gurdjieff in Constantinople. I saw the world as a four-dimensional sphere with space and time together. And I saw how this world was expanding, how everything was living in it. But I then saw that inside this there was a dark place where what was left behind, what had not kept up, was lost. I saw also a bright place surrounding this which was occupied by beings who had got ahead of the world, who were free from the world.

It was later I heard from Gurdjieff the notion of accelerated transformation and the difference between those who can keep up with the evolution of the world, and eventually reach completion; and those who do not keep up, who get left behind; and also those who can go ahead.[84]

This second account brings out, with greater clarity, that within the sphere of eternity, time and space are somehow unified. Further, Gurdjieff's comment explained a feature Bennett himself had missed, i.e. that there are three classes of what we must presume to be human souls: those who keep up with the evolution of the world, those who fall behind, and those who outpace it. Bennett referred to this as the "Rue de Péra" vision,[85] and took the sketch to Sabaheddin. Bennett vainly tried to express the vision mathematically: he wanted to be able to measure and therefore test, prove or disprove his fifth dimension theory. It appears that thirty years later he did succeed, to his own satisfaction.[86] Bennett tried to study the fifth dimension by inducing a different state of consciousness, fruitlessly experimenting over three consecutive days with hashish. He discussed this with Sabaheddin, who warned him off, saying that hashish could damage what he called "the astral body." To the Prince, this was: "a quasi-material organ having a special sensitivity

---

[84] Bennett (2006b) 8.
[85] Bennett (1997) 272.
[86] Bennett (1997) 38.

that enabled it to act as a link between the physical body and the higher parts of the self."[87] Bennett did not understand what was meant, being something of a Cartesian, i.e. thinking of body and mind as being separate. He followed the advice, and desisted from hashish.[88] He continued to visit the dervishes, and met people from Asia credited with extraordinary powers. However, nothing "could be made the subject of controlled experiments."[89]

This changed when he met a hypnotist calling himself "Radwana de Praglowski," who was able to put a sceptical British officer into a cataleptic state such that his head could be placed on one chair, and the feet of his rigid body on another, while someone stood on his stomach. This reminded Bennett of the Rifai dervish and the scimitar.[90] Bennett apparently wondered whether the Rifai did not use hypnotism. More extraordinary was how de Praglowski could put Mrs Beaumont and a Russian girl under hypnosis, for which purpose they foregathered once or twice weekly. They had significant success with "exteriorization of the sensitivity," where the subject was brought into a trance so deep that her skin lost its sensitivity, but she could still hear the hypnotist's voice. A screen was then placed around her head, so that she could not see what was being done, as an object (e.g. a gold ring) was suspended from a thread. Asked to report what she felt, the subject would cry out that she was being burned when the ring was brought near her, suggesting to Bennett that there were "zones of sensitivity over the body," which appeared "to take the form of a series of sheaths, the closest of which is a few millimetres and the outermost a metre from the skin ... (so that there is) "some field of force surrounding the human body that is linked to the nervous system within the body. This forced me to revise my unfavourable opinion of Sabaheddin's description of the astral body ..."[91]

Sabaheddin encouraged them to experiment with the "regression

---

[87] Bennett (1997) 38.
[88] Bennett (1997) 39.
[89] Bennett (1997) 39.
[90] Bennett (1997) 39.
[91] Bennett (1997) 39.

of memory," such that the subject "forgets recent events, and does not know where he is. He appears to be living at a definite moment in the past. The voice and manners change and become younger and younger as the regression proceeds."[92] Mrs Beaumont, under hypnosis, fluently spoke the Hindustani she had known as a child, but which as an adult she had almost totally forgotten.[93] Although he tried to take them back to past lives, neither Mrs Beaumont nor the girl, had any memories prior to conception. Bennett observed that: "When either of them was living her life of five, ten or twenty years ago, she neither knew nor cared about any other time—past or future."[94] These experiments proved to be of no assistance in understanding the fifth dimension, and began yielding diminishing returns.[95] Then Gurdjieff entered the story. In a 1949 article, Bennett made clearer than in any other place, that what Gurdjieff said to him superseded for him, his earlier efforts to understand the fifth dimension, among which he numbered the experiments with hypnotism.[96]

2.6 GURDJIEFF

Through Sabaheddin, Bennett had met his second wife, and now he was to meet Gurdjieff. Referring again to fate and destiny, Bennett states: "The pattern of my life must certainly have required this meeting, for three distinct threads were leading me towards it."[97] He had used this same word, "pattern," in speaking of how he first met the Prince.[98] The three threads were (a) P.D. Ouspensky began giving lectures in Mrs Beaumont's drawing room.[99] Bennett befriended Ouspensky, without

---

[92] Bennett (1997) 39-40.
[93] Bennett (1997) 39-40.
[94] Bennett (1997) 40.
[95] Bennett (1997) 40.
[96] Bennett (1949b) 2.
[97] Bennett (1997) 41.
[98] Bennett (1997) 32.
[99] Bennett (1997) 41.

then becoming interested in his teaching.[100] (b) He met Thomas de Hartmann, and both Mrs Beaumont and Bennett were impressed with the idea that "he had access to some secret knowledge."[101] (c) Sabaheddin invited him to meet Gurdjieff at dinner. While awaiting Gurdjieff, Bennett learned that: "the Prince had met him by chance when he was returning from Europe to Turkey after the Young Turk revolution of 1908."[102] Bennett continues:

> He (Sabaheddine) had met Gurdjieff only three or four times, but he knew that he belonged to a group of occultists and explorers with whom he had travelled far and wide. The Prince regarded him as one of the very few men who had been able to penetrate into the hidden brotherhoods of Central Asia ...[103]

In a piece written in 1947, as the prologue to his lecture series published as *The Crisis in Human Affairs*, Bennett reported the rumour of Gurdjieff's appearance in Constantinople, and his first meeting with him, in terms which supplement what he later wrote in *Witness*. There, he described Gurdjieff as:

> the most remarkable man I have ever met.... He was said to be a great traveller and a linguist who knew all the Oriental languages, reputed by the Moslems to be a convert to Islam, and by the Christians to be a member of some obscure Nestorian sect. He proved to be neither, and his linguistic attainments stopped short near the Caspian Sea, so that we could converse only with difficulty in a mixture of Azerbaijan Tartar and Osmanli Turkish. Nevertheless, he unmistakably possessed knowledge very different from that of the

---

[100] Bennett (1997) 42-43.
[101] Bennett (1997) 43.
[102] Bennett (1997) 44.
[103] Bennett (1997) 44. This suggests that Bennett understood a Tartar dialect.

itinerant Sheikh of Persia and Trans-Caspia, whose arrival in Constantinople, had been preceded by similar rumours. It was, above all, astonishing to meet a man, almost unacquainted with any Western European language, possessing a working knowledge of physics, chemistry, biology and modern astronomy, and able to make rather searching comments on the then new and fashionable theory of relativity, and also on the psychology of Sigmund Freud.[104]

Around 9:30pm, Gurdjieff arrived, speaking "with an accent that was a strange mixture of cultured Osmanli and some uncouth Eastern dialect."[105] Sabaheddine invited Bennett to explain his experiments with hypnotism. Gurdjieff listened intently, giving the impression he understood Bennett's conversation better than Bennett himself. Then Gurdjieff offered his interpretation of the phenomena:

> He spoke as a specialist to whom the theory and the practice of hypnotism were equally familiar. Afterwards, when I tried to translate his explanation to Mrs Beaumont, I found to my dismay that I had forgotten nearly all he had said. Later, this experience was to repeat itself many times, and not for many years did I understand its true significance. In one state of consciousness we see, hear and understand with different faculties from those which are active in another state. When we pass from one state to another, memory does not provide a link, for the nature of memory is to confine our attention to one narrow stratum of our experience, that is, to one line of time.
>
> Gurdjieff spoke about levels of experience in relation to hypnotism. He began by defining various substances or energies, the existence of which he said, could be demonstrated,

---

[104] Bennett (1954) 15-16.
[105] Bennett (1997) 44.

but which natural science had not yet discovered. There were yet other substances so fine as to be beyond detection by any physical means. Every possible action depended upon these substances. For example, if we are to think, we must use the substance of thought. If we are to have any kind of supranormal experience, this will be possible only in so far as the appropriate substance is available.

There are ways of separating and controlling the finer substances. One of these ways is what we call hypnotism. There are many varieties of hypnotism, differing according to the substances that are brought into action. Gurdjieff explained the regression of memory as the property of a particular substance present in all living beings and capable of being, as he put it, "crystallized in the form of a kind of finer body within the physical body."[106]

I shall omit Bennett's report of what Gurdjieff said to Sabaheddin's comment about reincarnation. Then, Gurdjieff:

spoke of the experiments I had made with the exteriorization of the sensitivity and the different responses of a hypnotized subject to different metals. With every metal, a particular fine substance is associated. The same substances also exist in man, although they are on a lower level than the true human substance. Each substance has a definite psychic property. As a subject is brought into a state of deep hypnotic trance, the different substances begin to separate—like iron and brass filings under the action of a magnet. In this condition, the subject can respond to the influence of substances to which he is usually insensitive. So, one can use

---

[106] Bennett (1997) 45.

different metals to induce different psychic reactions such as anger, fear, love, gentleness, and so on.[107]

From this point, Bennett lost the thread of the exposition, and could not absorb what was said.[108] Impressed by Gurdjieff's speaking only of what he had verified for himself, and also by the range of his knowledge, he felt that Gurdjieff could answer his questions, if only he knew which questions to ask. Bennett did not speak about the experience of March 21, 1918, but rather of the "sphere of sense perception vision," showing him the diagram, saying that he believed that the fifth dimension was the region of free will:

> Once again, Gurdjieff listened very seriously, and examined the diagram which I drew to indicate the "upper" and "lower" levels of existence outside of our space and time. He said: "Your guess is right. There are higher dimensions or higher worlds where the higher faculties of man have free play. But what is the use of studying these worlds theoretically? Suppose that you could prove mathematically that the fifth dimension really does exist, what use would that be to you so long as you remain here?" He pointed to the diagram and sphere representing the whole of space and time. "If you remain here you will have to go down. If you wish to ascend into the world of freedom, then you must do so in this present life. Afterwards, it will be too late."
>
> He reminded me of what he had said about the crystallization of a finer body and added: "Even that is not enough, because that body also is under material laws. In order to be free from the laws of space and time, you yourself must change. This change depends on you, and it will not come about through study. You can know everything and yet

---

[107] Bennett (1997) 45-46.
[108] Bennett (1997) 46.

remain where you are. It is like a man who knows all about money and the laws of banking, but has no money of his own in the bank. What does all his knowledge do for him?

Here Gurdjieff suddenly changed his manner of speaking, and looking at me very directly he said: "You have the possibility of changing, but I must warn you that it will not be easy. You are still full of the idea that you can do what you like. In spite of all your study of free will and determinism, you have not yet understood that so long as you remain in this place, you can do nothing at all. Within this sphere there is no freedom. Neither your knowledge nor all your activity will give you freedom. This is because you have no ..." Gurdjieff found it difficult to express what he wanted in Turkish. He used the word *varlik*, which means roughly the quality of being present. I thought he was referring to the experience of being separated from one's body.[109]

Neither Bennett nor the Prince could grasp Gurdjieff's meaning, and Bennett did not know how to continue the conversation, although later in this volume, Bennett rephrases what Gurdjieff meant in this way: "that it was not enough *to know*, but that one also had *to be*."[110] Gurdjieff invited the three of them to see a demonstration of Temple Dances, important he said for the study of ancient wisdom, at the Yemenedji Sokak on Saturday.[111]

Bennett and Mrs Beaumont, but not the Prince, duly attended. Ouspensky and de Hartmann arrived, which surprised Bennett, as he had not then known of their connection with Gurdjieff. When Gurdjieff entered, all his pupils rose and began the dances. The most impressive of the dances was one introduced with the words: "The exercise that will follow represents the Initiation of a Princess. It comes from a cave

---

[109] Bennett (1997) 46.
[110] Bennett (1997) 77.
[111] Bennett (1997) 46-47.

temple in the Hindu Kush."[112] There followed some men's dances, and a dramatic "Stop!" exercise. Despite the impact made by the movements, neither Bennett nor Mrs Beaumont "felt drawn to find out more about him for ourselves."[113] They had the impression that they had stumbled across "a closed circle—almost a secret society" and that they would have no place in it. Although Gurdjieff remained in Turkey for around a year, departing for Germany only in the autumn of 1921, and Bennett saw him on a few occasions, he has nothing further to report of these meetings.[114] However, the themes which we sketched in the Introduction have all been touched by Bennett and Gurdjieff: the reality of the goal of the mystic search, the need for struggling in accordance with a path to achieve, and the need to develop something almost indefinable, here he speaks of "being present," in order to realise the possibilities.

2.7   P.D. OUSPENSKY

It may not be unfair to say that, in *Tertium Organum*, P.D. Ouspensky takes up the challenge of Kant's critique of reason, and finds that the solution must lie in the direction of what he calls the "Tertium Organum," or a mystic way of thinking. In Ouspensky's interpretation, Immanuel Kant (1724-1804), did not propound a system, but posed a question that the world has yet to answer. That is, how it can be that:

> *The whole of our positive science—physics, chemistry and biology—is based on hypotheses contradictory to Kant's propositions.* We do not know in what manner we ourselves impose upon the world the properties of space, i.e. extension, and we do not know in what manner the world—earth, sea, trees, people—could *not possess* this extension. We do not know how we can see and *measure* this extension *if it does*

---

[112] Bennett (1997) 47.
[113] Bennett (1997) 48.
[114] Bennett (1997) 48.

not exist, or what the world can be like if it has no extension.[115] (italics in the original)

After a lengthy disquisition covering philosophy, scientific subjects, psychology, and literature, some of it mystical, Ouspensky concluded that our existing consciousness was a "transitory" one, which would lead to a "higher consciousness," already making an appearance on the earth. Citing Carpenter and Bucke (section 0.6),[116] he linked this idea to that of "Superman."[117] The Superman who has this "higher," or "cosmic" consciousness will have a sense of four-dimensional space (a "spatial sense of time"), and will have a logic which is not bound by the law of non-contradiction, he will have a "logic of the unity of all."[118] When Ouspensky gave Bennett a copy of *Tertium Organum*:

> The book opened my eyes for the first time to the possibility that mankind was about to pass through a great change, which would bring once again into active use faculties and powers latent in man but long buried under the weight of our logical thinking.[119]

This suggests that Bennett had not yet read Bucke's *Cosmic Consciousness*. He was ready for the idea of a new consciousness, in which the dimensions of time and space would be more fully and truly seen by the new man, after all, he had studied non-Euclidean geometry in the lines, and discoursed on higher dimensions of geometry while recovering from shrapnel wounds. In "about 1921" Ouspensky allowed him to read "the original preface" to what would become *In Search of the Miraculous*, which Bennett much valued.[120] Ouspensky must have had

---

[115] Ouspensky (1981) 8.
[116] Ouspensky (1981) 263.
[117] Ouspensky (1981) 277-78.
[118] Ouspensky (1981) 282-85.
[119] Bennett (1997) 48.
[120] Bennett (2016) 120. He was later given a copy, and included it in Bennett (1973).

quite some confidence in Bennett to allow this, and, given its contents, may have been trying to encourage Bennett to become a student of Gurdjieff.

Ouspensky departed for England shortly before Gurdjieff and his entourage left Constantinople. Bennett seems to have been quite fully engaged at that time with his intelligence work. He stated in *Witness* that, together with his obsession with politics, he had a lack of feeling, and that the Prince said to Mrs. Beaumont: "*Notre enfant génial a le coeur encore glacé*" (our inspired child still has a frozen heart.")[121] However, he had a fallout with his superiors, and was returned to England in 1921, travelling with Mrs. Beaumont, to whom he was now firmly attached. Of this connection, he wrote:

> Why was I so sure that the link with Mrs Beaumont would never be broken? It seems to me now—looking back forty years—that my certainty came neither from my head nor from my heart, nor was it connected with my body. It had much more the character of a premonition, a seeing ahead into the future, which had nothing to do with my thoughts or my wishes.[122]

Bennett adds that he had a certain indefinable awareness that his life was following a pattern which was independent of his own will, and that Turkey and its people figured in it.[123] He also had an awareness and acceptance which came to him at "critical moments" of his life, that he himself was in fact unimportant.[124] In the autobiographical essay, he placed even more emphasis on the tolls taken upon his health: "I was twice mentioned in the Commander in Chief's dispatches and recommended for accelerated promotion. The severe overwork caused by carrying chief responsibility for the work of a secret service organization,

---
[121] Bennett (1997) 50.
[122] Bennett (1997) 52-53.
[123] Bennett (1997) 53.
[124] Bennett (1997) 53.

the ramifications of which covered more than a million square miles of territory between Persia, Arabia, Soviet Russia and the Balkans, resulted in a breakdown of my health and I was invalided back to England in 1921."[125]

On February 4, 1921 he reached London, where he saw his nearly six-month-old daughter Ann for the first time. However, he lacked any emotional connection with his wife. Then, although he was in England on sick leave, and he badly needed rest and recreation, he was invited to perform some work for the government at a conference which would include a Turkish delegation. Bennett wrote that as the request for his services was being made:

> I experienced that strange state of unreality which came over me whenever I saw that some future action was inevitable, and that my own will was powerless to influence the course of events.... I should have refused, and yet I knew before he had finished speaking that I would accept.[126]

By now, Bennett has built up a picture of his life as being lived according to a pattern fated for him, not chosen, but with a purpose which transcended him and his own private activities; hence his statement that he knew himself to be unimportant. This suggests that the pattern which supported the aim was important. In his work for the conference, with its opportunities to view major world leaders up close, he saw that these "famous people were moved by the same petty motives as the rest of us," and that although it ended on an ostensibly happy note, it had been an exercise in futility.[127]

With his duty to his country discharged, Bennett was obliged to decide where his future lay. He realised the strength of his attachment to Mrs. Beaumont, while he was an outsider in his own family. He had

---

[125] Bennett (1957) 4.
[126] Bennett (1997) 54.
[127] Bennett (1997) 55.

no wish to return to Oxford, although he was senior mathematical postmaster at Merton College, and his scholarship was being held open: despite the fact that he said he had already resigned it.[128] As he expedited the resignation of his commission, aware of how much he had changed, he had the sense that "Nothing was real … (but) I knew with an uncomfortable clarity that I was going to do many foolish things before finding my own destiny."[129] Here follows an important passage:

> [A]ll my values had changed. I was beginning to learn that we live by values in the timeless eternity of my fifth dimension, and not by facts in the time of clocks and calendars which cannot adapt themselves to the hide-and-seek of Value. Life as we live it flows in more than one track of time. The tracks are separated by our different states of consciousness, and our memory tends to run back along one track to the exclusion of the others. In this way, we lose touch with a great part of our past life, especially those events which contained experiences alien to our present mood. This is not to be wondered at, since values are what we care about and respond to, whereas facts are indifferent. It is probable that we scarcely ever remember the facts of our past life, unless they happen to be connected with some value. Not all values please, but all do matter to us in one way or another. One result is that life in retrospect usually seems interesting to us, though our story of it may seem quite uninteresting to others.
>
> Another consequence of the "one-track" character of memory is that it is quite impossible to be completely honest and sincere in our attempts to reconstruct the past. The tantalizing, though not surprising, conclusion is that the greater

---

[128] Bennett (1997) 28. Perhaps the resignation had not been received or processed.
[129] Bennett (1997) 56-57.

the significance of an experience, the less we are capable, even if we wish to do so, of telling the whole truth about it.[130]

This shows the influence of *Tertium Organum*, while going beyond it in the importance attributed to values. The first of Bennett's books was *Values: An Anthology for Seekers*, privately published in 1943. As we shall see (section 5.4), the foreword to that volume bears the unmistakable stamp of *Tertium Organum*. However, the last word of this chapter properly belongs to a concise statement about the Constantinople period of his life, found in the autobiographical fragment, which indicates the direction he would take to realise a state wherein, as Gurdjieff said, "the higher faculties of man have free play:"

> I also met in Constantinople P.D. Ouspensky, Thomas de Hartmann and other pupils of Gurdjieff in whose system for the Harmonious Development of Man I found the intellectual satisfaction and the practical methods of self-development that I had been seeking.[131]

---

[130] Bennett (1997) 57.
[131] Bennett (1957) 3-4. I refer to Gurdjieff's comments at Bennett (1997) 46.

Bennett (standing) watches outdoor Movements, at Coombe Springs.

CHAPTER 3

WITH GURDJIEFF AT FONTAINEBLEAU

3.1 THE THIRD VISION: DESTINY

Bennett recalls that he was only back in London for six weeks in February and March of 1921. While there, he acted as an unofficial liaison officer assisting the British in their dealings with the Turkish delegation at the first stage of the "Conference of London" (February 21 and March 12, 1921). He had himself costumed by a high class couturier, so as to make "a creditable imitation of a diplomat."[1] Mingling with international figures, he saw some of the men who had caused problems for the British when he was working in Turkey.[2] Perhaps the most telling lesson from this close contact with the movers and shakers of international diplomacy, was that: "famous people are moved by the same petty motives as the rest of us."[3] Bennett then tells how, solely through his knowledge of the personal interests of one of the Ankara delegation in farming, and a timely word to Lloyd George, the Turk was moved to deliver a conciliatory speech.[4]

The now inevitable separation from his wife, his daughter Ann, and his father-in-law David McNeil came to pass. His values had changed, and Bennett maintained that our values, more than anything else, determine the course of our lives. We do not always see this, according to Bennett, because we live in different tracks of time (that of events, and

[1] Bennett (1997) 54.
[2] Bennett (1997) 54-55.
[3] Bennett (1997) 55.
[4] Bennett (1997) 56.

that of values), and we have separate "states of consciousness" for each of these tracks. In one state of consciousness, we can recall only what relates to that track of time.[5] Bennett does not exclude himself when he concludes that this makes it effectively impossible to "be completely honest and sincere in our attempts to reconstruct the past."[6]

At this time, Bennett met Ramsay MacDonald (1866-1935), who would become Prime Minister in 1924 and again between 1929 and 1935.[7] He considered entering party politics, and endured an unpleasant post-election debriefing from his father-in-law. Bennett states:

> I knew I would go away, not because of my father-in-law, not because I could not be a husband and a father, not because I was disgusted with politics, not even because of Mrs Beaumont or some mystical call of the East, but simply because I had to. I had no power to choose.[8]

If he was disgusted with politics, and I do not suggest that he was not, it is strange that he sought preselection for the United Empire Party in 1931. A notice appearing in the *Liverpool Echo* and other United Kingdom newspapers on May 12, 1932, states that Bennett had been a candidate for the United Empire Party, an ephemeral political party launched by two "Press Barons," Lords Beaverbrook and Rothermere in February 1930.[9] Bennett was unsuccessful, and in the event brought a defamation action against Mrs Joynson-Hicks and her husband for comments she had made about him at a United Empire Party meeting. When she publicly apologised, and paid his legal costs, Bennett withdrew the action.[10] In *Witness*, Bennett passes over the entire incident. Perhaps there was a connection between Bennett and Lady Rothermere, who had brought Ouspensky

---

[5] Bennett (1997) 57.
[6] Bennett (1997) 57.
[7] Bennett (1997) 58-59.
[8] Bennett (1997) 58-59.
[9] Boyce (1987) 106.
[10] Furnished by Michael Benham, by email, July 9, 2022.

to England and visited Gurdjieff,[11] but speculation would be pointless. If Bennett was ambivalent about a political career, then in *Witness* he effectively denied that ambivalence, by omission. Immediately following this, Bennett significantly mistakes his dates:

> By one of those coincidences that mean more than our carefully planned actions, I went that afternoon to visit Ouspensky, then living at a hotel in Russell Square. It was our first meeting since he had left Turkey several months earlier, and he told me of the success he had met with in London and of lectures he was giving to a group of theosophists and psychologists. I told him that I had decided to leave England and return to Turkey, but I said I would like to hear some of his lectures. He said: "Come if you like. But you cannot decide. If you go to Turkey, it is not because you decide. You have no power to choose. No one has power to choose."[12]

According to this account, Ouspensky's words "impressed (him) strangely."[13] However, Ouspensky did not arrive in London until August 1921.[14] On August 7, 1921, Ouspensky wrote to Claude Bragdon from "Constantinople-Marseilles," that: "I am going to London and I am writing this on the way to Marseilles."[15] It seems that Bennett is confused here, in a manner to which he was predisposed: his memories would be rearranged in order to paint what he saw as the fated trajectory of his life. Rarely, I think, does Bennett lie about the past (however, see the Lewis episode in section 6.6). But it may be that in his search for meaning in the events of his life, his memory was sometimes pliable. Here, I suspect that what has happened is that a conversation which probably

---

[11] Webb (1980) 185, 218-20, 230, and 253.
[12] Bennett (1997) 58-59.
[13] Bennett (1997) 59.
[14] Webb (1980) 218.
[15] Michael Benham provided me with a copy of the handwritten letter on September 11, 2021.

took place in Constantinople in 1920 has been transposed to London in 1921, possibly under the influence of his own realisation that: "I knew I would go away ... simply because I had to. I had no power to choose."[16] Just as he imitated Ouspensky and relied on his authority in his group work, Bennett drew on Ouspensky to verify his conclusions in more personal spheres (sections 4.8 and 4.9). I am fortified in this conclusion by his later stating in *Witness* that the first time he had heard Ouspensky's comment, it "had made so little impression."[17]

Further muddying the waters, Bennett told his Sherborne students that he was persuaded to meet Ouspensky in England through the effort of his friend Forbes Adam (incorrectly spelled "Adams"). In a talk from the 1970s, reproduced only in the posthumously assembled *The Sevenfold Work*, Bennett stated:

> When I made contact with the Work it had nothing whatever to do with anything that I did.... I simply met people, by sets of independent coincidences; Ouspensky, de Hartmann and Gurdjieff in Turkey, and Forbes Adams in London. Forbes Adams began talking to me about the Work—he had met Ouspensky—and was determined to bring me into the Work; he had no idea of my previous contacts.[18]

While Adam had a significant role in the peace conference of February and March 1921, there was at that time no "work" in England for Bennett to join. Again, a memory has probably been transposed.[19] It is noteworthy that Bennett omitted this from *Witness*, possibly to obviate questions

---

[16] Bennett (1997) 58-59. For Bennett's conversations with Ouspensky in Constantinople in 1920 or January 1921, see Bennett (1997) 41-43 and 48.
[17] Bennett (1997) 67.
[18] Bennett (1979) 117.
[19] The biographic note available online does not do justice to Adam's interest in spiritual ideas. https://www.findagrave.com/memorial/128968454/eric-graham_forbes-adam accessed May 31, 2022. Michael Benham has helpfully provided me with a good deal of material concerning Adam, which I had intended to include in an appendix, but ultimately I have decided it is too tangential to my purpose here.

about why Adam, a promising career diplomat, and a baronet, would suicide.[20] In the event, probably in April 1921, Bennett returned to Turkey, where he was welcomed by people convinced that he was a secret agent for George V.[21] Bennett was solemnly invited by a high-level delegation of Albanians to become their king, but declined. While he reflected that he would have "cut a better figure than King Zog,"[22] others had more cause to regret this caprice of history. In another strange incident, a deposed Egyptian *khedive* or viceroy sent Bennett one thousand sovereigns (probably a gold coin worth one pound sterling). The go-between begged Bennett to accept the gift and to allow him (the go-between) to keep half. Bennett agreed, noting that the unscrupulous intriguer would not miss the money. However, later that decade, his association with the former *khedive* would make him an object of suspicion to the British Legation in Athens. Bennett found a moral in the story:

> As time went on, the memory of this affair grew more and more distasteful, and it became a factor in making me understand that we carry the consequences of our actions within ourselves for years after the external events have disappeared. I came to realise that we can be free from the past only when we have so changed ourselves as to be no longer the same person who performed the action. A dishonest man does not become honest simply by ceasing to act dishonestly, but by an inward change that makes it impossible for him to act dishonestly.[23]

Bennett's disillusionment with the supposed wisdom of politicians and powerbrokers deepened as he travelled around Turkey, finding that: "Turks, Arabs, Kurds, Armenians, Greeks, each had good qualities lacking in the others. There was no hatred between the races except what

---

[20] See appendix 5.
[21] Bennett (1997) 59-60.
[22] Bennett (1997) 60.
[23] Bennett (1997) 60-61.

was stirred up by professional agitators and politicians."[24] In recounting a meeting between Mrs. Beaumont and himself with Sabaheddin, Bennett returns to Ouspensky's statement that we have no power to choose our actions. Mrs Beaumont felt that Ouspensky was probably correct, but that at the same time "she was certain that everything that happens to us is the consequence of our own actions," and that we are always responsible for our own suffering.[25] Bennett summed this up by saying: "It seemed to me that fate was a mystery which none of us could understand and that no formula could express."[26] Fate, destiny, and choice or free will were central themes in Bennett's mind. He saw in the incidents of his life the pattern of his fate, producing a sense of discovery, but also as we have seen, possibly distorting his memory. The difficulty of producing a philosophy which systematically covers all theoretical aspects of a question is notorious. But to write an autobiography which suggests rather than declaims produces a more accessible text, and allows the trajectory of the subject's life to reveal any larger meaning inherent in the details. Also, empathy makes for a better lesson, and the very need to be a sympathetic character may also affect the author's selection and presentation of material.

Bennett has arrived at a rather sophisticated position: we have no power of choice, yet our actions have prepared the path along which we hurtle, and we are responsible for our suffering. Perhaps these statements can be reconciled on the basis that we cannot change external events, but can adopt a conscious attitude to suffering and become receptive to higher influences.[27] Thus, Gurdjieff taught that *as we are* we have no choice, but we do not have to remain that way, and the first practical method for change is self-observation:

> [S]elf-observation itself brings about certain changes in (one's) inner processes. He begins to understand that

[24] Bennett (1997) 61-62.
[25] Bennett (1997) 62.
26 Bennett (1997) 62.
[27] A lesson taught by Gurdjieff, and grasped by Bennett: Blake (1996) 281.

self-observation is an instrument of self-change, a means of awakening. By observing himself he throws, as it were, a ray of light onto his inner processes which have hitherto worked in complete darkness. And under the influence of this light the processes themselves begin to change. There are a great many chemical processes that can take place only in the absence of light. Exactly in the same way many psychic processes can take place only in the dark. Even a feeble light of consciousness is enough to change completely the character of a process, while it makes many of them altogether impossible.[28]

Perhaps the very idea that we cannot choose can ignite a desire to acquire the power of choice. For Gurdjieff, much of our suffering is caused by the fact that we identify with our past and imagine ourselves responsible for our unconscious actions, not understanding that: "If *one* thing could be different *everything* could be different."[29] Yet, after a certain point, Bennett will cease to say that he could see that he had no choice.

The day after the talk at Scutari, in April or May 1921,[30] Bennett had a mystical experience, "in the graveyard of Haidar Pacha."[31] As he watched the sun sinking into the Sea of Marmora: "Slowly my attention turned inwards, and I was aware that my life was spreading out before me."[32] He states that he was sure his future was being shown to him, yet he neither believed nor disbelieved. He understood that:

> I was to be given seven years to prepare, and then my life would begin. I was to perform some great task, but not until

---

[28] Ouspensky (1949) 146.
[29] Ouspensky (1949) 21-22.
[30] This occurred after he had left London in March 1921 (the Woolwich by-election of 1921 was held on March 2), but before he met de Kay in May 1921: compare Bennett (1997) 55, 58, 60, and 68.
[31] This detail is found only in Bennett (1962) 343.
[32] Bennett (1997) 62-63.

> I was sixty would I know what the task was to be.... [Further,] I would not know my true destiny until I was seventy years old.[33]

This vision supplied him with hope through "long years of dry despair."[34] It returned with some vigour in Damascus in 1953,[35] and was evidently a factor in his concluding that he was destined to aid Subud. But he came to believe that the predicted future is not in fact inevitable,[36] while potential futures might be actualised in eternity.[37] At this time, a dentist alerted Bennett to the likely profits if the claims of the heirs of Sultan Hamid (from the House of Osman) to concessions over the Mosul oilfields were vindicated. This dentist's chair was fraught with consequences. Bennett was introduced to the Sultan's Chief Eunuch (sic) with a view to acting as the heirs' attorney.[38] In connection with this, he travelled to Berlin to meet John de Kay. As he travelled through post-war Europe, what he saw: "disposed me towards the doctrine of human impotence expounded by Ouspensky, which, when I first heard it, had made so little impression."[39]

3.2 "PRIVATE DREAMS"

Bennett opened the next chapter of *Witness,* "John de Kay," with a vivid portrait and sustained defence of the controversial adventurer (1872-1938, his name is also spelt "DeKay"), whose saga and history in the court, both civil and criminal, brought him notoriety. The *New York Times* obituary noted that, according to accounts, he had been at various times a rancher, a journalist, a newspaper publisher, and—as an agent of the government of Mexico—had organised their National Packing

---

[33] Bennett (1997) 63.
[34] Bennett (1997) 63.
[35] Bennett (1997) 238-239.
[36] Bennett (1978b) 26.
[37] Bennett (1956) 143-144, 168-169, and especially 277.
[38] Bennett (1997) 63-64.
[39] Bennett (1997) 67.

Company. He wrote a play named *Judas* in which Sarah Bernhardt starred, and also authored a number of books. The obituary observed that his "financial career ... contained several periods of apparently great affluence, and also several encounters with the law."[40] However, the play had a run of one night, notwithstanding Bernhardt's drawing power, and more indicative of his reputation was an ominous report in the *New York Times* from the Lausanne Conference of 1922:

> John de Kay, reputed American millionaire ... is a mystery to the Near East Peace Conference here. French secret police ... are investigating to find out why he is here and what he is doing. Wild rumors are current that he is liaison agent between the Turks and the Bolsheviki, and other reports state that he represents the Celonsal Oil Syndicate, which has immense interests in Mosul. When the correspondent visited him today Mr de Kay at first tried to conceal his identity and then expressed great surprise that it had been discovered.... He would not reply when asked if he represented oil interests.[41]

The article mentions his arms-dealing, his boasting of possessing diplomatic clout, and a case of breach of contract bought against him in England, where the court found against him.[42] Neither does de Kay emerge as an attractive figure from a study of his role in the Mexican meat industry: rather, his endeavours were marked by grandiloquence, deception, and lobbying the local dictatorship with a view to forcing Mexicans to rely on refrigerated meat rather than the fresh product they preferred.[43] Bennett's admiring sketch might be attributed to the fact that de Kay had been the employer, and the lover of Winifred Beaumont, and

---

[40] *New York Times*, October 6, 1938, 23, accessed April 15, 2022.
[41] *New York Times*, November 26, 1922, 2, accessed April 15, 2022.
[42] *New York Times*, November 26, 1922, 2, accessed April 15, 2022.
[43] Pilcher (2006) 122-126, 128-129, 132, 134, 138-140, 148, 168, and 170. However, de Kay made humanitarian objections to the cruel slaughter of bulls: 149.

had funded Prince Sabaheddin's plan to reconcile Turkey and England.⁴⁴ It must be clearly stated that almost everything Bennett asserts about de Kay by way of exculpation, is open to argument, and most probably wrong. However, I doubt that further study of de Kay would cast more light on Bennett's motives.⁴⁵ When appropriate, I acknowledge Bennett's naivety, blindness and unreliability in narrating the past. I might suggest, too, that his unsuccessful forced defence of de Kay is a part of the *apologia* for his life which is a secondary theme throughout *Witness*.

It is a mark of Bennett's naivety that he could be taken in by de Kay, of whom Thackeray's description of Captain Costigan could justly be applied: "the Captain was not only unaccustomed to tell the truth – he was unable even to think it."⁴⁶ The same could also be said of Bennett and Idries Shah (appendix 3). I suggest that Bennett's association with de Kay was, for him, a paradigmatic experience: it schooled him to ignore warning signs that he was engaged with a fast, if not a deceitful player, and to explain away de Kay's manifest faults (so too, with Shah).⁴⁷ However, the most insightful comment about Bennett's character was, I suggest, the one Gurdjieff made to Elizabeth Mayall, later to be Elizabeth Bennett:

---

⁴⁴ Bennett (1997) 68-70. On the relation between de Kay and Beaumont, see *The Illustrated Police News*, April 30, 1922, 4, provided by Michael Benham. Bennett indicates this without stating it explicitly: "Mrs Beaumont discovered that John de Kay— whose sexual morality had never been impeccable – was the father of two children by a mutual friend. She decided to withdraw from his life." Bennett (1997) 69.

⁴⁵ Michael Benham has uncovered a number of serious allegations against de Kay, and correctly contends that Bennett understated the extent of de Kay's crimes and misdemeanours, and his own defaults with the Estates: email communications of 8, 9, 12, 25 and 28 July 2022. On March 31, 1899, *The Waukegan Daily Sun*, Illinois, reported that as defendant in a fraud claim, de Kay's lawyers contended that people can be so obtuse that they cannot complain that they did not realise they were being deceived. The judge dismissed the argument. If this was de Kay's contention, and not one volunteered by his lawyer, this would indicate that de Kay was, at least in 1899, quite cynical. De Kay's criminal and extradition history was complex, e.g. he was cross-examined in England for six days or more in the extradition matter which related to an allegation of "participation in the commission of the crime of fraud by a baker or officer of a public company," said to have occurred in 1912 in the USA: *The Times*, October 1924. Provided by Michael Benham, July 10, 2022, no page reference.

⁴⁶ W.M. Thackeray, *Pendennis*, vol. I, chapter 5.

⁴⁷ Michael Benham and I independently came to the conclusion that Bennett's experience with de Kay eerily prefigured his being taken in by Shah.

"He *naïf*, like a little boy.... Can perhaps be good. Very perhaps."[48] That is, he was overly credulous, insufficiently sceptical, but, Gurdjieff added, there was still hope.

So, with Mrs Beaumont's encouragement, the naive Bennett steeled himself to accept as genuine what was bogus. De Kay now fired Bennett with his own enthusiasm for the alleged rights of the Osmanli family to property of the Sultan Abdul Hamid II (1842-1918), and furnished him with introductions to bankers in London.[49] This project was to prove disastrous for all concerned.

Back in England, Bennett attended Ouspensky's lectures, now held at 38 Warwick Gardens in Earls Court. Bennett characterised those attending Ouspensky's lectures as "theosophists and psychologists," yet people like Maurice Nicoll and Kenneth Walker, medical students, were probably neither, although they perhaps had some theosophical interests. Black remembered that, at the time Ouspensky began his lectures, the Theosophical Society itself was "under the cloud of the differences of Besant and Leadbeater," and so, for many "thoughtful people ... Gurdjieff had an instant appeal."[50] Psychology at that time was under the influence of William James, whose *The Varieties of Religious Experience* included a celebrated chapter on mysticism. Dorothy Phillpotts, who in 1941 married George Phillpotts, a scientist who worked with Bennett, was told that Bennett's lectures were "*psychological* lectures" (her italics), a discipline which did not have the "marked anti-religious prejudice" of psychoanalysis.[51] She relates that James' writings held an eminent place in Bennett's presentations.[52] Theosophy and psychology appealed to many, but, for a small number, Gurdjieff's Fourth Way was intriguing.

Ouspensky, Bennett said, was trying "to destroy in his listeners the illusions by which modern, civilised man is pleased to live."[53] Bennett

---

[48] Elizabeth Bennett (2015) 95.
[49] Bennett (1997) 70.
[50] Black (1941) 16.
[51] Phillpotts (2008) 20.
[52] Phillpotts (2008) 133-45.
[53] Bennett (1997) 70.

presents a lengthy paraphrase of this message, which reaches its climax thus: "Man has no power to direct his private affairs, and he is equally helpless in his social and political life."[54] Bennett also remarks on how, although he now found Ouspensky's analysis to be patently correct, some protested that the war had been only a hiccup "in the great march forward ... to universal peace and justice." Ouspensky did not agree, and, on one occasion, A.E. Waite, a poet and scholar of esotericism (section 0.6), had objected: "Mr Ouspensky, there is no love in your system."[55] Ouspensky's statements are best understood as having been formulated in absolute terms in order to make a point. Ouspensky said that taking statements literally when they are not meant that way is a mark of a low order of thought called "formatory thinking":

> Formatory apparatus has very definite limitations. One of its peculiarities is that it compares only two things, as though in any particular line only two things existed. Then formatory centre likes thinking in extremes; for instance it either knows everything or it knows nothing.... For instance, if I say, you must do this or you must do that, people say, 'But you said we cannot do!'[56]

Ouspensky also stated:

> [F]rom one point of view we are so mechanical that we can do nothing; but from another point of view there are several things which we can begin to do. We have certain possibilities in us, only we do not use them. It is true that we cannot 'do' anything in the sense that we cannot change what we *feel* at any given moment, but we can make ourselves *think* about a subject at a given moment. This is the beginning. We

---

[54] Bennett (1997) 70.
[55] Bennett (1997) 70.
[56] Ouspensky (1957) 63.

must know what is possible and begin from that, because then the possibility to do something, instead of letting things happen, will gradually increase.[57]

The statement that we cannot decide or do anything should not, therefore, be taken absolutely, but it is difficult to state the truth precisely and comprehensively.

Bennett notes that he saw his wife a little on this stop in London, and that his mother and Mrs Beaumont made friends. Of his mother's psychology, he said: "[She] prided herself, perhaps to excess, on not being able to suffer fools gladly."[58] However, he had accomplished what he needed in order to represent the Osmanli heirs, including "a draft contract drawn up by John de Kay that seemed to me eminently fair."[59] In Romania, Mrs. Beaumont displayed an uncanny ability to pick the winner of the horse races. This impressed upon him a sense that "gambling is a wrong activity for man. It was not a moral notion, but rather that there was a hidden danger which one would be foolish to incur."[60] This is rather characteristic of Bennett's points: he digresses in order to illustrate a moral principle, and to place it on a psychological foundation. The mission on behalf of the heirs of Sultan Hamid did not prosper, and after some months, he left for Berlin. It was now December 1921.[61] On the advice and with the assistance of de Kay, a company, Abdul Hamid Estates Incorporated was registered in the State of Delaware with a notional capital of $150 million, from which Bennett and his colleagues would harvest a ten per cent commission. Bennett travelled to Turkey to have nineteen out of the twenty-two heirs eventually vest all their rights in the firm.[62] Bennett then returned to Berlin after taking his final leave of Prince Sabaheddin, who eventually died in poverty in Switzerland,

---

[57] Ouspensky (1957) 76.
[58] Bennett (1997) 71.
[59] Bennett (1997) 71.
[60] Bennett (1997) 71.
[61] Bennett (1997) 72.
[62] Bennett (1997) 72-74.

an alcoholic. In Berlin he had discussions with de Kay about the great wealth and wide-spread estates of the Abdul Hamid heirs in Iraq, Tripoli and Palestine.[63]

On June 8, 1922, Bennett arrived in London, and unable to progress the Osmanli claims, returned to Ouspensky's groups. His comments are rather enlightening as to how Gurdjieff's work fitted into the contemporary world:

> At that time, many people were filled with high ideals—or rather dreams—of helping humanity. John de Kay had spent the past two years in working out the Constitution of an International Institute ... that would provide the means for realizing the programme of the Second Socialist International. He believed that nothing less than a great crusade for the rights of the common man, as against all the powerful organizations of State, religion, finance and industry, would secure peace and progress for mankind. ...
>
> John de Kay's enthusiasm and eloquence could not win me over to his ideas, for I was more deeply impressed by the dangers that stem from man's helplessness and ignorance than by the threat of power-seeking oligarchies. I was strongly drawn to Gurdjieff's ideas as they were presented by Ouspensky.... Gurdjieff's plans were no less grandiose than those of John de Kay. He also spoke of his Institute [for the Harmonious Development of Man] as destined to spread all over the world and to regenerate mankind. My own dreams were not unduly modest. I conceived world-wide research to establish the reality of the unseen world of the fifth dimension, bringing in on the one hand the social ideals of de Kay and on the other the psychological methods of Gurdjieff. All

---

[63] Bennett (1997) 75.

this was to be financed from the riches of the East in the form of the Abdul Hamid lands and concessions.[64]

This combined concern for the internal and external worlds was typical of Bennett. Grand philanthropic ideas were in the air. Like many others, Bennett was attracted by them, and thought that something practical was now possible through his project. In recounting his meeting with T.H Morgan and other renowned biologists who envisioned "the possibility of directing the future of life on the earth through artificially induced mutations,"[65] Bennett offers the wry comment: "Each had his own private dream."[66] Yet, he asserts that he: "deeply felt the unreality of what we were saying," and knew that both the Abdul Hamid Estates claim and the schemes for human betterment would never eventuate.[67]

Apart from the question of feasibility, how could Bennett have thought that it was good to earn money by vindicating the alleged rights of a despot to vast riches to which he had, at best, a tenuous moral entitlement? Abdul Hamid had followed the bloodthirsty model of despotism,[68] moonlighting as a rapacious thief. As a ruler, he is remembered, among other sanguine accomplishments, as one who had "reawakened and fomented that (Islamicist) fanaticism," bending his administration to the benefit of Muslims and the prejudice of non-Muslims.[69] Pursuing the "rights" of his heirs would be like helping descendants of Ivan the Terrible keep whatever they had looted from Novgorod. This is the point Sir Percy Loraine, the British government's representative made in a letter to the Secretary of State dated January 9, 1928: the Greek government had already rejected a Turkish government claim based on Abdul Hamid's actions, so how could anyone imagine they would not reject

---

[64] Bennett (1997) 76.
[65] Bennett (1997) 76.
[66] Bennett (1997) 76.
[67] Bennett (1997) 76.
[68] Morris and Ze'evi (2019) 60
[69] Morris and Ze'evi (2019) 116 also 36, 43.

these claims?[70] To accept the validity of gifts from a foreign tyrant would be inimical to the independence of Greece from Turkey.

3.3 STUDYING WITH OUSPENSKY

Bennett and Mrs Beaumont now studied with Ouspensky at 38 Warwick Gardens and with the associated groups in private residences. This was practically a full-time work: he would attend meetings three or four nights a week, and conduct research for the group during the day at the School of Oriental Studies or the British Museum Library. Bennett's facility with ideas led to his being appointed to repeat and to explain Ouspensky's lectures.[71] Bennett refers to the teaching as the "System," and states that he was fascinated by Gurdjieff's cosmology, and by "the penetrating psychological analysis (which) was an antidote to the unverifiable speculation that so greatly marred the teachings of theosophy and anthroposophy."[72] Bennett avers that only at this time, with Ouspensky, did he learn something of what it meant to "work on himself," an experience which "opened a new world for me."[73] The centre of his efforts was self-remembering, and with it, our inability to remember ourselves. This very inability showed him what Gurdjieff had been trying to say when, at their very first meeting, he had struggled to find the words to contrast "being" with merely "knowing."[74] Only with being, could there be choice:

> I was convinced that self-remembering and the power of choice are intimately linked. Ouspensky said: "How can you speak of power of choice in relation to a man who is asleep, who has no permanent I and who cannot remember himself?" I answered this question for myself: "I am and shall

[70] FO 371/12919, 140-141.
[71] Bennett (1997) 76-77 and 79.
[72] Bennett (1997) 77.
[73] Bennett (1997) 77.
[74] Bennett (1997) 77.

continue to be the helpless plaything of every chance influence until I can remember myself. Everything else is a waste of time."[75]

Ouspensky advised them to struggle with habits, such as smoking, for struggles could serve as "alarm clocks." Bennett was struck by the report of a man who was pleased that he had ceased from smoking, only to come to himself and realise that he was in fact smoking a cigarette at that very moment. This indeed, he said, was sleep.[76] Then, after Ouspensky had spoken of the value of sacrificing something precious, one woman confessed to being unable to break a cup of her heirloom china.[77] Bennett learnt from all this that the chief reason we cannot remember ourselves is that "we are too much attached to all the things that keep us asleep."[78]

Ouspensky urged his students to locate Gurdjieff's teachings within comparative studies. Equally persuaded of the value of Hindu and Buddhist teachings, and that neither could be accurately understood in translation, Bennett decided to learn Sanskrit from M.H. Kanhere, a Brahmin from Benares living and teaching in London, and Pali from Mrs Rhys Davids (1857-1942, born Caroline Augusta Foley). Each impressed him. Bennett cited his lengthy conversations with Davids, often about words for different psychic states, as significant in persuading him that "there is one underlying pattern common to all religious experience, quite irrespective of the forms of religious belief and worship."[79] This was Sabaheddin's favourite theme, and would also be heard from Subuh and Shah. Bennett also joined the Central Asian Society, and spoke at some of its meetings, supported by "that strange mixture of ardour and inconsequence, Commander Kenworthy, later Lord Strabolgi."[80]

---

[75] Bennett (1997) 77.
[76] Bennett (1997) 77.
[77] Bennett (1997) 77-78.
[78] Bennett (1997) 78.
[79] Bennett (1997) 78-79.
[80] Bennett (1997) 79. Joseph Montague Kenworthy, 10th Baron Strabolgi (1886-1953).

Promised funds from de Kay not materializing, Mrs. Beaumont and he sold or pawned everything, able to afford only one meal a day. Bennett recalled: "We knew hunger, and were thankful for this experience, which I regard as essential for the understanding of human nature."[81] Bennett differentiated involuntarily going hungry from voluntary fasting. He had no doubt that fasting can influence "the relationship between mind and body," but he never became used to, and even "dreaded" his regular fasts.[82] He continued:

> There is a serious disadvantage in voluntary fasting that I have observed in myself and other people. This comes from the inner sense of superiority that it engenders. When I discovered that I was beginning to pride myself upon fasting, and that I liked other people to notice and even speak about my austerities, I left them altogether. I believe that a man needs to be very free from self-love before he can safely allow himself to practise austerities. It is not enough to hide them from other people, for even this adds to the inner feeling of superiority which is a fault more deadly to the soul than greed. Involuntary hunger from real poverty has a different effect. It is a state we share with hundreds of millions of our fellow-men. For this very reason it does not isolate us from others, but engenders a sense of kinship.... Voluntary fasting is good only when it is practised by an entire community, as in Islam. The fast of Ramadan ... was instituted to enable the rich to participate in the feelings of the poor and understand the need for sharing their wealth.[83]

Bennett met Ramsay MacDonald, now leader of the opposition in the UK Parliament, at the Athenaeum, an exclusive Pall Mall members'

---

[81] Bennett (1997) 79.
[82] Bennett (1997) 79.
[83] Bennett (1997) 79-80.

club, founded by John Wilson Croker, an MP and the Secretary for the Admiralty, as a "club for literary men and artists."[84] Bennett was not immune to the consequence of the person and the site, but the meeting left a "vivid memory" because when MacDonald proposed that Bennett stand for election as a candidate at the next election, Bennett refused, since he was "guided by the vision of the future that had been shown to me in the cemetery at Scutari."[85] As he watched the "grave, elderly members of the club passing up and down the staircase ... I knew that all this did not fit the pattern of my life."[86] As we have seen, his later experience with the United Empire Party casts some doubt that it was so simple and definite.

Bennett made a scene at a meeting with Ouspensky, and decided to devote himself to foreign affairs, but immediately "knew" that he would not: rather, he would follow Gurdjieff and Ouspensky. Despite this, he found himself travelling to Munich, with Samuel Untermyer (1858-1940, a celebrated New York lawyer) in connection with the Abdul Hamid legacy.[87] When Standard Oil offered $100,000 for an option on the concessions, de Kay advised Bennett to ask for one million dollars. This caused Standard Oil to pull out altogether, but now Bennett learnt that: "it does not pay to overcall your hand."[88] Bennett spent three months in Europe in these ultimately fruitless negotiations, but found a chance to visit Gurdjieff's Institute at Fontainebleau.

Although it occurred later, on February 20, 1923, it is more convenient to mention now that on February 20, 1923, Bennett met Sir John Shuckburgh (1877-1953), a high ranking Colonial Administrator. Bennett, already working with Maitland Edwards, discussed with him the Abdul Hamid Estates, and especially the claims to the oil-rich lands in what was then called "Mesopotamia." Apparently, Bennett said that he and the other British representatives could not continue in respect of the oil

---

[84] Davy (1925) 8-9.
[85] Bennett (1997) 80.
[86] Bennett (1997) 80.
[87] Bennett (1997) 81.
[88] Bennett (1997) 82.

territories if the British Government was against them, but their withdrawal would only lead to the claims being taken over by Americans. Shuckburgh regarded this as a threat, and was pessimistic that any commission would be established to enquire into the justice of the claims. Bennett was quite forthright in his criticism of the British government's attitude, but stated that he only intended to try and change, not to oppose it.[89] Sami, who has made the only full study of the oil claims known to me, states that: "Captain Bennett assured him that as regards the oil right, "he and his associates would agree to act entirely in accordance with His Majesty's Government's policy, whatever that might be."[90]

Now, Sami is a relative of Abdul Hamid, so his assessment of Bennett as "perfectly reasonable" occasions little surprise.[91] When he asserts that the contemporary British and Turkish governments viewed Bennett, Maitland, and associates with suspicion, there is no reason to doubt him.[92] Shuckburgh, took the view that Bennett and friends were only interested in their commission, although as Sami notes, that is legitimate.[93] However, the image of Bennett as an opportunist and speculator, would taint the British government's attitude to him even when he had ceased to interest himself in the Mesopotamian claims.[94] Further, I cannot see how an attempt to "try and change" could not be interpreted by those whose minds he was trying to change, as "opposition." Bennett seems naïve, here.

3.4 WITH GURDJIEFF AT FONTAINEBLEAU

At Fontainebleau, where Gurdjieff's Study House had just been built, he met A.R. Orage (1873-1934), and Katherine Mansfield (1888-1923) just

[89] Sami (2006) 60-61.
[90] Sami (2006) 61.
[91] Sami (2006) 62.
[92] Sami (2006) 62.
[93] Sami (2006) 62.
[94] Sami (2006) 62-63. See chapter 4 and appendix 2 for the subsequent history of the claims.

one week before her death from tuberculosis on January 9. This places Bennett in France at the opening of 1923.[95] Bennett spoke with Gurdjieff for a few minutes, and although Gurdjieff invited him to stay for a week, he was pulled away by his business commitments. Quite appropriately, perhaps, as Bennett returned to Paris, he said to himself: "This is your chief feature: always to be doing the thing that is less important, and neglecting what matters to you most."[96] He returned to the Abdul Hamid affairs, securing only a right to attempt to vindicate "the Princes' title" under Turkish law. The eight months of negotiating and manoeuvring evoked "a terrible reaction" in him, such that: "I could see that in this short time the means had overshadowed the end. I had lost touch with the spiritual aims which I had imagined that all my efforts were to serve. When I spoke to Ouspensky about my experiences, he advised me to go for a long visit to Gurdjieff's Institute in Fontainebleau."[97] When Bennett speaks about the "spiritual aims" he had hoped to pursue, he is barely doing justice to the grandeur of his aspirations: "...world-wide research to establish the reality of the unseen world of the fifth dimension, bringing in on the one hand the social ideals of de Kay and on the other the psychological methods of Gurdjieff."[98] But Bennett does not evince any suspicion as to the justice of these Turkish aristocrats' claim to vast properties.

The circumstances surrounding Gurdjieff's purchase of a stunning property at Fontainebleau on October 1, 1922, and the establishment of the "Institute for the Harmonious Development of Man" are set out by Taylor.[99] This visit marks, I suggest, the most significant experience in Bennett's adult life, for he had an experience which both Gurdjieff and he understood as Gurdjieff having connected Bennett to a source of higher energy. Fortunately, while he was at the Prieuré, Mrs Beaumont was in Biarritz with her mother, and retained the letters which Bennett

---

[95] Bennett (1997) 83.
[96] Bennett (1997) 83.
[97] Bennett (1997) 83-84.
[98] Bennett (1997) 76.
[99] Taylor (2020) 99-101.

wrote to her daily. As Ouspensky would comment about being with Gurdjieff in Essentuki, Bennett now states: "So very much happened to me that, if I had relied on my memory alone, I could not believe that I was there only thirty-three days."[100] Bennett does not give precise dates, but he spoke to Ouspensky in London after July 8, 1923, and he states that "at the beginning of September 1923" he left the Prieuré for the last time.[101] We can therefore infer that Bennett spent about three weeks in England before returning to France, arriving at the Prieuré either at the very tail end of July or the start of August 1923.

When he arrived, he saw how the Prieuré had changed over the eight months since his last visit. He had not long to wait before he met Gurdjieff, who told him, in oracular fashion:

> You have already too much knowledge. It will remain only theory unless you learn to understand not with your mind but with heart and body. Now only your mind is awake: your heart and body are asleep. If you continue like this, soon your mind also will go to sleep, and you will never be able to think any new thoughts. You cannot awaken your feelings, but you can awaken your body. If you can learn to master your body, you will begin to acquire Being.
>
> For this, you must look on your body as a servant. It must obey you. It is ignorant and lazy. You must teach it to work.... When you are master of your body, your feelings will obey you.... You cannot start with thoughts, because you cannot yet separate yourself from your thoughts.[102]

Gurdjieff later made another statement which presaged important concerns in Bennett's life: "Patience is the Mother of Will. If you have not a mother, how can you be born?"[103] At the Institute, Bennett

---

[100] Bennett (1997) 85.
[101] Bennett (1997) 84 and 98.
[102] Bennett (1997) 86.
[103] Bennett (1997) 91-92.

began as kitchen boy, later moved to sawing, and then to the stone quarry. Recounting how Gurdjieff spoke of "Conscious Labour and Intentional Suffering," Bennett said that Gurdjieff's words were often misunderstood, "with that comic literalness that overtakes Europeans and Americans when they are confronted with Asiatic subtlety."[104] Of relevance for the contemplative-exercises, when Gurdjieff gave the celebrated "Stop Exercise": "First the eyes were to fix upon the object of their gaze. ... every voluntary movement was to be arrested and held."[105] That the instruction began with fixing the eyes is, to the best of my knowledge, mentioned in no other account. The dysentery which Bennett had suffered in Smyrna now returned, but he "disregarded the objections of my body," and forced himself on.[106] Day by day, he weakened, until one day, which seems to have occurred after about three weeks,[107] was, Bennett said, the "most extraordinary and important day of my whole life."[108]

3.5   THE LOST LECTURE OF 1923

Before we come to that event, mention should be made of what we might call "the lost lecture of 1923," a lecture which Gurdjieff gave, and which no one other than Bennett could understand. Towards the end of his life, when speaking at Sherborne about how we live on a low level of ourselves, he said:

> In 1923, Gurdjieff gave a lecture about this theme. Unfortunately, most of it was lost, but I retained some notes and I remember the strange diagram that he drew of the different centres and the formatory apparatus. He said

---

[104] Bennett (1997) 89.
[105] Bennett (1997) 91.
[106] Bennett (1997) 92.
[107] I am here following the rough indications given in Bennett (1962) 121-122 and 129; (1997) 92.
[108] Bennett (1997) 96.

something like this: "You are taught that you are three-centred beings, that you have thinking centre, emotional centre, moving centre and this is how you live. But in reality man does not live like this – man lives with only one thing and that is with his formatory apparatus, because that is all his personality can live with." Then he drew the diagram in which there was a little piece of mechanism in the front rather like a fan with an axle behind it. It was simply blowing out whatever came from behind it; puffing it out into the open. He drew arrows showing that the intellectual centre had no means of expression through the personality. The personality can only express itself through the ready-made words, ideas, habitual expressions, and so on, that are stored up in formatory apparatus. Nothing comes directly from the centres; nothing goes directly to the centres.[109]

After fifty years, Bennett returned to the bleak picture of human beings functioning at a dismally low level, accepting that: "Man does not live even in the lower part of himself. He lives in an artificial shell that surrounds it."[110] This uncompromisingly grim picture can be related to the insights of his eighth vision (section 4.9), which also presented him with a way forward and out of it.

3.6 THE FOURTH VISION: THE GREAT ACCUMULATOR

As the dysentery gripped him, Bennett became feverish, and decided that he was so sick he had to stay in bed. However, as often happened with him, having resolved to do one thing, exactly the opposite happened: "I felt my body rising. I dressed and went to work as usual, but this time with a queer sense of being held together by a superior Will that was

---

[109] Bennett (2006) 14-15.
[110] Bennett (2006) 15.

not my own."[111] From what follows, we might infer that the operative will came from Gurdjieff. Bennett joined the work teams, but had no appetite for lunch, and so lay down wondering if this was his end. In the afternoon, they began working at a movement of such complexity that not even the most experienced pupils could maintain the independent sequences for head, feet, arms, and torso. After this tortuous prelude, Gurdjieff had de Hartmann play various rhythms for which they had to stamp the pattern.[112] Then, as pupil after pupil had sat out, the significant moment arrived:

> I felt very ill and weak. A deadly lassitude took possession of me, so that every movement became a supreme effort of will.... Soon I ceased to be aware of anything but the music and my own weakness.... Gurdjieff stood watching intently. Time lost the quality of before and after. There was no past and no future, only the present agony of making my body move. Gradually, I became aware that Gurdjieff was putting all his attention on me. There was an unspoken demand that was at the same time an encouragement and a promise. I must not give up—if it killed me.[113]

I see no reason to interpret this as a manner of speaking: Bennett literally meant that Gurdjieff was telepathically communicating with him, and that the demand was ruthless. Bennett rose to the challenge, and:

> Suddenly, I was filled with an influx of immense power. My body seemed to have turned into light. I could not feel its presence in the usual ways. There was no effort, no pain, no weariness, not even any sense of weight. I felt an immense gratitude to Gurdjieff and Thomas de Hartmann, but they

[111] Bennett (1997) 92.
[112] Bennett (1997) 92-93.
[113] Bennett (1997) 93.

had quietly gone off, having dismissed the class, and leaving me quite alone. My own state was blissful beyond anything I had ever known.... It was exultation in the faith that can move mountains.[114]

It must have been August 1923; a disproportionate number of Bennett's visions came in August. It may be that lengthy spells of warm weather disposed him to such experiences. Bennett did not join the others who were then having tea, but went into the garden and tested himself by digging. No one, Bennett affirms, can dig both quickly and for a long time, but he felt that he had to test this power which had entered him, and he dug for over an hour, in fierce heat, at a rate which ordinarily he could not sustain for two minutes, and yet he felt neither fatigue nor even a sense of effort. The diarrhoea and abdominal pains from which he had been suffering disappeared, and he experienced an extraordinary clarity of thought. In this state, he recalled his experience in the Grande Rue de Péra, and found that he could now be aware of the fifth dimension (the second vision).[115] He states:

> The phrase "in my mind's eye" took on a new meaning as I "saw" the eternal pattern of each thing I looked at: the trees, the plants, the water flowing in the canal and even the spade, and lastly my own body. I recognised the changing relationship between "myself" and "my pattern." As my state of consciousness changed, "I" and my "pattern" grew closer together or separated and lost touch. Time and Eternity were the conditions of our experience, and the Harmonious Development of Man towards which Gurdjieff was leading us was the secret of true freedom. I remember saying aloud:

---

[114] Bennett (1997) 93.
[115] Bennett (1997) 37-38.

"Now I see why God hides Himself from us." But even now I cannot recall the intuition behind this exclamation.[116]

This touches on certain themes, especially of the "pattern," which Bennett would return to through his life, but especially his mother's wisdom, cited at the close of the 1974 draft of *Witness*. Bennett interpreted his experience through the lens of what Gurdjieff had said to him when he met him at Prince Sabaheddin's, at Kuru Cheshme:

> [I]t is not enough to know that another world exists; one must be able to enter it at will. Now I was living in Eternity and yet I had not lost my hold on Time. I was aware that Life itself is infinitely richer and greater than all that our thinking mind can possibly know about it.[117]

Bennett then walked through the forest, "satisfied just to be as I was," when, turning a corner, he suddenly met Gurdjieff, who, without preliminaries, said:

> "There is a certain energy that is necessary for work on oneself. No man can make efforts unless he has a supply of this energy. We can call it the Higher Emotional Energy. Everyone, by a natural process, makes a small amount of this energy every day. If rightly used, it enables man to achieve much for his own self-perfecting. But he can only get to a certain point in this way. The real complete transformation of Being that is indispensable for a man who wishes to fulfil the purpose of this existence, requires a very much greater concentration of Higher Emotional Energy than that which comes to him by nature."
>
> "There are some people in the world, but they are very

---

[116] Bennett (1997) 93-94.
[117] Bennett (1997) 94.

rare, who are connected to a Great Reservoir or Accumulator of this energy. This Reservoir has no limits. Those who can draw upon it can be a means of helping others. Suppose that a man needs a hundred units of this energy for his own transformation, but only has ten units and cannot make more for himself. He is helpless. But with the help of someone who can draw upon the Great Accumulator, he can borrow ninety more. Then his work can be effective."

He let all this sink in, and then stopped, and looking into my eyes said: 'Those who have this quality belong to a special part of the highest caste of humanity. It may be that one day you will become such, but you will have to wait for many years. What you have received today is a taste of what is possible for you. Until now, you have only known about these things theoretically, but now you have experience. When a man has had experience of Reality, he is responsible for what he does with his life."[118]

This experience of "Reality," with Bennett's capital R, is one sign of the connection between Gurdjieff's work and mysticism, which I sketched in the Introduction. Gurdjieff then said that after a day or two, they would discuss his future plans, as Bennett might find a place in them. When Gurdjieff departed, Bennett remained in the forest where he discovered he had an extraordinary control over his feeling, including the ability to summon and experience the emotions of astonishment, fear, joy, and then love. But the mystery of love was so great that he had to leave the state, lest he plunge so deeply that he cease to exist.[119] Later that evening, Gurdjieff gave a lecture in Russian. Bennett could not only follow, but he could see where the translator erred. Gurdjieff was:

---

[118] Bennett (1997) 94.
[119] Bennett (1997) 94-95.

showing how our capacity for work depends on the way we are connected with the sources of energy inside us and beyond us. All that he said illuminated my own experience.... I saw a picture of all humanity thirsting for the energy that was flowing through me. Gurdjieff spoke of the Great Eternal Reservoirs, which are connected with Sacred Beings who have come to earth to help mankind. He then passed to another diagram showing how the Will of God in creation acts through energies of different density of fineness. I could see that such sources of help are really present and was aware of the great mistake that we men have made in breaking the contact that we could have with them.[120]

However, something which Gurdjieff said to him alone seems to have been omitted from this account. In the papers published posthumously as *Transformation*, he adds that the conversation with Gurdjieff was in Turkish, and that Gurdjieff said:

A man who wishes to change must have the necessary energy. Say he needs one hundred units, but with all his efforts he can only collect ten. He is helpless. Suppose he meets a man who has more energy than he needs for himself. That man can lend him ninety. Then he will do what he wants. Afterwards he must repay. Now you cannot do anything by yourself, so I must help you.

There is a special substance—let us call it "higher emotional energy" that you need. You do not know where to get this substance, but I know. Those who can give this substance to others who need it belong to a special section of the highest caste of humanity.[121]

---

[120] Bennett (1997) 95-96.
[121] Bennett (1978a) 34-35.

Bennett then asked Gurdjieff how he could obtain help, and he replied "When you say *amar* (mercy!) with all your being. Only then can you be helped."[122] This should be related to Gurdjieff's telling Bennett: "Nature hates vacuum. When you make empty, help will enter."[123] It is an important detail, and we shall return to it, together with mention of an important incident in 1948 or 1949 when Gurdjieff purported to "loan" Bennett some of his Hanbledzoin (the energy of the higher emotional centre, and the "blood" of the "being-body Kesdjan" or astral body).[124] In the 1957 essay, Bennett states that at Fontainebleau, he: "underwent unusual experiences which revealed to me new potentialities latent in the human psyche of releasing and controlling energies still quite unknown to science."[125] Perhaps this realisation fuelled his desire to take science towards that area, so far as it lay within his ability, and was one factor inducing him to write and publish in 1964, a slim but significant volume titled *Energies: Material, Vital, Cosmic*. It is noteworthy that Bennett makes the barest allusion to this remarkable incident in his later account of his Fontainebleau visits.[126] Perhaps he felt he could add no more to the earlier account.

3.7 RETURN TO LONDON

The next day, Bennett had the conviction that "somehow, I must not only taste, but make my own, the power to connect myself with the Great Accumulator that could endow man with such marvellous powers."[127] Although he had just experienced "the most extraordinary and important day of my whole life" he could not say anything about it to others.[128] A few days later, Gurdjieff spoke to him about his plans to purchase more land and to build an observatory to continue astronomical

---

[122] Bennett (1978a) 35.
[123] Bennett (1978a) 39.
[124] Bennett (1978a) 34.
[125] Bennett (1957) 4.
[126] Bennett (1973) 147-159.
[127] Bennett (1997) 96.
[128] Bennett (1997) 96.

investigations which he had commenced in Central Asia thirty years before. Bennett took this quite literally. Towards the end of August, Mrs Beaumont arrived for a visit, but Bennett's dysentery had returned: the great experience had only held it in abeyance. She insisted on taking him to Paris, but when he returned to the Prieuré, he was still "suffering a reaction after the prodigious experiences of the week before."[129] Having received an encouraging letter from de Kay, and needing to help his mother, he told Gurdjieff that he had to leave. Gurdjieff said:

> So far you have come here as a trial. You have been given something. But if you come here to work, you must understand that nothing is given.... You have the possibility of learning to work. The truth is, that very few people in the contemporary world have this possibility; for most people there are barriers they cannot pass. Everyone has these barriers; they are in human nature. You have seen that it is possible to be directly connected with the Great Accumulator of Energy that is the source of all miracles. If you could be permanently connected with this source, you could pass all barriers. But you do not know how it is done, and you are not ready to be shown. Everything is still in front of you to be done, but you have the proof that it is possible. It may take twenty, thirty or even forty years before you will be able to enter into possession of the power that was lent to you for a day. But what is a whole lifetime if such a thing is possible? Ever since I was a young boy, I have known of the existence of this power and of the barriers that separate man from it, and I searched until I found the way of breaking through them. This is the greatest secret that man can discover about the human nature. Many people are convinced

---

[129] Bennett (1997) 96-97.

that they wish to be free and to know reality, but they do not know the barrier that prevents them from reaching reality.[130]

Gurdjieff told Bennett that internal work could not pass a certain stage unless one could make contact with the "Great Accumulator of Energy," which seems to include the "Great Eternal Reservoirs." However, to the best of my knowledge, Gurdjieff disclosed no further information concerning the relation between the two. Although Gurdjieff asserted that this knowledge was "the greatest secret that man can discover about the human nature," Bennett had warned about falling into "comic literalness" when "confronted with Asiatic subtlety."[131] But even if this is not meant to be literally and absolutely true, it must still have some relation to the truth, and the circumstances taken as a whole suggest that Gurdjieff, on this occasion, meant exactly what he said. It is even more striking that these ideas correspond to contemplation-like exercises which, at the end of his life, he gave Bennett (the Four Prophets), and George Adie (the Four Ideals).[132]

In this conversation, to Bennett's surprise, Gurdjieff told him that he would need only two years before he could work alone; although this was predicated on the condition that Bennett "devote all (his) energies to the task," and be "ready for anything."[133] Gurdjieff invited Bennett to learn Russian, accompany him to the USA as his interpreter, and learn to deliver lectures to Gurdjieff's standards. Gurdjieff added: "Later you will be ready to give your last shirt to help the work – as I am ready to give mine."[134]

3.8 LEAVING GURDJIEFF AND THE PRIEURÉ

Bennett left the Prieuré, and was not to see Gurdjieff for twenty-five

---

[130] Bennett (1997) 97-98.
[131] Bennett (1997) 89.
[132] See Azize (2020), ch. 17.
[133] Bennett (1997) 98.
[134] Bennett (1997) 98.

years. When Bennett returned to London, he met Ouspensky, but could not speak of his experience of connection to the Accumulator, but he did describe Gurdjieff's lecture on "energies and the changes of speed," to him.[135] There is no mention of "changes of speed" in the original account, but one can conjecture that when the finer energies descend to a lower level, they slow down.[136] We must infer that Bennett was silent as to what Gurdjieff had said to him about the "greatest secret."[137] Yet, Ouspensky's subsequent comment to Mrs. Beaumont was penetrating: "I can assure you that Gurdjieff is a good man. But Bennett was right to come away: he is not yet ready for that work."[138] Bennett continued attending Ouspensky's groups, and promoting the Sultan Abdul Hamid Estates. It is perplexing that he should describe de Kay's advocacy of the Estates to Ramsay MacDonald's Labour government as "a plea for the oppressed."[139] Their new-found poverty in Europe could equally be seen as a karmic turnaround. Eventually, de Kay was extradited to the USA on unrelated matters.[140]

At this point, Ouspensky called a special, and limited meeting, at which he declared that he had decided to break relations with Gurdjieff, and offered them all a choice to work with Gurdjieff or himself. The only condition was that if they elected to remain with him, they would "not communicate in any way with Mr Gurdjieff or his pupils."[141] When Ralph Philipson asked why, Ouspensky replied that he believed Gurdjieff was passing through a crisis, and that they in London could be of no use to him, and neither could he to them, adding that this did not mean that Ouspensky was "against him, or ... consider that what he is doing is bad."[142] Ouspensky stated that Gurdjieff had "only two 'I's; one very good and one very bad" but if he took the wrong path for the future, he could

---

[135] Bennett (1997) 100.
[136] Ouspensky (1949) 317-18.
[137] Bennett (1997) 100.
[138] Bennett (1997) 100.
[139] Bennett (1997) 101.
[140] Bennett (1997) 101-102.
[141] Bennett (1997) 102.
[142] Bennett (1997) 102.

go mad or else "attract to himself some disaster in which all those round him would be involved."¹⁴³ Ouspensky's prediction was made, as Bennett reveals on the next page, after the motor vehicle accident of July 1924. Bennett then speaks about his own position in terms which remind us of other elements in this book, namely the importance of his connection to the Great Accumulator, and of Bennett's life following a pattern he could not change:

> I owed him [Gurdjieff] the greatest experience of my life. And yet as my feelings were surging this way and that, I knew that I would not go to Gurdjieff. I was bound to continue to live just as I was living. In later years, I was often asked why I had not followed Gurdjieff. I do not believe that I was influenced by Ouspensky's warning. It was much rather as if Gurdjieff himself had withdrawn from me, and would not let me follow him.¹⁴⁴

Bennett comments that only later did he see that the pattern of Gurdjieff's life obliged him "to drive away all those who could be most useful to him." He cites as examples Ouspensky, Orage, and Nicoll, and states that it was his good fortune that he lived long enough to be able to return to Gurdjieff.¹⁴⁵ I cannot see how Gurdjieff drove Bennett away. On his own account, Bennett freely decided to go, although Gurdjieff made quite a fair effort to persuade him to persevere. However, it does make sense as an *apologia* for the perceived spottiness of his relations with Gurdjieff, for later in *Witness* he seems to regret that: "I had left Gurdjieff and the Prieuré in order to follow Ouspensky."¹⁴⁶ That is, Bennett was being defensive, meeting in advance the criticism that he should have stayed with Gurdjieff. However, within terms of Gurdjieff's teaching, the most critical point of this chapter, and perhaps of the entire study, is

---

¹⁴³ Bennett (1997) 102.
¹⁴⁴ Bennett (1997) 103.
¹⁴⁵ Bennett (1997) 98-99.
¹⁴⁶ Bennett (1997) 168.

what Gurdjieff said to Bennett about the Great Accumulator of Energy and about Great Reservoirs, and about these being "the greatest secret that man can discover about the human nature."

The framework of the Djamichunatra

CHAPTER 4

WITH OUSPENSKY

4.1   SEEKING A CAREER, AND A SECOND MARRIAGE

Bennett states that in 1924 he helped Ouspensky translate his books into English, and took an active part in his groups. A rather noteworthy incident, nonetheless omitted from *Witness*, occurred at this time when Ouspensky asked Bennett to draw the Enneagram (a symbol used by Gurdjieff in his teaching):[1]

> I remember vividly when I first saw that the Enneagram was a picture of myself. Mr Ouspensky was giving a lecture on the Enneagram ... and asked me to put the diagram on the blackboard. As I was drawing the familiar lines, I felt myself going out of myself and entering the diagram. I noticed that I was facing myself and grasped for the first time the essential difference between the two sides of our bodies. How long this lasted, I don't know, but from that evening, I was convinced that the Enneagram is a living diagram and that we can experience ourselves as Enneagrams. I was particularly struck by seeing that I understood the point 6, although not with my mind.[2]

Yet, his mature opinion was that, touching what was most

---

[1] Ouspensky (1949) 289, 293.
[2] Bennett (1983) 32.

important, his inner work and his self-observation, he (Bennett) then had no real understanding of what he was about.[3] To an extent, this is a question of comparison with the relative clarity and insight he was to later achieve. However, Bennett was in truth pouring his energies into international intrigues. Although de Kay had not, for whatever reason, honoured his agreement with the heirs of the Sultan, Bennett persevered, travelling over Europe, meeting potential backers, and being put in funds to "entertain the Princes, and where necessary to make them small advances of money." This embraced drinking, cabarets and the "women of the strange half-world." He disarmingly confesses that: "I could only justify the way I had been living as a necessary part of my education. To this day I do not know if this is true or not.... between July 1924 and February 1925 my way of living was quite incompatible with the high ideals I had set before myself."[4] Once more, *Witness* evinces its secondary theme as an *apologia pro vita sua*.

When this business threatened to demand his absence from England for months if not years, he sought Ouspensky's advice, who answered indirectly with an enigmatic tale of a knight who is offered one of three paths. If he heads to the right he will lose his horse; if to the left, he will lose himself; but if he proceeds straight ahead, he will lose both his horse and himself. The paradox was that it would not matter in the end which path of the three he took, *provided he persisted*.[5] Later, Bennett says something which alters our understanding of the riddle (section 4.5). But for now, Bennett must have enjoyed Ouspensky's confidence, because Ouspensky arranged for Bennett to share with Dr. Maurice Nicoll—a clear favourite of Ouspensky's—the answering of questions at group meetings when Ouspensky himself was absent. Also, Bennett taught English to Madame Ouspensky, while she taught him Russian.[6] Bennett recounts a conversation in which he said to Ouspensky: "I am

---

[3] Bennett (1997) 103.
[4] Bennett (1997) 103-4.
[5] Bennett (1997) 104.
[6] Bennett (1997) 104-105. For Ouspensky's regard for Nicoll, see Pogson (1961) 108-109. Bennett had met Mme Ouspensky in Constantinople in 1920: Bennett (2000) 9.

sure that this work can lead to the attainment of Consciousness and Immortality, but I am not sure if I can reach it myself ... in the last year I have gone back rather than forward."[7] This statement together with Ouspensky's reply are significant not only for what was to happen to Ouspensky's groups after his death, but also for Bennett's actions after Gurdjieff's death, and yet more, I think, as adumbrating a theme which looms large in *Witness*:

> He sighed deeply and said: "... I am not sure. I am sure of nothing. But I do know that we have nothing, and therefore we have nothing to lose.... I will not give up the struggle. In principle, I believe that it is possible to attain what we seek—but I am not sure that we have yet found the way. But it is useless to wait. We know that we have something that has come from a Higher Source. It may be that something more will come from the same Source."[8]

Touched by Ouspensky's sincerity, Bennett declared that the confessions "gave me far more confidence than any positive affirmation."[9] Perhaps this honesty, together with Ouspensky's other qualities, persuaded him both that something substantial was possible following the teaching, and also that there was a real chance that assistance would come from the "Higher Source." When Subud appeared, after the deaths of both Gurdjieff and Ouspensky, Mme Ouspensky echoed her husband's words, saying: "Since Mr Gurdjieff went, I have been waiting for someone to come. I still wait, but he has not come, perhaps he will not come in my lifetime." But she would not be drawn on how to recognise a new teacher.[10] This expectation disposed Bennett towards the idea of further dispensations.

In a vain hope of raising funds, Bennett left for Athens in April 1925,

---

[7] Bennett (1997) 105. As ever in quotations, the capitals are present in the original.
[8] Bennett (1997) 105.
[9] Bennett (1997) 105.
[10] Bennett (1962) 332; (1997) 262-63.

where now being divorced, he married Mrs Beaumont.[11] She had been warned by friends not to marry a man twenty years her junior, but they enjoyed the support of Bennett's mother.[12] Bennett feared, probably correctly, that the British Legation in Athens had conceived a fixed suspicion of him:

> I did not like to visit the Embassy [in Athens], although we had friendly introductions, being embarrassed over the publicity that had accompanied my divorce. In the sequel this proved very foolish as we had been expected and our failure to make ourselves known was misinterpreted as hostility towards our own Government. My task was hard enough without the need to alienate the sympathies of the British colony in Greece.[13]

Now, the publicity which had accompanied his divorce was indeed bad. The *Nottingham Evening Post* of 10 May 1924 included this piece:

> 'My Love Is Like A Lion.'
> Woman Co-Respondent's Parody on Song of Solomon
> Decree Nisi against R.E. Officer
> Some extraordinary letters from a woman, 50 years of age, were read in the Divorce Court yesterday, when Mrs. Evelyn Bennett ... was granted a decree nisi against her husband, John Godolphin Bennett ...
> The misconduct was alleged with a Mrs. Winifred Beaumont ... writing to Captain Bennett in one letter: "My

---

[11] Bennett (1997) 106. Michael Benham advises that in fact she was twenty-two years his senior, having been born on 24 March 1875, and Bennett on 6 June 1897.
[12] Bennett (1997) 105. These brief mentions of his mother set the background to the "Help for the Deceased Exercise" which Gurdjieff taught Bennett in 1948 or 1949.
[13] Bennett (1997) 106.

love is like a lion. He walks on silent feet like a young lion with loose strides."[14]

This is the context against which Bennett decided not to call upon the consular office. The Abdul Hamid business did not prosper, and de Kay, while pursuing his own agenda, had "turned implacably" against Bennett. The text of *Witness* states: "The autumn and winter of 1926 passed, and the dispute with John de Kay ended with the return of his emissary to America. In the spring of 1926."[15] This last year must be an error for "1927" as no northern hemisphere spring follows the autumn of the same calendar year. At this point, Bennett received some of the Abdul Hamid title deeds, and hoping to take possession, went to view some of the properties.[16] The Bennetts were fascinated by local features, such as the "physical perfection" of a Bulgar peasant woman who naturally and with balanced movements, walked uphill with a load of wood on her head while she span wool. Other experiences, like witnessing the explosion of the volcano on Santorini, were extraordinary.[17] In both cases, Bennett's interest is in larger issues: the relationship between people and their communities and societies, and the development of the planet. But although Bennett saw some signs that his Abdul Hamid project was advancing, he still had to wait for the authorities to act, and, as he wrote: "I am by nature so impatient that any kind of waiting seems endless."[18] With apparently gratuitous candour, Bennett recounts that one evening, when his frustration boiled over, he began screaming, and then struck his wife with his fists when she tried to calm him down.[19] I

---

[14] Michael Benham forwarded the newspaper extract to me with a note that similar pieces appeared in other United Kingdom papers, on July 9, 2022. I have edited the piece, wishing only to show the sensational tone. It also noted the twenty-two years of age difference between Bennett and Beaumont.
[15] Bennett (1997) 109.
[16] Bennett (1997) 109-10.
[17] Bennett (1997) 108-9. The incident which Bennett wrote "probably" occurred in May 1925, more likely happened on or shortly after 11 August: https://www.santorini.com/santorinivolcano/volcaniceruptions.htm accessed January 13, 2022.
[18] Bennett (1997) 110.
[19] Bennett (1997) 110-11.

suspect that he discloses this partly in order to make clear that he was, at that moment, weak; but also to indicate that he was remorseful, so that he became quite a different person.

4.2 THE FIFTH VISION: THE PAST IS UNDYING

The boiling frustrations prompted his wife to suggest a holiday, during which they visited the ruins of Mycenae. Most likely in or soon after August 1925, Bennett stood on the battlements, from where he could survey the plains, and received another epiphany:

> The essential history of the Greek legends is imperishable. I could see returning Agamemnon and his weary followers and sense the turbulent emotion of Clytemnestra far more vividly than in Aeschylus' presentation of the tragedy. In Greece, I first began to experience the undyingness of the past. I saw that history is more than fact, and that it cannot be made by the mind alone.[20]

Implicit in this is that on later occasions, too, he experienced "the undyingness of the past." Yet, when he recounts that he became aware of the ancient city of Babylon and its people during a visit to its ruins in 1953, he does not speak quite the way he does of the vision at Mycenae.[21] In a letter dated November 26, 1955 to Marjorie von Harten, a long term pupil of his, who was visiting Central America, he wrote:

> Whenever I have visited ancient sites I have found it possible to sense the quality of the existence of the people who lived

---

[20] Bennett (1997) 111. In some only partly published lectures delivered in 1974, Bennett refers several times to the reality and significance of his preternatural and accurate perception of past events. Interesting as they are, those references await fuller study. Bennett used them in conjunction with a Sufi-inspired teaching of different "worlds" in which we exist at one and the same time.
[21] Bennett (1997) 240, also but less vividly, Bennett (2000) 104-7.

there, and in this way to understand their history, as it is said 'with all three centres'.[22]

All this suggests that Bennett literally meant that he saw the ancient warriors returning from Troy and sensed Clytemnestra's turmoil. If so, was the vision objectively faithful to the historical kernel of the epic, or, if the tale were purely legendary, did he see and feel something projected from inside himself? Ancient Greek literature, and in particular, Homer was a major influence upon the Edwardians. Ogilvie's study of the influence of Greek classics on English intellectual life from 1600 to 1918 concludes that: "in Homer the Edwardians found an author who responded to them and who served to canalize and voice their felt but unspoken impulses."[23] Steeped in Homer from his childhood, could Bennett's revelations have been subjectively true? Certainly, he felt something quite deeply, hence the unusual observation that history "cannot be made by the mind alone." I suspect that Bennett means that a higher centre than his ordinary mind was operating to enter the past as if it were present. This was no play with words: Bennett claimed the same for his vision of Judas at the Last Supper.[24] Bennett goes on to suggest that some of the architectural marvels of ancient Athens may have been due to the influence of the mystery cults, and states that, while sitting in an Orphic shrine, he "felt the power" of that "form of worship."[25] Yet, despite his enjoying what could fairly be accounted preternatural showings, he reached this conviction:

> I should have disregarded every other consideration and stayed with Gurdjieff. He at least has a method—but I have only theories. He spoke to me of *Being* the first and last times

[22] von Harten (1978) 2.
[23] Oglivie (1964) 143.
[24] Bennett (1997) 213. In Gurdjieff circles, it is thought that while one's visions may be persuasive for that person, but there is no good reason for anyone else to accept them.
[25] Bennett (1997) 111.

that I saw him. I *know* more and more, but I still *am* nothing. I must be free from all this and return to work upon myself.[26]

4.3   IMPRISONMENT, MARCH 1928

Given his experiences with Gurdjieff, especially the connection to the Great Accumulator, and his being made an assistant teacher by Ouspensky, this statement "I still *am* nothing" is rather unexpected. However, there is no reason to doubt Bennett's sincerity: he was still enmeshed with the Abdul Hamid Estates, and fixated upon the huge financial reward he expected to reap, and so he did not return to Gurdjieff.[27] Bennett travelled to London, where he met Ouspensky, who urged him to help Ferapontoff and Ivanoff, two of the most promising of Gurdjieff's former pupils.[28] He returned to Greece, where he received his mother for a visit. There, the once-promising business conditions soured, and in March 1928, he was arrested upon charges of having been concerned in forging title deeds.[29] In prison, he grimly realised that he could neither establish his innocence nor expect help from any quarter. Then:

> At that moment my state of consciousness changed, and I saw that all this had no importance. I had allowed myself to be drawn away from my real aim, and anything would be better for me, even prison than continuing to engage in affairs that involved so much intrigue; affairs which, even if successful, would never give me any true freedom. I lay on the bed and went peacefully to sleep.[30]

In this condition, his wife, together with his mother, visited him,

---

[26] Bennett (1997) 112.
[27] Bennett (1997) 112.
[28] Bennett (1997) 112 and (1973) 236.
[29] Bennett (1997) 113.
[30] Bennett (1997) 113.

although his "poor little mother was terribly distressed."[31] She was bustled off to a sister in Florence, fearing that he had "inherited my father's weakness and got myself into trouble, as he had so often done when we were children."[32] There are no further details, but the picture seems to be that his mother and he were still emotionally entangled in their family history. Bennett's position in the Greek gaol seemed hopeless until his wife devised a plan for him to feign illness by swallowing iodine, manoeuvring the authorities to peremptorily release him, presumably because the prison medical facilities were inadequate.[33] Bennett could only take the iodine in the latrines, and these were, without any exaggeration, horrible. However, take the iodine he did, and he suffered all the effects of a fever, only to find that the doctor had been unable to attend that day. In the morning, he felt better, and his wife had to procure yet more iodine. He wrote:

> I felt the utmost nausea at the very thought of returning to the latrines. But such disagreeable experiences also produce some degree of separation of the inner from the outer man. I was beginning to feel inwardly detached from the body that was being so unkindly treated, and by this time, found myself able to go through the whole process as if it were happening to a stranger.[34]

He took the second dose, and was subsequently released. Much later, in 1957, he reflected that in the gaol, he had met and studied "types of humanity with whom I had never previously been in contact," and understood at first-hand what it was like to be locked up, unsure if he would be released. Most significantly, he states: "from this time, I began

---

[31] Bennett (1997) 115.
[32] Bennett (1997) 115.
[33] Bennett (1997) 115.
[34] Bennett (1997) 116.

slowly to acquire the virtue of patience which until then had been sadly lacking in my make-up."[35]

4.4 THE FOREIGN OFFICE FILES

Throughout this account, Bennett says nothing of the issues he and his wife had with the British Consular Office, or its head, Sir Percy Loraine (1880-1961), affectionately known as "Pompous Percy" for personality traits such as his being appalled that an embassy where he served lacked a grand staircase. As Ambassador to Turkey from about 1933, Loraine exhibited an unseemly fury, giving due warning of his "dismissal, voluntary retirement, suicide, or other form of promotion."[36] He stubbornly kept the Istanbul embassy going and manned all year round, despite being ordered to maintain his embassy at Ankara in keeping with Turkish requirements, and practical problems and expenses.[37] Both Loraine's character and his strategic views disposed him against Bennett's activities, and explain the lack of official assistance when Bennett was arrested and gaoled. Loraine became "a great admirer" of Ataturk, arranging for Edward VIII to visit Istanbul in 1936, which visit was naturally interpreted as the mountain calling on Muhammad. He became so close to Ataturk that a spoof telegram in which a dying Ataturk offers to make Loraine the next president of Turkey, was thought to be genuine when it emerged thirty years later.[38] It was thought that Bennett was arrested due to Turkish intrigue. Loraine was not one to sympathise with a concession hunter representing the interests of the former Turkish regime. If his desire to see Britain and Ataturk's Turkey enjoying cordial relations already existed in 1928, he would have deprecated the occupations of a freebooter, a divorcee who had married another divorcee, had not

---

[35] Bennett (1957) 5.
[36] Berridge (2009) 142 and 153 does not provide the specific dates of Loraine's appointment or arrival in Turkey.
[37] Berridge (2009) 154-55.
[38] Berridge (2009) 155-59.

contacted the Legation on arrival in Athens, and was probably putty in the hands of de Kay.

Bennett could, in *Witness*, have excoriated Loraine who had died on May 23, 1961. The Foreign Office was well aware that Loraine's indiscretion in speaking badly of the Bennetts was producing the impression in diplomatic circles that the sole or real reason for his inactivity was his dislike of Bennett, and counselled him to be more discrete.[39] The British diplomat Orme Sargent (1884-1962) frankly admitted in a note dated March 30, 1928, that, although he suspected Bennett was in fact guilty of using "dubious facts and documents ... we [do not possess] any definite evidence against Bennett himself. Our suspicions are chiefly based on the shady and dishonest company he is known to keep."[40] Given what is known of de Kay, and Bennett's suggestibility, that suspicion was not without some justification. Mrs Bennett's letter to the Foreign Office in London, dated March 28 (1928), highlighted the hostility of both the Turkish Government and that of the British Consul, Sir Percy Loraine: two hostilities which I conjecture were related. It relevantly reads:

> <u>Private</u>
> Sir,
> To whom shall I appeal for help if not to you? Pray be so good as to read this letter and if it seems to you that I have reason and justice on my side, give me your help.
>
> I am British, as is my husband. He is in prison here, arrested, and kept in prison under a law created by Pangalos, when Dictator, which permits any juge d'instruction to arrest anyone "on suspicion" alone.
>
> It is now two weeks since he was arrested and we have not yet had access to my husband's papers and letters, taken from his office, and which would establish his complete

---

[39] FO 371/12919, 218-23.
[40] FO 371/12919, 223, an almost identical comment is typed up at 236, and 242 as part of the letter where Sargent expressed his "concern" about Loraine's comments.

innocence. Not that he is accused of any crime. The accusation is – that one of his employees <u>might</u> have committed an offence and that <u>if</u> he did so, then my husband must have incited him to do it. During these 2 weeks witnesses have been heard and the Minister of Justice the Juge d'Instruction and the Public Prosecutor have admitted that he is not guilty – and have printed this in the newspapers.

Yet he is still in prison. We have appealed to our Consulate to ask the Minister of Justice <u>why</u> this British subject is not allowed out on bail, which is his right, but their reply is that they must take their instructions from the Minister and he doesn't see fit to interfere.

Note that we did not ask for any <u>interference</u> with Greek justice, but for the support that a mere demand would give, asking the <u>reason</u> for the undue detention of a British subject.

Sir – I must draw your attention to the attitude of our Minister here. Sir Percy Loraine has shown himself so biased against us, that I must suppose his conduct over this affair to be due to a personal hostility.

On other occasions the Consuls of the various countries here exert themselves energetically on behalf of their compatriots – and the other day the French Consul obtained bail in 48 hours for a wretched French sailor who had grievously injured a Greek by stabbing. Yet <u>we</u> can get no help.

I must firmly bring before your notice certain facts.

It has come to our knowledge that Sir Percy Loraine has on several occasions, covering some months, spoken very ill of us in society – before Greek ladies. In one house – Mme Kapodistria who regularly receives the various Embassy people he said

> 1. that we were not fit people to know,
> 2. that he would have to cut off from his visiting list people who chose to know us,
> 3. that he had been obliged to ignore a couple staying at our house, because they were our friends (a Colonel and Mrs Maitland Edwards)
> 4. that he did not believe we were even married.
>
> These remarks were repeated again, and were <u>volunteered</u> on each occasion, when our names happened to be mentioned. On one such occasion they were heard and repeated to us by MME Rascano, wife of the Roumanian Minister.
> Our lawyer, Mr Damarchino, who has been a Judge and Procureur General here, has heard such remarks made—and repeated in several houses.
> Not long ago, my husband called at the Embassy, asking to see Sir Percy Loraine.[41]

She states that Bennett saw an underling, and when Bennett said he had heard of Sir Percy's hostility to them and their friends, was assured that this was not the case. But he was making these statements at the time, and there is no one in Greece to appeal to. She continues:

> His attitude and words have added infinitely ... and have caused us grave prejudice.... It is <u>because</u> (my husband's business here) is so great that this trouble has arisen, for we are in direct opposition to the Turkish Government which seeks by this attack to lessen our prestige and drive us from the field.

She then provides character references, including Lady Malcolm,

[41] FO 371/12919, 201-204.

and ends with an appeal for aid.[42] Mrs Winifred Bennett née Elliot emerges as a formidable, intelligent, and indomitable woman, conveying a sense of outrage while presenting a judicious case on her behalf of her husband, combining verve and reason. When its contents are compared with Bennett's account, it emerges that Bennett passed over the role of the Turkish government and the British Consul. Nothing in the Foreign Office files indicates or even hints that Mrs Bennett was inaccurate in what she said of Loraine: rather, Harvey wrote on April 2, 1928 that Loraine had attributed "undue importance" to "Bennett's antecedents."[43] Nor was she wrong to point to the injustice of the bail law, and to attribute it to the Pangalos dictatorship of 1925-1926. She sought access to letters which, as Edwards stated, would show that Bennett never doubted for one moment the soundness of the heirs' title, and that being so, would hardly instigate forgeries.[44]

Neither Bennett nor his wife can have known that Loraine apparently lied to the Foreign Office. On March 26, 1928, he wrote: "No request that I should assist in obtaining bail has been received by me or reported to me."[45] This was in answer to a memorandum from the Foreign Office dated March 24, 1928, reporting that Mrs. Bennett complained that she had made repeated requests to him for this, but had received no answer.[46] Although one might object that the FO memo itself does not constitute "notice," a Foreign Office memorandum notes this request made by the Aegean Trust on March 3.[47] This mendacity, taken together with the consoling reassurance to Bennett, leaves little alternative but to conclude that the Consul was playing a double game. Winifred Beaumont was divorced on the grounds of her adultery with de Kay, her purple poetry was made public in Bennett's own divorce proceedings, and de Kay had established a reputation for deceit and

[42] FO 371/12919, 204-205.
[43] FO 371/12919, 289.
[44] A letter dated 10 March 1928 from Anglo-Hellenic, signed by Edwards: FO 371/12919, 213-214.
[45] FO 371/12919, 248.
[46] FO 371/12919, 178.
[47] FO 371/12919, 154.

profiteering. Loraine was justified in being wary of the Bennetts, but he did not allow them the chance to defend themselves, and as Harvey stated, he attached "undue importance" to these factors.

It is all the more remarkable, then that Bennett passes over the Consul's defamation of his wife and himself, except to obliquely hint at some sort of misunderstanding, and to blame himself for it. He does not even mention the energetic measures taken by his wife. He also passes over the putative role of the Turkish government. Rather, he speaks of other matters such as how, at this time, he saw the Greek tendency to dream of a greatness which was beyond any present evidence. A signal example of that was the notice-board in the small seaport of Kavalla, which proclaimed the presence of the "Pan-Cosmic School of Dancing."[48] While there, he made a concordance of the Upanishads, from the Sanskrit, which enabled him to understand the "psychological significance of the peculiar sequences of ideas," which was not that of either Shankaracharya or Schopenhauer.[49] He could have travelled to Mt Athos, but kept postponing it until cooler weather might arrive, however, he was recalled to England before that eventuated: "I left the next day with Mount Athos unvisited, enriched only by the lesson that we should take our chances when they present themselves and not wait for a more convenient "tomorrow."[50]

4.5 RETURN TO ENGLAND

Back in England by Christmas 1928, he came to an agreement with the Abdul Hamid Estate backers, whereby his shares were purchased and the costs of his defence were paid, and he resigned from the project.[51] He passed time by playing chess, at a very high level:

---

[48] Bennett (1997) 116-17.
[49] Bennett (1997) 117.
[50] Bennett (1997) 117.
[51] He refers a little later to "generous compensation (on) the termination of my contract," Bennett (1997) 117-18.

> This experience helped me to see better a serious defect of my nature. I could evaluate positions as well as really good players, but my impetuosity made me lose games that I should have won. Such I was, and such I have remained. It is not true to say that seeing one's defects is half-way to remedying them. Human beings do not in general learn from their own mistakes, any more than from those they see made by others. To a small degree, we are *conditioned* by experience—like Pavlov's dogs—but we do not *learn* from it.[52]

"Impetuosity" here is rather a close relation to the impatience he has previously noted. Again, Bennett's candour can fairly be considered impressive, and he draws a general moral from it. This is part of the reason that *Witness* can be seen as an educational autobiography, as well as an *apologia pro vita sua*.

His mother had by now returned and had "recovered her usual calm."[53] He began writing: "trying to express my conviction that the invisible world of eternal potentialities is continuously connected with the world of actual events," which pursuit reignited his interest in mathematics.[54] He remained in London, living quietly, apart from Ouspensky, until he returned to Greece for his trial in September 1929, before the Court of Appeal in Salonika, Macedonia (the city of the Thessalonians in the letters of St. Paul). He and his wife returned via the Orient Express for the sixteen-day trial, three of which he spent in the witness box, being examined and replying in modern Greek since he had dispensed with the services of any interpreter. He had been fortified in running that risk because from the opening of the prosecution case it was manifest that there was no evidence against him: the only danger was that he might incriminate himself. But he was acquitted, and costs were awarded against the Greek government.[55]

[52] Bennett (1997) 117.
[53] Bennett (1997) 118.
[54] Bennett (1997) 118.
[55] Bennett (1997) 118.

In his biography, *Gurdjieff*, James Moore asserts: "Public Record Office papers indicate that, under continued Foreign Office pressure, reluctantly applied, all charges against JGB were dropped on 13 August 1928."[56] He expresses surprise that Bennett could say that he had faced any trial in 1929. However, there is grave reason to doubt that Moore actually read those records, for the very records include a note, dated August 29, 1929 by Sir Oliver Harvey, that Bennett was in Athens, and the proceedings against him had not yet been heard.[57] So as not to break the flow of the narrative, I consider Moore's assertions in appendix 2. Although Bennett was acquitted, the cause of the Estates was lost. It is curious that this lengthy period of four years is passed over so quickly, almost foreshortened in the telling, but this is not because he was trying to paint himself in bright colors:

> I felt much worse about myself than others felt about me. A phase of my life that had lasted eight years had ended in failure. Since the age of twenty-four, I had been engaged in the affairs of the Abdul Hamid succession. I was now thirty-two and Ouspensky's prophecy that I would lose both my horse and myself had been fulfilled.... I had grown very weak physically; the tuberculosis that was to invade my lungs four years later had probably already taken root and I had an emaciated appearance that alarmed my friends. I had lost confidence in myself, feeling that everything I touched must fail. I wanted very much to return to the work with Ouspensky, but I had no prospect of making a living in England.[58]

The lack of confidence in himself is specifically related to the fact that, until that time, his undertakings had not prospered. Yet, Bennett

---

[56] Moore (1991) 355.
[57] FO 371/13611, 4-8. On April 12, 2022, I wrote to a Greek Government information office seeking any evidence available as to the proceedings, the charges, and the trial if any. I have received no reply to date.
[58] Bennett (1997) 118.

displayed a certain self-confidence when he had passed up Ramsay McDonald's offer, and especially Gurdjieff's proposal. His reference to Ouspensky's prophecy clarifies the earlier account, i.e. that Ouspensky was warning him that if he went ahead on his intended road he would lose everything. This explains the riddle: if Bennett took the right hand road he would lose his horse, meaning his property, but not himself (because he would have kept true to the inner work). If he took the left hand road, he would become wealthy, but not develop his being. So, in this enigmatic fashion, Bennett suggests that he had returned after four years with nothing to show for it, either externally or internally, except the determination to take Ouspensky's advice and persevere in pursuing his chief aim.

In an aside which relates to the "King's College revelation," (chapter 6), Bennett remarks that: "According to an ancient tradition, a man's soul is ready to be born only when he reaches his thirty-third year."[59] Bennett turned thirty-three in 1930, but we need not take this as an ineluctable mathematical formula. He returned to Greece to help out with a coal mine, touched by the confidence shown in him: other than this, he states, he surrendered, for a time, his connections with the Near East.[60] At the mine, witnessing the ancient carbonized tree trunks, his interest was aroused, and he quickly returned to England, stirred by "The picture of immense reserves of energy preserved for millions of years under the soil, and waiting for man to come and use them, [which] was a challenge of a kind I had never met before."[61] Perhaps he was more sensitive to this sight because he had had the extraordinary experience of connection with the Great Accumulator, and had been writing about "potentiality." However, his relationship with Ouspensky suddenly bottomed. When Bennett had been arrested in Greece, some of Ouspensky's letters to him had been seized and forwarded to the British Embassy in case there was some Bolshevik connection. The Home Office in England had

---

[59] Bennett (1997) 119.
[60] Bennett (1997) 119.
[61] Bennett (1997) 120.

called Ouspensky in for questioning, which had upset him. He resented Bennett, blaming him for the entire incident.[62] Bennett then went to Paris, searching for Gurdjieff, but his enquiries were fruitless.

4.6   THE SIXTH VISION: THE FUTURE OF HUMANITY

Accordingly, Bennett returned to England, made his base in inexpensive lodgings, and set off once more to Greece, on the "Greek Lignite" project, enjoying the necessary research. At the Ostrovo swamps at Vevi in Greece (now Lake Ohrid), Bennett saw a massive flock of storks taking off and flying as if one organism. He saw in this the manifestation of a "collective consciousness" through which "the great Stork Being" becomes "visible as an articulated whole and then disperses again along the river banks of Egypt and Ethiopia."[63] It was, he said, evidence of: "an intelligence that operates quite differently from the mind of man."[64] This exhibits a feature of Bennett's mind: he did not merely feel astonished at a sight, he perceived at once the intelligence behind it. This led to the following:

> As I stood in the deep silence left by the great birds, I caught a glimpse of the future of mankind. One day, we shall become aware of the collective consciousness of humanity…. In this vision, there was also a promise that the time was not so far distant when the human race would make a step forward and begin to look beyond the narrow loyalties of nation, race and religion, towards the distant goal of human unity.[65]

This will have been late in 1929 or just possibly early 1930. Bennett himself twice describes this as a "vision" and saw in it a verification of the teaching of Gurdjieff and Ouspensky. Yet, it is hard to reconcile this vision with Gurdjieff's teaching: human evolution, for Gurdjieff,

---

[62] Bennett (1997) 120-21.
[63] Bennett (1997) 121-22.
[64] Bennett (1997) 122.
[65] Bennett (1997) 122.

is towards individuality. The idea of a controlling super-mind seems to me to be a less individuated, and hence, a lower stage than anything Gurdjieff envisaged for humanity. This is exactly the criticism which Ouspensky made of these ideas of human evolution when they circulated in the wake of Darwin.[66] Rather, Bennett's interpretation bears the influence of Blavatsky and Bucke (section 0.6).

However, the idea that individuals could combine and affect humanity as a whole, is quite different. In a series of lectures he gave in 1962, Bennett disclosed that Ouspensky had several times told them that: "something had gone wrong in the first decade of this century, and the war, the so-called great World War had marked the failure of a high purpose."[67] When Ouspensky had travelled to the East: he had found evidence of groups of people, isolated one from the other, who were aware of what was happening in the world at the start of the twentieth century. Ouspensky had thought that it had been their destiny to link up. Had they done so, he conjectured: "a really big transformation would have occurred in the life of man, but something or other had gone wrong."[68] This sense that isolation was damaging to humanity may have contributed to Bennett's willingness to make contact with teachers from outside the Gurdjieff tradition. He decided to take pupils and to "share my vision with others."[69] His wife encouraged him, saying: "You have been given this vision because you have your own task to do." She suggested that Ouspensky may have been indirectly nudging him in this direction, adding "You must gather your own people round you and make your own school. You make a mistake in not trusting yourself and your own powers."[70] Characteristically, Bennett promptly rejected her advice, then went and acted on it. By early 1930, he had started a small study group to study esoteric ideas. He sent reports of each meeting to Ouspensky,

---

[66] Ouspensky (1934) 120-22.
[67] Bennett (2014) 82. The lectures were chiefly on the Shivapuri Baba. So far as I am aware, Ouspensky never reduced this opinion to writing.
[68] Bennett (2014) 81-82.
[69] Bennett (1997) 122.
[70] Bennett (1997) 122.

with the note that he (Bennett) would stop the groups if Ouspensky disapproved.[71] Meanwhile, his Greek Lignite project was warmly greeted in England, and the "Grecian Mining and Development Company" was formed with Bennett as Managing Director.[72]

4.7 OUSPENSKY ON OBJECTIVE CONSCIOUSNESS

Unexpectedly, in October 1930, Madame Kadloubovsky, Ouspensky's secretary, telephoned to invite his wife and himself to a lecture at Warwick Gardens. This was the first of a series called "The Search for Objective Consciousness."[73] Maintaining a sphinx-like silence as to the recent past, Ouspensky asked Bennett to read some of the lectures aloud, while he listened. The aim of these lectures was to expand his own groups beyond the forty or fifty people then studying with him. The lectures were successful, and Ouspensky's relationship with Bennett warmed. Ouspensky confided in him that Gurdjieff's work had not prospered as Gurdjieff had hoped, a fact to which Gurdjieff himself averred.[74] Ouspensky then returned to the idea of a "Higher Source" from where help might come (section 4.1):

> I am still as certain as ever that there is a Great Source from which our System has come. Mr Gurdjieff must have had a contact with that Source, but I do not believe that it was a complete contact. Something is missing, and he has not been able to find it. If we cannot find it through him, then our only hope is to have a direct contact with the Source. But there is no chance for us to find it by looking, of that I have been convinced for nearly twenty years. It is much better hidden

---

[71] Bennett (1997) 123.
[72] An online search of UK corporate records found nothing for this company.
[73] Bennett (1997) 124.
[74] Gurdjieff (1981) 4, "I had not, when in full strength and health, succeeded in introducing in practice into the life of people the beneficial truths elucidated for them by me," writing of events in 1927; also Bennett (1997) 124.

than people suppose. Therefore our only hope is that the Source will seek us out. That is why I am giving these lectures in London. If those who have the real knowledge see that we can be useful to them, they may send someone.... The essential secret is still missing.[75]

Bennett later came to agree that something had been missing, but it was supplied when Gurdjieff instigated the teaching of contemplation-like exercises (section 8.3). Bennett states that he found it hard to reconcile his new responsibilities with his desire to renounce self-will, that he was "too easily distracted by worldly affairs," and that he had a major failing: "lack of persistence." He decided that he should keep a diary, as "something in my nature objected to anything that would bind me to the past."[76] This is unexplained: why does keeping a diary "bind" one to the past? For some people it may be the opposite, the diary commits the past to paper, allowing one to cease ruminating. He made a vow to keep it from New Year's Day 1931, for one thousand days. He succeeded in this, yet he felt, on October 1, 1933, that he had gained "no tangible results."[77]

On the other hand, he made a major advance with the Greek Lignite project: one of the drawbacks of the resource was "the evil smell of the lignite charcoal," but tests showed that this was caused by the burning of sulphur compounds, which could be destroyed if the lignite was charred at above 900 degrees centigrade. Bennett's report on this, *Problems of the Greek Fuel Industry*, was his "first appearance in print," and it made him proud.[78] On a visit to Greece in connection with the project, he went gold-prospecting. The finding of some "tiny yellow grains" brought tears to his eyes: "There is a special kind of excitement in finding gold that must be connected with the perennial quest of men for this enigmatic metal.... I felt an unreasoning urge to go on searching until I found real

---

[75] Bennett (1997) 124.
[76] Bennett (1997) 125.
[77] Bennett (1997) 125.
[78] Bennett (1997) 125.

gold for myself.... The lust for gold is an incommunicable experience, but none the less real for that."[79] Although this urge passed at once, it persuaded him that the impulse was real, and that unless one has experienced it, one cannot rightly judge others' experience.[80] He utilised this realisation when he wrote about elementals, e.g. as recorded in *Creation*. There, Bennett said that, in 1923, Gurdjieff gave a lecture on elementals:

> Elementals are not living. They are not beings or individuals.... These elementals are the spirit of materiality or the unmanifested powers of the material forces. These have no consciousness.... I (earlier) spoke of the spirits of living things—tree spirits, monkey spirits and so on. There are also the spirit of the mountain, the spirit of a river, and the spirit of the sea.... We can be aware of the elemental force in a great storm. Though it lasts a short time, we can be aware of its effect on the psyche.
>
> One of the strangest elemental forces is connected with money. Why does gold have such an extraordinary effect on the human psyche? There is something in this elemental that attracts people. There are rarer and more precious metals than gold.... some of mankind's oldest and most beautiful works of art are made in gold.[81]

The project folded when Venizelos' government fell, and the suspicious Tsaldaris regime taxed lignite and brown coal at levels which made mining unfeasible. Bennett spent all his own money, and fought on until, he says, June 1932, when the cause was lost.[82] However, there must be some confusion: Venizelos served as Prime Minister on eight occasions. Only once did Tsaldaris succeed him: that occurred on November

---

[79] Bennett (1997) 126.
[80] Bennett (1997) 126.
[81] Bennett (1978b) 45.
[82] Bennett (1997) 126-27.

4, 1932. Perhaps the project folded in June 1933. Bennett now returns to his work with Gurdjieff's system:

> The satisfaction I had felt in working with my small group of pupils for more than a year since I had started in October 1929, gave place to the constant exposure of my deficiencies in my work with Ouspensky. I watched with nostalgic memories of my own beginnings, the enthusiasm of the hundreds of newcomers to his groups. In ten long years, I had gained nothing but profound disillusionment. Many of those who had studied with Ouspensky since 1922 were in the same condition.[83]

Ouspensky's wife, Sophia, had rejoined him in 1929. Ouspensky himself would write, lecture, and teach, and she would "create conditions for work," a division of labour which became more marked with the passing of time.[84] They eventually leased a grand property, Gadsden in Hayes, Kent, where some pupils went to live and work with her. Bennett was encouraged to attend on Sundays and sometimes for weekends.[85] Oddly, and for reasons he never understood, his wife was only once allowed to attend. For three years he could not be with her on his one free day. The practical work was relocated to Lyne Place near Virginia Water in 1934, an even more splendid site.[86] Bennett candidly admits that in committing his weekends, and thereby allowing his wife to suffer, there was "something radically awry in my attitude," but he viewed Ouspensky as the "superman I myself aspired to become one day. I was completely blind to his limitations."[87] Bennett assumed that the Ouspenskys were

---

[83] Bennett (1997) 127.
[84] Bennett (1997) 128.
[85] Bennett (1997) 128-29.
[86] Bennett (1997) 129.
[87] Bennett (1997) 129.

"almost infallible," and there had to be good reasons for this arrangement.[88] His reflection on this is illuminating:

> When I found myself in the position of a spiritual teacher and saw that my most ill-considered suggestions were taken as inspired utterances, I became aware of the necessity for anyone who has the task of guiding others in spiritual matters to abstain from hiding his own defects and mistakes, and to make sure that no one shall look upon him as an "authority" in his own right. In this respect, Gurdjieff was an example to us all; he set himself to shock and even to disgust those who came to him for teaching.[89]

At this time, Bennett's attitude to the Ouspenskys was influenced by his desire to deny his self-will by unquestioning submission to his teachers. He thus missed out on the friendship which Ouspensky offered: "I was ridiculously stiff, not realizing that Ouspensky was a human being who enjoyed human companionship."[90] Further, his internal attitude was rebellious. At the same time, his wife confronted him with the observation that he was upset because his business was not doing well. Bennett initially expressed outrage, precisely because she was right, but he recovered himself and thanked her.[91] Now, Bennett recounts: "By one of the coincidences that play so great a part in shaping our destiny, the next evening Ouspensky introduced a new theme that was to have a great influence on my life for the next twelve years."[92] The theme was memory exercises, which Bennett at once related to religious practices of committing scripture to heart. This practice was, he concluded: "a survival, not of an illiterate age, but of a time when men understood the danger of living too much

---

[88] Bennett (1997) 129.
[89] Bennett (1997) 129.
[90] Bennett (1997) 130.
[91] Bennett (1997) 130.
[92] Bennett (1997) 131.

in their thoughts."[93] However, Ouspensky administered a shock to him: while everyone else was given a specific memory exercise, Ouspensky said that no such exercise was suitable for Bennett. The next week, Bennett was able, with calm and gratitude, to hear others speaking about their efforts. Then, at the end of that meeting, Ouspensky allowed him to start the exercise.[94] This was still 1931, and over the next four years, Bennett proved able to recite the Our Father:

> simultaneously in Greek and Latin at different rates, and even for a very brief spell, to add also the prayer in German or Russian. This produced a state of controlled dissociation, the usual connection between my intellectual, emotional and instinctive functions was suspended, and a link of a new kind—a condition of pure consciousness—held them together.[95]

While Bennett went on to learn the Gospels, Ouspensky soon dropped the theme, as he often would with a new practice.[96] This apparently casual comment about Ouspensky's changes of course marks his incipient questioning of Ouspensky, and the book's secondary genre as an *apologia*, here explaining his separation from Ouspensky. Another sign of Bennett's increasing independence is his initiating periods of intensive work for his group over periods of up to four weeks, when they would live and work together.[97]

4.8 THE SEVENTH VISION: THE ENERGY OF LIFE

About some time, between August 1931 and August 1932, I can be no more precise, Bennett had a vision in Finsbury Square, Central London:

---

[93] Bennett (1997) 131.
[94] Bennett (1997) 131.
[95] Bennett (1997) 132.
[96] Bennett (1997) 132.
[97] Bennett (1997) 132.

As had happened in June 1920, I began to "see" the world in its five-dimensional form. As I entered the fifth dimension, time stopped but life went on. I saw life as energy or rather a quality of energy. Rising into the fifth dimension, the quality changed, growing finer and also more intense. Nothing was happening and yet everything was changing. I saw that there was no degradation of energy. In a flash, I realised that this was to be expected if time stood still. The formula took shape in words: "In eternity the laws of thermodynamics are reversed. Within a closed system, entropy is eternally conserved, but energy itself has many values."[98]

Bennett was reminded of Gurdjieff's insight: "Two men may look outwardly the same, but one may have incomparably more Being than the other, You cannot see this because you are still blind to Being."[99] Ouspensky dismissed Bennett's report of this, as he had all Bennett's other attempts to speak of his visions, even the connection with the Great Accumulator in 1923. The distance between them grew, for, as Bennett said: "I could not deny my own vision."[100] Also important for his development as a teacher, in September 1932, his wife brought him face to face with his own unfeeling responses to his own students: "They spoke from their hearts, but you answered from your head. Could you not see how much they were suffering and why?"[101] The Grecian Mining Company folded. His financial affairs were disastrous, and they had to sell many valued possessions. A period of his life had ended: "something in me had died and nothing was yet reborn in its place."[102] However, he accepted a moderately paid position with H. Tollemache and Company, a coal-related firm, which was the occasion of his making some name

---

[98] Bennett (1997) 132-33.
[99] Bennett (1997) 133.
[100] Bennett (1997) 133.
[101] Bennett (1997) 133-34.
[102] Bennett (1997) 134.

for himself as an industrial researcher, and touring England to sell coal dust.[103]

Ouspensky tried, throughout 1933, to teach him discretion: Bennett admitted that as soon as he heard anything interesting, he felt compelled to speak about it.[104] It was perhaps at this point that Ouspensky told Bennett that he reminded him of a Chinese fable where a man lives in a graveyard, believing that the dead were alive. As Bennett understood it later, the message was that he could not discern reality from his fantastic speculations.[105] As Bennett set off for one of his intensive work periods, Mme Ouspensky urged him not to imitate Ouspensky, but to "try to be yourself." Apparently, he was even copying Ouspensky's mistakes in speaking English. When Bennett replied that he could not trust himself, she answered:

> Of course you cannot trust yourself; you cannot trust anyone else either. There is only one way to learn what you can trust in yourself, and that is by your own actions proceeding from your own intention. When you imitate others, you learn nothing about yourself, and you can never grow strong. You have in you the possibility of being of great value to the Work, but for that you must prepare yourself and gain your own experience.[106]

In the aftermath of this conversation, and the collapse of the Greek Lignite project, he found himself at war with himself, and distrustful of anyone who spoke well of him.[107] This could not be the whole truth of his self-image, but the converse may have been true: he may in fact have been suggestible to people who spoke down to him.

---

[103] Bennett (1997) 134-35.
[104] Bennett (1997) 135.
[105] Bennett (1997) 283.
[106] Bennett (1997) 136.
[107] Bennett (1997) 136.

4.9 THE EIGHTH VISION: SELF-OBSERVATION

Bennett then describes an out of the body experience which took place in the presence of Ouspensky. By 1933, Bennett states, Ouspensky was given to staying up for much of the night drinking claret and talking. Bennett thought that Ouspensky: "seemed to be obsessed with the need to put himself back into the life he was living before he first met Gurdjieff in 1915." Then, on an occasion at Lyne Place which can be dated to August 1933:

> That night the two of us were alone. The whole night passed. Towards morning, when we had drunk between us four or five bottles of claret, I was speaking and expressing my opinion about some question … as I spoke I went quite outside myself and heard my own voice and even watched my own thoughts as if they were going on in someone else. I saw myself as completely artificial; neither my thoughts not my words were my own. "I"—whoever at that moment "I" might be—was a completely indifferent spectator of the performance.
>
> Quite suddenly the spell broke, and I was back "inside" myself. I said to Ouspensky: "Now I know what self-observation really is. In all these years I have never seen Bennett as he really is until this moment." He replied very seriously, saying: "Was this worth sitting up all night for?" I said: "Yes, indeed, or for twenty nights if necessary." He continued: "If only you can remember what you have just seen you will be able to work. But you must understand that no one can help you in this. If you do not see for yourself, it is impossible for anyone else to show you."[108]

---

[108] Bennett (1997) 136-37. For the date, see the top of 136. The reference to the summer morning is on 137.

As he was returning home, filled with a rare joy at the beauty of the summer morning, Bennett realised that: "One vision does not make a conscious man." However, at the seminar he then held, "I got further than ever before in reaching a sense of unity with those I worked with."[109] The final comment is designed to show that he was changing since his wife had rebuked him for his coldly intellectual approach to the suffering of others, and now a change had been effected not by any direct effort, but simply by observing himself with an extraordinary degree of separation. Given the number of visions which occurred in the month of August (see Table 1), the reference to the beautiful summer morning may point to a favourable sensitivity to warmth.

In a talk to his Sherborne pupils towards the end of his life, Bennett told the same story. On this occasion, he said that he was then going to a Summer School with Ouspensky, and they had decided to spend a night at Gadsden, Kent, and proceed to Shoreham in the morning. On this occasion, he stressed the conclusions he drew from his experience:

> At one moment the whole thing became clear to me. I saw how I was living my life in an unreal way, that everything was just words and I had no contact with reality at all. I saw that there was nothing I could expect; that nothing could happen to my personality. It didn't matter whether it was good or bad, clever or stupid, it had no potential.... until that moment I had no real understanding of the difference between "personality" and "essence."[110]

Bennett's visions are mutually illuminating. They are the warp and weft of *Witness*. In about May 1934, Dr Francis Roles, perhaps Ouspensky's most trusted recruit, and an authority on tuberculosis, diagnosed Bennett with that disease, and prescribed three months of complete rest. His regime included extract of aloes, taken on the advice

---

[109] Bennett (1997) 137.
[110] Bennett (2006) 15-16.

of a solicitous Ouspensky. In retrospect, Bennett saw this illness as "a phase in the process of dying and rebirth, which had started in 1929,"[111] a process which had begun after his acquittal in Greece and his reaching the age of thirty-three, when he had lost both his horse and himself.

This coincided with his becoming first director of the Coal-burning Appliance Makers' Association in 1934.[112] By 1937, when its fourth annual meeting was being held, it was known as the "Combustion Appliance Makers' Association (Solid Fuel)." Bennett's efforts prospered. With the incisive intelligence which characterised his scientific undertakings, Bennett was surprised that so common a practice as the burning of solid fuel had been little studied for greater efficiency and cleanliness, despite the smog which it caused.[113] He interested Lord Ernest Rutherford (1871-1936), who spoke at what must have been their first annual meeting, in this research.[114] A note in the *Journal of the Society of Chemical Industry*, of March 27, 1937, opines that the Association was a "young body rapidly attaining an important position," and pointing to the benefits of cooperation, as opposed to "internecine warfare."[115] An article in a later number of the journal, dated April 10, 1937, states: "The Director of the Association, Mr J.G. Bennett, presented a paper entitled *The Progress of Solid Fuel Burning Appliances*.... The paper was divided into three sections."[116] Lord Rutherford's assistance led to the founding of the British Coal Utilization Research Association, of which Bennett became the first director. However, while he gives the impression that this was in 1934, the BCURA was founded in 1938. Bennett dates to 1936 his being invited to join the Coal Research Club, where he met Drs Marie Stopes, Margaret Fishenden, and Clarence Seyler, who had founded "Coal Systematics."[117] This may be the source of Bennett's later use of the term "systematics."

---

[111] Bennett (1997) 138.
[112] Bennett (1997) 138-39.
[113] Bennett (1997) 139.
[114] Bennett (1997) 139.
[115] *Journal of the Society of Chemical Industry* 56 (1937) 316.
[116] *Journal of the Society of Chemical Industry* 56 (1937) 353-54.
[117] Bennett (1997) 140. For Seyler and "Coal Systematics," see https://biography.wales/article/s2-SEYL-ART-1866 accessed July 16, 2022.

4.10 COAL RESEARCH

Bennett skims over the next two years, which seem to have been occupied with his coal research. However, by 1936, while he was becoming closer to Mme Ouspensky, he had lost Mr Ouspensky's confidence. From October 1937, he was able to join what Bennett calls Madame's "Gurdjieff exercises" class, a movements class. Although his wife was now allowed to join in the work with Mme Ouspensky, she (his wife) began to express a fear that he needed a younger woman who could bear him children.[118] Her being invited to join the work after the earlier "harsh decision" to exclude her, seems to have caused her to feel that she was only being invited because she was his wife.[119] She said that he cared more for his work with Ouspensky than for anything else, and that "it would be much better if I disappeared altogether."[120] This brought Bennett right up against his "sense of an almost hopeless inadequacy in front of my own inner problems."[121] Then, on January 24, 1937, she attempted suicide by an overdose of sleeping tablets. After decisive medical intervention, she spent three days in a coma, with him by her side, until she briefly opened her eyes, spoke a word, and fell into a normal sleep. The next day she disclosed to him that she had left her body and gone to a place where she had heard a heavenly music, and knew that Jesus was present. Although she wished to remain, she heard Bennett calling her, and had no power to resist his summons. She had to return to her body, understanding that she had to see her life through, and that Bennett really did want her.[122] Ouspensky had been solicitous for her welfare, and asked to see her as soon as possible. In a private conversation, he told her: "I know that something important has happened to you." She said she would wait a year before telling him of her experience, as she needed

---

[118] Bennett (1997) 140-41.
[119] Refer back to Bennett (1997) 129, and also 141.
[120] Bennett (1997) 141.
[121] Bennett (1997) 141.
[122] Bennett (1997) 141-42.

the time to be convinced of its reality.[123] It is not explicitly stated, but it seems implied that Ouspensky had intuited that she had had an extraordinary experience, yet Bennett simply reports this.

In 1938, Evelyn, Bennett's first wife, died. He arranged to see his daughter Ann, for the first time in nineteen years. He regretted his decision to "make no attempt to see her or interfere in her life."[124] Once more, he felt that he could not understand people, but could arouse their interest in his own "visions."[125] And now his wife had had an illuminating vision. Ouspensky reminded them when the year was ended, and she told him of what she had seen. When she returned, she said to Bennett that Ouspensky had been longing to experience the reality of the other world, but in vain. She expressed sympathy for him, but stated that she had seen what she did only because she had been "willing to die."[126] This willingness, I think, is the key. His wife stressed how very lonely Ouspensky was, and how much he suffered.[127] An equally poignant aspect of this was that her vision had embraced Bennett and his own future, but she knew that he would not believe her. Later, Bennett realised that she was correct, that he was "dominated and ruled by my own stupid cleverness."[128] This is a rather telling and insightful phrase which Bennett had applied to himself.

In the spring of 1939, Ouspensky said that his hopes of finding the source of Gurdjieff's ideas was fading. Bennett wrote to the head of the Mevlevi Order, who invited Bennett to visit him. Ouspensky was delighted, and the Bennetts planned to travel in the spring of 1940, but WWII prevented this.[129] During the war, Bennett returned to his studies of the fifth dimension, and a desire to connect Gurdjieff's system with "contemporary discoveries in science and pre-history."[130] Mme

[123] Bennett (1997) 142.
[124] Bennett (1997) 142-43.
[125] Bennett (1997) 143.
[126] Bennett (1997) 143.
[127] Bennett (1997) 143.
[128] Bennett (1997) 143.
[129] Bennett (1997) 143-44.
[130] Bennett (1997) 144.

Ouspensky left for the U.S., and Bennett's wife commented on the despondency of those who farewelled her. What, she enquired, was the value of their inner work, if they were so dependent upon her? A fortnight later, Ouspensky declared that he, too, was leaving. Bennett records Ouspensky's reasons: he was certain that Germany would win the war, and that Communism would sweep over Europe. The only hope, he said, "lay in America keeping aloof."[131] Bennett makes no comment on this: he does not need to, Ouspensky was utterly wrong. But his mentioning it is a further reason to see an *apologia* in the subtext of this book.

This serves as a prelude to his last meeting with Ouspensky, which was "more than a physical separation." In answer to Bennett's three questions, Ouspensky told him that he made no advances in the work because he kept returning to the start, only to make another false start, and that if he (Bennett) were to try and reduce the system to writing, its only value would be to persuade him that it could not be done.[132] As for himself, he had no intention of publishing a written account, but he might change his mind.[133] Bennett's comments about how much he had learnt from Ouspensky ("He has taught me everything ...") are perhaps a little surprising: he treated Ouspensky as practically on the same level as Gurdjieff, but so too did Maurice Nicoll. One can only conclude that, in person, Ouspensky made a huge impression.[134] Bennett continued his groups, while his internal reciting of the Our Father gave him a curious sense that he "was not destined to die in that way and at that time."[135] Surviving the Blitz, Bennett and his wife had the shared sense that "the destruction of the physical body need not be a disaster to the soul."[136] He ends this chapter, the fifteenth in *Witness*, recalling that he now had to

---

[131] Bennett (1997) 144. Presumably, after the Nazi victory, the Communists would triumph.
[132] Bennett (1997) 144-45.
[133] Bennett (1997) 144.
[134] Bennett (1997) 145.
[135] Bennett (1997) 145.
[136] Bennett (1997) 146.

search for new purposes both to life and work.[137] That is a rather artistic way to close the account of his time with Ouspensky: his two teachers had left the United Kingdom, and he now had to begin in a new place both literally and metaphorically.

---

[137] Bennett (1997) 146.

The Spring House at Coombe Springs. Fortunately, it is still extant as it has been heritage listed.

CHAPTER 5

COOMBE SPRINGS

5.1   THE BCURA

In the brief 1957 autobiographical note, Bennett provided some details of his career during WWII which had been omitted from *Witness*; once more, the narrower scope of the note obliged him to jot down the central facts, while the more expansive recollections of the book freed him to wander into a wider and less precise narrative:

> With government support, the British Coal Utilization Research Association was founded in 1937. A scheme that I had started with one typist as an information bureau in 1934 grew by 1945 into the largest cooperative research association in England with an annual budget of 750,000 pounds. I was the first Director General of the Association which made, during the Second World War, important contributions to conserving our overstrained fuel resources. I was appointed a member of the British Government Committee on the efficient use of fuel and became Chairman of the Sub-Committee on Industrial Fuel Efficiency.
>
> I also held office as Chairman of the British Standards Institution Industrial Committee on Solid Fuel and as Chairman of the Conference of Research Associations of the Department of Scientific and Industrial Research. During

this time I published a number of scientific papers on coal research.[1]

So far as David Seamon and myself have been able to ascertain, those papers were published between 1936 and 1944.[2] On May 5, 1941, the Bennetts inspected a property at Coombe Springs to assess its suitability as a site for this work. It was derelict, the grounds overgrown, and the owner a fantasist living on the memory of past glories. But the Bennetts saw the potential and "were convinced that we should come and live there, and that it would become a great centre of spiritual life."[3] A lease was taken for the BCURA. Probably in mid-1941, the BCURA nominated him to represent it on the prestigious Parliamentary and Scientific Committee ("PSC") which consisted of nearly four hundred persons selected from both Houses of Parliament and more than one hundred scientific societies.[4] It appears that he was appointed honorary treasurer of the Committee, a post he held until 1948 when he resigned from the Committee. Bennett notes, almost in passing, that this honorary post provided him with opportunities to speak to audiences of influential people.[5] For a scientist who had not studied science at any university, let alone Cambridge or Oxford, this was a tremendous testament to his native talent and powers of application. The amount of information he was able to process for Britain was prodigious, and other honours and significant posts came his way.[6] It may be fair to conclude that he was not impeded by the guilt by association with de Kay which had permeated government circles.[7]

[1] Bennett (1957) 6. On March 17, 2022, I wrote to BSI for information, but have as yet received no reply.
[2] Bennett (1936), (1941) and (1944); Bennett and Brown (1940), and Bennett, Brown and Crone (1941).
[3] Bennett (1997) 147.
[4] Bennett (1997) 148.
[5] Bennett (1997) 148 and 156.
[6] Bennett (1997) 148.
[7] Michael Benham forwarded me, by email on August 3, 2022, an excerpt from an article in *The Daily Telegraph* of June 22, 1943, about Bennett's directorship of the BCURA, including details of an interview with him. It states: "At Oxford he took high honours

Bennett says little about the Committee, but it has been an important institution in Britain, and exerted an international influence.[8] In November 1939, Captain Markham, the Honorary Secretary of the Parliamentary Science Committee, requested Lieutenant-Commander Powell to provide a secretariat for what was to be the PSC. The first Chairman was Sir Arthur Wilson. In 1940 a constitution was drafted. The original Aims and Objects, which stood unchanged even when Powell and Butler came to write a book on the Committee in 1979, read:

> The Parliamentary and Scientific Committee is a non-Party body formed with the object of providing a permanent liaison between scientific bodies and Parliament. It seeks to become a centre for the consideration and discussion of scientific information bearing on current proceedings in Parliament.[9]

This provided members of the Committee with direct input into major issues. The central feature of its activities was probably the regular monthly meetings at the House of Commons, followed by a dinner "at which the talk can continue between scientists and parliamentarians."[10] Bennett passes over it in *Witness*, but, on February 12, 1946, he was appointed to the Scientific complement of the first Steering Committee to plan future activities.[11] On December 7, 1943, with Professor I.M. Heilbron (who worked on the development of penicillin, among other projects), Bennett delivered a talk setting forth "A programme for the

---

in mathematics." It is not stated that Bennett made this claim. If he did, it would show that he was hypersensitive about not having studied at a tertiary institution. I would be slow to infer that he did make the claim, because it could easily have been disproved. A similar error in the *Middlesex County Times*, March 5, 1949, where he is also said to have graduated from Oxford, does not refer to an interview with Bennett.
[8] On the interest throughout the British Commonwealth, see Powell and Butler (1980) 46-48.
[9] Powell and Butler (1980) 11-12.
[10] Powell and Butler (1980) 13.
[11] Powell and Butler (1980) 64.

more comprehensive application of science to our national life."[12] When it is possible to obtain external information about his activities, it appears quite remarkable how much Bennett omits, all in the direction of modestly failing to mention achievements and honours. It seems that, through the PSC, Bennett was an active influence upon British approaches to energy and scientific research and education, and through Britain, upon global trends.

Bennett's work for the war effort by making the most efficient use of coal, was effective, despite his lack of tertiary qualifications for these senior appointments: "My strong point was my ability to see more deeply and more quickly than others into the potentialities of a situation."[13] If any of his staff were brought before the Conscientious Objectors' Tribunal, he would testify on their behalf, although he himself took the attitude:

> that a consistent pacifism is impossible. We have the right to criticize and oppose violence only if we neither allow ourselves to be violent nor to profit from the violence of others. I could claim neither justification.... My dominant conviction was rather of the stupidity than of the wrongness of war. I did not have the passionate belief in the sacredness of human life that converted many into pacifists.[14]

At this time, Bennett and his wife became close friends with the pianist and composer Tobias Matthay (1858-1945), and he took piano lessons from one of Matthay's pupils. Bennett was charged with scattering the former's ashes over the countryside when he died. Bennett stated:

> I have never doubted that he had attained to that degree of liberation from terrestrial influences which enables the soul

---

[12] Powell and Butler (1980) 69.
[13] Bennett (1997) 148.
[14] Bennett (1997) 148.

to enter into a fuller existence after death. Such a soul continues to transmit good influences after its departure from the earthly scene.[15]

This runs counter to the sentiment that the good men do is often "interred with their bones" (Shakespeare, *Julius Caesar*, III ii 55). Further, this is another sign that one of the aims of this volume was to present a "teaching autobiography." In 1942, he was elected a member of the Athenaeum Club (section 3.3).[16] Sitting among their august number, Bennett felt that he could see what they had missed: "that human cleverness will never solve the fundamental problems of life."[17] Bennett was certain that the Allies would win the war, not so much because their cause was right, or they were better strategists, but because "every attempt at universal domination must eventually fail."[18] Bennett also noticed that he and his small crew seemed little affected by the war. He found in this a principle, not only that an individual or small group could find a safe place in turbulence, but that: "there may be an invisible protection for those who are called to serve a great purpose."[19]

Meanwhile, he was reducing to writing what he had understood of Gurdjieff's system, reading it to his pupils, and amending it in the light of their comments and questions. He took one "central theme to give coherence and structure," and this was the triad, "the theory that everything that exists or happens in the universe is the conjunction of three independent factors."[20] With Ouspensky's blessing, Bennett had researched ancient Indian philosophy, and found an idea that corresponded closely with Ouspensky's deduction from Gurdjieff's indications, that: "the variability inherent in all existence is ascribed to the six possible combinations of the three *gunas* or qualities of nature: Sattvas

---

[15] Bennett (1997) 149.
[16] Bennett (1997) 149.
[17] Bennett (1997) 149.
[18] Bennett (1997) 149.
[19] Bennett (1997) 149-50.
[20] Bennett (1997) 150.

or purity, Rajas or dominance, and Tamas or inertness."[21] Ouspensky initially encouraged Bennett to report the results of his research to the group, but dropped the topic after a few months. Bennett conjectured that this was because: "he had reached the point where some quite new notion was needed in order to bring the abstract law into closer contact with concrete facts, and this notion would not reveal itself before its time."[22] The implications of this comment are that human discoveries are not simply a question of human intelligence or ingenuity, although these have a part: the idea itself may not be ready to be realised in any human intellect. This implies that ideas exist among us, perhaps in an overlapping dimension. Bennett was persuaded that the strange way they had found and leased the house at Coombe Springs was due to the working of "a triad that I had never been able to understand."[23] He mused that, if destiny works through triads, then perhaps they attract "coincidences."[24] Bennett was granted permission to take his group to Coombe Springs on weekends to clear the grounds.

At this time, Bennett was working at his relationship with his daughter Ann. In retrospect, he drew a distinction between being a good father and a good parent.[25] If I understand him correctly, the "father" is in a loving connection with the child, while the parent raises and educates the child. However, Bennett is vague, and even my conjecture presents but two different perspectives on the one reality. Shortly after a twenty-first birthday party for Ann, on August 13, 1941, he and some others went to camp out in Wales for twelve days. This set the scene for what he considered to be his most important creative work in philosophy: "the elucidation of the six fundamental laws of existence and the manner in which they produce secondary laws in passing from one level to another."[26]

---

[21] Bennett (1997) 150.
[22] Bennett (1997) 151.
[23] Bennett (1997) 151.
[24] Bennett (1997) 131.
[25] Bennett (1997) 151.
[26] Bennett (1997) 151.

5.2 THE NINTH VISION: REDEMPTION OF THE UNIVERSAL ORDER

We have arrived at mid-August 1941, again, late summer. To set the context for what follows, Bennett refers the reader to volume 2 of *The Dramatic Universe*. There, in chapter 28, "The Six Fundamental Laws," he sets out what he saw as laws of Expansion, Concentration, Identity, Interaction, Order and Freedom. These "laws" (perhaps, "regularly observed patterns" based on a self-limiting will),[27] are the key to the twelve day stay near Pen-y-pas in Wales.[28] On the very first morning, he was alone, walking, struck by the sublime peace of the Wales countryside, and mentally contrasting it with war-struck London, when:

> I began to see the laws that governed all these processes. I saw involution and evolution: the descent of Power from Above, and the struggle of Existence to return to its Source. I saw how all that exists is what it is eternally and indestructibly and yet is always changing, merging with everything else and filling the universe with endless activity. I saw the universal Order and finally, I saw how Love and Freedom redeem everything. I shouted for joy in my aloneness, thanking God that I had been shown such wonders. ... The next morning I went out again, and this time I saw how every law has a pure and impure form. Then I understood why we had failed to make headway with triads eight years before. Ouspensky had failed to recognise the true cosmic character of several of the triads. ... This continued day after day. Sometimes the complexity of what I saw was too much for me, and I could not transcribe it. I saw how out of the simplicity of

---

[27] Bennett (1998b) 56.
[28] Although it is usually spelled "Pen-y-Pass", Bennett has "Pen-y-pas."

the triad arises all the intricately interwoven patterns of our experience.[29]

The consonance of this with many mystical visions, e.g. those of Mother Julian of Norwich, should appear obvious to the student of mysticism. However, it is marked by Bennett's intellectual sophistication. Soon after, during a long and uncomfortable train journey, he awoke with the realisation that there are "negative triads," which he named Imagination or Negative Involution; Self-Worship or Negative Evolution; Fear, or Negative Identity; Waste, or Negative Interaction; Subjectivism, or Negative Order; and Identification or Negative Freedom.[30] As Bennett states: "These visions were different from any that had come to me before. This time I was being shown truths that were not for me alone."[31] The Wales visions comprised ideas which Bennett could have deduced, but which burst upon his consciousness with an invigorating access of feeling. Although he heard no voice, there is a certain affinity to the second vision (Rue de Péra). If that earlier one showed him the picture of reality, this one gave him the patterns or codes, so to speak, which produced it.

It is impossible to be definitive as to how Bennett had these visions, but it seems to be analogous to the way that some mathematical prodigies simply perceive solutions to problems. Inglis writes of G.P. Bidder (1806-1878) that he was unable to explain how he would instantly be able to multiply numbers like 337 x 53 except that the answers "rise with the rapidity of lightning."[32] Also striking is that there were a series of such visions. Although the first—like those before and after—simply occurred without Bennett's consciously producing them, the subsequent visions were induced in regular order when he went out for morning walks.

---

[29] Bennett (1997) 152.
[30] Bennett (1997) 152. For a vivid account of the external circumstances see (1994) 180.
[31] Bennett (1997) 152-53.
[32] Inglis (1989) 122. Inglis mistakes the prodigy for his son, the QC, who had the same name.

On his return to London, Bennett suffered from impetigo. Reflecting in *Witness*, he wrote:

> I believe that there is a close connection between the condition of our bodies and that of our psyche. If I was brought for a time into a state where I could be aware of great truths, my coarse body, which reflected my psychic impurity, had to suffer the consequences. Looking back, I saw that I had suffered unaccountable physical ailments each time that I was passing through some psychic experience of a higher reality.[33]

I only record that this was Bennett's view. Even on Gurdjieff's principles, this may not be the correct explanation in all such cases. Bennett's idea of a "coarse body" reflecting "psychic impurity" strikes me as possibly influenced more by his mother's "puritanical New England upbringing," than anything else.[34] In correspondence with Jean Toomer, he indicated an alternative explanation, that each of our natures feeds on the one below, i.e. the growing astral body has to take some of its food from the physical body.[35] My sense that there was a puritanical element in Bennett receives some confirmation in the fact that he now attempted to write a chapter about "the Higher Centres in man," but found that he was baffled by what he was coming to believe was a "secret connection with the sexual function and mystical experience."[36] When he wrote a section on the question, his wife told him that there may be more to the sexual function than we realise, and he (Bennett) had a negative and inauthentic attitude towards sex.[37]

---

[33] Bennett (1997) 153.
[34] Bennett (1997) 8.
[35] Letters from the Beinecke Rare Book and Manuscript Library: Toomer's letter of January 19, 1953, under the note dated January 20 on the second page, and the first page of Bennett's reply of January 27, 1953.
[36] Bennett (1997) 153.
[37] Bennett (1997) 153.

5.3 MISUNDERSTANDINGS BETWEEN BENNETT AND OUSPENSKY

In November 1941, Ouspensky sent a message about the progress of his work in the United States, and a desire that his English students continue on the "highest possible level."[38] Bennett was doubtful, believing that:

> the Work was something dynamic that was alive only when it was expanding. The history of religion and spiritual movements shows that, when the impulse to search and move forward gives place to the impulse to hold on and preserve, the death knell has been sounded.[39]

Ouspensky received reports that Bennett was writing a book on the system and giving lectures. He prohibited him, and Bennett tried to comply, but finding that his writing was a necessary help, he resumed it, and expanded his own teaching of the system and the methods. Although his work with the BCURA prospered, he could never see "coal research as an end in itself," while his groups "could make a contribution, however modest and imperfect, to the eternal welfare of those who were seeking for spiritual values."[40] Meanwhile, his visionary perspective on meeting the UK's long-term energy needs aroused jealousy; and yet he felt that his external success was threatening his inner aspirations. In a train carriage, at the end of the year 1941, Bennett wrote a prayer:

> O Lord Creator, and all you Conscious Powers through whom the Divine Will is manifested, let me be liberated from sleep, mechanicalness and slavery, and find refuge in Conscious Action from which no evil can come. Let me turn

---

[38] Bennett (1997) 153-54.
[39] Bennett (1997) 154.
[40] Bennett (1997) 154.

from the part to the Whole; from the temporal to the eternal; from myself to Thee.⁴¹

After some "very bitter experiences," he states, his prayer was answered. He ends this chapter with the ominous comment: "My whole world had to crumble before I could return to the path which, in the depths of my conscience, I knew to be right."⁴² While the prayer is reminiscent of passages in the Upanishads, it bears distinctive marks of Bennett's abiding concern to understand Will, time and eternity, and to be active. He was now introduced to M.W. Thring and R.L. Brown, with whom he studied the geometry necessary to represent eternity as a fifth dimension. A draft paper was submitted to an authority, who was interested, but challenged the fundamental assumption that "time and space were merely conditions of existence."⁴³ Bennett adds that his work with Ouspensky and with his own groups felt quite separate from his own "interest in the geometry of higher dimensions, and my conviction that Eternity was as real as Time,"⁴⁴ and also from his life with his wife and his daughter.

At this time, he led a group of twenty-five to the Lakes District, where they went hiking and practised the movements.⁴⁵ Bennett was interested in the "Orders of Beings," an aspect of the "scale of being" which had been developed by Cuvier [Jean a.k.a. Georges Cuvier, 1769-1832] from Aristotle, but neglected for Darwinian evolution. This led to the chapter "The Spiritualization of Existence," in *The Dramatic Universe*.⁴⁶ That chapter, appearing in volume 2, is perhaps most memorable for its thesis that there exist "demiurgic intelligences," spiritual powers or essences which stand between nature and the divine essence as instruments for fashioning creation.⁴⁷ The clearest explanation of these essences and

---

⁴¹ Bennett (1997) 156.
⁴² Bennett (1997) 156.
⁴³ Bennett (1997) 157-58.
⁴⁴ Bennett (1997) 157.
⁴⁵ Bennett (1997) 158.
⁴⁶ Bennett (1997) 158.
⁴⁷ Bennett (1961a) 313.

their role is perhaps that found in *A Short Guide and Glossary to The Dramatic Universe*, written by Bennett and Marian Kaminski in 1970, but not published until 2021:

> Hitherto it seemed that there was a simple choice between 'fundamentalism'—that is, belief in the literal truth of the story of Genesis—and 'evolutionism'—that is, belief that life appeared by the working of blind chance. In *The Dramatic Universe* … I have proposed a theory of the origin and development of life that seems to avoid the pitfalls of both extreme views. This is the theory of Demiurgic Intelligences. In Vol. II … I have developed the conception taken from Gurdjieff of 'Reciprocal Maintenance' according to which every kind of being feeds upon another kind and is food for yet another kind. This leads to a Scale of Being in which animals feed on vegetables and are food for a level of being higher than man that I called the Demiurges.… Let us … assign to the Demiurgic Intelligences the task of guiding the evolution of the earth from its first lifeless beginning towards a future state when it will be the instrument and vehicle of a Great Will.[48]

Thus he sought to reconcile two apparently inimical views: direct creation of life and mechanistic evolution. Bennett's writing possessed the potential to reach that reading public for whom *Beelzebub's Tales* were incomprehensible; the challenge was to make his own treatment full and precise without sacrificing clarity and readability. Bennett increasingly overworked himself in efforts to reach the public, but his London lecture series *Man and his World*, was successful, and his group continued to grow. Extensive notes from these lectures were published in 2008.[49] Yet, he was pouring so much effort into the Gurdjieff work,

---

[48] Bennett and Kaminski (2021) 11-12.
[49] Phillpotts (2008).

that his relations with the Mining Association and its chairman Herman Lindars, became increasingly strained. He was, he knew, acting foolishly, but he could not change.[50] He perceived within himself the symptoms of self-will, although, for nine years, he had been incessantly praying "Thy Will be done," and spoke eloquently on the topic at one of his lectures.[51] Yet, Mme Ouspensky had often said to him that he was "too kind" to himself.[52] This may be the equivalent of Gurdjieff's later comment that Bennett never struggled with *himself*: his work was external, not suffering to confront and oppose his inner weaknesses and contradictions.[53] When he sent Ouspensky a copy of his revised geometry paper:

> He summarily dismissed the paper on five-dimensional physics with: 'If successful it will only amount to a new theory of Thermodynamics, and nothing more." He then went on to say that nothing new can be found by intellectual processes alone, and that there is only hope: that we should find the way to work with the higher emotional centre. To this he added the sad comment: "And we do not know how this is to be done."[54]

This was the last direct correspondence he ever had with Ouspensky.

5.4 VALUES

In February 1943, Bennett wrote the preface for, and then privately printed a selection of mystical and philosophical literature, *Values: An Anthology for Seekers*. It was reprinted in 1951 by Unwin Brothers, and again in 1963 by Bennett's own Coombe Springs Press, and in 2018 by the J.G. Bennett Foundation. Bennett passes over it in *Witness*, but it merits

---

[50] Bennett (1997) 158.
[51] Bennett (1997) 158-59. Gurdjieff warned against taking one exercise for too long, lest one become habituated to it and it become a futile obsession: Gurdjieff (2021) 101. Perhaps this is what Bennett did with the prayer "Thy Will be done."
[52] Bennett (1997) 159.
[53] Bennett (1997) 217.
[54] Bennett (1997) 159.

mention. Although it was issued in a limited number, Bennett nonetheless approached the copyright holders for permission to publish, so he doubtless intended a wider publication after the war. Perhaps he intended that *Values* would help to promote his groups. There is a large selection of material, which is prefaced by Bennett's statement that:

> The sacred literature of all ages and the speculative writings of the philosophers abound in passages which endeavour to express the ultimate values which form the goal of human striving. Some of these passages are well known—the most perfect are to be found in the Gospels … The object [here] has been to give ready access to a few of the more precise and also the more pregnant statements in Eastern and Western literature.[55]

Twice in this preface he refers to teachings of "self-creation," and cites David Hume and Buddhist teaching for the proposition that it is difficult to assert that we have any self or soul.[56] The unstated philosophy which led him to speak thus is, of course, Gurdjieff's. The anthology opens with a little-known letter from John Keats to his brother, "The Vale of Soul Making," which anticipated some of Gurdjieff's ideas: "Do you not see how necessary a world of pains and troubles is to school an Intelligence and make it a Soul? … thus does God make individual beings, Souls, identical Souls of the sparks of his own essence."[57] The second and the thirty-eighth extracts are the story of Moses told by Rumi. The first of these is almost a collection of proverbs, while the second may have commended itself to Bennett because there the intellectually proud Moses, who condemns the ignorant devotions of shepherd, is rebuked by God: "So far as thou canst, do not set foot in separation: of all things the most hateful to me is divorce."[58]

---

[55] Bennett (2018) 1.
[56] Bennett (2018) 1. Compare Ouspensky (1949) 156 and 308 on suffering.
[57] Bennett (2018) 8.
[58] Bennett (2018) 138.

Other selections are taken from Plato's Republic, the Upanishads and Patanjali in Bennett's own translation, St. Macarius, Boehme, Chuang Tzu, the Dhammapada, Eckhart, the Tao Te Ching, other Christian and Buddhist texts, and Attar's *Conference of the Birds*. There is an absence of Jewish, Theosophical, and Occultist material. In 1954, Bennett said that there was "very little teaching, very little significant content" in Blavatsky's books.[59] The material in *Values* is judiciously selected to be substantial but not formidable; long enough to grapple with but not so long as to become tedious. Although he did not refer to *Values* by name, when he was delivering some lectures on his meetings with the Shivapuri Baba, Bennett stated:

> This is something that I realised a very long time ago, when I found in reading modern books about the traditions—whether the Christian, or the Muslim, the Hindu, or the Buddhist—that these books were somehow hollow—no authentic ring sounded from them. That is why I was driven back to studying as far as I could the original sources; and how I acquired a taste for going back to the source whenever possible.[60]

This is a characteristic feature of Bennett's mind: the drive to learn the original languages of great literature and be able to drink directly from the spring.

5.5   THE TENTH VISION: *FIAT VOLUNTAS TUA*

Bennett said that when he first met Ouspensky, the latter had "preached the gospel of *grow or die*."[61] This shines a fresh light on Ouspensky's teaching, even if it serves as an *apologia* for Bennett's writing about the

---

[59] Bennett (1995) 80.
[60] Bennett (2014) 28.
[61] Bennett (1997) 160.

system, for Ouspensky had categorically forbidden this time and again. Bennett spoke with some of the senior pupils at Lyne Place, but a gap was opening between their philosophy of "conservation" and his own of "development."[62] A vision followed at Coombe Springs, relieving his anxiety about this widening rift:

> Early in the morning of Thursday, 14 April 1944 ... I had slept badly and was in a rebellious state, seething with resentment against Ouspensky and his pupils; against Lindars and the Council of the BCURA; even against my own group because they could not understand my difficulties.... I said to myself: "Now is the moment to sacrifice all this self-love and self-pity." I said aloud the words *Fiat Voluntas Tua*,[63] and for the first time in my life I was conscious of speaking them with no reservation of any kind. With the incredible speed of conscious vision that leaves thought limping lamely far behind, I saw the future; not one future, but all possible futures. I saw myself losing my job. I saw myself triumphantly successful. I saw Ouspensky repudiating me, and all his pupils shunning me in the streets. I saw myself followed by people who loved and trusted me. All this and much more was presented to me in the merest moment of time. And I accepted it all. Whichever the future God might send, I was ready to follow it without question.
>
> In the same moment that I made the decision, I was flooded through and through with love. I said aloud: "Jesus!" Jesus was everywhere. Each new-born spring leaf on the willow trees was full of Jesus, and so were the great oak trees, still bare of green. The spiders' webs glistened under the morning dew. The eastern sky glowed with the coming sun.

---

[62] Bennett (1997) 160.
[63] The Vulgate of Matthew 6:10, "Thy will be done," from the "Our Father."

> Jesus was everywhere, filling all with love. I knew that Jesus is God's love.
>
> I saw also that each separate part could contain so little of God's love just because it was so small. I said to myself: "Unless concentration can occur He is as if not there." As I spoke the words they were full of meaning, but now I have forgotten what they meant, except for one thing: that in order to live in the Love of God—that is, in union with Jesus—we must pray without ceasing. This practice, which for many years I had followed so conscientiously, had been as nothing, because without love, prayer is empty.[64]

Bennett returned to the house, and told his wife of the experience. She stated that when she had been as dead, she too, had known that Jesus was God's love, and that the "vision" had "never quite" been lost. On this occasion, what Bennett called his "ecstasy" lasted for three days.[65] Confirming that Bennett had at least some contemporaneous notes, he adds:

> If I had not written down my experiences during those days, I should not now trust my memory. For a short time, I was able to see and even to enter that realm in which Divine Love is a reality. But when I could no longer see, I returned to myself, and many years were to pass before I again became directly aware of that reality.
>
> Even now, I can scarcely believe what I wrote in my journal concerning the real Presence. I find the words: "We can see the literal truth of 'Take, eat; this is My body' ... We must see literally, as I have seen, how Jesus is the uttermost reality of personal existence and yet is not a person in any sense that has meaning for human conception". I had made the

---

[64] Bennett (1997) 161.
[65] Bennett (1997) 161.

step which leads from understanding of symbols to participation by way of gesture.⁶⁶

This experience would be resumed, so to speak, many years later at the monastery of St. Wandrille. There, a celebrant bearing the Sacrament passed Bennett, and he felt Christ first approaching then passing Him, "present in the Host."⁶⁷ It can also relate to the fourth vision, at Fontainebleau, and to what he was later to write of Jesus in *The Masters of Wisdom*. Further, the reference to the need to have some "concentration" of the divine is significant: he came to believe that architecture could be an aid in this, and he realised his insight in the Djamichunatra, a building which at times operated as if it were conscious (section 8.7). There is one consequence which marks this tenth vision as one of the truly significant ones in Bennett's life: from this point, Bennett speaks in terms of his own decisions, and ceases saying that he had no choice. He had made this comment about the situation he felt in, tugged between Lindars and industry, and his students and the Gurdjieff Work. Paradoxically, by submitting, at least in principle, to the Will of God, he ceased to oppose his own small will to larger currents. This, I suggest may have been the opposition which led him to feel that what he may have wished, he had act differently.

Bennett now delivered the J. Arthur Reavell Lecture of the Institution of Chemical Engineers, an honour which unsettled the old guard, who saw Bennett as an outsider to their guild.⁶⁸ Such was Bennett's state, and his native ability, that he was able to win over the hostile audience. A subsequent series of lectures on Gurdjieff's ideas (not naming Gurdjieff) attracted large audiences, and he saw the need to found a society in some form.⁶⁹ Plans were made to move the BCURA

---

⁶⁶ Bennett (1997) 161-62.
⁶⁷ Bennett (1997) 286.
⁶⁸ Bennett (1997) 162. For Reavell https://www.icheme.org/about-us/people/presidents/james-arthur-reavell/ accessed 8 February 2022. https://archives.dundee.ac.uk/ms-50-13-51. It seems that Bennett may have been the first person to be so honoured: a matter he does not mention.
⁶⁹ Bennett (1997) 162.

activities to a new property at Leatherhead, and even to provide him with a "private Director's laboratory." At the earth-turning ceremony, he had a clairvoyant experience where, separated from his body, he surveyed it "from another dimension" and knew that he would not go to work at Leatherhead. There were several problems in his involvement with BCURA, precisely because his research was so successful that it was heading beyond his original remit.[70]

At this time, May 1944, he became ill through the tension between his desire for worldly position and success, and his desire to surrender self-will, as he had in the act of self-abnegation which had been the catalyst for the tenth vision. As he pondered his options, one of which was to resign from the BCURA with a generous parachute, he wrote the last chapter of his book on the Gurdjieff system, which he called "Salvation."[71] This is extant both as an unpublished paper titled "Soteriology," and in an edited form as Book Two of *The Way to Be Free*.[72] It is a bold paper, contemplating religious history and possible human spiritual development: issues he would return to in *The Dramatic Universe*. Together with the liberation he found in the abandonment of self-will and in the prospering of his Gurdjieff-group work, he nonetheless felt that there was a darkness in the world, and he saw his task as that of a modern-day Noah, preparing "an Ark in which one could take refuge from the destruction that seemed inevitable."[73] Just at that moment, he was offered an even more attractive full-time position combining science and business. Of course, he turned it down. Immediately, another offer was made to work part-time on a well-remunerated coal-related project. This one, he accepted, and he closed a deal with Mrs William to purchase the property at Coombe Springs.[74]

Anticipating a practice he would find decisive in his spiritual development, he decided to spend "half an hour every morning, after waking

---

[70] Bennett (1997) 162-63.
[71] Bennett (1997) 164.
[72] Bennett (2006).
[73] Bennett (1997) 164.
[74] Bennett (1997) 165.

up, in quiet self-collection."[75] The impulse for this was his realisation that although he had driven himself very hard, he could not remember himself any better than he had when he had first met the ideas. At this time, too, he learnt that Gurdjieff was still alive and resident in Paris.[76] On New Year's Day 1945, he and his group celebrated the occasion together; the first time in twelve years that they had not been invited to the Ouspensky premises at Lyne Place. His state of depression and distress soon passed, for his work, both in coal and with his groups, was going swimmingly.[77] With other scientists, he produced a new form of carbon, "delanium," and he came to be joint holder of a number of patents, British or foreign. Bennett does not elaborate on his procedures, but says that: "By using unorthodox methods, I was able to get some young men of exceptional originality and was building up a team from which I hoped for great results."[78] Perhaps this contributed to the later development of "Systematics."

While the groups were growing, there came the final misunderstanding with Ouspensky. Bennett gave some of his pupils, Americans, letters of introduction to Ouspensky, then teaching in New York. They mistakenly told him that Bennett had been speaking from his (Ouspensky's) lecture notes. Ouspensky had his solicitors demand the return of all his material, and his group in Lyne Place were instructed to break off all relations and communication with Bennett. The cut was peremptory.[79] Bennett writes:

> It was a bitter day for me. I had left Gurdjieff and the Prieuré in order to follow Ouspensky and had tried for so many years to conform to his discipline.... I was determined not to justify myself or to explain what I had done.... I can now see,

---

[75] Bennett (1997) 166-67.
[76] Bennett (1997) 167.
[77] Bennett (1997) 167.
[78] Bennett (1997) 167.
[79] Bennett (1997) 167-68.

only too well, how in this reasoning, there was an element of self-martyrdom.[80]

This is significant for its inconsistency with his own earlier account, which we had doubted, that Gurdjieff had forced him away (section 3.8). This is the more truthful account: Bennett had left Gurdjieff. Bennett's own group, now over one hundred strong, largely elected to remain loyal to him as opposed to Ouspensky. To Bennett himself, full of self-doubt, this was sobering. He recalled how Ouspensky had told him that he, Bennett, and Madame Ouspensky likewise, were "young souls" who had not had the experience of many lives on earth; however, he (Ouspensky) believed that in "some previous existence" he had taken his own life.[81] This disclosure, is so far as I know, quite unique. Bennett seems to imply that Ouspensky told them this in relation to Winifred Bennett's belief that she too had once suicided. Bennett briefly mentions Ouspensky's theory of Eternal Recurrence, distinguishes it from reincarnation, and adds that he (Bennett) came to theorise that there is a third kind of time, which he called "Hyparxis," which he defined as "ableness-to-be."[82] In volume 1 of *The Dramatic Universe*, Bennett states that, for Aristotle, *hyparxis* meant the "ableness of a given animal to approach the ideal existence of its species," and that for Proclus, it seemed to be a sort of "determining-condition."[83] If I understand him correctly, Bennett is distinguishing potential from being itself, and also pointing out that this potential is limited, not endlessly open: hence "hyparxis" cannot be present in every moment of time, but only some, and when it is present, it means that an external force is entering our world to provide the opportunity of exercising free choice. I could be quite mistaken, but it seems to me that, towards the end of his life he tended to speak not only about "hyparxis" but also, with much the same meaning, about "pattern." Thus, at Sherborne, he said:

[80] Bennett (1997) 168.
[81] Bennett (1997) 169.
[82] Bennett (1997) 169.
[83] Bennett (1956) n.2, 137-38.

If we are talking about pattern in the objective sense, then we don't see it because it is unmanifested. The pattern itself does not exist and therefore we cannot know it. But the pattern is that which gives existence the possibility of having the right form, being as it should be. Our task as human beings is to enable the two to fuse together so that what is happening in the manifested world really corresponds to what is happening in the unmanifested world.[84]

The hyparchic pattern can be received in a human mind (perhaps through the instinctive centre), for "Intelligence in the Hyparchic Future can influence the present by acting upon the minds of creative beings like man."[85] This remained central to his purpose in writing *Witness*. He relates these meditations to our third vision, and to Gurdjieff's words of 1923 that "You already know too much, but your knowledge is useless without Being," and to Shakespeare's lines: "Men must endure their going hence, even as their coming hither. Ripeness is all. Come on."[86] This blend of thoughts led up to the reflection that he would not meet his "true destiny" before he was sixty. So although "outwardly all was going well, I was still secretly anxious and insecure, wondering where I was being led."[87] When news of the dropping of the atomic bomb on Hiroshima arrived, Bennett saw the end of an Epoch of confidence in human reason, and the dawning of one of madness. Still, he believed, there had to be some remedy, and for this, the Gurdjieff work had to spread.[88]

---

[84] Bennett (2006) 28.
[85] Bennett and Kaminski (2021) 16. For reasons I cannot understand, David Bohm (1917-92) who enjoyed an intellectual exchange with Bennett in the early 1960s, took "hyparxis" to be "the time of repetition," or "renewal": Blake (2016) 7 and 15.
[86] Bennett (1997) 169. The lines are spoken by Edgar in *King Lear* V.ii.9-11.
[87] Bennett (1997) 169-70.
[88] Bennett (1997) 170.

5.6 THE *INSTITUTE FOR THE COMPARATIVE STUDY OF HISTORY, PHILOSOPHY AND THE SCIENCES*

He now started learning Tibetan, and founded the *Institute for the Comparative Study of History, Philosophy and the Sciences*.[89] The Memorandum and Articles of Association show that it was incorporated on May 2, 1946. The first object of the corporation was:

> 3(a) To promote research and other scientific work in connection with the factors which influence development and retrogression in man and their operation in individuals and communities; to investigate the origin and elaboration of scientific hypotheses and secular and religious philosophies and their bearing in general theories of Man and his place in the universe; and to study comparative methodology in history, philosophy and natural science.[90]

The balance of the objects relate to teaching and research, and introduce the term "psychokinetics" (but do not define it). Bennett held ambitious, long-term plans. His ability justified some optimism, and his view of the global situation required action. When he celebrated his forty-ninth birthday, and opened Coombe Springs as his group base with twelve residents: "It was an electrifying day for us all; for the first time we had a place of our own, to be devoted wholly to the creation of a centre for spiritual studies."[91] Bennett took in his mother, who had suffered a stroke the year before. Life for the residents was marked by heavy demands, inspired by memories of his time with Gurdjieff at the Prieuré. Hence for their first retreat, they worked intensively, in dust and heat, on the theme of "Being and Consciousness."[92] Bennett enthused that

---

[89] Bennett (1997) 171.
[90] Memorandum and Articles of Association, *Institute for the Comparative Study of History, Philosophy and the Sciences*, clause 3.
[91] Bennett (1997) 171.
[92] Bennett (1997) 171-72. Bennett describes it as a "seminar," but that is hardly an

some of the participants, had an experience of "breaking through to a different state of consciousness by means of extreme physical exhaustion."[93] I discern here the influence of his fourth vision, which he experienced at Fontainebleau after intense physical efforts in the movements class. Bennett also applied what he called "emotional stress," and later produced "daily topics" as aids to mental alertness. He later wrote that there is another side to such practices:

> They easily degenerate into what Gurdjieff used to call "working to avoid work," that is, making efforts that are easy in order to hide from oneself that one is shirking the sacrifice that is really called for.... I am doubtful whether I did any good to myself or others by devising various spiritual exercises. Though their purpose is to provide a fulcrum through which our desire for perfection can exert its pressure, they can easily become ends in themselves.[94]

One important milestone was the 1946 report of the Parliamentary and Scientific Committee on *Universities and the Increase of Scientific Manpower*.[95] Of this audacious paper, recommending increased expenditure on higher scientific education, he comments: "We live in an age where it is seldom wrong to have a bold approach to the problems of the future."[96] On that score, he practised what he preached. Yet, important as that work was, he felt his value for the Committee was running its course, and as he wished to pour more of his energies into the new Institute, where life was "varied and full of colour," he "ceased to be a member" of the Committee only much later, in 1948.[97] The spring of 1945 saw the end of WWII. As the fighting had been drawing to an end,

---

adequate term. He does not specify how many days it lasted.
[93] Bennett (1997) 172.
[94] Bennett (1997) 173.
[95] Bennett (1997) 173. Mentioned in Powell and Butler (1980) 20.
[96] Bennett (1997) 173.
[97] Bennett (1997) 173.

Elizabeth Mayall, later to be his third wife, joined the group. In her posthumously published memoirs, she wrote:

> Release [from the armed forces] came at last. After four and [a] half years of wearing uniform every day I had to learn how to wear flowery hats again and to let my hair grow. But not for long. At his wife's insistence, Mr Bennett gave reluctant permission for me to join his household of eight to ten people at Coombe Springs ...[98]

Neither she nor Bennett state why he was reluctant; in fact, Bennett does not mention this at all. I am unclear why this meant the end of long hair and flowery hats for Elizabeth. It is not as if there were no amusements at Coombe.

5.7   THE "UNKNOWN BUILDERS"

Bennett was interested in the possibilities of theatre for group and individual work. He organised a production based on Ouspensky's *Strange Life of Ivan Osokin,* and initiated attempts to stage "live theatre" according to the indications in the chapter "Art" of *Beelzebub's Tales.*[99] He mentions a play he was inspired to write, and which, having been lost for some seventy years or more, was rediscovered by A.G.E. Blake in February 2022. In *Witness,* Bennett omits to name it. Appropriately enough the title pages reads: "Unknown Builders." Concerning it, he writes:

> I wrote a play based on the burning of Chartres Cathedral in 1187, and its rebuilding by a prodigious effort of the entire countryside. This was rehearsed during the autumn and produced at our New Year party at Coombe Springs. In it I tried to represent the power that enters a human community

---

[98] Elizabeth Bennett (2015) 65.
[99] Edwards (2009) 30 and 43.

when all are joined by a common aim beyond all personal gain. There came to me, when I was writing this play, the conviction that the Virgin Mary began to influence human destiny with the beginning of the second millennium of the Christian Era. I tried to convey some feeling of the love that grew between mankind and the Blessed Virgin in the rebuilding of Chartres.[100]

Although the title page reads "January 1st 1949," the narrative in *Witness* is quite ambiguous as to whether its first performance was on January 1, 1948 or 1949. However, the play itself is of some interest. It opens with a prologue delivered by the Angel of Eternity of Chartres Cathedral, who declares, *inter alia*, that:

> The destiny of mankind is an everlasting tapestry. Warp and weft are the visible and invisible, the eternal and temporal. Unseen powers stretch the invisible warp on the loom of eternity. Men of inward vision are vouchsafed glimpses of these powers and a little understanding of their purpose. To those who serve the temporal, it is given to move with the shuttle with which the invisible tapestry is woven, but since they cannot see the invisible, eternal pattern upon which they are working, they come to weave patterns of their own imagining.[101]

These reflections seem autobiographical. The angel seems to say that the true pattern is understood by "the servants of the eternal," but we materialists here on earth are largely "the servants of the temporal." However, some of us serve the "Great Purpose," and are tasked with

---

[100] Bennett (1997) 173-74.
[101] Bennett (1949a) 1.

healing or rectifying the temporal distortions of the eternal pattern.¹⁰² These last are the "builders" of the title, for:

> they labour unceasingly to build on the crumbling foundations of time a bridge to the eternal, and by this bridge every man may pass over, if he is willing to do so, and discover with his fellows the common understanding of a single purpose.¹⁰³

The play, with its elevation of those who selflessly work for a common aim is as much a statement of purpose for the new Institute as anything in the official document which was registered in London. There is a Master Builder and three apprentices, the young Luke, the more advanced Damien, who is working as a brother in an Order of Ransom, and Peter the Mason.¹⁰⁴ They know that some great building work awaits them, but the land at Chartres is already built upon. Damien reports on events in the East, and the need for devotion to Mary in the West, where its lack is sorely felt.¹⁰⁵ When the old church goes up in a conflagration, the Master declares:

> The moment has come. The Virgin Mother has been carried in safety from the crypt. Go, Damien, tell the Father Abbot we are ready. And do you, Luke, go with him and do his bidding. Many stout hearts and strong arms will be needed. For now eternal power will again be poured through the channel of human strength; and the church we shall build will last for a thousand years.¹⁰⁶

---

¹⁰² Bennett (1949a) 1.
¹⁰³ Bennett (1949a) 2.
¹⁰⁴ These orders, dedicated to ransoming captives from the Muslims, were founded in the late twelfth and the thirteenth centuries. In Bennett' day they most likely meant the Guild of Our Lady of Ransom, founded in 1887, and still active: https://www.guild-ransom.co.uk accessed April 25, 2022.
¹⁰⁵ Bennett (1949a) 2-6.
¹⁰⁶ Bennett (1949a) 8.

The Angel of Eternity proclaims:

> [A]ll that is revealed to man is incomplete; and being incomplete, it is impermanent; and being impermanent, must be renewed; and that which is revealed is the source of his faith and the mainspring of his endeavour; and every revelation is for a time. And so there is a time when the Son is revealed, and a time when the Mother is revealed. And since the least revelation of eternal truth is beyond conceiving by the mind of man, so the revelation of the Mother has power to raise men above the foolishness of their own wisdom; and the vision of the Mother comes in its season to these who have freed themselves from the bond of creaturely pride. And by this vision is created a new Heaven and a new Earth.[107]

This last sentence alludes to the Book of the Apocalypse (Revelation) 21:1. But the statement that even a revelation is only for a time and must be renewed, is striking as an anticipation of his later concept of "hazard" (section 12.6). The Master Builder declares that every action of wisdom is done for seven reasons. The two pupils recount the first five:

> *Luke* We build that we ourselves may learn to live; and that we may wake from the sleep which binds those whose purposes are within themselves; and…
>
> *Peter* We build that we may help one another to awaken and live the good life.
>
> *Damien* We build because we love beauty and serve the Truth.
>
> *Luke* We build because the secrets of our craft must be preserved and handed to those who come after.

---

[107] Bennett (1949a) 8-9.

Peter We build that our craft may be honoured, that men may come to it and its future be assured.[108]

The Master then discloses the sixth reason:

> We build to serve a purpose higher than ourselves. A purpose which is only made manifest when its time is ripe. Today that purpose is to renew in men's hearts the hope and trust without which art and religion are both in vain. For the outward eye observes the world of changing forms, but the inward eye observes the changeless symbols. Our task is to create a symbol which all men can see. A symbol of the union of the eternal with the temporal. A symbol which will rouse in men the longing to take part in the Everlasting Work.[109]

The essence of each of the six reasons might be paraphrased in terms of Gurdjieff's teaching, as (1) an individual's awakening from waking sleep; (2) aiding others to do so; (3) to serve Beauty and Truth; (4) to pass on the understanding of their school; (5) to attract others to their school; and (6) to advance all these goals by producing, in time, objective art. Over and above this, there is a presentiment of what he would write about how a *sacred image* facilitates a "return to the Source," by focussing human energies in the direction of their aspirations and thus "accumulate reservoirs of this sort of energy centred around the focal points of prayer and devotion."[110] Bennett now depicts the way that a "Great Crusade" came to build the cathedral:

> So rich and poor, young and old, moved by the same impulse, burning with the same zeal, set forth thronging the roads. Winter and Summer, Autumn and Spring, the pilgrimage

---

[108] Bennett (1949a) 9.
[109] Bennett (1949a) 9-10.
[110] Bennett (1994) 164. For the Four Ideals Exercise, see Azize (2020), ch. 17.

goes on. Round the great church now rising off its roots are camps and stores, taverns and stalls. Leaving their farms, their homes, their crops, their trades, their families, the comfortable pattern of their ways, they come, bringing their strength and skill, their wealth or power. And when they leave to do their necessary tasks others replace them, so that in the space of ten short years the Virgin has been welcomed to her home, the roof is set, the floors laid, and the great doorways open.[111]

The Angel of Eternity states in terms which remind us not only of Gurdjieff's teaching on symbolism, but also of Bennett's proud family connection to the Arthurian legends:

The eternal truths cannot be expressed in the language of human wisdom. None the less it is given to some to teach the ancient legends and underlying myths, the heritage of all mankind, in simple thoughts, more true than any creed, wiser than any philosophy. In legends of the Quest is shown the undying search of man for the highest good. In myths of the blind man restored to sight is shown the opening of the inward eye, which sees things to which the eye of flesh is blind. Thus all things which are visible are signs and symbols of things that are invisible, and the invisible is the meaning and goal of things which are visible. Whosoever, therefore, aspires to become the servant of the Great Purpose, must learn to read as symbols all things that present themselves to the eyes and ears of flesh.[112]

When young Luke remarks that some of their carvings will be so placed that the details will be effectively invisible, Peter replies: "The

---
[111] Bennett (1949a) 10.
[112] Bennett (1949a) 11, for Gurdjieff on symbolism see Ouspensky (1949), 278-98.

mason is working for love of Our Lady. He would not be saddened even if his work were hidden where no mortal eye would ever see it."[113] Brother Damien praises the invisibility of the unknown builders, and the Master adds: "It is not our acts, but our understanding that ennobles or debases."[114] The Master points Damien to the carvings depicting the active and the contemplative lives, and teaches him not to think about these two as opposites. The figures come to life, and express their mutual gratitude, then the Master declares:

> The fruit of Contemplation is the union of our will with that of Our Lord. The fruit of union is the manifestation of His purposes in the world. The Active and the Contemplative Life are united and reconciled in Love. Neither is nobler nor better; for neither can be complete except in Union with Her Lord. Union has no end and no beginning; it is what it is beyond all worlds.[115]

The Four Seasons circle the Angel of Eternity, who speaks about the renewal which has featured in this play, leading up to two mystical declarations: "All perish and all is renewed and yet there is no renewal and no perishing," and "The Eternal seeks a Body and the Temporal seeks a Soul. So, neither is complete without the other, and their Marriage is the weaving of the Tapestry of Life."[116]

The Master observes that: "Our work is finished, but it is not complete. We have come to the end and we have made a beginning."[117] This provides the occasion for Peter the Mason to ask whether they can now learn the seventh reason of their work or whether it is beyond human understanding, or even that it is for others to learn of it. The Master responds that the hardest lesson of all is that:

---

[113] Bennett (1949a) 12.
[114] Bennett (1949a) 12-13.
[115] Bennett (1949a) 14.
[116] Bennett (1949a) 15.
[117] Bennett (1949a) 15.

The Eternal has power and no strength, but the Temporal may receive the power of the Eternal, so that which is without a body may be given a body, and the Great Purpose may be fulfilled. But the ultimate secret that man must learn is that the strength of the Temporal is as the strength of water, which is only felt when it flows. Nothing is permanent, nothing is for ever. Only in the sacrifices of all purposes can the Great Purpose be fulfilled."[118]

The last word belongs to the Angel:

The Temporal is the realm of means, the Eternal is the realm of ends. The ultimate truth for man is the undying sacrifice, for the Temporal must sacrifice its means that the Eternal Purpose may be fulfilled, and the Eternal Pattern must be sacrificed, for even in its fulfilment there can be no final perfection. On the Loom of Eternity, the everlasting tapestry is woven. In the warp are the Divine Purposes, revealed by glimpses to mankind. In the weft are deeds and sufferings, success and failure. Each is sacrificed to the other, the invisible to the visible, no less than the visible to the invisible. But the supreme sacrifice is ineffable, beyond Eternity as it is beyond Time. The tapestry itself is but a veil beyond which is the Unknown, of which nothing is nor ever shall be revealed; where goodness, truth and beauty, the uttermost perfection, are but motes in the Sunlight. The Sunlight is all.[119]

That is the last word of the play. It is impossible not to contemplate it in the light of Bennett's autobiographical disclosures, and discern the influence of what I have counted as the fourth and tenth visions. First, I would consider the fourth vision, that of August 1923,

[118] Bennett (1949a) 16.
[119] Bennett (1949a) 16-17.

at Fontainebleau, when Gurdjieff, having caused Bennett to experience what he saw as a connection to the Great Accumulator, taught Bennett what he (Gurdjieff) considered to be "the greatest secret that man can discover about the human nature."[120] I would suggest that the power which Bennett claimed to have experienced could be understood as the "sunlight" of the closing peroration of "The Unknown Builder." I see the influence of the tenth vision (*Fiat Voluntas Tua*) in the idea of constant renewal, and that even our own achievements must be sacrificed.

I am told by A.G.E. Blake, that Bennett had the play performed once at Coombe Springs, but that it was otherwise neglected. Several who have read it since its rediscovery have commented that some of the writing of the play is ponderous, and that the language and action are not natural. I wonder, according to what criterion is it to be judged? It is not written according to contemporary standards or in a modern genre: it is a Mystery Play, like the celebrated *Everyman*. One might suggest that "The Unknown Builders" represents an extraordinary and inspiring achievement for a scientist's first attempt at writing drama. But Bennett did more than write about creating "a symbol which all men can see. A symbol of the union of the eternal with the temporal. A symbol which will rouse in men the longing to take part in the Everlasting Work." He and his pupils built it in the Djamichunatra at Coombe Springs.

---

[120] Bennett (1997) 98.

The completed Djamichunatra, with a body of water in the foreground.

CHAPTER 6

THE KING'S COLLEGE VISION, 1947

6.1   THE DEATH OF BENNETT'S MOTHER

Bennett now comes to the death of his mother. The old lady knew she was dying, and after watching "The Unknown Builders" from her wheelchair, started to be interested in Bennett's spiritual quest. Previously, she had been anxious only that he succeed in the world. She had disliked Ouspensky, dismissing him as "your Kouspensky," but she now asked Bennett what he understood about eternity, death, and the soul. He tried to "make her see for herself that the relationship between her and my father and us children could never be broken."[1] It may follow from Gurdjieff's teaching about "essence," that parents and children have an eternal relationship. Bennett records:

> She died in the lodge at Coombe Springs. I had been with her half an hour before and had gone out for a walk. When I returned she had ceased to breathe. I sat beside her for a long time and for the first time in my life became aware of a kind of mystic participation in the condition of a dead person. I could sense her bewilderment, and a heart-rending sadness took hold of me that had nothing to do with myself or with past or future. It was the sadness of her own dawning realization that she had put her trust in the wrong things

[1] Bennett (1997) 174.

and would have to learn all over again to live according to her true destiny.

The experience suddenly lifted, and I felt that I had lost touch with her. The sadness vanished and a peaceful quiet took its place. It was not until two years later that I was able to make a step towards understanding what the experience signified.

Looking back over the intervening years, I connect my mother's death with the beginning of a change in myself that was to lead, a few months later, to experiences so overwhelming as to give a new direction to my whole life.[2]

Here, I see an allusion to the King's College Vision, when Bennett would again participate "in the condition of a dead person." The "step towards understanding" is related, I think, to the eleventh vision, when he was working with Gurdjieff's exercise of "Helping the Deceased."[3] Although Bennett does not make an explicit connection, his inner work now shifted into a higher gear, and it may be legitimate to see his mother's passing as allowing Bennett space to be more himself, so to speak. Perhaps there is a pattern of learning associated both with attachment to and separation from a teacher or other figure, especially a parental figure. Bennett chose some remarkable teachers and also made some remarkable separations, in both processes acquiring something for himself. About this period, he writes:

From the beginning of 1947, I introduced the practice of early morning meditations, which any resident or visitor at Coombes was free to attend. I also initiated some of the members of my groups into the practice of repetition as I had learned it from Ouspensky. We also worked regularly at Gurdjieff's rhythmic movements and ritual dances. The life

[2] Bennett (1997) 174.
[3] See Azize (2021).

at Coombe grew ever richer and more varied, but some of the original members of the community were beginning to feel the strain. Interest in our groups was growing, and the meetings I held weekly in London in the spring of 1947 were attended by men and women who were beginning to take the ideas and methods of Gurdjieff's System very seriously indeed.[4]

Two years later, after he had met Gurdjieff again for the first time in 25 years, he was to be swept up into the rejuvenation of Gurdjieff's methods, and through the new methods, to see his mother once more (sic). Intriguingly, his instigation of morning meditations anticipated the Morning Preparation (Collected State) Exercise which Gurdjieff had, unknown to Bennett, been teaching for up to ten years (section 7.2).[5]

6.2   THE CRISIS IN HUMAN AFFAIRS

Bennett now signed a contract with his publishers, Hodder & Stoughton, for what would become the first volume of *The Dramatic Universe*. At this time, it was to be called *The Foundations of Natural Philosophy*. However, each revision led to further revisions, and they agreed to publish, instead, *The Crisis in Human Affairs*.[6] In *Witness*, he records:

> It was a bold venture to agree to publication, for it was the first book to appear with an account of some of the main features of Gurdjieff's System. It was also the first publication of my conception of Eternity as the domain of potentiality, both material and spiritual. It would be more accurate to say

---

[4] Bennett (1997) 174-75.
[5] It is my thesis that Gurdjieff came to believe that his system needed such practices: Azize (2020) *passim*. That Bennett independently began morning meditations is another indication that he may have been correct.
[6] Bennett (1997) 175.

that, through understanding Eternity, we can recognize that spirit and matter differ only in their form of consciousness.[7]

This was not the first published work to explicitly mention Gurdjieff and outline his ideas. That honor belonged to Rom Landau, who in 1935 included chapters on Gurdjieff and Ouspensky in *God Is My Adventure*, although more of Gurdjieff's ideas are found in the Ouspensky chapter than in that devoted to Gurdjieff. Landau suggests that Ouspensky's most distinctive teaching came from Gurdjieff, although he was not certain of the teaching as a whole.[8] There had also been two earlier books influenced by Gurdjieff, King's *The Butterfly: A Symbol Of Conscious Evolution* (published in 1927 under a pseudonym), and Cosgrave's *The Academy For Souls* (a novel published in 1931).[9] Given his prominent position in British scientific and industrial circles, Bennett was courageous to declare himself a convinced student of these unusual ideas. Landau, in contrast, was an outsider to the teaching, and his book included chapters on others such as Meher Baba and Rudolf Steiner. Landau's book was very successful, and Bennett's volume must have sold pleasingly, for a third edition was published in 1954.

The Crisis in Human Affairs was organized in two parts: "The Origin of the Crisis," in approximately ninety pages, and "The Coming of the New Epoch," in about seventy. The text comprised the lectures Bennett gave at the foundation of the Institute. They bear the mark of material delivered without notes, and phrased to strike an audience, rather than to be pondered in solitude. A young woman, then named Joan Cox, was invited by George Cornelius to attend these lectures. She recalled the crowded hall, and Bennett's handsome and magnetic presence, a "tall man with cornflower-blue eyes ... energy vibrated from him."[10] Mrs.

---

[7] Bennett (1997) 175.
[8] Landau (1935) 131 and 147.
[9] Driscoll (1985) 20-21, 46, 94.
[10] Edwards (2009) 212-13.

Bennett invited her to visit the community at Coombe Springs, which she soon joined with her son.[11]

Although the influence of Gurdjieff is marked, Bennett's personal contribution predominates, especially in the introduction of his concept of "Epochs." Against the background of WWII, the series of talks had been successful, because Bennett acknowledged that the world stood on a razor's edge, but offered hope. Behind the book lay the first vision, that of March 1918, and the string of revelations which had followed, each contributing to Bennett's ever developing sense of mystery but also of enlightenment, two states which nourished each other.

Bennett must have been pleased at the idea of scholars and scientists reading his work; it is one of several works from the Gurdjieff tradition mentioned by E.F. Schumacher in *A Guide for the Perplexed*.[12] However, the lectures and the book in particular were aimed at the ordinary person, who could appreciate a new way of thinking about human affairs, "if he feels the need to see the world and his own life in a more positive light than that given by most modern modes of thought."[13] Bennett does not deny the horrific global conflict which had followed hard upon the heels of the "war to end all wars." But his goal is transformative, hence he writes: "Our aim in these studies has been not merely to sound the knell of a dying epoch, but to seek for a positive understanding of the human problem."[14] Bennett resisted the temptation to offer a quick fix, promising only the necessity to work so that humanity can accept what must, he says, come:

> If I am right in the conclusion that we are witnessing the

---

[11] Edwards (2009) 13.
[12] Schumacher (1977) 96. See especially 45 (Gurdjieff and levels of being), 14-15, 44, 57-58, 77, 80, 81, and 111-112. Bennett introduced Schumacher to Gurdjieff's ideas when they met through the BCURA: Wood (1984) 231. They remained in contact to the end of Bennett's life: Bennett (1990) 85. Schumacher's debt to Gurdjieff and Nicoll is quite substantial. In fact, he occasionally lectured on Gurdjieff, and for a period of about a year after a particularly successful lecture led a group studying the ideas of Gurdjieff and others: Wood (1984) 233-34, and 256-57.
[13] Bennett (1954) 20.
[14] Bennett (1954) 181.

> end of an Epoch and not the transition from one form of civilization to another, we must place the hope of the world in a fresh Revelation of the Divine Purpose to Mankind and prepare ourselves to be ready to receive it.[15]

The idea of "Epochs," and that we are on the cusp of a new one, allows Bennett both to candidly admit the mistakes and the horrors of the past, and to set out a vision of a possible future which is a fresh departure and not just a continuation of past failures. He frankly acknowledges his debt to Toynbee's *A Study of History*, with its division of human history into diverse but often related "civilizations."[16] *A Study* was a sprawling twelve-volume series which appeared between 1934 and 1961. By 1947, the first six volumes had been published, dealing with what Toynbee called the "Geneses" (the plural of "Genesis"), Growths, Breakdowns, and Disintegrations of Civilizations. The work was influential:

> The immense readership of *A Study of History*, helped in part by its wide press coverage, meant that the work had a significant cultural and intellectual influence on British society in the late 1940s and 1950s. Its main focus, analysing the growth and decline of 28 separate civilisations over history, meant it was used by many readers and commentators as a prism for analysing contemporary society and Western civilisation as a whole.[17]

The six volumes which had been published by the time of Bennett's lectures had been generally well-received.[18] Later volumes met increasing criticism, for Toynbee's wide-ranging and abstract approach to human history as a whole: "defied preconceived notions about the specific limitations of a historians' work to a specific period and geographical

---

[15] Bennett (1954) 194.
[16] Bennett (1954) 24-25.
[17] Hutton (2014) 405.
[18] Hutton (2014) 406-7.

location."[19] Like Toynbee, Bennett was prepared to boldly speak outside of his areas of expertise, and in doing so adopted the tone of a "sage."[20] Both would have been driven to adopt such a role, for where one lacks specialist qualifications, one can claim authority by appealing to a higher wisdom. Further, Toynbee saw religion as "a central mechanism of history", and a force for renewal,[21] as did Bennett. Even to some Oxford history students: "Toynbee's expansive approach to history was deeply appealing over the suggestion that historians should be cautious, conservative and limited in their judgment."[22] The same was doubtless true of the approving members of Bennett's audience.

According to Bennett, the civilizations of the last 5,000 years fall into two equal periods, the first being from about 3000 to 500BC; the "ritualistic-sacrificial period."[23] Bennett prefers to call this the "hemitheandric period" because, he asserts: "its really significant character (was) that the meaning of human life was conceived in terms of the doings of certain men, demi-gods or heroes."[24] The Greek roots of the word "hemitheandric" will be "half," "divine" and "man" respectively. He continues: the "Megalanthropic Epoch" ("great man") succeeded around 500BC, the essential message of the great teachings which then appeared being that *"the individual matters."*[25] This Epoch has now run its course, hence the bankruptcy of modern values.[26] A new or "psycho-kinetic" view is needed to replace the obsolete "psycho-static" one: that is, human nature must be seen as dynamic and changeable, with a possibility of transformation.[27] Here, Bennett reformulates an idea in Ouspensky's chapter on "Superman" from *A New Model of the Universe* (section 0.6).[28] As Bennett phrases it in *Crisis*, our importance lies not so much in what we are as in

[19] Hutton (2014) 410.
[20] For Toynbee as a "sage," see Hutton (2014) 408.
[21] Hutton (2014) 413-15, citing 414.
[22] Hutton (2014) 412.
[23] Bennett (1954) 24-25.
[24] Bennett (1954) 25.
[25] Bennett (1954) 26-27.
[26] Bennett (1954) 107-9 and 113.
[27] Bennett (1954) 114-15.
[28] See specifically Ouspensky (1934) 119.

what we can become.[29] For Bennett, Gurdjieff showed how to change in a positive direction.

Bennett was influenced more by Toynbee's method and example than by his conclusions. Toynbee does not divide the past into epochs: his categories were "civilization" and "society," which concepts Bennett disavowed. For Toynbee, his twenty-one societies which made up "Western society" were "so many representatives of a single species of the genus."[30] Bennett, being a self-taught historian, did not possess the breadth of knowledge to critique Toynbee's historiography, just as he was not able to sufficiently critique his own historical work. Thus, Bennett explicitly presents his system of epochs as based on Toynbee's with "a little adaptation," when it is rather a misreading of Toynbee.[31] I can find no evidence at all that Toynbee held any such view of the past five thousand years. The phrase "ritualistic-sacrificial period" does not appear in Toynbee, or in any other scholar I can locate. Once more, this imprecision is that of the autodidact. But the idea of developing human consciousness is found in Bucke and Hegel. Hegel's school of thought may have influenced Bennett both directly, and indirectly through Schopenhauer.[32] One interpretation of Hegel sees him as having drawn up a scheme of Oriental, Greco-Roman and Germanic cultures. In the oriental, the despot only, not man as such, is conceived of as free; in the Greco-Roman liberty is allowed only to some (free men) but not to others (slaves). Then, the Germanic peoples "under the influence of Christianity first arrived at the conscious awareness that man as such is free."[33]

This brings Bennett to a discussion of Gurdjieff's ideas, influenced by Ouspensky's presentation and his innovative understanding of time and eternity.[34] Bennett contends that the type of Fourth Way School he

---

[29] Bennett (1954) 34.
[30] Toynbee (1935) 172. I use the second edition of this work.
[31] Bennett (1954) 24.
[32] Bennett (1973) 202 seems impressed by at least one aspect of Schopenhauer's philosophy.
[33] Copleston (1963) 221-22.
[34] Bennett (1954) 160-64.

was experimenting with at Coombe Springs was needed to prepare for a new revelation:

> we are all asleep, but ... our responsibility towards ourselves, towards other people, and towards those things which are beyond our personal concern, is that we should seek a way to ensure that our ears shall not be closed and that our eyes shall not be able to see when the time comes. This is the aim of the psychokinetic attitude to man, the opening of possibilities in our essence, the opening of the inward eye and of the inward ear, which are able to perceive indications coming from a different level.... we entirely depend upon the help of a very different kind from any that we can see around us today. The essential difference between an Epoch and Civilizations is that the former originates in Revelation from beyond humanity, while the latter are the work of schools within humanity itself. If I am right in the conclusion that we are witnessing the end of an Epoch and not the transition from one form of civilization to another, we must place the hope of the world in a fresh Revelation of the Divine Purpose to Mankind and prepare ourselves to be ready to receive it.[35]

As we shall see, *Crisis* was almost a dry run for *What Are We Living For?* and a curtain raiser for *The Dramatic Universe*. There is a continuity in Bennett's work which shows an original mind working out and developing insights over the course of an eventful life.

6.3   THE ELEVENTH, OR "KING'S COLLEGE" VISION

The emphasis on Revelation with a capital R may sound an unexpected note for a pupil of Gurdjieff and Ouspensky, but Bennett called his next direct contact with the supernatural, occurring on 15 September

[35] Bennett (1954) 193-94.

1947, "the King's College revelation."[36] His scientific career was advancing swimmingly, and his lectures were attracting larger audiences. His wife was effectively operating as a spiritual guide, finding that she had "scope for her power to awaken and inspire people."[37] Helena Edwards (née Joan Cox) remembered her as "an extraordinary woman with clairvoyant powers."[38]

Bennett's new work was heavily indebted to Gurdjieff, and he made attempts through various people to locate Gurdjieff in Paris: but even the French police were of no assistance.[39] Writing in 1941, Ian Black stated that he had met no one who could tell him of Gurdjieff's fate, and he regretted that "we had lost touch for ever with a man, the like of whom we would not meet again."[40] Bennett was not alone in being unable to satisfy his curiosity as to whether Gurdjieff had disappeared into the darkness of Occupied France.

Bennett was now deeply touched by a *shared* mystic experience, rather a *rara avis* in the literature. On the last day of a seminar which followed soon after the lectures, while meditating what form an ideal community might take, and the position of man and his relationship with the planet, a sort of epiphany dawned on Bennett and those with him:

> That day was strange, for though the fifty people present afterwards agreed that it was supremely important, not one could remember just what was said. My recollection is that we saw all life on the earth as a female Being who passes through great cycles of fertility and sterility in her spiritual receptiveness. When her moment of fertility comes, the cosmic male Power descends upon earth and all life is inseminated with a new spiritual power. From this is born a new

[36] For the date see Bennett (1997) 175-76.
[37] Bennett (1997) 175.
[38] Edwards (2009) 29.
[39] Bennett (1997) 175.
[40] Black (1941) 20.

Epoch. Not only man, but everything that lives, takes part in this cosmic ritual.[41]

Bennett says little more about this experience.[42] In his wife's circle was a young physician, Bernard Courtenay-Mayers, who "had played a heroic part in the French Resistance movement, but had escaped with his nerves shattered by concentration camp horrors and other heart-rending experiences."[43] At the end of 1947, he was suffering from some sort of guilt associated with a perceived personal failure during the war. Bennett tried speaking with him, but to no avail. Bennett was himself "restless, almost feverish," and decided to head outside for the walk he often took on Wimbledon Common.[44] However, on this occasion, he found himself walking across to his former school, King's College for the first time since 1917, and wondering why he now returned there. At the College playing fields, Bennett made his way, "half in a dream up to a monument" which proved to be a memorial for the fallen in WWI:

> I started reading the names. One after another I saw the names of boys with whom I had played Rugby or cricket. Hardly one seemed to have escaped. I knew then why I had never returned; I had never reconciled myself to the loss of so many of my best friends. I was all alone in the great playing field; but, as I stood, I was no longer alone. All these boys were still there, still living with their powers undiminished. A Great Presence enveloped us all. An immense joy flooded through me. Past all understanding, it was yet true that premature death is not necessarily a disaster. *Potentialities are not destroyed by death*. I was, quite irrationally, convinced that an angel had been sent to make me aware of this truth.

---

[41] Bennett (1997) 176.
[42] This was not the only occasion when Bennett had an epiphany of a "super-intelligence" operating on the planet: see sixth vision (section 4.7).
[43] Bennett (1997) 175.
[44] Bennett (1997) 177.

When referring to an angel having been sent, Bennett is probably alluding to the Greek etymological root: an *angelos* is a "messenger." He continues:

> I walked back across the Common quite aware that the angel was still with me. I understood that I must speak that evening of death, of what it can and what it cannot destroy.
>
> When I came to the door of Coombe Springs, Elizabeth was waiting for me: "Mrs B. wants you at once." My wife was at the head of the stairs: "Bernard needs you at once." I went into his room. He was writhing on the bed, his face distorted, uttering pitiful moans and sudden screams. I stood at the head of the bed for a few moments, and then said: "Bernard, you need not suffer—they are all right." He lay still, gave a deep sigh and went to sleep. I knew that I had told him what was necessary, and that he had believed.[45]

Striking as this is, another strange experience awaited:

> That day, Coombe Springs was visited by some Great Presence. It might have been some angel or an even greater Being. When I spoke that evening at Denison House, it was neither I nor my own voice that spoke. I was, during the whole of that day, completely certain that in some utterly incomprehensible way the boys who had been with me at school, and had died on the battlefield, were as much alive as I was. The experience was quite different from that of my own state when I nearly died. It was not a personal experience nor remotely resembled any kind of direct communication with them, for I had no notion, no picture, of how and

---

[45] Bennett (1997) 177. Elizabeth Mayall, to be his third wife, was by now part of the household at Coombe: see section 5.6 above.

> where they were living. Only I was aware that their potentialities had been preserved intact and undiminished.
>
> I cannot remember what I said that evening, not was any record made of it, but afterwards several who had lost sons in the war came up to me and said that all grief had been lifted from them.
>
> The next day all of us at Coombe Springs were subdued, and many were awestruck. I discovered, as the days went by, that several others had been aware of a Great Presence and of a blessing that had come to us.[46]

There was a coda to this experience, for when Bennett had shortly afterwards gone to South Africa:

> I could not sleep that night but prayed that I might see what was right.... Slowly the night grew quiet. I was aware again of the same Presence that had spoken to me of death in the school field at King's a few months before. This time it was a personal message or instruction: "You are not meant to stay in Africa. Your place is in London. Trouble will come, not as you imagine, but differently, and you have to be in the midst of it. There is no need for Noah's Ark, for this time there will be no flood. The task before you is quite different from what you suppose."
>
> I have expressed what came to me in words, but it was an unspoken message, the meaning of which was clearer than words could make it.[47]

So, as Bennett understood it, he was thrice visited by the same presence, but on the first occasions, in England, the experience had been shared. On his view of the matter, there must be disembodied

---

[46] Bennett (1997) 177-78.
[47] Bennett (1997) 182.

intelligences which have some sort of identity, and can choose when and how to communicate with us. The conditions in which such a presence can manifest, or to whom, are obscure. Yet some but not all of those at Coombe Springs that day felt the Great Presence. In connection with a conversation on telepathy, in 1953, Bennett told the Sufi *murshid* Emin Chikhou of this vision, and asked whether the telepathic connection between the living, which Chikhou said was based on "love, and calling on the name of Allah" was like what and how he had learnt of his school fellows continued existence. Chikhou replied:

> Yes, you had a bond of love from youth, which is the strongest. For many years you had felt the separation, and Allah on that day guided you to the spot where He could reveal to you the true existence of the spiritual nature of man.[48]

6.4 THE DEATH OF P.D. OUSPENSKY

Ouspensky died at dawn on October 2, 1947.[49] As Bennett was leaving the house to take his morning dip in the springs, his nephew delivered the news.[50] Bennett had known Ouspensky was ill, and had written requesting permission to visit him, but his letter had not been answered. In London, Bennett called on Janet Collin-Smith, wife of Rodney Collin (also known as Collin-Smith), who was within Ouspensky's inner circle. She told Bennett of Ouspensky's last hours.[51] Bennett felt a greater love than he had known for Ouspensky, without feeling any nearer to his former teacher. In terms reminiscent of Bennett's recent epiphanies, he wrote:

> I was strongly aware of the difference between death after a long life on earth and a premature departure. Ouspensky's

[48] Bennett (2000) 59.
[49] Webb (1980) 458.
[50] Bennett (1997) 178.
[51] Bennett (1997) 178.

potentialities had been brought into time, and they had undergone an irreversible transformation. There was something that I could not understand and should not try to understand. A great cycle of my life which had lasted nearly twenty-seven years had closed.[52]

I read this in the light of the King's College vision. Bennett is implicitly comparing Ouspensky's life with that of his fellow school students who had died young. This comparison proved to be significant for Bennett's later understanding: that there is, let us say, "a cosmic dispensation" by which souls which have not explored their potential somehow retain it. What is not clear, and what perhaps Bennett himself could not have clarified, is at what point has a person's potential been "brought into time"? Is it a question of age, some sort of inner development, something else, or a combination of these? Bennett seems to be trying to articulate an ineffable insight.

6.5 AFRICA, FROM BENNETT'S PERSPECTIVE

Bennett was now fifty years old, and the concept of "Psychokinetic Philosophy" which he had formulated in *The Crisis in Human Affairs* was earning him invitations to lecture in England and in France. When he travelled to Paris, he made fruitless enquiries about Gurdjieff. His "psychokinetic" teaching was going well, and his industrial research was promising to handsomely reward him. But like many others, he feared that another outbreak of war was imminent – he does not say so, but the great foe was now Stalin's Soviet Union. Reflecting in *Witness*, Bennett makes the pregnant comment: "Ouspensky was dead, Gurdjieff had disappeared. There was nothing to hold us in Europe."[53]

He pondered much on Noah's Ark, and was sure that he could lead a community to safety where they might "weather the coming storm

---

[52] Bennett (1997) 178.
[53] Bennett (1997) 179 and 180.

and afterwards return and help in the rebuilding of a new civilization."[54] He mentions that: "Two friends, Cecil Lewis and his wife Olga, had decided to emigrate and offered to explore the possibilities of Rhodesia and South Africa and send us their report."[55] They flew down the week after Ouspensky's death, and promised to report back to him.[56] Then, in January 1948, he was offered the opportunity to go there himself. On the way, they stopped in the Sudan, where he visited Omdurman, and was struck by how the entire life of the city was "regulated by [Islamic] religious observance."[57] Then follows an elusive passage which seems suggestive of another vision:

> As I stood upon the bridge that crosses the Nile, where the waters from Ethiopia and Uganda flow together, I was transported into the past; an age even more remote than ancient Greece. The Baharian colonists, who had descended into Egypt from the mountains eight thousand years ago, must have gone past this spot.[58]

The reference with ancient Greece implies that he is comparing this experience with his fifth vision, at Mycenae; but when he says that the ancient people "must have gone," he is musing, not seeing. Bennett had thought, at one time, that a new race of humanity might have been developing in Africa, with powers of extra-sensory perception, but he is now "less and less inclined to attach any importance to this notion."[59] We have already reviewed how this idea which could naturally be deduced from that of evolution, was prominent in Bucke's *Cosmic Consciousness* and in Blavatsky's *The Secret Doctrine,* but rejected by Ouspensky (section 0.6).

[54] Bennett (1997) 179.
[55] Bennett (1997) 179.
[56] Bennett (1997) 179.
[57] Bennett (1997) 180.
[58] Bennett (1997) 180.
[59] Bennett (1997) 181.

Bennett had several insights and impressions while in Africa, but I would suggest that the most important of these was hearing the Presence which had spoken to him in the King's College vision, which passage I have already excerpted above. He wrote:

> "You are not meant to stay in Africa. Your place is in London. Trouble will come, not as you imagine, but differently, and you have to be in the midst of it. There is no need for Noah's Ark, for this time there will be no flood. The task before you is quite different from what you suppose."
>
> I have expressed what came to me in words, but it was an unspoken message, the meaning of which was clearer than words could make it. I slept almost at once and woke feeling calm and assured. I did not know whether I should speak of what I had received. It seemed to me that the message was for me personally, and if others wished to go and fund (sic) a colony in Africa, I should help rather than oppose them.[60]

Bennett's writes that on meeting the Thorburns and Lewises: "There were cross currents of feeling, and I had not helped matters by my own change of plans."[61] Later that day, he led the experiment of a moderately extended meditation on the Beatitudes (in Matthew 5), shared by five others, and how the effects of this lasted among them for several weeks.[62] A moving incident occurred when he came upon a Basuto village during a walking trip:

> Their ages must have ranged from seven to seventy, and they were singing and hoeing to the rhythm of their own music. As they saw me they all stopped and stood up straight in

---

[60] Bennett (1997) 182. The word should be "found."
[61] Bennett (1997) 182.
[62] Bennett (1997) 183.

surprise. Then with one accord they began to laugh. I have never heard such laughter. It was pure joy and friendship, without malice and without thought.... This was one of the unforgettable moments of my life.... this happiness that I saw before my eyes was beyond all the others.[63]

Bennett then asks whether the Africans might not be "more firmly rooted in tradition than all the rest of us," and is pained at the fate of the Red Indians, "the bearers of a tradition perhaps twenty thousand years old."[64] By "tradition" he means more than just conventional repetition of inherited norms and mores, but does not elaborate. In a talk given between 1972 and 1974, Bennett adds the detail that the African tribespeople had migrated to that valley only one hundred years ago, "to get away from the white people."[65] This adds a poignancy to the reflection, in *Witness*, that: "No power on earth could save this happy Basuto tribe from civilization. It was only a matter of time before a kind government would start schools and shops and provide them with tools and tractors."[66]

Another pregnant observation comes in the form of a prayer: by the waterfall of the source of the Crocodile River: "In the thunder of its voice, I prayed that I might never forget that if man has created cities, nature is still God's handiwork."[67] He does not say that nature is God, but that it bears the signs of being His work. Towards the end of his life, he returned to this theme, and began to consider whether nature might not be understood as a sacred image (section 12.7). When he returned to England, Bennett raised funds to help the community which had started there, but it did not prosper and had to be sold up.[68] It is instructive to compare this account with that of Cecil Lewis himself.

---

[63] Bennett (1997) 186.
[64] Bennett (1997) 187.
[65] Bennett (1975) 14. This has the strange corollary that the village in question was a relatively modern experiment, and not a representative of an ancient tradition.
[66] Bennett (1997) 186.
[67] Bennett (1997) 187.
[68] Bennett (1997) 187.

6.6 AFRICA, FROM LEWIS' PERSPECTIVE

In the introduction, I briefly treated of Cecil Lewis' mixed attitude to Bennett. I suspect that a significant part of this is due to his having found, in Jeanne de Salzmann and Henriette Lannes, new and steadier teachers of the Gurdjieff work. But behind the decision to seek further guidance from them and not from Bennett was possibly disappointment in the African venture. Bennett distinctly states that the Lewises had decided to emigrate, and when he had the vision which told him that the world situation was not as he envisaged, he felt unsure as to whether to tell them, but said enough to produce "cross currents of feeling." Lewis' account is sufficiently different to make it appear that Bennett was simply lying in two important particulars: according to Lewis it was Bennett who had taken the initiative and induced them to decide to "emigrate" to South Africa, on the basis that he would be living with them; and second, even after he had returned to England, Bennett maintained to them that the decision to move to South Africa was correct. Harder than this, their staying in South Africa meant that they missed meeting Gurdjieff in person, for by the time they eventually returned to England, Gurdjieff had died.

Lewis recalls how Bennett impressed upon them their own "awesome responsibility" for the world situation: Ouspensky had died, Gurdjieff was believed dead, and "He, Bennett, alone remained as the custodian of these tremendous possibilities." This raised the question: "How could we preserve them for posterity?"[69] Although he does not mention the atomic bomb, this was probably at least part of the reason that Lewis considered that "in the next conflagration" the Gurdjieff ideas could be entirely lost. Significantly, he continues:

> With practically no further investigation, or what would today be called a feasibility study, Bennett swept us all off our feet by deciding that something must be done at once. He

---
[69] Lewis (1993) 137.

suggested that South Africa was our best choice and somehow convinced us that this was a wise, simple and logical solution to finding a refuge for our El Dorado. A nucleus was formed of those who trusted him and were ready to uproot their lives and set up this survival centre in a strange country that none of them knew, but which – such was the faith and hope Bennett inspired – was to become the taproot of this sacred trust placed in our hands. Because of its very nature it would be bound to succeed. My part in this adventure was typical, exciting, romantic and quite unnecessary.[70]

Lewis' wife, his son and his wife, his daughter, a family of weavers, and "an enthusiastic local spinster" all accompanied him.[71] Lewis draws a heavy curtain of silence over Bennett's trip to South Africa and his withdrawal from the project. He does, however, record that the news Gurdjieff was teaching in Paris struck them like a "bombshell."[72] Lewis also takes pains to explicate that Bennett and the others had to find a "new balance" with the teaching. Further: "That it was done at all was largely due to the remarkable influence of Mme de Salzmann."[73] Lewis saw the Gurdjieff system as now revealed to them to be different, if complementary with the more intellectual one taught by Ouspensky and Bennett.[74] Lewis appends some letters which Bennett then wrote to him. The most important is that of November 18, 1948:

> The truth is that everything is so exciting here at the moment that hardly anyone can bear the thought of being separated from it. At the same time, if and when disaster strikes, the very people who are reluctant to do anything to share in building

[70] Lewis (1993) 137.
[71] Lewis (1993) 137-38.
[72] Lewis (1993) 138.
[73] Lewis (1993) 138-40, quoting 140.
[74] Lewis (1993) 138-41. Again, Lewis is coy about Bennett's own standing here, but Bennett did not have the current teaching, as de Salzmann did, so his comments on the Ouspensky dispensation must also apply to Bennett.

up a home for us to go to, will be only too ready and anxious to take advantage of what has been done.... I am equally certain that within two or three years we shall enter that period of acute nervous tension which Beelzebub calls 'solioonensius'. Such periods induce intense incentive to work in those who are capable of it, but they engender madness in those who have lost touch with the real aim of life.... As I understand it, the next Solioonensius will be the most intense of all. As an outcome, either mankind will change to a different mode of existence or there will occur the most terrible process of mutual destruction. So our decision to seek a place in SA remains just as valid as it was three years ago.[75]

It is difficult to see how this can be reconciled with the account that the Presence told Bennett, while he was in South Africa, that: "There is no need for Noah's Ark, for this time there will be no flood." At the best, Bennett had forgotten this in November 1948. On the other hand, he may have been disingenuous when he wrote *Witness*, or when he wrote that letter, or on both occasions. In either event, we see once more that *Witness* serves, among other purposes, as Bennett's *apologia pro vita sua*. After detailing certain weaknesses he did admit to (including a fondness for women, morally worse when "the relationship of teacher and pupil also existed"), he wrote:

> Those who had to deal with me were above all exasperated by my habit of agreeing with almost anyone who might urge upon me some course of action and then, upon further reflection, feeling it to be mistaken and doing something quite different, without either warning or explanation. I could see all these and other defects and was under few illusions about myself.[76]

[75] Lewis (1993) 142-43.
[76] Bennett (1997) 188.

Yet, the correspondence of November 1948 shows that it seems he was under an abiding illusion about his responsibility for the South African adventure, and the fact that a small number of his friends would lose the opportunity to meet Gurdjieff. Further, in a letter dated 6 June 1967, written to John Allen, Bennett wrote:

> the year 1967 has for a very long time been predicted as a year when there would be critical events determining [the] course of history for a long time to come. For this reason, it now becomes important for us to consider what geometrical locality we shall find ourselves in at a given moment. Fifteen years ago, I was earnestly advised to make my way straight to Damascus as soon as the signs of the end of the world were fulfilled. I must say that I have not taken this advice seriously, nor do I think it likely that anything catastrophic will happen just now. It is, however, not wholly irrelevant to consider the prophecies of Edgar Cayce, which seem to have been made quite independently and in ignorance of the earlier prophecies of important events about this time.[77]

"Geometrical" is probably a mistake for "geographical." That he was concerned about this as late as 1967, when he was now ambivalent about precise prophecies of catastrophe, tends to confirm that he had been entirely behind the South African venture.

6.7 MRS. BENNETT, AND MADAME OUSPENSKY

The next phase of Bennett's life is marked by the prominence of two remarkable women: Winifred (Polly) his second wife, and Mme Sophia Ouspensky, and the story of how they brought him back to Gurdjieff. On his return to England from South Africa, Bennett found his wife to

---

[77] Unpublished one page letter of June 6, 1967.

be quite ill, and decided upon a holiday in France, during which they visited the newly discovered cave paintings at Lascaux. He emerged from his visit, convinced that there had been esoteric societies in those most ancient periods.[78] His wife returned happier, but still in pain. When travelling to the U.S. to investigate coal research there, he was welcomed by Mme Ouspensky, who stunned him—on Bennett's account—by telling him that Gurdjieff was alive in Paris and had never gone mad.[79] However, as we have seen, Bennett already knew that Gurdjieff was alive, he had just been unable to find him.[80] I suspect that what was stunning was the implication that Mme Ouspensky had remained in touch with him, and knew how to locate him. Bennett enjoyed close relations with her: it was he who suggested the title *The Fourth Way* for her magisterial collection of materials from Ouspensky's lectures and their subsequent question and answer sessions.[81] Her strength, as Bennett expressed it, was that: "She looked beyond Ouspensky to Gurdjieff, and beyond Gurdjieff to the Great Source from which comes every good gift and every perfect gift."[82] This brings to mind Bennett's statement on July 1, 1962, that he once heard Gurdjieff say: "I am only a bridge; when you have got over the stream you can kick me away."[83] At this point Bennett makes an incidental observation which sheds some light on how, at the time he wrote *Witness*, he saw what was to happen:

> Turning again to the lessons of the past, we can see how all the followers of a great man are convinced that they are doing justice to his memory. It is only in the perspective of history that we can clearly see the factions separating. In the long run, the passive preservers die away, as did the Jewish Christian Community in Jerusalem.... It is the near heretics

---

[78] Bennett (1997) 188.
[79] Bennett (1997) 188-89.
[80] Bennett (1997) 175.
[81] Moore (2005) 29.
[82] Bennett (1997) 190.
[83] Bennett (2004) 252.

like St Paul ... who see beyond the outer form to the inner grandeur of the message and make it live and give fruit in the lives of men.[84]

To a degree, Bennett is offering a defence of his own "near heresy" from Gurdjieff. Before he returned to Europe, his coal related work in the U.S. was the occasion of his coming across a herd of wild bison at the foot of a mountain glacier. They so reminded him of the bison depicted on the walls of the Lascaux caves that: "I became convinced that the American Indians were a link with remote antiquity—perhaps the ice ages—and that we had perpetrated a hideous crime in destroying their culture rather than learning from it."[85] Visiting Mme Ouspensky again, she made him apprehensive as to what superhuman demands Gurdjieff might make on him, were they to meet again. Bennett sent his wife a cable expressing his fear that Gurdjieff might send him to a monastery in Persia: a comment which suggests that Bennett had read *Herald of Coming Good* in which Gurdjieff wrote of just such a practice.[86] She sent one in reply advising him to do whatever Gurdjieff required. Bennett wrote: "This was an heroic reply, because I knew well enough that she would not survive my going."[87] It was not to come to this, but on his return, he found her condition much worse, and the mystery of her ailment aggravating an already alarming situation. Yet, when he crossed the channel on August 6, 1948 to see Gurdjieff, she insisted on accompanying him, although Dr. Courtenay-Mayers feared she would not survive the rigours of travel. First, they went to the Rue du Bac where they met Jeanne de Salzmann. To their surprise, she asked them if they would like to lunch with Gurdjieff. As Bennett states, part of their astonishment was that they "had been expecting to be kept waiting for days, and to meet all kinds of demands before

---

[84] Bennett (1997) 190.
[85] Bennett (1997) 191.
[86] Gurdjieff (1933) 59-60.
[87] Bennett (1997) 192.

we were allowed to see him."[88] Perhaps Mme Ouspensky had surmised something like this might happen, or perhaps she had not. Even she may not have had the measure of Gurdjieff.

[88] Bennett (1997) 192.

Bennett, possibly in Africa.

CHAPTER 7

WITH GURDJIEFF IN JERUSALEM

7.1   THE REUNION WITH GURDJIEFF

It is often said in Gurdjieff circles that Bennett overstated the extent of his contact with Gurdjieff, and attributed to Gurdjieff things which he had not and could not have said. However, Bennett did in fact spent a good deal of time with Gurdjieff in the last fifteen months of Gurdjieff's life, just as he describes. Apart from the testimony of Elizabeth Mayall (later to be Elizabeth Bennett), Paul Beekman Taylor, who remembers the period of August 1949 well, writes: "Bennett had arrived from England, and he and Gurdjieff talked a good deal together".[1] The evidence is that Gurdjieff immediately considered Bennett to be one of his most promising and responsible students.

Bennett's wife (Winifred, his second wife) forced herself to attend the meetings, notwithstanding that her health was badly failing: "My wife's fortitude seemed unnatural, rather as if she were possessed by that mysterious strength that sometimes enters those who are about to die."[2] They entered Gurdjieff's apartment at 6 Rue des Colonels Renard, an unexpectedly small and dingy apartment of pungent odour, where the windows were forever shuttered, and the lighting was electric. Then Gurdjieff appeared:

> He was old and sad; but his skin was smooth and he held

[1] Taylor (1998) 180.
[2] Bennett (1997) 193.

himself as erect as ever. I felt a sudden warmth towards him, very different from the youthful awe and the timidity with which I had approached him at the Prieuré.... His open shirt and untidy trousers were more in keeping with his whole appearance than the smart French suits he wore in 1923. He moved, as always, with a grace and an economy of gesture that were in themselves enough to induce in those near him a sense of relaxation and well-being.[3]

Although Jeanne de Salzmann said that Gurdjieff would remember him, he silently sized Bennett up, saying: "No, I not remember." Then after a pause added: "You are Number Eighteen. Not big Number Eighteen but small Number Eighteen."[4] The number possibly refers to the toasts to the idiots. The literature dealing with the toasts should be supplemented with the full list of idiots, published in 2007 from George Adie's notes.[5] Adie's notes reveal that number 18 is:

Merde de merde qui en même temps s'imaginer roses de roses.
= who consider others shit of shit but themselves R. of R.[6]

In an unpublished and unattributed paper, which is known to have been by Bennett, titled "The Science of Idiotism," he states that at this time of his life, Gurdjieff used the toasting of idiots as a way of achieving several aims at once: it included a teaching on human destiny and on inner aspects of human life, thus helping people to see something about themselves.[7] Moore describes the toasting as "perhaps Gurdjieff's strangest and most innovative method of teaching."[8] Speaking of the meals as a whole, Gurdjieff said to Helen Adie: "You think that these are

[3] Bennett (1997) 193.
[4] Bennett (1997) 193.
[5] Adie (2007) 241-46.
[6] Adie (2007) 245.
[7] Bennett (undated and unpublished) "Science of Idiotism," 1.
[8] Moore (1991) 353.

just ordinary meals, but actually they are intended for your work and for me to watch you."⁹ On Saturday, October 9, 1943, he asked one of his French pupils whether, during the break, he had thought of drinking to the health of the idiots. When he said he had not, Gurdjieff replied:

> You have not understood (it). There is a science of idiotism. When you have chosen your category, in drinking to the health of idiots of your category, you can enter into contact with them, and you have the ability (faculté) of uniting yourself (vous fondre) with their substance. It is necessary to do this seriously. If you wish to receive without joking, it is necessary to give without joking. Throughout humanity there are different categories of idiots. There is even the Unique Idiot? Who might the Unique Idiot be? God. But you (can) never go (all the way) up to God. Between you and God there are twenty categories of idiots. You have not yet been (sufficiently) perfected to be able to see God. You can see only up to Zig-Zag Idiot. (From when you began) until today you cannot even sense my category: I am in the eighteenth category of idiots.¹⁰

This is the only reference known to me wherein Gurdjieff speaks of this "merging" or "uniting" of the members of a given category, and tells a pupil that he should have continued the toasts when not at Gurdjieff's table; at least for his own class of idiot. Bennett insisted that the toasts were part of the "sacred" meal at Gurdjieff's apartment. Newcomers would hear the toasts and the description of so many idiots as were toasted—often no more than the toasts one to six were given,¹¹ which does suggest an ascending hierarchy of idiots. On their second visit, they

---

⁹ Adie (2015) 50.
¹⁰ Gurdjieff (2020a) 219.
¹¹ Moore (1991) 354 states that "toasts beyond twelve were seldom even approached," but Adie's contemporanous notes for use as director extend from One to Twenty-One: Adie (2007) 242-45.

would nominate their "idiot." One had to drink at each and every toast, but individuals were acknowledged only at their proper place. Gurdjieff always referred to himself as Eighteen.[12] I will set them out in seven triads:

1. Ordinary; 2. Superior; 3. Arch;
4. Hopeless; 5. Compassionate; 6. Recalcitrant;
7. Square; 8. Round; 9. Zig-Zag;
10. Enlightened; 11. Doubting; 12. Swaggering;
13. Full of Remorse; 14. Born; 15. Patented;
16. Imagining; 17. Stinking; 18. Shit of Shit;
19. Vermin (or "maleficent"); 20. Indifferent; and 21. Unique.[13]

The question arises what Gurdjieff may have meant by "small Number Eighteen." Moore states that: "Idiot 18 represented the highest development which a human being could reach, but in order to attain it, he had first voluntarily to descend from 17 to category 1, the ordinary idiot."[14] Moore does not explain what is meant by this "voluntary descent," but taking the material as a whole, I would conjecture that it is meant that a person has to experience all the difficulties of the path, and then revisit their experiences, but this time consciously. Adie's notes suggest two slightly different types of Eighteen: a first who is shit of shit but sees himself as rose of roses, and a second who thinks others to be shit of shit but himself to be rose of roses. The difference would then be that the second looks down on others, but the first does not. However, on another occasion, Gurdjieff toasted Bennett at Number Eleven, "Doubting Idiot."[15] Had Bennett started to descend? It is futile to conjecture.

At that first meal, Bennett was seated to Gurdjieff's right. Interrupting the toasting ritual, Gurdjieff asked Mrs Bennett whether she was not in

---
[12] Bennett (undated and unpublished) "Science of Idiotism," 1-3.
[13] Adie (2007) 242-45.
[14] Moore (1991) 354.
[15] Bennett and Bennett (1991), 50.

bad pain. She replied that she was. He left the table, to return with some pills which she took. After a little, Gurdjieff again stopped the ritual, and:

> turning to my wife, (he) said: "Where is your pain now?" She answered: "It is gone." He insisted: "I ask where *is* it now?" Her eyes filled with tears and she said: "You have taken it." He replied: "I am glad. Now I can help you. After coffee, Madame Salzmann will show you an exercise."[16]

After the meal, Gurdjieff invited Bennett to a private meeting, where he told Bennett that the first commandment of God to man is "Hand wash hand!... You need help and I need help. If I help you, you have to help me." Gurdjieff indicated he needed money. Bennett was ready to oblige, and asked him to teach him how to work for his being, to which Gurdjieff responded: "Now you have much knowledge, but in Being you are a nullity. If you wish, I will show you how to work, but you must do as I say."[17] Given that Bennett states that their conversation "was the exactly fitting continuation of what he had said to me at the Prieuré," one can only speculate that Gurdjieff recollected how Bennett had previously not done what Gurdjieff had advised, despite his having been shown something which Bennett considered preter- if not supernatural.[18] Gurdjieff told him that he understood the distinction between sensation and feeling only with his mind, and told him to ask de Salzmann to teach his wife and himself "the exercise of sensing and feeling."[19] I return to the question of this exercise in the next section. It is interesting to note Bennett's words that he soon located de Salzmann, but:

> When I said that we were to learn the exercise of sensing and feeling, Madame de Salzmann asked if I was sure I had

---

[16] Bennett (1997), 194.
[17] Bennett (1997) 194-95.
[18] Bennett (1997) 195, compare 97-98.
[19] Bennett (1997) 195.

understood rightly, as this exercise required preparation. However, it proved to be what he wanted, and she explained very simply and clearly what the exercise was, and how often and how long we should do it.[20]

Given later developments, none of this is without significance, in particular, it subtly indicates de Salzmann's under-estimating Bennett's development, and understanding of Gurdjieff's instructions. She also gave Bennett copies of the "Ashiata Shiemash" chapters from *Beelzebub*, as directed, and which he was to read thrice. Bennett's wife began a speedy recovery and eventual cure of her mysterious illness, and the next day had a conversation with Gurdjieff about Bennett, which persuaded her that Gurdjieff could assist him in his search.[21] Some of Bennett's pupils, such as Dr. Courtenay-Mayers, came over to Paris, although they entertained little hope of meeting him, as Mme Ouspensky had told Bennett not to ask for permission to bring any of his pupils.[22] Gurdjieff set out on a touring trip, with Bennett due to follow the next day. However, on the morning he was to depart, Bennett learnt that Gurdjieff had been in an accident, and was returning. Bennett arrived at the apartment at the same time as Gurdjieff, whom he saw alight from the car with bloodied clothes and blackened face: "It was a dead man, a corpse that came out of the car, and yet it walked."[23] Inside, Gurdjieff declared: "Now all organs are destroyed. Must make new."[24] Even as blood flowed from his ear, possibly due to a cerebral haemorrhage, Gurdjieff invited him to dinner that same night, and the meal did in fact proceed. Gurdjieff went to bed early, but nonetheless dispensed with the morphia which had been procured, on the basis that he had found how to live with pain.[25] Despite Mme

---

[20] Bennett (1997) 195.
[21] Bennett (1997) 195.
[22] Bennett (1997) 195-96.
[23] Bennett (1997) 196.
[24] Bennett (1997) 196.
[25] Bennett (1997) 196-97.

Ouspensky's apprehension, Elizabeth Mayall and Dr. Courtenay-Mayers were invited to eat with Gurdjieff.[26]

Gurdjieff knew about Bennett and Mayall. A confrontation which he engineered with her is of the first importance for understanding Bennett's psychology and the way Bennett would prove gullible in the Abdul Hamid scheme, and when confronted with the sincere but overly confident Pak Subuh and the insincere and fraudulent John de Kay and Idries Shah. One day, in his Paris apartment, Gurdjieff asked Mayall: "Tell. Why you want this man?" She asked whether she did in fact want him. Gurdjieff was not at all taken in: "Yes. You want. He *naïf*, like a little boy. What you want with little boy?" He passed on, then turned around and added: "Not always so. Can perhaps be good. Very perhaps."[27] It seems to me that Gurdjieff was helping both Elizabeth and Bennett himself by preparing her for the future, by pointing to Bennett's chief character flaw. Tellingly, Shah had much the same view of Bennett, whom he described as "an innocent" in "this business" (section 10.5). Indeed, the sharp knew his mark, and played on Bennett's lack of a healthy scepticism.[28]

To return to Bennett's account of events in Paris: in an observation fraught with deeper meaning for those who understand his development of Gurdjieff's idea of the Ray of Creation and the inter-related worlds, Bennett wrote:

> For four or five days after the accident, it seemed that he either could not or did not feel the need to play a role, to hide himself behind a mask. We then felt his extraordinary goodness and love for humanity. In spite of his disfigured face and arms—he was literally black and blue from head to foot—and his terrifying weakness of body, he was so beautiful that

---

[26] Bennett (1997) 197.
[27] Elizabeth Bennett (2015) 95.
[28] In old but venerable and colourful Australian slang, the "sharp" was a swindler who preyed on "flats" or newly arrived immigrants.

we felt we were looking at a being from another and better world.[29]

This means, in Bennett's terms, that Gurdjieff was conscious not only of his life in the shared world of sensitivity to material objects, but also of higher worlds (section 2.1). We all live in World 48, but a person with their own individuality, who has their own "I," also lives in Worlds 24 and 12, because they can "concentrate conscious energy," and that allows this person's will to be an "agent of the creative power" behind our universe. One might not be able to maintain the sublime life of World 12, but yet be able to experience, by moments, the life of World 24, in which our inner life is real, not subject to fantasy, and we can say: "I am aware of myself; I am aware of my surroundings."[30]

Bennett believed that the Gurdjieff they saw at this time was "the real Gurdjieff," who could no longer artificially maintain the "strange and often repellent behaviour" which was intended to impede people from idolising him.[31] Gurdjieff told Bennett to invite to Paris those eighty pupils of his who were gathered at Coombe, so Bennett returned at once to England to call them back, but oddly, gave his own warning "that there will be many difficulties."[32] So, Mme Ouspensky's "prophecies of problems" were twice confounded. Bennett was still under their influence, but by the time he came to write *Witness*, he was free. Although Bennett does not draw out the lesson that a real teacher is easier of access than one might think, he includes these details in the text: the only reason I can see for this is that he is subtly making the point that Mme Ouspensky's warnings were unduly ominous. Bennett seems to have detailed transcripts of the address he gave to his pupils in England. The chief point was that:

---

[29] Bennett (1997) 197-98.
[30] Bennett (1994) 104-7.
[31] Bennett (1997) 210 provides examples of this behaviour, and observes that: "the advice that he gave older men and women resulted in many irregular relationships being formed."
[32] Bennett (1997) 198.

he can show us the way to work effectively so as to get results from our work. He has shown me an exercise that has completely transformed my understanding of self-remembering. Whereas I went to Paris convinced that self-remembering is both indispensable for man and impossible of attainment, I am now sure that it can be attained, and moreover by the very simple means of involving the powers latent in our own bodies.[33]

In an unpublished lecture which Bennett delivered on March 17, 1949, at Livingstone Hall, he said:

> There is one thing I advise you all to work on persistently until you have mastered it, and that is the distinction between sensing and feeling. This is one of the foundations of the practical method which Mr Gurdjieff is now giving people to help them in their work, and there are many things which cannot be done until you are able to make this distinction in your own immediate experience; he calls this the distinction between "je" and "moi", between "me" and "myself". By "je" we mean that experience of ourselves which comes from our feelings; by "moi" we mean that experience of ourselves which comes through our bodily sensation. Ordinarily, both of these are outside or below the threshold of our conscious experience, they both belong to our sub-conscious, and only affect what we call our conscious state indirectly through associations, or directly when there is a process of particular intensity, such as physical pain or strong, powerful feeling, and even then, we fail to realize that these things belong to kinds of "self" feeling which we do not ordinarily experience.
>
> Try, above all, to see how from this there comes a certain kind of "self" feeling; this is what Mr Gurdjieff calls "je." Try

[33] Bennett (1997) 198-99.

> to see if you can bring together into your experience both "moi" and "je"—in other words, try to see if you can sense the whole of the life of your body, and then also have the experience of feeling yourself present in it; have the experience directly and not merely as something which colours your thoughts—have the experience directly of the succession of emotional states which is present in you.

The vividness of this advice, given as Bennett was travelling to and fro across the Channel, at least matches the quality of his later recollections in *Witness*. This idea of a distinction between "I" and "me" also appeared in the first lecture he delivered at Conway Hall in Red Lion Square, in 1955.[34] However, Gurdjieff had not only introduced the concept of this separation in 1943, he had taught a "Separation Exercise" (more precisely, a series of exercises) as a form of contemplation-like evidence, which, so far as I am aware, was not taught to anyone who had not been in the WWII French groups.[35] One of these exercises, assuming a knowledge of the basic process is found in Gurdjieff's answer to the first question at the Saturday meeting of October 16, 1943.[36] The dangers of dissociation as a result of such exercises must have been high. However, I would have thought that was a reason to carefully prepare balanced and mature pupils before teaching the exercises: not to fail to pass them on altogether, which seems to have been what happened.

---

[34] Bennett (2016) ii, 1-12.
[35] This was evidently one of Gurdjieff's major exercises. If we peruse the 1943 transcripts alone, we find it mentioned for a sustained period, in both the Thursday and Saturday groups: Gurdjieff (2020a) 80-85, 92-96, 101, 115, 130, 169, 186-94, 218. Further, the explanation Gurdjieff gives of the separation, while not inconsistent with Bennett's explanations, are much more developed: e.g. at 246. Since writing the final draft of this volume, I have seen an published letter which provides a fuller but still incomplete explanation of the basic Doubling or Separation Exercise, and unpublished notes which seem to contain the full Exercise. However, to include these here is not feasible.
[36] Gurdjieff (2020a) 232-33.

7.2 GURDJIEFF TEACHES BENNETT CONTEMPLATION-LIKE EXERCISES

What was this exercise of sensing and feeling, which Gurdjieff assessed as capable of helping Bennett, which de Salzmann queried as requiring a preparation which evidently she did not believe Bennett to have had, and was *the exercise* which he told his own pupils made self-remembering a reality and the work possible? George Bennett, son of J.G. Bennett, has generously provided me with Bennett's own final texts of the exercises he wanted passed on, with a title page "Catalogue of Inner Exercises." There is no exercise titled "The Exercise of Sensing and Feeling" in those papers. However, other Bennett students have passed on to me their notes, and among these are two exercises titled "Sensing and Feeling."[37] The first of these is described as "for beginners." It assumes knowledge of the "collected state," which is described as "becoming aware of one's entire presence by sensing, feeling, and in the head brain 'I am here now'." If this is the exercise which Gurdjieff had de Salzmann teach Bennett, it would bear out de Salzmann's concern that the exercise needed some preparation, and yet it would also indicate that Gurdjieff assessed Bennett and his wife as having had sufficient experience of the collected state. The exercise is expressed as "confined to the limbs," although it notes that the "vital organs" will nonetheless be affected by the exercise. Like the authentic Collected State Exercise used in the Morning Preparation, it begins with relaxation of the body, and comes to sensation of the spinal cord, and arousing feeling in the solar plexus.[38] The notes add that it was given in the first Sherborne course (that of 1971-72).

But it soon becomes more sophisticated, involving the desire to feel "remorse of conscience." There also appears the striking statement: "Sensitive energy is the 'etheric double'." This is related to Bennett's philosophy of energies, and is somewhat in accord with the surviving notes of the various "Separation Exercises." The chief difference is that

---

[37] These notes were sent to me under the collective title "Morning Exercise Project."
[38] See chapter 17 of Azize (2020).

there, Gurdjieff refers to the feeling energies as being the "etheric double." However, words like "sense" and "feel" were often interchanged, Gurdjieff tried, very carefully to establish distinctions between them, over the entirety of his career.[39] Taking all the material together, I suspect the reference is in fact to the *theoretical underpinning* of the Separation Exercises. However, those actual exercises with their distinctive features were not, so far as I can see, taught to Bennett, and certainly, they feature neither in his own or his pupils' notes.

The second exercise of this name ("Sensing and Feeling") was given in the third course (that of 1973-74). It adds nothing to the first, but rather takes it in two stages, separated by a few days, so that only two thirds is attempted over the first days, before it is completed. If this exercise does in fact reflect the exercise of the same name taught in 1948, it shows three new developments in Gurdjieff's methods over the previous twenty-five years:

> 1. The introduction of a practical exercise to become consciously aware of sensation, and of feeling. Previously he had only given examples of the difference and invited people to become more aware of the differences in life: see for example the talk of 20 January 1923, where Gurdjieff provides many of the elements which would be reassembled into this exercise.[40]
>
> 2. The use of relaxation as a prelude to the raising of sensation and then of feeling, in that order, with all three held

---

[39] For 1923, see Gurdjieff (2014) 203-5; and Bennett (1997) 203, when Gurdjieff was leaving for the U.S. in October 1948, his "last parting message" was "Before I return I hope with all my being that everyone here will have learned the difference between sensation and feeling."

[40] Gurdjieff (2014) 203-9, see especially the paragraph on 207 commencing "When you pronounce the word 'I' you will have a purely subjective sensation in the head." If Gurdjieff had taught this as part of a seated contemplative exercise, then together with the other content of this talk, it would have approximated to the "Exercise of Sensation and Feeling."

together. This was a feature of the Morning Preparation, as Gurdjieff taught it to George Adie in 1948 and 1949.[41]

3. The idea of coming to "remorse of conscience" was linked with the exercise.

This bears out Bennett's observation that the exercise helps one to remember oneself through "the very simple means of involving the powers latent in our own bodies." Previously, Gurdjieff had been sending his pupils into life to make these efforts. By now he has concluded that, while these efforts were necessary, they were not sufficient. That method alone was too difficult, and so, to produce the results he had hoped for, it was helpful to begin in a quiet state, temporarily cloistered. Then, having more clearly and uninterruptedly become conscious of this state, one goes into life with a benchmark against which one's decline from this conscious state can be judged.

Finally, two facts combine to persuade me that in the compilation of Contemplative Exercises which he bequeathed, Bennett was not attempting to leave a record of all the exercises he had learnt, but to pass on his own contribution to the spiritual life; omitting what was purely Gurdjieff, but within a Gurdjieff-framework, so to speak. These are, first, the inclusion of exercises from other traditions, but not from Gurdjieff, such as the Vayu Prana Meditation and the *zikr*.[42] Bennett evidently felt that he had made them part of the regime at Sherborne, which can be related to the comment that it is the "near heretics" who look beyond the form and keep the teaching innerly alive (section 6.7). The second is the omission from this collection of the authentic Gurdjieff exercises known from *Life Is Real Only Then When "I Am,"* the Paris transcripts, the "exercise of sensing and feeling," and another concerning appointments (section 8.4). Bennett does not even refer the reader to them, he simply omits them. I conclude, therefore, that the "Catalogue of

---

[41] Azize (2020) 298.
[42] He mentions learning the *zikr* from Shushud at Bennett (1997) 296.

Inner Exercises" is a collection of Bennett's own take on exercises from Gurdjieff and other sources.

Around this time, Bennett is not precise, there occurred an incident, of critical importance for understanding the difficulty of working at the Gurdjieff exercises, the need for assistance of someone with more experience, and the significance of Bennett's experience of what he believed to be connection with the Great Accumulator (section 3.6):

> Once Gurdjieff showed me an exercise which required that one should remember to say "I am" every hour at the exact moment, neither a minute early nor a minute late. I struggled desperately to do this exercise and failed completely. At most, I remembered five or six times out of sixteen waking hours. I tried all kinds of devices for reminding myself, but they only worked for a short time and none of them enabled me to carry out the exercise completely. Then one day Gurdjieff called me into his room and said: "You cannot make the exercise. I will lend you some of my *hanbledzoin*." For the next three days without any effort, I remembered almost to the second. I had such confidence that I put the exercise right out of my mind in the intervening time and yet I never forgot.[43]

It will be recalled from section 3.6, that at the time of the fourth vision at Fontainebleau, Gurdjieff said to Bennett:

> There are some people in the world, but they are very rare, who are connected to a Great Reservoir or Accumulator of this energy.... Those who can draw upon it can be a means of helping others. Suppose that a man needs a hundred units of this energy for his own transformation, but only has ten units and cannot make more for himself. He is helpless. But

[43] Bennett (1978a) 34.

with the help of someone who can draw upon the Great Accumulator, he can borrow ninety more. Then his work can be effective.[44]

The continuity is noteworthy: in one he speaks of "borrowing" and in the other of "lending" the energy (with the implication that it must somehow be repaid), and the phrase "cannot make" appears in both passages. Bennett learnt from this the necessity of receiving higher force from someone who could loan it to him. In section 8.4, I set out Clive Entwistle's understanding of what Bennett experienced, and how it influenced him.

7.3 THE RETURN TO PARIS AS A GROUP LEADER

When Bennett returned to Paris now, he came with up to sixty of his pupils, some of whom assisted Gurdjieff with the transcription of *Beelzebub's Tales to his Grandson*. For example, Rina Hands, who worked a good deal for Gurdjieff during this last fifteen months of his life, had been a member of Bennett's group.[45] In the autumn of this year, which means very soon after his return to Gurdjieff, Bennett began to establish groups in various parts of England in addition to those he had in London and Coombe Springs. They were led by his more experienced pupils, but apparently, he visited each group "in turn."[46] Were there more material available, it would be interesting to know whether it was not in fact Bennett who at this time laid the seeds of the success the London Gurdjieff Society was to enjoy under Henriette Lannes. It seems that even this slight contact with Gurdjieff had affected a substantial shift in Bennett. When one considers events such as the tenth and eleventh visions, it seems that Bennett had already arrived at the threshold of a more permanent shift in consciousness: perhaps it only needed a

---

[44] Bennett (1997) 94.
[45] Hands (1991) details her time with Gurdjieff. She had been with Bennett before this: Bennett (1997), 175.
[46] Elizabeth Bennett (2015), 75.

nudge so that the state of being which had been induced by exceptional circumstances could now be accessible by reason of his own methodical efforts. Bennett wrote that, at Gurdjieff's apartment, those who had been with Ouspensky (e.g. Kenneth Walker), and those who had not (e.g. Jane Heap), all learnt:

> the deep significance of the physical body of man and its latent powers. Gurdjieff showed us exercises so new and so unexpected in their effects that we all felt that a new world was opening for us…. At every meal, the director was called upon to propose the toast of All Hopeless Idiots and to clarify the distinction between those who are subjectively hopeless, inasmuch as they are fully aware of their own nothingness and those who are objectively hopeless, inasmuch as they are unable to repent of their sins and are therefore doomed to perish like dogs.[47]

When Bennett speaks of being unable to "repent of sins," I am not certain that he is quoting Gurdjieff. George Adie's contemporaneous notes state for the fourth toast:

> To the health of all without hope, subjectively and objectively. That is to say, to the health of all those who are candidates to die honourably and to all those who are candidates to burst like a dog, and I should say, by the way, that no one can die honourably who has not worked on himself.

The idea of "sin" is not necessarily wrong: Gurdjieff had said that the concept does have a meaning for someone on or approaching the way, i.e. sin is what stops a person's progress and allows self-deception and sleep.[48] But Bennett's use of the word here may reflect something of his

[47] Bennett (1997) 199-200.
[48] Ouspensky (1949), 357.

mother's distantly Puritan influence. Bennett then recounts how, immediately after these evenings with Gurdjieff, those who had been there would often repair to a café to compare notes. There, they would find that they not only had different recollections, their memories of what Gurdjieff had said and done were often contradictory. Bennett comments that to provide any all-round account, forty or more perspectives would be needed from all the periods of his life, but that most of those students who could have written had passed away, without writing anything of substance.[49] This again, I suspect, is part of Bennett's apology for writing.

It was probably around this time when Bennett heard a woman tell Gurdjieff that during one of the exercises, she had been conscious for fifteen minutes together. Gurdjieff replied that that was not possible, and when she insisted, he said: "It is not possible. Even not possible for God's Mother. You wish to be more than God's Mother?"[50] Bennett recounts this in connection with his insight, possibly also given at this time by Gurdjieff, that to continually have full consciousness we would have to be liberated from time, and our physical body could not stand this.[51] It will be remembered that in the aftermath of the fourth vision, when Bennett was able by his will to experience love, he had to leave the state because he feared he would disappear.[52] The upshot is that the student can, with proper humility, not berate themselves for sharing in our human imperfection.

7.4 THE TWELFTH VISION: HELPING THE DECEASED

Bennett now explains that he is "reluctant to describe any of Gurdjieff's spiritual exercises, as I am sure that they should never be undertaken without supervision by some experienced guide. Herein indeed lies

---

[49] Bennett (1997) 200.
[50] Bennett (1998b) 38.
[51] Bennett (1998b) 38.
[52] Bennett (1997) 94-95, section 3.6.

the chief obstacle to the spread of Gurdjieff's method."⁵³ He goes on to explain that it takes so long to prepare guides in the Gurdjieff method, and there are such difficulties before them, that few are formed to the requisite degree. Bennett adds that "a new field of understanding" was opened to him by the exercise I call "Helping the Deceased," and about which I have published a study. It is noteworthy that this exercise was taught not only to Bennett but also to others, always with slightly different features.⁵⁴ One day, Bennett relates, Gurdjieff asked about his mother, when she had died and how he felt about her. Bennett continues:

> [Gurdjieff] then said: "She is in need of help because she cannot find her way by herself. My own mother is already free, and I can help her. Through her, your mother can be helped, but you have to bring them into contact." He gave me a photograph of his mother who had died at the Prieuré twenty-four years earlier, and said: "Every day for half an hour you practise what I say. First look well at this picture until you can see my mother with your eyes shut. Then place two chairs side by side, and on the right chair picture my mother and on the left your own mother. Stand in front of them and keep your attention fixed upon the wish that they may meet and your mother may receive help. This is a very hard exercise, and you must have a great wish to help your mother. You cannot help her yourself: but through my mother I can help her."⁵⁵

Bennett reminds us that when his mother had died, he had felt that she needed help.⁵⁶ He worked harder at this exercise than he had at any of the others. Bennett uses the plural "others," so, clearly, by this time he had learnt at least several exercises. He continues:

⁵³ Bennett (1997) 200.
⁵⁴ Azize (2021a).
⁵⁵ Bennett (1997) 201.
⁵⁶ Bennett (1997) 174. See section 6.1.

The task proved to be unexpectedly painful. After a few weeks, the effort of standing before two empty chairs became almost intolerable. To my surprise, I found myself bathed in sweat from head to foot, as if I had been doing heavy manual work. One day, I burst into tears and sobbed for the entire half-hour.... I was invaded with doubts and a feeling that the whole affair was a cruel joke that Gurdjieff had played upon me. Then a change began. After I had done the exercise for a month, I began to be aware that t h e r e were presences in the room. These presences, which at first were fleeting and nebulous, took the shape of my mother and Madame Gurdjieff. I felt distinctly that my mother was resisting, and would not turn her head to the left. Then, one day, the contact was unmistakable. A wave of relief and gratitude flowed through me.[57]

I count this as the twelfth vision in what I see as Bennett's "book of visions," it is so intimately related to his theme that experience of death and resurrection are possible in this life. In this case, the outcome can as readily be described as "redemption." The redemption of his mother illuminates the significance of the many details Bennett has disclosed about her, as if casually and incidentally. Although Bennett adds that it seemed that Gurdjieff was then with him in his bedroom, Gurdjieff had not known of the outcome until Bennett saw him a few days later. Gurdjieff said: "Now you are part of my family, and we will not be separated."[58] Bennett felt "towards him as a son," and made to kiss his hand, but Gurdjieff swiftly withdrew it and said that it was he who should kiss Bennett's hand.[59] Again, there is an apologetic undertone in the light of the later criticisms to be made of Bennett as a maverick who strayed from the true teaching. Bennett also takes care that the reader should

---

[57] Bennett (1997) 201.
[58] Bennett (1997) 201.
[59] Bennett (1997) 201.

know that: "From that day, I was unable to repeat the exercise, although I often became aware of some delicate and almost imperceptible contact with my mother."[60] It may, partially, be this that gave Bennett the conviction that:

> People who are fixed in the spirit realm when they die, form a whole world around them. They are quite convinced that they are living in an ordinary world with their friends and other people who have died. We can know this because it is possible to communicate with people in that state. They may even be able to recognize real things because part of them is really there. What neither they, nor the people who attach importance to communicating with them, see is that they are prevented from making further progress. They are not able to enter the third world where transformation is possible. They cannot leave things behind.[61]

This last quoted material is not precisely datable, but must hail from after 1966. Where it provides details of continued existence going beyond what is in *Witness*, this raises the question whether there was more to the 1948/49 experience than is reported, or whether Bennett had other sources of knowledge. However, certain things said by Bennett at a series of lectures, posthumously published as *Making a Soul*, are suggestive:

> It is not possible for me to pay the debt of my existence without at the same time paying my part of the debt of my parents. Therefore, the work that I do must be for my parents also ... a man can finally become himself, and such a man is a source from whom possibilities radiate. The possibilities he creates enter into his parents also.... People who do not

---

[60] Bennett (1997) 201.
[61] Bennett (1978) 13. This is an edited version of an unpublished talk from February 1974.

accept and love their parents are cut off from possibilities. I have heard Gurdjieff say that many times, and I myself have seen it with my own eyes in hundreds of cases, and now it is for me an established truth. Not to love one's parents is an almost insuperable handicap in the work.[62]

The "Helping the Deceased Exercise" which Gurdjieff taught Bennett adds a strikingly concrete element to this teaching of honouring one's parents.

7.5 WITH GURDJIEFF IN NEW YORK

Bennett was able through his contacts, both direct and indirect, to obtain for Gurdjieff the necessary travel documents to cross the Atlantic to the U.S. in 1948, and to also return to France.[63] Bennett's subtlety is also evident in his remarks about Gurdjieff's departure for the port on October 30, 1948. The words of his farewell were: "Before I return I hope with all my being that everyone here will have learned the difference between sensation and feeling."[64] This was doubtless true, but I suspect that it struck Bennett, and he may even have included it, to remind us of the importance of this, and that the first of the contemplative exercises Gurdjieff had de Salzmann teach Bennett was "the exercise of sensing and feeling."[65] Bennett states that when he returned to London, some members of his group were affronted by Gurdjieff's drinking, obscene language, and the rumours, which he stoked, of his womanising.[66] However, I am yet to find such a first-hand account to that effect.

Bennett travelled to the U.S., arriving only a few weeks after Gurdjieff, and was with him on January 13, 1949, when Gurdjieff celebrated what he

---

[62] Bennett (1995) 98.
[63] Bennett (1997) 202 and 203.
[64] Bennett (1997) 203.
[65] Bennett (1997) 195.
[66] Bennett (1997) 204.

said was his eightieth birthday.⁶⁷ Taylor recalls that, after dinner, Bennett was one of those "honored" pupils who would read from the manuscript of *All and Everything*.⁶⁸ Here, Bennett saw some remarkable examples of how Gurdjieff tried to "break down all [the students'] personal attachments" to teachers, whether that teacher should be Ouspensky, Bennett, or himself.⁶⁹ Then occurred one of those remarkable events which Gurdjieff could produce. Gurdjieff had asked his pupils how to word a letter announcing the publication of *Beelzebub* and seeking funds for this purpose, but had dismissed all their suggestions.

The following morning, Bennett met Gurdjieff at Child's Cafe. After a silent interlude drinking tea, Gurdjieff simply said: "You now write letter," and Bennett duly wrote something out. Gurdjieff took it up, not even proofreading it. At lunch that day, Bennett was given the letter to read, to general approval. Bennett remained silent as the assembled "adepts" (the unusual word used in the letter) commended Gurdjieff's writing: "I had been made the subject or the victim of one of those tricks of thought transference, or suggestion, that Gurdjieff loved to play."⁷⁰ Gurdjieff then appointed Pentland as his representative for America, Zuber for France, and Bennett for England, and later that afternoon promised him that if he followed Gurdjieff to France, and followed his instructions he would "soon have soul."⁷¹

In *Concerning Subud*, Bennett provides one small fact which he omitted from *Witness*, that when he joined Gurdjieff in New York on this trip, he hoped to meet Alice Bailey (1880-1949).⁷² However, she was in the final year of her life, and so he never met her, although he did read her books, and knew some of her friends.⁷³ He then sets out her ideas about the "Avatar of Synthesis," citing them as a reason for his accep-

---

⁶⁷ Bennett (1997) 204-5. Bennett states that Gurdjieff was in fact younger, and that the date, New Year's Day according to the Old Style, was symbolical.
⁶⁸ Taylor (1998) 169.
⁶⁹ Bennett (1997) 205.
⁷⁰ Bennett (1997) 206-7.
⁷¹ Bennett (1997) 207.
⁷² See Hanegraaff (2006) 158-60.
⁷³ Bennett (1958) 35.

tance of Subud.[74] Given the evident importance Bailey had for Bennett, it is surprising that he does not mention her in *Witness*. It invites one to wonder what else was omitted.

7.6   PARIS, 1949

Unlike 1923, Bennett now honoured Gurdjieff's offer to study with him, being dutifully present at Gurdjieff's disembarkation at Cherbourg. There, Gurdjieff gave him some pills, and an exercise. This inaugurated:

> a period of eight months which was the hardest and most painful of my life…. On the one hand, Gurdjieff taught me a sequence of exercises for the control and transformation of the psychic energies in man. On the other, he set to work to destroy my closest and most precious relationships.[75]

This did not except his relationships with his wife, and with Elizabeth Mayall.

Although Bennett does not descend into detail, he states Gurdjieff deliberately situated him as a pupil, and not a teacher, although he had his own substantial group, and was still being told to form new groups. To an extent, Bennett did not understand what was happening, but was obliged to "read between the lines and guess at his intentions."[76] In one strange incident, Gurdjieff told Bennett to start a group in Holland. Bennett thought this was one of Gurdjieff's soon-to-be-forgotten whimsies, and was stunned when Gurdjieff railed at him on the grounds that he needed a Dutch group for contact with Dutch India. Rightly or wrongly, Bennett connected this with the subsequent appearance of Subud in Indonesia.[77] Intense learning of inner exercises continued:

---

[74] Bennett (1958) 35-38 and also 9.
[75] Bennett (1997) 208.
[76] Bennett (1997) 208-9.
[77] Bennett (1997) 209.

At that time, Gurdjieff had set me to work upon a spiritual exercise that completely baffled me, for it required the attainment of a state of motionless equilibrium of all the psychic functions, and yet the absence of any constraint or effort of attention. When he first explained it to me, it seemed simple compared with the complicated and very difficult exercises, connected with the control of the energies of sensation, feeling and thought that I had been working on before. Its very simplicity made it supremely difficult to accomplish.[78]

It is impossible to be certain now, but this may well be the exercise which Bennett called "The Permanent Immovable Point." Something similar is known to have been given to other pupils. The exercise seems to have led Bennett to see that rather than taking his own Coombe Springs groups for a summer seminar, he should remain with Gurdjieff: and now he concluded that he had been wrong to try to dominate all his bodily and psychical functions, and this through "long and painful exercises."[79] This new insight seems to be related to what he was witnessing in Gurdjieff: a "direct awareness of the unity of all life and our dependence upon the Mercy of God."[80] When someone told a malicious story against someone else, Gurdjieff interrupted with: "Every breathing creature has self-love, and this we must not offend."[81]

Bennett's relationship with Gurdjieff was deepening: when he was offered a five year contract as Advisor on Industrial Development in Ceylon (Sri Lanka), Gurdjieff said that a one year contract might be

---

[78] Bennett (1997) 210.
[79] Bennett (1997) 210.
[80] Bennett (1997) 210. Our dependence on the mercy of God is not an easy concept for Gurdjieff students to understand, especially if one comes to the Gurdjieff tradition having been disillusioned with the religions one has met. But in higher stages of the Gurdjieff work one not only comes to feel something of the reality to which it refers, but the phrase "Lord Have Mercy" can, if used properly, be a practical aid in self-development. See also section 3.6.
[81] Bennett (1997) 210-11.

alright, but not a five year, for he would need Bennett in Europe and America after a year.[82] Yet, at the same time, Bennett was finding it hard to abandon his addiction to self-torture, hence in August 1949 he insisted on reading all three volumes of *Beelzebub* for his own students, to the point that his tongue swelled and was being cut by his teeth.[83] In retrospect, Bennett concluded that such efforts were of little or no abiding value, but that the exercise Gurdjieff had given him was more important, although he did not realise its "true significance" until many years later.[84] I suggest that this is a reference to his realisation that the Subud exercise of *latihan*, in which he had placed almost messianic hopes, was not enough, whatever its short-term merits, and he needed to return to Gurdjieff's exercises.[85]

He also reports that, beginning from August 7, 1949, Gurdjieff tried to show him that what he needed was an (external) "Reminding Factor," rather than to torture himself: a lesson he began to learn, seeing that he needed to be able to say no to absurd demands that he push himself. As Bennett states, Gurdjieff did not explain that he was doing this, because had he done so: "the task itself would have vanished."[86] One might suggest that the task was more than simply refraining from certain efforts: it was to see for himself why and how he needed to discipline himself.

7.7   THE THIRTEENTH VISION: OUT OF BODY

On August 14, 1949, Bennett had what I count as the thirteenth vision. A favorable climate had been prepared from August 7, and especially on August 13 when Gurdjieff, like Ouspensky, told Bennett that his academic work on the geometry of higher dimensions was useless, saying: "When you have Being you will know all these things without the need

---

[82] Bennett (1997) 211.
[83] Bennett (1997) 211-12.
[84] Bennett (1997) 212.
[85] Bennett (1997) 283-84.
[86] Bennett (1997) 212. The precise date, 7 August, emerges from Bennett and Bennett (1991) 26-27.

for Mathematik."[87] Gurdjieff also then told him "Physical efforts are unnecessary," and then gave him "explanations about the inner life of man that were beyond price."[88] Interestingly, the next day according to the diaries, but "two or three days later" according to *Witness*:

> I had the experience of leaving my body without the special conditions of previous occasions. I was reading aloud before the evening meal. Suddenly, without any warning, I found myself several feet away from my body. My voice was still speaking, but it was not "my" voice any more, but a stranger's. I said to myself: "How can *he* read?" He can't possibly give the right intonation!" I could see the other people from quite a different perspective and wondered if anyone else knew that an empty shell was reading. I wondered if Gurdjieff knew, and at the same moment the body's eyes looked up from the reading and saw him, and, without knowing how, I was back in my body again and the reading continued. The sense of separation from the body persisted for several hours, although I remained inside it.[89]

Oddly, what seems to be the same incident is related in an inconsistent manner in the Sherborne talks which were preserved in *Deeper Man*:

> I also remember a very special occasion during the time that I used to read from *Beelzebub's Tales* before the meals in Gurdjieff's flat, which used to happen twice a day. The place was full of cigarette smoke and Gurdjieff, as usual, was sitting facing me in his chair. Suddenly I found myself up in the corner looking at my body – which continued to read

[87] Bennett (1997) 212.
[88] Bennett (1997) 212.
[89] Bennett (1997) 212-13.

as if nothing had happened! I remember thinking to myself, "How intelligently he reads even when I am not there!" Then Mr G. looked up at me and gave me a look—so—and I closed my eyes and found myself back in my body, still reading.[90]

A little later in the same talk, he adds:

When I had that experience of being out of my body while reading, I still remember the sly look that Gurdjieff gave me and how it is to be outside of this physical world and yet able to look on what takes place in it. Even the same kind of thinking can go on as when in a body—one can even wiseacre![91]

These two accounts have significant differences: the chief is that, in the earlier, the astral body deprecates the physical body's reading, in the latter it praises it. Even if one attempted to reconcile the accounts by conjecturing that the astral body thought something like "How well he reads, but he can't get the right intonation," the plain fact is that the two accounts are different, and can be harmonised only by producing a third account. Further, the earlier account does not mention Gurdjieff's memorable sly look, it mentions the astral body's wondering whether Gurdjieff could see him, not that he did, let alone that he gave a "sly look." Also, in the one account the physical body looks at Gurdjieff then the experience ends, while in the latter the closing event is the astral body closing its eyes.

As we have discussed, the fact of such phenomena, or at least that Bennett maintained that they were factual and informative, is central to the "witness" he wanted to present. But no phenomenon is an end in itself: it has to serve some aim, hence Bennett's dwelling upon the nature of the astral body, and its relation to the physical. Generally speaking, neither Gurdjieff's exercises nor any of his methods were taught with

---

[90] Bennett (1994) 173.
[91] Bennett (1994) 175.

a view to inducing mystic visions. The fourth vision with the stated connection to the Great Accumulator, and the fourteenth (section 7.8) are exceptions. It is implicit in Gurdjieff's system that the goal of union with God can occur without such visions, Yet, Bennett states that he did experience them, and he relates this vision to the first one, that of March 21, 1918, and the sequelae to the fourth vision (August 1923 at Fontainebleau):

> This was only the beginning of an avalanche of amazing experiences that continued for four weeks. I became conscious of internal organs such as my liver and how they worked. The condition of complete command over my emotional states that had come to me at the Prieuré returned unexpectedly one morning. This time I found that I could be aware of events happening in another place.[92]

First, Bennett lightly stresses that the emotional control he had once experienced after Gurdjieff had, on his understanding, connected him to "the Great Accumulator" now returned, but not as a result of Gurdjieff's direct action. Second, it appeared "one morning," augmented by a sort of clairvoyant knowledge. This and the understanding of how his liver worked both describe what he witnessed and also bear out Gurdjieff's statement that "When you have Being you will know all these things"[93] by direct insight. In *Deeper Man*, Bennett draws out more lessons from these diverse experiences.[94] We shall return to this later.

7.8 THE FOURTEENTH VISION: JERUSALEM IN 33 AD

Then comes the fourteenth vision, when Gurdjieff repeated to him what he had already written in *Beelzebub*, that Judas was the closest of the

---

[92] Bennett (1997) 213.
[93] Bennett (1997) 212.
[94] Bennett (1975) 175-182.

apostles to Jesus, and understood his mission better than the others. Gurdjieff called on Bennett to give his own opinion: was Gurdjieff correct, or was the Church? Then:

> The crowded dining-room disappeared, and it seemed as if Gurdjieff were leading me back through the centuries to the Jerusalem of A.D. 33. It seemed that I had been there before, but this was not at all important. I was strongly aware of the prodigious forces at work—good forces and evil forces at war. Judas was unmistakably on the side of the good forces. That was all that I needed to know. In a moment we were back in the flat and I was speaking to Gurdjieff: "You are right, Judas was the friend of Jesus, and he was on the side of good." Gurdjieff said in a low voice: "I am pleased what you understand."... He (added): "... One day Mr Bennett will give a conference on the Last Supper, and many people will be thankful to him." This was but one of many enigmatic prophecies about my future.[95]

Elizabeth notes, in her diary entry of August 27, 1949, what she overheard of this. Bennett's diary omits it altogether, but the entry about a conversation of August 28 leaves little doubt that it had occurred on August 27.[96] It seems that Bennett intends us to understand that Gurdjieff facilitated his (Bennett's) somehow placing himself in Jerusalem at the time of the Last Supper, where he became aware of the true relationship between Jesus and Judas, and that there was some sort of metaphysical struggle between good and evil. The episode also provoked a later experience wherein Bennett "had a kind of vision of the horror of reincarnation."[97]

However, no explanation is given of this. Also, between 1972 and 1974, in a talk to students at the Beshara centre in England, he was

---

[95] Bennett (1997) 213.
[96] Bennett and Bennett (1991) 59-60.
[97] Bennett (1997) 216.

asked about Abdul Qadir Gilani (1078-1166), founder of the Qadiriyya Sufi order. Bennett said that his knowledge was incomplete, but added: "I suppose I could put myself into Baghdad at that time and tell you something about the story."[98] George Bennett tells me that on one occasion at Sherborne, someone asked a question about Neanderthal Man; that Bennett went silent, and then stated something to the effect that Neanderthals did not "have the same difficulty as we do in their intellectual centre, but that they suffered from a similar problem in their emotional centre."[99] One wonders whether having been "taken" into the past by Gurdjieff (at least in his own understanding of what transpired), Bennett believed he could now do so by himself.

Finally, on an undated occasion, Gurdjieff said that Bennett would be like Judas for himself (i.e. Gurdjieff), working to ensure that his work not be destroyed. Gurdjieff also once said: "Judas is universal type; he can enter into all situations—but he has no type of his own."[100] Bennett found it illuminating, and applied it to himself, without explaining why. I suspect that Gurdjieff intended to indicate by this that Judas, and Bennett like him, were versatile: that is, they would respond with more spontaneity than a person with his own defined nature. To put it another way, I would conjecture that Gurdjieff meant, and Bennett understood him to mean, that he (Bennett) was unpredictable.

Bennett was present on Gurdjieff's last car journey, to Vichy and Lascaux. Gurdjieff made some comments, significant for Bennett, at the meals on this trip:

> Once he spoke of the "Inner God who can be the directive power in all our actions. He said: "If you learn to obey Inner God, this is a thousand times better than the Ten Commandments, which only tell us how to live, but cannot help a man to work." The same evening he spoke about

---
[98] Bennett (1975) 49.
[99] Email communication from George Bennett, January 24, 2021.
[100] Bennett (1997) 213.

immortality, saying: "Unmortal is very big thing but is not all. If a man works he can become of use even to God." He pointed to me and added: "There are two kinds of unmortal. He now has already Kesdjan Body. This is unmortal, but not real unmortal. Real unmortal only comes with higher body. He have body for soul—but must also have body for "I."

He then went on to speak of the difference between Paradise and what he called the Sun Absolute. "You can go to Paradise with Kesdjan body.... Must not be satisfied with Paradise—must find way to *Soleil Absolu*." ... To me (this) meant that a great step had been taken towards the fulfilment of the promise he had made to me in New York, eight months before.[101]

It will be remembered that Gurdjieff had said to him that he would "soon have soul."[102] What Bennett mentioned later, but not in *Witness*, is that he had already been able to discern, "by certain signs" that his "body kesdjan had been formed."[103] I suspect that he is referring to the thirteenth and fourteenth visions. On the return journey, Gurdjieff separated his car from Bennett's, and the latter visited a site at La Grande Paroisse which Gurdjieff was negotiating to purchase. Gurdjieff had, on some other occasion, told Bennett that his method could not give its best results unless there was a place where people could live and work together.[104] Bennett took this as programmatic, and his experiment in communal life, already begun at Coombe Springs, developed at Sherborne. This is also interesting because the Fourth Way is said to be a way in ordinary life, not in monastery or ashram;[105] yet Gurdjieff did say, even in Russia, that:

---

[101] Bennett (1997) 215. "Soleil Absolu" is French for "Sun Absolute."
[102] Bennett (1997) 207.
[103] Bennett (1994) 189.
[104] Bennett (1997) 216.
[105] Ouspensky (1949) 48 and 313

> On the fourth way it is possible to work and to follow this way while remaining in the usual conditions of life, continuing to do the usual work, preserving former relations with people, and without renouncing or giving up anything. On the contrary, the conditions of life in which a man is placed at the beginning of his work, in which, so to speak, the work finds him, are the best possible for him, at any rate at the beginning of the work.[106]

Gurdjieff twice qualifies the principle of "work in life" by making clear that he is referring to the beginning of the process.

7.9 THE PASSING OF GURDJIEFF

Gurdjieff was not pleasant with Bennett, making him feel his scorn for Bennett's failure to understand something. When Bennett told Gurdjieff that he could never repay him for his helping his wife and himself, Gurdjieff said nothing. But much later, after conversations with other people, he turned to Bennett and said, apparently quite deliberately:

> "What you say about never repay – this is stupidity. *Only* you can repay. Only *you* can repay for all my labours…. Only *you*"—with great emphasis—"can repay me by work. But what you do? Before trip I give you task. Do you fulfil? No, you do just opposite. Never once I see you struggle with *yourself*. All the time you are occupied with your cheap animal."[107]

The only guidance Gurdjieff gave Bennett was that if his conscience had been brought into consciousness by an intense inner struggle, he would have realised what was required. In his attempts to understand

---

[106] Ouspensky (1949) 48-49.
[107] Bennett (1997) 217.

exactly what he had not understood and done wrong, he turned to Jeanne de Salzmann for help. She offered him a general principle, and this was the occasion of Bennett's recording how much and how generously she had helped him and others.[108] To add to his confusion, Cornelius then reported to Bennett that, at a lunch, Gurdjieff had said: "Bennett is my best pupil: I need him in America. But everyone takes his energy!"[109] This is consistent with Gurdjieff's earlier advice that were he to go to Ceylon, it should not be for more than a year, because he needed him in America.[110]

However, in *Concerning Subud*, published in 1958, Bennett wrote of this statement that he counted upon me alone to ensure that his work was not lost: "I knew Gurdjieff well enough to realize that he had told perhaps fifty other people the same thing, and none could ever guess what he really intended."[111] I would not doubt Bennett's sincerity at the time of writing this, but a different impression is given in *Witness*.

Reflecting on the difficulties which were emerging with his scientific work at Powell Duffryn, where he was suspected of favouring those who joined his Institute, Bennett stated: "I had no stable attitude.... [I was like] a chameleon that takes the colour of every background."[112] When he reported this to Gurdjieff, the latter agreed that it contained a significant amount of truth, but that it was changing, he was acquiring his own "I" and "when you know it has come, you will have such happiness as you cannot imagine."[113] It is implicit in this that Gurdjieff knew that happiness. Together with this, Gurdjieff manifested other sides, abruptly changing from a harsh to an extraordinarily gentle tone when offering help to his wife, and offering this advice to a deeply wounded Russian woman:

---

[108] Bennett (1997) 217.
[109] Bennett (1997) 218.
[110] Bennett (1997) 211.
[111] Bennett (1958) 8.
[112] Bennett (1997) 218.
[113] Bennett (1997) 218.

He described the state of the father and mother: how they lie together in bed and experience the sounds and scents coming from the garden and are happy; and so a human seed is sown that is destined for happiness. But if they are full of passion, angry with one another or with anyone else, or if the father is thinking only of his cheque book and how much the baby will cost—then all these influences will enter the seed and the essence is formed with tendencies to hatred and avarice. God is not responsible for this. He made man to be clean.[114]

This strange reflection on destiny and conception "brought peace and comfort" to the poor woman.[115] On his return to London, Bennett began a series of lectures with the title *Gurdjieff: The Making of a New World*. De Salzmann flew over, and gave a movements class for 183 people.[116] This was the last month of Gurdjieff's life. When Bennett saw Gurdjieff for the last time, in a cafe on October 22, Gurdjieff adopted Bennett's phrase: "The next five years will decide. It is the beginning of a new world. Either the old world will make me 'Tchik' (i.e. squash me like a louse), or I will make the old world 'Tchik'. Then the new world can begin."[117] This is perhaps a little perplexing: did Gurdjieff really believe that what he had done was a force to be reckoned with on such a scale? If so, then he almost certainly conceived that there was a mystic element to what he was doing, such as Bennett was later to write, in *The Masters of Wisdom*, about the work of Jesus.

It seems, Bennett said, that Gurdjieff was indifferent as to whether he lived, since he had seen the American proofs of *Beelzebub*, and his work was proceeding in England. The latter country had now become very important to him, but he also urged his students to promote *Beelzebub*.[118]

---

[114] Bennett (1997) 219.
[115] Bennett (1997) 219.
[116] Bennett (1997) 219. The tacit point is that this is an large class.
[117] Bennett (1997) 220.
[118] Bennett (1997) 220.

On October 29, 1949, Gurdjieff died. Given the thesis of Bennett's book, these comments concerning his experience at the side of the corpse of Gurdjieff are significant:

> I was certain that though he himself had left us for ever, his power remained, and that his work would continue. I noticed one phenomenon that I have since observed at least three times. I was convinced that he was breathing. When I shut my eyes and held my breath I could distinctly hear a regular breathing—although no one else was in the chapel.
>
> Later still, I returned to see his death mask taken. This broke the last link with his body. I could not feel the slightest value to myself or to him in seeing or thinking of it again. The best death is that which is the most complete separation of the mortal and the immortal parts of man; everything told me that Gurdjieff had gone away completely and finally, never to return.[119]

Behind all this seems to be the idea that the real history of the world we know is made by forces operating on a different level, and that what seems small to us here may represent something of significance in that other world, which Bennett sometimes called the *alam-i arvah*,[120] although to judge by *Deeper Man*, and the unpublished lectures that book is drawn from, he taught this together with the scheme of worlds which Gurdjieff had taught Ouspensky.[121] This terminology was one of many he experimented with. In the next chapter of *Witness*, Bennett added:

> Over the years, the conviction had grown in me that dying is a process far more complex and diversified than people

---

[119] Bennett (1997) 221.
[120] See Bennett (1975) 173.
[121] See the diagram Bennett (1994) 162, which relates to the earlier scheme to that in *Beelzebub's Tales*.

suppose. It is hard to express just what had been added to this conviction by the manner of Gurdjieff's passing. His was a clean, decisive dying to which he gave his willing consent and for which he was fully prepared. There were no loose ends, no sense that any part of him remained attached to some unfinished experience. Each element had gone to its appropriate place. If I were asked what I meant by this, I could not have replied; but much later, I began to understand it better.[122]

7.10 WHAT ARE WE LIVING FOR?

The London talks delivered under the title *Gurdjieff: The Making of a New World* were published as *What Are We Living For?* The book published as *Gurdjieff: The Making of a New World* in 1973 was quite different. The first edition of *What Are We Living For?* was issued by Hodder & Stoughton in October 1949, and reprinted by the Coombe Springs Press in 1965 and 1973. A Bennett Books edition appeared in 1991 with "new material." Apart from the 1991 foreword by A.L. Staveley, a comparison of the two texts does not immediately reveal any differences.[123] It rehearses much of the material in *The Crisis in Human Affairs*, which stands to reason as both sets of lectures were intended to interest an English audience in Gurdjieff's ideas and the groups Bennett was conducting. The introduction helps to make the transition from lecture notes to an integrated volume. Bennett declares that the book was written with one aim, to ground the hope that, impossible as it may seem, a balance between "the inner and the outer life" can be established, despite the baleful influence of Western Civilization.[124] Bennett envisaged a change in human nature. Staveley put the matter concisely in her 1991 foreword to the book:

---

[122] Bennett (1997) 222.
[123] See the copyright page of Bennett (1991a).
[124] Bennett (1991a) 5.

We earn or lose our souls, Gurdjieff says, by the way we live our lives, and he calls man a self-creating being. Man and only man in all creation has the possibility of choice, of choosing whether he will live and die as he is, a thinking animal perishing, as animals do in the end, or of choosing by his actions to create in himself that which is real and imperishable.[125]

In his introduction, Bennett excludes from consideration two types of imagined change in human nature: external change through some agency for an object external to the person changed; and "internal change without external objective."[126] Bennett offers penetrating insights into mystical experiences which regard external work as "secondary in importance" and "belong to the category of the inner life for the sake of the inner life or being for the sake of being."[127] Bennett's concern, rather, is for the "deeper and less accessible tradition of schools that possess knowledge of a higher order concerned with "being for the sake of doing"."[128] This, he says, is the substance of Gurdjieff's teaching, upon which the book is based.[129] Bennett notes that modern scientific thought treats us as purely governed by physical laws but that we strongly feel our power of choice, yet if we have souls and are free, we nonetheless act like slaves. However:

> I have not encountered any more convincing explanation of these contradictions than that which is given by Gurdjieff. It is very simple. The confusion arises because we fail to distinguish between what man is and what he might be. According to Gurdjieff, man does not possess a pre-existent immortal soul, but in the course of his life a soul becomes formed, to a

---

[125] Bennett (1991a) 4.
[126] Bennett (1991a) 14.
[127] Bennett (1991a) 14.
[128] Bennett (1991a) 16.
[129] Bennett (1991a) 20.

greater or lesser degree of perfection, according to the way in which his life is lived.[130]

The determinist and free-will positions are, on this view, based upon a false dichotomy. Neither does religion as we know it provide a complete solution. Bennett states that a person can engage in religion for non-religious motives, such as enjoying ritual or seeking a certain emotional stimulus.[131] Despite the history of human religion and science, people are becoming more dependent upon governments to organise their civic lives, and advertising to prompt and control their choices so that life is "virtually determined."[132] In developing Gurdjieff's insights into the significance of suggestibility in the operation of the human psyche, Bennett introduces some ideas which still have reference to the modern psyche even today:

> Modern newspapers are divided mainly into three parts—advertisement, sports, and news.... The ability to read about sports induces another peculiar and dangerous passivity in the use of leisure. It leads also to a quite artificial system of values whereby men who have acquired some special physical skill are accorded the status of national heroes.... [I include the] artificial hero worship the "buildup" of movie stars and other particularly automatized, helpless individuals whose owners use them for expressing entirely unreal situations and for stimulating an artificial sexual response in very large numbers of people at a small cost.[133]

Bennett identifies three disastrous developments in modern thought which have led us to exalt human reason and to disregard the possibility of divine revelation: the influence of Aristotle ("the notion that the

[130] Bennett (1991a) 28.
[131] Bennett (1991a) 36.
[132] Bennett (1991a) 47.
[133] Bennett (1991a) 48.

human mind is capable of making ultimate judgments on the truth or falsity of propositions regarding the nature of reality"),[134] Descartes (identifying people with their thinking processes, and rigidly dividing matter and experience in a "dualistic metaphysics"),[135] and the doctrine of evolution "explained in terms of blind, accidental processes."[136] Succinctly put, the difference between Hegel, Marx, and Darwin on the one hand, and Gurdjieff on the other was that the latter did not credit any "automatic necessary evolution" but said that "progress in the upward direction" had to be purposive, and could be attained only through conscious labour and intentional suffering.[137] This was the teaching as Gurdjieff had reformulated it in *Beelzebub's Tales*.[138]

Curiously, in the light of his future conversion to Catholicism, Bennett speaks of the degeneration of religions, wherein philosophy and theological speculation grow up to "sanction" the blossoming faith as an organization.[139] In an interesting study, he contrasts Christianity as it has become with what it was in its original kernel of truth, and concludes that the substance of the pristine faith was equivalent to Gurdjieff's teaching of conscious labour, and the necessity to work upon ourselves.[140] He also sketches the idea he would later develop, that humanity had been static for two hundred thousand years until "a conscious intervention from a higher level" transformed humanity and ultimately "laid the foundations of the modern world."[141]

These passages among others show that, at every point of his thesis, Bennett is not simply reiterating what he has heard Gurdjieff say, but attempting to digest it, and then apply it to modern problems in an original manner which shows the value of Gurdjieff's system. Unlike Ouspensky's lectures published as *The Psychology of Man's Possible*

---

[134] Bennett (1991a) 63.
[135] Bennett (1991a) 65-66.
[136] Bennett (1991a) 69.
[137] Bennett (1991a) 70.
[138] See Gurdjieff (1950) especially 808, but also 292, 322, 350, 384 and 1106-7.
[139] Bennett (1991a) 83.
[140] Bennett (1991a) 85-87 and 98-99.
[141] Bennett (1991a) 102-3.

Evolution, which could be described as purely Gurdjieff's ideas presented systematically, these lectures are unmistakably Bennett, using what he has learned from Gurdjieff. One of the lessons Bennett wanted to transmit was, I suggest, the comment made apparently tangentially in *Witness*, that touching human vices: "God is not responsible for this. He made man to be clean."[142] (the context is given in section 7.8).

7.11 A LOST GURDJIEFF LECTURE

On July 16, 1951, Bennett referred to talks Gurdjieff had given in Paris "about seven years ago" on the topic of dreams and their relation to inner work:[143]

> During these talks he explained that there is a certain transformation of energy which can liberate us not only from dreams but also from slavery to our associations. There is a substance from which our own active force—the active principle in us—can be nourished. If we being to struggle with 'ourselves'—with our own passive principle—the effect is to divide the substance into three parts. One part is consumed in the struggle itself. It is the attention which we have to use in order to work. The second part is not for us at all; it is needed for cosmic purposes. When it is liberated by our struggles, it is radiated, and goes to its destined place. Only the third part remains for the growth of our own Being. This part can settle in us, and then it enables our Second Body to grow.
>
> Now this substance is produced in us anyhow, whether we transform it or not. If during the day we accomplish this transformation, when we sleep at night our organism can rest properly and assimilate what is necessary for the growth

---

[142] Bennett (1997) 219.
[143] Bennett (1951) 1.

of our Being. If we do not work to accomplish this transformation, some of the substance remains unused, but its nature is that it cannot remain inactive. So when we go to sleep it begins to combine and set in motion the material of our associations—chiefly those of the preceding day's experience. Out of these our dreams are made, and during the daytime we find ourselves unable to liberate ourselves from automatic associating.

It can even happen under certain conditions that in sleep this substance can awaken the higher centres. Then people have dreams of a special kind which are called 'higher emotional centre' dreams. Such dreams seem to people to have an enormous significance—as if they were revelations of some higher truth. In reality they may be quite subjective, but their quality of importance and power comes from the nature of the energy which enters into them. If people are not warned against this, they can attach exaggerated value to such experiences and imagine that they prove that something is being achieved. It is really just the opposite, for if we are awake in our sleep, we shall certainly be asleep in our waking state.

One very characteristic difference between Gurdjieff's teaching and nearly all other current ideas about the possible inner development of man, is that he teaches us to be on our guard against confusing *subjective experience* with a real *change of Being*. Subjective experiences can be very attractive; when they are the result of a higher energy, they give us a taste of a different world. At some stage in our work such experiences are continued beyond their rightful purpose in giving us the foretaste I mentioned.[144]

On my reading of this unpublished transcript, it seems that up

[144] Bennett (1951) 1.

until this point he has been summarising Gurdjieff's ideas, as delivered either in a formal talk or in a group meeting. What follows next sounds more conversational, and to be from Bennett: that such experiences can provide encouragement since they give us a much-needed taste of something higher, but the danger is that one substitutes dreaming about the goal for working towards it. He adds that what has been said about dreams during night-sleep is also true of daydreams: this is standard Gurdjieff and Ouspensky.[145] He concludes from this: "The result is that the very substance which is most needed for the formation and growth of our Higher Bodies is lost to us through associations by day and dreams at night."[146] This material was used in a lecture Bennett gave at Sherborne, although he does not cite Gurdjieff.[147]

Bennett continues, giving examples of how to struggle with associations (e.g. by occupying the mind with useful material or to direct one's attention to one's physical sensations.[148] That work is done during the day, but in addition:

> Mr Gurdjieff advised us that, the last thing before we go to sleep, it is good to occupy our minds—or even our feelings—with something. In particular, it is the best moment to pray for those who have died whom we have loved. One evokes in oneself the clearest memory one can and directs towards them an impulse of love from ourselves, and the wish that it may be well with them.... If we do this sincerely, it uses up the energy which would give us dreams.[149]

Gurdjieff did answer questions to his students about dreaming in 1944,[150] however, no talks which cover this material are known to me.

---

[145] Ouspensky (1950) 32.
[146] Bennett (1951) 1-2.
[147] Bennett (1977b) 113.
[148] Bennett (1951) 2.
[149] Bennett (1951) 3.
[150] Gurdjieff (2020b) 159-62.

This suggests that either Bennett was told of the talks, by Gurdjieff or one of his pupils, or else that he saw a transcript which is otherwise unknown. In either case, the fact that Bennett was given this rare material suggests that he may have been shown it because Gurdjieff believed that it had a special application to Bennett, who was wont to hear "inner voices" giving him directions, as in the third vision in the graveyard at Scutari, and in South Africa, and have doubtful revelations of the future of humanity, as in the sixth vision at the Ostrovo swamps. In terms of Gurdjieff's ideas, whatever value such experiences may have had for Bennett, it is another thing altogether to imagine that they possess objective value.

The advice about praying for the dead not only shows how Gurdjieff became more patently religious in his Paris years, but it also has some connection with the Helping the Deceased Exercise. It is possible, given the continuity in Gurdjieff's teaching, that in his early years with Ouspensky and others in Russia, he had placed the emphasis on outlining the theoretical basis of the practical work so central to his system. Then, in later years, the emphasis was on the practical implementation of that system and, as has been mentioned, in the more advanced stages of that practice, human dependence on the mercy of God became more necessary to move beyond a certain plateau, hence the "Lord Have Mercy Exercises" of the 1940s. In Gurdjieff's system, "Lord Have Mercy" signifies, I think it fair to say, not that one appeals for compassion but is otherwise passive, but that one actively prepares oneself to receive the grace or "mercy" always flowing from God, and to bring the application of the third or reconciling force to digest and assimilate it.[151]

---

[151] See Azize (2020) chapter 12.

Working on the Djamichunatra at night. This picture gives some indication of the scale and eerie power possessed by this most remarkable and unique building, when it stood.

CHAPTER 8

THE SECRET OF EVERLASTING LIFE

8.1   THE FIFTEENTH VISION: THE SECRET OF EVERLASTING LIFE

Despite the quarrels which sprang up among the students after Gurdjieff's death, and which affected Bennett's state, he felt that, on the day of the funeral, they were vouchsafed "a foretaste of the benefits that multitudes would receive from his (Gurdjieff's) life of devotion to the welfare of mankind."[1] Bennett notes that some of the civil strife among Gurdjieff's pupils arose because Gurdjieff would "give two or more people, without telling the others, authority to act for him in a particular matter."[2] One of the bones of contention was the "authority" of Jeanne de Salzmann, upon whom Bennett relied to learn more of the exercises; especially important because he believed that he had "not received from Gurdjieff the final teaching which he had promised."[3] Bennett was certain that the lacking lesson concerned "an action so profound that it would enable me to die to the old man and to be born again.... All that I had done up to that time might enable me to die awake, but it could not give me the secret of death and resurrection."[4]

I suspect that Bennett was correct in this, that his trust was misplaced, and that the lesson lay in the direction of being able to make contact at will with the Great Accumulator, perhaps by a route connected

[1] Bennett (1997) 222-23.
[2] Bennett (1997) 223.
[3] Bennett (1997) 222-23.
[4] Bennett (1997) 223.

with the Separation Exercises and a practical understanding of the mercy of God. Properly understood the prayer "Lord Have Mercy" is, I suggest, a prayer that God lift one up and to be united to himself, in the sense referred to in section 0.3 above, where I have gathered some of the pertinent references from Gurdjieff. I shall not pursue it at length here, but this is connected with what I might call the "esoteric" understanding of "nothingness." In brief, the Separation Exercises aim to facilitate a completely new understanding of myself and my nothingness, realised in the very act of praying it with all available faculties and centres, so that "Lord Have Mercy" becomes a practical means of union with higher levels, perhaps even with God. Gurdjieff had lifted Bennett, so to speak, into contact with the Great Accumulator at Fontainebleau (section 3.6) without much preparation, and Bennett had not returned for the further two years which Gurdjieff had told him were needed to be able to make that contact himself.[5] The unexpected intensity of the experience may have disturbed him.

Now, Bennett had been with Gurdjieff for only fifteen months, and he had made some important discoveries, and experienced what I count as the twelfth, thirteenth, and fourteenth visions.

However, the matter does not rest there. *Witness* is based on the premise that Bennett had discovered the secret of death and resurrection, and the entire logic of the book is that he discovered it through his visions, the nature of which changed as Bennett's work on himself progressed. That is, notwithstanding the failure to pass on exercises which could have intensified and accelerated his inner work, when Bennett was once travelling to Paris by the Golden Arrow (the train/ferry service which was then operating), he experienced a revelation which he could not date when writing *Witness* for lack of a contemporaneous record:

> I ... was drinking coffee. As I put my cup down my attention was drawn to my breathing, and in the brief instant when the flow of breath changed from inspiration to expiration, I

[5] Bennett (1997) 98.

became aware of Eternity. This was the first time in my life that I lived through a timeless event.... This was not at all like a dream—there were no visions, no images, nothing happened, not even a thought. It was a state of pure cognition, a luminous certainty. The central truth was the imperishability of the will. Body perishes, all the functions that depend upon the body turn into dreams and eventually fade away. Even my very self, my own existence and the feeling of "I" that accompanies it, could endure only for a time. But my will was out of time and space, and nothing could destroy it. So long as the will was the prisoner of my functions, that is, of my sensations, my thoughts, feelings and desires, it must be involved in their fate. If they perished, it must perish with them. But if my will were free from all these, especially from "being" anything at all, then it would be truly imperishable, immortal and able to create for itself whatever vehicle it might need in order to exist and work. This freedom is the will to do God's Will, and I understood once and forever that this is the secret of everlasting life. All the mysteries of the Christian creed, and not those of Christianity alone, but of all that has been revealed to men through the ages, became one clear consistent truth. All this and infinitely more was revealed to me, age upon age and world upon world, and yet the entire experience did not occupy the time of a single heart-beat.[6]

Feeling that what he had witnessed was "the secret of everlasting life," he was left with a conviction that "consciousness of eternity is possible for man."[7] Bennett then muses that painting might be the only art which "can express eternity."[8] I am not sure if he excludes sculpture,

---

[6] Bennett (1997) 224-25.
[7] Bennett (1997) 225.
[8] Bennett (1997) 225.

especially given the impression made on him by a Pieta by Michelangelo (section 1.1). However, the real lesson which he learned from this and several later and similar experiences, was that: "Eternity is always here and now."[9] He nonetheless found ongoing difficulties with the leadership of the Gurdjieff groups, of which he was part, although he reiterates his admiration of de Salzmann's optimism and example.[10] This vision exhibits, to a high degree, all four of William James' "handy marks" of mysticism: ineffability, noetic quality, transiency, and passivity, and so once more illustrates the coherence of the themes of *Witness* within the Western mystical tradition.[11]

Bennett then turns to his work at Powell Duffryn Research Laboratories, and the difficulty of allowing scientists to exercise their originality in their early years. Firms usually subordinate their young workers to a larger team until they have proved themselves, by which time their most creative years may well be spent.[12] Because of the curious combination of his employing a capable scientist who was also a communist, his association with Gurdjieff (thought to have been a Russian spy), his "very queer secret society" (the Gurdjieff groups), and the fact that their research was connected with atomic energy, his career at Powell Duffryn ended in drama and the suspicion that he was a communist plant.[13] His wife now suffered an attack of coronary thrombosis so serious as to disfigure her face.[14] It was painful to leave his beloved laboratory, his novel methods of unleashing young talent not fully tested, while tending to his wife, who had been given little time to live.[15] Mrs Bennett made a "spectacular recovery" under the care of Dr Salmanov, who had been recommended to them by de Salzmann, and who was providing directions through Dr Courtenay-Mayers. Bennett took his wife to France, although it had been thought she was too ill to survive the

[9] Bennett (1997) 225.
[10] Bennett (1997) 225.
[11] James (1902) 322, chapters XVI and XVII.
[12] Bennett (1997) 226.
[13] Bennett (1997) 226-27.
[14] Bennett (1997) 227.
[15] Bennett (1997) 227-28.

ambulance from the hospital back home.[16] However, she had a relapse and again nearly died. Bennett swiftly brings the narrative to the year 1952.

8.2 THE SIXTEENTH VISION: NO POWER OF ACTION

While preparing to participate in a public movements demonstration on May 17, 1952, Bennett's health declined by stages into a serious illness. Afterwards, he was diagnosed as having again succumbed to tuberculosis. He travelled to Paris to see Dr. Salmanov, but failing to follow the doctor's advice upon his return to Coombe Springs, he sustained some sort of physical shock. With a conviction that the illness was "not ordinary," and that he was "intended to die," he lay in pain for three days, when:

> Without any warning, I found myself leaving my body. I no longer felt pain or any other sensation. I went out of my body very gently and can clearly remember a kind of wordless recognition that could be expressed in the words: "This is death and I had no idea it was so peaceful." I was aware that my body was on the bed.... I looked for my own breathing and it was there—but not a physical respiration. I could not think, but only be aware of my experience. This is hard to describe; it was rather as if my experience was being presented to me. I ceased to hear, think, or breathe voluntarily. I knew that I was in some kind of body, but it was certainly not the body I had just left.
>
> I do not know how long this state lasted, but I heard my wife call my name. I felt a sharp stab of pain and I was once again in my body.... [I]n a week I was well again. I have never understood what happened to me so far as the illness is concerned, but I surmise that the "out of the body" experience

---

[16] Bennett (1997) 228.

> belonged to what Gurdjieff calls the second, or Kesdjan, body of man. This taught me something of what he meant by the need to build a different body for the "Real Unchangeable I." While I was out of the body I had no "I," only an awareness that was blissful and peaceful – but in which there was no power of action.[17]

This seems to confirm rather than to extend what he had learnt from previous visions: that he would survive the death of the physical body, but his astral or Kesdjan body had no power of initiation.

This was his fourth out-of-body experience. In the first, eighth and thirteenth visions, there had been the same lack of will-power, but this feature had not come to his attention. What, it seems to me, is significant with the sixteenth vision, is that on this occasion he realised that he had no will-power. In Gurdjieff's teaching, becoming aware that we lack a feature is the first step to acquiring it.[18] Given Gurdjieff's system, Bennett would have understood that the sixteenth vision showed that he had begun to develop will-power. He was now persuaded that he could find a way to furnish the astral body with that power.

8.3 TEACHING GURDJIEFF'S CONTEMPLATIVE EXERCISES

Bennett was summoned to present lectures on the Gurdjieff System at Carnegie Hall. That Mme Ouspensky and de Salzmann should have invited him shows that Gurdjieff was not alone in thinking he needed Bennett in the U.S. A transcript of a meeting beforehand, with Jeanne de Salzmann, Henriette Tracol (née Lannes), Lord Pentland, Sir Clifford and Lady Norton, and other senior members of the Gurdjieff groups, shows Bennett taking a leading role, and being asked questions about the system by those present. Even de Salzmann deferred to him on

---

[17] Bennett (1997) 230. The awareness of some sort of breathing without respiration may relate to what he experienced when Gurdjieff's body was laid out (section 7.9).
[18] See for example Ouspensky (1949) 104-5, and 311.

occasions. Interestingly, they discussed among themselves what the central idea of the system might be, and how it differed from religions and other systems.[19]

Although he enjoyed their esteem, Bennett did not feel that he belonged among them, although he wished to be united with those spreading the ideas and the work: "I was as convinced as ever that Gurdjieff had brought to the world the most powerful instrument of self-perfecting that has ever been known. He was in the best sense a Master."[20] He felt that the annual Russian Orthodox requiem service for Gurdjieff enabled them to renew their bond, but he was haunted by the predictions of both Gurdjieff and Ouspensky that another teacher would come to them.[21] This feeling would not be weakened by his own expectation of a further "revelation" (section 6.2). Bennett summed up his attitude thus: "If our task was to prepare and not to fulfil, then even our disunity made sense. We should keep alive what we had received and be alert for whatever might come."[22] This insight does not simply deprecate the differences among the students, but contemplates that these could be valuable. Some sort of "union of purpose" seemed possible, marked by certain significant gatherings rather than a close and continuous collaboration. But was that enough to enable them to stimulate one another, and share insights and methods learnt from the master?

I wonder if Gurdjieff had not intended his pupils to individually retain without interference what they had learnt from him, yet remain close enough to learn from each other. I might call this "communication without domination." Bennett does not consider whether the prophecies might be realised through this very situation, i.e. that no external teacher or teaching was needed (assuming they would be realised at all). Yet, as we saw in section 2.4, in the last years of his life, he asserted that the really important events of our life are sourced in higher worlds, and

---

[19] Unpublished thirteen page transcript dated November 15, 1952.
[20] Bennett (1997) 230.
[21] Bennett (1997) 231.
[22] Bennett (1997) 231.

that: "These events are not mechanical and do not belong to the predictable future."[23]

Further, in the posthumously published *Creation*, Bennett declared that because of the nature of reality, no prophecy can be certain of fulfilment:

> When (God) comes into the existing world, He is subject to the limitations of the existing world.... in the incarnation of God as Jesus, He came under the laws of this world. His body went through transformations like any other body.... He was also limited in what He could know.... He did not foresee how things were going to happen. He said: "You will not have gone through all the cities of Israel until the Kingdom of God—or the Son of Man—be come. It did not happen like that.... We cannot know about the future because there are factors which are unknowable, that are not within the existing world.[24]

Bennett came to this insight later in life, for when he had visited Islamic countries in 1953, he was impressed by their apocalypticism (section 8.4). Bennett's work in the U.S. met with success. In addition to the new people interested in Gurdjieff's ideas, Jean Toomer (1894-1967), one of Gurdjieff's celebrated former pupils, met Bennett at Mendham where Mme Ouspensky was living, and on January 19, 1953 wrote to him, hoping for a meeting.[25] Taylor correctly summarises the situation, saying that Toomer now returned to following Gurdjieff's ideas due to:

> the influence of John Bennett in New York, remarking that, in listening to Bennett speak, he felt that Gurdjieff had taught new things during and since the war, things that he

---

[23] Bennett (2006) 8, see also (1998b) 26.
[24] Bennett (1978b) 26.
[25] Taylor (1998) 204.

had withheld from Orage and himself in the 1920s.... After a few meetings in New York, Bennett invited him to join his group in England, but Jean didn't think his health was up to the move.[26]

The correspondence between Toomer and Bennett shows that the "new things" were the inner exercises. When I wrote *Gurdjieff: Mysticism, Contemplation, and Exercises,* I set out my reasons for saying that when Gurdjieff had first known Bennett, between about 1919 and 1924, he had not been teaching what he was to call "Aiëssirittoorassnian-contemplation" and "Transformed-Contemplation." The exercises, I suggested, were introduced only later, probably from around 1930 and developing particular during WWII when he produced a series of exercises for his Paris groups.[27] This is confirmed by correspondence between Bennett and Jean Toomer which only became available to me in the course of 2021. The first letter is from Toomer to Bennett.

> 19 January 1953, Doylestown, PA
> Dear John,
> I wonder if you received the joint letter written to you by Fred and myself. I wrote my letter the evening of Dec 17th, when you were on the first lap of your return to England. Fred wrote his the following morning. We had hoped it would ... serving among other things to give immediate continuity to one of the finest things that has happened to me, to Fred, in a long, long time—our meetings with you. Though I tried to say it in that letter, I can't begin to say all that those meetings meant to me, but at this moment I think of one thing particularly. I was again started in the work. That was and is the big thing—plus the promise, yes the certainty of continuing working and sharing the life with you. But this

---

[26] Taylor (1998) 205.
[27] Azize (2019) 110-11, 171-74, 182-84, and 187-209.

happened too: my faith was revived that my pattern was still in operation. I had more than begun to doubt that it was. So little of any real meaning had come my way, so little help, so few "combinations." ...

At the bottom of the letter, is an addition of January 20:

(p. 3, paragraph 6) The inner practice you taught Fred and me—if that other body is in fair to good state, I can at least try to do that exercise, and usually with some result...

(final paragraph) When I was with you, and Jeanne, my feelings, my inner life, was evoked.

(p. 4, paragraph 2) The inner exercise you conveyed to Fred and myself.... during the past month, having these new inner practices, I also have a new interest in people around, testing out to see if this one, that one, might be interested in the work, and more than interested. It could be that a very good group could be formed of people round abouts here, when I am ready to conduct one, which will only be after I've learned more than I know now, and become more proficient in the inner exercises, and get more energy and power into life, my life. The power is within, I know it, have experienced it. Energy too.... And I remember your telling me what G. told you: a force can come into your life and when it does you feel joy...

(p. 6, paragraph 1) Again about that inner exercise. Though I've yet to experience sensations moving down the arms, leg, etc., to clear out tensions, I have at times experienced some sensations. More life in the arm, a sort of fullness in it, the leg, etc. Sometimes tingling sensations, particularly in the hands, fingers, feet, toes. Sometimes sensations of pulsing.

The next relevant letter is that of Toomer to Bennett on February 17, 1953:

> I've known for some years that my chief current need is for relaxation. What I did not know, until first you and then J. de S. said so, is that right in the Gurdjieff work are to be had inner exercises and practices that gradually enable one to relax and relax down to the deep relaxation. What good news! Difficult to do it, yes; but what very good news that the means exist and that it is possible to do it. I know, deep inside myself, that once I have attained the ability to induce even a measure of the deep relaxation, the entire tone, temper and current of my energies, and of my being too, will change so decidedly that things impossible to me now will be possible then.... It is deeply true to say that whatever has come to me through you and J. de S. is a Godsend.[28]

On page 3 of the same letter, speaking about attending a group of new students in New York, who were being taught by Jeanne de Salzmann and Henriette Tracol (née Lannes), Toomer wrote:

> And I felt about the people—You can't really appreciate what you are receiving. If want (sic) you are receiving now had been available to me, and to others including Orage, ten, fiften (sic) years ago!

The case is overwhelming that, if Gurdjieff was teaching the exercises while Orage was his pupil, it was to a circle so select that it did not include even Orage, the chief representative of his teaching. This is most unlikely. The simplest explanation is that he had not then devised the exercises, and this is why he was not teaching them. It also emerges from

---

[28] Beinecke collection, p.1, the entirety of paragraph 2, with fifth sentence of paragraph 4.

this correspondence that Bennett was, at that time, teaching the same exercises as de Salzmann and Lannes. Later, he was to develop what he had received, especially by incorporating Sufi practices. However, Bennett always retained a certain reticence about the exercises in his public works and statements. In this he was following Gurdjieff's lead:

> Gurdjieff regarded breathing exercises as particularly sacred and at the same time perilous. He was shocked at the way in which breathing exercises, particularly those of the Indian Yogis, had been introduced into the West and employed to produce states of ecstasy and to develop certain powers of perception and experience.[29]

It is open to conclude from this that the danger Gurdjieff saw was not the teaching of the exercises in itself, but their abuse for the purposes of inducing abnormal states and manifesting phenomena. Bennett made further oblique reference to Gurdjieff's exercises:

> [He] certainly had a deep respect for Lamaism. In *Beelzebub's Tales*, he asserts that a group of seven lamas possessed both knowledge and spiritual powers unparalleled elsewhere on earth, and that the accidental death of the chief of the group had destroyed one of the hopes of mankind. A further point is that in one of his most remarkable spiritual exercises Gurdjieff placed "Lama" on the same footing as Muhammad, Buddha and Christ, and asserted that there was a special concentration of spiritual power in a certain place between Tibet and Afghanistan.[30]

No details are given of this exercise, however it must have been related to the Four Ideals Exercise which featured just those four "ideals": Christ,

---

[29] Bennett (undated) *Introduction to the Third Series*, xxxii-xxxiii.
[30] Bennett (1973) 96.

Buddha, Muhammad, and Lama.³¹ I return to Bennett's teaching of contemplative exercises in the final chapter.

8.4   FURTHER SEARCHING IN THE EAST

Although Bennett wished to cooperate with the others who had also been with Gurdjieff in Paris, he saw his own task as being to build up what he had at Coombe Springs, for Gurdjieff had said that theory had no value unless "it opens the door to practice," and that "a place was necessary where people could live and work together, thereby gaining experience which would be later called upon when they had to go out and work with others."³² But how to find unity without uniformity? A place with others, without losing his integrity? To experiment with new ideas, while keeping to the fundamental principles? He found that the majority of his pupils were advancing, especially through the practical work which he arranged at Coombe Springs. Groups and teachers were needed, he concluded, to help develop a permanent "I" which was more than "the ever-flowing stream of consciousness." The annual seminar of 1953, possibly in August, ended safely, but there had been alarming moments, of which no details are given. Bennett wrote a paper on "The Dimensional Framework of the Natural Sciences," a sort of promotional summary of the ideas which would go into his *Dramatic Universe*. It was published in the proceedings of the XIth International Congress of Philosophy, but I have been unable to locate any record of Bennett attending that Congress: he is not listed as one of the speakers.³³

Bennett's account makes it sound like when, during a meditation, he heard a voice in his breast say "Go to the East," it was to obtain some form of assistance.³⁴ Before passing to Bennett's departure for the Middle

---

³¹ Azize (2020) chapter 13.
³² Bennett (1997) 231.
³³ Bennett (1953). For the speakers, see https://www.pdcnet.org/collection-anonymous/browse?start=0&fq=wcp11%2fVolume%2f8986%7c14%2f&fp=wcp11 accessed August 10, 2022.
³⁴ Bennett (1997) 232. Although Pittman (2012) 126 states that Bennett was looking for "the sources of Gurdjieff's teaching," I am unaware of the basis of this claim. At

East, we must ask what he was seeking. The autobiographical note of 1957 states:

> After Gurdjieff's death, I worked for some years with his closest pupils, but it became clear to me that some vital factor was missing and that, although valuable and important results could be obtained by a large proportion of those who followed the System under experienced teachers, the great step which takes men through the barriers of time and space in their own eternal self could be achieved by only a very few. I was able, from what I myself had reached, to prepare many people for this step and even bring them to the verge of it, but I could not from my own power give them the strength to make it. Nevertheless, I felt obliged to continue with my own pupils some of whom had been with me up to twenty years and even to accept new pupils and to give public lectures on the Gurdjieff System. These series of lectures became known in London and when I gave them I could count on an audience of 500 or more.[35]

Bennett means that he knew the *goal* of the inner work – he could hardly doubt that after the fourth, tenth and fifteenth visions (at Fontainebleau, Coombe Springs, and on the train to Paris). He also knew the methods which would lead in that direction: the exercises Gurdjieff had taught him in 1948 and 1949 seemed to be the final piece in the puzzle. However, those practices could only take him to the threshold of what he had seen and experienced in his fourth vision. He lacked the "power" to pass over and into that higher reality at will, as Gurdjieff had

---

Bennett (1997) 256, he speaks of seeking evidence that the ancient teaching had not been lost: that is not the same thing as seeking the source of Gurdjieff's teaching, for "ancient teaching" and "Gurdjieff's teaching" are not coterminous.
[35] Bennett (1957) 7.

told him should be his real aim, at their very first meeting.[36] Neither could he take others beyond, as Gurdjieff had taken him at Fontainebleau.

Clive Entwistle (1916-76), whom Bennett noted as having been in Paris with Gurdjieff in 1948 and 1949,[37] wrote to Jeanne de Salzmann on April 24, 1975:

> It is my impression that the work of self-transformation as described by Gurdjieff, is, within the Foundation both here and in England ... <u>not going forward along a road but turning in a closed circle.</u> This circle can be defined as DO-RE-MI-DO-RE-MI-DO-RE-MI, etc. For a group as for an individual, the passage to FAH requires a shock from outside, that is <u>from above.</u> The nature of this necessary shock is quite specific and real and in its absence the further inner growth of an individual, at least in the fourth way ... <u>cannot take place.</u>... I write <u>from my own experience.</u>... Bridging the MI/FAH interval in the work requires the shock of a flooding in of Higher Emotional Energy. This can occur exclusively and only by a connection with the Great Accumulator, or universal reservoir of higher psychic energies...
>
> This of course was Bennett's experience, that is, after forcing B. to a certain pitch of effort, G. established the connection. Then for a few hours Bennett lived in that extraordinary paradise of miracles in which nothing seemed impossible. Then he was sent to bed, and Gurdjieff "switched him off". The next morning he woke up back in his old everyday world and level of functioning - though with a clear <u>memory</u> of that <u>other level</u> on which it is possible for man to live and function. As a result of conversations with Bennett it is my impression that his endless chase after teachers was

---

[36] Bennett (1997) 46.
[37] Bennett and Bennett (1991) 107, 109 ("Mephisto"), and 110. Donna Sherwood, Entwistle's widow, informed me that he was called "Mephisto" by Gurdjieff (telephone conversation, July 20, 2020).

<u>in the hope of re-experiencing this connection</u>, but that this hope was never again fulfilled.[38]

This is significant: from their conversations, Entwistle concluded that Bennett sought people who could re-establish him in contact with the Great Accumulator.[39] Indirect support for this view is drawn from a passage Bennett wrote in 1968, published only posthumously in *Transformation* (section 7.2), wherein Gurdjieff loaned Bennett some of his *Hanbledzoin*,[40] for it shows that Bennett was well aware that he lacked direct access to this "higher emotional energy" which he craved. Alan Tunbridge, a pupil at Coombe Springs from 1964 to 1966, recalls that Bennett taught them of three accumulators or reserves: the first, which we use in normal life; second, the "second wind" well-known to athletes; and third, the Great Accumulator "which could be accessed directly by performing a super effort which drained the other two." The third could sometimes be accessed by "super efforts" (understood here as persevering when it seems impossible).[41]

It is characteristic that, in setting out for the East, Bennett took account of the fact that this would mark that he was not indispensable for his group.[42] He left England on September 15, 1953.[43] The autobiographical note concisely states that:

> in response to a new impulse to seek fresh contact in the Moslem World. I spent about three months travelling in Turkey, Syria, Jordan, Lebanon, Iraq and Kurdistan. During this time, I met several Dervish brotherhoods and was initiated into some of their spiritual exercises and rituals. I found

---

[38] Unpublished letter of Clive Entwistle made available to me by Donna Sherwood. The underlining is in the original.
[39] Entwistle (1976) 378-383; for Entwistle in Paris, see Bennett and Bennett (1991) 103, 104 (under the nickname "Mephisto"), 107-110, and 28 (his wife as "Mrs Mephisto").
[40] Bennett (1978a) 34.
[41] Tunbridge (2015) 77.
[42] Bennett (1997) 233.
[43] Bennett (1997) 234.

among these Sufis a general conviction that the end of the world, as had been prophesied by Muhammad, was near and that a new prophet was about to appear. I was even given detailed information about the signs by which this event would be preceded. In 1955, I made another journey, reaching northern Persia, and this time met with two Sufi saints, one in Damascus and one in a remote Persian village, who told me that I was destined to prepare the way for a Great Messenger from God who was to come to Europe and begin his mission from my own house. Several signs obliged me to take the prophecies seriously, and in 1956 I began a project to construct at our centre at Coombe Springs a great hall of uniquely original design, all the dimensions of which are based on the symbol of the Enneagram. While this building was in progress I first heard of Subud, which from the end of 1956 became the dominating factor in my life.[44]

Here the autobiographical note ends. Ominously, Bennett forgot his own warning about the "comic literalness that overtakes Europeans and Americans when they are confronted with Asiatic subtlety"[45] (section 3.4), for he took the prophecies seriously, believing that they had been fulfilled in Subud (chapter 9). However, as we saw in section 8.3, Bennett was to be disabused, and later came to conclude that no prophecies made in this world could be counted upon. Further, he is no longer saying that he had no choice; so far as I am aware, he ceased to say this after the tenth vision (*fiat voluntas tua*).

He also departed with the intention to "discover, if possible, the way in which enclosed spaces can concentrate psychic energies,"[46] a study which would tie in with his deepening understanding of sacred images (section 12.5). To realise his vision of "a really fine tekke at Coombe

---

[44] Bennett (1957) 8.
[45] Bennett (1997) 89.
[46] Bennett (1997) 234. For his detailed examination of religious buildings see for example (2000) 10-12 and 14-15.

Springs, built by our own hands,"[47] he took copious notes, measuring the dimensions of the religious buildings, and making sketches, finding that the proportions expressed in the dimensions of diverse *tekkes* could be identical.[48] He even studied the acoustics of the buildings, and concluded that in the Suleimaniye mosque in Istanbul: "the architect had built a spiritual temple within an earthly temple."[49] In this, Bennett was perhaps following up a lead given by Gurdjieff, who wrote that in ancient Babylon there had gathered sages who understood how to apply in architecture what he called the law of "Daivibrizkar," or "the law of the action of the vibrations arising in the atmosphere of enclosed spaces," for: "the size and form of enclosed spaces and also the volume of air enclosed in them influences beings in particular ways."[50] Gavin Perry, an architect, concluded that "Mr B. knew more about architecture than I would ever know."[51]

Bennett's diary notes were sent back to the Coombe Springs groups and read aloud.[52] They are full of meetings with teachers, and sundry insights, such as that: "To create tradition, it is necessary to repeat. Repetition gives strength and strength is the force of tradition."[53] In a Kurdish village near Mosul, he saw two young women spinning mohair "with exactly the gestures of the women's spinning dance of Gurdjieff's occupational series [of movements.]"[54] Bennett also had some type of inner experience of the "Reality of Existence," which he did not describe.[55] Early in his trip, he discovered that: "The possibility of meeting a real *murshid* [Arabic for "spiritual guide"] has become much less important for me. I know that my *murshid* is within and I only need to learn to listen."[56] It was a lesson he would often forget and often recall.

[47] Bennett (2000) 20, and (1997) 236.
[48] Bennett (1997) 234.
[49] Bennett (1997) 235.
[50] Gurdjieff (1950) 466-67.
[51] Perry (2020) 8.
[52] Elizabeth Bennett's preface, Bennett (2000) 5.
[53] Bennett (2000) 18.
[54] Bennett (2000) 142.
[55] Bennett (2000) 96.
[56] Bennett (2000) 20.

Bennett returns to his belief that an "Epoch" had closed and a "New Dispensation was about to begin."⁵⁷ There are numerous references in the book to this idea and to Muslim apocalyptic, centring around the second coming of Jesus.⁵⁸ As Sedgwick notes, although Bennett was, to a point, impressed by Naqshbandi Sufi Emin Chikhou (Muhammad Amin Shaykhu), the latter interpreted the "New Epoch" in terms of the Last Days of traditional Islamic eschatology.⁵⁹ However, perhaps Bennett's most important conclusion was that, if his contacts had not withheld anything important: "they have far less than we have learned from Gurdjieff about methods of inner work. They make up by the intensity and continuity of their work for the more effective methods we have been taught."⁶⁰

8.5   THE SEVENTEENTH VISION: FIRST DO YOUR DUTY

Bennett enjoyed some remarkable experiences in the Middle East; after a display of his own stubbornness, he was watching the sun setting over clouds and the pale blue mountains of Kurdistan, and discovered a "complete stillness ... an intense happiness as I became aware of my own inner consciousness, still and unmoved even by the manifestation of my own stupidity."⁶¹ In Aleppo, he met Farhad Dede, a Mevlevi who belonged to an order which Bennett calls "Dedeghian," a rare Muslim order dedicated to the contemplative life, poverty, and chastity.⁶² Among the many disclosures he made to Bennett, one of the most pregnant was that knowledge of and living the true dervish way was disappearing because a true Sheikh or leader was rare, and there were too few.⁶³

Of significance for Bennett's development of the contemplative exercises, was his experience at Ceyhan, some twenty-seven miles east

---

⁵⁷ Bennett (2000) 95.
⁵⁸ Bennett (2000) 54, 64, 95, 99, 106, 120 and 174.
⁵⁹ Sedgwick (2016) 195-96.
⁶⁰ Bennett (2000) 174, also Bennett (1997) 239.
⁶¹ Bennett (1997) 241.
⁶² Bennett (1997) 242, and (2000) 159-77.
⁶³ Bennett (2000) 177.

of Adana. Here he met Hadji Hassan Effendi, a young man who struck him as possessing "powers connected with Hanbledzoin that I have not so far encountered on this journey."[64] Their talks covered certain powers, and "spiritual experiences," by which I think Bennett means mystic experiences and visions, such as the Hadji's vision of Muhammad.[65] Then, in a passage which is paraphrased in some of Bennett's contemplative exercises from Sherborne, he states:

> [Hassan] spoke about the heart, and said that there is a place under the left breast which has the power of knowing God. Our first task is to open the way to this place. It is very small in the bodily sense, but in the spiritual it is immense.... (That is the point of the heart where the higher emotional centre is situated).... Hadji Hassan also gave explanations about the place of the soul under the right breast, but he did not complete them.[66]

Bennett never states that Gurdjieff had said anything similar, and the idea is presented as being novel to him. Therefore, when this instruction appears in Bennett's "Catalogue of Inner Exercises" (section 7.2) it doubtless represents a dervish influence. Before retiring for that night, the Hadji advised him to make certain preparations, confident that in the night God would send him an answer about whether to accept an invitation from the United Nations in New York to work as an adviser to the Turkish coal industry for a princely salary. In these contemporaneous notes, Bennett wrote:

> When I awoke at 4:30 the others were sleeping. I was wide awake and sat up and did my inner work. As I was working I saw before me a well and a man leaning over it, but there

---

[64] Bennett (2000) 182. For "Hanbledzoin," see section 3.6.
[65] Bennett (2000) 182.
[66] Bennett (2000) 183.

was no bucket. In my hand there was a bucket and a voice said to me, "First do your duty and then see to yourself." I understood that this meant that I should stay in England where people need me and not spend further time in searching in Asia. At least not yet.

When I sat down to do my own inner work, I could feel myself back at Coombe Springs and realized very well that my work is there. This journey is for me a very necessary step, without which I could not have seen where I stand and what I must do. But it is an episode—it does not lead me to any place where I must stay.[67]

After the visionary experience of being at Coombe Springs passed, he came to himself once more, back in Ceyhan. It was the morning of Friday, November 13, 1953. His friends agreed that it meant there would be a "new dawn" at Coombe Springs, and that his place was there.[68] This vision has certain parallels with the third vision overlooking the Sea of Marmara, when Bennett believed that he heard a voice telling him something about his future. However, in this seventeenth vision, there is a narrative, the apparent meaning of which is that it was Bennett's duty first to help the man who sought water, and then to look to his own desires. After this, Bennett headed for the north, and the land of Gurdjieff's birth, although this is not covered in *Witness*. This could be related to his admission that he had been boasting he would be the first pilgrim to Gurdjieff's early home.[69] Perhaps Bennett decided to mortify his pride by omitting from *Witness* all but the most perfunctory reference to that leg of his travel. However, Bennett never made it to Kars, the city of Gurdjieff's early life, and much of the travelogue is of interest only because of his reflections about his inner world, such as the reflection on the last page:

---

[67] Bennett (2000) 184-85.
[68] Bennett (1997) 245. As is usual, *Witness* has some details not found in the diaries.
[69] Bennett (2000) 212.

I asked myself what is the chief lesson I have learned in these eleven weeks. Rather to my surprise, I found myself saying that the most important of all is the realization that work means being in the Presence of the Higher consciousness; and the respect of that consciousness is what we must cultivate chiefly and most urgently. Without that feeling of reverence, the work can have no momentum to carry it over our inevitable lapses of consciousness.... I am conscious that a Greater Power is present here and everywhere, and the consciousness of that power is the greatest of all joys.[70]

This hearkens back to the critical fourth vision, and is redolent of the King's College vision (section 6.3), when he and others also sensed a "Great Presence."

8.6 SEPARATING FROM THE GURDJIEFF SOCIETY

Bennett returned to several challenges at Coombe Springs. First, his wife's situation had deteriorated, and she was suffering from dementia. Bennett considered that: "her true self remained unchanged, and that what seemed to be a disintegration of the self was, in reality, only a failure of the machinery of communication,"[71] or even "the unveiling of a hidden wisdom that the ordinary self of man fears and does not wish to recognize."[72] He discerned an element of purgatory in these conditions.[73] Shortly afterwards, a Sheikh in Damascus would say to him that the help they were giving her was wrong, because it did nothing but "disturb the work that God is doing in her soul."[74] Bennett's insight, and the Sheikh's advice present different perspectives on dementia.[75] At

---

[70] Bennett (2000) 237.
[71] Bennett (1997) 246-47.
[72] Bennett (1997) 247-48.
[73] Bennett (1997) 248.
[74] Bennett (1997) 251.
[75] Bennett makes further comments along these lines at (1997) 249.

this time, Elizabeth Mayall returned from France with her boys, whom Bennett describes as "her two sons."[76] This is not strictly inaccurate, for they were also his children.[77]

The second challenge was his relation with Jeanne de Salzmann and the Gurdjieff groups. Bennett's comments on this are restrained and diplomatic: he critiques himself as exasperating and given to changing his mind after having promised to devote himself to a particular course.[78] Although some of those who had been with Gurdjieff would always be friendly, they were the minority. He had introduced his own pupils to Gurdjieff, and now many had become attached to the Gurdjieff Society in London, established by de Salzmann and others. The numbers are not known, but those who left Bennett included Bernard Courtenay-Mayers, Med Thring, Rina Hands, George and Dorothy Phillpotts, Cathleen Murphy, and Cecil Lewis.[79] Some of these ceased to speak with Bennett at all (e.g. Lewis), while others never disowned Bennett or denied their debt to him although they remained with the Society (e.g. Courtenay-Mayers). No detailed history of their relations is available. Bennett treasured his contacts with those who shared his history with Gurdjieff: he met the Adies at Gurdjieff's table, and retained an amiable correspondence with them at least up to and after October 1965 when he gifted the Coombe Springs property to Idries Shah.[80] These people were tangible links with the precious and poignant times in Paris. To have been slowly cut off from them was a suffering.

However, Bennett took a stand on principle: the work at Coombe Springs, which was now attracting visitors, was a microcosm of the Gurdjieff tradition, needing to expand and attract more people or else collapse. He desired unity with the others, but only if "spontaneous and

---

[76] Bennett (1997) 249.
[77] See the "Final Note" by George and Ben Bennett, Bennett (1997) 310.
[78] Bennett (1997) 248-49.
[79] Moore (2005) 45 makes the same point. Murphy was one of the pillars of the Society: Moore (2005) 39-40.
[80] Bennett (1997) 291-92. I have seen correspondence between Bennett and Adie after this date. However, it cannot now be located.

unforced."[81] As he tactfully puts it: "there were considerable divergences of opinion as to the desirability of lectures or indeed of any action that might arouse a wider interest in Gurdjieff's teaching."[82] Gurdjieff's pupils were on the horns of a dilemma: if they relied on personal contacts alone to interest people in the Work, the groups would remain small, and limit their possibilities even for work. But with a public profile, the groups could become too large for effective work, if only because unsuitable people might be admitted and even the others might lack sufficient guidance. Anecdotal evidence is that, for about forty years, the interest aroused by *In Search of the Miraculous* was so great that the groups continued to grow at a pleasing rate (e.g. the actress Diane Cilento learnt of the Gurdjieff work through this book, and first met Bennett at his lectures on it).[83] Hopes that the movie *Meetings with Remarkable Men* would produce a large influx were unrealised,[84] and from some point around and after 1990 when Jeanne de Salzmann died, the groups have, with some exceptions, been contracting. Bennett was not imagining the policy which valued confidentiality and secrecy: when, in 1975, de Salzmann decided to produce the film *Meetings*, she wrote to the groups under her direction: "The moment has come when the Work has to emerge, appear in the world in a certain way. The period of Work secrecy is over whether we like it or not. The time has come to meet the confused, inaccurate, and sometimes hostile ideas about the Work."[85]

Rightly did she use the word "secrecy." Moore observes that: "the standard de Salzmann policy line towards 'unofficial' Work publications (even including René Zuber's recent memoir *Qui êtes-vous Monsieur Gurdjieff?*) was one of thinly coded disparagement."[86] Zuber was so senior

---

[81] Bennett (1997) 246.
[82] Bennett (1997) 248.
[83] Cilento (2008) 309-12.
[84] Moore (2005) 253-54 and 258.
[85] Moore (2005) 215. The date of 1975 is based on Moore's comment on 208. When de Salzmann made the decision and exactly why is unknown to me. I have seen a transcript in which Henriette Lannes says that they are not to discuss *Beelzebub's Tales*, and that this rule comes from Mme de Salzmann.
[86] Moore (2005) 248.

that Gurdjieff pronounced him his representative for *Beelzebub's Tales* in France.[87] This coolness towards publishing even extended to *Beelzebub's Tales*: Bennett felt that it was handled by the de Salzmann groups like "a disreputable elderly relative, best kept in the background."[88]

8.7   THE DJAMICHUNATRA

In March 1955, Bennett travelled to Baghdad via Cyprus, where he received a message from a Turkish dervish to visit his *murshid* Sheikh Abdullah Daghestani in Damascus.[89] Bennett declared that it would not be possible, but when he eventually arrived in the city, he found that he had time for the visit.[90] Daghestani told him that he had seen an angel with messages for Bennett: one concerning his wife (noted above); a second one concerning Elizabeth;[91] and a third answering his question whether he should go his own way or "follow others," which in context means the Gurdjieff groups. The message was that he must trust himself, and attract people, although "the Armenians" would persecute him. Bennett states that he was stunned by the aptness of the messages, especially the latter, as he was already planning a public series of lectures. Then Daghestani produced a coda:

> God has always sent Messengers to show the way ... and he has again done so in our present age. A Messenger is already on earth, and his identity known to many. Before long he will come to the West. Men have been chosen to prepare the way for him.[92]

Daghestani stated that the Messenger would go to Bennett's own

---

[87] Bennett (1997) 207. The book was published in France in 1977, then translated into English and published as Zuber (1980).
[88] Bennett (1997) 248.
[89] Daghestani was a "Turkish-speaking Naqshbandi shaykh": Sedgwick (2016) 195.
[90] Bennett (1997) 250.
[91] Bennett (1997) 255.
[92] Bennett (1997) 251.

house, for he (Bennett) was one of those chosen to prepare the way, and God had appointed two angels to help him. He added his own advice: practise submission to the will of God.[93] Bennett interpreted the third message as a prophecy that "Gurdjieff's people" would turn against him.[94] His experience just before the King's College Revelation had already persuaded him of the existence of angels, and the knowledge Daghestani had shown of Bennett's own situation seemed to have come in some preternatural way. Might not other information which had come through the same paths likewise prove true?[95] In North Iran, he confessed to a dervish, Ahmad Tabrizi, that he did not know the will of God, to which the latter replied: "Then you must wait patiently. Your patience is your submission, and it is the proof of your faith."[96] In the presence of Tabrizi he learnt, simply by experience, that there is a difference between accepting the Will of God, and surrendering one's own will.[97] This question of "Will" was to loom large in Bennett's final synthesis.

When Bennett returned to England, he resolved to build a "great hall" at Coombe Springs, and deliver the contemplated series of public lectures. He was sure that these two steps would lead to a separation from de Salzmann and her groups,[98] from which I conjecture that she had opposed the erection of the hall, perhaps as being in competition with the Society's premises. In July 1955, he visited her near Como, on behalf of the Gurdjieff family, but the meeting did not go well. In October 1955, she came to London and arranged the splitting of the groups: no longer could people in one group join in activities with those from the others.[99] I have made mention of this incident in section 0.5. He proceeded with the building. In terms which reflect his play, "The Unknown Builders," he wrote:

[93] Bennett (1997) 251.
[94] Bennett (1997) 252.
[95] Bennett (1997) 252.
[96] Bennett (1997) 254.
[97] Bennett (1997) 254.
[98] Bennett (1997) 256.
[99] Bennett (1997) 256.

The group of architects, under the leadership of Robert Whiffen, was delighted with the decision to build. The money was made available by loans made by our pupils in amounts from one pound to two thousand. A new life seemed to inspire Coombe Springs.... The team formed itself. In addition to English residents at Coombe, we had Americans, Canadians, Australians, South Africans, and a Norwegian. Whenever a specialist was needed, he appeared from somewhere.

The work of the architect's group was out of the ordinary. Twelve to fifteen men, with sharply differing tastes and views on architecture, worked together without either pay or personal credit. No single feature was incorporated in the building that all did not accept. This sometimes meant waiting for weeks or months before some part of the building could go forward. I took some part in all this, but we were all convinced that no one person could do anything. The building seemed to have a plan and a purpose of its own, and all we could do was to wait until one part after another of the plan was revealed.[100]

This was the building which was known as the Djamichunatra, after the "Djameechoonatra" in *Beelzebub's Tales*, which Gurdjieff describes as "a kind of terrestrial "monasterial refectory" in which the second being-food is collectively taken."[101] The "second-being food" is air.[102] That is, it was a venue for the conscious reception and contemplative transformation of air, a feature of many of Gurdjieff's exercises, and especially of the Collected State Exercise, the basis of the Preparation.[103]

---

[100] Bennett (1997) 256-57.
[101] Gurdjieff (1950) 1160.
[102] Gurdjieff (1950) 647.
[103] Azize (2020) chapter 17.

8.8 BENNETT AS TEACHER

A number of accounts of life at Coombe Springs have been published. Anthony Bright-Paul wrote *My Stairway to Subud*, and Raymond van Sommers published *A Life in Subud*, to promote Subud. Bennett is therefore bracketed as a stage in the writers' journeys. Patsy Foard produced *Rabbit Blue: Autobiography of a Painter*. Alan Tunbridge, who left Bennett for Idries Shah, self-published *A Noose of Light*. But they are not alone: for example, there are reminiscences in Gladys Remde's *A Life in Search of Meaning*.[104] These illustrate how newcomers, interested in the Gurdjieff ideas, found life at Coombe Springs. The earliest is Bright-Paul's, who was ushered into Bennett's study in September 1950:

> Sunlight streamed in through the bay window on to the pale green walls, where there were prints of dancing dervishes, coloured pictures of Sufi Saints, and two remarkable frames with Arabic writing written diagonally.... We waited for some minutes ... when an enormous man in carpet slippers entered suddenly, and without introduction took his seat in another armchair. For some minutes he sat quite still, then uttered the one word, "Well?"[105]

Bright-Paul and his friend put eager questions about the Gurdjieff system to everyone at Coombe Springs they could find, but these were not quick to answer. Later, he saw the gap between his confidence with ideas he did not really understand, and the "inner discipline" of the students who "put upon themselves a demand always to relate the

---

[104] Remde's book was written in advanced old age, and there are signs of confusion: e.g. she mentions a "guru" from "India" named "Subud," in a context which suggests this was before they met Gurdjieff in 1948/1949, or made the experiment of an African "ark": Remde (2014) 53. Of course, Subuh was from Indonesia, "Subud" was the name of his movement, and the contact with him was after both Africa and Gurdjieff's death.
[105] Bright-Paul (2005) 57-58.

words they used to the facts of their own experience."[106] This shows that Bennett must have had some success in leading his pupils in some inner discipline such that they were able to refrain from talking automatically. Bright-Paul relates that Bennett could often discern the true question behind something which had sounded rather inadequate when spoken. One young man said that he wanted to ask a question but at the same time did not, and ended by posing: "Why am I speaking?" To this Bennett "answered with great force and gravity: "because you were created to be free."[107]

Another, complementary impression of the life at Coombe Springs and its charismatic lord was written by Raymond van Sommers. Upon arrival, he was immediately invited to lunch:

> The rest of the dining room was set up with bare, scrubbed timber trestle tables, laid with simple cutlery. There were two large glass bowls of salad and one of fruit on each, and wholemeal bread on a table near the entrance door. There were chairs for about forty people. I was alert with excitement. I was, I felt certain, in the sanctum of the world's most secret school and among those who had discovered the purpose of our life on earth and how to wake up in a world that was asleep. It was the equivalent no less than being sighted in a land of the blind. It was 1 May 1955.[108]

Van Sommers continues to describe the lunch, and Bennett's administering a shock to the diners by calling a "Stop!"[109] This is a practical method, introduced by Gurdjieff, where the teacher calls "Stop!" and everyone within hearing stops at once, allowing them to see themselves in transition between one mechanical posture and another.[110]

---

[106] Bright-Paul (2005) 60.
[107] Bright-Paul (2005) 66-67.
[108] van Sommers (2004) 4.
[109] van Sommers (2004) 7-8.
[110] Ouspensky (1949) 351-56.

Bennett invited the students to speak about their inner experiences, and if appropriate, made a comment. For example:

> "What did you see?" asked Mr B, addressing the question at large. There was an air of command about him, but charisma as well.
>
> An attractive young women with a Dutch accent and a red and white Lapland sweater started to speak. "At that moment", she said, "I was thinking: 'I am now remembering myself.' But when the Stop! came I was startled. I saw that 'I' wasn't awake. It was just my thoughts."
>
> "Ah, yes!" said Mr B. "That is how it is. Often we are nothing but our thoughts."[111]

He then describes how Bennett drove the conversation at lunch, asking about how his indications had been received, and what people had found. Van Sommers states that by the end of this he felt "stimulated, alert and alive."[112] Among other matters, he records that they would conduct cold water ablutions at 5:00am each morning, even in winter (a regime Gurdjieff often recommended).[113] Van Sommers joined the Coombe Springs architects' group which was designing the Djamichunatra. He wrote:

> The group of twelve professionals worked together with Mr B to develop a building with an atmosphere appropriate to its sacred use such as Mr B had seen during his travels in the Middle East. The proportions were calculated according to the symbolism of the Gurdjieff Enneagram, a mystical symbol portraying the transformation of man's spiritual energies.

---

[111] van Sommers (2004) 7.
[112] van Sommers (2004) 8.
[113] van Sommers (2004) 41.

We all believed the building was very special, both for its aesthetic design and for its symbolism.[114]

As part of The Work Mr B made everything as difficult as possible. We had to dig and screen our own gravel for the concrete from within the grounds. At first he insisted we build a crane instead of hiring one. When this proved dangerous and unworkable, he allowed us to hire one, but only on condition that we erected it ourselves piece by piece. Our trust was exceeded only by our sincerity and commitment. We worked physically until we almost dropped from exhaustion and then continued on with our psychological exercises. We forged a brotherhood through sacrifice and common desperation—the need to remember ourselves. Every detail was constructed with loving care. Scrolls containing information about The Work were sealed into the large redwood frames for posterity.[115]

... In appearance the building shape was unique and striking. It had nine sides with large slanting cedar walls rising from a fifteen metres diameter concrete base. It stood twenty metres high with a sloping faceted roof. Inside, subdued light filtered down through slots in the top of the walls, and three large stained glass windows high up on the timber walls lit the space above. There was no furniture except for a seat for about eighty people around the inside perimeter. The timber floor was covered with rugs for large meetings. Although the building did not appear large from the outside, the height and vaulting ceiling inside created a sense of inner space. Even with three hundred people seated it did not seem crowded.[116]

---

[114] van Sommers (2004) 43.
[115] van Sommers (2004) 45.
[116] van Sommers (2004) 46.

The size of the Djamichunatra does not well appear from the generally available photographs, but van Sommers has a striking one which shows it illuminated at night, and people standing in its doorway, making its significant dimensions quite apparent.[117] Tunbridge mentions the building as the site of meditation, movements, the Subud *latihan*, the performance of plays, and other meetings.[118] Two of Tunbridge's recollections of the practical work with Bennett are particularly illuminating. First, on Sundays:

> sometimes Mister B. would devise an exercise in which all could participate, such as a memory exercise involving touching your ear when anyone gave you something, or perhaps maintaining a continuously repeated prayer in your thoughts as you were working.[119]

Secondly, Tunbridge had had a stutter since his childhood, when a V2 rocket had exploded too close to him. At Coombe Springs, he was once asked to read at lunch: listening to an edifying reading while eating has long been a monastic custom. Tunbridge was assailed with doubt when one of the senior men offered to read it for him. Tunbridge rejected the offer, deciding that he had to go through with it himself. In the result, he read for half an hour without stuttering: "I had somehow been helped to do it."[120] It seems that Bennett arranged for someone to put Tunbridge in a position where he was reading because he himself wanted to read, and not only because he had been asked to. It is simple, but it also required wisdom to choose a method which brought enough pressure to induce new behaviour, but not so much as to induce new problems.

Foard notes some other aspects of Bennett's organisation of the work at Coombe Springs, e.g. when some South Africans who had

---

[117] van Sommers (2004) 50.
[118] Tunbridge (2015) 68, 71, 72, 83, 84, 104, 195, 200 and 320.
[119] Tunbridge (2015) 74.
[120] Tunbridge (2015) 76-77.

servants waiting on them at home arrived, Bennett put them on cleaning the toilets. They "left in great anger to be so degraded."[121] Also, when Bennett was away, Elizabeth would take their group.[122] The memoires make so much mention of Elizabeth that it is apparent she was a major presence. One person's criticism of Bennett as being in it for the money elicited a smile: the residents made the absolutely minimal contribution, the income was basically what Bennett earned from lectures, seminars and books; besides, he was a scientist and writer who dedicated the bulk of his time to teaching and helping large numbers of people.[123] Bennett invited the "Chief of the Druids" over to speak about modern druidism.[124] While Foard has more details about love interests and the personalities of the residents, her formulation of what she learnt from Bennett about artistic creation possesses merit:

> [T]he Creative Power stems from this life force: that is, the capacity to Create in any field is above the Conscious level. After an accumulation of knowledge—mental, physical and emotional—something beyond us puts it all together and produces the result. This is the same in science and all fields, art perhaps on a more unconscious level or accepted to be so.[125]

Later, Bennett recommended to the complement of artists that they try clearing their minds for three minutes, then, with eyes closed for a further three minutes, see what mental images "the artist inside us produced."[126] Foard reported that the experiment appeared to have succeeded, and that some of the artists persevered with it for some time, so fruitful did it seem.[127] These snapshots from three separate books

---

[121] Foard (1991) 190.
[122] Foard (1991) 214.
[123] Foard (1991) 234-35.
[124] Foard (1991) 257.
[125] Foard (1991) 202.
[126] Foard (1991) 218.
[127] Foard (1991) 224.

present a rather pointilistic picture, but there is, nonetheless, a coherence. Of her own progress, Foard wrote:

> My painting is the best it's ever been, really strong now and the will to work is becoming stronger all the time. I am also becoming far more sure in myself of the meaning of what it is to create. There is definitely an energy-making atmosphere at Coombe, an indefinable source, but something which actually pervades the whole place.[128]

Not the least striking is Anthony Blake's recollection that in his very first meeting with Bennett:

> I waylaid him on his way to lunch at the big house in Coombe Springs with a most serious question: "Mr Bennett. What is original sin?" He paused and appeared to consider the question with full attention. His answer was surprising but has never gone from me: "It is not to do what one can do, and strive to do what one cannot."[129]

The meaning would appear to be that, in eating of the Tree of the Knowledge of Good and Evil, Adam and Eve were aspiring to something beyond their reach, and neglecting their duty. I do not doubt that it was surprising, and yet, once formulated, it seems obvious. Bennett emerges from this and the other accounts as a capable teacher in his own right. Yet, he himself considered that he did not begin teaching in his own voice until the Sherborne courses of the 1970s.[130] I see this as a sign of Bennett's deep ambivalence about himself: the difference between what he was doing at Coombe Springs and at Sherborne was one of degree, not in nature. For example, the teaching in *A Spiritual Psychology*, based

---

[128] Foard (1991) 246.
[129] Blake (2017) 12.
[130] Bennett (1997) 300-1.

on lectures delivered in 1962 and revised and published in 1964 (section 12.4) show someone who refers, often, to Gurdjieff and Subuh, and yet, I would say, teaches in "his own voice." So too does the collection of talks in *Sunday Talks at Coombe Springs*. I might select but one example not only for its originality and penetration, but also for its relevance to this study of Bennett as a witness to death and resurrection:

> The Death, Passion and Resurrection of Jesus Christ seem a unique event: so extraordinary and so incomprehensible that it seems to be something which we can only look at from afar, not something concerning us personally. Yet in reality all great notions reproduce themselves again and again on all scales; so that if we cannot understand something on a very large scale, we may be able to see and understand it on a smaller scale nearer to our own experience.
>
> Sometimes people have said ... that the very idea of death and resurrection is no more than a relic of an ancient fertility cult.... This kind of attitude is quite mistaken. I mean the either-or attitude that *either* death and resurrection is a sublime notion belonging only to theology and concerning God, *or* it is something concerning Nature only.... This is wrong. We are all part of one single manifestation. There is, in the way this world is made, a principle of dying and being born again which runs right through the whole process of the world.[131]

8.9 THE DRAMATIC UNIVERSE

In May 1956, the first volume of *The Dramatic Universe* appeared. It was probably, for Bennett, his most important book: he kept a leather-bound gold-tooled set of it.[132] It received little notice, but that included a

---
[131] Bennett (2004) 181-82.
[132] Roth (1998) 37.

favourable review in *The Times Literary Supplement*. In an unpublished forward, written in 1952, Bennett explained that:

> A situation is dramatic when there is a need accompanied by the uncertainty as to whether it will be satisfied. The greater the need and the more impressive the scale on which it is experienced, the greater is the dramatic content.... Though immeasurably removed in scale and in cosmic significance, man and the galaxy are joined by the bond of suffering and compassion.[133]

Bennett's purview could hardly be more expansive. The book merits a full study, but this book is not the place for that study. Bennett was keenly aware that his style, and his coining of the phrase *hyparxis*, "the sixth dimension which permits free choice" when it enters our world, mystified some and annoyed others.[134] Yet, he stood by the book, for he expected criticism and incomprehension, because it was both new and opposed to modern thought. He knew that "the majority" would find it "inaccessible,"[135] even if, I would venture to say, parts would be clear enough for the majority of readers. I contend that *Witness* is primarily an extended reflection upon Bennett's visions. He evidently saw *The Dramatic Universe* in a similar light:

> If what I had seen in 1920 was right, then the reality of the fifth and sixth dimensions inevitably followed. Many of the experiences described in this book had confirmed and extended my first vision. If it were right, then sooner or later scientific research would lead to the same discovery. It did not matter if this should happen during my lifetime or after my death.[136]

---

[133] Bennett (1991b) 3.
[134] Bennett (1997) 257. I set out my understanding of hyparxis in section 5.5.
[135] Bennett (1997) 257.
[136] Bennett (1997) 257.

I count the vision of 1920 at the Rue de Péra as his second vision, not the first. Bennett felt committed to this project, and he worked hard at the second volume, to be called *The Foundations of Moral Philosophy*. He had begun with a plan for one volume, then extended it to two.[137] Eventually, four would be published, volume 3 being subtitled *Man and his Nature*, and volume 4 *History*. The scope of volume 2 would embrace, in some fashion, "all human experience and endeavour to show that there is a great harmony underlying all the diversity and chaos of our sense experience."[138] In volume four, he states:

> According to our reckoning, the change of Epoch can be detected in the seven-year period from 1844 to 1851. There was no sudden, and certainly no catastrophic, occurrence. The causal influences in history operating on the economic, political and social levels, prevent sudden changes.... Nevertheless, the influx of a new and immensely powerful influence can be recognised as having reached its maximum intensity in the year A.D. 1848.[139]

Bennett asserts, then, that between 1844 and 1851, there appeared a new "focus of Intelligence" for humanity. His concept of this, I contend, indicates those elements within his intellectual milieu which had most affected him. Bennett sees the new epoch as being "the Synergic Epoch," and probably destined to "dominate history for the next two or three thousand years."[140] This epoch is typified by an impulse to "**structural cooperation** ... a stage of integration in which the parts of a whole surrender some of their independent existence, in order to participate in a higher gradation of being."[141] (bold in the original)

---

[137] Bennett (1997) 247.
[138] Bennett (1997) 257-58.
[139] Bennett (1966) 385-86.
[140] Bennett (1966) 386.
[141] Bennett (1966) 386.

According to Bennett, the chief intellectual elements in this new epoch are these ideas:

1. The doctrine of "Universal Evolution and the Unity of Life."
2. The "theory of Relativity and the rejection of Absolutism."
3. The "belief in Cooperation and the need for large-scale organization."[142]

A little later, he spoke of three new basic concepts: "**Evolution, Relativity** and **Probability**."[143] (bold in the original) I shall not examine these ideas in detail here. Those studies of *The Dramatic Universe* which are available tend to be glib, e.g. Monserud's 120 page Masters thesis spends as much or more time on other writers (e.g. Loveday and Barbour), and is given to unsubstantiated assertions such as: "The work of J.G. Bennett is heavily flawed. He held opinions that were incredibly superficial and his life was far from perfect."[144] I am not sure this is enlightening, either as to Bennett's work or his life.

What is perhaps more to the point is that *The Dramatic Universe* is often found disappointing by students of Gurdjieff's ideas because it is not always directly addressed to questions of the inner, spiritual work. The gap between the ideas in Bennett's four-volume study, and Gurdjieff's system, is well-indicated by Gurdjieff's comment to him in August 1949: "When you have Being you will know all these things without the need for Mathematik"[145] (section 7.7). That is, Gurdjieff's system aims at development in *being*: in these books, Bennett's chief concern is elsewhere. There is, however, an indirect connection: after all, there is probably nothing that cannot somehow be tied in with concepts of being. But the connection can be so remote as to be effectively non-existent. One might say that Bennett had experienced certain visions which communicated to him something of unique value about life, death, and

---

[142] Bennett (1966) 386.
[143] Bennett (1966) 390.
[144] Monserud (2003) 53.
[145] Bennett (1997) 212.

eternity. Although Gurdjieff told him that the critical point now was to be able to experience the state of being in which those visions had been vouchsafed, much of Bennett's effort went into describing in scientific terms the basis of his visions.

In the summer of 1956, Elizabeth and he went to climb Mount Blanc, no less. They returned to a seminar with three hundred people at Coombe Springs, and initiated an "unforced effort" to complete the Djamichunatra by June 1957. In a development which again reminds one of "The Unknown Builders," he wrote:

> Several of us felt and declared that the building had come to life and was directing its own construction. It was communicating its own form and construction to the minds of the architects and attracting the specialists it needed. It was clear that my own role in relation to it was, for the time being, at an end. It would complete itself in its own way, and in its own time.[146]

The Djamichunatra, its windows, and the scrolls carefully placed within the redwood posts, would be destroyed by one of Bennett's post-Gurdjieff masters (Idries Shah), but first it would be opened by the first of this series (Pak Subuh). Yet, it may be that Bennett and his group had created, in wood and glass, a sacred image (section 12.5).

---

[146] Bennett (1997) 259.

1957: Frank Lloyd Wright surveys the Djamichunatra. Bennett stands to his left, and the profile of Robert Whiffen can be seen to Bennett's right. I have not been able to identify anyone else. Unfortunately, we do not know how F.L.W. assessed it.

CHAPTER 9

THE SUBUD CHAPTER

9.1 BENNETT'S INTRODUCTION TO SUBUD

Up to and including chapter 24, the various editions of *Witness* are identical. However, Bennett made significant changes from that point on. In the 1962 volume, chapter 25 is titled "A Prophecy Fulfilled," chapter 26 is "Subud Comes to Coombe Springs," and the final chapter, the 27th, "The Decisive Experience." In later editions, chapter 25 became "The Subud Experience," chapter 26 was "Elizabeth," chapter 27 became "Service and Sacrifice," and the new final chapter, the 28th, "Life Begins at Seventy." The changes are substantial, and hence I shall quote the earlier text in some detail. For the sake of clarity, I shall indicate when a text is found only in one edition, and until we have come to the end of the first edition, the footnotes disclose where a passage is found in both editions.

Bennett had heard "rumours" of Subud in 1955, but did not pay attention to them until Ronimund von Bissing, a former pupil of Ouspensky, disclosed that he had received the Subud initiation known as the *latihan* (see below) from one Husein Rofé, and believed that "Subud might be the key to solving all our spiritual problems."[1] Bennett's first meeting with Rofé, which took place at Coombe Springs, was not decisive, and even at the second meeting, in London, he found Rofé's stories of "premonitions fulfilled and psychic phenomena" to be "anathema."[2] Given his predilection for the same, this is difficult to accept at face value. I

[1] Bennett (1962) 328; (1997) 260.
[2] Bennett (1962) 328-29; (1997) 260.

would conjecture that this comment is related to the secondary aim of *Witness*, to provide an *apologia*: it inclines us towards the view that Bennett was not suggestible, but properly sceptical, to be persuaded by experience. Bennett omits from the second edition that Ethel Merston, who had been with Ouspensky and Gurdjieff, felt, from her first meeting with Rofé, that Subud was worth studying; and that he returned to see Rofé on two further occasions, although it was "hard to explain why." He also omits some of his character analysis of Rofé, and his musings on the prophecies of his past being fulfilled.[3] As would happen with Idries Shah, the endorsement of former fellow pupils of Gurdjieff and Ouspensky carried some weight with him.

In constant demand at Coombe Springs, and with his wife's dementia worsening, Bennett accepted Madame Ouspensky's invitation to join her at Mendham to work on his next volume of *The Dramatic Universe*. His relationship with his own group was ambivalent: he stated that he had promised himself to stay at Coombe while his wife was alive, but he felt that he himself: "veered between leadership of the most obnoxious kind – that is, dictatorship – and an equally unsatisfactory repudiation of responsibility that left everyone guessing."[4] Across the Atlantic, his writing went extremely well. Madame Ouspensky asked him about Subud, and vouchsafed to Bennett: "Since Mr Gurdjieff went, I have been waiting for someone to come. I still wait, but he has not come, perhaps he will not come in my lifetime." But she would not be drawn on how to recognise a new teacher.[5] The Gurdjieff groups in New York were "cold and suspicious," accusing him of betraying de Salzmann.[6] Bennett does not murmur, but it must have pained him to find himself "for the fourth or fifth time in my life ... ostracized by old friends."[7] That passage was removed from the 1974 edition. Perhaps the supercilious judgments of his peers in the Gurdjieff groups predisposed him towards his eventual

---

[3] Bennett (1962) 330-31.
[4] Bennett (1962) 331-32; (1997) 261-62.
[5] Bennett (1962) 332; (1997) 262-63.
[6] Bennett (1962) 332-33; (1997) 262.
[7] Bennett (1962) 333.

tryst with Subuh. He admired Madame Ouspensky all the more because she was true to herself, showing him unfailing hospitality.[8]

Back in England, caring for his wife and students, he began to develop his insight into God as the Supreme Will, and that we entertain an "anthropomorphic fallacy" about God.[9] Having decided to not bother about Subud until the book was completed: "the very same inner voice that I had learned to trust interrupted me and said: "On the contrary, you must go now." On November 25, 1956, Rofé told Bennett to declare faith in God and submission to His Will, then performed the "formal opening, or initiation, that gives contact with the Life Force that operates in Subud." Bennett felt "an almost unbroken consciousness, free from all mental activity and yet intensely alive and blissful." He later said that the state was redolent more of "the prayer of diffuse contemplation than of Gurdjieff's self-remembering."[10] "Diffuse contemplation," a seldom-used term, was suggested to him by a monk of St Wandrille's.[11] Catholic contemplatives usually compare "infused contemplation" with "acquired contemplation." Passive contemplation is "infused," while active contemplation is "acquired."[12] Bennett means that this state came to him through no effort of his own (other than his declaration and submission); and that it was different from the effort which Gurdjieff had demanded of him in August 1923 at Fontainebleau.

Bennett did not wish to let others know, saying that while some would be for and others against, there would be those who "would conclude that I had lost my faith in Gurdjieff's methods."[13] The next statement is rather tendentious:

> The *latihan* as we practised it ... was an altogether new experience for me. In all Gurdjieff's exercises, there was a result

---
[8] Bennett (1962) 332-33; (1997) 262.
[9] Bennett (1962) 333-34; (1997) 263.
[10] Bennett (1962) 334; (1997) 263-64.
[11] Bennett (1962) 372; (1997) 281.
[12] Butler (1927) 13, 37-39, 42-43 and 61.
[13] Bennett (1962) 334-35; (1997) 264.

to be achieved, a predetermined state to be reached by an intentional act of will. Here all was spontaneous. No two *latihans* were the same; there was always something new to be learned; but there was also a striking recapitulation of all I had learned before. All that I had learned and taught of Gurdjieff's psychology over so many years came to life in the *latihan*.[14]

This arguably presents a caricature of Gurdjieff's exercises in order to heighten the difference between those exercises and the *latihan*. It depends upon what one means by a "predetermined state." Certainly, Gurdjieff's exercises were never as open-ended, even formless, as the *latihan*. But when a pupil said that she worked at them with a "predetermined aim," Gurdjieff replied that it should not be like that.[15] He insisted that they not work at the exercises expecting results. Only by not expecting any specific result, and above all by not identifying with immediate results, could they achieve the desired result: the accumulation of the substances needed to coat the higher bodies.[16] In a passage omitted from the 1974 edition, Bennett disclosed that of the ten or so who then tried the *latihan*, the only five who persisted were those who had been former pupils of Gurdjieff or Ouspensky.[17] Perhaps he meant to imply that they were better prepared than the others. Bennett and the men were allowed to initiate their wives, although one of the conditions of the *latihan* was that the sexes separated for it.[18] In describing the vicissitudes of Elizabeth's and his approach to Subud, he wrote:

> The greatest stumbling block was Rofé's suggestion that all effort is useless, and that no good can come from struggling

---

[14] Bennett (1962) 335; (1997) 264 with very minor changes).
[15] Gurdjieff (2009) 176, May 10, 1945.
[16] By way of example, see Gurdjieff (2009) 4 (December 7, 1941), 18 (July 22, 1943), 71 (October 21, 1943), 176, and 180 (December 9, 1946).
[17] Bennett (1962) 335.
[18] Bennett (1962) 335-36.

with our own faults and weaknesses. He said blithely that all these are purified by the Grace of God, and that any effort to improve ourselves is misplaced self-will. This contradicted what was for me an unassailable truth: the principle that we can possess only what we have earned.[19]

Bennett wrote to Subuh, who replied, refining Rofé's rigid principle by indicating that "efforts coming from the mind alone are useless."[20] Gurdjieff, too, said that purely mental efforts were insufficient: one has to struggle with one's whole, with mind, feeling, and organic instinct.[21] Subuh's advice was provisionally accepted since, Bennett said, he found that his conscience was being "awakened." This, he said, enabled him to maintain his acceptance of Gurdjieff's teaching on the importance of conscience, and further, to experience conscience as a reality.[22] However, the issue was a fundamental one, and could not be dismissed so easily: when it had to be faced, it would lead to Bennett's separation from Subuh and Subud.

In February 1957, Rofé disclosed that in 1934 Subuh had prophesied he (Subuh) would travel the world teaching Subud, that England would be the first land he visited, and that when Rofé came to England, he would meet spiritually prepared people. He believed that Bennett and his friends were the predicted group. When Bennett and colleagues discussed their experience, they discovered that they all considered the *latihan* to awaken conscience, and that it worked more rapidly and effectively than the Gurdjieff exercises. They were accordingly "anxious" that others from the groups should have the chance to try Subud.[23] Bennett flew to the U.S. to meet Madames Ouspensky and de Salzmann, who agreed that Subuh should be invited to England; de Salzmann saying

---

[19] Bennett (1962) 336.
[20] Bennett (1962) 336.
[21] The number of references would be endless, but see Gurdjieff (2014) 364 and 388; (2017) 159; and (2009) 178.
[22] Bennett (1962) 336-37.
[23] Bennett (1962) 337; (1997) 264.

that she would be glad to meet him, "as only in this way could she form any opinion as to whether or not he might be the expected Teacher."[24] Bennett had said Mme Ouspensky was waiting for another "teacher,"[25] but this is the first indication that de Salzmann shared the expectation. Then follows another telling passage, also significantly omitted from later editions:

> Until that time I had attached far less importance to Pak Subuh as a man than I did to the *latihan* as an experience. However, I recognized that he must be the best exemplar of the results given by the *latihan*, and perhaps something more beside. Madame Ouspensky again asked me, at our last meeting, how I would expect to recognize if he were a true Teacher. I replied ... by the effect that one experiences within oneself in his presence. I did not think that I could easily be taken in by an impressive exterior. She did not find my reply convincing, and said: "You cannot judge someone who is on a higher level of being than yourself. I advise you to pray. Only by prayer can you hope to be shown what is right."[26]

The full import of this becomes apparent later, when Bennett meets Idries Shah. But Shah was unknown to Bennett at the time of the first edition. As he completed volume 2 of *The Dramatic Universe* while awaiting the arrival of Subuh, Bennett completely recovered from the sequelae of his dysentery and his tuberculosis infection. He considered that this healing was possibly due to the *latihan*.[27] Then Bennett comes to the "kind of moral regeneration" which was "of far greater importance": over about fourteen days, he underwent the "truly purgatorial" experience of recalling everything from his past, "especially those episodes which

---

[24] Bennett (1962) 337; (1997) 264-65.
[25] Bennett (1962) 332; (1997) 262.
[26] Bennett (1962) 337-38.
[27] Bennett (1962) 338; (1997) 265.

I had wished to forget." These included his seductions of women, his faithlessness to males, and "above all, my insensibility to the feelings of others and my consuming self-will," to the extent that he "could not sleep for remorse and self-loathing."[28] Omitted from the revision is that he wrote to Subuh about this suffering:

> On the day I received his reply and before I had opened the letter, it had lifted. I knew that God is merciful, and that I was forgiven. I read Bapak's letter, in which he assured me that what I was passing through was a true purgation ... and that it would not last longer than I could bear.[29]

Bennett then reveals what was removed from the 1974 edition, that as he was awaiting the arrival of Subuh, he taught his pupils Gurdjieff's "Practice of the Collected State" and had them study how to distinguish "essence" from "personality."[30]

In Gurdjieff's terms, "essence" can be taken as what is real and permanent in us, while personality is the superficial layer formed in us by education, imagination, and the imitation of sleeping role-models.[31] Bennett was assimilating Subud's *latihan* to Gurdjieff's "collected state."[32] At this time, the actress Eva Bartok, who was a pupil of Bennett's rang from Hollywood to say that she was very ill. Bennett invited her to come over, sensing that "she was destined to be cured through Subud, and that through this, Subud would become known far and wide."[33] And so, on about May 22, 1957, Pak Subuh arrived in England.

---

[28] Bennett (1962) 338-39; (1997) 265.
[29] Bennett (1962) 339.
[30] Bennett (1962) 339-40.
[31] Ouspensky (1949) 161-65.
[32] Bennett (1962) 340, this passage is lacking in (1997) 266.
[33] Bennett (1962) 340; (1997) 266. She was cured, apparently miraculously.

9.2   PAK SUBUH

Muhammad Subuh Sumohadiwidjojo ("Pak Subuh," 1901-87) had begun to teach the practices which would become organised as Subud in 1933.[34] Two studies have placed Subud within the Javanese mystical tradition.[35] Subud is related to Javanese Islam, specifically to Sufism: Subuh studied with a Javanese Naqshbandi teacher, his first pupils were from that milieu, he performed Muslim prostrations, recited the *shahada*, recommended observing the Ramadan fast, cried *Allahu akbar*, and like Muhammad he claimed to have experienced an "ascension," and identified the divine light as the "Nur Muhammad," (Arabic for the light of Muhammad).[36] However, the very name "Subud" comes from three Sanskrit words, although it is striking that whether by accident or otherwise, the word "Subud" and the name "Subuh" are so similar in English as to often be confused. In a non-Islamic vein, Subuh used the concepts of *karma* and *jiwa*,[37] and did not insist on his followers complying with the pillars of Islam, or use the Qur'an to any significant degree. Whatever the origin of Subud, the system which Bennett met may have used Islamic or even Sufi terms, but it was universalistic, claiming that it was neither a religion nor a teaching.[38]

When Subuh arrived, Bennett was impressed by his calm self-possession and independence of his surroundings. When he asked him whether those admitted to Subud should cease to work according to Gurdjieff's methods, he replied:

> No. Change nothing. Bapak is not a teacher. Gurdjieff is your teacher, and once you have a real teacher, you are never separated from him whether he is alive or dead. But Bapak tells

---

[34] Geels (2021) 568 and 571.
[35] Sedgwick (2016) 196-98, who also notes the influence of Theosophy in Indonesia, strong in the 1930s and vigorously continuing into the 1950s.
[36] Geels (1997) 123-25, 134, 148 and (2021) 570-72. There are other points of contact with Islam, but these are sufficient to show that the contacts are not trivial.
[37] Geels (1997) 148-49. On *jiwa*, see Geels (2021) 577-78.
[38] Geels (1997) 174-78.

you if you sincerely practise the *latihan* you will understand Gurdjieff's teaching quite differently.... [L]ater on you will learn from your teacher Gurdjieff many things that you never heard him say before.[39]

The 1962 version of chapter 25 closes with the observation that Bennett much later realised that Subuh had told him what he had wanted to hear, something he often did.[40] Only the 1962 edition mentions that when Ibu Subuh, Pak's wife, arrived at Coombe Springs, she declared that she had seen the house and grounds in a vision, so that: "When Pak Subuh told me of Ibu's premonition, I could not but offer our hospitality."[41] On June 1, 1957, amid much excitement, the Subud crew moved into Coombe Springs. Within the space of but one month, over four hundred people, almost all of whom were Bennett's pupils, were initiated, and attended regularly for the *latihan*.[42] However, not all who came from the Ouspensky tradition shared this favourable view; e.g. Joyce Collin-Smith queried certain features of Subuh's style, and to criticise Ibu for her shoplifting and sense of entitlement.[43]

Found only in the first edition is that Subuh began prompting Bennett to write something "so that all people can understand what Subud means." Bennett began to dwell on his third vision, the "prophecy ... [which] had predicted that I would meet my real destiny in my sixtieth year." He turned sixty shortly after Subuh arrived. He thought of Gurdjieff's comments about one to come, and Daghestani's prediction, and how all these prophecies were apparently now being fulfilled.[44] Given what was to happen, it is not to be wondered at that Bennett would remove these passages when he edited *Witness*. But a prudent

---

[39] Bennett (1962) 341; (1997) 267.
[40] Bennett (1962) 341.
[41] Bennett (1962) 342.
[42] Bennett (1962) 342-43; also in (1997) 267.
[43] Collin-Smith (1988) 94 and 101. She notes, there, that the main Ouspensky pupils were initially cool and then frigid in their attitude to Subud.
[44] Bennett (1962) 343.

editor, even in 1962, might have drawn the line at this passage, also later deleted:

> [T]he coming of Pak Subuh had been attended by strange signs and portents. In the week that he accepted our invitation, a brilliant comet appeared in the sky. As I watched it on a moonless night ... I was seized with a sense of awesome expectancy. Common sense would have dismissed as foolish superstition the old belief that comets are harbingers of great events.... [T]he eastern sky was filled with wonder as if an immense Presence overshadowed the earth. Something said to me: "That is the coming of Subud to the West."[45]

Recalling that Bennett saw signs of the Parousia in his own time,[46] it is scarcely possible to overstate the extent to which Bennett relied upon the fulfilment of prophecy in accepting Subuh and Subud: prophecy features on the very first page of his apologetic treatise *Concerning Subud*.[47] Contending that "Subud and Gurdjieff's ideas were indissolubly linked" and that Gurdjieff and Subuh were "in some way connected," he arranged for two meetings between de Salzmann and Subuh. However, neither de Salzmann nor her close associate Henri Tracol found any affinity between Gurdjieff's system and Subud.[48]

Bennett came to be embarrassed by the next event. In three pages found only in the 1962 edition, Bennett described the violence sometimes provoked or occasioned by the *latihan*. One man practiced *latihan* long beyond when he had been told to stop, and for twenty days would neither eat nor wear clothes, smashed doors, and broke one of Bennett's ribs. Then, he went into an abnormally quiet state, and a few days later, died.[49] Bennett and Subuh were both present either as he

---

[45] Bennett (1962) 343.
[46] Bennett (1975a) iii, cited in section 0.2.
[47] Bennett (1958) 7-8.
[48] Bennett (1962) 343-44.
[49] Bennett (1962) 345-46.

died or just after, it is unclear. A "charnel stench" arose, so strong that Bennett vomited. As he knelt to pray, he felt as if the deceased man and himself had become one in a combat between good and evil powers. Time ceased, and he felt he was being dragged down by an evil force, then there arose a great peace, then the miasma returned, and so on.[50] When Subuh returned, he declared the event unprecedented, and said that for the deceased "this purification was the only way. For the rest, a veil will be drawn over the event."[51] In the 1974 edition, the text loses all continuity. There, immediately after the apparently miraculous cure of Eva Bartok,[52] he writes: "Pak Subuh said afterwards: "Mr Bennett is very strong."[53] This is a reference to his situation after the strange death, and not to Bartok's cure. On the other hand, Bennett did not delete how he attributed the recovery of his wife's gentle and intelligent nature to her initiation by Ibu Subuh,[54] and he always remained sensible of his debt to her and to Subud.

9.3 OPENING THE DJAMICHUNATRA

The next two pages were removed for the 1974 edition. In August, the summer seminars were held, and many international visitors were initiated into Subud. Probably soon after this, Subuh travelled to Holland and Rofé to Morocco. Bennett was more persuaded than ever that Subud could directly benefit tens of thousands of people, and "perhaps all mankind" indirectly."[55] Subuh returned for the opening of the Djamichunatra, which Bennett saw as "a material link between Gurdjieff and Subud." The central axis pointed to Fontainebleau where Gurdjieff was buried:

---

[50] Bennett (1962) 346-47.
[51] Bennett (1962) 347.
[52] Bennett (1962) 344-54; (1997) 267-68.
[53] Bennett (1997) 268.
[54] Bennett (1962) 347-48; (1997) 268.
[55] Bennett (1962) 348.

He had spoken of a nine-sided building which exemplified in its proportions the Laws of World Creation and World Maintenance, and as the plans of the new hall came to life, we found in it an expression of the laws of which Gurdjieff wrote in *All and Everything*.[56]

When Pak Subuh came to Coombe, someone asked him if there was any significance in a nine-sided building. He replied that there are nine spiritual powers, and that we should see for ourselves their significance when our spiritual consciousness was more developed. We felt that we had been preparing for the coming of Subud even before we knew of its existence.[57]

On October 29 that year, they commemorated the ninth anniversary of Gurdjieff's passing, including an orchestral arrangement of some of Gurdjieff's music:

This occasion was for men an end and a beginning. It carried me back to October 1920, when I heard Thomas de Hartmann play Gurdjieff's music in Istanbul. It was a promise that Gurdjieff's life work should find at least one of its modes of fulfilment in the coming of Subud. I was asked to give a name to the building, and chose the word Djamichunatra, taken from Chapter 46 of *All and Everything*, where it is used to describe the place where the soul receives its spiritual nourishment.[58]

Bennett states that the name seemed "strangely appropriate" to Subud, without venturing why.[59] The element "Djami" represents the Turkish *cami* for "mosque," pronounced as *jami*. Bennett confesses to

---

[56] Bennett (1962) 348.
[57] Bennett (1962) 348.
[58] Bennett (1962) 348-49.
[59] Bennett (1962) 349.

having felt some diffidence: "Who was I to proclaim the consanguinity of Gurdjieff and Subud, which others, more qualified than I, so hotly denied?"[60] This is striking for three reasons: first, as an example of his reticence, for he has not hitherto indicated that there was "hot" denial from either de Salzmann or anyone else, only rejection. Second, it is unclear how naming the hall the Djamichunatra meant anything about a relation between Gurdjieff and Subud, unless, and this is the third matter, the status of Coombe Springs had changed: it was now not merely hosting Subuh and his initiations, it was a Subud establishment. Bennett was now convinced that Gurdjieff's teaching and Subud had both come from the same Source (Bennett's capital S) and were "manifestations of one and the same Providential Action."[61] In that deleted section, Bennett had written:

> [W]e invited Pak Subuh and his family to the Djamichunatra where, on behalf of the Institute, the architects and builders, I offered it to Subud for any purpose it might serve. During the short talk that Bapak then gave, I became convinced that the building itself was contributing to the sense of harmony that we all felt. My mind went back to the Mevlevi Tekkes, to the Byzantine churches of Greece and Turkey, to the Gothic chapter houses of France and England – all of which were of similar shape and size, and many of which produced the same sense of quiet harmony. The effect was not merely one of sound and light, but rather of a concentration of psychic energies. There were "presences" in the Djamichunatra the reality of which I could not doubt, but the nature of which I certainly could not perceive. Pak Subuh spoke often of these "presences," and said that we only fail to be aware of them

---

[60] Bennett (1962) 349.
[61] Bennett (1962) 349.

because we are conditioned to rely exclusively on sense perceptions.[62]

Both Subuh and Bennett's publishers suggested that he write a book on Subud. This book, which Subuh approved, was *Concerning Subud*.[63] I shall not deal with the differences between the original 1958 and the revised 1959 editions of this volume.

9.4 BENNETT IN AUSTRALIA

Now commenced what Bennett appropriately termed a "stream of surprising events."[64] Together with Elizabeth and their sons, they travelled with or in advance of Subuh to the U.S., especially the West Coast, to Honolulu, Fiji, and then to Australia where—on his account—after an initially inauspicious start, Elizabeth and he initiated successful openings for respectable numbers of men and women in the Adyar Hall, Sydney.[65] Having been in a state of revolt, Bennett found a sense of "immense peace" in which he felt the hall to be filled with a "Presence":

> Nearly all the men in the room were responding to the *latihan*. More had happened in a quarter of an hour than I had seen in England in a month. In that moment, I became convinced beyond all doubt that the Power that works in Subud has nothing to do with me or with any other person. I could not understand why or how I should be a channel for its transmission, but I could no longer question its real—that is, its objective—presence.[66]

Bennett reported that Elizabeth's experience had been identical,

---

[62] Bennett (1962) 349.
[63] Only in Bennett (1962) 350.
[64] Bennett (1962) 350; (1997) 268.
[65] Bennett (1962) 350-51; (1997) 269.
[66] Bennett (1962) 351; (1997) 269-70.

even to awareness of an overshadowing numinous Presence which made the openings.[67] I do not count this among the visions because nothing was seen – there was an experience, but no revelation. Also dropped when Bennett revised the book is the story of their travelling with Subuh in Australia and Java, and especially, how Subuh told them of how, on June 22, 1933, he had experienced an illumination and made a journey "through and beyond the solar system," and described the mysteries he saw.[68] As he spoke, Bennett experienced a change of consciousness in which the difference between himself and others disappeared. He termed this "the crowning experience of my entire contact with Subud up to that time."[69]

9.5 THE DEATH OF THE SECOND MRS BENNETT AND MARRIAGE TO ELIZABETH MAYALL

The text of the two editions again converges from the end of chapter 26 in the 1962 volume and of chapter 25 in the 1974. Bennett returned to England via Ceylon, to find his wife much weakened, but calm and "most truly herself."[70] On the morning of July 25, 1958 she died, but gave him a signal that:

> she remained conscious through death.... She was finally liberated from the personal attachment, and had found the union of the soul that neither death nor any other creature can dissolve. I have never felt separated from her since that time.[71]

After Polly Bennett's death, Bennett returned to his draft of the second volume of *The Dramatic Universe*. He typified the entirety of the

---

[67] Bennett (1962) 351; (1997) 270.
[68] Bennett (1962) 352-53.
[69] Bennett (1962) 352.
[70] Bennett (1962) 354; (1997) 270.
[71] Bennett (1962) 355; (1997) 270-71.

study as a working out of the insights gained from the second vision.⁷² Bennett had a moment's glimpse of something, but to work out its consequences would be the work of a lifetime. The enduring value he found in his draft of *The Dramatic Universe* surprised him, because while he had changed, his old ideas were still valid. He wrote the following in 1962, but the sentence underlined was excised from the later edition:

> Beyond all doubt, I myself had changed. <u>One year of Subud had done more for me than the previous thirty</u>. One change that I was aware of had been a shift in the centre of gravity of my experience, from my head to my heart.⁷³

The underlined sentence sounds extravagant, but its excision indicates that he came to believe that the first edition was unduly zealous for Subuh. Further, if he strictly meant to speak of the period from about 1928, it is consistent with the interpretation offered in chapter 8, first suggested by Clive Entwistle: that Bennett was seeking re-connection to the Great Accumulator, such as he had known in August 1923 (the fourth vision). When he speaks of the "centre of my experience," he alludes to Gurdjieff's idea of the different "men," where:

> *Man number three* means man on the same level of development but man in whom the centre of gravity of his psychic life lies in the intellectual centre, that is, man with whom the thinking functions gain the upper hand over the moving, instinctive, and emotional functions; the man of reason, who goes into everything from theories, from mental considerations.⁷⁴

With "man number one" and "two" the "centre of gravity" is in the

---

[72] Bennett (1962) 356; (1997) 272.
[73] Bennett (1962) 356; cf. (1997) 272.
[74] Ouspensky (1949) 71.

moving/instinctive and emotional functions, respectively.[75] Bennett adds that Prince Sabaheddin had told his wife that Bennett's heart was still frozen, and that this "had remained true through all the changes of the years. Subud had melted my frozen heart, and nothing could ever be the same again."[76] That is in both versions, but only the first bears this:

> I had revolted against my old researches and theories; against my tendency to live in abstractions and ignore facts. I had been inclined to cast my manuscripts into the flames and write no more until I could write from the heart.[77]

Bennett avows that for the first time, now, he was able to rely on his own judgment when evaluating it as "an important book that had to be published." He had leaned upon Ouspensky, Gurdjieff, and his second wife, but Subuh had "done for me what no one else had been able to do. By refusing to allow himself to be used as a prop, he made me stand on my own feet."[78] Omitted from the revised edition is that Bennett had begun to separate his own authority from Subuh's, noting that when he had left Indonesia, he found that he had no questions for Subuh, even as to whether there were anything he (Subuh) wished him to do for Subud in the West.[79] In 1962 he saw the "absence of questions" as evidence that a deep change had occurred within him:

> (My) weaknesses were still there, but I was not longer dominated by them.... I was able to face what I had always been too timid to acknowledge; the truth that I had been given an insight into cosmic mysteries that was my own, and did not derive from any teaching that I had received from others. These musings, which I had never before dared to admit into

---

[75] Ouspensky (1949) 71.
[76] Bennett (1962) 356; (1997) 272.
[77] Bennett (1962) 356-57.
[78] Bennett (1962) 357; (1997) 272-73.
[79] Bennett (1962) 357.

my waking consciousness, brought with them the awareness that I had been reborn. I was filled with joy and thankfulness to know that ... 'Now, verily I Am'. Gurdjieff had said to me at a prophetic meeting in his café shortly before his death: "now you have the taste of real 'I', but one day it will enter you and remain permanent. Then you will experience such happiness as you cannot imagine." After nine years, his promise was fulfilled. I knew that I was at last myself. But I also knew that this was only a beginning.[80]

The 1974 text abruptly rejoins the narrative with: "I said: Now I must marry Elizabeth".[81] She told him a strange story about seeing a phantom woman in blue, whom Subuh and Ibu Subuh told her was the "true wife of Mr Bennett" who would enter into Elizabeth, uniting their souls, for "the mutual completion of the male and female natures can be realized between more than two souls," and that it was Elizabeth's destiny to be Bennett's companion.[82] Bennett accepted the reality of the vision, and welcomed the change he saw in Elizabeth and their children, writing:

> I realized that I not only admired her, but loved her in a way that was quite new to me. I had never before wished for the life of a family. Indeed, it had not occurred to me that I might find satisfaction in having a wife and children round me.... I had travelled, moved from house to house, and when we finally settled at Coombe Springs, it was not to make a home but a centre for my work.[83]

They married on October 27, 1958. The changes he was finding in himself, and the marriage and family life were two aspects of his progress

---

[80] Bennett (1962) 358.
[81] Bennett (1962) 358; (1997) 273.
[82] Bennett (1962) 358-59; (1997) 273-74.
[83] Bennett (1962) 360; (1997) 274-75.

through life, because he had not previously been "ready and able to live with a wife as a husband and a father."[84] He confessed:

> I suppose that the greatest test of our true condition is our attitude to fear. I had always been deeply afraid, because I was not living in my true self. It seems to me that this fear is almost universal among men and women, though usually hidden from their waking consciousness. We are afraid because we do not really live, and our fear is of having our unlivingness exposed to ourselves and others.[85]

Bennett sets out half a page of further meditation on marriage. The material is striking, and use the concept of the dyad, as a dynamic stage, to help explain how harmonious spouses can through their spiritual union share one soul and also come closer to other people.[86]

9.6   THE EIGHTEENTH VISION: CHRIST CRUCIFIED

Bennett's narrative returns at once to Subud. As Subud assumed a global profile, and Subuh indicated that an international conference should be held in London, Bennett offered to organize it. As part of the preparation, he travelled to Mexico, where he arrived on March 9, 1959. Subuh joined them on March 26. Bennett had a remarkable experience at Coyoacan on Good Friday. In 1959, the feast fell on March 27:[87]

> I went to do the *latihan* with a man in a state of deep distress…. In the midst of the *latihan* I became aware of Jesus on the Cross and was raised up and entered into His body, and looked through His eyes on the maddened and uncomprehending crowd below. I became aware of the dreadful

---
[84] Bennett (1962) 361; (1997) 275.
[85] Bennett (1962) 360; (1997) 275.
[86] Bennett (1962) 360; (1997) 275.
[87] https://www.calendar-12.com/holidays/easter/1959 accessed March 26, 2022.

stench and of swarms of flies over the Body. Everything in me was outraged and disgusted. There was no mercy anywhere; nothing clean. And I knew that Jesus was aware of it all and infinitely more: of all human uncomprehendingness stretching away and away in time and place. I was aware also of the immensity of the love that could see all and forgive all. I noticed that my arms had been raised, and I could feel that I was involved in the Crucifixion. Then I fell into a kind of unconsciousness in which everything became remote, and out of the darkness a brilliant light emerged, growing brighter and more and more glorious. In this radiance I was aware of the Other Nature of Christ; the glorious Divine Nature, untouched by anything that exists. Gradually the radiance rose higher and higher above me, and I was left behind. I became myself again, wondering what might be the meaning of what I had lived through.

When the *latihan* was finished, I felt myself as weak as if I were about to die. I could not bear the presence of others, and went away and hid until my usual condition returned. As I sat in solitude, I understood that I must learn to live with the reality of the Christian beliefs, and to accept that there is here a mystery that the mind of man can and never will penetrate.[88]

I consider this to have been one of the central visions in *Witness*, because it included something which went beyond anything he could have worked out for himself. In this case, the dual and simultaneous reality of the divinity and humanity of Jesus is pre-eminent, with the inescapable corollary that this is something the ordinary mind cannot understand. While the light he saw was "untouched by anything that exists," yet it manifested among them. Bennett passes from this to some recollections of comments made by Subuh both about healing and other

---

[88] Bennett (1962) 363-64; (1997) 277. That it was at Coyoacan appears only at (1962) 375.

signs, and in answer to some questions posed by Aldous Huxley, who was opened in the *latihan*.[89] Within three months Bennett was to have a related vision.

9.7 THE NINETEENTH, TWENTIETH AND TWENTY-FIRST VISIONS: THE LOVE OF GOD

One must wonder that Bennett skips quickly over the Subud Congress at Coombe Springs, omitting even the brief note he wrote in 1962 from the 1974 edition.[90] It is known that some people were disappointed and left Subud after it. Bennett passes to his June 1959 visit to the Benedictine monastery of St. Wandrille in France. Three of the monks received the *latihan*. Bennett now describes what I count as the nineteenth vision:

> During my stay in the monastery, I was aware, for the second time in my life, of the state of the Love of God. I had known only too well that, although I believed in God and was obedient to His Will, I had never been able to love God.... I was convinced that God is the Supreme Will that is beyond individuality, even in its purest and most perfect form.... It seemed impossible for me to *love* a Will that I could never hope to comprehend.
>
> Now the marvel had happened. I was aware that the Love of God could be experienced without any image or thought. To love God means to participate in God's Love. That awareness was delicate and fleeting. It was a ray of hope and not an attainment.[91]

If this was the second occasion on which he came to an awareness of the "state of the Love of God," the first was the tenth vision, at Coombe

---

[89] Bennett (1962) 364-65; (1997) 278.
[90] Bennett (1962) 365. Absent from (1997) 278.
[91] Bennett (1962) 365-66; (1997) 279.

Springs on April 14, 1944 (section 5.5). The description of this as "hope" is interesting: for Gurdjieff, hope was not just wishing, but was based on the apprehension of something real and present which could return and become more lasting.[92] Later, in the 1962 edition, Bennett notes Subuh's clarification for the monks that the "Great Life Force" which features in the *latihan* is "a created thing, and that the contact with it was, therefore, a natural process."[93] Bennett returned to St. Wandrille's at least once. On a later stay, while he was practising *latihan*:

> I heard a voice within me saying: "Surrender to the Will of God is the foundation of all religion." Then I became aware of the Presence of Jesus, and saw that He is the manifestation of the Love of God. The thought entered my mind: "Then Christianity is the one true religion." At the same moment, I found myself intoning the opening chapter of the Qur'an.... Then the same voice said: "It is my Will that my Church and Islam should be united." I said in astonishment: "Who can accomplish such a task?" and the reply came: "Mary."[94]

Neither this visit nor the next are dated. But during one of these he was meditating on how the Will of God is that we love our neighbour, when:

> I was overwhelmed with love. The love I felt towards Elizabeth transformed itself into a love of all humanity. Then everything human and personal vanished. I was aware that God's Love and my love were one and the same. I stood trembling, taking in deep breaths like sighs. I could no longer bear the love that flowed through and through me, and I fell to the ground. As I lay prostrate, I became aware that

---

[92] Gurdjieff (1950) 358, 362, 801, and 1131.
[93] Bennett (1962) 370.
[94] Bennett (1962) 372; (1997) 281-82.

> something more was being shown to me.... that I must be satisfied at present to know the Will of God in general. I was not yet ready to know it in any particular instance.... These are lame words; they cannot convey the assurance that a promise had been made to me that would surely be kept. If I for my part could achieve the love of my neighbour, then I would be received into the Love of God.[95]

After this vision, with a joy which, he stated, had never since left him, Bennett had a certainty that he could not have received this vision had he been alone.[96] He related this to Subud in that it showed him that "every action and every thought that does not come from the love of God is sinful, and this means that I am nearly always in a state of sin."[97] That knowledge made him suffer, but the joy remained, and "this state of simultaneous awareness of joy and suffering is the condition that makes it possible for us to be aware of our own individuality."[98] It may not be accidental that it was in the monastery at this time that he wrote seven chapters, presumably the first seven of "this account of my own life."[99] Also strangely absent from the revision is his witnessing the birth of his daughter, Hero:

> In *The Dramatic Universe* I have written hundreds of pages to prove the contention that Life is the central fact of existence, the vehicle of the Reconciling Will of God as Manifested in Creation. No words can express the miracle of life so effectively as the birth of a child. It is the sign and symbol of the descent of spirit into matter and of the ascent of spirit towards its origin in God.[100]

---

[95] Bennett (1962) 373; (1997) 282.
[96] Bennett (1962) 373; absent from (1997) 282.
[97] Bennett (1962) 373-374; absent from (1997).
[98] Bennett (1962) 374; absent from (1997).
[99] Bennett (1962) 374; absent from (1997).
[100] Bennett (1962) 374.

This reflection on life leads Bennett back to the religious thoughts he had experienced at St. Wandrille about the need for religion, despite our incapacity to know the "Purpose and Plan." Subud, which was enriching the monks, seemed to provide a simple means of directly experiencing "the reality of religious faith."[101] One of the fruits of this was a short book, *Christian Mysticism and Subud,* which he would soon criticise as "failing to render Pak Subuh in his own terms."[102] After recounting his early readings in Underhill, Inge, and other Edwardian literature of mysticism (section 0.6), Bennett states:

> One thing that struck me very much when I returned to these books after perhaps twenty or thirty years, and noticed, in my old margin notes, what I had then approved and what I had disliked, was that I too missed the essential point that the mystical action and experience do not come from man himself.[103]

The mystics who were cited neither referred to themselves as mystics, nor claimed to understand their experiences. However, accepting the term, Bennett said that mysticism aims at a state of Union between the will of the individual with that Will of God. Christian mysticism, he said, is centred on union with Christ, and declares a need for self-discipline and asceticism; while in Subud, it is purely a question of "complete submission" to God's Will.[104] Bennett only briefly mentions mystic experiences of becoming "one with the powers of nature," a theme to which he would return at the end of his life, when he started to believe that a sacred image could be seen in, or perhaps through, nature (section 12.5).[105]

---

[101] Bennett (1962) 375.
[102] Bennett (undated) "Subud – The Sufi Background," V.
[103] Bennett (1961b) 11.
[104] Bennett (1961b) 10-11 and 47.
[105] Bennett (1961b) 65.

9.8 BENNETT'S DISAFFECTION FROM SUBUD

On December 18, 1964, Bennett wrote to Subuh, offering his resignation, and that of Elizabeth, as helper-openers in Subud. On January 13, 1965, Subuh accepted the resignations. How did it come to this? A clear trajectory of re-evaluation, even disillusionment is evident from the heyday of Subuh's stay at Coombe Springs in 1957. In *Concerning Subud*, there was little mention of any harmful consequences of Subud, even entirely accidental ones. In the second edition, written barely four months after the first, Bennett brought out "more explicitly the difficulties and the hazards of Subud,"[106] in the new section VII.4, titled "The Hidden Forces in Man." Bennett declares that, because Subud exercises all aspects of one's nature, and some of these can be violent and grotesque, the results can appear "disconcerting and even alarming."[107] Bennett then presented at some length the objection of a man who was reminded, during the *latihan*, of barbaric sights he endured at the end of WWII. However, Bennett, answered him, and the man decided that he would try the *latihan* again, and he eventually came to believe that Subud offered hope for a real and lasting change in humanity.[108]

A less sanguine case study is found in *Witness*, published in 1962,[109] and with quite some force in the original prologue to *A Spiritual Psychology*, in 1964. Bennett was aware of, and made oblique reference to correspondence in the pages of *The Lancet* about Subud. So far as my research discloses, the first of these was a letter, printed on December 30, 1961, from Drs. Francis and Kiev from Maudsley Hospital, a psychiatric hospital in London:

> We have recently encountered two patients, showing gross disturbance of behaviour, who expressed delusions evidently derived in part from their experience in a spiritual sect known

[106] Bennett (1959) 179.
[107] Bennett (1959) 121.
[108] Bennett (1959) 122-24.
[109] Bennett (1962) 344-47.

as Subud. It was difficult to tell whether these were shared beliefs of the sect or autistic productions of the individual.... A central feature of Subud is a group exercise called the Latihan, aimed at removing conscious control of emotions, thoughts, and behaviour, to allow their free expression and self-knowledge. In Subud it is believed that these exercises, particularly if they are over-indulged in, may be dangerous to certain individuals. "Subud crises" are described, in which individuals display in their everyday life behaviour normally reserved for the Latihan.... They neglect their appearance, adopt bizarre postures, speak with "strange tongues," and experience intense subjective changes. Our two patients would come in this category.... Latihan may possibly precipitate psychotic illness, as certain psychotherapeutic procedures resembling it do occasionally.[110]

On April 28, 1962, Dr. E.K. Janzen from Holland reported a "Subud crisis" in a middle-aged woman.[111] On May 19, 1962, Dr. Gabriel Jaffé reported that he had been present when Subuh (not named) "was himself present and exercising his powers." He continued:

[T]he Subud crises are psychogenic.... most of the participants were people conspicuous by their suggestibility.... although major delusions are not common, some degree of persistent mania or elation followed the "exercises" in most of the "disciples." The overall impression was predominately one of group hysteria and hypnosis.[112]

The response came on May 26, 1962 from Richard Mackarness, a medical journalist. The nature of his reply can be gauged from its final

---

[110] *The Lancet*, December 30, 1961, 1452.
[111] *The Lancet*, April 28, 1962, 916.
[112] *The Lancet*, May 19, 1962, 1073.

salvo: "In a world in danger of going down before the advancing tide of Communism, any movement like Subud which emphasises spiritual values deserves encouragement in the West."[113] Bennett was aware of these controversies and of the reality of the "Subud crises." It may have taken some time, but it should not occasion surprise that Bennett had completely refigured his attitude to Subud by the time he wrote the Introduction to the 1974 edition of *A Spiritual Psychology*, where he was saying: "The strongest influence in my life has been George Gurdjieff, and much of the spiritual psychology developed in this book has been learned from him."[114] Then, a little further on he mentioned his issues with Subud:

> In 1962, I came to the conclusion that the *latihan* is too limited in its action to provide a complete way of life. This was confirmed by the observation that those who practised it with enthusiasm and conviction tended to become narrow in outlook and loyalty. Subud was becoming a new cult or, at best, a Moslem sect.... As a method the *latihan* works, but it does so in a very specific manner by unblocking the channel that leads from the outer to the inner parts of the self. This action cannot take more than one to two years. In fact, I think it can be completed within six to ten months, and to continue longer is non-productive and finally counter-productive. I can recommend the latihan especially to those who are overactive intellectually and emotionally shut in.[115]

These two passages show the nature of Bennett's final views: that the Gurdjieff methods come first, but that Subud can be a help if used for one to two years at most. Not all issues with Subud had to go so far as a crisis in order to be problematic. Tunbridge recalls that Subud helpers

---

[113] *The Lancet*, May 26, 1962, 1125.
[114] Bennett (1999) 20.
[115] Bennett (1999) 29.

came on weekends, although the residents of Coombe Springs irreverently referred to these as "helpless helpers" because of "their inability to organise anything whatsoever." They would, he said, hold group meditation sessions (which must have been "testings") to determine who would peel the potatoes, leaving it for the residents to take matters into their own hands so that they might eat.[116]

The practical effect of the *latihan* had persuaded Bennett to accept and to spread Subud. He had been instrumental in having his own students purchase a nursing home at Brookhurst Grange where standard medical practices would be augmented by the *latihan*.[117] More than anyone else, he had made Subud an international phenomenon. Time and again, he cites, in his own vindication, people's experience of Subud. If he now admitted that Subud's practical value was mixed, then his position within Subud became precarious. Unlike Gurdjieff's intellectually satisfying system, Subud claimed to have no doctrine, a notion which Bennett admitted was "almost meaningless" in the West, as it surely did have one.[118] Bennett's reticence renders it hard to reconstruct the development of his disaffection; for example, only in the 1974 edition of *A Spiritual Psychology* does he refer to meetings which he had with the Maharishi Mahesh Yogi, in and after 1959, intense Subud periods, where he learnt the Maharishi's form of meditation:

> It consists in the use of a mantra repeated silently in the breast in much the same way as the prayer of the heart of the Russian Orthodox monks.... The method of Transcendental Meditation is much gentler and more controlled than Subud. It is now very well known throughout the world and its value as a natural and effective means for removing psychological

---

[116] Tunbridge (2015) 66.
[117] Mitchell (2018) locations 595-65. The nursing home had to close, but I can find no details about this.
[118] Bennett (undated) "Subud—The Sufi Background," VII.

tensions and for awakening the mediator to the reality of a spiritual world.[119]

Bennett means that there are diverse ways of providing a spiritual energy, some of them like Transcendental Meditation (T.M.) are gentle and deliver a low current, while others like Subud are more vigorous and deliver a higher current. I read Bennett as implying that while the stronger charge delivered by Subud is instantly effective, it is too strong for some people. This is a development of the critique of Subud which had appeared in that book's 1962 edition but was removed from the 1974 edition, together with some of the praise.

In the 1962 original, he wrote that he went into the Subud Congress not understanding how Subud worked, and aware that it had "an action that was illogical, effects that could be terrifying, bewildering or imperceptible. And yet it had an appeal that meets the needs of our modern world."[120] What he says about "bewildering" effects supports my interpretation of his comparison of Subud and T.M. In *Christian Mysticism and Subud*, he offered the related idea that the necessary transformation not only does not require any mystical experience (doubtless including the *latihan*), but can be impeded by these and "any kind of eccentric satisfaction or even the minor consolations of religion."[121]

In 1962, however, Bennett had favourably contrasted the "sturdy independence" of the Subud followers with the "passive conformism" of those in the Gurdjieff groups.[122] This led him to ask whether Subud might not be providing "just the shock required to save Gurdjieff's work from becoming its opposite?"[123] The inherent implausibility of a position that to be true to Gurdjieff one had to follow Subud, must have been apparent to Bennett. Further, he saw inadequacies in those guiding Subud.[124]

---

[119] Bennett (1999) 29-30.
[120] Bennett (1962) 367.
[121] Bennett (1961b) 69.
[122] Bennett (1962) 367.
[123] Bennett (1962) 367.
[124] Bennett (1962) 367.

The root problem, as he saw it, was that although people were changing, they remained isolated from each other. They were less dependent on others, but no more related. The more they sensed a divine power, the less they valued any human influence in their lives.[125] On the one hand, Subuh would not be a leader, but on the other hand, a leader was needed most particularly because those aroused by Subud rejected external authority.[126] Bennett now introduces the theme which briefly reunites the 1962 and 1974 narratives, and which while not a critique of Subud shows that he had lost his belief in the uniqueness of Subud:

> The true nature of harmony is to be neither active nor passive, but in a third state which embraces such diverse qualities as Love, Freedom and Order, Reconciliation and Truth. This third state is so unfamiliar to our modern thought that our languages lack a word for it. I recognized it in Pak Subuh's references to the Roh Ilofi, or the Spirit of Reconciliation. I had known it as the Tao of the Chinese, as Sattva of the Hindus, as the Harmony of the Greeks, as the Holy Spirit of God of the Old and New Testaments, and as the Zat Ullah, the Divine Essence of Islam. All my life I had sought for this Third State. The need to understand and experience it lay at the very root of Gurdjieff's teaching, and all his exercises were directed towards its attainment.[127]

This led Bennett to reflections on "Individuality" as "a single undivided will that is independent of time and space."[128] He had known individuality, he says, in the restaurant car as he travelled to Paris: the fifteenth vision (section 8.1). This once more demonstrates that these

---

[125] Bennett (1962) 367-68. The idea that *latihan* conducts a "divine power" contradicts Subuh's advice to Christian monks that the power was a natural one. Perhaps Subuh was once more telling his hearers what would please them: Bennett (1962) 341.
[126] I am summarising the effect of Bennett (1962) 366-68.
[127] Bennett (1962) 368; Bennett (1997) 279.
[128] Bennett (1962) 369; Bennett (1997) 280.

visions not only had a great significance for him, but weave a cohesive narrative which often sourced his theory. He now knew that his Individuality possessed "its own vessel," and that vessel would "house," so to speak, his unity with Elizabeth, Polly, and perhaps others.[129] Subud, he said, shows that our isolation is not due to an "inherent atomism" as humans, but to "the closing of the doors of perception."[130] Bennett always remained grateful to Subud and to Subuh: on January 4, 1960, when "convulsed" by "revolt," and even wishing to close and sell Coombe Springs and to destroy his writings, Subuh had shown him the "wounded animal" inside himself.[131] On one occasion, Subuh told him that he would write a book which would "make people understand in a new way about the worship of the One Almighty God," and advised him to return to the piano as a help in learning "not to think so much."[132] Yet, even when praising Subud as a means of directly experiencing faith, Bennett hesitates: "I would not dare to say that Subud is the keystone of the great work of spiritual regeneration. It may be that other and more wonderful manifestations are being prepared."[133]

When he was revising *Witness* he was able to formulate the nub of another aspect of the problem: his excessive expectations of Subud. Bennett does not put it so concisely, but I submit that this is a fair summary: "All my geese are the Archangel Gabriel," he told Elizabeth "in a moment of disillusion."[134] It was not just the feathery appearance. Gabriel was the angel of the Annunciation of the birth of the Messiah and of the conception of John the Baptist, and the voices of geese were celebrated as prophetic. Bennett possibly meant that he was forever imagining he was receiving good tidings of great joy. In 1974, he suggested that this was his chief feature: in Gurdjieff's terms, the central axis around which

---

[129] Bennett (1962) 369; Bennett (1997) 280.
[130] Bennett (1962) 369-370; Bennett (1997) 280.
[131] Bennett (1962) 370-371; Bennett (1997) 280-81.
[132] Bennett (1962) 371; absent from Bennett (1997) 281.
[133] Bennett (1962) 375.
[134] Bennett (1997) 283.

a person's ideas of himself (called "false personality"), faults and blindness, rotate.[135] As a prelude to his fullest critique of Subud, he stated:

> As I look back to 1961, I see how I persisted in believing that Pak Subuh was "the Archangel Gabriel," long after I should have understood that Subud was far more limited in its action than he had led us to believe. I could not help seeing that I myself was losing my grip. Coombe Springs was in disorder. I had abdicated its direction.[136]

Then follows a critical comparison of the effects of the Subud and Gurdjieff method:

> By the autumn of 1960, the realization came to me that I had ceased to work on myself and had relied upon the *latihan* to do what I should be doing by my own effort. Without telling anyone, I resumed the discipline and the exercises I had learned from Gurdjieff and almost at once found that my state changed for the better. Some of my old friends and pupils came to me and told me that they felt that something was wrong and described symptoms similar to my own. I suggested that we should quietly resume our early morning exercises and especially set ourselves "will tasks" that would require effort and sacrifice.[137]

This incidentally illuminates the nature and purpose of Gurdjieff's contemplative exercises. Bennett concluded that the *latihan* was "excellent as a means of opening the heart, [but] did nothing for the will." For the requisite balance, they needed to return to Gurdjieff's work. The numbers of those doing so quickly increased, and when the Subud group

---

[135] Ouspensky (1949) 226.
[136] Bennett (1997) 283.
[137] Bennett (1997) 283-84.

in London learnt of this "many were terribly shocked and upset."[138] Subuh was notified and someone, it is not clear who, concluded that Bennett had fallen under "Satanic influences." Subuh was persuaded that Bennett was trying to assume his authority, and Bennett was once more ostracised "from old friends."[139] He obliquely refers to a dispute after the Subud Congress, but provides no details.[140] Bright-Paul published a letter of 18 December 1964 from Bennett to Subuh, together with Subuh's reply of January 13, 1965. I set out only portions of each. Bennett writes:

> Will Bapak kindly give me a decision about my position as a Subud helper? Elizabeth joins me in asking this question.... Bapak made me a helper-opener.... I have heard—thought not directly from Bapak—that Bapak does not agree with the way the work is now going at Coombe.... I would, therefore, like to explain what has happened. After nearly five years' experience of Subud during which time I was relying exclusively on the *latihan* for my spiritual development ... I discovered that things were not going rightly with me. I was growing weak and lazy and not fulfilling my duties in life properly. I tested about this and received a very clear indication that I should return to the spiritual disciplines that I had ... learned mainly from Gurdjieff. When I began once again to practise these disciplines my state improved and after a few months I was convinced that this was the right thing for me.[141]

"Testing" is a Subud technique of posing a question and receiving an answer. Bennett then goes on to tell Subuh that others, too, benefitted

---

[138] Bennett (1997) 284.
[139] Bennett (1997) 284.
[140] Bennett (1997) 287.
[141] Bright-Paul (2005) 282. The date of Bennett's letter appears in Subuh's at 284.

from returning to the Gurdjieff exercises. Bennett then adds this detail which he omits from *Witness*:

> [I]n the last year and a half, I have come into contact with a Source of the ancient Sufi Tradition, which has strengthened my conviction that the work requires something more than the practice of the *latihan* alone, and this is the chief reason that I am writing to Bapak now.[142]

Bennett then offered on his own behalf and on that of Elizabeth to resign as a Subud helper-opener if he could not continue as he now was. It seems that Idries Shah, the "source" Bennett referred to, appeared when he could function as a dissolvent to prise Bennett free from his devotion to Subud. This seems to be how Bright-Paul understood the effect of Shah's appearance. Bright-Paul was, and at the time of writing still is, devoted to Subud, but he is quite critical of the handing over of Coombe Springs to Shah when it "had already been given to Subud," as he put it.[143] Subuh, of course, accepted the resignation of the Bennetts on the basis that all they needed was the *latihan* and if they did not find this to be so, then there was something wrong with their practice.[144]

A more fundamental critique was that the experiences of many in Subud were "largely self-deception and wishful thinking," such as he had seen with the "Oxford Group" which later became "Moral Rearmament."[145] To his credit, Bennett realized that he rejected the testimony of others that they had received "messages and guidance direct from God" yet he himself "could communicate with a source of wisdom that was within myself but beyond my consciousness."[146] The conclusion he came to was:

> Whenever I deliberately "tested," that is put myself quite

---

[142] Bright-Paul (2005) 283.
[143] Bright-Paul (2005) 286-87.
[144] Bright-Paul (2005) 283-84.
[145] Bennett (1997) 284. He provides no details of his knowledge of that movement.
[146] Bennett (1997) 284. I have reordered Bennett's words, but not unfairly.

passively into the *latihan* and asked specific questions, I got ambiguous answers or no answer at all. But, if I allowed the slightest wish for a particular answer to colour my asking that answer came, and did so, often, in a subtle and indirect way that made self-deception very easy. On the other hand, if I did not ask at all but prayed for guidance, the indication of what I should be doing came unexpectedly and unpredictably without the *latihan* and especially when I was not thinking about it.[147]

Having seen the limitations of the *latihan*, his time with Subud was done. Later, he admitted, he had "failed to find" a "spiritual reality" in Subud.[148] But he formulated three criteria for discerning when to accept or reject suggestions from this "inner voice":

1. They must not be contrary to common sense.
2. They must be surprising or at least unexpected.
3. They must be unprompted and unsolicited except in very general terms of "asking for help."[149]

Bennett did not use the *latihan* in any open way at Sherborne, but I have been informed by students who had been opened before Sherborne that he would meet them privately at another location for *latihan*. However, this was very rare, and they do not recall that he ever mentioned either Subud or Subuh at Sherborne.

9.9 BENNETT, SUBUD, AND GURDJIEFF

At some point in the spring of 1958, Henriette Lannes had Dr. Courtenay-Mayers read to the London Gurdjieff Society, which was affiliated with

---

[147] Bennett (1997) 284.
[148] Bennett (1997) 287.
[149] Bennett (1997) 284-85.

de Salzmann, a paper she (Lannes) had written titled "About *Concerning Subud*." It "constituted a finely tuned metaphysical counter-thrust against that newly published book; and implicitly, against its author J.G. Bennett."[150] There is a curious factor here: the doctor had come to the Gurdjieff work through Bennett, and had even lived at Coombe Springs. He had been an integral part of the events around the King's College Vision: it was he who had suffered acute depression until Bennett was able to share the insight from his revelation (section 6.3). Why would Lannes have asked him, of all people, to read this? It is little wonder that Moore describes him as being "melancholy-faced" and a "troubled reader."[151] Moore states that he had studied the relationship between Bennett and Lannes, "episode by episode" over twenty years, and it was: "inescapably antithetical." He continues:

> Like Madame Lannes, Bennett was a big stick. He possessed charisma, energy, flair, and exceptional abilities.... These great gifts Bennett dedicated (and this was the sheer pity of it) to inconsistent messianic and millenarian fancies. If any novelty item sufficiently glittered with spiritual chic, Bennett would infallibly swoop and jackdaw away with it.... his powerful but ungovernable imagination moved into overdrive. Was the advent of Subud better foreshadowed by the Arland-Rouland (sic) comet or by the Third Secret of Fatima? Was Pak Subuh himself conceivably the 'Avatar of Synthesis' predicted by Alice Bailey? Or was he—here Bennett could scarcely breathe his hope—a token of *Parousia* the Second Coming of Christ ... very difficult to say.[152]

Moore's prose is so affected it is often difficult to be sure of what he means. It would be easy to dismiss his glib comments about Bennett as

---

[150] Moore (2005) 43-44. At my request, the Gurdjieff Society kindly searched for but was unable to locate a copy of Lannes' paper.
[151] Moore (2005) 44-45.
[152] Moore (2005) 44, also 53-54.

"jackdaw," but he does have a point: there were significant differences between the practices of Subud and Gurdjieff, and there was something fanciful and messianic about Bennett which suggested wish-fulfilment.[153] Moore also relays the sense that within the Society it was considered that Bennett had descended "from the sacred to the profane."[154] In the end, Bennett returned to Gurdjieff's methods, but with a new philosophical approach influence by Subud, and a deeper appreciation of Gurdjieff's contemplative exercises.

However, there is more to the said "divagations" than appears on first glance. Bennett was not the first "esteemed" pupil of Gurdjieff who had gone seeking other teachers after 1949, and neither was he to be the last: the final irony is that de Salzmann and Tracol themselves "divagated" in precisely the direction Bennett had—of introducing into the Gurdjieff work an element that might be described as "passive," or even as Pauline de Dampierre said, "feminine."[155] Bennett was initiated into Subud, and some who had been with Ouspensky and Gurdjieff had begun to investigate Subud.[156] Even Madame Ouspensky had wondered about Subuh, and was "waiting" for a new teacher.[157] Moore says of the 1960s, when one of his friends from the London Gurdjieff Society was "losing faith in the Gurdjieff Work," and went to Saanen to see Krishnamurti (1895-1986):

> This painless and elegant Krishnamurti option was in fact attracting a clutch of people who recoiled from Bray's physicality.... Where would these divagations end? Was some serious schism or re-alignment pending? Kenneth Walker was disconcertingly throwing bouquets in the direction of the

---

[153] Moore (2005) 45-46.
[154] Moore (2005) 46. One of the defects of Moore's overwriting is that one must wonder whether he is being accurate or exaggerating for the sake of effect.
[155] Pauline de Dampierre had been a pupil of Gurdjieff and was one of the leaders of the Paris Institut in the 1980s and 1990s. She said to a third party: "Mme de Salzmann introduced a feminine element into the Work." (personal communication). She died in 2003: https://www.gurdjieff.org/childe1.htm accessed March 27, 2022.
[156] Bennett (1962) 328; (1997) 260-61.
[157] Bennett (1962) 332; (1997) 262.

Maharishi Mahesh Yogi; Lizelle Reymond—a new director of Comonaim and future group leader in Switzerland—openly professed her indebtedness to the Samkhya teacher Sri Anirvan; and Bennett was yet again at oriental sixes and sevens. In all this, Madame Lannes stood like a rock for Gurdjieff and Gurdjieff alone, but since Madame de Salzmann herself sat in the front row at Saanen, my teacher was subtly outflanked.[158]

Bray was a location for Sunday work which was and is maintained by the Society. It seems that very many of those who had been with Gurdjieff, even his closest disciples, including de Salzmann, felt a need to supplement his teaching, and to replace his presence by sitting at the feet of a "Master." Moore names others, also eminent in Gurdjieff-Ouspensky circles who did likewise, and notes that Bennett by now was interested in "Idries Shah with his pseudo-Sufism."[159] After the death of Lannes in 1980, de Salzmann tempered Gurdjieff's insistence upon the need to struggle:

> Fronting the new doctrine was an oligarchy-led modulation of idiom from active to passive voice: the pupil no longer 'remembered himself' but 'was remembered'; no longer 'awoke' but 'was awoken'. Pupils did not, need not, could not, work: they were 'worked upon' (even while they literally slept!).[160]

Despite her criticism of Bennett for his unfaithfulness to Gurdjieff, de Salzmann introduced a "New Work" which owed a good deal to Krishnamurti, Roshi Kobori, Dürckheim, and Zen in general.[161] This suggests that perhaps Bennett was simply ahead of the race in seeking

---

[158] Moore (2005) 88.
[159] Moore (2005) 97.
[160] Moore (1994) 12.
[161] The evidence is presented in Azize (2020) 220-25.

to supplement Gurdjieff's teaching. That so many of Gurdjieff's personal pupils should feel this need shows how hard it is to realise inner development, and also, perhaps, how strongly quick results are desired. Elizabeth Bennett states that when he first met Rofé, Bennett had been "wholly satisfied" with Gurdjieff's system.[162] However, one can be fully satisfied with a system yet feel that something is missing in oneself. Her memoires end at that point. Her thoughts would have been valuable for, as we have seen, she also became a helper-opener in Subud, and likewise tendered her resignation in December 1964. Although her husband gained a great deal from his time with Subud, he puts it curiously when he says that he eventually had to "extricate" himself from it, and return to Gurdjieff's methods[163] Bennett concluded that, even as a student of Subud, he had relied upon his prior work with Gurdjieff: without that background, he may not have experienced Subud the way he did.[164] I was told by someone who had been with Subuh and Shushud, and also with Pierre Elliot (Bennett's nephew through Winifred Bennett née Elliot, and a pupil with Gurdjieff in Paris), that Subuh himself said that he had found Bennett's pupils well prepared for Subud. But the problem for him was that he had had so little acquaintance with Westerners that he had not realised these people were the exception rather than the rule in the West. Subsequently, he said, he found those who came to him less ripe for the *latihan*. This suggests that perhaps neither Bennett nor Subuh understood each other as fully as they thought they had.

---

[162] Elizabeth Bennett (2015) 143.
[163] Bennett (1997) 287.
[164] Bennett (1962) 335.

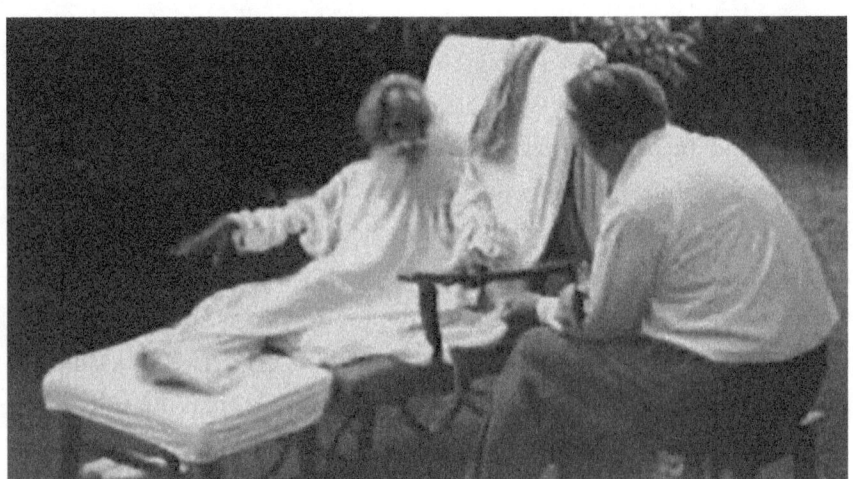
Bennett visiting the Shivapuri Baba.

CHAPTER 10

BENNETT'S SEARCH IN THE 1960s

10.1 THE SHIVAPURI BABA

The sexagenarian Bennett was now establishing a family, quite a novel experience for one who had been exclusively eccentric. Without wishing to indulge in sentimentality, his sons George and Ben Bennett have provided me with information about his virtues as a father. For example, Ben recalls that in spring 1957, when they spent four months in a two room cottage in Wales:

> He cooked us really delicious scrambled eggs for breakfast, and cut the toast into strips setting them in the egg to look like the funnels of a ship, to our delight. I also recall him holding me in his arms outside at night, to see the Arland-Roland comet.[1]

Elizabeth Bennett, writing the foreword to the original edition of *The Masters of Wisdom*, expressed regret at not having recorded the "fantastic fairy stories" he spun for his children, in which a hedgehog, prince, or magic starfish might pass between worlds and dimensions, thus "making a picture of the possibilities open to man."[2]

As young children arrived, the type of travel he had undertaken for Subud would cause ongoing difficulties for his family. Bennett does not

---

[1] Email from Ben Bennett dated 29 March 2020.
[2] Bennett (1977a) 5.

mention this as a reason for leaving Subud, but then neither does he mention the fact that he personally knew at least twenty people who suicided. He wrote that he did not believe that they could all have been psychopaths, and that when he raised this with Icksan Ahmad, one of Subuh's helpers, he had been assured that this could not happen to anyone who practised the *latihan*. Yet, Bennett notes, it did happen, and it happened many times: "I do not say that these people were not suicidal before they came to Subud, but the point is that the *latihan* could not help them to bear life."[3]

Then, one day in January 1961, at Coombe Springs, when Bennett and his group were working on the Gurdjieff morning exercise to which they had returned, he heard the Shivapuri Baba telling him to come soon or it would be too late.[4] Bennett had first learnt of the Baba through Professor Ratnasuriya, a Sanskrit expert who was then a member of Ouspensky's groups, and was to meet Gurdjieff in 1949.[5] In 1955, Bennett had been visited by Hugh Ripman, a fellow-pupil of Ouspensky, who had also briefly met Gurdjieff. An enthusiastic Ripman shared with Bennett his diary notes of his meeting with the Baba that year.[6] Ripman's memories are quite consistent with Bennett's.

Concerning Bennett's apparently telepathic contact with the Shivapuri Baba, there are two unanswered questions: how can Bennett have known who was speaking to him, since he had only barely heard of the Baba and presumably had never heard his voice? And, how did Baba make the contact? It is not as if the Baba was ever an international celebrity. Even today, the majority of references to him are in connection with Bennett's two books on him, and a search of a university library database yielded only six hits, none of which were substantial. We are left to speculate that the Baba was able to tell, by some sort of intuition, that Bennett existed, should come to see him, and could be contacted by

---

[3] Buddhist (1964) 22.
[4] Bennett (1997) 285.
[5] Bennett and Manandhar (1965) 31-33.
[6] Bennett and Manandhar (1965) 33-35 and 137. Ripman's account circulates as an undated typescript: Ripman (undated and unpublished).

this means. There is more than something of the marvellous about the incident as reported, but as with Ouspensky knowing that his second wife had experienced something remarkable when she had almost died (section 4.10), Bennett simply mentions it, without comment.

In 1961 and again in 1962, Bennett visited the Baba in Nepal, where he was given the task of writing about him. Bennett considered this useful as renewing his acquaintance with Indian spirituality, although the sage himself was "universal ... beyond the distinctions of teachings and religions."[7] Born in 1826, he had followed his grandfather, a hermit, into the forest, to become a *sannyasin*, i.e. one who has abandoned the world to seek *Jiwaanmukti* or "God-Realization."[8] He took the name Govindananda Bharati and travelled the world, meeting Queen Victoria,[9] Theodore Roosevelt, and many others.[10] He himself related that he met George Bernard Shaw, who chided him: "You Indian saints are the most useless of men; you have no respect of time." To which, he said, he replied: "It is you who are slaves of time. I live in Eternity."[11] He eventually returned to India, and finally retired to Nepal, where he died in 1963.[12] I should add that I have looked for corroboration of these stories, as has Michael Benham, but neither of us has been unable to locate a single piece of evidence other than the Baba's own accounts. Bennett accepted the veracity of his travels and encounters, but I would prefer to reserve judgment.

The message which the Baba wanted Bennett to make known, however, was of quite another order, and needed no colourful autobiography to commend it: briefly, the teaching was how to work towards the "sole purpose of this human life [which] is nothing but the realization of God":[13]

---

[7] Bennett (1997) 285.
[8] Bennett and Manandhar (1965) 11, 15-17.
[9] Although it is believed that pertinent records were deliberately destroyed: Bennett and Manandhar (1965) 25.
[10] Bennett and Manandhar (1965) 17-27.
[11] Bennett and Manandhar (1965) 26.
[12] Bennett and Manandhar (1965) 36.
[13] Bennett and Manandhar (1965) 112, 116 and 86.

> Let the thought of God be alone in your mind, destroy every other thought. You will see God before you and all your problems are solved. This is the first business. Now, unless you live a disciplined life, this meditation is not possible. There is this body.... How much to eat, how much to sleep, what to see, what to hear? All this should be controlled and commanded. This is one duty. Another duty is towards home, society, nation, etc. Find out what we have to do. A third duty concerns material needs. Without material wealth, we cannot do these things. For that we have a professional duty. These are the duties one has got to do. They should be found out and practised properly, without any failure, without commission or omission. Then life becomes steady. In the steady life, meditation is very easy.[14]

This message is repeated in many ways, with certain variations and additions, in the book Bennett produced with the help and notes of the Baba's long time pupil, Manandhar, and in the more recently published lectures which Bennett delivered in 1962.[15]

The Baba spoke of "three primary divisions of Right Living": "duty," its guiding principle being intelligence, "morality" needing discrimination, and "worship" with "spiritual longing."[16] In the Baba's teaching, "spiritual longing" reaches its apogee in "thought of God" or meditation, which, he said, needs preparation and a strong mind,[17] so that it can eventually become an element in ordinary life.[18] When specifically asked about problems which had arisen while practising Subud, Baba stated that they resulted from a lack of any practice of "moral discipline."[19] Bennett agreed: "although "submission" in the Subud sense is needed, it

---

[14] Bennett and Manandhar (1965) 46.
[15] Bennett (2014) and Bennett and Manandhar (1965).
[16] Bennett and Manandhar (1965) 86.
[17] Bennett and Manandhar (1965) 50.
[18] Ripman (1999) 127 and 139.
[19] Bennett and Manandhar (1965) 51.

will not work without self-discipline."²⁰ Bennett apparently lacked confidence in himself to the extent that even when he had realised something for himself, he needed the authority of the Baba in order to depart from Subuh's indications. As mentioned above, the emergence of Idries Shah also played a role in weening himself from Subud.

Further, the Baba gave him to understand that his destiny might lie in teaching the transformation of being which Gurdjieff had said was possible for him. As Bennett put it, what had been an "audacious quest" for immortality became more than a distant vision.²¹ At the very end of *Long Pilgrimage*, Bennett quotes the Baba as having said:

> The sum and substance of my teaching is this: live the minimum life possible, subjecting body and mind to strict discipline. Again, how a very hungry man longs for meat, how a man suffering from intense cold longs for heat, so long for God, meditate on Him continuously.... this is for the whole world. It is by this that I saw the Truth, and I am happy. Yes.²²

The Baba's teaching was universalist.²³ He used the question "Who am I?" as an instrument for enlightenment,²⁴ but the crux of the teaching was meditation. He stated that there are three stages in meditation: *dharana* (steadiness), *dhyan* (meditation) and *samadhi* (diffuse contemplation).²⁵ The last term will have been Bennett's translation, based on a hint given by a monk at St Wandrille.²⁶ Baba recommended having a separate clean and tidy room for meditation, with pictures of "realized souls ... for the sake of inspiration," where one could burn incense or sacrificial fires "for they purify both air and mind."²⁷ Like Gurdjieff, he

---

²⁰ Bennett (1997) 285.
²¹ Bennett (1997) 285-286.
²² Bennett and Manandhar (1965) 176.
²³ Bennett and Manandhar (1965) 112.
²⁴ Bennett and Manandhar (1965) 150.
²⁵ Bennett and Manandhar (1965) 110.
²⁶ Bennett (1997) 281.
²⁷ Bennett and Manandhar (1965) 110.

stated that the morning was the best time for meditation, after "answering the call of nature and taking a bath," and, when seated, adopting an erect posture. However, he recommended *pranayama* or breath control twice or thrice but not more than ten times a day,[28] whereas Gurdjieff only recommended becoming aware of the breath, not trying to control it.[29] Other details of the meditation practice were culturally Hindu, e.g. visualising God as Vasudeva and offering him flowers and incense.[30]

The Baba also made some comments about present day life being difficult, and destined to become more so. He even suggested that about two-thirds of the population of the world would be destroyed in 1972.[31] I have seen a vague allusion to this prophecy by Bennett, who always retained traces of the apocalyptic imagination which had impelled some of his pupils to move to South Africa. However, the Baba also said to him that the important thing was to study the conditions of life in England, to get on with what he was doing, and to help his pupils understand their duties in the contemporary world.[32]

In the 1962 lectures, Bennett related the Baba's message to his own abiding concern for values. A moral quality such as fearlessness or dignity necessarily expresses a value: and a quality as such cannot be neutral. Therefore, Bennett said, our higher nature is in some ways a system of values. In terms reminiscent of the Baba's teaching, he added that: "Mind should be so formed that it will contain a certain stable system of values by which one lives."[33] To a significant extent, *The Dramatic Universe* and the work of Bennett's later life, especially the residential courses at Sherborne, can be seen as an attempt to actualise a way of life based on stable values, and so to form the students' minds. When he refers to his own "duties" he means those which he had neglected at Coombe Springs.[34] The Baba impressed upon Bennett that we can only

---

[28] Bennett and Manandhar (1965) 110.
[29] Azize (2020) 281.
[30] Bennett and Manandhar (1965) 112-13.
[31] Email communication from Anthony Blake, January 25, 2021.
[32] Bennett (2014) 87 and 90. Bennett and Manandhar (1965) 54-55.
[33] Bennett (2014) 49.
[34] Bennett (1997) 283.

know what is immediately before us: our duty, the right action, and that we must put everything else aside. Because we can only see one step at a time, faith is needed.[35]

Leaving Nepal, Bennett returned to England via Turkey. When he revisited Hagia Sophia, where he had been so moved in 1919:

> I saw how my confidence had been shattered by successive blows. One after another of my props had been removed and I was once again face to face with my secret world. My repeated mistakes and misjudgements rose before my inner vision and I could see the wretched combination of weakness and arrogance, false humility and inward stubbornness that had led me from one disaster to another. But I could also see a sure guiding hand. Each disaster had been the death of part of myself, but, in every case, it had been followed by resurrection. Outwardly my life had been a recurrence of promises unfulfilled; inwardly it had been a step-by-step liberation from a false belief in the outer and a growing confidence in the inner. The Shivapuri Baba had tipped the balance in my favour.[36]

When Bennett had asked about Catholicism, the Baba had assured him that his growing sense that he should become a Catholic was right: "I would find ... God-realization through Christ."[37] Bennett mentions in this respect his appreciation of periods spent at the monastery of St Wandrille, but not for some reason, his fourteenth vision of Jesus in Jerusalem, or the eighteenth of Christ Crucified. But those visits were significant, not least because they began when he was opening some of the monks into the *latihan*, but continued after the separation from Subud. I cannot see that Bennett was accepted into Catholicism

---

[35] Bennett (2014) 76.
[36] Bennett (1997) 286.
[37] Bennett (1997) 286.

"evidently feeling that he had been tricked into practising Sufism against his wishes," (meaning by Subuh) as Sedgwick muses, for his reception was based more upon his experiences at the monastery, and the confirmatory advice of the Shivapuri Baba.[38]

I suggest that the Baba possessed another magnetic quality for Bennett: by focussing on a few simple lessons for use in everyday life, he provided a practical and accessible template for the student. Gurdjieff brought many ideas and techniques, but from his unsystematic way of teaching no practical and realisable paradigm emerged, to be impressed upon his students. Bennett eventually would learn how to do this at Sherborne. Therefore, in his applied study of the Baba's methods, he was also developing Gurdjieff's heritage, in continuity with Gurdjieff's purposes and ideas.

10.2 THE TWENTY-SECOND VISION: CHRIST IN THE SACRAMENT

In the summer of 1961,[39] Bennett stayed at St Wandrille, praying for guidance, when:

> One day I was at High Mass, sitting as a guest of the Monastery behind the choir, but in front of the rail at which communion was distributed to the laity. This means that the celebrant had to pass me as he brought the Sacrament. My thoughts were wandering, when I felt a shiver pass through my body. I became completely aware that Christ was coming towards me in the sacrament. I could feel Him go past and felt the deepest reverence and pure joy. As I knelt, I understood beyond doubt that God could be and was present in the host. I saw in a flash how the doctrine of the Real Presence is free from the anthropomorphism that so distressed me in most

---

[38] Sedgwick (2016) 201. Sedgwick is, I think, correct to see limitations in Bennett's acquaintance with the literature of the Sufis, although the evidence of *Values* shows that it was not as poor as Sedgwick surmised.
[39] Email communication from Ben Bennett, March 29, 2022.

Christian theology. If God is pure Will, then He can manifest in and through any vehicle. I saw how the second Person of the Trinity must be manifested and, indeed, is a person by reason of manifestation. All these and many other understandings poured into my mind, while I felt at the same time joy and gratitude that this should be shown to me. Above all, I was aware of the Love of God as beyond all the limitations of existence—of "name and form"—in terms of which we think. I was sure that this omnipresent love was able to reach me as the small being kneeling unnoticed in the aisle of the chapel.[40]

In a lecture delivered in 1962, Bennett adds the detail that when "Christ in the flesh ... was passing me ... I heard a voice inside me saying as clearly as possible: "You see I am present"."[41] Bennett seems to have understood this vision as, in Gurdjieff's terms, higher intellectual centre becoming active, so as to directly grasp the reality before him, while the lower centres were sufficiently balanced and active to be able to accurately remember the impression. Gurdjieff had said that:

> In most cases where accidental contact with the higher thinking centre takes place a man becomes unconscious. The mind refuses to take in the flood of thoughts, emotions, images, and ideas which suddenly burst into it.... The memory retains only the first moment when the flood rushed in on the mind and the last moment when the flood was receding and consciousness returned.... Only very seldom does it happen that a mind which has been better prepared succeeds in grasping and remembering something of what was felt and understood at the moment of ecstasy. But even in these cases the thinking, the moving, and the emotional centres remember and transmit everything in their own way, translate absolutely new and

[40] Bennett (1997) 286.
[41] Bennett (1964) 27.

never previously experienced sensations into the language of usual everyday sensations, transmit in worldly three-dimensional forms things which pass completely beyond the limits of worldly measurements; in this way, of course, they entirely distort every trace of what remains in the memory of these unusual experiences. Our ordinary centres, in transmitting the impressions of the higher centres, may be compared to a blind man speaking of colours, or to a deaf man speaking of music. In order to obtain a correct and permanent connection between the lower and the higher centres, it is necessary to regulate and quicken the work of the lower centres.[42]

Bennett then prepared himself for reception into the Catholic Church, and a year later his wife and children followed suit. At some time, Elizabeth also had a "personal revelation" of the Real Presence of Christ in the Eucharist, which reconciled her to some aspects of Catholicism which she did not understand. Bennett himself believed in the validity of the Catholic sacraments and its claim to the Apostolic Succession, but he also saw that there was much "human speculation and even human fantasy" in the teachings of the Church.[43] At least after the fourteenth vision, Bennett had formed a new view of some of the events recounted in the Gospels, notwithstanding that he had to depart from the Gospel text. Arguably, his fresh perspective on the Incarnation was both consistent with and also transcended previous Catholic understanding. He believed the Church to be equally astray in its modernist, conservative, and centrist currents. In short: "The Catholic Church is the custodian of a mystery that it does not understand, but the sacraments and their operation are no less real for that."[44] This is reminiscent of Gurdjieff's asserting that: "The Christian church is—a school concerning which people have forgotten that it is a school."[45]

[42] Ouspensky (1949) 195.
[43] Bennett (1997) 286-87.
[44] Bennett (1997) 287.
[45] Ouspensky (1949) 302.

Bennett recalls that the combined effect of his visit to the Baba and his experiences at the monastery had lifted his depression and given him hope that he might "find the spiritual reality that I had failed to find in Subud."[46] He had thought that he was at the end of his search when, through Subud, he was "reborn with a real capacity for compassion and understanding of others."[47] But as he articulated it now, this reborn child had to mature. Inspired with confidence, he organised a seminar at Coombe Springs for the summer of 1962, to adumbrate his personal understanding of Gurdjieff's psychological teachings.[48] The lectures and the questions and answers which followed them were to be revised and published as *A Spiritual Psychology*.

10.3 THE BOHM-BENNETT CORRESPONDENCE

The chief significance of this correspondence for my study is, paradoxically, the fact that Bennett does not mention it in *Witness*. This signal fact shows that *Witness* was not an average autobiography, and that its contents, especially touching post-Subud events, were directed to his chief aim: bearing witness to death and resurrection, that they were possible during this life, that we had no need to fear either life or death, and that all could be redeemed through the mystic search for union with God (in so far as such union is possible).

The only source for this correspondence is Anthony Blake's book *The Bohm-Bennett Correspondence, 1962-1964*, which he has made available on the internet. At the time, Bohm was Professor in Theoretical Physics at Birbeck College, London. One of his research students was Henri Bortoft, a pupil of Bennett. Anthony Blake had studied under Bohm when the latter had been at Bristol University. Bortoft and Blake introduced Bohm and Bennett to each other.[49] The published correspondence begins with a letter from Bohm to Bennett, dated February 3, 1962, setting out ideas

[46] Bennett (1997) 287.
[47] Bennett (1997) 287.
[48] Bennett (1997) 287.
[49] Blake (2016) 5.

which he related to volume 1 of *The Dramatic Universe*.[50] The next letter, also from Bohm, is dated February 12, 1962 and refers to a recent conversation with Bennett.[51] There then follow six letters from Bennett, and four in the reverse direction. The last letter is that from Bohm, dated March 31, 1964. He expresses scepticism about "the role of Gurdjieff's observing consciousness." He doubts that any consciousness is able to "stand back" from "sensitivity," believing it just as likely that: "it fails to see certain hidden reciprocal relationships between them."[52] Bohm closes by expressing a happy expectation of discussing these ideas with Bennett, but there are no further letters. In his letter of March 28, 1964, Bohm having read Bennett's paper on "Energy and Scientific Creativity," states:

> I found it most interesting indeed, with certain similarities to my own point of view on the subject, and certain differences.... Firstly, creativity is certainly based on a kind of mental energy, which has some deep source, far beyond consciousness. I go along with your division of this energy into four main aspects:
>
> Creative Energy in its Totality: 1. Creativity as Such. 2. Consciousness (Judgement as to what is True and False). 3. Sensitivity (in the Form of the Specious Present). 4. Automatic Nervous Activity.[53]

It is intriguing that Bohm, like Bennett, postulates a creative energy higher than consciousness. I am not competent to pursue this area any further, but, I repeat, the fact that Bennett omitted any whisper of his friendship with Bohm and this correspondence is a remarkable reminder that *Witness* was written to testify to mystical realities through selectively telling the story of one John Godolphin Bennett.

[50] Blake (2016) 6.
[51] Blake (2016) 9.
[52] Blake (2016) 38.
[53] Blake (2016) 34.

10.4 THE TWENTY-THIRD VISION: WORK AS THE WILL TO REALITY

This revelation is recorded not in *Witness*, but in the epilogue to *A Spiritual Psychology*. It is dated January 1964, although the later editions incorrectly show "1974," an understandable error, since it seems remarkably broad in outlook for Bennett in his Subud years. In the epilogue, Bennett deprecates Kant's idea of Reality as the "Categorical Imperative from which life derives its meaning," as a weak way of conveying the proper sense of urgency.[54] He continues: "I was impelled to write this Epilogue by the impact of a vision or vivid dream that woke me from sleep a few nights ago."[55] In that vision, he was among ghosts who "wanted to turn into real people." He then found himself among another community of ghosts, but these did not know they were ghosts. He told them that they could go to the other place by aeroplane, but they insisted that one of the planes come and guarantee that it was possible. He explained that "once an aeroplane had gone over, it would never return." They considered this to be both "illogical and unreasonable," and lost interest in what he had to say. Bennett pitied them, and as he began to wake up, he also wondered why their ghost life was not good enough, and if it was not after all, necessary.[56] Then:

> I awakened completely and saw, in a flash, the infinite significance of Work. It is the imperative of all imperatives, the source from which all life takes its meaning, the way to Reality and even Reality itself. Work takes many forms; but all forms have one common character: the *Will to Reality*. Whether active or passive, whether in solitude or in society, work is always one and the same; it is the dedication of the will to the realization of Reality. This dedication carries with

---

[54] Bennett (1964) 249; (1999) 182.
[55] Bennett (1964) 249-50; (1999) 182.
[56] Bennett (1964) 250-251; (1999) 182-83.

> it the obligation to *share* understanding with others and to *serve* the Work in its universal significance.[57]

I have abbreviated it somewhat. At this point he fully awoke and saw that all forms of Work comprise the will to reality.

The story owes a good deal to C.S. Lewis's *The Great Divorce* (1945), which Bennett praised. While the conclusion owes everything to Gurdjieff, yet the tale is distinctive Bennett throughout. That Bennett felt compelled to make this the final word of his *A Spiritual Psychology* indicates how essential he felt it to be to his life's work. However, that work was to take an unexpected turn with the emergence of Idries Shah.

10.5 IDRIES SHAH

Idries Shah (1924-96) was something of a publishing phenomenon in the 1960s and 1970s, when high sales were reported for his books. Although confirmed figures are lacking, the many translations of his writings into foreign languages are at the very least consistent with significant success. His assertion that Sufism is a universalist and not a purely Islamic phenomenon has lost whatever currency it once had. There is a similarity with Subud which has likewise declined in influence, although not quite so much as Shah's school. Mark Sedgwick has considered Shah's career at some length;[58] while James Moore has contributed one article. But, in general, when Shah is mentioned in scholarly works, it is only tangentially, and the author either takes Shah's claims at face value or else curtly dismisses them. In a modern academic study of Sufism, Nile Green wrote about what he called "fusion Sufis" who sideline the Sufi tradition by abstracting it from its Muslim context, while drawing on selected aspects of that tradition.[59] He continued:

---

[57] Bennett (1964) 250-251; (1999) 183.
[58] In Sedgwick (2016).
[59] Green (2012) 224.

> The most fascinating early case study is Idries Shah ... who was raised in England after being born to a Scottish mother and an Indian father of Afghan descent. After publishing an occultist manual on *Oriental Magic* in 1956 and a book of travels to Mecca in which his persona was very much that of the sardonic imperial Briton, in the early 1960s Shah became the secretary to Gerald Gardner, the impresario of neo-pagan witchcraft. Then, as the hippy enthusiasm for Morocco and India shifted fusions towards eastern religions, Shah played on his family background to reinvent himself as the heir to an ancient lineage of Afghan aristocrats and Sufi masters that stretched into the ancient past of Persia. By "translating" digestible nuggets of doctrine from classical Sufi works into best-selling compendia, and attracting such avant-garde acolytes as the novelist Doris Lessing and the poet Robert Graves, Shah by the end of the 1960s acquired not only a wide following but also an institutional basis by way of his own publishing house and a charity he named the Institute for Cultural Research. While Shah was widely disparaged, he was, as a brilliant self-publicist, more responsible than anyone for the growth in Western awareness (if not always understanding) of Sufism.[60]

Green concluded that Shah exemplified the appropriation more than the continuation of the tradition.[61] I agree with the essence of Green's view, although, for reasons given in appendix 3, I would go further. To anticipate, I would suggest that the keys to understanding how Shah came to dominate Bennett are threefold:

1. Shah was a plausible pretender to esoteric knowledge, who would use deception when it suited his purposes, being careful to leave himself pretexts and rationalisations should the target person come to suspect

---

[60] Green (2012) 224-25.
[61] Green (2012) 226.

him. He was equally adept with flattery and attack, often defensive attack, using people's self-questioning to maintain his own position.

2. Because he belonged to no authentic Sufi tradition, he had to keep his (Western) sources secret, base his authority as a teacher and Sufi shaykh upon his family history, and then fashion an unfalsifiable and therefore unassailable doctrine: i.e. that no one else understood anything and did not even know how to learn. If everyone has to learn how to learn (and even to learn how to learn how to learn, *ad infinitum*), they have no standing to criticise him. Thus, his particular claim to authority dictated his teaching. Further, people need to be "deconditioned." Criticism was dismissed as evidence of a need for deconditioning.

3. He exploited Gurdjieff's myth by fitting himself into it at two points: as a Sayyid or descendent of Muhammad, and as a pretended representative of the Sarmoun(g) monastery.

So how did Shah come to figure in the Bennett story? In June 1962, Bennett received a letter from Reggie Hoare, who had been a colleague when studying with Ouspensky, Gurdjieff, and Subuh, but had left Subud in 1960 having been alienated by disputes after the Congress.[62] Hoare disclosed that he had made contact with Idries Shah who had come to England avowedly to teach, to those who were interested in Gurdjieff's ideas, what was needed to "complete their teaching."[63] Bennett claims that he was wary, but Elizabeth and he met Shah, who was almost but not quite an "English public school type." Initial impressions were unfavourable but during the evening they came to believe that he was "unusually gifted ... (and) had the indefinable something that marks the man who has worked seriously upon himself."[64] After a few months, Hoare persuaded Bennett to see him again, stating that he had "verified his credentials," apparently meaning by this the claim that Shah had been sent to the West by "an esoteric school in Afghanistan, probably the very one which

---

[62] Bennett (1997) 287. George Adie said that he had introduced Hoare to Gurdjieff. There is an eye-witness mention of him at Gurdjieff's table: Edwards (2009) 45 and 48.
[63] Bennett (1997) 288.
[64] Bennett (1997) 288.

Gurdjieff describes in the last chapter of *Meetings with Remarkable Men*."[65] According to Hoare, Shah had told him far more about the Enneagram than Ouspensky had ever disclosed.[66] Given Hoare's reputation for caution and his Intelligence Service background, Bennett took this seriously. At some point, Shah gave Bennett a document which on its face authorised Shah. This "Declaration of the People of the Tradition" was copyrighted by Octagon Press. It spoke of the "Path to Truth," and of the difficulties but also the possibility of transmission."[67]

Bennett was astonished to think that there was someone in England, "no charlatan or idle boaster" who was "entitled" to speak on behalf of the "Invisible Hierarchy," (as no one from the hierarchy appeared to speak in their own person, this was sheer hearsay). Shah would insist that Bennett travel to meet him, and then spent hours lecturing about *baraka* and other topics.[68] In Islam, *baraka* can be understood as a blessing, and especially in Sufism, as a blessing based on sanctity which transmits a power.[69] Bennett understood this to be the same as "Higher Emotional Energy" or "Hanbledzoin."[70] Significantly, he never states that Shah could actually transmit *baraka* as opposed to talking about it, and the sort of story he told about Gurdjieff's "loaning him" Hanbledzoin were never told about anyone else (section 7.2).

These meetings seem to have continued for two years, until in January 1965, when, as he was praying, he asked for a "clear indication" as to Shah's trustworthiness. The reply came "For that you must pray together." When Bennett said that they should pray together, Shah agreed, and Bennett was satisfied, only realizing later—he does not say when—that they had not in fact done so.[71] This may be an echo of Bennett's memory of Madame Ouspensky's statement that we cannot

---

[65] Bennett (1997) 288.
[66] Bennett (1997) 288. When Bennett asked him about the Enneagram, Shah would deflect his questions, speaking about the "octagon": Blake (2018) 123 n.46.
[67] Bennett (1997) 288-90.
[68] Bennett (1997) 290.
[69] Schimmel (1975) see the index under *baraka* but especially 82 and 234.
[70] Bennett (1997) 290.
[71] Bennett (1997) 290-91.

see a person who stands on a higher level than ourselves but something can be made known through prayer.[72] Mme Ouspensky's advice is found only in the 1962 edition. It is difficult not to think it might have been omitted from the later edition as too embarrassing to remember. The fact that he was satisfied with Shah's agreeing with the principle suggests to us, even if Bennett did not himself draw the conclusion, that at some level he wished to invest his trust in Shah. Bennett was quite taken by Shah's talk of working with the "Higher Source" to reach people in authority, "to help mankind survive the coming crisis."[73] Saying that he needed to reach more people, Shah wanted Bennett to gift him Coombe Springs, and was discontented even with the offer of placing it entirely at his service. "The time is short. The caravan is about to set out. Those who are not ready to join it will be left behind," Shah warned.[74]

Subuh had been content when Bennett made facilities available for the use of Subud. Now Bennett was asked to alienate the entire property. The more Bennett felt that he was attached to Coombe Springs and his hopes that the Gurdjieff work would continue there, led by his sons, the more he felt he had to hand it over. In June 1965, he persuaded the Council of the Institute to gift Coombe Springs to Shah, unconditionally. Tunbridge, a student at Coombe Springs, recalls Bennett telling them to read Shah's book *The Sufis*, and the declaration of "The Guardians of the Tradition," on the basis that: "he believed Shah to be directly linked to and authorized by the ancient source of wisdom from which Gurdjieff himself had gained his knowledge. Further, Mister B. implied that he would step aside to allow Shah to become leader of studies."[75] Shah came down, and produced a sense of urgency, speaking to the students of the significance of his mission.[76] Shah was offered half the proceeds of sale, but he insisted on "all or nothing."[77] Shah drove

---

[72] Bennett (1962) 337-38.
[73] Bennett (1997) 291.
[74] Bennett (1997) 291.
[75] Tunbridge (2015) 81.
[76] Bennett (1997) 291.
[77] Bennett (1997) 291-92.

the Bennetts with a whip: "his work would brook no delay." On January 13, 1966 they gave the last demonstration of Gurdjieff's movements in the Djamichunatra. Bennett is quite definite that he had moved out of Coombe Springs before Shah moved in. This is consistent with the absoluteness of Shah's demand.[78] With understatement, Bennett wrote that:

> The next few months were hard to bear. No sooner was Shah in possession, than he banned our people from visiting Coombe. He complained vehemently of any delays in vacating. He made me feel unwelcome, so I stopped going there.... His behaviour could be accounted for if it was adopted deliberately to make sure that all bonds with Coombe Springs were severed.... In 1966 we heard that Shah had decided to sell Coombe Springs ... to be developed by building 28 luxury houses.... The only wrench was to see the Djamichunatra destroyed. Some effort was made to save Rosemary Rutherford's beautiful stained glass windows, but this proved impossible and all went for scrap.[79]

Bennett rationalized this by saying that the new property Shah purchased, in Kent, was "undoubtedly more suitable for his purpose."[80] He provides no details of how he concluded this. Afterwards, Mme de Salzmann asked him what he had gained from his contact with Shah, to which he replied: "Freedom!"[81] I have not found any specification of this "freedom"; either what it was from or what it was for. But a clue to his meaning can be found in an undated transcript from a talk given to students at Sherborne in the 1970s. He must have been speaking of the tenth vision (section 5.5), when he said:

> Many real troubles came in my life in every way. I suddenly

---

[78] Bennett (1997) 292.
[79] Bennett (1997) 292-93.
[80] Bennett (1997) 293.
[81] Bennett (1997) 293.

found myself in total misunderstanding with Ouspensky and cut off from all contact with his work. I had no contact with Gurdjieff and my life was going badly. I was turned out of my job. I was struggling with how to make things come right and suddenly I saw that if all goes wrong then I am free from the whole lot.[82]

If this is a fair parallel, then alienating Coombe Springs to Shah was a case of "all goes wrong," and the loss was welcome because it freed Bennett from his obligations, perhaps his teaching function even more than the property. But Shah did not let the matter end there. Blake recalls:

When Bennett left Coombe Springs and went to live in the nearby town of Kingston, Shah staged long weekend parties and would sometimes send some of Bennett's previous students who had gone over to Shah with leftover food: an obvious symbolic act one might say, but also a challenge. The turning point was when Bennett said to such an offer: "no, thank you. I have enough of my own."[83]

When friends offered a seventieth birthday party and a gift subscription, he refused it in a gesture which he later realised had been "boorish and unkind."[84] When Bennett established his Institute at Sherborne in October 1971, Shah was invited to some meetings, on a casual basis. However, so far as I am aware, this was only for the First Basic Course. It seems that after 1972, Bennett' attitude to Shah underwent the final shift, possibly as a result of further correspondence from Hasan Shushud. On 1972, Bennett wrote to Shushud:

A book on Idries Shah has just been published which claims

---

[82] Bennett (1979) 117-18.
[83] Blake (2017) 37.
[84] Bennett (1997) 293.

him to be the "King of Mystics", the "Kutb-ul-Ahtol", accepted as such by all the "Tarikats." It is even said that seven years ago (1965) there was a grand reunion at Karatas, near Izmir, where Mr. Shah was elected chief of the Naqshbandis, the Kadiris, the Chishtis etc. etc.

I would like to find out if possible whether this story is authentic or if it is pure invention. It would prove whether Idries Shah is serious and whether I would have to be on my guard with him. If, on the contrary, he is truly the Sheikh ul Mesheikh of all the Tarikats, he is an important personage. Yet even if he is important I do not feel it necessary to be in contact with him since it seems to me that the "baraka" of Sherborne came to us directly without intermediaries.[85]

The reference to "Karatas" is part of Shah's trawling for Gurdjieff students: it is the home planet of Beelzebub in *Beelzebub's Tales*. We do not, unfortunately, have Shushud's reply. It is quite significant, however, that Bennett states that the *baraka* or spiritual force at Sherborne came without any "intermediaries." It is a mark of Bennett's naivety that he could fancy there could be truth in such an outlandish tale. When Bennett died, Shah was informed, attended the funeral, and told Anthony Blake that Bennett had been "a rarity in 'this business' because of his innocence."[86]

10.6 UNDERSTANDING BENNETT AND SHAH

The casually disclosed assumption that he was engaged in a "business," and that Bennett was an "innocent" in it, reveals how Shah really thought. It also comes close to reconciling the diversity of views of Shah, which turn around two inconsistent views: that he was indeed a Sufi *shaykh* sincerely passing on Sufism in the West, and that he was a deliberate fraud, an interloper in the Sufi tradition, for to be a *shaykh* implies

[85] Bennett and Shushud (1971-74) 18.
[86] Blake (2017) 37.

having been trained and being accepted in the Sufi tradition. That is, Shah regarded the traditions, past and present, as a disguised commerce, and himself as simply a smarter trader. On this assumption, it would be possible, but for unmistakable evidence of deceit, to take Shah as a "teacher" on the lines that Will Rogers spoke of 'artists": "If a man ain't nothin' else, then he's an artist. It's the only thing he can claim to be that nobody can prove he ain't."[87]

To some, it was unthinkable that Bennett could have been deceived by Shah; while Shah's apologists defended his mendacities as having been necessary to "decondition" people. It may be beyond human ability to conclusively demonstrate that a person is a sincere spiritual teacher with something valuable to communicate: who is to judge, and how? On the other hand, to demonstrate deceit may be possible; one need only find betrayal or intent to cheat. A true believer can always rationalise deceit or even oppression: it could have been for the other person's own good. But then, why assert that it was, in fact, just that? To say that a deceiver *could* have acted with benign intent still concedes the fraud, but calls for an act of faith as to the motive. It is possible to establish that Shah was disloyal on one signal occasion (the Khayyam deceit of Graves), and did engage in deceit (posing as having been sent by Gurdjieff's teachers and in his plans for Coombe Springs), and hence that he was not merely a *poseur* or a pretender, but one who was aware that he was deceiving in pretending to "Gurdjieff's mantel."[88]

Shah was born in Simla, India, in 1924, but raised in England. His father was an Afghan Muslim, his mother a Scotswoman of a background assumed but, so far as I am aware, not stated, to be Anglo-Celtic.[89] He attended high school, but never university.[90] Shah emerged into the public eye as a student of magic, became a colleague of Gerald Gardner, and ghost wrote probably the first two thirds of Gardner's "autobiography,"

---

[87] https://www.azquotes.com/quote/1428818 accessed April 22, 2022.
[88] Thompson (1995) 24-26.
[89] Sedgwick (2016) 209.
[90] Moore (1986) 5.

Gerald Gardner Witch.[91] In 1960, he vouchsafed to a colleague that while he (Shah) had it on the authority of what he implied were "inner planes" that Gardner's movement "will be the cornerstone of the religion of the coming age," he could not "rationally" see "it."[92] Gardner's biographer considers it to be "perhaps, a slight exaggeration" to suggest that "Shah dropped Gardner like a stone."[93] But drop him Shah did, after involving Gardner in an elaborate hoax about how, since one of Gardner's forbears had married a "descendant of Genghis Khan," he (Gardner) was "entitled to the rank of Indian Prince, but he needed to go to India in person to claim the title."[94] I would not disagree with Heselton's conclusions that: "It is clear that the Shahs had a long history of deception and subterfuge, which makes their relationships with Gerald Gardner more understandable,"[95] and that Shah "decided that, as Gerald had lost his usefulness to him, he would play Gerald at his own game and wind him up with an elaborate story with very little basis in truth."[96]

So, becoming increasingly disappointed with Gardner, Shah wrote to Robert Graves (1895-1985), leading to a meeting in January 1961. Their common point of interest was, initially, magic mushrooms and "ecstatic religions." At the time he was attaching himself to Graves' rising star, he had been declaring that the Eastern tradition was the source of the pagan witchcraft of the West. He now also began seeking out pupils of Gurdjieff, claiming to know the source of Gurdjieff's teaching, just as he had done for witchcraft. Although Hayter makes some errors and is given to overstatement, yet his position as a student and continued champion of Idries Shah and his brother Omar Ali-Shah, means that he had access to some information not otherwise available. It is, however, wise to be careful in using him. Hayter states that in 1962 that the two brothers:

---

[91] Heselton (2012) 610-15, for an analysis of Shah's distinctive style in the first two thirds of the book.
[92] Heselton (2012) 612.
[93] Heselton (2012) 623.
[94] Heselton (2012) 625-26.
[95] Heselton (2012) 623.
[96] Heselton (2012) 625.

began their teaching with a group of vaguely dissident Gurdjieffians, (dissident in the sense that they worked with Vera Milanova and not with Jeanne de Salzmann), although this may ascribe more thinking and intention than is justified to the bunch of Parisian expatriates that we were at the time....

As well as talking to us in Paris, through John Bennett and the Hoares, the two brothers encountered a number of people who had been connected to the Indonesian teacher Pak Subuh. I myself joined up in 1964, and was privileged to be able to work with both teachers until 1977, which was when the two brothers announced the separation of their teaching activities.[97]

Howarth adds that Vera was herself American, and the group she had in Paris was of English-speakers.[98] A little later, speaking of the year 1960, Hayter wrote:

Vera Milanova Page, who had been the widow of the famous French poet René Daumal, who was the wife of the British landscape architect Russel (sic) Page, had refused to submit to the rule of her contemporary Jeanne de Salzmann, and had organised a small group of students based on Gurdjieffian ideas. She had been close to Gurdjieff herself...

Vera Page came down with cancer in 1961 and died the following year. The future of the study group in Paris became a matter of great concern.... It was about this time that Reginald Hoare read a travel article about Afghanistan in *Blackwood's Magazine*: in this article there was a description

---

[97] Hayter (2002) 177.
[98] Howarth (1998) 331-32.

of a Sufi exercise that was known only to the top ten ranked Gurdjieffians of the period.⁹⁹

The exercise in question was the "Stop Exercise." as that had been published in 1949, its knowledge was hardly restricted to some imagined "top ten ranked Gurdjieffians."¹⁰⁰ Hoare wrote to the magazine, and Idries Shah replied. Hayter puts it like this:

> It was Idries Shah who replied to Hoare's letter as author of the article, which he himself was later to describe as "trawling." Reggie ... introduced him to various Gurdjieffians in London and Paris, and through John Bennett, to others who had been connected to the Indonesian teacher Pak Subuh.... Although Russel Page was under considerable pressure to take on the leadership of the Paris group himself, to his great credit he asked Shah to take on this drifting group whose leader had just died, and Shah accepted. The first meeting between Idries Shah and the Paris group took place in the spring of 1962.... Shah's instructions were to write a personal letter stating why one was in the group and what one expected from it, to cease reading the canonical literature by Gurdjieff and Ouspensky, and to stop the practice of the *mouvements*.¹⁰¹

Howarth adds that some of these young people moved to London to study with Shah. When Howarth shortly after met up with some of these:

> the Shaeffers admitted to me that Shah was constantly disparaging the work they had done for years in Paris.... He complained that he had to "undo" all that they had learnt there. I asked them why then, if this were so, Shah was so actively

---

⁹⁹ Hayter (2002) 186-187.
¹⁰⁰ Ouspensky (1949) 351-56.
¹⁰¹ Hayter (2002) 187-88.

proselytizing specifically Gurdjieff followers when he had even more accessible to him millions of unpolluted English who had never heard of Gurdjieff. They couldn't find an answer.

Alice and Shaef took me to have Sunday tea with Idries Shah and his family and group members. I found him tall and good-looking, a completely Anglicized Afghan. But afterwards, in spite of not wishing to hurt the Shaeffers' feelings, I admitted that although he would certainly make a fascinating dinner guest, he didn't convince me as a teacher.[102]

Hayter states that in 1962 and 1963, Shah was conducting "basically parties" at Coombe Springs. However, this is inconsistent with *Witness*, and I have been assured by George Bennett that Hayter is simply wrong on this point.[103] Hayter adds that the groups in Paris would listen to the mantra *Om Mane Padme Om* (sic), then tapes of Shah reading "Sufi texts and stories," but "the Lataif came later."[104] What the latter involved is not said, but the comment is too vague to make much of except that Shah must have at least mentioned the *latā'if* of Islamic thought. The Naqshbandi are known to have used exercises "of the five *latā'if*, five subtle points in the body upon which the mystic has to concentrate his recollection until his whole being is transformed."[105] Within Islamic traditions, there are differences: in one tradition there are five, in another there are seven *latā'if*.[106] As I show in appendix 3, Hayter makes serious errors in his attempts to exculpate Shah from charges of callousness and duplicity in his dealings with Bennett, and vandalism in his causing the destruction of the Djamichunatra, a building Shah described to Tunbridge as "the Hitler bunker,"[107] a rather bizarre comment, given the nature of Bennett's above-ground temple, and that bunkers were underground fortresses.

---

[102] Howarth (1998) 332.
[103] Email from George Bennett, April 24, 2022.
[104] Hayter (2002) 188.
[105] Schimmel (1975) 175.
[106] cf. Schimmel (1975) 379.
[107] Tunbridge (2015) 94-95.

The comment Shah made to Blake at Bennett's funeral shows that he saw himself as one of a tribe of entrepreneurs. Even this cannot explain two matters, Shah's role in deceiving Robert Graves over the non-existent Khayyam manuscript, and the destruction of the Djamichunatra as an incident of his deceit of Bennett over the donation of the Coombe Springs property. There is a third matter I consider equally significant, and that is the deception around the idea that he was sent to "complete" Gurdjieff's work. However, that third fraud can be read as Shah sincerely entertaining the belief that Gurdjieff was likewise in the "business" of being a teacher, that he (Shah) was no less a teacher than Gurdjieff, and that anyone gullible enough to believe that he had been sent by the same school wanted to be taken in. The other two deceits cannot be explained on that basis.

The details of the Graves deception are in appendix 3. The incident shows how Shah not only changed course over his career, but reversed it in some respects which cannot be explained other than by a deliberate career move prepared in the libraries of the West, and not in the *tekkes* of the East. Never in his life did he appear as a practising Muslim. He was probably not even lapsed, because that would imply he had at one time been a sincere Muslim, while the available evidence shows that he only ever viewed Islam with detached bemusement. He initially presented himself as an outsider to Sufism, which he saw as an Islamic phenomenon. He began as a student of magic and Western "pagan witchcraft," but he reversed the tables on the then-dominant Murray thesis by asserting that those traditions had their roots in the Muslim East.[108] The value of being able to speak in the name of an ancient tradition no one else knew anything about was not lost on Shah, and so he invented a universalist Sufism lacking any sense of reverence and love for God, yearning for unification (*tawhīd*), or other classic marks of Sufism.

The second significant matter is how Shah insisted that Bennett had to give him the entire property, and not just funds. He asserted that he

---

[108] Hutton (2019) 282. For Hutton's critique of Murray's thesis, her "mistake" being more wilful than ignorant, see (2019) 290-92, 300 and especially 375-76 for the final demolition of the Murray "thesis" by Keith Thomas and Norman Cohn.

needed just that property for his pressing work in dealing with the "coming crisis."[109] As we have seen, he soon made Bennett unwelcome, and then sold the property, although it meant the Djamichunatra was demolished with its embedded scrolls, stained glass, redwood timber, and all its appurtenances in order to make money from the sale of luxury residences. A building which Bennett described in terms perfectly suited to the erection of Chartres Cathedral, and which he said had actually exerted a conscious influence upon those within it, was brought down to the dust so that the wealthy might live in style at green and pleasant Kingston-on-Thames.

This was a grave act of destruction, and should not be glossed over: the property was sold so quickly, and the demolition of the Djamichunatra so gross an act of vandalism, that it is difficult not to conceive that Shah intended from the very start to sell the property, careless of the destruction of an extraordinary work of spiritual architecture which he was unable to appreciate. Now, had his intention to sell the property been disclosed, it would not have made the already difficult task of persuading Bennett and the trustees to gift it to him any easier. One suspects it would, rather, have ruled it out of court, and Shah knew that.

Neither did any "caravan" set out. Neither did Shah take steps to deal with any "crisis." It is hard to see what Bennett had been thinking. Richard Graves suggested that Shah had astutely reflected back at his uncle Robert his own ideas.[110] Shah shrewdly seized on the apocalyptic sense which had led Bennett to South Africa, and levered him through the powerful emotions it aroused. Bennett does not explain how giving property to Shah was a way of paying his debt for help received by others so that he might pay his debt to the Creator.[111] That is, one wonders how the Creator or anyone else was repaid by a gift to Shah. For such a purpose, one might suggest donating it to a children's charity or a hospital; or to the Gurdjieff work. Besides, the dichotomy between a debt to humanity and one to the Creator is unconvincing. As with the incident of Cecil Lewis and the

---

[109] Bennett (1997) 291.
[110] Graves (1995) 326.
[111] Bennett (1997) 293.

colony in South Africa, the only conclusion can be that Bennett is prevaricating. At what Blake described as "the turning point," when Bennett refused to accept leftover food which Shah sent to him through his former students, no less, saying that he had enough of his own, he had finally realised that Shah was indeed a charlatan: "a mountebank who descants volubly in the street; ... who pretends to wonderful knowledge or secrets, *esp* in the healing art; an impostor, a quack."[112] However, in keeping with his book's secondary purpose of an *apologia pro vita sua*, Bennett would admit to some mistakes, but not too many.

It also worked in Shah's favour that Bennett had a weakness for the Sufi tradition, and was later to publish a full-scale thesis that Gurdjieff was basically a Sufi.[113] He specifically declared his intention of relating Gurdjieff's methods to "those of the Khwajagān,"[114] the "Masters of Wisdom."[115] Cusack has noted that Gurdjieff did not state that Sufism was his root tradition, rather it was Shah and his brother Ali-Shah who made that claim for him, and then critiqued Gurdjieff on that basis.[116] In fact, as she concludes, notwithstanding Bennett's theories: "[I]t is manifestly the case that Gurdjieff was *not* a Sūfi and did *not* teach Sūfism."[117] It also helped Shah get past Bennett's critical faculties that his variety of Sufism went back to the dawn of human history, and was universalist: both features of Bennett's idea of the esoteric tradition. Ultimately, however, Bennett's gullibility was a function of the naivety which Gurdjieff had identified in him.

When Bennett speaks of his time with any of his teachers, he is fulsome about what he learnt from them and how the practices they taught him changed him: Ouspensky had taught him much about himself, a great deal of the Gurdjieff system, and the hesychast method of prayer, with which he had worked for years until his return to Gurdjieff. He is generous

[112] *Shorter Oxford English Dictionary*, 317a.
[113] Bennett (1973) especially 135, 157 and 256.
[114] Bennett (1973) 217.
[115] Bennett (1973) 26.
[116] Cusack (2021) 623.
[117] Cusack (2021) 627.

in praise of Subuh, the Baba, and Shushud (section 11.1) But there is not one single word of what he learnt from Idries Shah, nothing of any technique, any knowledge, any experience he was shown.[118] With Shah it was all a question of whether Shah had established his "credentials" or not.

The third matter I averted to, and perhaps the most serious, is the confusion Shah has sown among people searching for an authentic spiritual teaching. His attempts to "trawl" among those interested in Gurdjieff, as Hayter recalls him phrasing it,[119] were cynical: they mean that he did not believe that Gurdjieff had brought any real knowledge, or at the least not so much knowledge as he (Shah) possessed, and so it did not matter if people abandoned the Gurdjieff system for his own "teaching." It seems to me that Moore was quite correct to say that in *Destination Mecca,* Shah displayed "a mind embarrassingly superficial and banal, lacking the least resonance of religious feeling."[120] Shah never demonstrated any respect for Gurdjieff and Bennett, whose efforts he exploited, or even to Islam which he misrepresented in a search for books sales. Moore's observation of a lack of "religious feeling" supports the suspicion that he was insensitive before the work done at the Coombe Springs property and what we might call "the sublimity" of the Djamichunatra.

Edwards later recalled Shah's first appearance, when he was: "endeavouring to accomplish ... the destruction of an image, which we had clung to for many years."[121] She believed that this gave them "a possibility of gaining greater understanding of ourselves and of our purpose."[122] She goes on to describe how Shah showed her a picture called "The Key Diagram," and how it made quite an impact upon her. She then gives some examples of Shah's imperturbable demeanour, and the feeling that she failed in that she never understood what he required of her.[123] Edwards twice reports, with apparent approval, Shah's statement that one cannot observe oneself

---

[118] Pittman (2012) 135-36 makes the same point, if more tentatively.
[119] Hayter (2002) 187-88.
[120] Moore (1986) 5.
[121] Edwards (2009) 117.
[122] Edwards (2009) 117.
[123] Edwards (2009) 117-21.

in the present moment, one can only, in retrospect, remember and see how an incident could have gone differently.[124] Strangely, she had already furnished examples from her first days at Coombe Springs where, especially through the use of the Stop Exercise, she had seen herself as she was, at the moment.[125] However, these comments shows that Shah himself had never been capable of observing himself while he was speaking or acting, and that he had a knack of making some people, at least, believe what he said despite their experience to the contrary.

Bennett had practical experience not only of Sufism but of the Naqshbandi way in particular. Shah was forced to yield that territory, refuse to speak of his past, and to move into areas like "deconditioning," telling stories, and "learning how to know" to hide his own ignorance. That is, it is my contention that since Shah realized he knew nothing of Sufism beyond what he had picked up in some books, the best strategy to bolster his authority was a triple one of making the most extreme claims to authority possible, attacking anyone who could be a critic, and finally, asserting that others had to submit to him before he could teach them anything. Shah found security in his claim that he was above judgment: if only the ignorant would criticise him, then the fact of criticism only proved the ignorance of the critics.

At the end of the day, Bennett's suggestibility before Shah cannot be rationally explained. Perhaps Shah was able to play on Bennett's belief that a crisis was coming but that a special revelation would be sent to save humanity. Bennett was predisposed to see this coming from an "Eastern" source. Shah was able to tease Bennett by claiming knowledge of *baraka* (which Bennett related to the higher energies of the Great Accumulator). He also made much of being a Sayyid from Afghanistan, and hence somehow connected with Gurdjieff's own posing as a Sayyid as he travelled in Central Asia.[126] That he was warmly recommended by Reggie Hoare, who insisted that Bennett meet him more than once,

---

[124] Edwards (2009) 121.
[125] Edwards (2009) 20-21.
[126] Gurdjieff (1963) 228-31.

awakened Bennett's occasional willingness to defer to others. While he never publicly admitted to having made a mistake with Shah, I see that as a subtext in *Witness*, e.g. when he admits that Shushud's advice not to gift the property to Shah had been correct,[127] and most especially in his comments about the sale of Coombe Springs and the destruction of the Djamichunatra. Even today, those who were at Coombe Springs see it as an act of vandalism and treachery: that is exactly how they have expressed it to me.[128] But Bennett must have seen this, too, for it must eventually have occurred to him that if the Coombe Springs property was not so "suitable" for Shah's "purpose" as another,[129] that Shah must have realised this before insisting on the Coombe Springs property, and therefore always intended to sell and demolish it.

10.7 SYSTEMATICS AND EDUCATION

By way of prelude to one of Gurdjieff's more colourful comments, Bennett states that when children are edged on to follow their likes and dislikes, they are only being educated "for slavery." He then reports that Gurdjieff once said of such parents: "Right to kill. Stick knife in back."[130]

Bennett opened "Life Begins at Seventy," the final chapter of the revised edition of *Witness*, by returning to the question of education, one which he had pursued while with the BCURA (section 5.1). He declared that our universities were medieval in both origin and outlook, expending energy on children and adolescents who do not have any sense of purpose or aim in life, so that much of what is learned is obsolete by age forty. Education should be, he contended, continuous, and at least in technical fields, not close-ended, that is, open-ended rather than being concerned for "precise operations and results."[131] Between leaving

---

[127] Bennett (1997) 295-96.
[128] Email and Zoom meetings with certain persons who request that their names not be put to their criticism of Shah.
[129] Bennett (1997) 293.
[130] Bennett (1994) 77.
[131] Bennett (1997) 294-95.

Coombe Springs and inaugurating almost four golden years of teaching at Sherborne, Bennett returned to education, and in particular, to an educational method he called "Systematics." Bennett's educational initiatives included a "deconditioning course," a teaching machine called the "Systemaster," and a journal *Systematics*, the journal of his Institute, which, he states, was "well-established in academic circles."[132]

Two useful volumes of Bennett's work on *Systematics* have been published: perhaps the most useful of all is *Elementary Systematics: A Tool for Understanding Wholes*, edited by David Seamon, a personal pupil of Bennett. The volume comprises six lectures delivered at Coombe Springs in 1963, with the article Bennett published as an introduction to the topic in the very first issue of the journal *Systematics*, in 1963. There is overlap between the contents of that and the volume published by the J.G. Bennett Foundation in 2017, *"Systematics,"* being a compilation of his essays from the journal, published between 1963 and 1972.[133] However, the latter volume includes lengthy essays on topics extraneous to Systematics, e.g. "The Hyperborean Origin of the Indo-European Culture," and two essays on Asian Sufism. Also valuable, is the work of Anthony Hodgson, who worked closely with Bennett as a Senior Research Fellow at the Institute for the Comparative Study of History, Philosophy and the Sciences.[134] Hodgson states that Bennett drew on many sources for his Systematics, not only the ideas of Gurdjieff and Ouspensky, but also on mainstream scientific work including Russell and Whitehead's celebrated *Principia Mathematica* of 1910-1913.[135]

Bennett states that Systematics is "an instrument of understanding," based on the idea that "all structures in the world, be they things, living beings, events or processes," manifest a certain limited number of patterns. These patterns can be expressed by reference to "one characteristic quality," and that quality is numerical.[136] As Hodgson expresses it: "The

---

[132] Bennett (1997) 295.
[133] Bennett (2017a)
[134] Hodgson (2006) 2.
[135] Hodgson (2006) 2.
[136] Bennett (1993) 8.

principle is that the number of terms in a system determines its structure, its qualities and its behaviour."[137] So, we can anticipate that if we take each of the numbers one to eight, abstracting from them "systems," we will find distinctive structures, qualities and behaviour. Were we take the numbers "one" and "two," we can see without any need for experiment, that the structure which corresponds to "one" will be a unity, while that corresponding to "two" will necessarily be a composite. But which qualities and behaviour would correspond? Bennett takes, as a start, one-term systems, the "monad," two-term systems, the "dyad," three-term, the "triad," four-term, the "tetrad," five-term, the "pentad,", six-term, the "hexad," seven-term, the "heptad," and eight-term, the "octad."[138] To commence with the monad, this system refers to "the special qualities of a thing that make it what it is rather than something else."[139] Hence, it is easy to see "learning" is one monad, and "government" is another.[140] Bennett produced diverse explanations, but in 1963, he provided this table:

System	Attribute	Term Character
monad	universality	unity in diversity
dyad	complementarity	positive and negative
triad	relatedness	affirmation, receptivity, reconciliation
tetrad	reciprocity	unity, quantity, quality, diversity
pentad	potentiality	inner, higher, centric, lower, outer
hexad	significance	self-realization
heptad	integration	completedness
octad	individuality	transcendence[141]

[137] Hodgson (2006) 4.
[138] See the table at Bennett (1993) 111.
[139] Bennett (1993) 18.
[140] Bennett (1993) 19.
[141] Bennett (1993) 111.

Parallels with Pythagoras and Plato are patent. In many descriptive systems, such as astrology, one category often overlaps with others, blunting the value of the taxonomy. This would appear, at first glance to be the case with Systematics, e.g. one finds "unity in diversity" characterising monads, "unity" for tetrads, and "completedness" for heptads. But, Hodgson developed a table, which differentiates these three systems as referring to "universality," "field of action," and "completedness," respectively.[142] The research is complex and difficult. So eminent a student as Anthony Blake opined that Bennett had tried to communicate the discipline of Systematics, but failed.[143] Elsewhere, Blake added:

> Mr Bennett himself struggled to make us aware of the inherent unity of all valid doctrines and understandings through his scheme of *Systematics*. Without the direct contact in oneself, systematics must remain an external complication.[144]

Perhaps Systematics, like *The Dramatic Universe*, falls under Gurdjieff's stricture that: "When you have Being you will know all these things without the need for Mathematik."[145] But if one has a direct contact with the ideas, a mixture of intellectual comprehension and emotional sympathy, the words come to life. The effort to develop Systematics was bold, and it may well, at some time in the future be found to have substantial practical value, and someone shall emerge who can promote it in a more accessible form.

---

[142] Hodgson (2006) 3.
[143] Blake (1980a) xii.
[144] Blake (1980b) 18.
[145] Bennett (1997) 212.

Elizabeth and John Bennett.

CHAPTER 11

"I AM" AND ALWAYS WILL BE

11.1 HASAN SHUSHUD

In 1962, the Bennetts had met Hasan Shushud (1902-88), who had a reputation as "an accomplished Sufi" who expounded what he called the "Way of Absolute Liberation." This was, he said, a system of "annihilation," by which he meant not "becoming unconscious of oneself" but "the real experience of detaching oneself from attributes and actions and confirming that God is the real doer."[1] Portions of his teaching, and certain reminiscences of him are readily available to the English language reader in Shushud's *Masters of Wisdom of Central Asia*, and his pupil Nevit O. Ergin's, *The Sufi Path of Annihilation*.

When Bennett was agonizing over whether to give everything to Idries Shah, he had written to Shushud, who indicated that he should not. Bennett ignored the advice, but later realized that Shushud had been correct.[2] When Shushud eventually came to England, possibly in 1968, he told Bennett that he (Bennett) "had gone beyond all those whom I regarded as my teachers."[3] Shushud spoke only Turkish and an eccentric version of French, so a translator was needed to help with most students.[4] He taught Bennett an exercise which he called *zikr-i-daim*, literally "perpetual remembrance," but rendered by Bennett as the more descriptive "perpetual prayer of the heart. Of this, Bennett wrote:

[1] Shushud (2014) 107.
[2] Bennett (1997) 295-96.
[3] Bennett (1997) 296.
[4] Cilento (2006) 341.

> It includes a method of breath control that is more effectual than anything I had previously encountered. I did not, at first, take to the *zikr* because I was suspicious of breath control exercises that worked differently from those I had learned from Gurdjieff. However, after a few weeks I became aware of a most reliable beneficial action. The breath control transfers the action of the *zikr* from the physical body to the *kesdjan* or astral body which becomes perceptibly stronger and more effectual.[5]

However, Shushud also told him that he would "live to a great age," which prediction, not surprisingly, pleased him.[6] On November 20, 1971, Shushud wrote to him: Providence will not fail to keep you a good while longer in this world. You have to leave a Work, surpassing that which there is to surpass."[7] Bennett's death three years later at the age of seventy-seven would seem to have falsified this, the latest of a long line of prophecies which Bennett trusted in. Once more, Bennett was predisposed to believe an auspicious omen. Cilento recalls:

> Occasionally, Hasan would give active advice but he would always dispense 'baraka' (blessing) by blowing his breath onto their heads. At times, he would hold their hands or write something on a slip of paper. He would give them a protection to wear around their necks for a week or so, and he always listened with the utmost care that took in the entire person as he did so. Hasan also had an infallible sense of the physical state of each individual who entered the room and would insist vehemently that some give up smoking or

---

[5] Bennett (1997) 296. Ironically, this is also the effect of certain of the esoteric exercises Gurdjieff had taught in the 1940s, but which were, so far as I can see, not passed on to anyone else by those who had learnt them.
[6] Bennett (1997) 296.
[7] He also confidently predicted a long and healthy for Bennett in an undated letter from 1971: both letters at Bennett and Shushud (1971-1974) 3.

that others visit a doctor ... I saw that he gave those people something very valuable that they desperately needed.[8]

Shushud also introduced an element of the concrete into Bennett's theories about a New Epoch and "synergism," or cooperation with "Higher Powers," so that Bennett concluded that these forces can only act in the world through humanity, and not outside of it. Bennett had already set out, theoretically, that a person could become what he called "a demiurgic intelligence," and Shushud persuaded him that it was indeed possible.[9] Incidentally, he also credited Shushud with having freed him from a conditioning which had been instilled by Ouspensky: the fixed conviction that: "higher levels of being (are) far away and that objective consciousness (is) no concern of ours."[10] It would be impossible to contradict Bennett on this, as he was so close to Ouspensky. But given the visions Bennett had been vouchsafed, one would think that he already had his proof. Bennett was predisposed to accept Shushud's views on Sufism and of esoteric history.

Shushud at first told Bennett that he should not be teaching because he was above that. Shushud came to see the sense in what Bennett was doing, and even in the methods he was using, for Shushud had insisted that only fasting and *zikr* were needed for perfection.[11] Bennett began experiencing visions and auditions, becoming convinced that he had once lived in Central Asia at the time of Khwaja (Master) Ubaidallah Ahrar (1404-90), with whom Bennett believed himself to be in contact (sic).[12] Although *The Masters of Wisdom* covers Ahrar, it sheds no light on this. Shushud purported to confirm at least some of this, and Bennett mentions Ahrar in the last book he worked on, his posthumously published *The Masters of Wisdom*.[13]

---

[8] Cilento (2006) 342.
[9] Bennett (1997) 297.
[10] Bennett (1997) 297-98.
[11] Bennett (1997) 304.
[12] Email communication from Anthony Blake 25 January 2021.
[13] Bennett (1997) 141-46, 153-55, and 304; and (1977a) 141-46 and 153-56.

Their correspondence is noteworthy, but is, in general, tangential to my purpose here. However, there are two letters, those which Bennett wrote to Shushud, which shed light on Bennett's dependence on Shushud when he heard "voices." Incidentally, it shows that he was learning that, despite what is said in *Witness*, he could not always trust such "communications." The first is dated January 21, 1973:

> Dear Master,
> Help me to understand an involuntary 'Hal' and (I will) never again experiment.
>
> For several days now, whenever I do the *Zikr* in time to the *Haps-i-Nefes* I often hear a voice in my chest which replies to my questions. I had asked, "Why do I not reach *fena'i mutluk*? What is it I lack?" The voice replied: "You have nothing more to do for yourself. You have arrived." It seemed to me that something else was expected and I asked "What do you want from me?" Then came the reply which flabbergasted me. "Accept to be everyone." I understood clearly that it was required of me to accept being unified with all other human souls and to share their (*soit*). I revolted. I wanted to be free of all that: to go alone toward the One. I was made to understand that the choice was up to me; but that my destiny could not be fulfilled if I turned my back on the human race. I saw clearly in myself that I could not tolerate the idea of my being chained in this human prison along with other prisoners. I was even unable to conceive of my Infinity other than in Will.[14]

Unfortunately, Shushud's reply is missing. On January 31, 1973, Bennett replied:

> Dear Friend and Teacher,

[14] Bennett and Shushud (1971-74) 23.

> Your letter, if I understand it correctly, implies that this 'communication' I received was illusory. This I willingly accept. It seemed too difficult and too enormous a task to take on myself the chains of imprisoned humanity. However, I have understood something important for myself: that one cannot retreat before any improbability whatsoever.
>
> I know a certain stage is over. I am aware of a profound freedom in relation to existence. I do not know whether that is the *fena'i sifat* although I am sure it is not the *fena'i zat* or *fena'i mutlaq*. I see in front of me a total liberation which I had not expected.[15]

That is, Bennett believed that, so far, he had experienced significant but not total liberation. However, he now "saw it in front of him." We now have to go back some four years to what I count as Bennett's twenty-fourth vision, one which occurred before the "illusory communication" of 1973.

11.2 THE TWENTY-FOURTH VISION: "I AM" AND ALWAYS WILL BE

Shushud advised Bennett to look after his health and not work so furiously.[16] When Shushud returned to Turkey in December 1968, Bennett fell seriously ill, and although he was too weak for the prostate operation he needed, he still forced himself in to the office to work on "Structural Communications," an aspect of Systematics. On January 28, 1969, he collapsed. Separated from his consciousness, he was out of his body for sixteen hours. In this state, he realized that his blood was "full of poison" which could destroy his brain, leaving him in a state of imbecility, but that:

---

[15] Bennett and Shushud (1971-74) 25.
[16] Bennett (1997) 298.

> I was fully and directly aware that "I" was, and would always be, exempt from it all. "I myself" would remain free ... I was very close to irreparable damage. Nevertheless I was filled with joy and confidence, for I knew for certain and forever that I could lose not only my "body," but also my "mind," and still remain "myself."[17]

The Bennetts had not long before purchased back into the family a cottage in Somerset which had been alienated in 1919. He had convalesced there in that year, and now returned after fifty years:

> I could look at my life as having completed a great cycle. In March 1919, I had seen that I could be without a body; now I had seen that my mind was also expendable. It was possible to be in a state of consciousness consisting of pure "seeing," without any mental process and without any external manifestation. This state of consciousness was not "in" space and time; more exactly, it was free from the conditions of space and time. It was neither "here" nor "there," neither "now" nor "not-now."[18]

Bennett accordingly described this as "one of the most important and instructive experiences of my life."[19] He then passes over some eighteen months of corporate work, and his contacts with "some of the greatest corporations in the world," as being "not relevant to the main theme of my life."[20] I have formed the impression, from what he was able to do afterwards, that it must have been quite lucrative. There may be an element of modesty in his sliding so quickly from this topic. But it would be nice to have seen set out here, what he means by "the full power of

---

[17] Bennett (1997) 299.
[18] Bennett (1997) 299.
[19] Bennett (1997) 299.
[20] Bennett (1997) 300.

Sytematics" and the practice of "Shared Participation."[21] He met a number of young Americans through Paul and Naomi Anderson, who had been pupils of Gurdjieff. It is unclear whether the meetings were in the USA, but perhaps not as they assured him that if he "were to come over and stay for a year in Boston or New York" he would have "thousands of followers."[22] But where should he be, England or America, and what should he be doing?

11.3 SHERBORNE HOUSE

At St. Wandrille, praying for guidance, he heard a voice announce in his breast: "You are to found a school." This put him in mind of all Gurdjieff's hopes for him as a teacher. He reflected that he had hitherto been a mouthpiece, so to speak, for Gurdjieff, Subuh and the Shivapuri Baba. He had leant on their authority not from fear but because "my time had not yet come" (an allusion to Jesus' words in John 7:6).[23] Yet, the school he opened would not be an imitation of any of the many he had seen, but would be original and fresh. Recalling how Gurdjieff would send people away after he had given them the material he believed they needed to find their own way, Bennett planned something similar, and said that: "if this was what the Higher Powers intended, they would provide the means."[24] He chose the title "International Academy for Continuous Education," acknowledging the inspiration of Plato, and that it would be "a teaching for the whole of life," the idea of continuous education appealing to him.[25]

A promotional event in England and a tour of the U.S. were successful, and they decided to open at Sherborne House in the Cotswolds. He was given the money to purchase Sherborne, and they were substantially assisted by Lord Sherborne's gift of furniture and equipment from

---

[21] Bennett (1997) 300.
[22] Bennett (1997) 300.
[23] Bennett (1997) 300-1.
[24] Bennett (1997) 301.
[25] Bennett (1997) 302.

the King's School which had occupied the premises until 1966.²⁶ They opened with ninety candidates, sixty from the U.S., and twenty-five from the U.K.²⁷ In the past, he said, the feasible had been rendered impossible but now the impossible had been made possible.²⁸ The academy opened on October 15, 1971. As Bennett wrote to Gavin Perry on June 28, 1973: "[W]e follow Gurdjieff's method here."²⁹ Further, although he does not provide details, Bennett felt that he was:

> in communication with a Higher wisdom and it was a real two-way communication. I could ask for help and guidance and receive them. I could even argue and insist upon the message being clarified.... My own weaknesses and stupidities no longer mattered. In my delirium a year before, I had seen that I could be myself *without* my mind. As the work no longer depended on my ability to do it, I could be confident it would succeed.³⁰

The basis of the discipline at Sherborne was the schedule, which had daily and weekly components. Although it struck students as reminiscent of an ordinary school, the institution was so large that it was a practical necessity.³¹ The day was structured by ablutions (to animate the body with the shock of cold water),³² the daily contemplative exercise, the meals, the practical work in the house and the grounds, the movements, and weekly themes and meetings with Bennett to discuss the themes. The initial daily schedule was to be:

6:00 a.m.	Cooking breakfast
6:30	Waking Bell

---

[26] Bennett (1971a) 8.
[27] Bennett (1971a) 8.
[28] Bennett (1997) 302.
[29] Perry (2020) 2.
[30] Bennett (1997) 303.
[31] Blake (2018) 110.
[32] Roth (1998) 30, 44; Cilento (2006) 330-31; Chromey (2022) 62 and 127.

7:00	Exercise
7:30	Breakfast
8:30 a.m. to 1:00 p.m.	Work period
[Lunch, not listed in the schedule]	
3:00 to 6:30 pm.	Work period
[Dinner, not listed in the schedule]	
9:00 to 10:30 p.m.	Work period

The schedule also notes that during the designated "work periods," all students would work at movements for one and a half to three hours, the same for gardening, one and a half hours on art and music, and three to four hours on "group work in psychology, communication, history, role playing and other group exercises, will-type study, creative thinking, systematics, cosmology and social studies."[33] Each of the "basic courses" was arranged in three stages which he called Exoteric, Mesoteric, and Esoteric, one feature of which was that more advanced inner exercises would be added in what must have been the mesoteric stage.[34] In his inaugural address, Bennett addressed the difference between the three stages in theoretical terms:

> The exoteric work is largely concerned with our functional mechanisms: the work by which man becomes balanced, harmonized in his inner and outer life, by which he develops powers that are latent in him, by which he learns how to relate himself to the outer world, to use his body, his senses, his sensitivity, his capacity for communication with others, and all the skills that are required for the effectual conduct of life....
>
> The second or the mesoteric stage ... is concerned with our being. This means a transformation of our being from

---

[33] Bennett (1971a) 8. A slightly different schedule, possibly due to changes made from course to course, is in Chromey (2022) 104-6.
[34] Bennett (1971a) 9.

its present ephemeral, fragmented condition, to a stable, permanent, and unified condition.... Above all, this second stage does bring a man in contact with his conscience ... the true link between the material and the spiritual sides of our nature...

Now I can say very little about the esoteric or third stage, which is the development of the will which leads to birth of the soul in man. It is here that man finds his own I, his own will. This comes from commitment and decision.[35]

Bennett's inaugural address for the Fourth Basic Course of 1974/1975 sketched the aim of the course and the outline of its activities. It seems that they had been engaged in a contemplative exercise, because Bennett begins by saying: "We have been sitting in silence and both you and I could tell that we are together as one whole."[36] This comment shows the central role of Gurdjieff's Aiëssirittoorassnian-contemplation for the practical methods, and also that the sense of being (the sense of "I Am") had to precede and remain at the center of all else.

Bennett then points out that while they had been together, now that he has begun speaking, they have become "separate people" because "thought and speech separate."[37] This is the second point, that while it is possible to be united in silent contemplation, when we begin to think and speak, as we must, we lose that unity and become lost in our own dreams and associations. We over-estimate the value of our thought because it has brought us "mastery over things in the material world."[38] This leads Bennett to the importance of working with clear sense perceptions, being conscious of the body and our feeling; that by attempting to "do" things (e.g. acquiring new skills) rather than "know about" them, we can learn.[39] They will study the symbolic discipline of

---

[35] Bennett (1971b) 2.
[36] Bennett (1974) 1.
[37] Bennett (1974) 1.
[38] Bennett (1974) 1-2.
[39] Bennett (1974) 2.

the Gurdjieff movements, which lead to a change in perception through exercising the power of attention.[40] The body cannot awaken, he states, "unless some restraint it put upon it," and especially upon its reactions.[41] Central disciplines include being conscious while eating, not consuming food unnecessarily, and not making unnecessary movements.[42] The energies the body uses in moving and eating unnecessarily use up the force needed for the inner work, Bennett states.[43] The mind, too needs to be restrained, so at the start of the course, he will ask people not to read any books, unless and until they are asked to use the library for study purposes: this should allow the faculties of sensation and feeling more room in their lives.[44]

Now, just over half way through the address, he comes to the foundation: the possibility of receiving help and perceptions from the higher world. I would suggest that what he says in this regard is also the chief rationale for the writing of *Witness*:

> The foundation of this whole work that we do together is the confidence that this is really possible. The main contribution that I can make is to convey to you my own confidence that this can be done.[45]

That is, the open-endedness of the revised ending of *Witness* aligns the purpose and contents of that book to the purpose and discipline of the Sherborne course. I find support for this in his comments about teachers and the "barrier" which I believe to be the barrier Gurdjieff mentioned when speaking of the Great Accumulator (section 3.7):

> [Many people] hope that something will happen and go from

---

[40] Bennett (1974) 2-3.
[41] Bennett (1974) 3.
[42] Bennett (1974) 4.
[43] Bennett (1974) 4-5.
[44] Bennett (1974) 5-6.
[45] Bennett (1974) 6.

> teacher to teacher hoping that someone will tell them how to do it. This is a very pathetic feature of the spiritual quest in the Western world. So many people look for a spiritual reality and so few pass through the barrier that separates it from this ordinary world.... it is mostly my business that it is really possible, because I can speak from having seen it made possible.[46]

That is, his own witness can instil the confidence (he also speaks of "faith") which they need to persevere, and to trust in their own efforts rather than in the *deus ex machina* intervention of a teacher. Timothy St. Clair-Ford, who studied with Bennett at Sherborne, recalls that Bennett often counselled them to: "Trust more and more, count less and less."[47] Part of the basis of the confidence Bennett urged is that just as we need transformation, so too do Higher Powers (his capitals) need us.[48] He then brings all these ideas together, including that of the invocation they say before meals, returning to the idea of an inner unity based on "being" which is more real than any external union.[49] To hold the energies necessary for transformation of being, a vessel is necessary, and that is the group and the grounds, hence the practical requirement to be at the Institute unless given permission to leave them for a purpose.[50] Even the periods of recreation are to allow the necessary energies to move freely in the organism, to reblend, and to be transformed.[51] The necessary discipline should not make them glum or unfeeling: "You have only to get past certain resistances and you are much freer and able to enjoy things."[52]

That provides a general introduction to the nature of what the

---

[46] Bennett (1974) 7.
[47] Email communication to me from St. Clair-Ford dated July 15, 2020.
[48] Bennett (1974) 8.
[49] Bennett (1974) 9.
[50] Bennett (1974) 9-10.
[51] Bennett (1974) 10-11.
[52] Bennett (1974) 11.

Bennetts attempted at Sherborne. Touching the specific practical discipline of the ablutions, Cilento wrote:

> the infuriating bell clanged pre-dawn and we lined up in the ablutions block to wash. The ritual ablution we followed was eyes and nose first, then one hand over the forehead while the other hand cleaned the ear as we repeated, either aloud or silently, 'Lord, have mercy. Increase my knowledge.' Next, the other hand went to work on the other ear with the same supplication and then it was hands, genitals, underarms and, lastly, the tired old feet.[53]

People who attended at Sherborne tell me that her account is basically correct. Some people clearly recalled some of the details, while others remembered different aspects of her account. However, someone was able to verify every part of it, except that some insisted that washing under the arms was not part of Bennett's instructions. However, I would not discount the possibility that Bennett included the armpits when speaking to some people. Bennett insisted on this ablutions discipline with cold water, telling at least one person that the washing removes certain invisible substances which form on the skin overnight (and which presumably have to be removed with cold water).

Roth provides details of the morning exercise, especially using it to explore sensation in the body, e.g.:

> He directed us to put our attention into the right hand. "Put" is an accurate way of expressing it: we easily make the mistake of "thinking" our attention, that is, forming a mental image of the object instead of directing our attention upon it. It's like picking up an object, transporting and depositing it in another location. I knew I was there when sensation made its own response.

[53] Cilento (2006) 330-31.

> Bennett took us through a number of experiments with this newly objectified aspect of ourselves. I confirmed that it was mobile, stretchable, having its own slow pace that could not be hurried. I experimented with drawing sensation up my arm, filling it like a vessel.[54]

People who were with Bennett both at Coombe Springs and later at Sherborne, recalled that his way of showing changed the exercises changed over time. At Coombe Springs he was passing on exercises as he had learned them, but at Sherborne years, he was speaking as someone who could see that, as he himself worked with the exercise, what he was saying was so. This was reflected in how, at Coombe Springs, Bennett would interrogate them about their experience with the exercises, because he needed to know what was happening. At Sherborne, on the other hand, he could see how they were. After the exercise, they would have breakfast, and Bennett himself would ladle out the porridge. As he did, would regard his students. They had the impression that he could see their state.

This brings us to the meals. The communal meals were a focus for their efforts: the paper on "Food" which was published alone and also with several other "Theme Talks" hails from these years.[55] The prayer or "Grace before Meals" which he composed in 1972, and initially intended only for limited use, lest it become mechanical, has spread into the Gurdjieff world, and beyond Bennett circles:

> All Life is One, and everything that lives is holy.
>   Plants, animals, and men; all must eat to live and nourish one another.
>   We bless the lives which have died to give us our food.
>   Let us eat consciously,

---

[54] Roth (1998) 45.
[55] Bennett (2006b).

Resolving by our work to pay the debt of our existence.[56]

Bennett was the central figure at Sherborne, to the extent that when he died soon after one course began, Elizabeth said that it was to be the last.[57] However, Elizabeth Bennett was herself a foundation of Sherborne. She spent a lot of time working with women, and in this respect produced a "Women's Leaflet," which dealt with issues to do with menstruation, pregnancy, childbirth, and after.[58] She also had daily work sessions for the housekeeping team, and in her interactions with the students was able to help them as the need arose.[59] She even taught the Bates method for vision improvement.[60] Tony Ingram shared with me this recollection: "One of her sayings which I have taken to heart was 'You can always do something' (i.e. with at least one of our centres and as long as one was awake).[61] It seems that four of his children, Hero, George, Ben, and Tessa were there at least sometimes.[62]

Of course, exotic visitors like the Cambodian monk Bhante (Dharmawara Mahathera) attracted more attention, and Bennett allowed him to teach meditation in the evenings (a practice which Gurdjieff never countenanced).[63] Bhante had heard of Bennett when Michael Sutton, Tim St. Claire-Ford, and Allen Roth were staying at his Indian temple, and mentioned that they intended to go to England to study with Bennett.[64] When Bennett visited India, a little later, they met. This was followed by an invitation in the Northern Hemisphere spring of 1973 to travel to Sherborne and teach meditation. Bhante went and taught his "Green Meditation" for healing, for a month at a time. Since

---

[56] Blake (2018) 114; Roth (1998) 53. George Adie was dubious about the phrase "the lives which have died," preferring something like "We bless those who have lived so that."
[57] Blake (2018) 118-19.
[58] Elizabeth Bennett (undated).
[59] Roth (1998) 36.
[60] Chromey (2022) 83.
[61] Email communication, October 7, 2023.
[62] Cilento (2006) 336.
[63] Blake (2018) 116.
[64] Dharmarwara (1991) 19.

Bhante was at Sherborne not long before Bennett's death, he can only have attended three courses if he was present towards the end of the second course, and during the third course, as well.[65]

As we have seen, Hasan Shushud was also an important and regular visitor (section 11.1). But when one of the students passed out during a "silent *zikr*," Bennett ceased the practice.[66] Anthony Blake, Henri Bortoft, Saul Kuchinsky, Arnold Keyserling, Edith Wallace, and others, gave sundry talks to the students.[67] Roth has preserved a perspicuous teaching phrase: "make, bear, take, care." This refers to how different students find the work: some make work, others must bear it, some care for it, and others take from it. He speaks with admiration of Michael Sutton, who was a "caretaker."[68]

In section 12.2, I deal with Bennett as a teacher of Gurdjieff's Aiëssirittoorassnian-contemplation or contemplation-like exercises, but it must be noted that, at Sherborne, he taught his students up to one hundred inner exercises.[69] Of all the exercises which were not contemplative, but still inner, the most important was the "Decision Exercise."[70] Anyone who wished could join him at Sunday Mass in a nearby Catholic church, or learn the Alexander Technique, but attendance was never mandatory.[71]

On January 13, 1972, they held quite a celebration for Gurdjieff's birthday, even reviving the toasts of the idiots,[72] something very rare in the Gurdjieff world. The students acquired substantial skills, e.g. in building, repairing, and maintaining a large house and its garden. At the end of the year, Bennett set them to teach the others what they had learned, on the basis that we can only share what we possess.[73] This was

---

[65] Dharmarwara (1991) 19-20. On his "Green Meditation," see Chromey (2022) 279-82.
[66] Blake (2018) 116.
[67] Perry (2022) 5; Chromey (2022) 251.
[68] Roth (1998) 81.
[69] Blake (2018) 103.
[70] Roth (1998) 64, 65, 66; and Chromey (2022) 174-75, 224-28, 234, 295-97.
[71] Blake (2018) 113.
[72] Cilento (2006) 336-37; and Bennett (1997) 303.
[73] Bennett (1997) 304.

a prelude to the time when they would be sent into the world to do likewise. Pondering what the students had really taken with them, he concluded that:

> The one sure method, the value of which became more vividly evident with each passing month, was "the decision exercise." This is my own adaptation of a technique I had learned almost casually from Gurdjieff and to which he refers almost casually in the Third Series of his writings ... I will not describe it here, because I have found that it cannot be transmitted effectively except by personal contact between teacher and pupil.[74]

Bennett's intention was to commence the fifth of five basic courses in 1975 and then to invite back those students who had shown they could transmit something of what they had made digested, and were "ready to make a step forward."[75] He was planning a sort of "master course" for the most serious of his former students; an idea perhaps inspired by what Gurdjieff had told Ouspensky about "schools of repetition," where graduates would return to their school to revive within themselves the feeling of their connection with the school, and to recall what they had learnt.[76]

At the end of 1975, Bennett would have had about 500 former students out in the world. That most were from the U.S. was no disadvantage: the influence and prosperity of their country would help them as Bennett went about establishing largely self-sufficient "New World Societies," as he wrote in his "Open Letter to Sherborne Graduates" of March 23, 1974.[77] He proposed various means of arousing interest, e.g. by publishing small books based on his Sherborne talks.[78] These communities would

---

[74] Bennett (1997) 305.
[75] Bennett (1997) 305.
[76] Ouspensky (1949) 302-3.
[77] Unpublished.
[78] Bennett (1981) is one such book.

include farms using "natural and biodynamic" methods, and be supplemented by, *inter alia*, craft centres, groups engaged in the Gurdjieff work including the movements, and individuals too far from these centres for regular attendance, but who would visit them and try to arouse interest. Clearly, Bennett's ideas had matured since the South African Venture. The purchase of a property at Claymont, West Virginia, still a Bennett-line centre of Gurdjieff work at the time of writing this book, was part of this bold proposal. There, George Bennett and a number of others have continued Bennett's work as exemplified at Sherborne, albeit with certain ongoing adaptations.[79]

I do not deal with Bennett's *Gurdjieff: Making a New World*, although I have made use of its contents where useful.[80] I do not consider the book, a biography of Gurdjieff with a study of his teaching, to have succeeded. In my view, it was far too much influenced by Shushud's notions about "the Masters of Wisdom." It might have been more productive had Bennett been able to confront the fact that, as Blake put it: "I believe that behind Mr Bennett's intense search for the origin and sources of Gurdjieff's teaching was the realization that there was no source but God himself."[81] However, before closing this section on Sherborne, it is fit to note Roberta Chromey's reflection upon Bennett when she went to see him in his apartment:

> "Come in, come in." He looked up from his writing and smiled that toothy grin. The one where he looked at you, right into you, only you felt like he was looking through you because there was nothing solid in you for him to see, and you saw it too. And that was scary because he was always fully there, all of him – a presence emanating from everything about him.[82]

---

[79] Amaral (2009) *passim*.
[80] Bennett (1973).
[81] Blake (1980b) 17.
[82] Chromey (2022) 132.

11.4 BENNETT AND BEELZEBUB

Gurdjieff dedicated much effort, his own and that of others, to the writing of the book known as *Beelzebub's Tales to his Grandson*, or the "first series" of *All and Everything*. All the indications are that he desired it to be widely read.[83] Gurdjieff had appointed Bennett as his representative for *Beelzebub's Tales* in England.[84] After Gurdjieff's death, Bennett came to feel that de Salzmann and her groups handled it like "a disreputable elderly relative, best kept in the background."[85] When de Salzmann's pupils had almost completed a new translation of Beelzebub, this time from the French version, Bennett was one of those to object. I have set out the correspondence with my own comments and interpretation elsewhere.[86]

De Salzmann was able to counter some of his contentions by retailing a story about Gurdjieff making a last-minute correction to the Russian, of which Bennett did not know. For the reasons set out in my article, I consider her account to be untrue.[87] We have seen that de Salzmann and Bennett did not always agree, and they were certainly at odds over her proposed translation. I have contended that the fuss was about the authority to make changes to what was effectively "scripture."[88] Fortunately, we are able to delve into Bennett's valuation of *Beelzebub's Tales*, due to the publication of some of Bennett's talks, with commentary, by A.G.E. Blake.

For this volume, Blake gathered the Prologue which Bennett had prepared for a projected volume of Gurdjieff's ideas, from the manuscripts of which, he edited those lectures which pertained to *Beelzebub's Tales*.[89] The bulk of the text is from Bennett's lectures in the 1970s at

---

[83] For details, see Taylor (2012) 55-78.
[84] Bennett (1997) 207.
[85] Bennett (1997) 248.
[86] Azize (2021b).
[87] Azize (2021b) 171-73.
[88] Azize (2021b) *passim*.
[89] Bennett (1977b) ix.

Sherborne.[90] In 1949, Bennett told them, Gurdjieff had been planning to visit London, but stated that he "would be able to say what he wanted to only to people who had thoroughly studied *Beelzebub's Tales*."[91] This is but one example of the value Gurdjieff attached to it, and which Bennett shared. Blake's transcript included the questions and answers at the end of each lecture. These are particularly effective as examples of how "each one of us has to create the meaning in ourselves by our own work."[92] Some of Bennett's interpretation is delivered as if it were so and could not be otherwise, even when we might find them doubtful today, e.g. his proposed etymology of the word "Heropass."[93]

It is the merest assertion to say that Gurdjieff "undoubtedly" drew the concept of the Heropass from the Zoroastrian Zurvan.[94] One would first need to know that Gurdjieff had even heard of Zurvan, and then exclude the possibility of coincidence. He then goes on to speculate that "Heropass" may be a translation into Greek of "Zurvan," and that the name of the Sarman (Sarmoung) monastery, celebrated from *Meetings with Remarkable Men,* may have been a dialectal rendering of "Zurvan."[95] On other occasions, however, Bennett's commentary presents plausible perspectives, and leads into other questions, e.g. in writing of Gurdjieff's creation account, he states:

> One of the most significant notions that Origen expressed was of this privation, *sterisis*. This privation has been introduced into the cosmos so that *the creation can create itself*. If it were not aware of being separated from its Source there would be nothing to make it return to its Source. Hence privation is the beginning of the creation.[96]

---

[90] Bennett (1977b) xi.
[91] Bennett (1977b) ix.
[92] Bennett (1977b) xi.
[93] Bennett (1977b) 93. Reading *Beelzebub's Tales*, I cannot see how the Heropass can be "the Holy One who is All."
[94] Bennett (1977b) 48.
[95] Bennett (1977b) 93.
[96] Bennett (1977b) 67.

At this time, Bennett continued to develop his understanding of the centrality of values to human life, hence in these lectures he said:

> The invention of money had the result of fixing people's attention on visible, measurable values so that things began to be valued not directly in terms of their use to us but in terms of some token.... when there had been exchange of goods, everything was in tangible form related to what was needed for the support of life. Now a step was taken away from life and there began to be fixed in people the belief that there were values existing outside of them which were to be measured in terms of wealth of money and acquisitions.[97]

It may well be that he was also meditating on his obsessive quest for riches in the 1920s. Of course, the solution he adopted was not to despise money, but to cease to identify with it. As Bennett said in another context, it is not the aim of the work to do away with human nature (or its needs); rather, the aim is to transform so that our nature comprises a whole in which each part plays "does what it should do,"[98] and, I suggest, legitimate needs are met.

Bennett made another contribution to making Gurdjieff's books accessible, this time in the publication of what is called *The Third Series*, or *Life Is Real, Only Then, When I Am."* In June 1972, Valya Anastasieff, one of Gurdjieff's nephews asked him to help the family see the Third Series into print. If the approach was indeed made by Anastasieff, and there is no reason known to me to doubt it, it was a remarkable sign of both how they must have felt unable to progress with de Salzmann and how much they esteemed Bennett. Perhaps of all the former pupils, he and Entwistle alone could speak with her as peers, and were independent enough to be willing to do so should there be a need. Characteristically, Bennett could see both sides of the dispute and the sincerity of both

---

[97] Bennett (1997b) 145.
[98] Bennett (1994) 66.

parties. The work of editing the writing brought Bennett into a closer understanding of some of Gurdjieff's most subtle ideas:

> I had reached the conclusion that Gurdjieff was more than a Teacher and less than a Prophet. He was a man with a true mission and he devoted his entire life to it. He needed people who could understand his message, and yet he was compelled to make the message obscure and hard to understand.[99]

Bennett always referred to such as Jesus, Buddha, and Muhammad as prophets. He was ranking Gurdjieff but one level beneath these.

11.5 DEATH

When asked whether Bennett had known he was dying, Elizabeth replied: "His essence knew, his personality did not."[100] There is a strange story circulating that Bennett died very suddenly, the only notice of his death being when his ghost appeared to Dr Sharma who said to him: "You haven't have you?" to which Bennett replied "Yes, I have," before he vanished with a smile. The doctor then called Sherborne. Elizabeth answered the telephone, unaware that Bennett was unwell, but found him dead, in his arm chair.[101] Both Anthony Blake and George Bennett assure me that this is untrue: Bennett had been quite unwell, and on the morning of his death, had been doubled over in pain. He had not been left alone from that time until his death. In the days before his death, Bennett had seemed to Gavin Perry to be "angelic and unearthly … [although] his mind was as strong and sound as ever!"[102] Bhante, who had left Sherborne only about fifteen days before Bennett's death,

---

[99] Bennett (1997) 306.
[100] Wallace (1991) 30.
[101] Cilento (2006) 385-86.
[102] Perry (2020) 16.

recalled that Bennett did not look at all well, and that he was worried about his health.[103]

There is a notion current in the Gurdjieff tradition, that at the moment of death, a person is exposed to extraordinarily high fine energies (what Gurdjieff once called "hydrogens").[104] It is, perhaps, as if a barrage of higher force is experienced. To the degree that a person has formed their higher being bodies, and only to that degree, those higher being bodies can retain their integrity and individuality, and join the wave of unimaginably fine power, in their journey. The teaching, which was given orally by Ouspensky, was first published by Rodney Collin, a close associate of the latter:

> [W]e have every reason to believe that the impact of ever higher energies at successive stages of development does not end at point 8 [in principle, the age of 35], or the prime of life. At point 9 of a logarithmic scale, which is equivalent to about seventy-five or seventy-six years, a still higher and more penetrating energy is projected into man's existence by nature.
>
> But this energy differs from the others in that it is *too intense* to be contained within a body of cellular structure.... This final cosmic energy is of such a nature that at its impact the cellular body of man is immediately split off from any more enduring life-principle which may exist in him, and is left to disintegrate. This phenomenon appears to him as death.[105]

Nowhere is Bennett as clear as Collin. He does, however approach

---

[103] Dharmarwara (1991) 21.
[104] Ouspensky (1949) 90.
[105] Collin (1956) 9. George Adie, who studied with Gurdjieff and Ouspensky, and knew Collin apparently considered the first chapter of this book to be based upon, if not plagiarised from, Ouspensky. He said this to others, not to me, however, on my reading of the book, it is plausible.

this teaching, perhaps implying the influx of an external higher force, in the 1954 lecture posthumously published as *Making A Soul*, in a rather densely written passage:

> The separation that comes at death between this part [of conscious being] that continues and our ordinary mechanical functions is a very big shock. At death, all from that part of us that belongs to the world of facts from that which has some connection with the world of possibilities is separated. It is separated exactly at that point through which our attention passes.[106]

An obscure hint of this teaching may be found in some memoires of Gladys Remde, who was introduced to Gurdjieff and his leading disciples by Bennett:

> I had the privilege of listening to Laurence Rosenthal play Gurdjieff's Hymns from a Great Temple. Although I could no longer hear it through my ears, the music resounded in my body as though it were coming from inside me. The great powerful chords made me tremble. Afterwards I asked Laurence if those powerful chords represented a great force that someday we would have to meet. He said, "Yes, it is true."[107]

Whether Remde had first heard this from Bennett, or came to it herself, I do not know. However, the tradition was clearly known to him.

The tone on which Bennett closes the final edition of *Witness* is rather different from that of 1962:

> For myself, I am aware that death is a phenomenon of the

---

[106] Bennett (1995) 92.
[107] Remde (2014) 96.

conditioned world. "Survival" or "life after death" is also a conditioned state and not a very desirable one, for it is a state of dreaming without awakening. One needs a body to wake up in and where is a body to come from! (sic)

The path of reality does not lead into the future, but out of time and space altogether. Once one realizes this simple truth, life and death go into a different perspective. Life and death, time and space do not cease to exist, but existence itself is seen as a mirage.

Meanwhile, there is this human world and its predicament. For mankind the future is real enough. We cannot turn our backs on the needs of the world.... It is my hope and intention that before I depart from this conditioned world, I shall have helped many to find their way.

More than seventy years have passed since I began to ask questions and remember the answers. I asked my mother: "Why can't we see God?" to which she replied, "I expect he doesn't want us to." This did not satisfy me then, but it satisfies me now. I can understand much better why some mysteries must remain mysteries and why others can be revealed. I am wholly convinced that there is a Providential Power at work in the world, but it cannot help us without our consent. I finish this new edition of *Witness*, as I did the first, by quoting Gurdjieff: "Only two things have no limit—man's stupidity and the Mercy of God."[108]

I quoted that last paragraph near the opening of the book, and it is a fine place to end before attempting to review the entirety of this study.

---

[108] Bennett (1997) 307.

Bennett was interested in Morris Dancing: Henri Bortoft and A.G.E. Blake are center.

CHAPTER 12

. . . AND WE HAVE MADE A BEGINNING

12.1 THE WARP AND THE WEFT

In "The Unknown Builders," his modern mystery play, Bennett wrote: "We have come to the end and we have made a beginning." In this study, we have explored the two-level writing of *Witness*, his "book of visions," his "Art of Dying," his *Apologia pro vita sua*, his instructive autobiography and testament. The warp of *Witness*, the lengthwise basis of its fabric, is eternity, while the weft, the threads woven across the warp, are the narrative of his earthly experiences. Together, they make up his life; which means that to the extent that they are unseen or unknowable, so too is the subject life.

The weft has been quite impressive: Bennett was a tremendously talented person, who as a youth excelled both in sports and in studies as diverse as geometry, chemistry, and languages. He showed sustained evidence of great shrewdness and practical ability, e.g. as an Intelligence Officer in Constantinople and a member of the Parliamentary and Scientific Committee. But he also demonstrated considerable naivety, even suggestibility, e.g. his fond "get rich quick" plan with the Abdul Hamid Estates, and his even more foolish gullibility for the opportunistic Idries Shah. The eccentric brilliant graduate of King's College, formed in an elite school which equally valued traditional classical and contemporary scientific studies, was well suited to mix with any class of society, from the patricians of the House of Lords to the levelling attitudes of the American campers who descended on Sherborne. His work on higher dimensions was published academically, and his research in coal has been folded into the annals of science. His many books have for the most part never been out of print, or have been reissued; and a great number more were produced by his pupils from his papers and recordings of his formal lectures and occasional talks. His most substantial work, *The Dramatic Universe*, is still read and studied, although there is little evidence that it is being read by scientists: Bennett's appeal is most definitely sustained by those with an interest in the Gurdjieff system of ideas and methods. His very openness to new ideas and teachers left many of his students fair game for a confidence trickster (Chicoine),[1] and any fad from Medjugorje to crystals, but arguably lacking the compass that enabled Bennett to right himself.

Even more impressive, I would contend, is the warp of the cloth Bennett wove. I expand on this in the next five sections of this chapter, which are thematic rather than chronological.

But first, it remains controversial that Bennett, best known as a student of Gurdjieff and Ouspensky, took up with and endorsed a miscellany of gurus, notably Pak Subuh, Idries Shah, the Shivapuri Baba, and Hasan Lutfi Shushud. It has been suggested, throughout this study, that there were several factors at work here. First, how was he to know that the latest adventurer had not been, as Gurdjieff had claimed for himself, in an esoteric school (as he understood the latter term)? Then, there is the compelling thesis of Clive Entwistle that Bennett was searching for someone who could connect him with the Great Accumulator, as Gurdjieff had, when precipitating the fourth vision.[2]

---

[1] I have a good deal of information about G.B. Chicoine. Suffice to say, I consider him a grandiloquent fraud in the tradition of Idries Shah, whose writings he recommended and whose ideas about the Gurdjieff teaching being defunct, he parroted, e.g. in his unpublished letter of November 25, 1980 addressed to "Dear Institute Member." In that letter he bitterly complains about Elizabeth Bennett and sundry others. He also quotes a letter from Shushud dated September 26, 1979 which, Chicoine says, states that a letter Chicoine had written on August 23, 1979 shows to Shushud "the sign awaited" of "a strong spiritual master who could be appointed only by the Almighty." No one could ever accuse Chicoine of false modesty.

[2] Materials edited after his death describe Bennett, in the 1970s, saying that energy of the sex center can enter other centres, providing them with "extraordinary powers,"

In addition, I have suggested that Bennett's relation with these people echoes other relationships in his life, especially that with his mother: namely, there is a pattern whereby Bennett would learn a great deal through his attachment to a parental figure or teacher, and then learn a good deal more from the separation which followed. The process is somewhat analogous to the way that one goes to a university or college to acquire a skill, and then has to go into the broader world to put it into practice, and in doing so, tests one's self as well as one's knowledge. The analogy breaks down in that it is widely recognised that one must go out into life when the course has been completed; whereas with teachers such as those Bennett met, leaving may be seen as treachery. However, this way of looking at Bennett's life is productive, and has the virtue of explaining why he instituted a series of year-long courses. The Gurdjieff work is seen as a lifetime commitment, despite the fact that Gurdjieff seems to have clearly separated some of his most advanced pupils from him at least for lengthy periods: a practice which he articulated when sending Olgivanna Lloyd Wright to the USA, explained to Ouspensky, and effectively implemented with Orage and de Hartman, and possibly with the de Salzmanns and others. With his courses, Bennett followed and adapted Gurdjieff's example, in a gentler, less personal way, to teach the lesson of attachment then separation. It is a dangerous path, because the risk is that one will attach oneself to a charlatan; but given Bennett's views on hazard, he must be understood to have seen the danger and deliberately taken the risk – although it meant he could be mistaken.

Despite all this, when one looks back over the course of the years from 1897 to 1974, the figure of Gurdjieff emerges significantly larger than any other actor in both the warp and the weft of Bennett's life work. Perhaps most who read Bennett today do so because of their

---

and that this is what Gurdjieff meant by the "Great Accumulator": Bennett (1981) 46. This is not easily reconciled with the statements Bennett made that Gurdjieff described the energy as "higher emotional." I suspect that if Bennett did make the statement in question he meant that the sex centre force can have the function of igniting the higher emotional energy. I do not see how sex centre energy being released into the body can actually be the Great Accumulator.

interest in Gurdjieff. When they turn to Bennett, they learn a good deal about Gurdjieff and his system, but they also find something else. I suggest that this something else is, at bottom, Bennett's own individuality. In this, he was true to Gurdjieff's encouragement to develop one's own essential individuality. It may even be that Gurdjieff's system was intentionally left as it was so that each of his pupils had to complete it according to their own individuality. I would suggest that Bennett, like Ouspensky, Nicoll, and Orage, concluded that something more was needed, and was quite candid about what he was doing and what he was adding. It strikes the writer as ironic that the other major pupil, Jeanne de Salzmann, criticised Bennett as not remaining true to the line which Gurdjieff had brought, but herself later introduced a "new work," but would not acknowledge the differences.[3] Anthony Hodgson (section 10.6) wrote me an intriguing email in which he said:

> In the last months at Sherborne before he died JGB sketched out a sevenfold work. Blake cobbled together some related fragments around it to make the little book. I was not there at time. Quite some years later I realised that it is neither affirmation (Ouspensky) or receptivity (de Salzmann) but a triad where the reconciling factor is the living structure of the enneagram, especially the 142857 inner lines as Will. This changed my entire orientation to inner and outer work.[4]

This understanding of Will is a chief feature in Bennett's idiomatic continuation of Gurdjieff's system. In seeing that there had to be an individual development of the Gurdjieff system, Bennett was visionary. He had also shown boldness in his work for Britain during WWII, and then for scientific education with the Parliamentary and Scientific Committee. The great danger was that his development might proceed so far and in such a direction that the connection to his sources would

---

[3] Azize (2020) 220-25.
[4] Email dated March 27, 2020.

become tenuous, and effectively disappear. I do not think that happened with Gurdjieff, although he approached that point in the late 1950s with Subud. It seems to me that Bennett made a creative contribution to the Gurdjieff tradition. I would suggest that while *The Dramatic Universe* was important, and may yet be seen to be more valuable than I have understood, Bennett's contribution reached its apogee in *Witness*. After that, I would add two other books as particularly significant: *A Spiritual Psychology* and *Hazard*, a posthumously edited volume. In my opinion, these volumes, more even than *The Dramatic Universe*, demonstrate his achievement.[5]

In spite of, or even partly due to his eccentricities, Bennett had friends among his fellow Gurdjieff pupils. Martin Benson, for example, recalling Bennett's investigations in Islamic countries, launched into this appraisal:

> The smoke of the incense goes up into the tower and collects as a heavy soot from which they make their ink, because it comes from a holy temple. Isn't that fantastic? ... Bennett spent a lot of time in Turkey.... he went to all the temples and everything.... You know I almost died listening to this. And he said that's where they make their ink. I like Bennett, you know, because he was full of these tales. He listened, he watched, he heard, and he remembered. He remembered many, many things, Bennett had more vision than a hell of a lot of people in our work here have. He does fantastic things and he gets involved and I don't hold anything against him no matter what the hell he does.[6]

---

[5] Beryl Pogson (1895-1967), who had the carriage of Maurice Nicoll's groups after his death, enthusiastically quoted Bennett's writings, even *The Dramatic Universe* which she had evidently studied. Pogson (2002) 160-64, 272, 335, 410-12, but especially 165, where she says that "people should write down on their hearts and remember" a passage which Bennett had written about the will.
[6] Lehmann-Haupt (2011) 229.

12.2 AS A TEACHER OF CONTEMPLATIVE EXERCISES

All those who were at Coombe Springs or Sherborne, with whom I have spoken, state that even with Bennett's own exercises, the first stage was to prepare oneself with the Collected State Exercise (the Preparation), which came from Gurdjieff.[7] That exercise is critical for understanding Gurdjieff's contemplative exercises. In an unpublished piece, Bennett said:

> In the Collected State, one's attention is neither outward nor inward, but in the shape of the body itself. One must try to do this twice a day. In four or five weeks you will experience something that is with you throughout the day. This is like trying to balance an eel on the end of your nose.[8]

The exercises were not an end in themselves, they were, in the first place, to help one come to a better state; so much so, that without certain states, Bennett said, it was impossible to understand certain ideas.[9] In the second place, the exercises are a true alchemy: the energies of the higher bodies are separated and then consciously blended, so that the higher bodies can be formed.[10] He even averred that some of the exercises he taught provided a preparation to enter a world he called "transfinite reality," the world of "a consciousness beyond our awareness of what is going on ... consciousness without any limitations.... It is popularly called "cosmic consciousness"[11] This "consciousness beyond our awareness" seems to have been one of the points at which he departed from Bohm (section 10.3), while the reference to "cosmic consciousness" shows the significance of Bucke even into the 1970s (section 0.6).

---

[7] Azize (2020) 271-92.
[8] Provided to me by Andrew Moyer.
[9] Bennett (1998b) 41
[10] Bennett (1994) 181.
[11] Bennett (1998b) 14-15.

Another aspect of this is that, in meditation, Bennett said, "we teach ourselves how to look and how not to think."[12]

This brings me to a matter which, in the Gurdjieff tradition, is rather controversial: to what extent did Bennett change the contemplative exercises he had received from Gurdjieff, even as he passed them on? Our resources are limited: we simply do not know everything said or taught by Gurdjieff and Bennett on this topic. But as we saw in section 7.2 above, there is unimpeachable evidence in *Witness* that Gurdjieff taught Bennett many of his contemplative exercises, beginning with one so advanced that Jeanne de Salzmann was dubious as to whether Bennett had not misheard. In section 8.3 we saw that, together, with de Salzmann and Lannes, Bennett taught Toomer these exercises. Clearly, in the years immediately after Gurdjieff's death, his major pupils were passing on one and the same set of authentic Gurdjieff exercises. The initial exercise taught to Diane Cilento, probably in 1972, is recognisably from Gurdjieff:[13]

> The exercise, called 'blending', is like learning the ABCs of meditation, using breath control to correlate the three centres – intellectual, emotional and body centre—so that they vibrate at the same level. It requires utter concentration, especially in the effort to direct one's attention to the various parts of the body involved.[14]

I have inspected Cilento's notes of exercises taught her by Bennett and they include both some which are patently from Gurdjieff, others which patently are not (e.g. the *zikr*), and some of which one could be unsure. However, I have now considered quite carefully, even anxiously, the exercises which Bennett himself collected, and passed on to his son George and to Anthony Blake. I have compared these with what I have

---

[12] Bennett (1998b) 15.
[13] Cilento (2006) 317-19.
[14] Cilento (2006) 319.

been able to learn of the Gurdjieff exercises, and have heard of the conclusions of Annie-Lou Staveley, who made a point of collecting as many of Gurdjieff's authentic exercises as she could. Without engaging in a full-length study, I might be permitted to state my conclusions:

1. Bennett never himself lost sight of, or ceased to teach the contemplative exercises he had learnt from Gurdjieff.
2. The longer he lived, the more he added other practices. Blake candidly states: "he added and changed a great deal."[15] He also at one time substituted for them the Subud *latihan*, a practice he never entirely abandoned to the end of his days (although it was not mentioned to Sherborne residents who had not previously been initiated into it). It seems to me, that his experience of the *latihan* shattered any dependence on Gurdjieff's exercises in a way that his exposure to Islamic practices in 1953 had not. The next critical stage was, I think, the introduction of a breathing exercise, a form of *dhikr*, which he learned from Hasan Shushud.
3. At the end of his life, after much editing, Bennett prepared a series of exercises, which he left to his son George as a critical part of his legacy. Although some of these exercises, such as the Six Point Exercise were doubtless based on an original exercise from Gurdjieff, Bennett passed it on in his own distinctive way. Even his form of the "Conscious Stealing Exercise," one of the exercises in Bennett's final series, was influenced by a suggestion from Idries Shah.[16]
4. Many other exercises and notes of exercises were taken down by students at the Sherborne courses. From my reading of these, there is considerable overlap here between those Gurdjieff exercises I consider to be authentic (such as

---

[15] Blake (2017) 18.
[16] A personal communication from A.G.E. Blake, who was told this by Bennett himself.

The Four Ideals),[17] and those which are not from Gurdjieff, but are in the final series (e.g. the Nine Point Exercise). This is not to say that there is no element of, for example, the Nine Point Exercise which is not from Gurdjieff. I think that there is. But it has been developed by Bennett and can no longer be reliably taken as a Gurdjieff exercise.

It is my view that, on the available evidence, the exercises Bennett wrote up and edited at the end of his life are precisely those which he himself devised or developed in his own individual way, so that he himself thought of them as representing his own contribution to the organic tradition.

At this point, it might be of interest to consider how Cilento provides an example of an exercise and how Bennett used it. She provides only these details:

> The evidence, called 'blending', is like learning the ABCs of meditation, using breath control to correlate the three centres – intellectual, emotional and body centre – so that they vibrate at the same level. It requires utter concentration, especially in the effort to direct one's sensations to the various parts of the body involved.... I set myself the task of remembering to do it assiduously.... At the end of the day, I was astonished. Instead of the weariness that enters the bones at around 4.30 p.m.... I felt a boundless energy inside me as though I had just leapt up from a great night's sleep.[18]

Cilento was also present when, later on, the entire group worked at it together. Interestingly, immediately after the exercise, they were given glasses of water as if to refresh them after the effort, and renew

---

[17] Azize (2020) 229-41.
[18] Cilento (2006) 319.

a palpable connection with the physical life. They then brought their observations of their experience. After several people had spoken:

> Mr Bennett whistled gently through his teeth (a characteristic I was to get to know very well). He looked up at last and said gently, 'You see, it's all about energy – whether one has enough of it to make the extra effort outside the simple procedure of handling our normal physical requirements like work, sopping, preparing meals and household chores. The 'blending' exercise allows the three centres, the intellectual, the emotional and the physical to start working together, to become compatible. We get tired because one of the centres is being overworked and the others are not exercised at all. It is all a question of learning to maintain equilibrium.[19]

That is the best description known to me of how Bennett taught the exercises. While that exercise requires conscious attention upon the breath, Bennett, like Gurdjieff, also warned of the dangers of breathing exercises:

> The human organism is so constituted that there is a delicate instinctive balance between the rate of breathing, the speed and volume of the pulse, and the discharge into the blood of hormones and other substances known and still unknown to science. The respiration is also closely related to the rhythms of the brain and nervous system. If the rate and pattern of breathing are intentionally altered, all the other functions connected with it must be adjusted, or harm to the organism will result.[20]

Bennett would have been aghast at the idea that his exercises might

---

[19] Cilento (2006) 320.
[20] Bennett (1958) 97.

ever be published. However, he would have been at least equally horrified by the thought that they might fall out of use. The question might not be a simple one of whether to maintain secrecy or not; perhaps the deeper question is how the need for this material is to be met. Cilento recalls him emphasising that, "in our age, esoteric knowledge was being disseminated as the need grew more crucial."[21] In my own opinion, Bennett's most important contribution to the Gurdjieff tradition may well be that he kept alive the tradition of teaching authentic Gurdjieff exercises, for without that inner work, the action of the ideas themselves never exceeds a certain point.

I suspect that, in terms of Gurdjieff's system, the reason for the necessity of the inner exercises is, or at least may be, something which Bennett referred to in talks given in July 1974 to his pupils about "experiences that usually occur when working with one's body and the energy of inner attention."[22] Bennett said:

> There is another element in doing that has always to be remembered. We can't do unless there is an ideal or a pattern. This presents itself to us.... in some cases the pattern itself has power. This is perhaps true in all cases, but in some cases the power of the pattern is the most important thing, as in certain exercises we do.[23]

I might suggest that, at its simplest, the one pattern behind all the Gurdjieff exercises, is the sevenfold pattern set out in my monograph on those exercises.[24] Individual exercises, based on that simplest pattern, then "ramify," so to speak into more complex patterns, e.g. I ventured to set out the pattern of the "Colour Spectrum Exercise."[25] However, Bennett also developed the idea of "pattern" in a manner significant for

---

[21] Cilento (2006) 318.
[22] Bennett (1989) 76, notes by A.G.E. Blake.
[23] Bennett (1989) 21.
[24] Azize (2020) 298.
[25] Azize (2020) 255-56.

the Gurdjieff tradition, by relating to the question of "real I." In a talk delivered in 1970 but only posthumously published in an obscure and defunct magazine in 1992, Bennett stated:

> The second dimension of time is the one I call eternity. I call it this because it is really basically my impression of timelessness. It accompanies us: it is there. If I say, "what am I," I am this eternal pattern that is in all my present moments. The present moments are constantly changing their contents in terms of memories and expectations, but this eternal pattern which is always there I call myself.[26]

This is possibly the very clearest statement made within the Gurdjieff tradition on this central mystery. It would go some way to explaining why, although philosophy seems to be against the concept of the "self," unless it is taken as a social and individual construct, yet belief in its objective reality stubbornly persists.[27] There has been a significant amount of philosophical discussion on the related concept of the "self," but I shall not enter into here, but as Bennett had included in *Values*, Hume's acid attack on concepts of self, it is a fair assumption that Bennett was here answering Hume (section 5.4). Bennett also stated in one of his last talks that the pattern was critical in the exercises, and I suspect, the movements:

> There is another element in doing that has always to be remembered. We can't do unless there is an ideal or a pattern. This presents itself to us.... But in some cues (sic) the pattern itself has power. This is perhaps true in all cases, but in some cases the power of the pattern is the most important thing, as in certain exercises we do.[28]

---

[26] Bennett (1992) 10.
[27] These issues are dealt with in chapter 5 of McIntrye (2007).
[28] Bennett (1989) 21.

This brings us to Bennett's concept of pattern in creation and history.

12.3 THE "WAR WITH TIME"

When reading Bennett, it is difficult to avoid the impression that his "epochs" and his overall take on human development owe a great deal to Hegel, with his emphasis on "will," while Schopenhauer's "idea" or "representation" (*die Vorstellung*) may have been a factor in Bennett's later appreciation of what he called "sacred images."[29] However, we would mislead ourselves if we saw all of Bennett's thought in terms of Western or even of world philosophy. His thought is larger than that, although he makes contact with world philosophy and other fields, besides. In volume IV of *The Dramatic Universe*, the volume I personally consider the most important of the four, he wrote:

> Let us start then with the hypothesis that life appeared and developed on the earth in response to a **plan** that arose in the hyparchic future of the earth's mind. The plan was not produced in time; it was rather a work of pure Illumination. We said also that it must be an **act** of the Creative Will of the Sun.... the operations of the will in the hyparchic state of **non-potential virtuality** have no power to bring about their own realization in the present moment of time. For this, they must take shape as an eternal **pattern**. This transformation of the solar acts takes place in the mind of the earth. The virtual pattern is effectual only if it is associated with potential energy, thereby passing into the eternity of the present moment.[30]

There are several footnotes to this passage. One notes that Bennett

---

[29] Bennett (1966b) 397. Some of his later ideas on sacred images are found in Bennett (1989) 37-47.
[30] Bennett (1966b) 115-16.

regards the earth as a "sub-creative entity," but the more important one, coming at the end of this passage, reads:

> The reader must remember that these are not arbitrary statements, or the result of an 'inner illumination'; they follow directly from the character of the geometry of six dimensions.... the application of these results to the sun and earth are suggested by observations unconnected with the geometry.[31]

A full analysis would be rather lengthy, but I think we can safely extrapolate the following: the creative will of the sun (the active force), brought intelligence of the planet Earth to foresee the possibility of terrestrial life upon it (the passive or receptive force). For this life to be actualized upon the earth, a third or reconciling force was needed: an eternal pattern allied with the potential energy needed to pass from eternity into the present moment.[32] Although the roles of the sun and the earth as the active and receptive forces, respectively, came to Bennett from other sources and research, the fundamental insight into the creation of life on earth comes from his understanding of higher-dimensional geometry, as set out in the previous volumes of *The Dramatic Universe*. I cannot pretend to any understanding of this geometry, but Bennett's pupil A.G.E. Blake, relates Bennett's six-dimensional framework (including eternity, time, and hyparxis) to Bohm's contentions about "a sub-quantum level of entities," in some of his notes to the posthumously published *Existence*.[33]

The life which is thus created upon the planet Earth is not the same as the already existing life of the planet, it is of a higher order. Hence, says Bennett:

---

[31] Bennett (1966b) 116 third footnote.
[32] Bennett does not say it, so far as I am aware, but just as he observed that matter cannot give itself form, so perhaps he would agree that life cannot give itself the purpose and direction which typifies it: Bennett (1998b) 42.
[33] Blake in Bennett (2010) 60-65.

> [T]he significant point about life on the earth is its ability to maintain a higher level of order than that of the energies and substances on which it feeds. It is this power, more than anything else, that distinguishes living from non-living matter.... [Life] can maintain order by drawing on the sun, but only on condition that it can renew its own power of transformation.[34]

That is, Bennett literally suggests that the pattern of life which is exemplified in human existence, comes from the sun, and brings a higher level or order than what would be possible from purely terrestrial conditions. After all, matter lacks order and cannot give itself form.[35] Also critical in the passage quoted at the beginning of this section, is the observation that the eternal pattern needs a certain energy so that it may pass "into the eternity of the present moment." The background of this may be that, for Bennett, and I think for Gurdjieff, too: "all actual experience is contained in the present moment and is not to be found elsewhere."[36] That is, only in the experience of the present moment, can the energy needed to actualise a design be localised where it is needed. This may be another reason why Gurdjieff could say that "Life is real only then, when 'I Am'," for only in one's experience of the present moment (I Am) can the pattern of the higher level be united with the energy of the lower, producing an order of life higher than the preceding lower.

This is *reality*, for a human being. As we are, we treat as reality what is in fact only one aspect. This is most evident in the case of time. For Bennett:

> Time is the name that we give to the disruptive influence that enters our present moment. In so far as we succumb to this influence, we find past and future separated from us and

---

[34] Bennett (1966b) 9.
[35] Bennett (1998b) 42.
[36] Bennett (1966b) 4.

from each other. We do not readily grasp that the disruption is due to the weakness of our own will. Hence we treat time as an objective reality and the temporal sequence as independent of man or any other mode of existence.[37]

Much of Bennett's work on higher geometry was intended to show that time is not "an ultimate category," and how this can help us – provided perhaps that we are geometers—come to a more objectively true understanding of creation and existence, or more fully, the "Cycle of Being" depicted in figure 33.2 of volume II of *The Dramatic Universe*.[38] What I think is of the first importance for Bennett, although he does not draw out all the results of his insight in this book, is that: "the various ways in which the present moment seeks to preserve its identity against the disruptive influences that enter it ... [are] collectively [known] as the *War with Time*."[39] That phrase—the war with time—understood as a higher order maintained in accordance with a solar pattern projected onto the earth, may be taken as a concrete description of the spiritual life, and especially of efforts made in accordance with the contemplative exercises and other practices taught by Gurdjieff and Bennett.

12.4 CHRIST AND THE "WAR WITH TIME"

Let us take one example of the "war with time" from human history: the work of Christ. Given Bennett's conversion to Catholicism, it is no overstatement to suggest that his understanding of this is surprising. To anticipate, Bennett's mature teaching was that while the redemption from sin of Pauline theology was real and important, the true secret of Christ's mission was primarily the "transmission of Divine Love."[40]

---

[37] Bennett (1966b) 6.
[38] Bennett (1961a) 248, but see also 243-61.
[39] Bennett (1966b) 6.
[40] Bennett (1977a) 64. Bennett had made an earlier essay into this area in Bennett (1948), but he never had it published, perhaps considering it in need of the further consideration he later gave the topic.

But this was not clear to Bennett in 1966. In volume IV of *The Dramatic Universe*, Bennett commences his treatment of "The Time of Christ," by reminding readers that, in volume II, he had suggested that Jesus Christ had incarnated "the Word of God," understood as "the Cosmic Individuality."[41] There are many possible ways to approach this topic, but in this volume, Bennett ascribes much importance to there being "local concentrations of sinfulness," meaning that not all the world is equally sinful.[42] Sin, he states, is "an act of wilful disobedience to an obligation of which we are conscious."[43] That human Will, we are linked with "the Cosmic Individuality: that is, with Christ," and so man cannot "be wholly absolved from responsibility if he accepted the 'evil suggestion' that he could become an independent creator in his own right."[44]

Hence, the work of Christ is inextricably linked with human sin, for: "a redemptive act by a non-sinful agent within humanity," directed towards the human situation, was necessary.[45] The Incarnation of Jesus was, according to Bennett, "possible only in an already perfected body-mind," with the result that, contrary to theosophical and similar ideas, Jesus neither developed nor grew in terms of his individuality (and hence, I suggest, his being).[46] The "Intervention" which was the Incarnation had to be prepared, and could only occur when the time was ripe. Bennett prepared the ground for this by his general theory of cycles and epochs in human history.[47] However, the Incarnation is beyond human understanding:

> chiefly because it belongs to the Realm of Impossibility that lies outside Existence itself. To unmake what had been made and to redeem mankind, an act of Will is needed that would not destroy Existence or even the smallest part of it. Within

[41] Bennett (1966b) 338 and the footnote.
[42] Bennett (1966b) 339.
[43] Bennett (1966b) 257.
[44] Bennett (1966b) 257.
[45] Bennett (1966b) 339.
[46] Bennett (1966b) 343 and the footnote.
[47] Bennett (1966b) 344-45.

the empty places of Existence a new power was to work and this was to be the Unitive Energy ... or the Power of love concentrated within a living man.[48]

Bennett then makes two quite extraordinary assertions, first, that the effects of the Incarnation would be felt through all human history, as they belong to the hyparchic (and thus non-time limited) aspect of reality.[49] Second, that although love was known to humanity before the time of Christ, it was only in his time that its significance penetrated into humanity. Pre-Christian Buddhist texts, he says, refer to causality and liberation, but only in post-Christian times, do ideas of compassion and redemption appear.[50] The same is almost entirely true, he suggests, of Hebrew texts on love, although the prophets knew of the redemption which was to come.[51] I am not endorsing, merely reporting Bennett's contention, but this would show the global significance of the Incarnation, whether one has heard of Christ or not, in Bennett's theory.

One of the more striking aspects of Bennett's theory is that he takes quite seriously the frequent references to the fulfilment of prophecies in the Gospel writers. This, he says, was a way of indicating to those with the requisite knowledge that there had been significant preparation for the Incarnation, as without such work: "it would not be possible to bring the enormous energies into play without disturbing the natural order."[52] Just as the Incarnation itself, with its concentration of higher energies, transcended the historical order, so too did Jesus's teaching. According to Bennett, this has not been understood. The limitations of the present moment can be transcended in the temporal future which we readily conceive and in the hyparchic future, which we do not, as it pertains to Will, and enters time from a non-temporal dimension. When Jesus spoke of the coming of the Kingdom of Heaven, his preparing a place for

---

[48] Bennett (1966b) 345.
[49] Bennett (1966b) 345.
[50] Bennett (1966b) 345.
[51] Bennett (1966b) 345.
[52] Bennett (1966b) 346.

his disciples, and so on, he is speaking of the hyparchic future. Hence, the standard dilemma between the promise of the early Parousia and its non-fulfilment, can be resolved if that promise refers to hyparxis.[53] Bennett deals with this in rather a short-hand way, but it seems to me that this is how he would interpret a text such as Matthew 16:28 "There be some standing here, which shall not taste of death, till they see the Son of Man coming in his kingdom."

In *The Dramatic Universe*, Bennett touches lightly on the Last Supper. It was, he states, "the concentration of Love and its transmission to the disciples to enable them to participate in the Resurrection."[54] I have much simplified Bennett's treatment so that the main outline might appear with some clarity. He was to return to the same topic within a decade in *The Masters of Wisdom*. Again, I must omit the great bulk of this unfinished work, but at least the chapter on "The Time of Christ" was completed. By 1974, when he is writing this material, Bennett has fallen under the spell of Shushud and his idea of the "Masters of Wisdom" from Central Asia. In 1966, the Magi of Matthew 2 were a "slender" indication that the "Hidden Directorate" sought to make contact with Jesus.[55] By 1974, they and the Essenes (or at least their inner circles), are members of the Masters of Wisdom, who "existed in central Asia from before the time of Zoroaster."[56] They were divided into exoteric, mesoteric, and esoteric castes.[57] As before, Bennett stresses that a "lasting change came over the whole world from the time of Christ."[58] He writes, with a new clarity that "we do not and cannot know what the event was in its full majesty because it took place in a region that human consciousness cannot reach."[59] The reason we cannot make sense of the Passion, Resurrection, and associated events is that: "We

---

[53] Bennett (1966b) 348-49.
[54] Bennett (1966b) 349.
[55] Bennett (1996b) 347.
[56] Bennett (1977a) 51.
[57] Bennett (1977a) 51-52.
[58] Bennett (1977a) 53.
[59] Bennett (1977a) 56.

seek to interpret an action that is beyond the mind of man in terms that derive from our human experience of this world."[60]

At this point, the temptation would be to follow Bennett into his discussion of various "worlds." Now, the temptation is seductive: Bennett developed a scheme of four worlds based, he said, on Sufi ideas, but consistent with mathematical ideas he drew from the work of Georg Cantor. I am unable to follow the arguments in *Georg Cantor: His Mathematics and Philosophy of the Infinite*, but it is notable that Cantor believed that: "in silence he could perceive the workings of a divine muse, he could hear a secret voice from above which brought him both inspiration and enlightenment."[61] This can probably be connected to Bennett's insistence upon *pattern* as a foundational element in the visible world, for the formative patterns belong to the subtle worlds.[62] However, the undertaking would be too large for this study, and also too tangential to the main themes of *Witness*. However, his conclusion at this point is intimately related with his eighteenth to twenty-second visions, vouchsafed between 1959 and 1961:

> I believe that the mission of Jesus as no less than an attempt to bring mankind to the next stage of human evolution when love will be an inherent property of the human essence as creativity has been for the past thirty-five or forty thousand years.[63]

In Bennett's scheme, the Transfiguration has a special place. Apart from his opinion that Judas was probably also present,[64] he sees the Transfiguration as "an action that embraced all worlds."[65] Suffice to say, this means that it did not only take place in time and eternity, but

---

[60] Bennett (1977a) 56.
[61] Dauben (1991) 289.
[62] Bennett (1958) 90.
[63] Bennett (1977a) 57.
[64] Bennett (1977a) 64 and 68.
[65] Bennett (1977a) 64.

also in hyparxis, for it opened "the channel of Divine Love to the other disciples and eventually to all who were capable of receiving it."[66] The Transfiguration is, for Bennett, the key to the Last Supper, for the latter transmitted to the disciples the power which had descended at the former event.[67] By the sharing at the Last Supper, the apostles entered the Kingdom of Heaven, and so passed "beyond life and death."[68]

12.5   THE SACRED IMAGE

I shall pass over Bennett's comments in *The Masters of Wisdom* about the mystery of despair and humiliation which Jesus, Judas and Peter had to endure, however, the idea that the resurrection body can only be seen by those who are able to love provides a link to his developed philosophy of the "Sacred Image," and his understanding of mysticism:

> From time to time, saints have visions of Jesus in his resurrection body, but they cannot approach him, as could the disciples who had been transformed into the resurrection world. This is where Paul fell into error. His vision of Jesus was not the same as the awareness of immediate presence that was possible for the disciples who had been initiated at the Last Supper.[69]

So far as I am aware, Bennett never makes this connection, but it does seem to me that his concept of what occurred through the work of Jesus fits in well with the ideas presented by Gurdjieff in the Four Ideals Exercise, namely, that an "ideal" of Christ really does exist, above the atmosphere of the earth, and is associated with an unimaginably fine energy, although an unprepared person cannot enter into contact with

---

[66] Bennett (1977a) 65.
[67] Bennett (1977a) 66.
[68] Bennett (1977a) 70.
[69] Bennett (1977a) 70.

it.⁷⁰ If one recalls that Gurdjieff spoke about these concepts at the time of the fourth vision (the Great Accumulator, section 3.6), one grasps the remarkable continuity between Gurdjieff's thought and Bennett's, even over a period of fifty years. In a lecture of May 14, 1974, after referring to Gurdjieff's "Conscious Stealing Exercise," which is quite similar to the "Four Ideals," Bennett stated, using the terms "sacred image" for "ideal":

> The sacred image is more than existing thing. The [sacred] image of Christ is more than any man, more even than Jesus was, because a power has been transmitted to that image which is then something very extraordinary. It is something which is more than this world. To bring it about very extraordinary things have to happen. Those who are concerned in the event, very often have to pay for it with their own lives and they have to return to the world that is beyond existence by way of a violent death.⁷¹

Bennett's development of the concept "sacred image" is of intrinsic interest; and is to be related to the comment he made in an unpublished letter that: "one of the problems that people were experiencing with the Gurdjieff Work was that they were so afraid of losing sight of their own nullity that they neglected a positive approach towards the higher powers."⁷² Incidentally, we saw that Gurdjieff told his pupils in Paris that they had the potential to be "micro-Dieu" (section 0.3). Further, pupils of George Adie in Newport, Sydney, would sometimes accuse themselves in trenchant terms. Adie would try to bring balance to their self-directed insults. On at least one occasion, he recalled that, in Paris 1948 or 1949: "someone had accused himself of being *merde* [shit], and Gurdjieff, who had himself used the word quite liberally, replied, "You are not tail of

---

⁷⁰ Azize (2020) 231-33.
⁷¹ Bennett (2017b) 62.
⁷² Blake (1980a) 179.

donkey, you are pupil of Mr Gurdjieff."[73] Gurdjieff was aware of the danger, as was Bennett.

In the same lecture, Bennett had said that "the sacred image is a picture or a mental image of God," but that we do not understand what an image *simpliciter* is, and its power.[74] He then offers the example of a man standing before a mirror and shaving. We think of the reflected image as less than the man, but viewing the image shows the man what remains to be done, and in this way the image influences the action.[75] This can be taken further, for example, the image of a doctor is a large influence on whether we trust the doctor or not, and perhaps even more than any prescribed medicine, contributes to healing.[76] Ten years earlier, delivering the lectures of *A Spiritual Psychology*, Bennett proposed that we consider the Guardian Angel as being similar to child who holds a pattern of the carpet to be woven before the workers, in the Eastern manner.[77] I suggest that the pattern helps because, in Bennett's later vocabulary, it presents an image. He explained the Guardian Angel's work thus:

> The Guardian Angel draws us towards spirituality and gives each of us the pattern of our spiritual life. If we can become aware of this, as it were *listen*, then we can receive both strength and guidance from it. In spite of all the mistakes a man may make in his life, the Guardian Angel still preserves his destiny for him and guards it. It always keeps open for him the path he should be following, and makes it possible for him to return to that path even if he has lost his way.[78]

A little later in the same lecture, in a passage which I suspect is related to the events around the King's College Vision, when he sensed

---

[73] Adie (2015) 147.
[74] Bennett (2017b) 59.
[75] Bennett (2017b) 59-60.
[76] Bennett (2017b) 60.
[77] Bennett (1964) 168-69.
[78] Bennett (1964) 168.

the presence of a power which he thought might be an angel (section 6.3), Bennett adds:

> the Guardian Angel exemplifies the ideal character to which our nature should conform. We can be very differently related to this ideal; it may be 'outside' or it may be 'inside'. So long as we live in the lower parts of the self, our Guardian Angel remains outside of us, a spiritual being alongside of our material being. This is how it is experienced when there is a moment of awakening which makes us aware of the presence of our Guardian Angel, as if it were really a voice speaking to us, other than our own.... The transition from the otherness of the Guardian Angel to its sameness, to its oneness with us is connected with the whole process of transformation of man.[79]

The following passage from lecture is noteworthy not only for its intriguing autobiographic comment, but more because by relating "conscience" to the "Guardian Angel" Bennett develops Gurdjieff's ongoing introduction of overtly religious elements into his teaching, and showing how what he had previously described in terms almost physiological or from engineering, could more properly be understood as referring or at least including reference to spiritual (angelic) entities:

> It seems very probable that our conscience is the material form of our Guardian Angel; that is, the form which is impressed upon our energies by the presence of a spiritual power that is part of ourselves. The Guardian Angel, being spiritual, has powers beyond conscience.... It is quite impossible to 'prove' it to the satisfaction of our reason; but I am convinced all the same that my Guardian Angel does help

---

[79] Bennett (1964) 177.

me, and has more than once got me out of very awkward situations.[80]

This then brings us to the sacred image in worship.[81] We have seen that just before he died, Bennett told Blake that: "he considered his main personal task consisted in finding a way of enabling the Western people he had to deal with to practise devotion."[82] He also told his son George that his aim was to introduce a new form of worship, and that "it might be related to nature."[83]

In his last years, Bennett saw the image as an instrument through which "existence is entered by what is beyond existence," and he related this to the biblical prohibition of idols, for the "true image is created without matter."[84] The process is one whereby "the spiritual can enter the material and ... we ourselves can be spiritualized."[85] Bennett relates this to worship:

> It must be said in all truth that there is a spiritual presence in the world and that in religious worship even by people who do not look beyond existence something does happen so that when they feel the presence of God in their worship this is not necessarily imagination. The presence of God can be felt and it is there. But that presence is adapted to our limitations.[86]

It is no problem, for Bennett, that we speak of an image when speaking of God, we have necessarily to speak of God as an image because:

---

[80] Bennett (1964) 190. Blake relates the ideas of pattern, hyparxis, and action in (1980a) 54.
[81] Bennett made some comments about "perfection" in the celebration of the Mass by Benedictine monks: Bennett (1998b) 50-51.
[82] Blake (1980b) 23, the fuller quote is in section 0.6.
[83] Conversation between George Bennett and the author, by Skype, June 28, 2021.
[84] Bennett (1998b) 24.
[85] Bennett (1998b) 24.
[86] Bennett (1998b) 24.

"God has too many dimensions to get into existence.[87] Further, by using a sacred image we are thereby protected from the mistake of thinking that we can know God in the same way as we know anything else.[88] When God comes into the existing world, He is subject to the limitations of the existing world." This leads to a discussion of the Incarnation, and how due to these limitations, there were things even Jesus did not know, and some of his prophecies were not fulfilled.[89] As we are, we *need* the help of sacred images, because we cannot *see* into higher worlds, but a sacred image:

> has been created around a very deep reality: the presence on this earth of a divine being. After the separation of the cosmic individual from this world through death ... the image is created that is a source of consolation and hope for people for a very long time.[90]

In a passage with striking parallels to Gurdjieff's "Four Ideals Exercise," Bennett states:

> The sacred image makes it possible to return to the Source. Because people's aspirations are directed towards the image, a concentrated flow of energy is produced. For those who can transform their energies with sufficient intensity and purity of intention, through their prayers and disciplines, it is possible to pass beyond and become directly connected with the source of the image. If there is not sufficient purity and intensity, the energies will only rise to a certain height, between Worlds 24 and 12. It is in this way that there accumulate reservoirs of this sort of energy centred around the focal points of prayer and devotion.[91]

---

[87] Bennett (1998b) 26.
[88] Bennett (1998b) 31.
[89] Bennett (1998b) 26; see also Bennett (2000) 76-77, and (2006) 8.
[90] Bennett (1998b) 30.
[91] Bennett (1994) 164. For the Four Ideals Exercise, see Azize (2020) chapter 17.

Blake recalls that in his last years, Bennett was approaching the question of a sacred image of nature, saying that we can and should learn to love nature, but that for this it was necessary that we realize that nature itself loves us.[92] This is connected with the sacred image of God, for: "We have knowledge of God in Nature, not as an all-powerful self-subsistent Being, but as the Source of goodness, mercy and redemption."[93]

12.6 HAZARD

This material came from *A Spiritual Psychology*, which together with *Hazard*, I consider to be the most important of Bennett's works after *Witness*. In *A Spiritual Psychology* Bennett shows why he believes that the inner work Gurdjieff taught is connected with and made possible with the help of spiritual intelligences. Bennett also stated that: "The earth itself is the body of the planetary spirit."[94] Now, Anthony Hodgson has suggested to me that Bennett's research sees the universe as intelligent, and "intelligence takes meaning from the capacity to navigate through hazard."[95] He stated that: "hazard ... is compounded of two things, one is a direction and the other is uncertainty."[96] A renewed understanding of this concept came to Bennett in the last ten years of his life.[97]

The crystallization of the astral body is a hazardous activity, in Bennett's terms, and part of the reason for writing *Witness* was to urge readers not to fear the dangers, and further, to indicate the general nature of the way forward: so that we do not fall "between false hope and mistaken hopelessness."[98] As noted in chapter 8, Bennett's idea of "dramatic" was that: "A situation is dramatic when there is a need accompanied by the uncertainty as to whether it will be satisfied."[99] Bennett says

---

[92] Blake (1996) 286.
[93] Bennett (2010) 81.
[94] Bennett (1983) 78.
[95] Email communication to me, April 13, 2020.
[96] Bennett (2010) 32.
[97] Blake (1980a) 101.
[98] Bennett (1998b) 28.
[99] Bennett (1991b) 3.

much about higher bodies, perhaps even as much as Gurdjieff, and in *Witness* he shares his experience of what he believed to be his astral or Kesdjan body, beginning with the first vision and through to the twenty-fourth. He related "hazard" to its etymological origin in the Arabic, an etymology found in Skeat, who derives the modern word directly from Middle English "the name of a game of chance, generally played with dice."[100] Einstein said that God does not play dice.[101] Bennett was not so sure. He elaborates his theory of hazard by reference to a board game:

> This game is really a representation of a cosmic doctrine that has been lost, rediscovered, and lost again.... and is being rediscovered in the twentieth century. The principle of the game of backgammon is that one has a certain path to traverse, and one traverses this path by moving from available hole to available hole, however, one does so under the control of an uncertain factor introduced by the throw of dice.[102]

I would conjecture, fairly confidently, that the "rediscovery" Bennett refers to is Gurdjieff's teaching of the "Law of Octaves,"[103] which was schematically represented in the Enneagram, and says that every process is subject to a law (or regular pattern) of discontinuity, making it necessary for action of an appropriate type to be taken at various points to keep the process moving as intended.[104] The point where action is needed is hazardous, and in *Witness* Bennett has provided many examples of where he did not do what he should have done, or did attempt but failed, and on occasions, where he succeeded, as with the critical fourth vision (at Fontainebleau), but also with the twelfth (helping his

---

[100] Skeat (1910) 265.
[101] See, for example, https://www.quantamagazine.org/pioneering-quantum-physicists-win-nobel-prize-in-physics-20221004/ accessed October 23, 2023.
[102] Bennett (1991b) 16.
[103] Ouspensky (1949) chapter 7.
[104] Bennett (1973) 196-97 makes the connection between Gurdjieff's "Law" and hazard. Gurdjieff's "Fourth Way" is aptly described as a "hazardous path," the title of Blake's two-part study Blake (2017) and (2018).

deceased mother), where all depended upon his own effort. Hence, in *Hazard* he declares: "So it is sufficient ... to say that what gives human life the character of enterprise, adventure, and even purpose is that there are crossroads at which there is an element of uncertainty."[105]

We might add that *Witness* also taught that *to the extent one is conscious, and to that extent only, one is aware of and able to choose at the crossroads*. Perhaps hyparxis can enter time only at the crossroads. This lesson must be related to Ouspensky's riddle of the knight offered three paths (sections 4.1 and 4.5). From this, Bennett learnt a hard lesson:

> Above all, I want you to grasp that hazard is not a negative state. It is not insecurity of the negation of security, nor is it disturbance or the negation of rest. It is a living potential and it is the gateway to a reality that is beyond security, beyond certainty, and that has no limits because it has no end.[106]

These words do not appear in *Witness*, but they belong to the same testimony. These ideas had been stewing in Bennett's brain for quite a while. His letter of January 7, 1963 to Bohm sketches a "universal principle of confusion":

> Perfect finite systems cannot exist, so that every finite system is imperfect. All imperfection is confusion. Consequently, in all finite situations, there must be some degree of confusion. It also seems probable that the confusion in a system of the Nth order can be resolved, or at least reduced, in the context of the (N + 1) the order.[107]

This referred back to a lost letter which Bohm had written Bennett on December 24, 1962, in which he offered as an example of confusion

---

[105] Bennett (1991b) 50.
[106] Bennett (1991b) 27.
[107] Blake (2016) 25.

"I wish and do not wish to get out of bed." As Bennett replied, they are two different "I"s.[108] If we pursued this, it would quickly take us right back to the foundation of Gurdjieff's system, both theoretical and practical. "The evolution of man," according to Gurdjieff could "be taken as the development in him of those powers and possibilities which never develop by themselves, that is, mechanically."[109] Evolution has been the super-idea of modern thought, and Gurdjieff related it, so far as humans are concerned, to conscious self-development. Bennett elaborated this concept by relating it to hazard:

> Evolution is more than development. True evolution is going into the dark. The Cosmic Life Principle is the principle into which life will enter. It needs the living, it devours it. Because it is empty it does not mean that it has no power. It is a very great power. It acts on all of us.[110]

Bennett has not used the word "hazard" here, but going into the dark cannot be anything else. We find ourselves in a hazardous situation, a dramatic universe, between order and chaos; as Gurdjieff told him, not with freedom itself but rather, with the *possibility* of freedom.[111] Bennett was, as noted, largely an autodidact. This both facilitated a tremendous breadth of research but also lead to limitations, especially in methodology. It was significant in his achievements, that he had an early and most remarkable strength in geometry, a wonderful discipline for a mystic, for over the doors of his Academy, Plato had written: "Let no person who is not a geometer enter."[112]

---

[108] Blake (2016) 25.
[109] Ouspensky (1949) 56,
[110] Bennett (1998b) 49.
[111] Bennett (2010) 33.
[112] My translation: Negropontis (2019) 3.

12.7 BENNETT'S ACHIEVEMENT

Most people with an interest in the life and thought of J.G. Bennett have come to him through their more fundamental interest in G.I. Gurdjieff. I have already stated that, in my view, Bennett was, at least in his intellectual formations, after P.D. Ouspensky, the most significant of Gurdjieff's pupils. He was indefatigable: there are extant written and audio records of over 1,120 talks, only 419 of which date before the Sherborne years which began in 1971.[113] It may be that at some point a previously unknown work will appear, but in the year 2024, that is how it appears to me. Gurdjieff's ideas and methods were intended to have a practical effect, and in particular, to lead to the crystallisation of higher being-bodies in its practitioners. No other student of Gurdjieff's ever produced the body of work on the formation and coating of the higher bodies which Bennett did, and in this respect, *Witness* is his greatest endeavour. I do not think that any other position is even fairly arguable. Ouspensky is sometimes criticised as preserving a form of Gurdjieff's teaching which Gurdjieff himself had superseded, just as Bennett is criticised for unrestrained development.

I doubt that either view is correct. They were different, and it was fruitful that they were. Had Ouspensky been like Bennett, he would have so mixed his own ideas with Gurdjieff's that we would not have any clear idea of which was which. But, at least in *In Search of the Miraculous*, Ouspensky was scrupulous in keeping his own ideas and Gurdjieff's separate.[114] Had Bennett been like Ouspensky, we would not have *Witness* with its ideas of death and resurrection, and the development of the concepts of hazard and the sacred image.

It is also, I suggest, to Bennett's credit, that in exploring and developing Gurdjieff's legacy, he would revise his own theses, sometimes in quite significant ways; not treating his own conclusions as infallible. David Seamon, who studied with Bennett at Sherborne, offers an interesting

---

[113] Perry (2022) 1.
[114] Ouspensky (1949) 208-13 and 329-40.

example of how Bennett made a study of what are called "triads," and in typifying them, departed first from Ouspensky, and then from his own earlier views.[115] The triads are a difficult topic, and Seamon attempts, with some success, to make the basic ideas more accessible. While dealing with Seamon highlights one matter which I had missed: that while Gurdjieff and Ouspensky spoke of the three "forces" working through each triad, Bennett substituted the term "impulses," for the word "force" suggests an energy which remains within itself, while "impulse" has the connotation of an energy "going out of itself."[116] This seems appropriate given the role of the triads of energies in the creation and maintenance of the world: they provide impulses.

Bennett tried to place Gurdjieff's teaching within the context of a "hidden directorate" or school of the "Masters of Wisdom," even if he died before he could complete committing his thesis to paper.[117] As Thompson formulated it, Bennett believed that: "Gurdjieff was not to be seen as an isolated phenomenon, but that his teachings should be understood in connection to a larger scale of action."[118] Bennett took Gurdjieff's system, including the Law of Seven, and summarised his findings with an autobiographical allusion:

> We do not have within us a principle of stable existence. What we find in ourselves, on the contrary, is a principle of renewal, of return, of being lost and found again. This principle we can really only understand if we experience it in ourselves; and we know its taste as the taste of rebirth: whenever we come back from a state of oblivion, of forgetfulness.[119]

But what of those who are curious as to Bennett's work apart from Gurdjieff? Perhaps Bennett's intellectual achievement lay chiefly in his

---

[115] Seamon (2020) 89 n.24.
[116] Seamon (2020) 87, quoting from n.21 on that page.
[117] See Bennett (1973) and especially (1977a).
[118] Thompson (1995) 45.
[119] Bennett (2004) 182.

attempt to place all of his quite considerable knowledge in the largest possible context. He saw human history as part of the unfolding of events occurring in higher dimensions. He saw the three-dimensional world which we perceive as a cross-section of a six-dimensional cosmos. He tried to establish a framework in which human life and smaller communities could be related to these higher forces and realms.[120]

Writing in the *Encyclopedia of Religion and Nature*, Bruce Monserud observed that Bennett had discovered methods for coal-burning which reduced pollution, and in *The Dramatic Universe* had produced a cosmic context for environmental ethics, which included but was not limited to this world and to eternity. This led to Bennett anticipating modern notions of a needed "radical reformulation of moral philosophy."[121] As stated, science was for Bennett more than just a way of earning money or of occupying his mind; he always related his science to what I must call his mysticism. Perhaps his achievement here is analogous to that of people in a cave. If there is no light whatever, they know only that the cave is mysterious. However, should one of them strike a match, they may see something of the cave's size and contours. That is, the mystery does not disappear, but rather they discover new dimensions of it. This, I suggest, is a way of thinking about how Bennett used his knowledge not to explain or demonstrate, so to speak, mysticism, but far more to reveal something of the sublime mystery.

It would be trite and hackneyed to say that Bennett's greatest achievement was his life. But I would venture to speculate that his greatest literary achievement was his autobiography. In about 1974, looking back on the fifteen years which had passed since the first edition, he wrote:

> I can see my life as a succession of "final revelations" all of which have carried me a step forward, but each of which

---

[120] I have not dealt with this in any detail, but see Bennett (1990).
[121] Monserud (2010) accessed from the internet, June 2020. No pagination shown.

proved to be a false crest from which I have seen new peaks to climb.[122]

One of the risks inherent in a book like this, a risk which it inherits from *Witness*, is that it might give the impression that unless one has visions and revelations analogous to Bennett's no progress on the spiritual path is possible. Bennett was quite aware that it was possible to "see into reality," and yet, to then stray "from some vision of things as they are into" inventions of their own.[123] Such people can run the risk, Bennett says, of mistakenly thinking that "what they have seen is all that has to be seen," and then interpreting their genuine perceptions according to what they have learned with their ordinary minds.[124] Perhaps what he then says of Gurdjieff can also, mutatis mutandis, be applied to himself:

> I say that Gurdjieff was a great man because having seen, he went on looking and never was satisfied until the end of his life. Nor did he ever set himself up for one who had reached finality. People with revelations are rare, but not very rare. Humble people are rare; but people who see something and remain humble are very, very rare.[125]

This connection of the Gurdjieff system to forms of worship was, for Bennett most advisable. Worshippers need a place to foregather, and the Djamichunatra, perhaps the ideal sacred place for the Gurdjieff tradition, had been wantonly destroyed. But having once been built, it can still inspire. My thesis is that Bennett's greatest achievement is found in his understanding of the twenty-four visions he had into life, death, eternity, the entry of higher energies of love into this world, the growth of being through the various spiritual disciplines he had learnt, so that

---

[122] Bennett (1997) 283.
[123] Bennett (1995) 81-82.
[124] Bennett (1995) 81-82.
[125] Bennett (1995) 82.

one could survive death as a conscious and active entity, and the relationship of these to traditional faiths.

This provides context to what I might describe as a profound and almost astonishing response Bennett gave in one his groups when a student asked him how he would answer "the Beelzebub question about how to save people on earth." That question occurs at the end of chapter 47 of *Beelzebub*: Hassein asks Beelzebub how he would reply to Our All-Embracing Creator Endlessness Himself, were he to ask him about humanity: "whether it is still possible by some means or other to save them and to direct them into the becoming path?"[126] Bennett stated that he would respond: "By allowing them to see the state of their own souls."[127] He was speaking from his own experience. If one vision was critical in this understanding, I would venture to say that it was the twenty-fourth when he saw "I am and always will be." Finally, he had achieved the certainty that at death he would lose neither his astral (Kesdjan) body or his mind: that he would remain *himself*.[128]

The penultimate word might be allowed to Anthony Blake's recollection:

> But an extremely important thing appears to have emerged in this [Sherborne] period of his life. While he was extending and speaking about communication with higher intelligences he was drawn to a sense of his own personal task or mission. It was to help discover or bring into manifestation a *new form of worship* mainly by creating a new sacred image.[129]

But the final word must be Bennett's: "Union has no end and no beginning; it is what it is beyond all worlds."[130]

---

[126] Gurdjieff (1950) 1182.
[127] Bennett (2006a) 62.
[128] Bennett (1997) 299.
[129] Blake (2017) 35-36, see also 28.
[130] Bennett (1949a) 14.

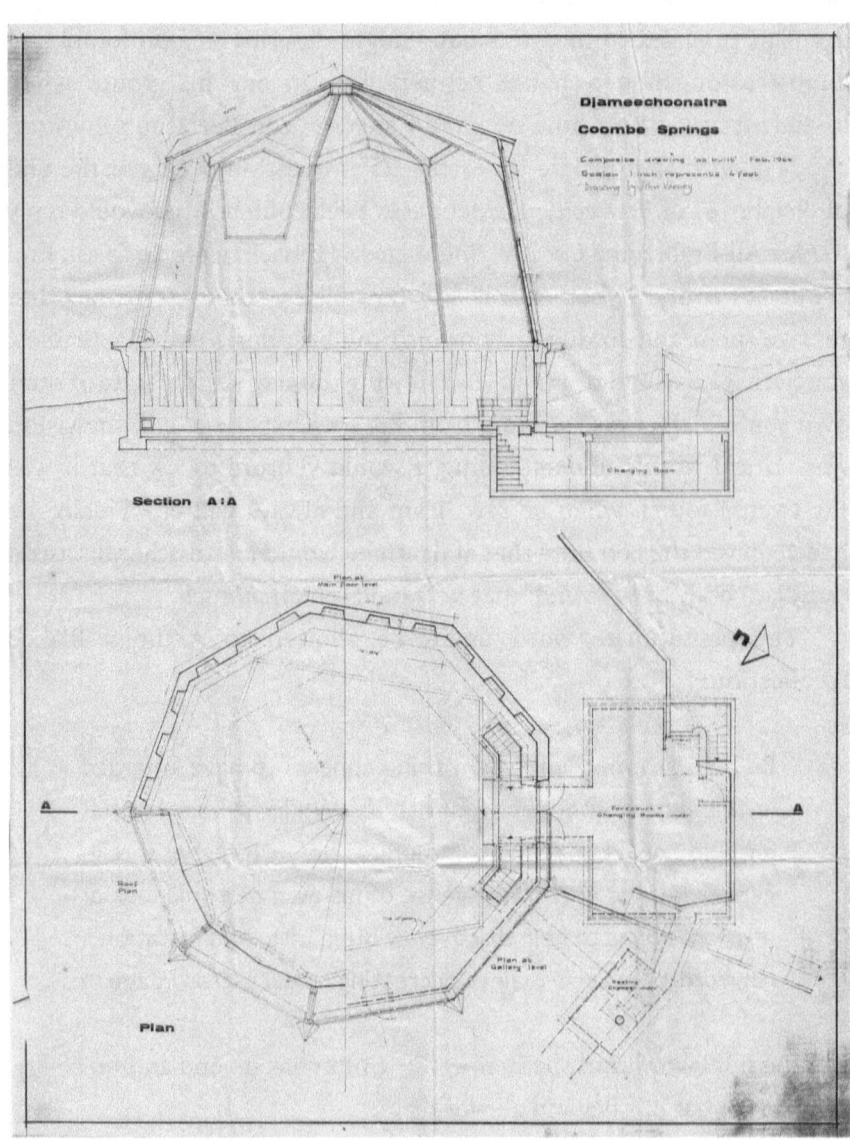

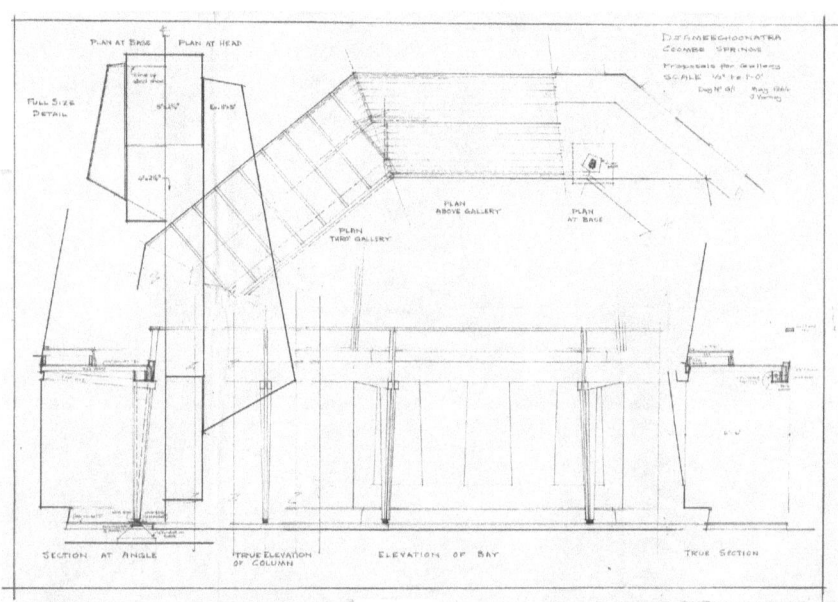

Architect's drawing of the Djamichunatra, Coombe Springs, from Raymond van Sommers, A Life in Subud, p.48 (freely available on the internet.) In the author's opinion, his preparation for and inspiration of this building may have been Bennett's greatest external accomplishment. Its wanton destruction was a crime against humanity and its spiritual welfare. As it was demolished through unconsciousness may another Djamichunatra be built through consciousness.

APPENDICES

APPENDIX 1   BENNETT'S FAMILY

Michael Benham has conducted a fair amount of research on Bennett's family. In some instances, I have been provided with the sources. In a straightforward biographical study, this would merit its being placed in chapter 1 with the sources fully footnoted. Given the nature of this study, I have decided to note the results of his research in this appendix, as a middle course between full inclusion and omitting it altogether.

In an email to me dated June 30, 2022, Benham stated that the earliest record available to him for J.G. Bennett's paternal ancestors refers to one John Bennett (1590 - ?). That "is as far back as available records go." His son William (1620-1707), his son John (1654-1704), and his son James (1685-1725), were all "born, lived and died in the village of Winsham, Somerset."

> His [son] James (1718-1791) was a Wine Merchant [with the] East India Merchants who lived at 163 Fenchurch St above their warehouses - a substantial building. (This is probably where the wealth came for his son James to purchase North Cadbury Court. Prior to this for at least three generation the Bennetts lived in the village of Winsham, Somerset and were not wealthy landowners.)
>
> Apart from James (1718-1791) baptising his son as a Presbyterian all the others were baptised and married in

the Church of England. His marriage to Elizabeth was in the Church of England.

James Bennett (1748-1815) [the father of J.G. Bennett's great-grandfather Henry Bennett] was born in London the son of James (1718-1791) and Elizabeth and baptised at their house in Fenchurch Street Sept 30th 1748 from Non-Conformist and Non-Parochial Registers Old Jewry (Presbyterian) London. [James] was the landowner in Somerset of the Cadbury Estate which included the village of Sparkford. Next to the house Cadbury Court was the church and above the church is a hill known as Cadbury Castle believed (by some) to have been the location of King Arthur's Camelot.

As for Bennett's claim that his ancestors owned this land for centuries see https://en.wikipedia.org/wiki/North_Cadbury_Court which traces the ownership and shows James Bennett bought the estate in 1796 from the Newman family.

Bennett's great-grandfather Rev. Henry Bennett (1796-1874) was admitted to Trinity College, Cambridge in 1814 graduating Civil Law 1st class 1822 and ordained deacon in the same year. (Possibly why his son William Henry became a solicitor.) Henry had one brother James and four sisters. He was married at the British chaplaincy, St Petersburg, Russia. 1821. He went back in 1826 to be the chaplain there. In 1827 he was chaplain at Dresden where William Henry was born. He was chaplain at Naples 1830-32 returning to England to become the rector in Sparkford, Somerset where he remained and is buried. He had 15 children.

... (Bennett' s grandfather) William Henry (solicitor) the oldest son (1827-1914) had four brothers, Edward, George, James and Charles. He was born in Dresden British subject. He lived at 5 Torrington Square, Bloomsbury, St George.

Bennett's mother (1869 Florence-1947 Kingston-on-Thames) retained her American citizenship. In 1901 she and Basil Wilfred, John Godolphin and Winfred Laura, with two servants (cook and maid) were living in a large house at 10 Ranelagh Avenue Barnes, Surrey. By 1911, Annie Craig, John Godolphin, Winifred Laura and Arthur Lancelot, with one servant (general domestic) were living at 1 Dunmore Road Wimbledon a much smaller nine room house.

Annie Craig's father was the painter Isaac Eugene Craig (1828 Pittsburgh - 1908 Florence).

Annie Craig's mother was Mary Argualt Brown (1830 Newport-1900 Florence. Her father was Major Thompson Skinner Brown (1806 Brownsville New York -1855 Naples) 1836; Chief Engineer New York and Lake Erie Railroad, 1836-38; Chief Engineer in the service of the United States superintending improvements on Lake Erie, 1836-46. Commissioned by the Czar of Russia as Consulting Engineer, and built the railroad from St. Petersburg to Moscow, 1849-54. His uncle was Major General Jacob Brown.

Bennett confuses his great-grandfather Thompson Skinner Brown with his great- great-grandfather Major General Jacob Brown.

Touching J.G. Bennett's father, Benham states:

Basil Bennett arrived New York, June 9, 1911 on the Mauretania, height 6' 3" light brown hair brown eyes. Final destination Havana, Cuba. He arrives back in New York from Havana on July 25, 1911, having stayed with an R.A. Gomez at 148 Camtranano Street, Havana. This is why he was not on the 1911 UK census.

On October 17, 1919 probate was granted to Annie Caroline Bennett, widow, [for the estate of] Basil Wilfred

Bennett of 105 Vassall Road, Brixton died December 20, 1918. [The value of his] effects was £233/10 [233 pounds stirling and ten shillings].

A more intriguing matter is the question of Bennett's relationship with his younger brother, Arthur Lancelot. On July 7, 2022, Benham wrote an email to me saying:

> Arthur Lancelot Bennett born December 5, 1904, obtained an M.A at Christ's College, Cambridge and later a PhD in Zoology. He went on to lecture in Zoology at Edinburgh University, before becoming Chief Fisheries Officer in Haifa, Palestine from 1936 to at least 1939. He served in the Royal Navy Volunteer Reserve during WWII. From at least 1946 he worked for the British Council as amongst other things Professor of Zoology, University of Libya and later in Somalia. By the time of his retirement he was Professor of Cell Biology at Glasgow University. He lived to the age of 80.
>
> The odd thing about his life is that he changed his surname by deed poll to Craig-Bennett on December 10, 1929 only a few months after JGB's trial in Greece, and three months before his first marriage in London. The marriage certificate was witnessed by his mother.

From an attachment to that email, it seems that Arthur made the name change by deed poll on December 7, 1929, while he publicly attested to the change of name on December 10. The Death Notice in *The Times* for July 17, 1985, stated: "Peacefully at home on 12 July 1985, Arthur Lancelot Craig-Bennett O.B.E. F.R.S.E. in his 81st year."

Benham's attachment also contains a good deal of information about A.L. Bennett's marriages and other matters which I do not think relevant even to this appendix. On July 7 and 10, 2022, I wrote to George and Ben Bennett about their uncle Arthur, and if they knew why the relationship between their father and uncle seemed to have been weak. On July 7, 2022, Ben replied with some of the information I had from Benham, adding this: "last saw him at JGB's funeral but he left without speaking." Benham and I have exchanged theories about why Arthur should have changed his surname to include his mother's name, but we have so little data to work with it is hardly worth speculating. However, while Bennett remained quite silent about Arthur's activities as a youth and adult, one of those silences is eloquent. In *Witness*, he wrote that despite his father's faults: "Not for anything would my sister and I have had him different."[1] The patent inference is that his brother Arthur, who changed his name to "Craig-Bennett," thus placing his mother's surname before his father's, had implacably taken his mother's part in the break-up, and would happily have seen his father other than he was.

One miscellaneous piece of Mr Benham's diligent research might be conveniently mentioned here. Concerning the recollection of being "chosen" to play against the New Zealand "All Blacks," Benham writes:

> The team was not the "All Blacks" but a New Zealand army team playing in an Inter-services Rugby Football Tournament. This was one of the sporting events to keep the men of the British and Dominions armed services occupied while waiting for demobilisation and transport home. The King presented the King's Cup to the winners, Australia.
>
> New Zealand and "The Mother Country" played twice. Bennett is not named in the Mother Country team for either match. The first match was at Inverleigh, Edinburgh, before 35,000 on April 5, 1919 (*The Scotsman*, April 7, 1919, page 3). The second match to decide the runners up was at Twickenham, London on April 16, 1919 (*The Times*, April 17, 1919, page 5).
>
> Bennett does say he was "chosen" for the team not he "played" in it, but it is odd he would mention it.

[1] Bennett (1997) 151.

Bennett may have been quite mistaken, however; it may be that he was selected to play but did not in fact do so. It is clear, however, that in some details at least, his memory was inaccurate.

APPENDIX 2   MOORE ON BENNETT

Moore unequivocally rejects Bennett's account of what he had done in the 1920s, and especially of the trial. In *Gurdjieff: Anatomy of a Myth*, Moore writes that Bennett:

> was held on remand in Athens central jail for approximately a month between 7 March and 4 April 1928. His apologia for this episode in *Witness* ... is at variance with anecdotal recollection in Work circles and with the primary documents in Foreign Office 371 (pieces 12919 and 12920), much as his account of prior military service is difficult to reconcile chronologically with War Office records.[2]

I pause to note that I have attempted to obtain the relevant War Office records, but they do not appear in an index search. I understand that documents from WWI have not all been digitalised. Further, Moore does not at all specify the documents and their contents (let alone extract them), or where they contradict Bennett's story; we are left to speculate at large. Therefore, I cannot check the veracity of this broad allegation. Now, Moore was writing a book on Gurdjieff, not Bennett, but then, why not either omit the allegation altogether or provide some material for support for it? Likewise, "anecdotal recollection in Work circles" would be of some value when the subject of the anecdotes is an internal group matter, because then they are recollecting the effect of events they were part of. But here it is events which took place either in Greece or in confidential government offices.

Moore continues:

[2] Moore (1991) 355.

> Combined together in an effort to extricate JGB were his second wife Winifred, powerful Work friends in London (including Lady Malcom), eminent business associates in the Aegean Trust Ltd, and the British Ambassador Sir Percy Lyham Loraine (who deprecated JGB but could not countenance a British national featuring as the protagonist in 'another Tichborne case with an oriental flavour'). ... Public Record Office papers indicate that, under continued Foreign Office pressure, reluctantly applied, all charges against JGB were dropped on 13 August 1928. JGB however claims that a year later, on 27 September 1929 he was tried on the original charge before the Court of Appeal in Salonika and, defending himself in Greek, was acquitted with costs awarded against the government.[3]

I have obtained copies of the Foreign Office files Moore refers to. At the outset, it might be stated that in a minute of April 2, 1928, Orme Sargent, at this time head of Foreign Affair's Central Department,[4] stated that it was not wise to give the impression anyone in government thought Bennett to be "a crook," even if we believe he uses dubious facts and documents, because:

> [I]f challenged to say what definite charge was made against Bennett we might be hard put to it as our suspicions when all is said and done are chiefly based on nothing more than the shady and dishonest company he is known to keep.[5]

This is the key point, and it is in no way contradicted in any of the

---

[3] Moore (1991) 355.
[4] *Oxford Dictionary of National Biography*, s.v. "Sargent, Sir (Harold) Orme Garton." accessed electronically on April 18, 2022.
[5] FO 371/12919, 235-39, quoting 236, see also 223 to like effect, and repeated in 242, the letter warning Loraine that he had made unwise comments.

Foreign Office material which has been made available to me. In addition, the FO files do show that Mrs Bennett and his associates in the Aegean Trust did try to have Loraine, the British representative, help Bennett, and that this included being granted bail, and being given access to certain documents for his defence. Even Mrs Bennett, when she sent a telegraph to the Prime Minister (at that time Stanley Baldwin), sought only release on bail.[6] However, the plain fact of the matter is that they either do not support or else flatly contradict Moore's account about Lady Malcolm (who is only mentioned in the letter of March 28, 1928 set out in section 4.3, by Mrs Bennett as a referee whom she has not spoken to beforehand so as not to influence anything she may say),[7] and Loraine who was absolutely determined not to help Bennett. I can find no reference to the "Tichborne case" in these documents. Not only was no Foreign Office pressure applied, reluctantly or otherwise, all British agencies resolutely refused to intervene.

Even more surprising, the files show that the case was continuing in 1929, and not that it had been dropped on August 13, 1928 or at any other time. File 371/13611, documents 4-8 comprise a letter dated August 29, 1929 from Oliver Harvey (1893-1968), first Baron Harvey of Tasburgh, at this time first secretary in Athens in the British diplomatic service,[8] wrote:

> A rather curious development has occurred in the activities of the notorious Captain Bennett in connection with the visit here of the Deputy Master of the Mint, Sir Robert Johnson, who came to secure an order for the new Greek coinage.... Shortly afterwards I was dining at the principal hotel here and observed Johnson dining at an adjacent table

---

[6] FO 371/12919, 177. See also documents 164-71, and 184 which specifies seeing Bennett "released, at any rate, on bail."
[7] FO 371/12919, 205 and the typed copy at 208-9.
[8] *Oxford Dictionary of National Biography*, accessed April 16, 2022. He was in charge of the Legation there: FO 371/13611, 15.

with a man who seemed to me to be suspiciously like our friend Bennett...

The next day ... I got hold of Johnson who spontaneously said he had met a man called Bennett at his hotel, who was particularly charming. Johnson had told him the nature of his business and Bennett had at once offered to take upon himself the negotiation of the contract as he knew exactly who was the man with the deciding influence ... whom it would be necessary to square. Bennett had undertaken to square him if provided with the necessary funds. Johnson had in fact interviewed certain officials at the Ministry in Bennett's company but before going further he wished to ask my advice.

... I had no hesitation in telling him of the dangerous character of Bennett, his antecedents in connection with the Aegean Trust and the fact of his actually being under trial for forgery. I said that ... he must at once sever all connection with him and make it quite clear that there was nothing doing as regards the contract.

Johnson was suitably horrified at the society into which he had fallen and undertook at once to bow off Bennett with whom he had arranged an interview for the next day to discuss the business...

I also understand that the reason why the proceedings against Bennett hang fire so curiously and he dares to flaunt himself in Greece, is that he is threatening, if proceeded against, to split on all the Greek officials who have received bribes from him at one time or another.

It is evidently necessary for those who sup with Bennett to have a very long spoon, but I think a Deputy Master of the Mint is a pretty good match even for Bennett![9]

---

[9] FO 371/13611, 4-8.

Moore's confident assertion that "all charges against JGB were dropped on 13 August 1928," is therefore demonstrably incorrect. I have set out a good deal from the letter so that it is apparent that Bennett did indeed enjoy a diabolic reputation among leading figures in the diplomatic service. His relations with them would be a study in itself, examining the curious culture of expatriate officials and the way that prejudices are formed and then confirmed by the fact that they are circulating, but that would be a different study.

The document continued:

> Sir P. Loraine is watching the case and will intervene as soon as the circumstances seem to justify him, but that up to the present there are no grounds which appear to warrant interference with the course of the legal proceedings. Bennett has a bad record and from what we know of him there is nothing inherently improbable in the charge. Although the Anglo-Hellenic Finance Corporation have now formed an impeccable Board, the fact remains that their business consists in exploiting ex-enemy interests in an ex-Allied country. On grounds of principle we have refused to give them support, as we know the promotion of the scheme at the hands of Bennett and his associates was of extremely murky origin.

Bennett was seen as an officer who resigned his commission to become "a concession hunter in Asia Minor," who associated with a former Khedive, with John de Kay (whose name is withheld) and was associated with "an apparently bogus gold mine."[10] Further, his profile was tarnished by fact that a claim on behalf of the heirs of a despot against a friendly nation must have seemed not only distasteful but opportunistic, even cynical. In retrospect, it seems natural that the British Legation should have formed such an impression of Bennett. However, they never

---

[10] 371/12919, 174.

allowed Bennett the chance to meet the allegations. I have referred to Mrs Bennett's telegraph to the Prime Minister.

When the Foreign Office drafted a memorandum to Sir Robert Vansittart, Principal Private Secretary to the Prime Minister, responding to the telegraph and to a visit from Burton Stewart of the Aegean Trust, the draft included this passage:

> We have been very careful to refrain from giving the impression that we have refused support because of Bennett's dubious antecedents. ~~Whilst his antecedents were in the back of our mind~~ ...[11]

Revealingly, the memorandum of April 10, 1928 omits the clause which was struck through in the draft. It was, therefore, their prepossession against Bennett which led them to take no action. It should be clear that Bennett was being detained while the investigation into any possible crime he had committed was being investigated. Even the Foreign Office asked Loraine why he had to be remanded on bail, and why the prosecution believed they had to oppose it.[12] There was, in fact, no evidence against him, not at this stage nor any other. Even "suspicion" may be putting it too highly: not one fact implicating Bennett in any fraud is ever found in these papers. Bennett had not helped by, on January 18, 1928, apparently telling someone at the Legation that he was not surprised that diplomatic support could not be given to the Aegean Trust in negotiations with the Greek government, and that the Trust had only hoped to "ensure that His Majesty's Legation offered no opposition to their activities." If he did say this, and Loraine's full memorandum states only that he was "understood" to have said it, then he richly deserved the retort that they did not see why there should be any opposition.[13] Such an attitude must have seemed dishonest, and if Bennett did so express

---

[11] 371/12919, 188.
[12] 371/12919, 178.
[13] 371/12919, 146-49.

himself, it was a grave and counter-productive error. When he was in need, the Legation considered him probably guilty, or at least undeserving of their aid, even if hard evidence was lacking.

A letter to the Secretary of State, Foreign Office, dated March 21, 1928, which is probably from Burton Stewart since it refers to relevant conversations with Mr Harvey and a visit to Mr Vansittart,[14] on Anglo-Hellenic letterhead, states that Tsanados, a former Minister of Government in Greece, gave evidence that he considered Bennett's arrest to be due to Turkish involvement.[15] There is no direct evidence, but the facts are suggestive; for Turkey was claiming the Abdul Hamid properties all over the former Ottoman Empire, and Loraine was a great friend of Kemal Ataturk.[16] This was the new factor disclosed in an unsigned memorandum of April 10, 1928 to Vansittart.[17]

But this is not at all the same as the picture Moore paints. The extent of his inaccuracies is such that the most charitable view is that he never saw the documents but was relying on hearsay. Finally, Moore states:

> PRO files in the FO 371 series present a composite picture of JGB's adventurism between 1921 and 1931 which is positively Buchanesque: in 1921 he was offered (as were others) the vacant throne of Albania; between 1921 and 1924 he was in virtual partnership with John Wesley de Kay (1872-1938) ... in 1922 JGB was appointed to represent the interests of the eight widows of Abdul the Damned; in 1926 he was suspected of smuggling hashish from Salonika; in 1927 of plotting a fraud involving a 'salted' gold mine at Avret Hissar near Kilkish; and in 1929 he attempted to compromise Sir Robert Arthur Johnson KBE, Deputy Master and Comptroller of the Royal Mint (piece 13661). JGB was abetted by Lt-Col. George

---

[14] 371/12919, 188.
[15] 371/12919, 184-86.
[16] Loraine states that Turkey had claimed the lands the Aegean Trust was interested in 371/12919, 140-41.
[17] 371/12919, 191-94.

Maitland Edwards (also known in Work circles). Embarrassed at various times by JGB were Ouspensky ... and the eminent British diplomat Eric Graham Forbes Adam, who committed suicide in Constantinople on 7 July 1925.[18]

Again, the files available to me do not at all show this. I could find nothing about the throne of Albania anywhere other than in *Witness*, nothing about smuggling hashish, or plotting a fraud. Bennett himself states that Ouspensky felt Bennett had drawn police attention to him, and no information is available to me about how Bennett may have embarrassed Adam. The files do, however, mention Johnson, but Moore has misstated their contents. But perhaps the crowning point is this: as we have seen, on April 2, 1928, Sir Orme Sargent wrote that they had to be careful about what they publicly said about Bennett because "if challenged to say what definite charge was made against Bennett we might be hard put to it as our suspicions when all is said and done are chiefly based on nothing more than the shady and dishonest company he is known to keep."[19]

What is perhaps most remarkable about *Witness* is how Bennett at no point criticises the British government or even Loraine, whose attitude of political propriety mated to moral rectitude, appears dubious.

APPENDIX 3   IDRIES SHAH

The purpose of this appendix is to deal with the controversy around Idries Shah in more detail than is possible in the narrative. It cannot be complete: but it can be comprehensive in that my view of Shah is now quite clear, and the more research I conduct, the more it strikes me as accurate. In chapter 10, I asserted that the keys to understanding how Shah came to dominate Bennett are threefold:

---

[18] Moore (1991) 355-56.
[19] FO 371/12919, 235-39, quoting 236.

1. Shah was a plausible pretender to esoteric knowledge, who would use deception or any other tactic when it suited his purposes.

2. He based his authority upon his family history, his past (which he kept secret), and the unfalsifiable doctrine that only he understood anything, that others did not even know how to know, and if they disagreed with him, it showed that they needed to be "deconditioned." In this way, the deception he had in mind suggested the "teaching."

3. He conjured up links to Gurdjieff's own stated history by being a Sayyid and claiming connection with the Sarmoun(g) monastery.

Here I shall deal with Shah under the following headings:

a. His early career

The first books he published were *Oriental Magic* (1956) and *The Secret Lore of Magic* (1957). The first of these is remarkable, not for its assertions about "Turanians," but for the way that, in speaking of magic, it anticipates his later approach to Sufism: "this strange identity of magic rituals and beliefs [across the globe] means that there is one single arcane science revealed to its adepts and handed down to every people."[20] He produced a diagram with two large boxes ("Siberia, Turanian shamanism" and "Babylonia: Accadians and Semites.")[21] From these boxes, arrows go in many directions to show the diffusion of magical arts. It presents as a sort of atlas of magic, drawing on much of the material which would feature in his next book. A review in *The Journal of Asian Studies* noted that Shah "obviously has a profound personal interest in the occult," but found him inconsistent, and given to naked assertion, although his writing style was praised.[22]

In *The Secret Lore of Magic*, he set out a number of magical texts and grimoires. Shah writes as a devotee of those arts, possessed of obscure knowledge, for example, he states that Eliphas Lévi was "greatly influenced by" Francis Barrett, "author of the much-quoted but almost never

---

[20] Shah (1956) 1.
[21] Shah (1956) 3.
[22] Elliott (1958) 255-56.

seen *Magus: The Celestial Intelligencer,* published in 1801." But Lévi, he continues, based his magic system on the *Key*, and in doing so was inaccurate, and so comparison [with the Key] is sorely needed," and he will be undertaking that work.[23] Likewise, he had spent over five years, he said, hunting in England and the Continent for the *Grimorium Verum*.[24] He mentions searching for arcane texts in the Library of Aya Sofia cathedral in Cyprus: "I examined the large collection of Persian, Arabic and other manuscripts there in 1951 without result."[25] He claims to have also searched libraries in France, India, Al-Azhar in Egypt, and the Library of Mecca.[26]

The third book he published was ostensibly a travelogue: *Destination Mecca*, also in 1957, although I shall make reference only to the version published in 1969 by Octagon, Shah's own press, because facing the copyright page we read: "Idries Shah's work is recognised as outstandingly important in current human life and thought." There is a good deal of this sort of thing in the Shah oeuvre; it reminds one of the saying that self-praise is dispraise. The book opens in a gentleman's club in London, where he has spent a lot of time.[27] He was later to rejoice in membership of the Athenaeum, and reside in a Georgian house in or near Tunbridge Wells.[28] Throughout his career, he cherished and collected the almost casual marks of English class distinction, hence:

> Saud speaks the most delightfully idiomatic English ... I could easily picture him as an Oxford tutor: with that precise, contained and unaffected phraseology that I once revelled in at many an Oxford occasion.[29]

This, it should be noted, was the Oxford School for Boys, not the

---

[23] Shah (1957) 12 and 226.
[24] Shah (1957) 80.
[25] Shah (1957) 234.
[26] Shah (1957) 234.
[27] Shah (1969) 11.
[28] Moore (1986) 6.
[29] Shah (1969) 115.

University, which would more naturally, perhaps come to mind, if one speaks of "Oxford" *simpliciter*, and an "Oxford tutor."[30] The book abounds with errors such as placing the Phoenicians: "several thousand years before Christ," and migrating as a nation "to Assyria from South Arabia," with a "tribal system, under the guidance of energetic and capable woman, [which] was entirely matriarchal."[31] This Phoenician fantasy continues through to p.166.

In a rather significant chapter, titled "Sorceror's Apprentice," he wrote: "Sufism is Islamic, and for that reason it is held to be impossible for a non-Moslem to become a Sufi."[32] This is exactly what he would deny later in his career, when he substitutes for his pose as an expert in magic, mastery of "Sufism." In making the move, he transferred his universalism and diffusionist tendencies. The Sufis, he noted claim they can contact each other and the dead telepathically.[33] He states that he went to Yeniburj in Syria to meet Sufis in practice. He presents as a bemused tourist, without the least indication of taking Sufism seriously. However, if the Sufis did not impress him, they were favourably impressed by him: "you are going to be a big man, an important man. I see you walking about in a large garden.... You are going in to a huge palace, there is a red carpet on the steps, you are asking for something, and it will be granted."[34]

As he left them, the *shaykh* said that Shah had witnessed "a divine form of magic. But the normal and worldly magi is to be found elsewhere. If you want to see that, why not amuse yourself by visiting Musa the Jew who lives in Damascus?"[35] And now we come to something Shah is interested in, even if the narrative becomes fantastic. Shah claims that he found Musa, who said that Shah must not teach the arts to anyone unfit to know them, and promise he will not exercise the Art "except you

---

[30] Moore (1986) 5. Moore also notes that the Shah of this book is quite a different man from the one who would later claim to be a Sufi.
[31] Shah (1969) 161.
[32] Shah (1969) 170.
[33] Shah (1969) 170.
[34] Shah (1969) 171-76.
[35] Shah (1969) 178.

are convinced that in so doing you will be in harmony with the destiny of people and of the world."[36]

Musa the Magician must have been naive indeed to teach magic on two minutes' notice with no preparation or security of good will but his own instruction. According to Shah, they performed some rituals and scenes from other places such as Cairo and Roda Island appeared to their sight, untill: "Suddenly, as I leant forward, my head projecting beyond the precincts of the circle, the picture snapped out."[37] Even in a Mecca travel book by a man later claiming to be a Sufi Master, indeed *the* Sufi Master of the Age, the most exciting part is the fiction about magic in Old Damascus.

Sometime around now, Shah mixed with Wiccans in London, and then became secretary to Gerald Gardner (1884-1964).[38] The career of Gardner, the most prominent person associated with the rise of modern pagan witchcraft, "the first fully formed religion which England has given the world,"[39] is treated in *Triumph of the Moon*. Hutton notes that Gardner's biography was written by Idries Shah, based on its subject's recollections.[40] To this point, Shah is not only clearly an enthusiast of magic, he is also distinctly not a Sufi, and sees it as an Islamic phenomenon. Shah's nimble change of career is the first clue that he believed in neither his pose as a student of magic, or as a Sufi. Shah was not one to follow Margaret Murray and her acolytes who, quite wrongly, argued that "pagan witchcraft" was a native European religion. He asserted that it had come from the Muslim East, via Spain.[41] From here it was a short step to claiming to speak in the name of that ancient tradition, and thus claiming an authority and a prestige greater than anything available through the eccentric Gardner. From Gardner he could have been

---

[36] Shah (1969) 180.
[37] Shah (1969) 182.
[38] Moore (1986) 5.
[39] Hutton (2019) vii and 247.
[40] Hutton (2019) 213.
[41] Hutton (2019) 282. For Hutton's critique of Murray's thesis, a mistake more wilful than ignorant, see (2019) 290-92, 300, and especially 375-76, the final demolition of the Murray "thesis" by Keith Thomas and Norman Cohn.

reminded of the value to one's career of being "devious, and capable of trickery and dissimulation."[42]

In 1960 or 1961, Shah wrote to Robert Graves (1895-1985), seeking to meet him on the basis that he, Shah, had written books on magical practices, and was now making a study of what he called "ecstatic religions" and have been "attending experiments conducted by the witches in Britain, into mushroom-eating and so on."[43] When Shah arrived for the appointment of January 17, 1961, he was accompanied by Gardner.[44] After a day together, Shah wrote a letter of blandishments to Graves, thanking him as a teacher and "stimulator."[45] A little later, Shah told Graves that his plan to rewrite and "de-code" *The Book of the Thousand Nights and One Night*, had been inspired by Grave's work on Greek myths.[46]

The three regrouped on January 22, then Shah and Graves alone on the next day. Graves' nephew and biographer opines that Shah became "one of Graves's most trusted and most influential friends" due to his ability to "reflect back to him a version of his own beliefs."[47] Rather surprisingly, given the divinity-free nature of Shah's later "Sufism," he enthused Graves with ideas of *baraka*, which he interpreted as "the sudden divine rapture which overcomes either a prophet or a group of fervent devotees … whom it unites in a bond of love."[48] Shah furthered his drug investigations, learning about mescalin,[49] and "soma," telling Graves that he had learnt through a cousin that it is still manufactured from a mushroom in India, and that he—Graves—could publish this discovery, he would not be doing so himself.[50] It might appear cynical to think that this "friendship offering" was made because Shah did not wish to publish his own fiction. However, the soma story was impossible, and

---

[42] Hutton (2019) 247.
[43] Graves (1995) 326.
[44] Graves (1995) 326.
[45] Graves (1995) 326.
[46] Graves (1995) 339.
[47] Graves (1995) 326.
[48] Graves (1995) 326.
[49] Graves (1995) 330.
[50] Graves (1995) 347.

Shah said "You'll never get the Brahman's secret acknowledged: it was stolen by Idries's cousin as Prometheus stole fire – *perhaps the same sort of fire?*"[51] Shah's interest in psychotropic drugs resurfaced in his pseudonymous essay "An Afghan Community," where he speaks of the "Sarmoun Community" (sic) growing *chungari* (sic) the "herb of enlightenment."[52]

Graves wrote an introduction for, and helped Shah find a publisher for, *The Sufis*.[53] However, although Graves was disappointed with the poor quality of the writing, he "so much wanted to believe Shah that he swallowed this explanation; though he did so with some difficulty," namely that the bad writing was an attempt to "decondition" his readers.[54] Little wonder that the nephew described his uncle as "increasingly gullible."[55] The need to "decondition" would be invoked to disarm any criticism. In the intervening years, Shah produced many more books of what he called "Sufism."

The frustration which scholars of Sufism and its literature, such as Elwell-Sutton, Schimmel and Green, expressed concerning Shah and his work can be understood.[56] Shah presents a "Sufism" devoid of Sufi practice, central Sufi doctrines such as *tawhid*, and Islamic content. That it could ever have been accepted as an authentic portrait only shows how keen people were to have a de-Islamicised Sufism which approximated more to Zen than to anything Islamic. Shah made a virtue of this by presenting Sufism as a universalist teaching.[57] Sometimes one wonders whether the very inconsequence and irrationality of his stated proofs saved him from mockery: e.g. his attempt to depict Francis of Assisi as "connected with the Sufis," (e.g. because he suggested twirling when lost, as a means of finding the right road, and this has some unstated

---

[51] Graves (1995) 348-49. The quote is from Graves, but the source of some or all of it is Shah.
[52] In Archer (1980) 41.
[53] Seymour-Smith (1983) 505-6.
[54] Graves (1995) 385.
[55] Graves (1995) 347.
[56] Elwell-Sutton (1972), Schimmel (1975) 9 n. 5, for Green, see section 10.4.
[57] Shah (1964) xxv-xxvi.

connection with the whirling dervishes.)⁵⁸ It seems so obviously wrong-headed that one wonders what was really behind it. As one example of his "Sufi teaching" books, I selected, at random, *Wisdom of the Idiots*. An unpaginated note explains the title:

> Note: Because what narrow thinkers imagine to be wisdom is often seen by the Sufis to be folly, the Sufis in contrast sometimes call themselves 'The Idiots'. By a happy chance, too, the Arabic word for 'Saint' (*wali*) has the same numerical equivalent as the word for 'Idiot' (*balid*).... This book contains some of their knowledge.

As often occurs, with Shah, his praise of the contents of his own books is placed side by side with criticism of "narrow thinkers." As with his comments to Graves about "hyenas," he was not slow to pre-emptively attack any critique of his own work. It is also stated on one of these early pages that:

> IDRIES SHAH belongs to the oldest and most famous noble family in the Middle East, bears four titles – and is a distinguished thinker who has achieved worldwide critical acclaim. …. His dozen books on human thought, travel, honour, folklore and literature have won a vast and constantly growing readership.

As an example of his honors, we are told that he was referred to in an Oxford university honours degree examination paper. We have seen his infatuation with Oxford, but to boast of being mentioned in an examination strikes me as pathetic. The book itself is 192 pages. It includes 94 pieces, the longest of which is barely five pages. Twenty pages are blank. There is no discernible order in the pieces. But there are common themes, e.g. his "Dispute with Academics" expresses a disdain for them

⁵⁸ Shah (1964) 258.

which, since he is so given to the theme, suggests a profounder respect for them.⁵⁹ A typical story is that of the dervish, who stopped a king in the street. The dervish said that the king could not even fill his begging bowl. As soon as the king filled it the gold, it disappeared. This happened so often that the king realised he was emptying his treasury. The dervish told him that he was illustrating a truth: the bowl is the desires of men and the gold is what man is given. "If you step into the bowl you will disappear," said the dervish. "Therefore, how do you hold yourself of any account?"⁶⁰

It is, to my mind, a mystery that Bennett could have taken such sententious moralising as in any way parallel to Gurdjieff's teaching. However, as I have indicated above, after the sale of Coombe Springs and the destruction of the Djamichunatra, Bennett realised that he had been had, but while unable to publicly admit this, cut down his dealings with Shah. Finally, *Wisdom of the Idiots*, ends with a note about twelve books by Shah, more about his lineage and his father (described as a "renowned savant") and more endorsements.⁶¹

b. "Trawling" in "Gurdjieff waters"

Bennett states that Hoare sent him newspaper clips in June 1962, which seems to refer to the article by "Omar M. Burke," in *Blackwood's Magazine* of December 1961, titled "Solo to Mecca." This, like "Major Desmond Martin," and sundry other names, I believe to be a pseudonym for Shah.⁶² Like Shah's own writing, this made a great deal of his descent, reaching its climax in praise, really self-praise, of Idries Shah:

---

⁵⁹ Shah (1970) 37-38.
⁶⁰ Shah (1970) 71-72.
⁶¹ Shah (1970) 180.
⁶² On April 18, 2022, I wrote the Idries Shah Foundation asking whether they could provide me with any information about the editor and a number of contributors to Archer (1980), as I could locate no details about them whatsoever, and asking whether these were not pseudonyms of Shah. They kindly replied on May 6, 2022: "As much as we would love to be able to help, I'm afraid we're unable to answer your questions. None of us were involved with the running of Octagon, which was dissolved some years ago."

On this earth the 'High Mantle' of Sufi supremacy devolved upon a member of the existing body of the descendants of Mohammed, for he it was who passed on the secret teachings of Sufism to a chosen circle. Sufism was the inner discipline of all religion, brought by all the prophets, including I was told, Jesus.

Who was the present-day Grand Sheikh of the Sufi Way; the member of the prophetic family recognised as the leader of the Sufis? He goes by the name and title of the *Idries Shah*, the Studious King, literally; and he is also known as The Bridge; the bridge between the old dispensation of Sufism and the new, for the projection of the teachings is always changing. This mysterious figure travels throughout the world, sometimes teaching, sometimes seeking. His is the greatest *baraka*; he is a prince as well as a Sufi. He is linked to Arabia, Afghanistan, and to India, in which country he is said to come from a princely family.[63]

Of course, it would be one thing if all Sufis said that Shah had been their leader. It would have been more impressive if Sufis had lined up to assert that Shah was their leader.

There is said to be another pseudonymous article in *The Times* on March 9, 1964. An online search of *The Times* did not locate it. I have also received information that it may have been the same or similar to a letter by "Major Desmond R. Martin," to the Editor of *The Lady*, "Below the Hindu Kush," vol. CLXII, No. 4210, December 9, 1965, p. 870.[64] Also, the "Declaration of the People of the Tradition" which Shah produced to Bennett is copyrighted by Octagon in 1966 and 1974.[65] The most significant effort Shah made to reach Gurdjieff's followers, and those

---

[63] *Blackwood's Magazine,* December 1961, 1754, vol. 290, 486-87.
[64] I wrote to *The Lady* on April 18, 2022. I have received no reply. The long-running magazine does not seem accessible through Australian libraries.
[65] Bennett (1997) 288. It is a sign of the times that the secret esoteric brotherhood should take care to protect their copyright.

interested in Gurdjieff's ideas, was the production of the pseudonymous *The Teachers of Gurdjieff* by "Rafael Lefort," published in 1966.[66] Moore summarises the volume as follows: "[Y]oung 'Lefort' pretends to have sought out Gurdjieff's teachers in Asia (a chronological absurdity), who demeaned their former pupil and pointed towards Shah."[67] Dushka Howarth recalls that Shah had, at some point in the 1960s, told two of his pupils, the Shaeffers: "that he was writing a book about Gurdjieff … to identify the sources of his teaching, but under an anagram pseudonym. So I was hardly surprised when the very imaginative *The Teachers of Gurdjieff* appeared authored by one 'Rafael Lefort' ('a real effort'?)."[68]

It appears fairly sure that *The Teachers of Gurdjieff* was written not by Idries Shah himself, but by his brother Omar Ali-Shah. Anthony Blake, my source, had this directly from someone who knew the Omar, his pupils, and family, and who stated that it was an open secret among the pupils, who laughed at how even Jeanne de Salzmann and Peter Brook had fallen for some of its account.[69] I suspect that Omar wrote it in collaboration with Idries: apart from abundant references to Shah tropes such as "the Guardians of the Tradition," to Nasruddin stories, to *baraka*, "deconditioning," and the need to learn how to learn,[70] it includes the following features which link it to Shah:

1. An emphasis on the "Syeds or descendants of Muhammed," especially the declaration, novel in Sufism, that: "There is no inheritance of the teacher's *baraka* save among the Syeds, the descendants of the Prophet."[71]

2. The idea of unsuspected Sufi influence in the West, e.g. that the books of Al Ghazzali "are believed to have influenced the thoughts of both" Francis of Assisi and Thomas Aquinas.[72]

3. Together with the obsessive fixation on Gurdjieff, and his Eastern

[66] Moore (1986) 5 and 8 n.25.
[67] Moore (1986) 6.
[68] Howarth (1998) 332.
[69] Email correspondence from A.G.E. Blake dated November 19, 2022.
[70] See for example Lefort (1966) 22, 55-56, 62, 84, 94, 113, and 146.
[71] Lefort (1966) 6 and 93.
[72] Lefort (1966) 72.

travels, criticism of him and especially of his ongoing pupils.[73] Also, criticism of all other non-Shah related teachings: "Pick Zen, Theosophy or Yoga, all are refuges for the incapable who want something to occupy their time and give them something both supernatural and seemingly rewarding to hold onto."[74]

A significant pointer to his agenda is a footnote in which, as authorities for the "Stop Exercise," Shah's *The Sufis* is placed on the same footing as *Meetings with Remarkable Men*.[75] I have already identified the question of authority as critical in determining Shah's course of actions, his tactics, and his "teachings." The cynicism of his approach to Gurdjieff's teaching and his cavalier preparedness to put people off it, is now extended to Zen, Yoga, and Theosophy, distinguished among other similarly superficial and supernatural systems. It is little surprise that the charlatan tars all competitors with his own brush: he really does not believe that it is anything but a business. But, for those who follow him, the dictum is expressed at the end of the book: go to a place in Europe and "immerse yourself in its baraka," and there: "Question nothing, obey all."[76]

With the *Blackwood's Magazine* article, Shah made a sustained "trawling" mission for Gurdjieff pupils (his word).[77] This serves as a good description of Shah's play for former pupils of Gurdjieff, which reached its apogee, perhaps, with the pseudonymous *The Teachers of Gurdjieff*.[78] It is striking that Shah never spoke of his own training: after all, given the contents of *Destination Mecca*, and the available evidence about his activities, it can only have come from books, and chiefly from English-language books. Tunbridge recalls that:

---

[73] Lefort (1966) 85. "Sarmoun" and its monastery are everywhere, see for example 105.
[74] Lefort (1966) 128.
[75] Lefort (1966) 112.
[76] Lefort (1966) 146.
[77] Hayter (2002) 187.
[78] Although he is enthusiastically pro-Shah, and accepts the thesis of *Teachers of Gurdjieff* as accurate, Hayter implicitly admits that Idries Shah wrote it: (2002) 229, also 188 and 261. Howarth's account of Shah's own comments leaves no doubt: (1998) 332. I wrote to the publishers for information on July 1 and followed up on August 9, 2022, and have received the reply that they have no relevant information..

In all his books, Shah never wrote a word about his own Sufi or other training and experiences. At one of the first meetings I had with him alone, he performed a boastful swaggering description of how he persuaded Mister B to hand over Coombe Springs. I say 'performed' because that's what it looked like. I felt quite sure he was doing it to test my attachment to my old teacher, so I was embarrassed. He strode up and down the room ... waving his arms about and puffing on his cigarette, saying something like, "I said to him, I said, look here *Bennett*, you claim to be connected to higher powers and have the interests of your people at heart? Well, here's your chance to prove it, *Bennett*. If you are sincere, you will give me this property, lock, stock and barrel, with no strings attached!"[79]

c. The Omar Khayyam Scam

In 1967, Robert Graves published what he asserted was a new and more accurate translation of the *Rubaiyat* of Omar Khayyam, made from a manuscript in the Shah family's possession for 800 years.[80] This would have taken it back to within a generation of the death of Khayyam in 1131. But experts disbelieved him, and although Shah's father died in an accident before he was due to produce the manuscript, "Idries prevaricated over providing proof of the document's existence."[81] Part of the issue was that Graves had accepted the assertions of Idries and his brother Omar that Khayyam had in fact been a "Sufi voice," and not, as the celebrated Fitzgerald translation implied, "anti-Sufi."[82] His nephew writes that: "the impression grew that Robert Graves had been guilty, at

---

[79] Tunbridge (2015) 323.
[80] Seymour-Smith (1983) 555-57.
[81] The Independent (London, England), 7 September 2014, Independent Digital News and Media Limited, https://www.independent.co.uk/arts-entertainment/books/reviews/invisible-ink-no-240-idries-shah-9715413.html accessed March 6, 2022.
[82] Seymour-Smith (1983) 557. Graves (1995) 446.

best, of extreme gullibility.... However, he could not allow himself to believe that the Shahs had deliberately deceived him."[83]

As his "Rubaiyat" came under increasing criticism, Graves "was certain that it would not be long before [Idries and Omar Shah], being honourable human beings, directly descended from Mahomet and from the final true Persian monarch would soon [produce the original manuscript]. In this, however, he was altogether mistaken."[84]

Seymour-Smith states that Idries had no part in this affair.[85] But this is not correct: Graves asked Idries to produce the manuscript in October 1970. Shah's response was remarkable for its irrationality and vitriol:

> Idries Shah ... argued that production of the MSS would prove nothing, because there would be no way of telling whether it was original, or whether someone had washed the writing from a piece of ancient parchment, then applied a new text, using inert inks. In his view, it was 'high time that we realised that the hyenas who are making so much noise are intent only on opposition, destructiveness and carrying on a campaign when, let's face it, nobody is really listening'.[86]

There was more in the same vein.

Even if production of the text would be futile, that was no reason not to produce it, it would rather have been reason never to have told Graves that he could produce a text to support his claims. Production, on the other hand, would at least show that the Shahs and Graves had acted in good faith, and that there was, at the least, some show of authenticity to the text. In this context, to attack one's opponents as "hyenas" is to immediately concede that no better argument is available, when the point was that many well-intentioned people were listening, and asking. How could the oldest manuscript of the *Rubaiyat* not be of interest to

---

[83] Graves (1995) 447.
[84] Graves (1995) 468.
[85] Seymour-Smith (1983) 558.
[86] Graves (1995) 471.

cultured people? The personal point, Graves asserted, was that Idries' new letter "completely contradicted two previous ones on the same subject in which he had promised to produce the manuscript if necessary."[87] There was further correspondence between Graves and Idries Shah, but it was no more satisfactory. Shah said they would discuss it in person.[88] Shah trusted, no doubt, to his oral powers of persuasion and Graves' gullibility. However, by 1987 it was known that the "authentic version" was a fraud:

> The manuscript was found to be Edward Heron Allen's notebooks collating the "Bodleian" and the "Calcutta" manuscripts, copied by some unknown person. The copying may have been done deliberately to deceive or just for copying purposes. The manuscript was given to the late poet Robert Graves, who knew no Persian nor anything about Eastern manuscripts, and had been led to believe he was translating the oldest Khayyam manuscript. Omar Ali Shah, a former General in the Afghan army, claimed the manuscript had been in his family for several generations.... He also maintains that Khayyam was not only a Sufi but an Afghani Sufi. The definitive scholarship on the Omar Ali Shah and Graves manuscript was done by the late L.P. Elwell-Sutton.[89]

Later, Ghani writes much the same of Elwell-Sutton's article unmasking the deceit:

> ELWELL-SUTTON, L.P. The Rubaiyat Revisited. Review of "The Original Rubaiyyat of Omar Khayam in a New Translation with Commentaries by Robert Graves and Omar Ali Shah'". ... A brilliant article that put to rest the

---

[87] Graves (1995) 472.
[88] Graves (1995) 472.
[89] Ghani (1987) 573.

authenticity of the alleged 1153 edition of Khayyam in possession of the Afghan General Omar Ali Shah. (The manuscript was supposed to have been written some 30 years after Khayyam's death.) The writer shows Omar Ali Shah's ignorance of Persian literature and language, and the naiveté of poor Robert Graves who was "used" in the charade. The alleged manuscript was a copy of Edward Heron Allen's note book (published in 1899) ... Further-more, the writer exposes the entire effort as "crude Propaganda for contemporary Pseudo Sufism". [90]

d. Scholarly Evaluation of Shah's Claims

Both Moore and Elwell-Sutton take issue with Shah's claim that descent from the Prophet confers some special authority upon him,[91] a claim on which Robert Graves placed a surprising amount of trust as establishing Shah and his family as "men of honour."[92] However, Graves was doubtless rendered more sensible to the prestige of descent from the Prophet since: "Graves himself ... states ... [that he was] led by Shah to claim descent from the Prophet – through his Irish connection."[93] My concern is, I think, more on the level of principle: first, if Sufism pre-dates and transcends Islam, why should descent from the Prophet count for anything? Second, from the mystic perspective, illumination is a divine gift in cooperation with personal efforts, it does not pass through family trees. That is, in making his claim to authority as a Sayyid, Shah undermines his own claims to authority as a sage. Shah went on to found several organizations, the more "esoteric" of which, the Society for Sufi Studies, is no longer active.[94]

Annemarie Schimmel (1922-2003), who was for a generation professor of Indo-Muslim culture at Harvard, wrote: "Idries Shah, *The Sufis*,

---

[90] Ghani (1987) 776.
[91] Moore (1986) 4; Elwell-Sutton (1972) 14.
[92] Seymour-Smith (1983) 558.
[93] Seymour-Smith (1983) 557.
[94] Kuçük (2008) 310. He does not explain what he means by "esoteric."

as well as his other books, should be avoided by serious students."[95] She does not give her reasons, but the fact that this was her opinion is typical of the general rejection of Shah's writings on Sufism by knowledgeable authors. Further, given the moderate and irenic tone of her scholarship, her reticence may be interpreted more as a desire to avoid offending than an inability to defend her position.

Laurence Elwell-Sutton, a professor of Persian and Middle Eastern studies, had produced a Persian Grammar and studies in Persian poetic metres, and proverbs, which are still in print. When it comes to his writings on Sufism, the salient points which Elwell-Sutton has grasped, is that Shah is unaware that Sufism is centred on the worship of God, and that it is a diversity which has changed quite significantly over time.[96] Yet time and again, Shah writes about "the Sufis" *simpliciter* as if there is only one Sufism. Even a glance at Schimmels' volume will show the range and development of Sufism. A deeper acquaintance with Sufism reveals that the relationship of Sufis with Islam, and even with each other, has been fraught with friction, criticism, and repudiation.[97]

Moore comments that the "Sufism" of Idries Shah is "a 'Sufism' without self-sacrifice, without self-transcendence, without the aspiration of gnosis, without tradition, without the Prophet, without the Quran, without the Prophet. Merely that."[98] Even Naqshbandi dervishes have criticised Shah. One such site states:

> There is evidence that Idries Shah was primarily an Occultist who used sufism as a cover, and that he deliberately promoted himself: as the foremost authority on sufism, as a great sufi shaykh, as the leader of the most esoteric circle of the Naqshbandi sufi order. However, the latter is contradicted by the fact that the Naqshband order is a very

---

[95] Schimmel (1975) 9 n.5.
[96] Elwell-Sutton (1972) 10-12.
[97] Sirriryeh (1999) *passim*, see especially ix for Sufi reprobation of other Sufis.
[98] Moore (1986) 7.

conservative Islamic sufi lineage, whereas Shah taught that sufism is a universal form of wisdom that predated Islam.[99]

Shah's "Sufism" is a fiction, maintained by mere assertion, as if one were to insist that the true Sussex is in the north of England and anyone who said otherwise did not know the true Sussex. I see no reason to depart from my conclusion in chapter 10 that Shah was obliged to engage in an aggressive strategy of saying that everyone else but himself had to "learn how to learn," and so rely upon enigmatic stories of uncertain interpretation. Had he been either clear or comprehensive, he would have been unmasked at once.

---

[99] Gamard (2005) no pagination.

ANNOTATED BIBLIOGRAPHY OF J.G. BENNETT'S WORK

BY DAVID SEAMON

This is an updated draft (June 2021) of an entry to be published in an edited collection on the work of British philosopher J.G. Bennett (1897-1974); includes book reviews and commentaries in *Systematics*, vols. 1-11 (1963-74); includes a new section on JGB's Subud writings.

J.G. BENNETT'S PUBLISHED WRITINGS:
AN ANNOTATED BIBLIOGRAPHY

This bibliography provides a listing of *published* works by British philosopher J.G. Bennett. They are organized in seven major categories for the most part each arranged chronologically by date of original publication:

> 1. Books by Bennett (for books and other entries on Subud, see category 6 below);
> 2. Edited compilations of Bennett's lectures, writings, and editorial works;
> 3. Entries by Bennett in the journal *Systematics*;
> 4. Entries by Bennett in the in-house "Work" journals *Enneagram* and *Impressions*;
> 5. Other entries by Bennett relating to the Gurdjieff Work;
> 6. Entries by Bennett relating to Subud;
> 7. Other entries: Travelogue and scientific and academic articles.

Entry format is as follows: title of publication, place of publication, publisher, date of publication; if the entry has been reprinted, place, publisher, and date are repeated. Also included when known are the entry's page length and International Standard Book Number (ISBN). Three caveats: First, I do not claim this list is comprehensive; some of Bennett's writings have been published in less well known venues difficult to locate; Second, a good number of Bennett's works have been reprinted several times in different editions by different publishers; for these entries, I have attempted a thorough listing of reprintings but have not been able to find complete information for some editions; Third, there exists a considerable number of unpublished works by Bennett; the J.G. Bennett Foundation is one major venue working for their eventual publication. See their website https://www.jgbennett.org/.

For assistance in locating, compiling, and clarifying entries, I thank Joseph Azize, Ben Bennett, George Bennett, Tony Blake, Carole Cusack, James Evans, and, especially, Gavin Perry.

1. BOOKS BY J.G. BENNETT

The Four Volumes of *The Dramatic Universe*

Considered Bennett's masterwork, *The Dramatic Universe* was published in four volumes between 1956 and 1966. The four volumes mark a search for a comprehensive description of the whole of human experience, including its less effable dimensions. Bennett aims "not to explain events but to formulate the rules that enable the possible to be distinguished from the impossible" (1956, p. 229). By the phrase, "dramatic universe," Bennett brings attention to "the character that all existence acquires through the presence everywhere of relativity and uncertainty, combined with consciousness and with the possibility of freedom" (1956, p. 20). He assumes that "behind the bewildering diversity and complexity of phenomena, there is an organized structure that holds them together" (1966, Vol. 2, p. 6).

The four volumes attempt a systematization of human experience, integrating science, philosophy, psychology, history, and religion. Bennett writes that his aim is "an ampler and more consistent account of the significance and purpose of man's existence on the Earth than was possible before recent advances in natural science, historical research and human psychology. One of the conclusions that I have reached is that we must regard the human race as it now exists on the Earth as being at an early stage of development toward true humanity" (1966, Vol. 2, p. xi). For Bennett's synopsis of *The Dramatic Universe*, in question-answer format, see "A Short Guide to 'The Dramatic Universe'," entry 5.4. A series of reviews of *The Dramatic Universe* were published in Bennett's journal, *Systematics*, Vol. 5, No. 2, pp. 135–174; reviewers were Leon Pompa, Roger Gentle, K. Steffens, Ernest Dale, and Oliver L. Reiser.

1.1. *Dramatic Universe, Vol. 1: The Foundations of Natural Philosophy.* London: Hodder & Stoughton, 1956, 534p., appendices, glossary of terms, index; Sherborne, Gloucestershire, UK: Coombe Springs Press, 1976, 1981, 534p., ISBN 0-900306-39-4; Petersham, MA: J.G. Bennett Foundation, 2018, 539p., revised edition with typographical errors corrected, appendices, glossary of terms, index, ISBN 1983509787.

In volume 1, Bennett examines the unity of the natural world. His aim is to bring scientific knowledge within the scope of one comprehensive theory of existence: "unless all knowledge can be brought into a coherent system, we shall have either to abandon the hope of finding man's place in the universe or else to accept with resignation, dogmas that disregard the lessons of natural science, and acquiesce in the continuing divorce of fact and value that has been the chief cause of our present bewilderment" (p. vii–viii). Bennett develops a conceptual framework that depicts "the totality of conditions that preserve the universe from chaos without reducing it to sterility" (p. 230). Drawing on his method of holistic understanding—what he calls "systematics"—Bennett proposes a twelve-term framework grounded in grouping phenomena "according to their level of existence; that is, according to the intensity of their inner togetherness" (p. 177).

1.1.1. *The Dramatic Universe, Vol. 1: The Foundations of Natural Philosophy*, abridged edition. Charles Town, WV: Claymont Communications, 1987, 182p., glossary, index, ISBN 0-93254-14-1.

Editor Eric Mandel's condensation of the first volume of *The Dramatic Universe*. In removing over half of the text in the original volume, Mandel aims to highlight "the important themes by carefully removing secondary material" (p. i). The major reduction is eliminating "the lengthy interpretation of the specific data of natural science that occupied most of the second half of the book. This was done out of the conviction that such interpretation must be renewed by each succeeding generation as knowledge grows and scientific hypotheses evolve" (pp. i–ii). A useful abridgement but necessarily studied alongside the original text.

1.2. *The Dramatic Universe, Vol. 2: The Foundations of Moral Philosophy.*

London: Hodder & Stoughton, 1961, 356p., glossary of terms, index; Sherborne, Gloucestershire, UK: Coombe Springs Press, 1976, 1981, 356p., ISBN 0-900306-42-4; Santa Fe, NM: Bennett Books, 1997, 356p., ISBN 1881408043.

In this second volume, Bennett shifts from the facticity of the natural world and the realm of fact to human experience and the question of values, about which "nothing can be known and where we must rely upon faculties other than sense-perception and mental constructs" (p. xi). The key concern is 'ought', which "does not express an element of knowledge: its meaning is not given in sense-experience or in any mental construct, and yet the word and all that it invokes is no less important than the word 'know'. Indeed, if we examine the situation carefully, we find that 'ought' comes first. Does it matter what we know or do not know unless there is some action that we ought or ought not to take in consequence?" (p. xi). As in volume 1, Bennett uses of the systematics approach to consider "the multi-term systems as far as the pentad" (p. xiii). Particularly significant is his presentation of three-ness, will, and the six triads of interaction, identity, expansion, concentration, order, and freedom. Bennett claims that, via these six triads, we can place "the extraordinary variety of patterns that we observe in the world around us" (p.98); we are able to "explore regions of experience that have hitherto been largely disregarded by philosophers of all schools and periods" (p. 93).

1.3. *The Dramatic Universe, Vol. 3: Man and His Nature*. London: Hodder & Stoughton, 1966, 315 p., glossary of terms, index; Sherborne, Gloucestershire, UK: Coombe Springs Press, 1976, 1981, 315 p., ISBN 0-900306-43-2; Charles Town, WV: Claymont Communications, 1987, ISBN 0934254184.

This volume continues Bennett's effort toward "a deepening significance of what is already there" (p. 78). His major questions remain "the problem of man and his nature, the problem of the universe and the natural order and scientific progress, and the problem of the ultimate purpose of our existence which is the heart of theology" (p. vi). He aims to demonstrate "that a unified world picture can be constructed that embraces all human experience and all human knowledge, as it presents itself to us in the second half of the twentieth century" (p. viii). By 1966, Bennett's Institute for the Comparative Study of History, Philosophy and Sciences had made considerable progress in perfecting Bennett's method of systematics, drawing on the concrete significance of number to study "structures as simplified totalities" (p. 9). The first chapter of this volume provides an updated understanding of systematics' systems from the one-term system of monad to the twelve-term system of dodecad. Following chapters present an integrated anthropology of human beings organized around human values, "various regions of existence or 'worlds'" (p. 122), and the "human life cycle" (p. 164). The final chapter considers "the ideal structure of human society according to systematic principles and what we can learn from history and the experience of the modern world" (p. vii).

1.4. *The Dramatic Universe, Vol. 4: History*. London: Hodder & Stoughton, 1966, 462p., glossary of terms, index; Sherborne, Gloucestershire, UK: Coombe Springs Press, 1976, 1977, 462p., ISBN 0-900306-44-0; Charles Town, WV: Claymont Communications, 1987, 462p., ISBN 0934254206; Santa Fe, NM: Bennett Books, 1997, 462p., 10-188140806X; Petersham, MA: J.G. Bennett Foundation, 2018, 588p., ISBN 10-1983509787.

In the last volume of *The Dramatic Universe*, Bennett considers history, particularly the history of the human mind: "History is the content of the mind, for all that has happened since the world began is present in the mind.... Conversely, it can validly be said that without mind there would be no history—nothing but an endless array of meaningless transformations of matter and energy" (p. 3). Bennett argues that the crux of the connection between mind and history is the *present moment*, which is "the totality of immediate experience both actual and possible" (p. 3). Bennett writes that "the Dramatic Universe is an historical universe. The human drama is the drama of history. The present moment with its immensely rich and complex content cannot be understood without reference to the content of the Greater Present Moment. But more important still is the enlargement of our world picture beyond simple 'past, present and future' to include other modes of existence that I have called the Eternal Fields and the Hyparchic Past and Future. With these, I postulate Higher Intelligences able to appreciate and act within a Present Moment of vastly greater duration and depth in all dimensions than of the human mind. I have tried in this volume to show that as body evolves toward mind, so does mind develop towards Intelligence and Intelligence towards some still higher Principle that we can scarcely conceive" (pp. viii–ix).

1.5. *The Crisis in Human Affairs*. London: Hodder & Stoughton, 1948, index, 238p.; 3rd edition, 1954, 238p.; Petersham, MAs: J.G. Bennett Foundation, 2016, 176p. index, ISBN 9781530893119.

Originally twelve lectures given in London in 1946 to mark the inauguration of Bennett's newly founded Institute for the Comparative Study of History, Philosophy and the Sciences, this book was the first publication of Gurdjieff and Ouspensky's ideas and resulted in the break between Bennett and Ouspensky, who distrusted Bennett's understanding of the "Work" ideas. In the preface to the 1954 Third Edition, Bennett evaluates the importance of Gurdjieff's contribution to "the inauguration of the New Epoch": "For more than a hundred years, new forces have been working in the life of man. Gurdjieff has perhaps been the first to give clear expression to these forces and to bring their mode of operation within the understanding of ordinary people of the Western world" (pp. 7-8). In indicating how this shift in understanding might proceed, Bennett writes that "man must not only know but also be thoroughly convinced that all existence is interdependent. Absolutism, individualism, isolationism, exclusivism are names that cover those tendencies by which in the past man has been set against man.... Gurdjieff's doctrine of the reciprocal maintenance of everything that exists, which he calls the *Trogoautoegocrat*, is, if not in itself the master idea, at any rate one of the most significance conceptions that have been formulated since the new epoch began" (p. 11).

1.6. *What Are We Living for?* London: Hodder & Stoughton, 1949; 167p.; New York: Coward-McCann, 1953, 167p.; Sherborne, Gloucestershire, UK: Coombe Springs Press, 1965, 1973, 1977, 167p.; Santa Fe, NM: Bennett Books, 1991, 113p., foreword by A.L. Staveley, ISBN 0-9621901-8-7; Petersham, MA: J.G. Bennett Foundation, 2016, 144p., ISBN 1532844883.

Bennett's focus is "the task of creating one's own being" (p. 28), which he argues is most possible via "the Work" of Gurdjieff and Ouspensky. The six chapters focus on education, science and philosophy, contemporary religion, and the aimlessness of contemporary human life. In a postscript, Bennett asks "Who is Gurdjieff?"

1.7. *Witness: The Story of a Search.* London: Hodder & Stoughton, 1962, 381p. index; New York: Dharma Books, 1962, 381p.,index; limited edition, Kingston-upon-Thames: Coombe Springs Press, 1971, 399p., index [includes "preface to limited edition" and "postscript April 1971"]; revised edition, Tucson, AZ: Omen Press, 1974, 380p., index [includes a new preface and four new chapters; subtitle altered to *The Autobiography of John G. Bennett*]; London: Turnstone, 1975, 380p, index.; Charles Town, WV: Claymont Communications, 1983, 380p., index, ISBN 0934254052; Santa Fe, NM: Bennett Books, 1997 [includes a "foreword" by George and Ben Bennett]; Petersham, MA: J.G Bennett Foundation, 2017, 415p., index [includes an "Epilogue" by Ben Bennett].

In some editions subtitled "The Autobiography of John Bennett," this book tells Bennett's life story, beginning with a near-death experience as an officer in World War I and ending with his founding the International Academy for Continuous Education, a "Fourth Way" school in Sherborne, Gloucestershire, England, that ran five ten-month residential courses from 1971 to 1976. In the new preface to the 1974 edition, Bennett writes: "For three thousand years and more, the world has lived by expansion and complexification. This trend has reached saturation. We must now turn again toward concentration and simplification. This does not mean throwing away the discoveries of science and technology that have real value, but it does mean abandoning all the results that threaten destruction. We shall have to give up the use of the automobile for private transport, the mass production of mechanical and electronic devices that are not necessary for life, the expenditure of fast resources on 'education' and 'defence'. I have put the last two words in quotation marks for they stand for two of the great frauds of our time. 'Education' does not educate and 'defence' does not defend. An enormous simplification of life, and with it a great increase in human happiness and prospect of survival, will come when mankind begins to base life upon the principle of satisfying needs rather than of gratifying the lust for more and more and more" (p. 2).

1.8. *Gurdjieff: A Very Great Enigma*, Kingston-upon-Thames: Coombe Springs Press, 1963, 1966, 1969, 70p., ISBN 0-900306-06-8; York Beach, ME: Samuel Weiser, 1973, 1984 (revised edition), 100p., ISBN 0-87728-216-1; Petersham, MA: J.G. Bennett Foundation, 2017, 109p., ISBN 9781546789291.

Originally three lectures given by Bennett at London's Denison House in 1963, this book overviews Gurdjieff's life and work. Chapter headings are: "Gurdjieff's Background"; "The Sources of Gurdjieff's Ideas"; and "Gurdjieff's Teaching and Methods." Bennett characterizes the Gurdjieffian tradition as "the Fourth Way," which he describes as "the fulfilment of all ordinary life obligations, coupled with a very exactly regulated and very intensive personal work" (p. 87). Bennett identifies two key principles: first, complete involvement in life externally; and, second, "acceptance internally of responsibility for certain work that is required for a great Cosmic Purpose" (p. 92). These lectures are included in *Lectures on Gurdjieff*; see entry 2.19.

1.9. *Creative Thinking.* Kingston-upon-Thames: Coombe Springs Press, 1964, 116p.; Charles Town, WV: Claymont Communications, 1989, 86p.; Santa Fe, NM: Bennett Books, 1998, 58p. ISBN 1-881-408-07-8; Petersham, MA: J.G. Bennett Foundation, 2017 [also includes *How We Do Things*—see entry 1.16], 114p., ISBN 1977683436.

Bennett examines the conditions for thinking creatively. He contends that "living in the medium" is one essential need, since no one can be creative in a medium with which they have no real contact. He presents several rules for creative thinking: First, seeking information about the matter one wishes to know; second, asking what one understands personally and directly about the matter; third, taking the aim for understanding seriously; fourth, finding a confidence that one can contribute to that understanding; and, fifth, emptying one's self so that understanding can enter and persevering until something genuine is seen. Includes questions and answers.

1.10. *Energies: Material, Vital, Cosmic.* Kingston-upon-Thames: Coombe Springs Press, 1964, 1975, 121p., ISBN 0900306009; Charles Town, WV: Claymont Communications, 1989, 121p., 0-934254-27-3 (cloth); Petersham, MA: J.G. Bennett Foundation, 2016, 109p., ISBN 9781539141020.

Based on seminars at Coombe Springs in the early 1960s, this book summarizes the theory of universal energies that Bennett laid out in *The Dramatic Universe*. In a scale of twelve energies ranging from mechanical to transcendent, Bennett argues that the energies available to human beings have an important place, standing on the threshold between the lower and higher. He emphasizes that self-development involves the choosing to participate consciously in the refinement of energies. Lecture headings are: "The Twelve Kinds of Energy"; "The Transformations of Energy"; "How Energies Do Their Work"; "The Secret of Creativity"; "The Last Question"; and "The Works of Love." Includes questions and answers.

1.11. *A Spiritual Psychology*, Kingston-upon-Thames: Coombe Springs Press, 1964, 251p., ISBN 900-30608; London: Hodder & Stoughton, 1964, 256p., index; revised edition, Lakemont, GA: CSA Press, 1974, 268p., index, ISBN

0-87707-128-4 [includes a new preface and new first chapter, "A Spiritual Psychology"]; Santa Fe, NM: Bennett Books, 1999, 187p., index, ISBN 1881408116 [includes new forewords by Charles Tart and A.G.E. Blake; first chapter now called "Introduction"].

This book is based on talks and questions from Bennett's summer program at Coombe Springs in August 1962. He defines "spirit" as "the essential quality of anything or any being... [I]t can be called the 'ideal' behind the actual; but the word *essential* is more appropriate by the sense it conveys of the opposite of *existential*, of the measurable and the knowable elements of our experience." In the original opening chapter, "Prologue," Bennett discusses differences between Subud [see entries in category 6 below] and the Gurdjieff Work: "In many ways, the action of Gurdjieff's method and that of the Subud latihan are opposite in their effects. Self-observation and persistent efforts to remember oneself generally lead to the destruction of most of the illusions that we have of our abilities and our value. They can lead to an excessive dependence upon the group leader or teacher and also a very strong tendency to hold together.... Subud, on the other hand, tends to produce self-confidence, a feeling that others are not necessary for our spiritual welfare, and with this a tendency to disunity and a belief that all is bound to be well if only one keeps regularly to the latihan" (pp. 29–30). This prologue was replaced in later editions by a new first chapter.

1.12. *Long Pilgrimage: The Life and Teaching of Sri Govindananda Bharati Known as the Shivapuri Baba* [in collaboration with Thakur Lal Manandhar]. London: Hodder & Stoughton, 1965; London: Turnstone Books, 1975; 191p., glossary, index, ISBN 0-85500-040-6.

Bennett's account of the life and teachings of the Indian holy man, the Shivapuri Baba, who was 135 years old when Bennett first met him in 1961 in Kathmandu, Nepal. The foundation of the Shivapuri Baba's teaching is "Right Living" (*Swadharma*), which he connects with the three disciplines of body, mind, and spirit: "The basic requirements of the three disciplines are the same for all people, all times and all conditions of life, but their practical application varies from age to age, from nation to nation, from individual to individual, and even for the same individual under different conditions at different times" (p. 8). Bennett calls him "a true saint who produced an immediate and uplifting effect on everyone who entered his presence.... I have met several truly remarkable men in my life, but none who so evidently belonged to a world different from ours" (p. 9, p. 11). Chapter headings: "The Quest," "Teaching and Method," "Right Life," "The Three Disciplines," "New Lights on Old Teachings," and "The Removal of Doubts." See entry 2.15.

1.13. *How We Do Things*, Sherborne, Gloucestershire, UK: Coombe Springs Press, 1965, 1974, 69p., ISBN 0-900306-04-1; *How We Do Things: The Role of Attention in Spiritual Life*, Charles Town, WV: Claymont Communications, 1989, 57p., ISBN 0-934254-25-7 (cloth). Published in French as *Comment nous faisons les choses*, Paris: L'Originel, 1978; 2nd edition, 1982, 64p.; Petersham, MA: J.G. Bennett Foundation, 2017 [also includes *Creative Thinking*—see entry 1.12], 114p., ISBN 1977683436.

A practical discussion of human energies and how we might draw on an understanding of how they work to use and transform them effectively. Bennett explains that "We have different instruments for the way we do things, of which our bodies, with our sense and limbs are obviously the primary ones. And within our bodies there are certain powers, such as thinking, feeling, wishing, which are used in different ways according to the energy which flows into them" (p. 8). Chapter titles are "Human Energies," "The Instruments of Function," "Sensitivity," "Consciousness," "Decision," and "Creativity." Includes questions and answers.

1.14. *An Introduction to Gurdjieff*. New York: Stonehill Publishing, 1973, 144p. A second printing was issued with the title *Is There "Life" on Earth? An Introduction to Gurdjieff*. 156p., ISBN 0-88373-008-1. The second printing includes an appendix, "International Academy for Continuous Education, Inaugural Address to the students of the Second Basic Course 1972/73," which was also published in entries 2.5.7 and 3.37.

Four lectures revised for publication and originally delivered in London by Bennett in October 1949, under the series title of "Gurdjieff—Making a New World." Lecture titles are: "The Needs of a New Epoch," "Gurdjieff—the Man and his Work," "Work on Oneself," and "Gurdjieff's Writings."

1.15. *Gurdjieff: Making a New World*. New York: Harper & Row, 1973, 320p., appendices, index, ISBN 0-06-090474 (paper); Santa Fe, NM: Bennett Books, 1992, 253p. appendices, index, ISBN 0-9621901-6-0.

Bennett's most comprehensive account of the life and teachings of

Gurdjieff. Bennett organizes his presentation via three themes: first, Gurdjieff's personal search for a "higher knowledge"; second, Gurdjieff's ideas and methods for transmitting them to his followers; and, third, a consideration of whether Gurdjieff is to be considered as an isolated phenomenon, or "whether he is a representative of a cultural tradition that has existed, does now exist, and is concerned with the present and future needs of mankind" (p. 3).

1.16. *Journeys in Islamic Countries*, Vols. 1 and 2, foreword by Elizabeth Bennett. Sherborne, Gloucestershire, UK, Coombe Springs Press, 1976, 123p. ISBN 0-900306-24-6; reprinted as one volume with the same title; includes a new foreword by Adrian Gilbert, editor's note, and introduction by George Bennett. Santa Fe, NM: Bennett Books, 2000, 243p., index. ISBN 1-881408-12-4.

These volumes reproduce Bennett's diary account of a ten-week journey through the Near East that he undertook in late 1953 with the aim of finding sources of Gurdjieff's teaching. The book's first part deals with his journey from Konya, Turkey, through Syria and the Holy land; the second part describes his encounter with the Mevlevi Dervishes and his visit to northeastern Turkey—Gurdjieff's homeland. While in Konya, he wrote that "The possibility of meeting a real *murshid*—spiritual guide—has become much less important for me. I know that my murshid is within and that I only need to learn to listen" (p. 7).

1.17. *The Masters of Wisdom*. London: Turnstone Books, 1977, 224p., index, ISBN 0-85500-052-X (cloth); New York: Weiser, 1980, 224p., index; Santa Fe, NM: Bennett Books, 1995, 178p., index, ISBN 18811408019; Petersham, MA: J.G. Bennett Foundation, 2018, 189p., index, ISBN 9781720853787.

Bennett aims to establish the existence of an inner circle of humanity by reconstructing a hidden, spiritual history guided by a group of men in touch with a higher wisdom. Identified by Bennett as the Khwājagān ("Masters of Wisdom' in Persian), these men are largely unknown in the West but are said to represent one of the most remarkable groups of human beings ever to have lived. Bennett writes that these individuals do not "work only on the external, visible level, but in domains to which ordinary people have no access. They are in contact with the higher wisdom that surveys life on this earth as a whole and can see whence it has come and whither it is destined to go" (p. 22). Includes a foreword by Elizabeth Bennett.

2. EDITED COMPILATIONS OF J.G. BENNETT'S LECTURES, WRITINGS, AND EDITORIAL WORKS

2.1 *Values: An Anthropology for Seekers*, privately printed 1943; London: Unwin Brothers, 1951; Kingston-upon-Thames: Coombe Springs Press, 1963, 169p.; Petersham, MA: J.G. Bennett Foundation, 2018, 143p., ISBN 9781985767768.

Compiled by Bennett in the early1940s, these thirty-eight entries are drawn from sacred literature and speculative philosophy. In a short foreword, he explains that the entries were used as an exercise in "Work" group meetings, with members "reading one passage every week and ending with a mediation upon the theme, 'Forms are different, but Truth is One'" (p. iii). He explains that "One way of liberating ourselves from old ways of thinking is to bring together different expressions of the same truth and exercise ourselves in the recognition of identity of content behind differences, and even contradictions, of external form" (p. iii). Entry authors include Plato, Jacob Boehme, Meister Eckhart, David Hume, John Keats, Jalaluddin Rumi, Zhang Zhou, and the Christian Desert Fathers.

2.2. *Intimations: Talks with J.G. Bennett at Beshara.* Swyre Farm, Aldsworth, Gloucestershire, UK: Beshara Publications, 1975, 100p., glossary, ISBN 0-904975-03-7 (cloth); New York: Weiser, 1975, 100p.; Petersham, MA: J.G. Bennett Foundation, 2014, 134p., ISBN 9781535108805.

Ten chapters based on edited transcripts of tapes made from talks with Bennett from 1972 to 1974 at Beshara, a Sufi community near Sherborne. Chapter headings are "The World Situation," "Self-Remembering and the Transformation of Energies," "The Seven Lines of Work," "Meditation and Will," "Suffering," "Creative Imagination and Intension," "Baraqah—St. George and the Dragon," "Khidr—the Four Worlds—Needs," "Beyond the Veil of Consciousness," and "Hu." Includes an introduction by Rashid Hornsby.

2.3. *Sherborne Theme Talks Series* (1976–77)
Four short monographs produced from transcripts of theme talks given by Bennett at the International Academy for Continuous Education between 1972 and 1975. Each talk relates to a specific theme for which students were to gather first-person observations to be reported in weekly theme meetings on Friday evenings. The monographs include questions and answers. They were reprinted

as one volume by Bennett Books in 2002 and entitled *The First Liberation: Working with Themes at Sherborne House, Volume 1*; see entry 2.4.

2.3.1. *The First Liberation: Freedom from Like and Dislike* (No. 1). Sherborne, Gloucestershire, UK: Coombe Springs Press, 1976, 35p.

2.3.2. *Noticing* (No. 2). Sherborne, Gloucestershire, UK: Coombe Springs Press, 1976, 48p.

2.3.3. *Material Objects* (No. 3). Sherborne, Gloucestershire, UK: Coombe Springs Press, 1977, 56p.

2.3.4. *Food* (No. 4). Sherborne, Gloucestershire, UK: Coombe Springs Press, 1977, 50p.

2.4. *The First Liberation: Working with Themes at Sherborne House, Volume 1*, Santa Fe, NM: Bennett Books, 2002, 83p. ISBN 1-881408-13-2.

A compilation of entries 2.3.1–2.3.4; includes an appendix, "Listening," which reproduces "extracts from a theme given by Bennett on 26th March 1973."

2.5. "The Transformation of Man" series (1974–77)
Seven lectures and portions of lectures given by Bennett, mostly between 1971 and 1974, and each published as a short monograph edited by Bennett associate A.G.E. Blake. The lectures' central aim is "to show a new view of the world, an utterly positive one, based on the firm conviction that man must transform himself and that this transformation is, to some degree, possible for every man and woman. Many of the ideas are taken from Gurdjieff but have been developed and sometimes superseded" (n.p.). Six of the seven lectures have been assembled in one volume, *Teachings from Sherborne*; see entry 2.21.

2.5.1. *Gurdjieff Today* (No. 1) Sherborne, Gloucestershire, UK: Coombe Springs Press, 1974, 47p. ISBN 0-900306-13-0.

Text based on a lecture given by Bennett at Caxton Hall in December 1973. Bennett asks how Gurdjieff understood the sense and purpose of life on the earth, especially human life. Bennett argues that the need is for human beings to see things as they really are via a direct perception grounded in "conscience." A key to developing conscience is what Gurdjieff called "conscious labors and intentional suffering." Includes questions and answers.

2.5.2. *The Enneagram* (No. 2) Sherborne, Gloucestershire, UK: Coombe Springs Press, 1974, 64 p.

Bennett overviews the *enneagram*, a symbol introduced by Gurdjieff and used to depict any organized process and to recognize and counter points of deflection. Bennett explains that the enneagram "is an instrument to help us to achieve triadic perception and mentation. Whereas our ordinary mental processes are linear and sequential, the world in which we live is threefold" (p. 1). According to Gurdjieff, threefoldness is one of the 'fundamental Sacred Cosmic laws' and must be studied by anyone who wishes to understand himself and the world in which he lives" (p. 1). This volume is edited by A.G.E. Blake, who later revised and expanded the original book as *Enneagram Studies*, published in1983; see entry no. 2.11. The original 1974 version is reprinted in *Teachings from Sherborne*; see entry 2.21.

2.5.3. *Sex* (No. 3) Sherborne, Gloucestershire, UK: Coombe Springs Press, 1975, 85p.; ISBN 0-900306-165.

Bennett discusses the significance of the sexual act and how it relates to perception and creativity. He considers the meaning of parenthood and marriage and asks what a realistic approach to sex might involve in our contemporary society. He emphasizes two main point: "First, that the primary normative function of sex for most people is neither procreation nor pleasure but the regulation of psychic energies. Second, that true marriage or union is possible only for the few who are able and willing to make the sacrifice of self involved" (p. 69).

2.5.4. *The Sevenfold Work* (No. 4) Sherborne, Gloucestershire, UK: Coombe Springs Press, 1976, 116p. Enlarged second edition, preface by A.G.E. Blake, Charles Town, WV: Claymont Communications, 1979, 156p.; ISBN 0-934254-01-X.

Bennett discusses seven lines of "the Work" that he identifies as *assimilation, struggle, service, manifestation, receptivity, submission,* and *purity*. He explains that "in the first line, we are *active* in taking into ourselves from outside; context: world. In the second line, we are *active* from inside from inside to inside; context: myself. In the third line, we are *active* from inside to outside; context: community. In the fourth line, we are *neither* active nor receptive; Context: action. In the fifth line, we are *receptive* in taking from outside; context: community. In the sixth line, we are *receptive* within, from inside to inside; context:

myself. In the seventh line, we are *receptive* to what is beyond us; context: world" (pp. 6–7). Includes questions and answers.

2.5.5. *The Image of God in Work* (No. 5), Sherborne, Gloucestershire, UK: Coombe Springs Press, 1976, 74p., ISBN 0-900306-27-0; five of the seven chapters republished in 1982 as *Sacred Influences* by Coombe Springs Press: Moorcote, Ellingstring, near Ripon, North Yorkshire, UK, 47p., ISBN 0-900306-96-3 [includes "introduction" and "bibliography and notes" by A.E.G. Blake]; the original 1976 text published in full as *Sacred Influences: Spiritual Action in Human Life*, Santa Fe, NM: Bennett Books, 1989, 86p., ISBN 0-9621901-0-1 [includes "publisher's notes" and "biographical note"].

This monograph is about finding "supra-personal realities in practice; so to say, in real life, in action" (p. 1). Bennett describes the remarkable power of sacred images as they can be a bridge between human beings and God and between this world and higher worlds. He suggests that the origin of these images is an invisible event initiated by higher worlds. He points to the important role that Nature and the natural world might have in activating a feeling of gratitude that "enables us to receive in the right way and to enter into the action of life in the right way" (p. 24). Includes questions and answers.

2.5.6. *J.G. Bennett's Talks on* Beelzebub's Tales (No. 6) Sherborne, Gloucestershire, UK: Coombe Springs Press, 1977, 147p, ISBN 0-900306-36-X; York Beach, ME: Samuel Weiser, 1977, 153p., ISBN 0-87728-680-9.

This monograph presents a series of Bennett's commentaries on Gurdjieff's *All and Everything: Beelzebub's Tales to his Grandson*. The majority of entries were given as Sherborne talks in 1974, although there are several items dating back to 1949 and 1950. The monograph is divided thematically into five parts: history, cosmology, cosmogony, Work, and Reality. Introduction by A.G.E. Blake. These talks provide some of Bennett's most penetrating commentary on Gurdjieff's philosophy.

2.5.7. *Needs of a New Age Community* (No. 7) Sherborne, Gloucestershire, UK: Coombe Springs Press, 1977, 99p., ISBN 0-900306-47-5; Santa Fe, NM: Bennett Books, 1990, 118p., ISBN 0-9621901-2-8 [incorporates additional material, including a foreword by A.L. Staveley; two appendices ("The Fourth Way" and

"Inaugural Address: International Academy, Second Basic Course"); a biographical note by George Bennett; and publisher's notes].

The entries in this monograph all engage the question, "How is it possible to have in a community genuine self-sacrifice and love that is not imaginary?" (p. 1). Chapters include "Spiritual Community," "The Three Orders of Human Society," "The Spirit of a Society," "The World Situation," and two chapters on "The Sermon on the Mount." Foreword by A.G.E. Blake. For the "Inaugural Address: International Academy, Second Basic Course," also see entries 1.17 and 3.37.

2.6. "The Dramatic Universe Series" (1976-78)
Three posthumous monographs assembled by A.G.E. Blake from Bennett's lectures and writings that focus on key themes in the four volumes of Bennett's *The Dramatic Universe*. The series was later retitled, "Studies from the *Dramatic Universe*" and republished by Bennett Books with new introductions by Blake.

2.6.1. *Hazard* (Vol. 1, "Studies from the *Dramatic Universe*"). Sherborne, Gloucestershire, UK: Coombe Springs Press, 1976, 112p. ISBN 0-900306-33-5; reprinted with new foreword by A.G.E. Blake, Santa Fe, NM: Bennett Books, 1991, 117p., index, ISBN 0-9621901-4-4; reprinted, Petersham, MA: J.G. Bennett Foundation, 2018, 99p., ISBN 13-978-1984279248.

A fundamental uncertainty in the very existence of the universe is a central theme of Bennett's *Dramatic Universe*. This fundamental uncertainty is what he called *hazard*, and this monograph includes portions of his lectures and writings on the topic: "As the years go by, I become more and more convinced that the doctrine of universal hazard must before long replace our belief in absolutes of any kind and that is why I have decided to speak about this doctrine at this particular stage of my life. Includes questions and answers.

2.6.2. *Existence* (Vol. 2, "Studies from the *Dramatic Universe*"). Sherborne, Gloucestershire, UK: Coombe Springs Press, 1977, 74p. ISBN 0-900306-40-8; reprinted with new foreword by A.G.E. Blake, Santa Fe, NM: Bennett Books, 2010, 96p. ISBN 188140822.

Bennett explains that "There is a growing awareness that we have to come to terms with the hazards of the world, and that we cannot do so without a different kind of understanding." Includes the 1960s working paper, "The Threshold of Existence," which considers "the consequences of retaining materiality but abandoning completely the notion of space-time as being more than forms of connectedness between material entities" (p. 44). This perspective requires that "we should revise the basic ontology of science, which assumes that objects exist 'in' space and time and that there is nothing 'outside' space and time. We postulate a material substratum—called *hylé* following the Greek usage—that is subject to conditions but does not require the notions of space and time for its definition" (p. 44). Includes questions and answers.

2.6.3. *Creation* (Vol. 3, "Studies from the *Dramatic Universe*"). Sherborne, Gloucestershire, UK: Coombe Springs Press, 1978, 77p. ISBN 0-900306-41-6; reprinted with new foreword by A.G.E. Blake, Santa Fe, NM: Bennett Books, 1998, 80p., glossary, ISBN 0-9621901-4-4.

In his original foreword, A.G.E. Blake writes that, "at every turn, Bennett brings us back to experience: what is it to exist, what kinds of consciousness are there, what are the possibilities of number, what is the essence of relationships, what is the essence of life?" (p. 6). Chapter headings include "Infinity and Beyond," "Deity," "Vitality," "Materiality," "Creation of Life," and "Evolution." Includes questions and answers.

2.7. *Transformation*. Charles Town, West Virginia: Claymont Communications, 1978, 198p. Santa Fe, NM: Bennett Books, 2003,135p., ISBN 1-881408-15-19.

Edited by Bennett associate Kenneth Pledge and originally written in the summer of 1968, this monograph is an unfinished longer volume on spiritual transformation, which Bennett defines in the first chapter as "the process by which a man can pass beyond the limitations of his own nature and become a 'New Man'" (p. 7). Bennett aims to describe "various ways that I myself have tried during the fifty years of my own searches" (p. 7). Chapter headings are: "The Four Sources"; "Necessary Knowledge": "Communication"; "Seeking and Finding"; "The Body and its Needs"; and "Harmonious Development."

2.8. *Deeper Man*. London: Turnstone Books, 1978, 254p., index, ISBN 0-85500-092-9 (cloth); Santa Fe, NM: Bennett Books, 1994; Petersham, MA: J.G. Bennett Foundation, 2019, 237p., index, ISBN 9781077845114.

Compiled and edited by Bennett associate A.G.E. Blake, this volume overviews and extends Gurdjieffian principles by asking what it might mean that human beings can live in multiple worlds, including the spiritual realm. The book is broken into three major parts: first, "Man": second, "Laws"; and, third, "Worlds." The ten chapter headings are: "The Three Worlds," "Energies," "Three-Centred Being," "Selves," "The Seven Worlds," "The Law of Three," "The World of Delusion," "Above and Below," "What is this Inner World?" and "Death and Resurrection."

2.9. *Idiots in Paris: Diaries of J.G. Bennett and Elizabeth Bennett, 1949.* Daglingworth Manor, Gloucestershire, UK: Coombe Springs Press, 1980, foreword by Elizabeth Bennett, 120p., ISBN 0-900306-47-5; New York: Weiser Books, 1991, 145p. ISBN 9780877287247; Santa Fe, NM: Bennett Books, 2008, 143p., ISBN 9781881408208; Petersham, MA: J.G. Bennett Foundation, 2016, 129p. ISBN 9781541113923.

These diaries by Bennett and his wife Elizabeth describe their time with Gurdjieff in the months before his death in Paris on October 29, 1949, where his apartment in the Rue des Colonels Rénard became the center of his teaching. A major daily event was the lavish meals, accompanied by Gurdjieff's "toast of the idiots," which Elizabeth Bennett pictures in vivid detail. In her foreword, she writes: "The ritual of the toasts was drawn from what Gurdjieff called the 'Science of Idiotism'…. The word idiot has two meanings: the true meaning given to it by the ancient sages was *to be oneself*. A man who is himself looks and behaves like a madman to those who live in the world of illusions, so when they call a man an idiot they mean that he does not share their illusions. Everyone who decides to work on himself is an idiot in both meanings. The wise know that he is seeking for reality. The foolish think he has taken leave of his senses. We here are supposed to be seeking for reality, so we should all be idiots: but no one can make you an idiot. You must choose it for yourself" (pp. vii–viii).

2.10. *The Way to be Free*. New York: Samuel Weiser, 1980; reprinted 1992, 201p. ISBN 0-87728-491-1.

Compiled and edited by A.G.E. Blake, this volume incorporates two parts: first, a series of lectures and lecture fragments mostly presented to students at the International Academy for Continuous Education in the early 1970s; second, a compilation of notes that Bennett made in 1944 as he was writing the final chapter of a book on the "System" of Gurdjieff. Blake explains that "these notes, made thirty years before the meetings recorded in the first part of this book, can be looked at as the theory behind the practical efforts of the succeeding years" (p. 159). Blake writes: "the main idea is that there is a complete organic whole of evolving humanity. If a man or a woman so will, they can participate in in this whole. The wish and efforts that can awaken in a man or woman can bring them to the point at which a real journey into their own essential self can begin. What lies ahead is perhaps unlimited. It cannot be predetermined. An unknown number of great human souls who have 'gone far ahead' are with us on this Earth here and now and through them we are helped in our own work of salvation" (p. 159). Preface by Elizabeth Bennett.

2.11. *Enneagram Studies*, York, ME: Samuel Weiser, 1983, 133p., ISBN 0-87728-544-6.

Edited by A.G.E. Blake, this volume is a revised and expanded version of *The Enneagram*, published in 1974—see entry 2.5.2. New material includes excerpts from the *Dramatic Universe* (Chapter 2, "The Overcoming of Hazard"; Chapter 6, "The Realization of Beauty"; and Chapter 8, "The Biospheric Symbiosis"). Also included, as a second appendix is Bennett's "The Sermon on the Mount," originally published in entry 2.5.7. Two chapters are by Bennett associates and reprinted from the journal *Systematics* (see entry 3): Clarence E. King's "The Manufacturing Process" (Chapter 4 and reprinted from *Systematics*, Vol. 1, No. 2 [September 1963]); and Kenneth W. Pledge's "Structured Process in Scientific Experiment" (Appendix 2 and reprinted from *Systematics*, Vol. 3, No. 4 [March 1966]). In the chapter on "The Realization of Beauty," Bennett uses the enneagram to illustrate the training of a professional singer and "the realization of beauty in sound" (p. 52). He pictures the process in three parts: first, a receptive impulse as contingency and "the accident of a good *voice*"; second, a reconciling impulse as hope and "*training* directed towards an aim not at first clear"; and, third, an affirming term as transcendence and "the *Art* of Music as a value beyond the person" (p. 52).

2.12. *Elementary Systematics: A Tool for Understanding Wholes*. Santa Fe, NM: Bennett Books, 1993. ISBN 0-9621901-5-2; foreword by Elizabeth Bennett.

Edited by David Seamon, this book is a compilation of six lectures on systematics that Bennett presented at Coombe Springs in 1963. Systematics is a method drawing on the qualitative significance of whole numbers to examine a phenomenon from different but complementary viewpoints. Chapters focus on the first five systems of *monad, dyad, triad, tetrad,* and *pentad*. The book includes as an appendix "General Systematics," Bennett's first in-depth account of the systematics method, originally published in *Systematics* in 1963—see entry 3.2.

2.13. *Making a Soul: Human Destiny and the Debt of Our Existence*. Santa Fe, NM: Bennett Books, 1995, 111p., index. ISBN 1-881408-00-0.

This text is based on a series of six London lectures given by Bennett, March 8 through April 12, 1954. The lectures were public and entitled "Man's Task and His Reward: A New Conception of Human Destiny Based on the Teaching of G. Gurdjieff." Titles of the six lectures are "The Reason for Man's Existence on the Earth"; "The Human Organism and its Functions"; "Consciousness and its Possible Transformations"; "Individuality—Fictitious and Real"; "The Debt of Our Existence"; and "The First and the Second Death of Man." Includes questions and answers. An earlier private edition using the title of the lectures was published in 1954 by Bennett's Institute for the Comparative Study of History, Philosophy and the Sciences. These lectures are most recently published in *Lectures on Gurdjieff* (2020); see entry 2.19.

2.14. *Sunday Talks at Coombe Springs*. Santa Fe, NM: Bennett books, 2004, 312p. ISBN 1-881408-14-0.

Edited by Bennett associate Ken Pledge, these are forty-one talks given during Sunday "Work" days at Coombe Springs—the research community near London that Bennett led between 1946 and 1966. Pledge explains that, though sometimes Bennett described these talks as informal "conversations," nevertheless "an overriding impression remains of his certainty and authority in domains ordinarily supposed impenetrable. Some talks emphasize the converse: how little is really known. Some are experimental essays at communicating principles and methods of work involved in human transformation; others are near perfect five-finger exercises in creative thinking upon some well chosen theme. The arguments are clear, their reasoning cogent" (p. xvi). Foreword by George Bennett.

2.15. *The Shivapuri Baba and His Message*. Petersham, MA: J.G. Bennett Foundation, 2016, 91p. ISBN 9781533489319.

This book comprises four lectures that Bennett delivered at London's Denison House in 1962. The lectures discuss the Indian holy man known as the Shivapuri Baba (1826–1963), who Bennett visited twice in Kathmandu, Nepal.

Lecture headings are "The Shivapuri Baba," "The Three Lives of Man," "The Way of Perfection," and "Looking to the Future." Introduction by Ben Bennett. A longer account of these meetings and the Shivapuri Baba's spiritual message is presented in Bennett's *Long Pilgrimage* (1965); see entry 1.15.

2.16. *Who Is Man?* Petersham, MA: J.G. Bennett Foundation, 2016, 128p. ISBN 9-781533-54629.

A series of six lectures given by Bennett in 1955 at Conway Hall in London's Red Lion Square. Lecture titles are "'I' and 'Me'," "Me and My Body," "Something Not Quite Right," "Man and Mankind," "Man and the Universe," and "Man—Actual and Potential." In summarizing the lectures, Bennett explains that "we have looked at man in different perspectives—very incompletely but enough perhaps each time to show us something of what we all know but never sufficiently face.... From whatever direction we look at man, we see a distinction between what he is and what he might be, a distinction between the actual man and the potential man. And it is in that direction that our search is leading us. If we are to understand what man is, we first understand also what it is possible for him to become" (pp. 109-10). Throughout the lectures, Bennett refers to Gurdjieff's method for "the Harmonious Development of Man" (p. 113). Includes questions and answers.

2.17. *The Great Human Problems: A Course of Study.* Petersham, MA: J.G. Bennett Foundation, 2017, 210p., ISBN 9-781542-923231; publisher's foreword by Ben Bennett.

Bennett defines the great human problems as "those that cannot be resolved by human ingenuity and common sense. They bring us fact to face with the limitations of our understanding and powers" (p. 1). Drawing on the structure of the enneagram and a method of study called "enquiry and discussion" (p. 3), Bennett aims to offer an accessible means for understanding these problems. The book is a compilation of papers resulting from a three-month period of work of Bennett and students in fall 1963 at Coombe Springs. The format is grounded in work on "structural communications" that became an important part of Bennett's research in the 1960s. The papers are organized in two parts: first, "Hazard as we find it"; and, second, "The Unconditioned." The book ends with a discussion of six "ways of life" based on the six fundamental triads of "Will" that Bennett developed in Volume 2 of *The Dramatic Universe*. He speaks of the "utilitarian man," "humanitarian man," "man of good will," "psychokinetic man," "man of destiny," and "man of freedom."

2.18. *Denison House Talks: Questions and Answers 1950–1, 1954.* Petersham, MA: J.G. Bennett Foundation, 2019, 393p., index, ISBN 9781095536391.

This volume provides twenty-six public talks that Bennett gave in Central London in two series, the first from September 1950 to July 1951; the second, during the summer of 1954. Emphasizing Gurdjieff's philosophy and system, at the time largely unknown, the talks were open to all interested parties and were well attended by audiences as large as three hundred. Recordings of the talks were made by a team of shorthand typists who would then transcribe the talks into written form. Includes questions and answers. Talks are marked by dates only and have no titles.

2.19. *Lectures on Gurdjieff.* Petersham, MA: J.G. Bennett Foundation, 2019, 335p., index, ISBN 9-781652-050261.

Subtitled "Fourteen Public Lectures in Four Series, 1949–73," Bennett gave these London talks to introduce Gurdjieff's teachings to a general audience, including those with no background knowledge. Entitled "Is there Life on Earth?" the first series of four lectures was given in October 1949, shortly before Gurdjieff's death at the end of that month. These lectures were originally published by Turnstone Publishing in 1973 (see entry 1.16). Entitled "Man's Task and His Reward," the second series of six lectures were given in March and April 1954 and originally published by Bennett Books in 1984 as *Making a Soul* (see entry 2.13). Entitled "Gurdjieff: A Very Great Enigma," the third series of three lectures were given in summer1963 and published in 1966 by Coombe Springs Press and in 1973 by Turnstone Press (see entry 1.10). Entitled "Gurdjieff Today, the volume's last entry is a stand-alone lecture Bennett gave in November 1973 to recruit students for his International Academy for Continuous Education and to announce publication of his *Gurdjieff: Making a New World* (see entry 1.17). This lecture was published by Coombe Springs Press in 1974 with the title *Gurdjieff Today* (see entry 2.5.1).

2.20. *The Study of Man.* Petersham, MA: J.G. Bennett Foundation, 2019, 168p. ISBN 9781699419601.

In early 1967, Bennett offered a course of seven lectures that clarified themes in the third volume of *The Dramatic Universe*. Students were asked to participate in field testing an experimental method of learning, "structured communication," whereby students responded to test questions on each lecture, making use of a "semantic matrix" of possible answers. One aim was using one's attention "on a higher level than that of ordinary thinking" (p. 1). Lectures include: "The Three Elements: Function, Being and Will"; "The Present Moment: Time, Eternity, Hyparxis"; "The Formation of Human Beings"; "Education: Four Selves"; "The Three Disciplines"; "The Stages of Development: Psychostatic, Psychokinetic, and Psychoteleois Orders"; "Last Things: Old Age, Death and Beyond." The volume is said to include all the lectures' study materials.

2.21. *Teachings from Sherborne.* Petersham, MA: J.G. Bennett Foundation, 2020, 425p., index, ISBN 9798622106361; foreword by Ben Bennett.

A compilation of six Sherborne talks originally published as part of the series, "Transformation of Man" (see entries 2.3.1–2.3.4; 2.5). Titles are "The Enneagram," "Sex," "The Sevenfold Work," "The Mask of God in the Work," "Talks on Beelzebub's Tales," and "Needs of a New Age Community."

3. ARTICLES BY J.G. BENNETT IN *SYSTEMATICS*

Published from 1963 until 1974, *Systematics* was an academic journal edited by Bennett and published by the Institute for the Comparative Study of History, Philosophy and the Sciences. Included here are thirty-three articles and reviews written or co-written by Bennett from 1963 until 1974. Many of these entries are reprinted in J.G. Bennett, *"Systematics" Papers, 1963–1972*; see entry 3.39.

3.1. "The Aims of the Journal," Vol. 1, No. 1 (June 1963), pp. 1–4.

As a research discipline, *systematics* is said to emphasize an "integrative principle that harmonises the sensible and suprasensible worlds." Journal entries relate to "the problem of human perfectibility, or the factors that determine progress or retrogression in individuals and communities" (p. 2). A guiding principle for all systematics research is "integration without rejection" (p. 3). No author is given but almost certainly written or co-written by Bennett.

3.2. "General Systematics," Vol. 1, No. 1 (June 1963), pp. 5–19; reprinted in *Elementary Systematics*, 1993, pp. 96–113.

One of Bennett's most lucid explications of systematics, a method of understanding that draws on the interpretive significance of whole numbers to facilitate a deepening familiarity with the phenomenon under study: "We perceive and understand in certain ways because we and the world are constructed in certain ways. These ways can be described in terms of *systems* and the study of all the possible forms of connectedness can therefore be called *systematics*" (p. 6). Reprinted, with added subheadings and edited notes, in *Elementary Systematics*; see entry 2.12.

3.3. "Discussion—[C. D] Broad's Lectures on Psychical Research," Vol. 1, No. 1 (June 1963) pp. 90–95.

Bennett discusses British philosopher C.D. Broad's *Lectures on Psychical Research*, a book considers philosophical aspects of psychical research. Bennett emphasizes that Broad "has performed a service of great importance in laying the foundations of a metaphysics that will take non-causal phenomena into account" (p. 94). Bennett calls for "the construction of a new metaphysics that will take all paranormal and non-causal phenomena into account [as] one of the best safeguards against dangerous confusion that is produced when theological conclusions are drawn from physical premises" (p. 95).

3.4. "Editorial: Systematics and General Systems Theory," Vol. 1, No. 2 (September 1963) pp. 105–10.

A comparison and contrast of Bennett's systematics with the General Systems Theory developed by biologist Ludwig von Bertalanffy. The article concludes that, "notwithstanding the marked differences in methodology and indeed in the very conception of a system, the two [approaches] are working upon converging lines, and … a comparison of the results obtained should be very fruitful" (p. 109). Systematics is said to assume that "the cardinal numbers bear significant qualities" (p. 106) and emphasizes "the importance of the qualitative elements in all experience as derivative from the qualitative significance of number" (p. 107). No author is given but almost certainly written or co-written by Bennett; see entry 3.32.

3.5. "Geophysics and Human History: New Light on Plato's Atlantis and the Exodus," Vol. 1, No. 2 (September 1963), pp. 127–56.

Bennett considers whether there might be similarity of pattern in geophysical and human events by arguing for a "historico-geophysical homology" relating to the "simultaneous disappearance of Plato's Atlantis, the destruction of the culture of Minoan Crete, the Exodus of the Israelites from Egypt, the flood of Deucalion recorded in Greek history, and a prodigious explosion of the volcanic island of Deucalion" (p. 128). Bennett emphasizes that his conclusions "are so startling that I put them forward at this stage only as striking illustrations of the general theme that there is a connection between geophysical occurrences and some of the major events in human history" (p. 128). See entry 3.6.

3.6. "What Is Time?" Vol. 1, No. 2 (September 1963), pp. 180–81.

Bennett discusses three kinds of time in human experience: first, ordinary, sequential *time*, which provides a sense of past, present, and future; second, *eternity*, which offers a sense of persistence, marks a "storehouse of potentialities" and means that "there can be many lines of successive time simultaneously present in eternity" (p. 180); and, third, *hyparxis*, which relates to "ableness-to-be" and points to situations where "we cannot only entertain purposes, but be deliberate and choose our actions with the aim of realizing them" (p. 181). Bennett explains that this threefold scheme of time is valuable because "it enables the whole range of human experience to be brought into a coherent system of explanation and understanding" (p. 181).

3.7. "The Hyperborean Origin of the Indo-European Culture," Vol. 1, No. 3 (December 1963), pp. 203–32.

Another article in which Bennett uses the systematics perspective to consider hidden connections between geophysical occurrences and events in human history (see entry 3.4), a possibility he considers here in examining the origin of the of Indo-European language and culture system. Drawing on Indian scholar B.G. Tilak's Arctic Home theory that the earliest Vedic hymns were written in the circumpolar regions, Bennett suggests that the Indo-European language and culture may have diffused from "an area in the Arctic Circle probably on the western Siberian hinterland of the Arctic Ocean" (p. 204).

3.8. "Total Man: An Essay in the Systematics of Human Nature," Vol. 1, No. 4 (March 1964), pp. 282–310.

Bennett writes that man is "a totality rather than a whole" and "is concerned with and lives in many different worlds at the same time. This association with a multiplicity of worlds, each making a different contribution to the total man, makes the task of describing human nature very complicated" (p. 282). To describe the diversity of the human constitution, Bennett draws on the systematic systems of monad, dyad, triad, tetrad, and pentad. For example, Bennett pictures the "human monad" as a family of eight overlapping curves that include energies, things, life, intelligence, values, history, space/time, and spirit. He pictures the essential "human dyad" as the tension between the "restricted concern" for meeting the inescapable needs of everyday life versus the "total concern" directed toward "the whole mystery of what is beyond our immediate reach" (p. 289). Drawing on the "human pentad," Bennett concludes that "The destiny of man, on any balanced view, must take account of his obligations as well as his rights. The systematic scheme of the pentad shows him as under three kinds of obligation. One is to himself, another to the ideal of human perfection…, and the third is to an objective purpose that is beyond humanity. If any of these three are neglected, man cannot attain to the complete significance which is his destiny" (p. 309).

3.9. "The Metabiology of Maurice Vernet," Vol. 2, No. 2 (September 1964), pp. 147–54.

Bennett overviews the work of French biologist and philosopher Maurice Vernet, who "treats biology not as a purely descriptive and utilitarian science, but as a discipline that makes it possible to apprehend human life and experience as a whole—that is, in their two-fold nature as animal and spirit. The method consists in search for the active principle of life itself while remaining within the framework of well-established biological data" (p. 147). Bennett concludes that Vernet's "critiques of heredity and evolution are of special value in view of the changing attitude of many biologists to the older theories of Darwin and Weismann" (p. 154).

3.10. "Review Discussion: *Man and Time* by J.B. Priestley," Vol. 2, No. 3 (December 1964), pp. 235–41.

Bennett discusses how this British writer's understanding of time contrasts with the current conventional view assuming that time is successive, irreversible, and single-valued. Bennett agrees with and extends Priestley's claim that "our lives are not contained within passing time, a single track along which we hurry to oblivion. We exist in more than one dimension of time" (p. 235). Bennett briefly mentions *hyparxis*, his temporal concept that allows one to "account for experience of a changeable future" (p. 241).

3.11. [Book review] *The Relevance of Science* by Carl F. von Weizsäcker (London: Collins, 1964), Vol. 2, No. 4 (March 1965), pp. 339-41.

Bennett describes this book as "a most important contribution to the debate on human destiny." He writes that the book's most important contribution is "to demonstrate that just as Christianity cannot be understood without reference to Judaism, and Judaism without reference to Mythology; so also is modern science incomprehensible without reference to the Christian tradition that made it possible, nurtured it and established its basic, though unavowed, postulate—that nature is knowable and passive, and man is knower and active in all their relationships" (p. 340).

3.12. "The Problem of Space and Time in Scientific Discourse," co-authored with Henri Bortoft, Vol. 3, No. 1 (June 1965), pp. 71-75.

At the time, Bortoft was a young researcher at Bennett's Institute and would go on to become a major figure in Goethean science and write the influential book, *The Wholeness of Nature* (Lindesfarne Press, 1996). This article overviews the Institute's efforts to construct "a language free from spatio-temporal presuppositions" and "able to communicate all that the scientist does and experiences, avoiding as far as possible inferences involving presuppositions as to the nature of the physical world" (p. 73). See entry 3.14.

3.13. "The Body and its Uses—The Gurdjieff System," Vol. 3, No. 2 (September 1965), pp. 127-33.

In probing the role of the body in human experience, Bennett emphasizes that bodily self-awareness is "a primary element of experience that is prior to knowledge of anything at all" (p. 127). In this article, he describes Gurdjieff's understanding of the body in terms of instinctive, motor, intellectual, and emotional functions. He makes connections between bodily possibilities and will, spontaneity, and creativity. Bennett emphasizes that full bodily potential is only available if "its operations are understood by the user himself and if he knows how to develop its powers to their highest efficiency and maintain them in good order" (p. 128).

3.14. "Towards an Objectively Complete Language," co-authored with Henri Bortoft and Kenneth W. Pledge, Vol. 3, No. 3 (December 1965), pp. 185–229.

The authors develop a symbolic language "for the purpose of describing the structural features of operations such as characterize the procedure of scientific investigation" (p. 185). Will and the Present Moment mark the foundation of this language, which is used to identify "six types of complex situations significantly exemplified in scientific work" (p. 185). The language is then used "to describe and clarify the operational procedure involved in the genesis and performance of a typical physical experiment" (p. 185). The authors conclude that this symbolic language "can easily be learned and used for describing experiments and…, apart from its philosophical importance, it proves to be of practical value for distinguishing the various stages of a practical undertaking" (p. 229).

3.15. "The Specification and Assessment of Human Beings," Vol. 3, No. 4 (March 1966), pp. 281–303.

Bennett presents a "scheme for specifying the characteristics required in people and in human activities, based upon the distinction of Function, Being and Will; the systematics and structures described in earlier issues of this journal; and the theory of energies" (p. 281). On one hand, Bennett highlights the threefold division of human function into bodily, affective, and intellectual aspects; on the other hand, he highlights four energies associated with life—automatic, sensitive, conscious, and creative. These designations lead to a three by four matrix in which are located twelve aspects of human being that can be developed, integrated, and educated. For example, sensitive energy associated with the intellectual function relates to strong analytic skills, a grasp of theory, and the ability to express ideas. In turn, conscious energy associated with the emotional function relates to emotional stability, self-criticism, self-confidence, and the ability to take responsibility.

3.16. "A Descriptive Model for Mental and Supramental Operations," Vol. 4, No. 2 (September 1966), pp. 135–42.

Bennett draws on twelve levels of energy to clarify the range of transcendent experiences such as precognition, clairvoyance, creative insight, and spiritual ecstasy. He focuses on what he calls *cosmic* energies, which are not subject to the limitations of time and space and "have us *within* them: they are everywhere, but they are also capable of concentration and transformation" (p. 137).

For example, *conscious* energy comes and goes and "is not controlled by the person who experiences it" (pp. 137-38). Conscious energy relates to a feeling of "I" and relates to judgment, insight, and "the combination of self-confidence and self-criticism that characterizes the good artist or scientist" (p. 138). Another example is *creative* energy, which is supra-mental and evokes a sense of unexpectedness and wonder: "No one is aware of creative steps except after they have been made" (p. 138).

3.17. "The Evidence for Intelligence other than Human," Vol. 4, No. 3 (December 1966), pp. 181-201.

Bennett overviews his argument for an "intelligent guidance in history," whereby the observation of temporal and historical processes leads to the conclusion that "intelligences other than human are operating upon a far larger scale than the human mind can grasp and that this must be postulated to account for the course of events" (p. 181). He concludes that the hope for the future of humankind requires "learning how to cooperate with the Higher Intelligence, making the fullest use of the powers that we now possess and other powers that we may be destined to develop" (p. 201).

3.18. "The Design of the School—Systems Integrated School Project: Paper 1," co-authored with Anthony M. Hodgson, Vol. 4, No. 4 (March 1967), pp. 289-303.

This article was originally a presentation given at a day-long seminar, "Systems-Integrated School," held at the University of Sussex in January 1967. Bennett and Institute colleague Anthony Hodgson describe an effort to use the method of systematics to envision a new kind of school that moves away from the traditional pedagogical hierarchy of administration/staff/students to provide "an integrated curriculum designed to enable the pupil to develop as an entire person while, at the same time, acquiring sufficient specialized knowledge and skill to embark upon a vocation in society" (p. 289). All articles in this issue of *Systematics* were originally Sussex-seminar presentations that "have been revised and amplified by the authors" (p. 285); also see entry 3.19.

3.19. "The Psychological Basis—Systems Integrated School Project: Paper 2," Vol. 4, No. 4 (March 1967), pp. 319-45.

Bennett marks out a pedagogical psychology "that will take account not only of man as a thinking animal, but also of his potential for developing higher functions such as creativity and judgement, charity and the spirit of service" (p. 319). He develops this psychology in terms of what the human being *does*, what he or she *is*, and *how* he or she acts—in other words, a focus on *function*, *being*, and *will*. This threefold understanding is said to offer one way whereby "the total assessment of the human being can be approached" (p. 344).

3.20. [Book review] *Catal Huyuk: A Neolithic Town in Anatolia* by James Mellaart (London: Thames and Hudson,1967), Vol. 5, No. 2 (September 1967), pp. 175-77.

Bennett's review of Mellaart's report on the excavation of this Neolitic site in south-central Turkey, described as one of the first true cities, with a fully developed agriculture and extensive trading. Mellaart argues that the Neolithic culture associated with Catal Huyuk belongs to a "Mother Goddess" culture, which Bennett concludes (in Volume 4 of *The Dramatic Universe*) was one of the four great culture systems "created in the last millenia of the last glaciation—i.e., about 12,000-10,00 years before the present" (p.176).

3.21. "Progress and Hazard," Vol. 5, No. 4 (March 1968), pp. 319-30.

Based on two lectures given in February 1968 at the University of Pennsylvania's Wharton School of Finance and Commerce, this article aims for an understanding of progress and hazard that is "reasonably free from ambiguity" (p. 319). Bennett argues that "progress cannot occur in the absence of hazard and hence, by the very nature of hazard itself, must be unpredictable and uncertain" (p. 319). He points out that this relationship is regularly ignored in human affairs because of an unfailing belief in the inevitability of human progress. Drawing on the systems of dyad, triad, tetrad, and pentad, he illustrates the relationship via two organizations that transform raw materials into socially useful products: an industrial enterprise and an educational institution.

3.22. "Outstripping Time" [transcript of a talk given to Institute members, Vol. 6, No. 1 (June 1968), pp. 50-64.

Bennett examines "psychological possibilities that arise on the assumption that the future may not be closed" and that time can be "outstripped" (p. 50). He argues that ordinary time relates to the loss of potential; that eternity relates to "the timeless conservation of potentiality" (p. 52); and that hyparxis "makes it possible to create potential and hence to change the world process" (p. 64). He describes hyparxis as that which "enables us to move across the streams of time and space, and even to change eternity. It is the inherent freedom associated with our will" (p. 62).

3.23. [Book review] *The Biological Time Bomb* by G. Rattray Taylor (London: Thames and Hudson,1968), Vol. 6, No. 1 (June 1968), pp. 71–72.

This British journalist's book heralded the development of current biotechnology, which Bennett emphasizes can benefit as well as undermine human life. Bennett points out that the deeper problem is that "man's ability to act intelligently has not kept pace with his capacity to interfere in natural phenomena.... In the past, man was aware of his weakness before the powers of Nature. We are now beginning to be aware that we are even weaker before the powers that reside in man himself. We have gained control of a wide range of extraordinary techniques, and we are quite unable to use them intelligently" (p. 71). Bennett concludes that the "basic problem concern's man's will.... [I]t is as true today as it ever was that man himself must choose between salvation and destruction...." (p. 72).

3.24. "The Progress of Educational Technology," co-authored with A.M. Hodgson, Vol. 6, No. 2 (September 1968), pp. 95–113.

An overview of Bennett's efforts in the 1960s to apply systematic principles to education, including the prescient recognition of the possibility of technological integration whereby the digital interface "itself becomes an active participant in communication" (p. 96). The authors consider the creation of "an effective curriculum and its operation in practice" (p.101) via monad, dyad, triad, tetrad, and pentad. The article includes a description of the "Systemaster data processing device," a digital teaching computer developed by the Hirst Research Laboratories. The authors conclude that such technologies point to "entirely new devices" that will "enable the higher capacities of the human mind and body to be developed by appropriate challenge and response exercises. The moral and emotional nature need not be regarded as inaccessible to technological help" (p. 113).

3.25. [Book review] *Ludwig Wittgenstein: His Place in the Development of Semantics* by Tulio de Mauro (Dordrecht: Reidel, 1967), Vol. 6, No. 2 (September 1968), p. 159.

Bennett criticizes de Mauro's study because "it does not carry the argument [regarding the foundation of language] beyond what is explicit in Wittgenstein's later conclusions.... He would have probably found a new light on semantics had he recognized that Wittgenstein was concerned in a progression of meanings that start with usage and go on through the usage of usage to [higher-level] meta-languages" (p. 159).

3.26. "Catholic Philosophy after Vatican II," Vol. 6, No. 2 (September 1968), pp. 163–66.

Bennett's comments on the June 1968 issue of *Sapienza*, the journal of the Dominicans of Italy, which published the proceedings of a congress of teachers of philosophy, held in Naples in December 1967. Bennett explains that the entries "convey the ferment of interest in philosophy that has been roused in the Catholic church, both by the impact of Vatican II and be debates initiated in many centres by informed teachers" (p. 163). Though Bennett sees this ferment in the church as hopeful, he concludes that "It still remains true that Christianity needs a modern Aquinas to lay the foundations of a new theology which will harmonize philosophy and science in a higher synthesis" (p. 166).

3.27. "The Educational Challenge of the Developing Countries," Vol. 6, No. 4 (March 1969), pp. 251–66.

Originally an address given in Monaco at the International Symposium on Development in February 1969, Bennett considers the weaknesses of current educational methods and advocates for self-teaching systems possible with developing computer technologies. He describes the learning system of "Structural Communication," which "introduces the tutorial mode and allows a full dialogue" between students and teacher "up to an extent never before possible. For this we make use of a highly specialized desk computer which is either used by one or shared by a number of pupils" (pp. 263–64).

3.28. "Review Discussions: What Can be Done about Intelligence?" [a commentary on two special issues of the 1969 *Harvard Educational Review* (Vol. 39, Nos. 1 & 2), which began with a lengthy article by controversial educational psychologist Arthur R. Jensen followed by seven responses by eminent psychologists, geneticists, and educators], Vol. 7, No. 1 (June 1969), pp. 41–53.

Bennett explains that Jensen's central question relates to "the nature of human intelligence and the possibility of raising its level by environmental influences. Jensen's central thesis is the diversity of factors that enter into the make-up of a successful human being and consequently the undesirability of subjecting all to an identical educational environment" (p. 41). Drawing on his Institute's work in Structural Communication, Bennett points to a new pedagogical model that incorporates and strengthens "the wealth of [learning] potentialities that escape from present methods of assessment" (p. 52).

3.29. "Review Discussions: The World Educational Crisis" [a commentary on *The World Educational Crisis* by Philip H. Coombs (New York: Oxford University Press, 1968)], Vol. 7, No. 1 (June 1969), pp. 54-62.

Written by an eminent American economist who studied systems of education, this book is said by Bennett to be "very important" because it presents crucial facts "lucidly described and supported by a wealth of statistical data not readily available elsewhere" (p. 54). Bennett highlights Coombs' seven principles of effective educational systems that include recognition of individual student differences; the power of self-instruction; the value of combining human energy and physical resources; and the principle that "learning objectives must be pursued beyond some minimum point of intensity and continuity, short of which the effort will have little pay-off" (p. 59).

3.30. "Sufi Spiritual Techniques," Vol.7, No. 3 (December 1969), pp. 244-60.

This entry was not written by Bennett but is his translation of portions of "a small pamphlet in Osmanli Turkish published in Istanbul and long out of print" (p. 244). Bennett explains that this pamphlet is "used as a manual by Dervishes of the Naqshabandi Order of Sufis" (p. 244). Bennett's translation presents the pamphlet's "collection of spiritual exercises, practical maxims and instructive anecdotes ... mostly taken from Persian manuscripts of the 15th and 16th centuries" (p. 244).

3.31. [Book review] *Orbis Pictus* by John Amos Comenius [reprint] (Detroit: Singing Tree Press/Gale, 1967), Vol. 7, No. 3 (December 1969), pp. 263-66.

Sometimes called the father of modern education, seventeenth-century Czech philosopher and theologian John Amos Comenius wrote *Orbis Pictus* (1658), a book using illustrations of everyday objects to teach children. Bennett admires the book because it applies the "Aristotelian dictum that understanding grows out of sense experience" (p. 264). Bennett also emphasizes that the book's

151 illustrations "are remarkable not only in their facts and the range of subjects they cover, but even more in the use of a structural or systematic presentation" (p.264) whereby there is developed "the child's power to pass from the recognition and naming of isolated objects to the understanding of their mutual relevance" (pp. 264-65).

3.32. "Systematics and System Theories," Vol. 7, No. 4 (March 1970), pp. 273-78.

This article contrasts Bennett's systematics with Bertalanffy and Rapoport's conventional general-systems theory. The latter is said to define any system in terms of interaction, which is a non-qualitative concept, whereas systematics defines any system in terms of mutual relevance, which is a qualitative concept. In this sense, the parts of a system "must acquire their very character from their presence within the particular system. They cannot be taken out of the system and remain what they are" (p. 275). No author is given but almost certainly by Bennett; see entry 3.3. Not included in entry 3.39.

3.33. "Cultural Streams from Ice Age to the 21st Century," co-authored with Jaroslav Krejčí, Vol. 8, No. 1 (June 1970), pp. 1-86.

This entry reports on a two-day 1969 seminar led by Bennett and Krejčí, a Czech sociologist. The seminar focused on "the cultural history of Asia, Africa and Europe since the end of the Ice Age and attempted to apply the principle of 'cultural levels' to forecasting the course of events during the next period of the evolution of the human mind" (p. 1). Includes questions and answers; the only entry in this *Systematics* issue.

3.34. "Review Discussion: Sufism for the Modern World—The Works of Sayyed Idries Shah," Vol. 8, No. 2 (September 1970), pp.175-81.

In discussing several of Sufi Idries Shah's writings, Bennett concludes that his ideas "are put forward with such discretion and so indirectly that their revolutionary character may be overlooked. He calls for no less than a revaluation of our basic values and for the development of new perceptions which will replace subject values by a direct understanding of what human life is really all about. There is no instant cure for the troubles of the world; but there can be no cure at all unless we accept the need to change our modes of thought" (p. 181).

3.35. "Mind and Matter" [four essays: Noosphere versus Biosphere; The Market of the Mind; Mind and Organization; and Minds in Communication], Vol. 8, No. 3 (December 1970), pp. 193-220.

The four entries in this article overview the state of the world and point toward potential futures, for which a key dimension is an accurate theory of communication that would "distinguish the levels of perception and decision-making at which communications operate" and establish "a classification of personal types as these have a decisive influence on interpersonal relationships and responses to situations" (p. 208). Drawing on a communication triad of "judgement," "message," and "response," Bennett delineates six communication strategies "primarily distinguished by the location of the act of judgement and secondarily by the way in which the informational content, or message, is developed" (p. 212).

3.36. "The Transformation of Man" [introductory address given at the Jubilee Conference of the Institute, April 21, 1971], Vol. 9, No. 1 (June 1971), pp. 1-7.

Bennett argues that "the self-realization of man must go far beyond what is commonly regarded as education" (p. 2). He suggests that" self-realization must include a far higher content of self-knowledge than is usually considered to be necessary" (p. 2). Bennett labels this transformative possibility *psychokenic*, which refers to the human possibility of "transforming into an integrated being whose knowable and unknowable natures have become one indivisible whole" (p. 4).

3.37. "International Academy for Continuous Education: Inaugural Address to the Students of the Second Basic Course 1972/73," Vol. 10, No. 4 (March 1973), pp. 227-36; also see entries 2.5.7 and 1.17.

Given in October 1972 to students beginning the second Sherborne course, Bennett focuses on two questions: first, what kind of person does each student wish to be and can the Sherborne experience make that wish more possible; second, what kind of world does each student want to live in and might what he or she learns at Sherborne contribute to creating that world. Bennett emphasizes that "the work has to come from within. It has to come from our own need, our own decision. Try to remember this: It is not easy" (p. 235).

3.38. "The Force Fields in an Organization: (1) The Dyad," Vol. 11, No. 4 (March 1974), pp. 235-47.

Based on a lecture given in February 1970, this article discusses the method of systematics in relation to institutional organization, giving particular attention to corporate enterprises. Bennett speaks of "force fields" because "dyadic tensions play a significant part in every organization. These tensions are necessary to produce the drive that makes and organization tick, but they are not produced by—nor can they be adequately recognized in—... measurable factors alone" (p. 242). Includes questions and answers. A note at the end mentions that there would follow a companion entry on the monad, but that article was not published, since *Systematics* ceased publication after Bennett's death in 1974. Not included in entry 3.39.

3.39. *"Systematics" Papers, 1963–1972,* Petersham, MA: J.G. Bennett Foundation, 2017, 529p. ISBN 13-978-1548659370.

Compiled by Ben Bennett, this volume includes twenty-six articles from *Systematics* authored or co-authored by Bennett. The one entry not included in the list above is "The Masters of Wisdom of Central Asia," authored by Hasan L. Sushud and perhaps revised by Bennett (Vol. 6, No. 4, pp. 310–29). Ben Bennett introduces the collection with a brief "publisher's note."

4.1. ENTRIES BY J.G. BENNETT IN *THE ENNEAGRAM* (1975–76)

Published at Sherborne House in Sherborne, Gloucestershire, *The Enneagram Magazine* aimed to "to provide a link of communication among past, present, and future Sherborne and Claymont students, Institute members, and interested friends." The magazine was to be "personal, informal, in a light tone, with news of each other and our activities. Issues will contain previously unpublished material from Mr. Bennett over the last four years and short Sherborne talks" (issue no. 1, March 1975, p. 1). Publication ended in1976 when Sherborne was sold to the Beshara Trust, a nearby Sufi community with which Bennett and several Sherborne students had had regular contact; see entry 2.2.

4.1.1. "The Master Idea of the New Epoch" [Part 1]. *The Enneagram*, issue No. 1 (March 1975), pp. 3–7.

The first part of a talk that Bennett gave at Sherborne on April 9, 1974, for the Third Basic Course. The focus is the "Master Idea"—"that attitude toward Man and his destiny which determines the entire value system of a culture" (p.

3). Today, "we are clearly passing from one world to another. Everyone can see that a world is dying and that a new world has to be born. What is not seen is that it is also a moment of very profound change in Man himself, in the whole mode of life of humanity" (p. 3).

4.1.2. "The Master Idea of the New Epoch" [Part 2]. *The Enneagram*, issue No. 2 (June 1975), pp. 3-7.

The second part of a talk that Bennett gave at Sherborne on April 9, 1974, for the Third Basic Course. "The future is a future of partnership, not of individualism—not merely partnership between people but partnership between the visible and invisible world to share the burden. We have first of all to learn to establish this partnership in ourselves. Very much of the work we do here together is concerned with enabling us to perceive what this partnership is" (p. 6).

4.1.3. [Review of] F. Schumacher's *Small Is Beautiful*, *The Enneagram*, issue No. 2 (June 1975), pp. 25-28.

Economist E. F. Schumacher visited Sherborne in June, 1974, and Bennett wrote a broadly favorable review of his best-selling book, which had been published the year before: "Schumacher ... brings us to the point where the reader is bound to agree that the new society to be viable will have to be based on smaller units, upon the rejection of quantity over quality, and upon the elimination of greed and fear as the main motives of human action.... He does not, however, deal with ... the means by which we can change our attitude to life and our modes of behaviour so radically that the welfare of our neighbour will truly be of an importance to us and equal to the satisfaction of our own desires" (p. 28).

4.1.4. "God—Nature—Work," *The Enneagram*, issue No. 3 (October 1975), pp. 2-5.

Extracts from talks Bennett had given relating to "Nature loves us" and drawn from a more comprehensive account published in entry 2.5, pp. 18-24. "We can open ourselves to what is coming into us from Nature. It is a kind of work to be receptive to this. What comes is not just 'good vibrations'. It is as if we become aware of the compassionate eye of Nature—who is aware of our difficulties and of what a task has been laid upon us—looking upon us. No matter how much we destroy, the compassion does not weaken" (p. 2).

4.1.5. "Other People," *The Enneagram*, issue No. 4 (January 1976), pp. 2–3.

Excerpts from a Coombe Springs Sunday talk given by Bennett on November 17, 1963; the complete talk is published in entry 2.14, pp.17–22. "We are only alone when as a person, we are unable to meet other people as persons. Of course, this is a very difficult thing, and we recognize only too well that even with those who are nearest to us ... there is still some gap between person and person, perhaps only bridged in moments. This is partly because we do not give enough importance to this truer kind of relationship in our lives, and we expect or imagine that we can be people with people without having done anything special about it. And yet experience shows us that something quite special has to happen so that this meeting of person with person can be a reality" (p. 2).

4.1.6. "The Hazards of Human Society," *The Enneagram*, issue No. 5 (April 1976), pp. 2–6.

Excerpts from one lecture of a series on hazard given both in London and New York in 1967; this series of lectures is included in entry 2.6.1, Chapter 5. "Can we look at the present world situation and ask ourselves whether this society, which by ordinary conceptions looks particularly disastrous, may not in reality be the kind of society in which something positive can arise?" (p. 5).

4.1.7. "Future Communities," *The Enneagram*, issue No. 6 (June 1976), pp. 4–10

One of a series of 1974 Sherborne talks eventually published as *Needs of a New Age Community*; see entry 2.5.7, pp. 46–66; and entry 2.21, pp. 374–88. "How many of us are really prepared to look for a way of life in which one would live with less instead of living with more? This lesson cannot be learnt by common sense because people close their minds to it: It can only be learnt by bitter experience, and that bitter experience will come.... [T]he transition from one system to another system can only come through the third force. It cannot come from either the passive majority or from an active minority. It can neither come from the governed nor from the power possessors" (p. 6).

4.1.8. "The Reconciling Force in History," *The Enneagram*, issue No. 7 (September 1976), pp. 2–7.

Originally from 1950, this work is republished *Talks on Beelzebub's Tales*, entry 2.5.6, pp. 31–42. "Man is powerless in his outer world and will remain so as long as he has no force in his inner world. It is only in the inner world that a reconciling principle can be found which will bring into harmony his desire for a better state and actions which make that better state attainable. It is necessary to distinguish between two apparently similar but really very different processes. The first is the striving to live in accordance with the significance and meaning of our existence; the second is the striving to live to accomplish a purpose which we believe to be rightly conceived" (p. 5).

4.1.9. "Responsibility," *The Enneagram*, issue No. 8 (November 1976), pp. 4-6.

This entry is identified only as a morning talk given in September 1964; it is not included in *Sunday Talks at Coombe Springs* (entry 2.14). "It is the principle of responsibility that the strong is responsible for the weak. Strength here means a will that is integrated on more levels, that is able to penetrate more deeply into things than the weaker will—a certain inner quality that one has that is closely connected with understanding and the power to choose" (p. 4).

4.2. ENTRIES BY J.B. BENNETT IN *IMPRESSIONS* (1981-92?)

Impressions was a journal published from 1981 to the early 1990s by the American Society for Continuous Education, headquartered at Claymont Court near Charles Town, West Virginia. The journal covered "Work" and related themes, with entries mostly provided by former Sherborne and Claymont students. The journal included several entries by Bennett. The last number is labelled the "Bennett issue" and provides no publication date, though probably it appeared sometime in 1992, since the issue includes a memoriam for Elizabeth Bennett, who died in August, 1991.

4.2.1. "Conscious Labor and Intentional Suffering," *Impressions*, Vol. 1, No. 2 (Fall 1981), pp. 5-8.

Excerpt from Bennett's lecture given at Sherborne in April 1974: "Intentional suffering is the suffering that one incurs in order to do one's duty. To accept a situation, knowing that it will, or may, result in trouble for oneself.... [W]hen we speak about intentional suffering in the terms that Gurdjieff uses, being-Part-kdolg-duty, he does not mean involuntary suffering, nor does he even mean voluntary suffering. He means this: To commit oneself to the future of mankind. We have to be like the air, to let everything breathe us, to let everything be transmitted through us" (p. 7, p. 8).

4.2.2. "Mercy," *Impressions*, Vol. 1. No. 4 (summer 1982), inside back cover following p. 30.

A one-page excerpt from a Sherborne talk, no date or title given: "Mercy is a special kind of transaction that does not belong to this world. It is giving and taking without counting, without any "how much" or why or wherefore. It is freedom.... The essence of mercy is giving what has not been earned; what is not deserved."

4.2.3. "Members of One Body," *Impressions*, Vol. 2, No. 2 (Spring 1983), inside back cover following p. 46.

A one-page excerpt from a talk by Bennett, no date, place, or title given: "It seems very strange that we have to be ourselves—unique and individual and yet as completely subject to the whole as my finger is to my body.... When we see the role we have to fill, every one of us becomes aware of our helplessness, but until we see that we do belong, that we are living members of a body and living *because* we are members of a body, then there is this other kind of despair."

4.2.4. "The Spiritual Hunger of the Modern Child," *Impressions*, Vol. 2, No. 3 (Fall 1984), pp. 3–5.

An excerpt from Bennett's introduction to a series of lectures in 1961 on childhood education. A central question is "whether there really are spiritual as distinct from psychic and materials needs, and if so, how these needs are to be satisfied" (p. 3). See entry 5.11 for the complete series of lectures, published as a book with the lecture-series title.

4.2.5. "Unity," *Impressions*, Vol. 3, No. 3 (Fall 1985), pp. 3–8.

A talk given by Bennett in 1965 at Coombe Springs' summer school: "The theme of this talk is unity, and this includes the process of unification—that is, how unity comes out of diversity." Bennett discusses three kinds of unity "that together when themselves integrated, make the complete organic unity": first, unity of function; second, unity of being; and, third, unity of will (p. 4).

4.2.6. "On Creative Thinking," *Impressions*, Vol. 4, No. 1 (Spring 1986), pp. 1–2.

An excerpt from Bennett's *Creative Thinking*; see entry **1.12**: "In order to have spontaneous thinking, there must not be interference from what is already present in us, which means that there must not be interference from words...."

If anything new is to come, it has to be outside of words or outside of any fixed symbols or images that are equivalent to words" (p. 2).

4.2.7. "The Characteristics of Psychokinetic Life," *Impressions*, Vol. 4, No. 3 (Fall 1986), p. 5.

A one-page entry drawn from Bennett's *Needs of a New Age Community*; see entries 2.5.7 and 2.21. "In living together, one has to play a role. One must know and judge—external considering—but be free inside so that one does not manifest exactly as one feels. This is the middle way. Only when one can put oneself in the place of another should one say things to them that may enter them deeply."

4.2.8. "The Planetary Enneagram," *Impressions*, Vol.4, No. 4 (Winter1986), pp. 8–9.

An excerpt from Bennett's *The Enneagram* and *Enneagram Studies*; see entries 2.5.2, 2.11, 2.21, and 5.18. The focus is "the application of the Enneagram to the study of our planet and the evolution of life" (p. 9).

4.2.9. "Guidance and Progress," *Impressions*, Vol. 5, No. 1 (Spring 1987), pp. 5–7.

An excerpt from Bennett's *Transformation*; see entry 2.7, Chapter 4. "The more we move along the path of transformation, the more evident does it become that our puny wisdom and our modern science fall very short of being able to understand how human history is being directed. Nevertheless, we all have our place in it, and we should never be satisfied until we have found it—and *know* that we have found it" (p. 7).

4.2.10. "What is This Inner Life?" *Impressions*, Vol. 5, No. 2 (Summer 1987), pp. 4–9.

An excerpt from Bennett's *Deeper Man*; see entry 2.8. "If we do not wake up from the dream world in this life, it is unlikely that we shall ever awaken, but we shall continue to dream until the substance of our souls dissolves. Gurdjieff said, 'It is necessary to work on oneself in this life; otherwise, early-lately one will perish like a dirty dog'" (p. 9).

4.2.11. "Points of Departure," *Impressions*, Vol 5., No. 3 (Fall 1987), pp. 4–6.

An excerpt from editor Eric Mandrel's condensed revision of the first volume of Bennett's *The Dramatic Universe*; see entries 1.1 and 1.1.1. The excerpt includes a description of Bennett's method of *progressive approximation*, which "starts with a total concept that is necessarily vague and faulty... We shall begin with the total givenness of all experience and, without forgetting the limitations of our powers of perception and thought, try to see that totality as one" (p. 6).

4.2.12. "Twenty Attributes of Wholeness," *Impressions*, Vol. 5, No. 4 (Winter 1987), p. 2.

Reproduced as the longhand copy that Bennett wrote at a 1960s educational conference in London, when asked by Bennett associate Ted Matchett to write down in twenty minutes twenty aspects of wholeness. Some of Bennett's descriptors: "A single undivided will;" "awareness of the illusory character of ordinary experience"; "freedom from sense of self"; "discrimination"; "ability to make and abide by decisions"; "total dedication to the sense and purpose of existence" (p. 2).

4.2.13. "This Is Not I," *Impressions*, Vol. 6, No. 1 (Spring 1988), pp. 1–3.

One of Bennett's "Sunday Talks" given at Coombe Springs, April 5, 1964. This talk is included in entry 2.14, pp. 225–32. "It doesn't matter if we fail to find "I" right away because "I" is not so easy to find as all that. This is a matter of trust—there is "I," it will do what it has to do, but it cannot be handled by its own instrument; that is, it is not able to be thought about by thinking or looked at by seeing. This is not the part that is conditioned. Therefore, never worry about "I" but make sure that you practice so far as you can detachment from your own instruments" (p. 3).

4.2.14. "The Second Domain," *Impressions*, Vol. 6, No. 2 (Summer 1988), pp. 3–4.

A talk in a series of three that Bennett gave in October 1965 to a Work group in Stoke-on-Trent: "One cannot lift oneself from one level to another without help from a higher level. This has to be grasped and grasped again, and assimilated, and remembered.... The help that we receive... is limited by one thing only, and that is our capacity to receive it.... This enlarging of the capacity to be able to receive is sometimes called the opening of the heart, because the heart is compared to a vessel. Heart here does not mean emotion—it is different. If you know what is meant in the language of the System by "the higher emotional center," that is the vessel that I am talking about, For most people, the higher emotional center is no larger than a thimble but is made of such material that it is capable of growing without limits. If only you could be given the power to see this—it is invisible to ordinary eyes" (p. 4).

4.2.15. "One Perfect Man Matters Even to God," *Impressions*, Vol. 6, No. 4 (Winter 1988), pp. 4–7.

A series of questions and answers that Bennett provided for the first in a series lectures given at London's Denison House, October 2, 1950; several question and answer are omitted. All lectures in this series, including all questions and answers, are published in *Denison House Talks*; see entry 2.18.

4.2.16. "Gurdjieff: Making a New World," *Impressions*, Vol. 7, No. 1 (Spring 1989), pp. 2–6.

A public talk given at London's Caxton Hall in November 1973, covering themes in Bennett's 1973 *Gurdjieff: Making a New World*.

4.2.17. "Consciousness and Its Possible Transformations," *Impressions*, Vol. 7, No. 2 (Summer 1989), pp. 4–8.

The third lecture in Bennett's series of six, given at London's Denison House, March 22, 1954. Bennett's theme is "the problem of reconciling belief in universal law with private freedom" (p. 4). Does not include questions and answers. This lecture, with questions and answers, is included in entries and 2.18.

4.2.18. "Pattern," *Impressions*, Vol. 7, No. 3 (Autumn 1989), pp. 2–4.

An excerpt from an article, Pattern/Intention," originally published as a pamphlet by Shantock Press in 1984. Bennett speaks of a particular manner of pattern that is "woven according to an intentional purpose that goes beyond this present. For each one of us, there is a pattern to our lives that is our destiny, and it is the realization of this that we do fulfill the reason for our existence here on earth" (p. 2).

4.2.19. "Food," *Impressions*, Vol. 8, No. 1 (spring 1990), pp. 5–9.

An excerpt from *Food,* the fourth volume in the "Sherborne Theme Talks," originally published in 1977; see entries 2.3.4 and 2.4. "You should always try to remember the significance of food: by remembering this, you will look at things in the right way and come towards an understanding—a painful understanding—of love" (p. 9).

4.2.20. "Struggle," *Impressions*, Vol. 8, No. 3 (autumn 1990), p. 9.

An excerpt from chapter 1, "The Four Sources," in Bennett's *Transformation*; see entry 2.7. Bennett points out that self-knowledge and struggle with oneself are linked by discrimination, which he describes via twelve "rules or guidelines" that include (1) remembering "always that you can only struggle within your own present moment"; (2) organizing one's struggle and "repeating the act as often as you become aware of the impulse you wish to struggle with"; (3) moderating overly ambitious aims by learning "to measure your own capacity"; (4) taking decisions "only when you are sure that you have both the intention and the ability to carry them out" (p. 9).

4.2.21. "Steps Along the Way," *Impressions*, Vol. 8, No. 4 (1992? special "Bennett issue"), pp. 2–6.

Excerpts from Bennett's autobiography, *Witness*; see entry 1.9. Excerpt headings: "An Early Vision: Istanbul, 1920"; "Vision of a Future Task: Scutari, 1920"; "Meeting the Remarkable Man: Constantinople, 1920"; "Sherborne House: Kingston, 1970."

4.2.22. "The Present Moment," *Impressions*, Vol. 8, No. 4 (1992? special "Bennett issue"), pp. 7–16.

One of six talks on "The Systematics of Organization," given by Bennett in Basking Ridge, New Jersey, in July 1970. "Everyone of us has this capacity for turning visions into realities, but some of you do it on a smaller scale; some of you do it on a bigger scale. What is required for this is the quality that we describe like decision, commitment, will; it's these particular qualities and the conditions under which they are able to operate that we want to examine now" (p. 7).

4.2.23. "Prayer," *Impressions*, Vol. 8, No. 4 (1992? special "Bennett issue"), p. 18.

"O Lord Creator and all your Conscious Powers through whom the Divine Will is manifested, let me be liberated from sleep, mechanicalness and slavery, and find refuge in Conscious Action from which no evil can come. Let me turn from the part to the Whole; from the temporal to the Eternal; from myself to Thee" (p. 18; no source given).

4.2.24. "Hearing the Inner Voice," *Impressions*, Vol. 8, No. 4 (1992? special "Bennett issue"), p. 26.

Another excerpt from *Witness* (entry 1.9) in which Bennett ends his association with Subud and returns to Gurdjieff's teaching and methods. Bennett explains that if one is to "take the guidance of Conscience seriously, one must be prepared to follow it wherever it may lead. It is not an imperative command, but a 'still, small voice' that is easily silenced. It does not strive nor cry, but if we trust it, it begins to trust us and to come more and more into the open—that is into our mental awareness" (p. 26).

4.2.25. "Resurrection," *Impressions*, Vol. 8, No. 4 (1992? special "Bennett issue"), pp. 27–28.

An excerpt from a Sunday talk at Coombe Springs, May 16, 1963. The full talk, including questions and answers, is published in entry 2.14, pp. 181–89, where the title of the talk is given as "Death and Rebirth" and the year of the talk is listed as 1965 rather than 1963. "We become lost or, as we say psychologically, identified with our feelings, thoughts or our activity, and we ourselves are lost. In that state of being lost, there is nothing we can do to find ourselves, but then it happens—we suddenly see that we are back again and alive: seeing, feeling, from something which is there in us, that was not there a moment ago. Something has come back which had been lost, someone has come back who had gone astray or was asleep" (p. 28).

5. OTHER ARTICLES, CHAPTERS, INTRODUCTIONS AND PUBLISHED LECTURES BY J.G. BENNETT RELATING TO THE GURDJIEFF WORK

5.1. "Living in Five Dimensions," *World Review, New Series No. 8* (September 1949).

Bennett asks how "the deterministic conclusions of physical science" might be reconciled with "our inner conviction that in some way we are free." He describes a sudden moment of insight in 1920 when he realized that "the physical universe must be five dimensional, and the causal mechanism of successiveness in time was no more than the presentation of our senses of a reality vast enough to permit every imaginable freedom, if only we could break down the limitations of our ordinary perceptions. Time itself could not escape from necessity, but we could escape from time.... Consciousness and freedom imply one another, but neither freedom nor consciousness is possible, so long as we suffer ourselves to continue in that mode of being which is bound in the chains of causal mechanism. It is the realization that inner freedom must be bought and paid for that is far more important than any theoretical explanation. Many people would agree with this, but very few reach a concrete—that is practical—understanding of all that is involved."

5.2. "Gurdjieff's 'All and Everything'" [review of *Beelzebub's Tales to His Grandson*], *Rider's Review* (London), Autumn 1950, pp. 30–38; reprinted twice in *Gurdjieff International Review*, Vol. II, No. 3 (Spring 1999), pp. 9–17; Vol. XI, No. 2 (Summer 2012), pp. 11–18.

Bennett contends that *All and Everything* presents "a new mythology, the power of which will be understood only by generations yet unborn.... In Gurdjieff's myth, the Universe comes into existence to ensure the perpetual self-renewal of the Most Holy Sun Absolute, or First Principle" (pp. 32, 34). Rejecting the age-old dualism of good and evil, Gurdjieff emphasizes "the Sacred Impulse of Divine Conscience," which replaces traditional moralities with an "inner self-judgement" and sense of duty whereby "understanding of the universal laws blends with an overwhelming compassion towards the suffering of mankind" (p. 36). Bennett concludes that Gurdjieff's radically new mythology centers on "a Universe which is the scene of a striving necessary to the Deity. It is permeated through and through with the consequences of the simple fact of successive actualization in Time" (p. 38).

5.3. "A Short Guide and Glossary to the 'Dramatic Universe'." Kingston-upon-Thames, UK: Coombe Springs Press, 1970, 32p.; Petersham, MA: J.G. Bennett Foundation, 2017, 32p., Kindle edition.

Twenty-six questions and answers via which Bennett describes major themes and conclusions of *The Dramatic Universe*. Questions focus on such topics as hazard, time, levels of being, values, energies, evolution, self-development, and the future of humankind. In answering why he calls the universe "dramatic," Bennett explains that "A dramatic situation is one whose outcome is important and yet uncertain. Hazard is the essence of drama. I believe that we should accept that the universe is through and through hazardous. We are only too well aware of hazard in our human experience; but it does not seem to occur to people that the whole world must be subject to hazard. Indeed, hazard is linked to importance. Only very unimportant events, such as ice melting when it is heated, are almost free from hazard. The most important events we know— such as the course of history during the past five thousand years—are the most hazardous.... Hazard and drama that it brings with it are the absolutely necessary conditions for the world to be worth living in. An undramatic universe would be dead: a clockwork mechanism predetermined to go nowhere" (p. 2).

5.4. "Radiations and Emanations, *Radionic Quarterly*, April 1971; reprinted, Ripon, North Yorkshire, UK: Coombe Springs Press, no date, 13p. ISBN 0-900306-20-3.

In this talk, originally given at a 1971 conference of the Radionic Association, Bennett emphasizes that there are different worlds, though, typically, human beings are only aware of "lower, coarser worlds, connected with physical, material phenomena" (p. 4). In fact, "man by his very nature is intended to be a bridge between the spiritual and material worlds" (pp. 4-5). More exactly, man can be "a transforming system for energies, a transmitter of influences from one world to another: a means of transmitting influences that come from the higher world to the lower world in order that the lower should be spiritualized, and that the higher should be nourished with their necessary sources. Through man, there should pass a twofold stream: a descending stream of influences from above and an ascending stream of substances refined from below, according to that principle of separating the fine from the coarse" (p. 5). Includes three diagrams: "Cosmic Transformations," "Levels of Phenomena," and "The Whole Man."

5.5. Introduction to P.D. Ouspensky, *Talks with a Devil*, London: Turnstone Press, 1972, pp. 1–18, ISBN 1-57863-164-5; York Beach, ME: Samuel Weiser, 2000.

Bennett's introduction to two allegories by Ouspensky: "The Inventor" and "The Benevolent Devil." Bennett first met Ouspensky in 1920 in Constantinople and became an active member of Ouspensky's London circle in 1922. In 1929, Ouspensky first told Bennett about *Talks*, explaining that the two stories "had been written to express his belief that man's chief error is to believe that the material world is the only reality. This belief, he said, is the source of most human troubles because people fight uselessly over unreal issues, disregarding the real problem, which is that of liberation" (p. 10).

5.6. Third Basic Course 1973/74: Inaugural Address [International Academy for Continuous Education]. Sherborne, Gloucestershire, UK: Coombe Springs Press/Institute for the Comparative Study of History, Philosophy and the Sciences, 1973, 18p. ISBN 0-900306-19-X.

"Gurdjieff had very strong ideas about what constitutes a perfect man. He said that the highest quality of a perfect man is impartiality. This is truly a divine attribute. It is ascribed by Christ to his Father when he says, 'He maketh His sun to rise on the evil and on the good and sendeth His rain on the just and on the unjust' (Mt. 5:45). Partiality is weakness and slavery, impartiality is freedom and strength. We have here to learn to translate this principle into a reality of our daily life.... We are in search of the significance of our lives, both individually and as a race, and of the means of bringing that significance to fulfilment. I am confident that if we work together properly we shall, in the next ten months, make a real step towards this goal" (p. 14, p. 18).

5.7. "Call for a New Society," originally 1974 [pamphlet], Charles Town, WV: Claymont Communications, 1979, 12p.

Bennett's prospectus for the Claymont Society for Continuous Education, established in 1974 at Claymont Court, a 418-acre rural property in the Shenandoah Valley, Jefferson County, West Virginia. Bennett described the task of this community to become "a fully integrated society, the members of which will be committed to self-perfecting and service to Nature and their fellow men" (n.p.).

5.8. Fourth Basic Course 1974/75: Inaugural Address [International Academy for Continuous Education]. Sherborne, Gloucestershire, UK: Coombe Springs Press/Institute for the Comparative Study of History, Philosophy and the Sciences, 1974, 11p. ISBN 0-900306-01-7.

"I want to say something about the foundation of it all, on which everything rests. I have spoken about another world and about different perceptions. All of you are interested in this and it was part of what attracted you here. It is possible for you to achieve something in the way of new perceptions and an understanding of the higher worlds and also to change yourselves. The foundation of this whole work that we do together is the confidence that this is really possible. The main contribution that I can make is to convey to you my own confidence that this can be done. But you must also understand that it is not easy. Many, many people set out on this path and the majority stay at the early stages or come to a point where they go round and round in circles getting nowhere.... This is not because it is unfairly difficult; it is more that people do not know how, and do not have the confidence that it can really be done. It is my job and of those who help in instructing you, to show you how. But it is mostly my business to convince you that it is really possible, because I can speak from having seen it made possible" (pp. 6-7).

5.9. "An Introduction to Gurdjieff's Third Series *Life is Real only then, when 'I AM'*." Sherborne, Gloucestershire, UK: Coombe Springs Press, 1975, 34p. ISBN 0-900306-14-9; Petersham, MA: J.G. Bennett Foundation, 2020, 22p. ISBN 9798637546442.

Bennett wrote this introduction for a longer version of Gurdjieff's Third Series, considerably different from the 1973 published edition produced by Triangle Productions (i.e., the Gurdjieff Foundation). Bennett describes the Third Series as "a strange work" that "contains a direct yet profound statement of the obligations which man must fulfill to deserve the name of man—a 'being made in God's image'. It gives a limited number of psychological exercises of little practical use unless they are placed within the framework of the entire method. What remains is largely a candid self-revelation, an extraordinary account of Gurdjieff's own handling of his pupils and of his own personal problems" (pp. 21-22). The book's central message is that "man can fulfill his destiny and achieve the purpose for which he exists here on the Earth, only if he is ready to suffer and make sacrifices ... in a very special way" (p. 23).

5.10. "What Makes Human Communication Possible?" *Communication*, Vol. 2, No. 1 (1975), pp. 23-29.

Bennett argues that "[C]ommunication requires some quality that could be called 'the ability to recognize what is being said and respond to it', for which we have no word in English. 'Communicability' refers to the message and not to the communicator. To avoid coining a neologism, I propose to use the word 'sensitivity' to express rather more than we usually imply by the word. I shall use the verb 'to sensitize' to designate the process by which a subject S is transformed from a state (S_i) in which he is insensitive (that is, in which he cannot recognize and respond to a message) to a state (S_r) in which he is responsive to it. The $S_i \rightarrow S_r$ transition may be temporary or permanent. We shall call the first "attentiveness" and the second "transformation" (p. 24). Bennett briefly describes how this approach has been used pedagogically with students at the International Academy for Continuous Education at Sherborne.

5.11. "Universal Dependence and Energies" [pamphlet]. Bovingdon, Herfordshire: Shantock Press, 1980, ISBN 0-946024-2-51.

An undated talk, probably from Sherborne, which begins with Bennett's asking students to report observations on making the effort to be aware of the moment of eating, "when the first mouthful enters." He explains: "It is the change of perceptions that is important here, that one becomes, for oneself, immediately aware that our dependence on life is a real thing that has to be reckoned on. If this one thing could really penetrate and people could understand this Universal Dependence that we people have on other forms of life, there would be great changes in the way we live."

5.12. "Living in Two Worlds" / "Sacred Influences" / "Breath" [pamphlet], Bovingdon, Herfordshire: Shantock Press, 1983, 16p., ISBN 0-946024-2-00.

Three Sherborne talks given by Bennett on April 8, April 26, and July 15, 1974. In his talk on breath, he explains that air "carries with it forces or energies or substances that enable us to pass from one world to another world. It is very extraordinary that air is really between this world of material, solid things ... and a different kind of world which is everywhere. Air is really the first of the universal states, the universal energies, and the most immediately present to us. Although we cannot see or touch it, we constantly experience it. We are aware of its action on us" (p. 14).

5.13. "Conscious Labour and Intentional Suffering" [pamphlet], Bovingdon, Herfordshire: Shantock Press, 1984, 14p., ISBN 0-946024-00-6.

Excerpt from a Sherborne talk given by Bennett in April 1974. With some editorial variations, also published as entry 4.2.1. Bennett identifies five kinds of useless suffering that include ill will toward others; doubt; fear of loss or privation; self-love, particularly self-pity; and suffering related to time—for example, impatience or regret.

5.14. "Intention" / "Pattern" [pamphlet], Bovingdon, Herfordshire: Shantock Press, 1984, ISBN 0-946024-40-5.

Two undated, unidentified talks. At the end of his comments on intention, Bennett asks students to attempt the following exercise: "See if you can prepare your going out of this room by picturing it, first of all, as a mental thing. Rising from your chair and see if you can actually sense a part of the body as you go through this door and find this sensation again when you reach the top of the stairs and again when you go out of the building.... Set yourself to see how far you can intentionally and consciously leave this place.... One should repeat this kind of exercise every day—that is, some simple action of this sort—to visualize and sense what it will be like to do."

5.15. *The Spiritual Hunger of the Modern Child: A Series of Ten Lectures.* Charles Town, WV: Claymont Communications, 1984, 220p., ISBN 0-934254-06-0.

Edited by Wendy Addison, these ten lectures were originally delivered in London in 1961 under the auspices of Bennett's Institute for the Comparative Study of History, Philosophy and the Sciences. Besides Bennett, lecturers included Mario Montessori, Clifford John Williams, Reverend Adam Bittleston, A.I. Polack, U. Maung Maung Ji, and Father Hugh S. Thwaites. As moderator of the event, Bennett presented four lectures: "A Survey of the Problem," "Begin from Afar—Gurdjieff's Approach to the Child," "The Subud Approach," and "A Summing-up and Practical Conclusions." In speaking of the role of a spiritual dimension in children's lives, Bennett writes: "We should not attempt to instill directly in children religious or spiritual truths, but rather should allow them to come towards them. We can do this by keeping alive in children the sense of wonder and the realization of how much there is that cannot be known and cannot be understood far better than by trying to impress upon them the extent of our own knowledge or of man's knowledge of the present time. We should make it clear to them that all we know is very little compared with the great wonder of the world in which we live, and that the great part of it is not to be explained by our scientific procedures. As far as the truly spiritual nature of the child is concerned, the opportunity should be taken for helping them develop the quality of true compassion; that is, a sense of the need of mankind and the desire to be able to do something for that need" (pp. 82-83).

5.16. "Work on Oneself" [pamphlet], Bovingdon, Herfordshire: Shantock Press, 1984, ISBN 0-946024-30-8.

One of four lectures delivered in London by Bennett in October 1949; also published in entry 2.19. Bennett discusses different kinds of energy, the understanding of which is important because "Work on ourselves has, as at least one of its primary purposes, the production in our organism of these higher forms of energy, which in the first place enable us to choose and take real decisions. These higher forms of energy are also able to transform our functions—thinking, feeling, and the rest, and raise them to a higher level. Finally, they can form something in us by which we can live entirely in a different world from the ordinary mechanical world of everyday life."

5.76. "Awareness of Others" [pamphlet], Bovingdon, Hertfordshire, UK: Shantock Press, 1988, 11p. ISBN 0-946024-15-4

A Sherborne theme talk given by Bennett on April 26, 1974: "This theme must take into account the respect that we must have for other beings; that is, to learn how to be open to people but not to interfere with them, not to try to act upon them.... [This theme] is one of the hardest things, because what man *is*, is almost impossible to see" (pp. 2, 4). Includes questions and answers.

5.18. The Planetary Enneagram." Santa Fe, NM: Bennett Books, 1990, 9p., and originally a chapter in *The Enneagram*, published by Coombe Spring Press in 1974; see entry 2.5.2.

Bennett draws on the enneagram to delineate the history, evolution, and potential future of the earth and humankind. The nine enneagram points he identifies as: (1) rocks, water, air; (2) soil; (3) biosphere; (4) vegetation; (5) invertebrates; (6) noosphere; (7) animals; (8) man; and (9) lithosphere. He writes: "We may now be in the presence of the Demiurgic action required to maintain the equilibrium of the earth. Man in his animal nature is a predator, he feeds upon all life, despoils his own home: the earth. The cycle of recurrence requires that the earth should be restored to its original state. Will this come about by the destruction of all life or by the transformation of Man? This is a question we cannot answer and it may even be outside the power of the Demiurgic Intelligence to resolve" (p. 6).

5.19. "Gurdjieff: The Unknown Teacher." *Gurdjieff International Review*, Vol.1, No. 1 (Fall 1997), pp. 22–24.

Taken from a typescript written in 1949, this entry is a brief account of Bennett's meeting Gurdjieff, and Bennett's dawning recognition that Gurdjieff's system offers a unique opportunity for self-transformation: "The hope that I might find a comprehensive and convincing world outlook became a certainty. I began to understand Gurdjieff's fundamental teaching that man is a helpless plaything of alien and indifferent forces until he creates in himself, by his own labours, an independent, conscious individuality.... Our present trouble is that man as an individual has lost his way. He does not know even where to place his hopes. Those who have understood this may be prepared to give serious consideration to what Gurdjieff has to say" (pp. 23, 24).

5.20. "Gurdjieff's Temple Dances." *Gurdjieff International Review*. Vol. V, No. 1 (spring 2002), pp. 19–22 [two excepts from *Wittness*, Bennett's autobiography; see entry 1.9].

Bennett describes the movements that Gurdjieff was teaching his pupils in Constantinople in 1920 and at the Prieuré in 1923. Includes description of the movement "Initiation of the Priestess" and the "Stop exercise."

5.21. "The Plight of the Soil." *Gurdjieff International Review*. Vol. XIV, No. 1 (winter 2019/2020), pp. 28–29 [an excerpt from *Gurdjieff: Making a New World*, pp.204-209; see entry 1.18].

Bennett illustrates how the earth's soil is what Gurdjieff termed an "essence class," characterized "by a pattern of possible experience." The earth's soil is crucial to the workings of nature because of its special property "of allowing matter in the three states—solid, liquid, and gaseous—to interact with high concentration of energy. The soil is less than one millionth part of the earth's mass and yet, with the equivalent surface layer of the oceans, it is the scene of nearly all the transformations upon which life depends" (p. 28).

5.22. "Nature Is Our Mother." *Gurdjieff International Review*, Vol. XIV, No. 1 (winter 2019/2020), pp. 30–35.

Originally a transcript of talks by Bennett at Sherborne in June 1974, a slightly different version of this entry was published in *The Image of God in the Work* and *Sacred Influences* (see entry 2.5.5). Bennett emphasizes that "we are not only part of Nature, but we have the special privilege of knowing this is so.... [Nature] is a mother and has the feelings of a mother. The important thing is to become aware of receiving help. We are ordinarily very blind to this, which prevents us from receiving what we could. Becoming conscious of the Love of Nature is a very big step, but we can make this step if we allow ourselves to" (p. 32).

6. ENTRIES BY BENNETT RELATING TO SUBUD

6.1. *Concerning Subud.* London: Hodder & Stoughton, 1958, 186p.; 2nd edition, New York: Dharma Book Company, 1959, 191p. [includes preface to 2nd edition and foreword to the American edition]; Petersham, Massachusetts: J.G. Bennett Foundation, 2016, 194p.[includes "publisher's note"], ISBN 1533606021.

An overview of the teaching of Dutch Indies spiritual leader Pak Subud, who Bennett thought might be the messianic figure hinted at by Gurdjieff. Bennett includes information about his contact with Gurdjieff and his pupils. On differences between Subud and the Gurdjieff Work, see 1.11. The "publisher's note" of the 2016 edition explains that this volume was Bennett's "best-selling book, but he refused after the second edition sold out, to allow his publisher to make any further impressions. The reasons for his decision are not known. Bennett left the Subud Brotherhood after 1960, although he continued until the end of his life to receive letters from readers of this book" (p. iv). On Bennett's experience with Subud, see 1.7, ch. 25.

6.2. "Subud: What ... How ... Why—Three Talks to Subud Probationers." Why. New York: Dharma Book Company, 1960, 13p.

These three talks were given in New York City on February 17, February 24, and March 3, 1959. In the first talk, Bennett explains that "there is inside us ... something like a little sac or vessel that has great possibilities of expansion, really unlimited possibilities, but if it is not used, it just grows smaller and smaller until it is just a light little thing in the middle of us."

6.3. "Subud: Introductory Talk." New York: Dharma Book Company, 1960, 12p.

A talk given in New York City on April 23, 1959: "This evening I am going to try to tell you something about Subud. It was taken from three words of the Sanskrit language: *Susila, Budhi,* and *Dharma. Susila* means, literally, right living or right action; *Budhi* means the inner nature, or spiritual powers of man; and *Dharma* means God's Law, or the Will of God. So that when these three words are put together, they mean the life of man rightly lived with the whole of his inner or spiritual powers conforming to the Will, or Law of God" (p. 1).

6.4. *Christian Mysticism and Subud.* London: Institute for the Comparative Study of History, Philosophy and the Sciences, 1961, 69p.

Based on four lectures on Christian mysticism give in 1960 at his Coombe Springs institute, Bennett asks whether "the Subud *latihan* is the same as the state of diffuse contemplation' described by Christian mystics or whether it is something new and different" (p. 8). Chapter titles are "The Meaning of Mysticism," "Subud and the Three Stages," "The Life of Pak Subuh," and "Mystical Experience and Mystical Action." The 2016 edition includes an unpublished 1961 monograph, "Subud—the Sufi Background," written after Bennett had resigned as a Subud helper after several years of service. See entry 1.7, ch. 25.

6.5. *Approaching Subud: Ten Talks by J.G. Bennett and a Discussion with Steve Allen.* New York: Dharma Book Company, 1962, 274p. and accompanied by a twelve-inch long-playing vinal phonographic record (33 1/3 rpm).

In the opening discussion with television celebrity Steve Allen, Bennett describes Subud as "a key that enables us to make a direct contact with the Supreme Source of Life. This is called in religion the Holy Spirit, the Giver of Life" (p. 11). The ten talks include "Beyond the Mind" (Talk 1), "Living Differently" (2), "Doing and Receiving" (3), "The Screen of Separation" (4), "The Essence of Religion" (5), "Whence Comes the Power" (6), "The Inner Instrument" (7), "The Power to Receive" (8), "The Meaning of Human Freedom" (9), and "Getting Disentangled" (10).

6.6. *Towards the True Self in the Practice of Subud.* New York: Dharma Book Company, 1963, 229 p; Petersham, MA: J.G. Bennett Foundation, 2019, 161p., ISBN 9781079993820.

A collection of twenty talks that Bennett gave to practitioners of Subud, a spiritual practice said to move one "towards the true self"—hence the volume's title. Bennett explains that "the word Subud comes from three Sanskrit words: *Susila*, which means right action; *Budhi*, which means the True Self; and *Dharma*, which means that which is objectively right and true—in other words, the Will of God. The point of this derivation of Subud is that only the True Self can perform right actions according to the Will of God" (p. 3). Titles of talks include "Submission and Understanding," "Training," "Apathy and Submission," "The Inner Certainty," "Inward Separation," and "Spontaneous Latihan."

6.7. *Christian Mysticism and Subud* and *Subud: The Sufi Background*. Petersham, MA: J.G Bennett Foundation, 2016, 130p. ISBN 9781546955207.

This volume is a compilation of two separate writings by Bennett: First, his *Christian Mysticism and Subud* (see 6.4); second, another 1961 writing, "Subud—the Sufi Background"—an unpublished pamphlet, "possibly because certain points refute arguments made in earlier lectures and would inevitably lead to controversy" (publisher's note, 2016, p. vi).

6.8. "Talks on Subud," 1957–62. During the time of his involvement with Subud (1957–61), Bennett gave many talks on Subud, of which some available entries are listed here (this list is *not* comprehensive). Some but not all these talks were published (apparently only in mimeograph) by the Institute for the Comparative Study of History, Philosophy, and the Sciences, Coombe Springs. Examples of these talks, without summaries, are as follows.

6.8.1. Talk of Mr. Bennett at the Hague in reply to the question, 'What is the deep connection between Gurdjieff and Subud?', September 21, 1957.
6.8.2. Mr. Bennett's Answers to Written Questions about the Subud Exercises, October 26, 1957 ("This transcript has not been corrected by Mr. B.").
6.8.3. Mr. Bennett's Answers to Questions about the Subud Exercises, January 4, 1958.
6.8.4. Self-Correction: A Talk by Mr. Bennett, October 11, 1959.
6.8.5. [1] Two Ways of Living; and [2] Nafsu and Djiwa. Sunday Talks, January 24 and March 20, 1960.
6.8.6. Beyond the Mind: Talk to Probationers, January 30, 1960.
6.8.7. About Inner Guidance and Lower Forces: Sunday Talks, January 31, 1960.
6.8.8. Doing and Receiving: Talk to Probationers, March 12, 1960.
6.8.9. The Inner Flow, Sunday Talks, March 1960.

6.8.10. About Testing, Sunday Talks, May 1960.

6.8.11. Talks on Subud, Series A (Kingston-upon Thames, Surrey: Coombe Springs Press, 1962). Nine talks that include "The Religious Experience" (Talk 2), "Receiving and Testing" (Talk 3), and "The Price of Purification" (Talk 4).

6.8.12. Talks on Subud, Series B (Kingston-upon Thames, Surrey: Coombe Springs Press, 1962). Seven talks.

7. OTHER ENTRIES BY J.G. BENNETT: TRAVELOGUE AND SCIENTIFIC AND ACADEMIC ARTICLES

7.1. "Gas Flow in Fuel Beds: A New Model Technique for the Study of Aerodynamic Processes," co-authored with R.L Brown, *Journal of the Institute of Fuel*, Vol.13, 1940, pp. 232–46.

This scientific paper considers the chemistry and physics of combustion in "fuel beds"—for example, the industrial burning of bituminous coal, a process that should be as controllable, efficient, and smokeless as possible. Recognizing that the major difficulty in studying fuel-bed combustion "is that everything is in a state of change" (p. 232), Bennett and Brown conduct a series of experiments, some of which use full-scale physical models. From the results of these experiments, the authors offer several practical implications relating to air-intake design; shape and structure of the combustion appliance; particle size and grading of the combustible; and placement of any subsidiary air-supply points. At the time of doing this research, Bennett was Director of the British Coal Utilisation Research Association; co-author Brown was a Research Officer with the BCURA.

7.2. "Broken Coal," a research report co-authored with R.L. Brown and H.G. Crone. Park Place, Cardiff: The Institute, 1941 [presented to the South Wales Institute of Engineers, Bridgend, Wales, March 20], 47p., includes responses from other coal researchers.

This research pamphlet summarizes the efforts by Bennett and colleagues to specify "the laws of coal breakage and to show something of their significance for the mining engineer and the manufacturer of coal breakage and also anti-breakage equipment" (p. 21). Like Brown, Crone was also a Research Officer with the BCURA (see entry 6.1). The men had begun research on coal breakage in 1933 with the aim to establish its "essential character ... and find out whether any great advances can be hoped for in the control of size as compared with what is possible today" (p. 21). A detailed summary of findings is provided in four articles entitled "Broken Coal," Parts I, II, III, and IV; Part I was published in the *Journal of the Institute of Fuel*, 1936 (Vol. 10); Parts II, III, and IV were published in the same journal in 1941 (Vol. 14).

7.3. "Science and Industry," *Nature* (London), vol. 153, Jan. 29, 1944, pp. 130–32.

Bennett clarifies the relationship between science and industry by describing the contrasting perspectives and efforts of scientists, engineers, inventors, and industrialists. He depicts scientific endeavor as a creative effort that discovers in natural phenomena "a meaning which they did not previously possess" (p. 130). The engineer's aim is "to make things work" and to "take all possible steps to ensure that the aim specified in advance is realized within a specified time, and at a specified cost" (p. 131). The successful industrialist must "have imagination and be receptive to new ideas," but, at the same time, he or she must be alert to how the new ideas might be actualized practically, being able to weight "successfully the favourable and the adverse factors in an enterprise" (p. 132).

7.4. "Unified Field Theory in a Curvature-Free Five-Dimensional Manifold." Co-authored with R.L. Brown and M.W. Thring. *Proceedings of the Royal Society of London. Series A, Mathematical and Physical Sciences*, Vol. 198, No. 1052 (July 22, 1949), pp. 39–61.

"Instead of identifying fields with the curvature of a metric, the present theory shows that they may be identified with the manner in which the four-way measuring system of the physical observer O is embedded in a flat five-dimensional manifold provided that due account is taken of the imperceptibility of the fifth dimension" (p. 39).

7.5. "The Dimensional Framework of the Natural Sciences," *Proceedings of the Eleventh International Congress of Philosophy: Philosophy and Methodology of the Sciences of Nature*, Vol. 6 (1953), pp. 102–7.

Bennett presented this paper in Brussels in August 1953 at the Eleventh International Congress of Philosophy. He presents "four fundamental determining conditions to which every phenomenon must conform if it is to be an authentic manifestation of normal experience": *presence*, in that "every whole has its own presence and therefore determines its own space"; *actualization*, in that every whole is fixed through selection and has its own time; *potentiality*, in that every phenomenon presupposes possibilities of actualization that range from determinism to freedom; and *correspondence*, which allows for a phenomenon's recurrent structures to be observed, classified, and compared (p. 103).

7.6. "An English Author's Impressions in New York," *Gentry*, issue 8, fall 1953, pp. 112–14.

Visiting New York City to lecture on "the problem of striking a balance between the inner and the outer world of man as outlined in the teaching of Gurdjieff" (p. 114), Bennett describes his impressions of the city and is particularly struck by "the frequency with which complete strangers spoke to me of dissatisfactions with material achievements for their own sake" (p. 114). Bennett associates this observation with two aspects of freedom—the freedom of having everything, and the freedom of wanting nothing. A future aim for humankind is "to harmonize, in the ordinary life of man, these two opposing impulses and to achieve a balance between outward freedom and inner freedom.... Americans realize that we cannot attain our inner ideals at the expense of denying our obligations in the outward life, and they are looking for a way that will show them how to keep a balance between an active, fruitful life in the world and inward freedom, happiness, and peace of mind" (p. 114). Published from 1951 to 1957, *Gentry* was a fashionable men's magazine founded, published, and edited by William Segal, a prominent figure in the New York Gurdjieff Foundation.

BIBLIOGRAPHY

The resources are listed by author. Each author's works are listed in chronological order. In the case of Bennett, I have taken the date of the first edition, unless the edition I am using may differ from that, in which case the date is that of the edition I use. For a fuller bibliography of Bennett's work, see the bibliography provided by David Seamon.

Anonymous, undated notes, titled "Morning Exercise Project" from a former student of J.G. Bennett.

Anonymous, transcript of a discussion between Bennett, Jeanne de Salzmann, Henriette Tracol (née Lannes), Sir Clifford and Lady Norton, and other persons, dated November 15, 1952.

Adie, George

2008   *George Mountford Adie: A Gurdjieff Pupil in Australia*, editor and co-author Joseph Azize, Lighthouse.

2015   *George Mountford Adie: A Gurdjieff Pupil in Australia*, revised and expanded, editor and co-author Joseph Azize, By the Way Books, Waukee, IA.

Amaral, John

2009   "Courses and Practica in the J.G. Bennett Tradition of the Gurdjieff Work," *Gurdjieff International Review*, https://www.gurdjieff.org/amaral1.htm.

Archer, Nathaniel P. (ed.)

1980   *The Sufi Mystery*, Octagon Press, London.

Atkinson, David Wiliam

1992   The English *ars moriendi*, Peter Lang, New York.

Azize, Joseph

2020   *Gurdjieff: Mysticism, Contemplation, and Exercises*, Oxford University Press, New York.

2021a "Gurdjieff's "Help for the Deceased" Exercise," *Alternative Spirituality and Religion Review*, 11 2 [2020], 1-22.
2021b "Did Gurdjieff Write Scripture?" *Postscripts*, 12.2, 151-87.

Bartok, Eva
1959 *Worth Living For*, Putnam, London. Bennett, Elizabeth
2015 *My Life, J.G. Bennett and G.I. Gurdjieff*, J.G. Bennett Foundation, Petersham, MA.
undated *Women's Leaflet*. Bennett, Elizabeth and John G. Bennett
1991 *Idiots in Paris: Diaries of J.G. Bennett and Elizabeth Bennett, 1949*, Samuel Weiser, York Beach, ME.

Bennett, George
1990 "Biographical Note," in John G. Bennett 1990, 104-12.

Bennett, John Godolphin
(undated and unpublished) "Introduction to the Third Series."
(undated and unpublished) "Subud—The Sufi Background."
(undated and unpublished) "The Science of Idiotism."
(undated and unpublished) "Introduction to *Gurdjieff: Making a New World*."
1936 "Broken Coal," Part I, *Journal of the Institute of Fuel*, 10.
1941 "Broken Coal," Parts II, III, and IV *Journal of the Institute of Fuel*, 14.
1944 "Science and Industry," *Nature* (London), 153, January 29, 130–32.
1948 "The Last Supper," unpublished manuscript.
1949a "Living in Five Dimensions," first published in *World Review*, 8, September 1949, downloaded from jgbennett.org.
1949b "The Unknown Builders," unpublished manuscript.
1951 "On Sleep and Dream," unpublished, July 16, 1951.
1952 *The Dramatic Universe: An Examination of the Significance of Human Existence*, unpublished draft.
1953 "The Dimensional Framework of the Natural Sciences," *Proceedings of the XIth International Congress of Philosophy*, 6, 102-7, North-Holland Publishing Co. and Éditions, E. Nauwelaerts.
1954 *The Crisis in Human Affairs*, 3rd edition, republished the J.G. Bennett Foundation, Petersham, MA, 2016 (first published Hodder and Stoughton, London).
1956 *The Dramatic Universe: Volume 1, The Foundations of Natural Philosophy*, The J.G. Bennett Foundation, Petersham MA, 2018 (first published Hodder and Stoughton, London).

1957   "An Autobiographical Essay," unpublished.
1958   *Concerning Subud*, Hodder and Stoughton, London.
1959   *Concerning Subud*, 2nd edition, J.G. Bennett Foundation, Petersham MA, 2016 (first published Hodder and Stoughton, London).
1961a   *The Dramatic Universe: volume 2, The Foundations of Moral Philosophy*, Claymont Communications, Charles Town, WV, 1985 (first published Hodder and Stoughton, London).
1961b   *Christian Mysticism and Subud*, The Institute for the Comparative Study of History, Philosophy and the Sciences, London.
1962   *Witness: The Story of a Search*, Hodder and Stoughton, London.
1964   *A Spiritual Psychology*, first edition, Hodder and Stoughton, London.
1966a   *The Dramatic Universe: Volume 3, Man and his Nature*, Bennett Books, Santa Fe, NM, 1997 (first published Hodder and Stoughton, London).
1966b   *The Dramatic Universe: Volume 4, History*, Bennett Books, Santa Fe, NM, 1997 (first published Hodder and Stoughton, London).
1971a   "Mr Bennett's Address to the AGM of the International Academy for Continuous Education," unpublished manuscript.
1971b   "Inaugural Address—First Basic Course," dated October 16, 1971, unpublished manuscript.
1973   *Gurdjieff: Making a New World*, Turnstone, London.
1974   *Inaugural Address: Fourth Basic Course, 1974/75; The International Academy for Continuous Education; Institute for the Comparative Study of History, Philosophy & the Sciences Ltd.*, Coombe Springs Press, Sherborne.
1975a   *Witness: The Autobiography of John G. Bennett*, Turnstone Press Ltd, Wellingborough.
1975b   *Intimations: Talks with J.G. Bennett at Beshara*, compiled and edited E. Bennett, A.G.E. Blake, and P. Gibson, Beshara Publications, Aldsworth.
1976   *Noticing*, Coombe Springs Press, Sherborne.
1977a   *The Masters of Wisdom*, Turnstone Books, London, reissued 1995 Bennett Books, Santa Fe, NM.
1978a   *Transformation*, compiled and edited Ken Pledge, Coombe Springs, Sherborne, reissued 2003 Bennett Books, Santa Fe, NM.
1978b   *Creation*, compiled and edited A.G.E. Blake, Bennett Books, Santa Fe, NM.

1979	*The Sevenfold Work*, compiled and edited A.G.E. Blake, 2nd revised edition, Coombe Springs Press, Daglingworth.
1981	*Sex*, compiled and edited A.G.E. Blake, Samuel Weiser, York Beach, ME.
1983	*Enneagram Studies*, compiled and edited A.G.E. Blake, Samuel Weiser, York Beach, ME.
1989	*Sacred Influences: Spiritual Action in Human Life*, Bennett Books, Santa Fe, NM. The 1989 edition includes some significant differences from the earlier Coombe Springs editions of 1976 and 1982, and includes the valuable notes which were omitted when it was reissued as *The Image of God in Work*, J.G. Bennett Foundation, Petersham, MA, 2017.
1990	*Needs of a New Age Community*, foreword by A.L. Staveley, compiled and edited A.G.E. Blake, Bennett Books, Santa Fe, NM (originally published, with less material, by Coombe Springs Press in 1977).
1991a	*What Are We Living For?* first edition Hodder and Stoughton, 1949, Bennett Books edition with a foreword by A.L. Staveley and other unspecified material.
1991b	*Hazard: The Risk of Realization*, 2nd edition, with new material, Bennett Books, Santa Fe, NM.
1992	"The Present Moment," *Impressions*, 8. 4, 7-16, transcript of a talk given in 1970.
1993	*Elementary Systematics: A Tool for Understanding Wholes*, ed. David Seamon, Bennett Books, Santa Fe, NM.
1994	*Deeper Man*, edited and compiled A.G.E. Blake, Bennett Books, Santa Fe, NM.
1995	*Making a Soul*, Bennett Books, Santa Fe, NM.
1997	*Witness: The Story of a Search*, revised edition, Bennett Books, Santa Fe, NM.
1998a	*Creative Thinking*, Bennett Books, Santa Fe, NM.
1998b	*Creation*, compiled and edited by A.G.E. Blake, originally published by Coombe Springs, Sherborne in 1978, republished by Bennett Books, Santa Fe, NM with a new foreword.
1999	*A Spiritual Psychology*, second edition, Bennett Books, Santa Fe, NM; originally published in 1974.
2000	*Journeys in Islamic Countries*, Bennett Books, Santa Fe, NM, originally published in two volumes, Coombes Spring Press.

2004	*Sunday Talks at Coombe Springs*, edited Ken Pledge, Bennett Books, Santa Fe, NM.
2006a	*The Way to Be Free*, compiled and edited A.G.E. Blake, revised edition of a 1980 original published by Samuel Weiser, Bennett Books, Santa Fe, NM.
2006b	*The First Liberation: The Sherborne House Theme Talks 1-5*, Bennett Books, Santa Fe, NM.
2010	*Existence*, Bennett Books, Santa Fe, NM, including material not found in the 1977 edition published by the Coombe Springs.
2014	*The Shivapuri Baba and his Message*, J.G. Bennett Foundation, Petersham, MA.
2016	*Who Is Man? Six Lectures by J.G. Bennett, 1956*, J.G. Bennett Foundation, Petersham, MA.
2017a	*"Systematics" Papers: Articles from "Systematics" The Journal of the Institute for the Comparative Study of History, Philosophy and the Sciences, 1963-1972*, J.G. Bennett Foundation, Petersham, MA.
2017b	*The Image of God in Work*, compiled and edited A.G.E. Blake, J.G. Bennett Foundation, Petersham, MA, revised edition with new material, based on *Sacred Influences*, Bennett Books, Santa Fe, NM, 1989, itself a revised edition of *The Image of God in Work*, Coombe Springs, Sherborne, 1976.
2018	*Values: An Anthropology for Seekers*, J.G. Bennett Foundation, Petersham, MA, first privately printed 1943, reprinted by Unwin Brothers, 1951; Coombe Springs Press, 1963.
2019	*The Study of Man*, J.G. Bennett Foundation, Petersham, MA, based on materials prepared in 1967.
2020	*Lectures on Gurdjieff: Fourteen Public Lectures in Four Series, 1949-1973*, J.G. Bennett Foundation, Petersham, MA; a revised omnibus edition of four earlier separate Coombe Springs Press publications: *Is There 'Life' on Earth?; Making a Soul; Gurdjieff: A Very Great Enigma;* and *Gurdjieff Today*.

Bennett, J.G and R.L. Brown

1940	"Gas Flow in Fuel Beds: A New Model Technique for the Study of Aerodynamic Processes," *Journal of the Institute of Fuel*, 13, 232–46.

Bennett, J.G; R.L. Brown and H.G. Crone

1941	"Broken Coal," Park Place, Cardiff: The Institute (includes responses from other coal researchers).

Bennett, J.G.; R.L. Brown and M.W. Thring.

1949   "Unified Field Theory in a Curvature-Free Five-Dimensional Manifold," *Proceedings of the Royal Society of London. Series A, Mathematical and Physical Sciences*, Vol. 198, No. 1052, July 22, 1949, 39–61.

Bennett, J.G. and Hasan Lutfi Shushud

1971-74   Unpublished correspondence.

Bennett, J.G. and Marian Kaminski

2021   *A Short Guide and Glossary to the Dramatic Universe*, J.G. Bennett Foundation, Petersham, MA.

Bennett, John G. in collaboration with Thakur Lal Manandhar

1965   *Long Pilgrimage: The Life and Teaching of Sri Govindananda Bharati known as The Shivapuri Baba*, Giridhar Lal Manandhar, Kathmandu, 2006 reprint with a foreword by G.L. Manandhar (originally published Hodder and Stoughton, London).

Benson, Robert Hugh

1910   *Non-Catholic Denominations*, Longmans, Green and Co., London.

Berridge, Geoff R.

2009   *British Diplomacy in Turkey, 1583 to the Present*, Martinus Nijhoff Publishers, Leiden.

Black, Ian E.

1941   *A Friend of France*, Jonathan Cape, London.

Blake, A.G.E.

1980a   *A Seminar on Time*, Claymont Communications, Charles Town.

1980b   "Mr Bennett and Daglingworth," *Bulletin of the Institute for Comparative Study*, 17-24.

1996   *The Intelligent Enneagram*, Shambhala, Boston.

2016   *The Bohm-Bennett Correspondence, 1962-64*, (editor), DuVersity Publications, Charles Town, originally published 1977, online version, accessed January 23, 2021, https://www.duversity.org/PDF/BBcorrespondence.pdf.

2017   "The Fourth Way: A Hazardous Path (Part 1)," *Religion and the Arts*, 21, 11-39.

2018   "The Fourth Way: A Hazardous Path (Part 2)," *Literature & Aesthetics*, 28, 101-56.

Blavatsky, Helena P.

1888   *The Secret Doctrine*, vol. II, *Anthropogenesis*, originally published Theosophical University Press, London, reprinted Theosophical University Press, Pasadena, CA, 1974.

Boyce, D.G.

1987   "Crusaders without chains: power and the press barons 1896-1951," in James Curran, Anthony Smith, and Pauline Wingate (eds), *Impacts and Influences, Media Power in the Twentieth Century*, Routledge, London, 97-112.

Bright-Paul, Anthony

2006   *My Stairway to Subud*, Undiscovered Worlds Press, Norwich, UK.

Bucke, Richard Maurice

1905   *Cosmic Consciousness: A Study in the Evolution of the Human Mind*, Innes and Sons, Philadelphia, first published 1901 by Innes and Sons.

Butler, Cuthbert

1927   *Western Mysticism*, 2nd edition, Fletcher and Son, Norwich, UK.

Campbell, Bruce

1980   *Ancient Wisdom Revived: A History of the Theosophical Movement*, University of California Press, Berkeley, CA.

Chromey, Roberta J.

2022   *Real People*, Red Elixir, Rhinebeck, NY.

Cilento, Diane

2006   *My Nine Lives*, Penguin/Viking, New York.

Collin, Rodney

1956   *The Theory of Eternal Life*, Vincent Stuart, London.

Collin-Smith, Joyce

1988   *Call No Man Master*, Gateway Books, Bath, UK.

Copleston, Frederick

1963   *A History of Philosophy, Volume 7: Modern Philosophy, Fichte to Nietzsche*, Burns and Oates, London.

Crilly, Tony

2006   *Arthur Cayley: Mathematician Laureate of the Victorian Age*, John Hopkins University Press, Baltimore, MD.

Cusack, Carole

2021   "Sūfism and the Gurdjieff 'Work': A Contested Relationship," in

Muhammad Afzal Upal and Carole M. Cusack (eds), *Handbook of Islamic Sects and Movements*, Brill, Leiden, 612-31.

Dauben, Joseph Warren

1991   *Georg Cantor: His Mathematics and Philosophy of the Infinite*, Princeton University Press, Princeton, NJ.

Davy, Thomas Humphry

1925   *History of the Athenaeum, 1824-1925*, William Clowes and Sons, London.

de Salzmann, Jeanne

2010   *The Reality of Being: The Fourth Way of Gurdjieff*, Shambhala, Boston.

Dharmarwara, Bhante

1991   "Bhante and Mr Bennett," *Impressions*, 8.4, 19-22.

Driscoll, J. Walter and the Gurdjieff Foundation of California

1985   *Gurdjieff: An Annotated Bibliography*, Garland, New York.

Edwards, Helena

2009   *All This—And Heaven Too?* Crucible Publishers, Bath, UK.

Ellenberger, Henri F.

1970   *The Discovery of the Unconscious*, Basic Books, New York.

Elliott, J.A.

1958   Review of *Oriental Magic*, Idries Shah, *Journal of Asian Studies*, 172), 255-56.

Elwell-Sutton, L.P.

1972   "Sufism and Pseudo-Sufism," *Encounter*, December 1972, accessed from https://pdfcoffee.com/sufism-amp-pseudo-sufism-pdf-free.html April 10, 2022.

Entwistle, Clive E.

1976   *Foundations for a New World View*, unpublished manuscript.

Ergin, Nevit O.

2014   *The Sufi Path of Anihilation: In the Tradition of Mevlana Jalaluddin Rumi and Hasan Lutfi Shushud*, Inner Traditions, Rochester, VT.

Evans, Jonathan

2021   *Secret Service: National Security in an Age of Open Information*, ed. Claire Foster-Gilbert, Haus Publishing, accessed April 13, 2022 from ProQuest Ebook.

Foard, Patsy

1991   *Rabbit Blue*, James Yeates Printing, Bairnsdale, AU.

Gamard, Ibrahim
2005 "Why Gurdjieff's "Fourth Way" Teachings are not Compatible with the Mevlevi Sufi Way," dar-al-masnavi.org/mevlevi-vs-gurdjieffism.html, accessed March 23, 2005.

Gardner, Brian
1973 *The Public Schools: An Historical Survey*, Hamish Hamilton, London.

Gathorne-Hardy, Jonathan
1978 *The Old School Tie: The Phenomenon of the English Public School*, Viking, New York.

Geels, Antoon
1997 *Subud and the Javanese Mystical Tradition*, Curzon, Richmond, Surrey.
2021 "Subud: An Indonesian Interpretation of Sufism," 568-88, in Muhammad Afzal Upal and Carole M. Cusack (eds), *Handbook of Islamic Sects and Movements*, Brill, Leiden.

Ghani, Cyrus
1987 *Iran and the West*, Routledge, London.

Graves, Richard Perceval
1995 *Robert Graves and the White Goddess: 1940-1985*, Weidenfeld and Nicolson, London (republished 1998, Phoenix, London).

Green, Nile
2012 *Sufism: A Global History*, Wiley-Blackwell (no place of publication shown).

Gurdjieff, George I.
1933 *The Herald of Coming Good*, privately published Paris, reprinted Sure Fire, Edmonds, WA, 1988.
1950 *Beelzebub's Tales to his Grandson*, Two River Press, Aurora 1993 reprint, original ed. Routledge and Kegan Paul, London).
1963 *Meetings with Remarkable Men*, Routledge and Kegan Paul, London reprinted Arkana, London, 1985.
1981 *Life Is Real Only Then, When "I Am,"* 2nd edition, Routledge and Kegan Paul, London.
2009 *Transcripts of Gurdjieff's Wartime Meetings 1941–1946*, 2nd edition, anonymously edited, Book Studio, London.
2014 *Gurdjieff's Early Talks*, anonymously edited, Book Studio, London.
2017 *Paris Meetings 1943*, Dolmen Meadow Editions, Toronto.
2020a *Groupes de Paris, Tome I: 1943*, Éditions Éolienne, Bastia, FR.

2020b   *Groupes de Paris, Tome II: 1944*, Éditions Éolienne, Bastia, FR.

Hands, Rina

1991   *Diary of Madame Egout pour Sweet*, Two Rivers Press, Aurora, OR.

Hanegraaff, Wouter J. (ed.)

2006   *Dictionary of Gnosis and Western Esotericism*, Brill, Leiden.

Hayter, Augy

2002   *Fictions and Factions*, Tractus Books, Reno, NV.

Heselton, Philip

2012   *Witchfather: A Life of Gerald Gardner*, vol, 2, Thoth Publications, Loughborough, UK.

Hodgson, Anthony

2006   "Qualitative Systems Thinking: A Fresh Look at J.G. Bennett's General Systematics," *Proceedings of the 50th Annual Meeting of the ISSS*, Sonoma, accessible at http://journals.isss.org/index.php/proceedings50th/article/view/323.

2007   *The Cosmic Vision of J.G. Bennett, An Appreciation*, (PDF supplied by the author).

Howarth, Jessmin and Dushka

1998   *"It's Up To Ourselves": A Mother, a Daughter, and Gurdjieff*, Gurdjieff Heritage Society, New York.

Hulme, Kathryn C.

1997   *Undiscovered Country: The Search for Gurdjieff*, new edition, Natural Bridge Editions, Lexington, KY, first edition Little Brown, New York, 1966.

Hutton, Alexander

2014   'A belated return for Christ?': the reception of Arnold J. Toynbee's A Study of History *in a British context*, 1934–1961," European Review of History, 21, 405-24.

Hutton, Ronald

2009   "The early Arthur: History and myth," in Elizabeth Archibald and Ad Putter, *The Cambridge Companion to the Arthurian Legend*, Cambridge University Press, New York, 21-35.

2019   *The Triumph of the Moon*, new edition, Oxford University Press, New York.

Inglis, Brian

1989   *Trance*, Grafton Books, London.

James, William
1902   *The Varieties of Religious Experience*, republished Folio Society, London, 2008, originally published Longmans Green, London.

Jeynes, William H.
2011   "Race, Racism, and Darwinism," *Education and Urban Society*, 43(5) 535-59.

Kinross, Patrick Baron
1964   *Atatürk: The Rebirth of a Nation*, Weidenfeld and Nicolson, London.

Küçük, Hülya
2008   "A Brief History of Western Sufism," *Asian Journal of Social Science*, 36, 292-320.

Landau, Rom
1935   *God Is My Adventure*, Ivor Nicholson and Watson, London, reprinted 1964, George Allen and Unwin, London.

Lefort, Rafael
1966   *The Teachers of Gurdjieff*, Victor Gollancz, New York.

Lehmann-Haupt, C. (ed.)
2011   *Martin Benson Speaks*, Codhill Press (no place of publication shown).

Lewis, Cecil
1993   *All My Yesterdays*, Element, Shaftesbury, UK.

MacIntyre, Alasdair
2007   *After Virtue: A Study in Moral Theory*, 3rd edition, University of Notre Press, Notre Dame, IN.

Macleod, Melissa Marston
undated *My Life: A Spiritual Quest*, privately published, Bramley, UK.

Mitchell, Rachman
2018   *Moments of Truth: Stories of a Doctor in Subud*, Balboa Press, Bloomington, IN.

Monserud, Bruce
2003   "The Meaning of Environment Ethics in J.G. Bennett's *The Dramatic Universe*," unpublished thesis, Master of Arts, University of Florida.
2010   "Bennett, John G." in Bron Taylor ed., *The Encyclopedia of Religion and Nature*, Continuum, neither place of publication nor pagination shown.

Moore, James
1986   "Neo-Sufism: The case of Idries Shah," *Journal of Contemporary Religion*, 3:3, 4-8.

1991   *Gurdjieff: A Biography*, Element, Shaftesbury, UK.
1994   "Moveable Feasts: The Gurdjieff Work," *Religion Today*, 9, no. 2:11-16.

Morris, Benny and Dory Ze'evi
2019   *The Thirty-Year Genocide : Turkey's Destruction of Its Christian Minorities, 1894-1924*, Harvard University Press, Cambridge, MA.

Nicoll, Maurice
1997   *Selections from Meetings in 1953 at Great Amwell House*, Eureka Editions, Utrecht.

Ogilvie, Robert M.
1964   *Latin and Greek: A History of the Influence of the Classics on English Life from 1600 to 1918*, Routledge and Kegan Paul, London.

Onions, C.T. (editor)
1973   *Shorter Oxford English Dictionary on Historical Principles*, 3rd edition, revised and reset, Clarendon Press, Oxford.

Opie, James
2011   *Approaching Inner Work*, Gurdjieff Books and Music, Portland, OR.

O'Prey, Paul
1984   *Between Moon and Moon: Selected Letters of Robert Graves 1946-1972*, Hutchinson, London.

Ouspensky, Piotr D.
1911   *Tertium Organum*, original Russian edition, republished 1992, Andreev and Sinovia, St Petersburg.
1931   *A New Model of the Universe*, Alfred A. Knopf, New York, reprinted by Dover Publications, Mineola, NY, 1997.
1949   *In Search of the Miraculous*, Harcourt Brace, New York.
1950   *The Psychology of Man's Possible Evolution*, Hedgehog Press, New York, reprinted Vintage Books, New York, 1974.
1951   *A Record of Meetings*, Stourton, Cape Town, reprinted Arkana, London, 1992.
1981   *Tertium Organum*, revised English translation, Routledge and Kegan Paul, London, from an earlier English translation published in 1923 by Kegan Paul Trench Trubner, London.

Perry, Gavin A.
2020   "My Sherborne Experiences with Mr Bennett," unpublished.
2022   "Talks, Themes, Exercises, Movements, Seminars," unpublished.

Phillpotts, Dorothy
2008   *Discovering Gurdjieff*, AuthorHouse, Central Milton Keynes.

Pilcher, Jeffrey M.
2006   *The Sausage Rebellion: Public Health, Private Enterprise, and Meat in Mexico City, 1890-1917*, University of New Mexico Press, Albuquerque, NM.

Pittman, Michael S.
2012   *Classical Spirituality in Contemporary America: The Confluence and Contribution of G.I. Gurdjieff and Sufism*, Continuum, London.

Pogson, Beryl
1961   *Maurice Nicoll*, Vincent Stuart, London.
2002   *The True Myth*, Eureka Editions, Utrecht.

Powell, Christopher and Arthur Butler
1980   *The Parliamentary and Scientific Committee: The First Forty Years 1939-1979*, Croom Helm, London.

Remde, Gladys
2014   *A Life in Search of Meaning*, By the Way Books, Richmond, TX.

Ripman, Hugh Brockwill
1999   *Search for Truth*, Forthway Center Palisades Press, Washington, DC.
undated "Hugh Ripman – Shivapuri Baba," unpublished 23 page PDF.

Robertson, Michael
2008   *Worshipping Walt: The Whitman Disciples*, Princeton University Press, Princeton, NJ.

Roth, Allen
1998   *Sherborne: An Experiment in Transformation*, Bennett Books, Santa Fe, NM.

Sami, E. Mahmud
2006   *The Quest for Sultan Abdülhamid's Oil Assets*, Isis Press, Istanbul.

Santipolo, Matteo
2003   *On the opposite sides of the continuum: Standard British English and Cockney. A Historical Outline of the Parallel Developments of the Two Varieties*, https://web.archive.org/web/20110206055350/http://www.humnet.unipi.it/slifo/articolosantipolo.pdf, accessed May 31, 2022.

Schimmel, Annemarie
1975   *Mystical Dimensions of Islam*, University of North Carolina Press, Chapel Hill, NC.

Schlieter, Jens
2018 *What Is It Like To Be Dead?Near-Death Experiences, Christianity, and the Occult*, Oxford University Press, New York.

Schlosser, Ulisses
2018 "Richard Maurice Bucke and the Modern Study of Cosmic Consciousness," in Mahmoud Masaeli, and Rico Sneller (eds), *Cosmic Consciousness and Human Excellence*, Cambridge Scholars Publishing, Newcastle upon Tyne, 15-39.

Seamon, David
2020 "Understanding the Esoteric through Progressive Awareness," *ARIES*, 20, 81-107.

Sedgwick, Mark J.
2016 *Western Sufism: From the Abbasids to the New Age*, Oxford University Press, Oxford.

Seymour-Smith, Martin
1983 *Robert Graves: His Life and Work*, Abacus, London.

Shah, Sayed Idries
1956 *Oriental Magic*, Philosophical Library, New York.
1957 *The Secret Lore of Magic*, Abacus, London, 1972 (originally published Frederick Muller).
1964 *The Sufis*, Doubleday, Garden City, NY, reprinted Anchor Books, New York, 1971.
1969 *Destination Mecca*, Octagon. London (first published 1957 by Rider, London).
1970 *Wisdom of the Idiots*, second enlarged edition, Octagon Press, London.

Shaw, Stanford J. and Ezel Kural Shaw
1977 *History of the Ottoman Empire and Modern Turkey*, Vol. II, Cambridge University Press, New York.

Shushud, Hasan Lutfi
2014 *Masters of Wisdom of Central Asia: Teachings from the Sufi Path of Liberation*, 2nd revised edition, Inner Traditions, Rochester, VT.

Sinclair, Frank R.
2005 *Without Benefit of Clergy*, Xlibris, no place of publication shown.

Skeat, Walter W.
1910 *An Etymological Dictionary of the English Language*, 4th edition, Clarendon Press, Oxford.

Sirriyeh, Elizabeth

1999 *Sufis and Anti-Sufis*, Curzon, Richmond, Surrey.

Stanley, Brian

2017 "Anglican Missionary Societies and Agencies in the Nineteenth Century" in *The Oxford History of Anglicanism, Volume III: Partisan Anglicanism and its Global Expansion 1829-c.1914*, ed. Rowan Strong, Oxford University Press, New York, accessed via Oxford Scholarship Online, January 12, 2021.

Staudenmaier, Peter

2014 *Between Occultism and Nazism: Anthroposophy and the Politics of Race in the Fascist Era*, Brill, Leiden.

Taylor, Paul Beekman

1998 *Shadows of Heaven: Gurdjieff and Toomer*, Samuel Weiser, York Beach, ME.

2001 *Gurdjieff and Orage: Brothers in Elysium*, Samuel Weiser, York Beach, ME.

2012 *Real Worlds of G.I. Gurdjieff*, Eureka Editions, Utrecht.

2020 *G.I. Gurdjieff: A Life*, Eureka Editions, Utrecht.

Thompson, William James

1995 *J.G. Bennett's Interpretation of the Teachings of G.I. Gurdjieff*, PhD thesis, University of Lancaster.

Toynbee, Arnold J.

1935 *A Study of History, volume I*, (second edition), Oxford University Press, London.

Tunbridge, Alan

2015 *A Noose of Light: Memories 1940-2015*, 2nd edition, self-published.

van Sommers, Raymond

2004 *A Life in Subud*, Dawn Books, Northbridge, AU.

von Harten, Marjorie

1978 *Walking in the World*, Coombe Springs, Sherborne.

Wallace, Edith

1991 "Elizabeth Bennett," *Impressions*, 8.4, 29-30.

Waugh, Evelyn

1928 *Decline and Fall*, Chapman and Hall, London.

Webb, James

1976 *The Occult Establishment*, Open Court Publishing, La Salle, IL.

1980   *The Harmonious Circle: An Exploration of the Lives and Work of G.I. Gurdjieff, P.D. Ouspensky and others*, Thames and Hudson, London.

Weikart, Richard

2004   *From Darwin to Hitler*, Palgrave Macmillan, New York.

Wertenbaker, Christian

2017   *The Enneagram of G.I. Gurdjieff*, Codhill, New Paltz, NY.

Wood, Barbara

1984   *Alias Papa: A Life of Fritz Schumacher*, Jonathan Cape, London.

Zuber, René

1980   *Who Are You Monsieur Gurdjieff?* Routledge and Kegan Paul, London.

Internet Sites

https://idriesshahfoundation.org (The Idries Shah Foundation)

https://www.proquest.com/docview/102506727?parentSessionId=LHWK7AEtxyU2v5AW3%2BzuEthRnW5iLkqxqVo52O%2Fd2r4%3D&pq-origsite=primo&accountid=14757 (*New York Times obituary*, "John de Kay, Author and Capitalist, 68)

https://www.proquest.com/docview/98766832?parentSessionId=rq2HUJj3XcOYWe%2Bp2xZ44cj%2F1U%2BglcNd%2FXXjSKvlBWM%3D&pq-origsite=primo&accountid=14757 (*New York Times*, "De Kay, At Lausanne, A Mysterious Agent")

https://www.independent.co.uk/arts-entertainment/books/reviews/invisible-ink-no-240-idries-shah-9715413.html *The Independent* (London, England)

Oxford Dictionary of National Biography, https://www-oxforddnb-com.ezproxy.library.sydney.edu.au/view

https://www.nmrs.org.uk/resources/obituaries-of-members/e/george-maitland-edwards/ (Northern Mine Research Society)

https://beezone.com/adi-da/gathering_honey.html (Gathering Honey—A. H. Almaas)

https://www.ngoadvisor.net/ong/susila-dharma-international (Subud)

https://www.santorini.com/santorinivolcano/volcaniceruptions.htm (The volcanic explosion on Santorini)

https://www.azquotes.com/quote/1428818 (Sayings attributed to Will Rogers)

https://www.guild-ransom.co.uk (The Guild of Our Lady of Ransom)

https://www.calendar-12.com/holidays/easter/1959 (The date of Good Friday in 1959)

https://www.gurdjieff.org/childe1.htm (Pauline de Dampierre)
https://www.findagrave.com/memorial/128968454/eric-graham_forbes-adam (Forbes Adams)
https://biography.wales/article/s2-SEYL-ART-1866 (Clarence Seyler and "Coal Systematics")
http://www.beatlesinterviews.org/db1980.0929.beatles.html (John Lennon's experience of self-remembering)
https://www.pdcnet.org/collection-anonymous/browse?start=0&fq=w-cpii%2fVolume%2f8986%7c14%2f&fp=wcpii (The XIth International Congress of Philosophy)
https://www.duversity.org/PDF/BBcorrespondence.pdf (*The Bohm-Bennett Correspondence, 1962-1964*)

INDEX

All references are to sections, not pages. Books by Bennett are listed at the end of the entry for him. Other books are indexed under their titles, not by author.

Bennett, John Godolphin
    partial amnesia claims 0.8
    autodidact 1.6
    birth 0.1, 1.1
    charwoman, Mrs Mursh 1.1
    coal 4.5-4.10, 5.1, 8.5
    chess 4.5
    childhood 0.8, 1.1, 1.2
    Christianity 1.1, 10.2
    collective consciousness 4.6
    contemplation-like exercises 7.2, 8.3, 8.5, 8.7, 9.1, 9.8, 9.9, 11.3, 12.2
    converts to Catholicism 10.1, 10.2
    death 0.1, 11.5
    near death 0.8, 1.5
    Decision Exercise 11.3
    on destiny 5.7
    disillusionment 4.7, 9.8 and 10.2 (with Subud)
    dissension between Gurdjieff's pupils 8.1, 8.6
    as educator 5.6, 10.7
    on elementals 4.7
    on epochs 5.5, 6.2, 6.3, 8.4, 8.9, 11.1
    on eternal pattern 2.1, 2.3, 2.6, 2.7, 3.1, 3.3, 3.6, 3.8, 5.2, 5.7, 12.2-12.6
    on eternity 2.5, 5.3, 5.7, 6.2, 8.1, 12.2
    expectation of another teacher 4.1
    family Appendix 1
    fate and choice 2.1, 2.7, 3.1
    father Basil 1.1, 1.2
    fifth dimension 2.5
    at Fontainebleau 3.4-3.8
    leaves Gurdjieff in 1923 3.8, 4.2
    searches for Gurdjieff 4.5, 5.5, 6.3, 6.5
    returns to Gurdjieff 6.6, 6.7
    delivers public lectures on Gurdjieff 7.9
    and the Gurdjieff tradition 0.7, 8.6, 12.7
    imprisonment 4.3
    on individuality 9.8
    integration without rejection 0.7
    possible King of Albania 3.1
    as leader of laboratory 5.5
    lectures, public 0.2, 0.8, 2.6, 4.6,

5.3, 5.4, 5.5, 6.2, 6.3, 6.5, 7.1, 7.4, 7.9, 7.10, 8.3, 8.4
marriage 2.1
meditation 6.1
mendacity concerning South Africa 6.6
travels to the Middle East 8.4, 8.5, 8.6, 8.7
mysticism 0.1, 0.2, 5.2, 6.1, 6.3
reciting the Our Father 4.7
assistant to Ouspensky 4.2, 4.6, 4.7, 5.1
Pali 3.3
parents 1.1, 1.6, 2.1
on the Parousia (Second Coming of Jesus) 0.5, 8.4, 9.2, 12.4
predictions and prophecy 8.3, 8.4, 8.7, 9.2
recuperation after WWI 1.6
sacred image 6.5, 8.4, 12.3, 12.5
Sanskrit 3.3, 4.4
scholarships 1.1, 1.3, 2.2
at school 1.1-1.3
secret of death and resurrection 8.1
Sherborne House 11.3
siblings 0.8, 1.1, 2.1
South Africa 6.5, 6.6
speculates that a "Turkish" soul may have replaced his original 0.8
"stupid cleverness" 4.10
suspicion of him as a former Intelligence officer 0.7, 4.4
systematics 4.9, 5.5, 10.7, 11.2
his task re devotion 0.5

Tibetan 5.6
on time 2.4, 6.2, 12.3-12.4
trial in Greece 4.5
tuberculosis 4.9
drawn to Turkey 2.1, 2.2, 2.7
travels to Turkey 2.2
learns Turkish 1.6, 2.1
on values 2.7, 3.1
visionary prophecies 4.6
on will 2.5, 8.1, 8.2, 8.7, 9.1, 9.7, 10.4
in WWI 1.4, 1.5
in WWII 5.1

Books:
"Catalogue of Inner Exercises" (unpublished) 7.2
Christian Mysticism and Subud 9.7, 9.8
Concerning Subud 0.1, 1.5, 7.5, 7.9, 9.2, 9.8
Creation 4.7, 8.3
The Crisis in Human Affairs 6.2, 6.5, 7.10
Deeper Man 1.3, 1.4, 2.1, 7.7, 7.9
The Dramatic Universe 0.8, 1.6, 5.2, 5.3, 5.5, 6.1, 8.4, 8.9, 9.1, 9.5, 10.1, 10.3, 10.7, 12.1, 12.3, 12.4, 12.7
Elementary Systematics 10.7
Energies: Material, Vital, Cosmic 3.6
The First Liberation 1.1
Gurdjieff: Making a New World 0.2, 2.5, 7.10, 11.3
Hazard 12.1, 12.6
Intimations 0.8
Long Pilgrimage 10.1

Making a Soul 7.4, 11.5
Man and his World 5.3
Masters of Wisdom 1.5, 5.5, 7.9, 10.1, 11.1, 12.4
Problems of the Greek Fuel Industry 4.7
"Science of Idiotism" (unpublished, and unattributed) 7.1
The Sevenfold Work 3.1
A Short Guide and Glossary to the Dramatic Universe (with Kaminski) 5.3
A Spiritual Psychology 8.8, 9.8, 10.2, 10.4, 12.1, 12.5
Sunday Talks at Coombe Springs 8.8
Systematics 10.7
Transformation 3.6, 8.4
The Unknown Builders (unpublished) 5.7, 6.1, 8.7, 8.9, 12.1
Values 1.1, 2.7, 5.4
The Way to Be Free 2.4, 5.5
What Are we Living for? 6.2, 7.10
Witness: The Story of a Search, passim and an apology 0.5, 0.8, 4.1, 4.5, 6.6, 10.6, 12.1
    editions 0.1
    genre 0.8

Visions:
Table 1
First ("Near Death," France, 21 March 1918) 1.5, 6.2
Second ("Vision of Eternity," Rue de Péra, c. September 1920) 2.5, 3.6, 5.2, 8.9
Third ("Destiny," Scutari, c. April 1921) 3.1, 5.5, 7.11
Fourth ("The Great Accumulator," Fontainebleau, August 1923) 3.6, 5.5, 5.7, 7.2, 7.3
Fifth ("The Past Is Undying," Mycenae, c. August 1925) 4.2, 6.5
Sixth ("The Future of Humanity," Ostrovo swamps, 1929/1930) 4.6, 7.11
Seventh ("The Energy of Life," Finsbury Square, 1931/1932) 4.8
Eighth ("Self-Observation," Lyne Place, August 1933) 4.9
Ninth (Redemption of the Universal Order," Wales, August 1941) 5.2
Tenth ("*Fiat voluntas tua*," Coombe Springs, 14 April 1944) 5.5, 5.7, 8.4
Eleventh ("The Soul Pool," King's College, 15 September 1947) 6.3, 6.4
Twelfth ("Helping the Deceased," Coombe Springs, 1948/1949) 7.4
Thirteenth ("Leaving the Body," Paris, 14 August 1949) 7.7
Fourteenth ("Judas," Paris, 27 August 1949) 7.8
Fifteenth ("Secret of Everlasting Life," en route to Paris, 1950?) 8.1

Sixteenth ("No Power of Action," Coombe Springs, 1952) 8.2
Seventeenth ("First Do your Duty," Ceyhan, Turkey, 13 November 1953 8.5
Eighteenth ("Christ Crucified and Divine," Coyoacan, Mexico, 7 March 1959) 9.6
Nineteenth ("The Love of God," St Wandrille, June 1959) 9.7
Twentieth ("Submission to God's Will, Mary," St Wandrille, 1959 or 1960) 9.7
Twenty-First ("Will and Love of God," St Wandrille, 1959, 1960, or 1961) 9.7
Twenty-Second ("Christ in the Sacrament," St Wandrille, Summer 1961) 10.2
Twenty-Third ("The infinite significance of Work, January 1964) 10.4
Twenty-Fourth ("I" am and always will be," England, 28 January 1969) 11.2

Premonitions, Out of Body Experiences, and Dissociations
Craiglockhart Military Hospital 1.6
London, wedding 2.1
Turkey 2.4
Coombe Springs, the "Great Presence" 6.3, 8.2, 9.2
Omdurman, Sudan 6.5
South Africa 6.5

A
Abdul Hamid estates 3.1, 3.3, 3.8, 4.1, 4.3, 4.5, 12.1, Appendix 2
Abdul Qadir Gilani 7.8
The Academy for Souls (Cosgrave) 6.2
Adam and Eve 8.8
Adam, Forbes 3.1
Adie, George 0.2, 7.1, 7.3, 8.6, 12.5
Adie, Helen 7.1, 8.6
Alexander Technique 11.3
Ali-Shah, Omar 10.6
All and Everything (Gurdjieff) 7.5
angelic communications 6.3
Apocalypse, Book of (Revelation) 5.7
apologia or "apology," the genre 0.8, 4.1, 4.5
"Archangel Gabriel" 9.8
Aristotle 5.5
Ars moriendi 0.1, 0.8
Ashiata Shiemash 7.1
astral body, see Kesdjan body
Athenaeum Club 3.3, 5.1

B
Bailey, Alice 7.5, 9.9
Bartok, Eva 9.2
BCURA (British Coal ...) 4.9, 4.10, 5.1, 5.3, 6.2, 10.7
Beaumont, Winifred 2.3, 2.5-2.7, 3.1-3.3, 3.8, 4.1-4.10, 5.1, 5.2, 6.3, 6.7, 7.1, 7.6, 7.9, 8.1, 8.2, 8.5, 8.7, 9.5, 9.8
  letter to the Foreign Office, 1928 4.4
  suicide attempt 4.10
Beelzebub's Tales to his Grandson

INDEX

(Gurdjieff) 5.7, 7.1, 7.3, 7.5, 7.6, 7.8, 7.9, 8.6, 8.7, 10.5
opposition to the revision 11.4
Benham, Michael 1.1, 3.2, 4.1, 5.1, Appendix 1
Bennett, Ann (daughter) 2.1, 3.1, 4.10, 5.1
Bennett, Annie Caroline née Craig (mother) 1.1, 2.1, 3.2, 4.1, 4.3, 4.5, 5.2, 6.1, 7.4
Bennett Basil (father) 1.1, 2.1
Bennett, Ben (son) 0.8, 8.6, 9.4, 10.1, 11.3
Bennett, Elizabeth (née Mayall) 0.8, 5.6, 7.1, 7.5, 7.6, 7.8, 8.5, 8.7-8.9, 9.1, 9.4, 9.5, 9.7-9.9, 10.1, 10.2, 11.3, 11.5
Bennett, Evelyn (wife) see MacNeil, Evelyn
Bennett, George (son) 7.2, 7.8, 8.6, 9.4, 10.1, 11.3, 11.5
Bennett, Hero (daughter) 11.3
Bennett, Tess (daughter) 11.3
Benson, Martin 12.1
Benson, Robert H. 0.6
Bennett, Winifred, see Beaumont, Winifred
Bergson, Henri 1.6
Bhante (Dharmawara Mahathera) 11.3
von Bissing, Ronimund 9.1
Blake, Anthony G.E. 0.5, 0.8, 5.7, 8.8, 10.3, 10.5-10.7, 11.3-11.5, 12.2, 12.3, 12.5
Blavatsky, Helena P. 0.6, 4.6, 5.4, 6.5
body and psyche connection 5.2
Bohm, David 0.8, 10.3, 12.2, 12.3, 12.6

The Bohm-Bennett Correspondence (Blake) 10.3
Bortoft, Henri 11.3
Bragg, Lawrence 2.5
Bright-Paul, Anthony 8.8, 9.8
Bucke, Richard M. 0.6, 2.6, 4.6, 6.2, 6.5, 12.2
Buddhism 5.4
The Butterfly: A Symbol of Conscious Evolution (King) 6.2

C

Cantor, Georg 12.4
Carnegie Hall 8.3
Carpenter, Edward 0.6
Catholicism 7.10
Cayley, Arthur 1.1, 1.6
Chicoine, G.B. 12.1
Chikhou, Emin 6.3, 8.4
Christianity 7.10
Chromey, Roberta 11.3
Cilento, Diane 8.6, 11.1, 11.3, 12.2
Collin-Smith, Janet 6.3
Collin-Smith, Rodney 11.5
contemplation 9.1
Coombe Springs 5.1, 5.5, 8.4, 8.5, 8.8, 10.5, 10.6
Cornelius, George 7.9
Cosmic Consciousness (Bucke) 0.6, 2.6, 6.5
conscious shocks, first and second 0.4
Courtenay-Mayers, Bernard 6.3, 6.7, 7.1, 8.1, 8.6, 9.9
Currer-Briggs, Michael 0.5
Cusack, Carole 10.6

D

Daghestani, Abdullah 8.7, 9.2
de Dampierre, Pauline 9.9
Darwin, Charles 0.6, 4.6, 7.10
Dede, Farhad 8.5
Dedghian (celibate dervishes) 8.5
Delphi 2.2
demiurgic intelligences 5.3
Descartes, Rene 7.10
Destination Mecca (Idries Shah) 10.6
Djamichunatra 5.5, 5.7, 8.4, 8.7, 8.8, 8.9, 9.2, 10.5, 10.6, 12.7
dreams 7.11
"druids" 8.8

E

Edwardian England 0.6, 9.7
    interest in Ancient Greece and Homer 4.2
Edwards, Helena (née Cox) 6.3
Edwards, Maitland 3.3
Einstein, Albert 2.5
The Elements of Non-Euclidean Geometry (Coolidge) 1.4
Enneagram 4.1
Entwistle, Clive 8.4, 9.5, 11.4, 12.1
eternal recurrence 1.6
evolution 0.6, 7.10

F

fasting 3.3
fate and destiny 2.1
fiat voluntas tua 5.5
Florence, Italy 1.1
Foard, Patsy 8.8
Foreign Office 4.4
formatory thought 3.2, 3.5
"Four Ideals Exercise" (Gurdjieff) 12.5
The Fourth Dimension (Hinton) 1.3
The Fourth Way (Ouspensky) 6.7

G

Gardner, Gerald 10.5, 10.6, Appendix 3
geometry 1.1, 1.6, 5.3, 7.7, 12.3
George, Lloyd 3.1
God 0.2, 0.3, 7.5
    only God has the right to say "I" 0.3
    realization of 10.1
    Will of God 5.5, 9.1, 9.7, 10.2
God Is my Adventure 6.2
Gospels 5.4
Grace before Meals (Bennett) 11.3
Les Grands Initiés (Schuré) 2.3
Graves, Robert 10.5, 10.6, Appendix 3
Great Accumulator 3.6, 3.7, 4.5, 4.8, 5.7, 7.2, 8.4, 9.5, 10.6, 11.3, 12.1
The Great Divorce (C.S. Lewis) 10.4
"Great Power, Presence or Source" 4.7, 5.7, 6.3, 8.5
Green, Nile 10.5
Groves, Philip 0.7
guardian angel 12.3
A Guide for the Perplexed (Schumacher) 6.2
Gurdjieff, George Ivanovitch, passim
    and
    meets Bennett in Constantinople 2.6
    advice to Bennett 3.4
    at Fontainebleau 3.4
    contemplation-like exercises 4.7, 6.1, 7.1 ("The Separation

Exercise"), 7.2-7.4, 7.11, 8.3, 9.8 (as different from the latihan), 11.3, 12.2
Help for the Deceased Exercise 4.1, 6.1, 7.4, 7.11
on higher centres 10.2
on higher dimensions 2.6, 4.8
lecture of 1923 on formatory apparatus 3.5
lecture of the 1940s on dreams and associations 7.11
as a mystic 0.2, 0.3
prophecy of Bennett's talk on the Last Supper 7.8
"I am only a bridge ..." 0.7, 6.7
movements 2.6
"Only two things ..." 0.1
"working to avoid work" 5.6

H
hanbledzoin 3.6, 7.2, 8.4, 8.5, 10.5
Hands, Rina 7.3, 8.6
von Harten, Marjorie 4.2
de Hartmann, Thomas 2.6, 3.6, 9.2
Hayter, Augy 10.6
Heap, Jane 7.3
Hegel, G.W.F. 6.2, 7.10, 12.3
Herald of Coming Good 6.7
higher being-bodies 2.6, 5.2
higher centres 2.5, 4.2, 5.2,. 5.3, 10.2
Hinduism 5.4
Hinton, Charles H. 1.3
Hoare, Reggie 10.5, 10.6
Hodgson, Anthony 10.7, 12.1, 12.6
Holy Grail 1.1
Howarth, Dushka 2.1, 10.6

Hulme, Katherine 0.4
Hume, David 5.4, 12.2
Huxley, Aldous 9.6
hyparxis 5.5, 8.9, 12.5
hypnotism 2.5, 2.6

I
idiots 7.1
In Search of the Miraculous (Ouspensky) 8.6, 12.7
Inge, Dean 9.7
Institute for the Comparative Study of History, Philosophy and the Sciences 5.6, 6.2
International Academy for Continuous Education 11.3
Islam 5.4, 6.5, 9.2

J
James, William 0.6, 3.2, 8.1
Jesus Christ 0.6, 5.5, 7.8, 7.9, 8.8, 9.6, 10.1, 12.4, 12.5
Judas 4.2, 7.8, 12.4

K
Kadloubovsky, Eugenia 4.7
Kant, Immanuel 2.7, 10.4
de Kay, John 0.7, 3.1-3.4, 3.8, 4.1, 4.4
Keats, John 5.4
Kesdjan Body 7.7, 7.8, 7.11, 11.1, 12.6
King's College School 1.1-1.3
King's College Vision, see the Eleventh Vision
Krishnamurti, Jiddu 9.9
Kuchinsky, Saul 11.3

L

Lancing College 1.1, 1.2
Lannes, Henriette 0.5, 6.6, 7.3, 8.3, 8.6, 9.9, 12.2
Lascaux Caves 6.7, 7.8
Last Supper 4.2, 7.8, 12.4
latihan 9.1-9.9, 10.1, 12.2
Lennon, John 0.4
Lewis, Cecil 0.5, 6.5, 6.6, 8.6, 10.6
Life Is Real Only Then, When "I Am" (Gurdjieff) 7.2, 11.4
London Gurdjieff Society 7.3, 9.9
"Lord Have Mercy" 81.
Loraine, Percy 3.2, 4.4
love 3.6, 9.7, 10.2

M

MacDonald, Ramsay 3.1, 3.3, 3.8
McNeil, Evelyn 2.1, 4.1, 4.10
Maharishi Mahesh Yogi 9.8
Marx, Karl 0.6, 7.10
Matthay, Tobias 5.1
Meetings with Remarkable Men (Gurdjieff, book) 10.5, 11.4
Meetings with Remarkable Men (film) 8.6
Merston, Ethel 9.1
Mevlevi dervishes 2.2, 4.10, 8.5, 9.2
Milanova, Vera 10.6
Monserud, Bruce 8.9, 12.7
Moore, James 4.5, 7.1, 8.6, 9.9, 10.5, 10.6, Appendix 2
"Moral Rearmament" 9.8
movements (i.e. Gurdjieff's "movements") 4.10
Murphy, Cathleen 8.6

Mycenae 4.2

N

Naqshbandi Sufis 8.4, 9.2, 10.5, 10.6
A New Model of the Universe (Ouspensky) 6.2
"New Work" 9.9
Nicoll, Maurice D. 0.5, 3.2, 3.8, 4.1, 6.2, 12.1

O

objective consciousness 4.7
Orage, Alfred R. 3.4, 3.8, 12.1
original sin 8.8
Ouspensky, Piotr D. *passim* and 0.5-0.7, 1.6, 2.7, 3.1-3.4, 3.8, 4.1-4.10, 5.5, 6.4, 11.1, 11.5, 12.1, 12.7
   Chinese fable 4.8
   on the failure of a high purpose 4.6
   the knight with three choices 4.1, 4.9, 12.6
   on his own previous existence 5.5
   suspicion of Bennett 4.5, 5.3
Ouspensky, Sophia 4.1, 4.7, 4.8, 4.10, 6.7, 7.1, 8.3, 10.5
   expectation of another teacher 4.1, 9.1, 9.9

P

Pan-Cosmic School of Dancing 4.4
Page, Russell 10.6
Parliamentary and Scientific Committee 5.1, 5.6, 12.1
Pentland, Lord 8.3

INDEX

Perry, Gavin 8.4, 11.3, 11.5
Philpotts, Dorothy and George 3.2, 8.6
Pittman, Michael 8.4
Plato 5.4, 10.7, 11.3
Pogson, Beryl 12.1
psychokinetic 5.6, 6.2, 6.5
The Psychology of Man's Possible Evolution (Ouspensky) 7.10
Public Schools, English 1.2
Pythagoras 10.7

R
racism 0.6
Ratnasuriya, Professor 10.1
Ray of Creation 2.1
real I 0.2, 0.3
Remde, Gladys 8.8, 11.5
Rifai dervishes 2.5
Ripman, High 10.1
Rofé, Husein 9.1, 9.2, 9.9
Rogers, Lionel 1.3
Rogers, Will 10.6
Roles, Francis 4.9
Roth, Allan 0.2, 11.3
Rumi, Jalal al-Din 5.4

S
Sabaheddin, Prince 2.3, 2.5, 2.6, 3.1, 3.2, 9.5
St. Clair-Ford, Timothy 11.3
St Joseph of Arimathea at Glastonbury (Lewis) 1.1
Saint Wandrille 9.1, 9.7, 10.2, 11.3
de Salzmann, Jeanne 0.4, 0.5, 6.6, 6.7, 7.1, 7.5, 7.9, 8.1, 8.3, 8.4, 8.6, 8.7, 9.1, 9.2, 9.9, 10.5, 10.6, 11.4, 12.1, 12.2
Santorini explosion 4.1
Schopenhauer, Arthur 6.2, 12.3
Schumacher, E.F. 0.8, 6.2
Seamon, David 0.8, 5.1, 10.7, 12.7
Second Body, see Kesdjan Body
The Secret Doctrine (Blavatsky) 0.6, 6.5
Sedgwick, Mark 8.4, 10.1, 10.5, 10.6
self-remembering 0.4
separation of "je" and "moi" 7.1
Shah, Idries 0.7, 2.3, 8.8, 9.8, 9.9, 10.5-10.7, 11.1, 12.1, 12.2, Appendix 3
    describes Bennett as "an innocent" in "this business" 10.5
    destruction of the Djamichunatra 10.6
Sherborne Courses 7.2
Sherwood, Donna 8.4
Shivapuri Baba 5.4, 10.1
Shushud, Hasan 10.5, 10.7, 11.1-11.3, 12.1, 12.2
sin 7.3
Smuts, Jan 1.6
van Sommers, Raymond 8.8
South Africa 6.3, 6.5, 6.6
spiritualism 0.6
Staveley, Annie-Lou 0.5, 0.7, 7.10, 12.2
Steiner, Rudolf 0.6, 2.3
Strange Life of Ivan Osokin (Ouspensky) 5.7
A Study of History (Toynbee) 6.2
Subud 7.5, 7.6, 8.4, 8.8, 9.1-9.9, 10.1
"Subud crises" 9.8, 10.1
Subuh, Pak 0.7, 8.9, 9.1-9.9, 12.1
Sufism 8.4, 9.2, 10.5

Sutton, Michael 11.3
Systematics (journal) 10.7

T
Taylor, Paul B. 3.4, 7.1, 8.3
Tertium Organum (Ouspensky) 0.6, 2.7
theosophy 3.2, 5.4
Thring, Med 2.5, 5.3, 8.6
Toomer, Jean 0.5, 5.2, 8.3, 12.2
Tracol, Henri 8.3, 9.9
Transcendental Meditation 9.8
Transfiguration of Christ 12.4
triads 5.1, 5.2
Tunbridge, Alan 8.8

U
Underhill, Evelyn 9.7
Upanishads 4.4, 5.4

V
The Varieties of Religious Experience (James) 3.2

W
Waite, A.E. 3.2
Walker, Kenneth 3.2, 7.3, 9.9
Waugh, Evelyn 1.2
What Is It Like To be Dead? (Schleiter) 1.5
witness, as Bennett understood the word 0.8
Worlds, theory of 2.1, 7.1, 7.9
worship 12.5
Wright, Olgivanna Lloyd 12.1

Z
zikr 2.2, 7.2, 11.1, 12.2
Zuber, Rene 8.6

www.ingramcontent.com/pod-product-compliance
Lightning Source LLC
Chambersburg PA
CBHW021129230426
43667CB00005B/75